CULTURAL ANTHROPOLOGY

The Field Study of Human Beings
2nd Edition

ALEXANDER MOORE

University of Southern California

COLLEGIATE PRESS

Collegiate Press
San Diego, California

Executive editor:
Christopher Stanford
Senior editor:
Steven Barta
Senior developmental editor:
Jackie Estrada
Designer:
John Odam
Production:
Chris Davis,
John Odam Design Associates
Cover photo:
Levon Mardikyan

Library of Congress Catalog
Card Number: 97-078022

ISBN 0-939693-48-8

Printed in the United States of
America

10 9 8 7 6 5 4 3 2 1

*This book is dedicated
to the memory of
Estanislao Coc,
informant, friend,
compadre. He guided
me to climb to the tops
of volcanoes and to hike
to his fields, but most of
all he guided me down
paths of local knowl-
edge. May he rest with
saints and angels.*

CONTENTS

ix Preface: A Personal Statement of Theoretical Position

PART I
1 ANTHROPOLOGY: UNDERSTANDING THE HUMAN PRIMATE

CHAPTER 1
5 ANTHROPOLOGY AS ENCOUNTER WITH UNKNOWN PEOPLES
9 Europe's Age of Discovery and Spontaneous Ethnographies
12 Interpretation of Ethnographic Facts
13 Ethnocentrism
17 Continuing Problems

CHAPTER 2
21 AN OVERVIEW OF CULTURAL ANTHROPOLOGY: A SUCCESSION OF CULTURES AND COMMUNITIES
24 Cultural Anthropology as Natural History
25 The Study of Communities
26 The Primate Troop: Chimpanzees
30 The Human Band
32 Tribal Communities
35 Traditional Civilizations
38 Modern Metropolitan Civilization

CHAPTER 3
45 FIELD WORK: ACCURATE DATA AND ADEQUATE THEORY
47 Pioneer Field Worker: Bronislaw Malinowski
51 The State of the Art of Field Work Today
61 Ethnographic Close-up: Freilich at Work Among the Brooklyn Mohawk
63 Attempting the Natural History of the Brooklyn Mohawk

CHAPTER 4
71 THE PRIMATE HOMO SAPIENS: OUR PLACE IN NATURE
73 The Living Cell and Human Beings: The Genetic Code and Anthropology
76 Humanity as a Species Among Related Species
79 Hominid Genuses: Australopithecus and Homo
89 Language, Genetic Codes, Human Speech, and Culture

PART II
103 BAND COMMUNITIES AND ELEMENTAL HUMAN INSTITUTIONS

CHAPTER 5
**107 THE BAND COMMUNITY:
SYNCHRONIZING HUMAN ACTIVITY CYCLES FOR GROUP COOPERATION**

108 *The Human Community*

111 *Cycles of Activities*

119 *Daily Speech Events: Managing Culture*

CHAPTER 6
127 RITUAL AND MYTH

129 *The Time Dimensions of Ritual*

130 *The Space Dimensions of Ritual*

133 *Rites of Passage: The Intersection of Ritual Space and Time*

134 *Ethnographic Close-up: Tiwi Rites*

138 *The Catalytic Power of Symbols in Ritual*

140 *Myths: The Narrative Dramas of Rituals and of Life Itself*

141 *Ethnographic Close-up: The Myth of the* Molimo *(Mbuti Pygmies, Itruru Rain Forest, Republic of the Congo)*

CHAPTER 7
151 THE HUMAN FAMILY: AN EMERGENT INSTITUTION IN BAND COMMUNITIES

152 *The Human Family and Culture*

154 *The Hearth and the Household*

155 *The Nucleus of Human Families*

158 *Ethnographic Close-up: The Marital Career of Nisa, a !Kung San Woman*

161 *Growth and Development of an Institution: Polygynous Extended Households*

162 *Human Sexuality, Gender Roles, Culture, and the Family*

166 *Consciousness, Norms, Tabus, Laws, and the Human Family*

CHAPTER 8
173 VALUES AND EXCHANGE: BANDS AND THE ORIGINAL ECONOMY

174 *Values*

178 *Ethnographic Close-up: The Tiwi Funeral*

180 *Values in Exchange: Systems of Giving and Giving Back at Various Life Stages*

182 *Sorting Out the Value of Goods*

183 *Reciprocity*

186 *Other Modes of Exchange: Redistribution and the Market*

187 *Band Communities and Emergent Institutions: The Concept of Culture Reconsidered*

PART III
197 **TRIBES AND EMERGENT INSTITUTIONS**

CHAPTER 9
203 *EXTENDING THE HUMAN FAMILY AND FORMING TRIBAL COMMUNITIES:*
HOUSEHOLDS AND DESCENT GROUPS AMONG TRIBAL PEOPLE

204 *Extending Households*

209 *Descent Groups*

212 *A Problem in Ethnology: Kin Terminologies and Marriage Exchange*

219 *Kinship and Community Among the Nuer*

CHAPTER 10
237 *TRIBAL WARFARE COMPLEXES:*
AGGRESSIVE SEQUENCES AND BALANCED NEGATIVE EXCHANGES

238 *Aggressive Sequences and Human Activity Cycles*

239 *Chimpanzee Aggressive Sequences and Chimpanzee Warfare*

242 *Social Drama: Aggressive Sequences in Band Society*

243 *Tribal Warfare*

245 *Ethnographic Close-up: The Tupinambá and Their Warfare*

249 *The Warfare Complex as Blood Feud: No True Redress and No True Outcome or Resolution*

251 *Warfare as Positive Exchange: Alliance Feasting*

CHAPTER 11
257 *FEASTING AND TRADING SYSTEMS:*
THE ECONOMICS OF REDISTRIBUTION AND TRADING RINGS

259 *The Big Man: Feastgiver and Redistributor*

263 *Ethnographic Close-up: The Siuai of Bougainville Island*

269 *Analysis of the Siuai Competitive Feast*

272 *Tribal Trading Rings*

273 *Ethnographic Close-up: The Trobriand Islanders*

278 *Brief Analysis: The Competitive Feast and the Kula Expedition Compared*

CHAPTER 12
285 *TRIBAL POLITICS: LEADERSHIP AND ITS REWARDS*

286 *Political Leadership*

291 *Ethnographic Close-up: An Elementary Leadership Pattern: Nambicuara Leaders and Their Followers*

293 *The Leader-Follower Unit: The Nambicuara Case*

296 *Tribal Republics*

297 *Ethnographic Close-up: The Cheyenne Tribal Republic*

301 *Overview of the Cheyenne Political System: Rule by the Few in Consultation with the Many*

CHAPTER 13
309 SHAMANS AND PROPHETS:
CATALYSTS FOR THERAPY AND CULTURAL CHANGE

311 *Ethnographic Close-up: Socorro Marroquín, Highland Mayan Shaman*

315 *The Dynamics of Shamanism*

319 *From Shamans to Prophets*

320 *Prophets and Revitalization Movements*

324 *Ethnographic Close-up: The Revitalization Movement of the Seneca Prophet Handsome Lake*

PART IV
335 **TRADITIONAL CIVILIZATIONS**

CHAPTER 14
339 URBAN CULTURES AND COMMUNITIES:
THE NATURE OF EARLY CIVILIZATION

341 *The Processes of Social and Cultural Evolution*

343 *The Urban, Civilized Pattern: Political and Economic Organizations*

343 *Mesopotamia: The Rise of the Nucleated, Walled City*

353 *The Nucleated, Walled City: An Ideal Form*

355 *The Green City: Ancient Egypt*

357 *Ethnographic Close-up: Understanding and Explaining Swaziland*

362 *Swazi Urbanism in Perspective: Civilization or Chiefdom?*

CHAPTER 15
369 THE ORIGINAL BUREAUCRACIES

372 *Royal Kinship and Households*

375 *Expanding and Differentiating the Original Bureaucracies*

376 *The Ottoman Turks: A Dynasty and Its Slave Bureaucracy*

385 *The Harem of the House of Osman: Slave Brides, Slave Mothers, and Lady Sultans*

394 *The Original Bureaucracy as a Dynamic Institution*

CHAPTER 16
401 FOLK CULTURES AND COMMUNITIES:
CIVILIZED "INSOLENTS" AND PEASANTS

404 *Insolent Civilized Tribes*

405 *Ethnographic Close-up: The Cruzob Maya: Resistance, Cultural Revitalization, and the Birth of a Folk Tribe*

407 *Open Peasantries and the Stem Family Household*

411 *Closed Corporate Peasant Communities*

415 *Ethnographic Close-up: Alotenango, a Maya Closed Corporate Community*

420 *Town- and City-Dwelling Peasants: Urban Agrarian Plebeians*

PART V
429 THE ANTHROPOLOGY OF MODERN LIFE

CHAPTER 17
435 THE MARKET AND THE MODERN METROPOLIS: A NEW SYSTEM OF EXCHANGE AND THE RISE OF COMMERCIAL INDUSTRIAL CITIES

436 *Markets and Marketplaces*

444 *Ethnographic Close-up: Whydah, Port of Trade*

446 *Modern Politics and Economics: The Nation-State and Market Systems*

450 *Industrial Market Systems and Settlement Patterns: The Succession of Modern Community Types*

CHAPTER 18
465 CORPORATE BUREAUCRACY AND THE CULTURE OF MODERN WORK

466 *Legal-Rational Bureaucracy: An Emerging Institution*

467 *The Baroque Capital: Monument to Absolute Royal Bureaucratic Power*

473 *The Modern Corporation and Bureaucracy*

476 *Corporate Bureaucratic Tables of Organization*

479 *Behavior in Modern Bureaucracies*

481 *The Culture of Corporate Work and the Cult of Efficiency*

486 *Ethnographic Close-up: The Worker and the Group*

487 *The Informal Group and Production*

CHAPTER 19
495 MODERNITY AND CULTURE

498 *Ethnographic Close-up: Mamachi, a Middle-Class Suburb of Tokyo*

502 *Analysis: Patterns of Modern Japanese Life*

509 *The Private World in North America: Differential Access to Modernity*

512 *Bridges Between Private and Public Worlds*

514 *Protest Movements*

525 *EPILOGUE: APPLIED ANTHROPOLOGY AND THE POLICY PROCESS*

528 *Anthropologists and the Policy Process*

530 *Ethnographic Close-up: Policy Recommendations and Kuna Democracy*

537 *References*

550 *Credits*

553 *Index*

viii

PREFACE: A PERSONAL STATEMENT OF THEORETICAL POSITION

To set the stage for what follows, let me discuss the theoretical background of this book. Its basic intellectual debt is to my doctoral mentor, Conrad M. Arensberg of Columbia University, and to Solon T. Kimball, his intellectual companion, with whom I enjoyed a close relation in the years I taught at the University of Florida (Moore, 1984). These scholars started with the premise that culture is explainable in human activity itself. This view is expounded in their *Culture and Community* (1965), a collection of their articles, but is not as lucidly presented as it might be. My point of departure, however, is their "community study method."

The community study approach has been unjustly neglected in recent years, partly because the name is misleading. To many readers it connotes the image of closed corporate communities, with their clear territorial boundaries and systems of physical and psychological defenses. In fact, the method had been formulated from a field study among the country people of West Ireland, as open a group, with the least barriers, as could be found. "*Network* study method" might be the better term. In this book the term *community* is applied, among others, to the simple, but pulsatingly dispersed and coalescing, hunting-and-gathering band; to the reticulated alliances of tribes; to the entire Swazi nation, assembled around king and queen mother through age grades and marriage networks; and to the archaic Ottoman slave bureaucracy with its slave schools and sultanic harem. None of these is a face-to-face, constantly activated, closed community; rather, each as a type, and in it individual examples, is a self-organizing and self-perpetuating network. In Arensberg's terms they are units of assemblage and dispersal, sometimes on yearly rhythms, other times on generational ones. These network/communities are capable of organizing and replicating themselves on generational and lifetime scales. As *cultures*, systems of ideas—mental templates, if you will, of how the network/communities must be organized—they are capable of regenerating themselves, transformed, after the pulsation of long cycles: 300 to 1,200 years. (See the discussion of revitalization prophets in Chapter 13, as well as the discussion of dynastic cycles in Chapter 15. See also Iberall and Wilkinson, 1987.)

Autobiography and reflexivity are avenues to understanding one's intellectual position. Thus I note that I came to graduate study in anthropology at Columbia University after majoring in history and literature (of Spain, England, and Russia since 1800) at Harvard College. The transition was the cause of considerable personal culture shock. Harvard was organized collegially, on the British manner, with tutors and teaching fellows and close faculty-student interaction (at least in those days). Columbia was organized on a central European model, with little collegiate life, and interaction with the faculty was a privilege that had to be earned. Harvard social science in those days was heavily Weberian and quite functionalist. Clyde Kluckhohn (from whom I took a graduate course on history and theory in anthropology the spring of my senior year) dominated the anthropology department with his talk of "values." (At Columbia "value" was something you bought or sold.) The younger Harvard faculty were of the same generation as Clifford Geertz, who holds a Harvard Ph.D., and who is, ever, a Parsonian functionalist.

Among the younger faculty at Columbia was Marvin Harris, whose career was just then emerging into the limelight. Harris was reworking the majority opinion of the Columbia department, which was neoevolutionist, more or less oriented toward cultural ecology, into explicit cultural materialism. Although I did subscribe to a neoevolutionary position, and although I enjoyed spirited talks with Harris over a coffee counter on Broadway, I was never converted to cultural materialism. Rather, I was bending all my wits to try to figure out what the admittedly difficult Conrad Arensberg was saying. To a lesser extent I was studying the work of Margaret Mead, from whom I took several courses, most notably the field methods seminar. My other doctoral mentors at Columbia were Charles Wagley and Ruth Bunzel, both pioneers in the ethnography of the Guatemalan highland Maya, among whom I was spending field work time my entire graduate school career. I have strived to emulate the lucid ethnographic writing style of both. Wagley, who had been a doctoral student of Ruth Benedict's, in particular gave me a sense of ethnography as an exercise in empathy and letters, in the sense of *belle lettres*.

I also supported myself for a semester as a field assistant to Julius Roth and Elizabeth Eddy, in a "qualitative sociology" project in a New York City hospital (Roth and Eddy, 1967). Eddy was later to work closely with Solon Kimball in a university seminar at Columbia, and in a later project was to provide me with the opportunity to research, write, and publish my first book, on inner New York City schools (Moore, 1967).

While Arensberg describes himself as an American functionalist, independently derived via the physiologist Walter Cannon as well as Pareto, Harris is a functionalist derived from Marx. Harris's (1979) neo-Marxist tripartite division of cultural-social phenomena into subsistence base, social structure, and ideology and belief (or "superstructure") grants theoretical priority to the first, subsistence base. Not so with Arensberg, nor with the approach followed here. Rather, for us social structure is composed of a number of actual behavioral patterns. These are grouped into institutions. I would describe them as *flows*. As institutions, they embody values, beliefs, and dispositions—in a word, *culture*. None is prior—except, perhaps, once it is emerged, politics, but politics compared to the rest of society is always unstable, given to faster turnovers.

Within the community/network view, the multiple institutional, holistic approach is key. I regard the task as one of rendering explicit what we already do well and valorizing that approach scientifically through inductive natural history. Bronislaw Malinowski's *A Scientific Theory of Culture* (1944) presents a "theory of organized behavior," but its organization is largely deductive, a priori, drawn by analogy with the individual organism, rather than from inductive observation from the ethnographic record. Malinowski's biology is by now quite antiquated as well. In 1942 Eliot Chapple* and Carleton Coon published *Principles of Anthropology*, which also attempted an institutional functionalist analysis that, while heavily influenced by the model of homeostasis in the individual organism, was far more empirical than Malinowski's approach. My own approach is closer to theirs than to Malinowski's. Chapple has continued the approach (1970, 1980), but his publications have not been in the anthropological mainstream. Perhaps he has been ahead of his time.

When I came to the University of Southern California in 1978, I had the pleasure of working closely with Barbara Myerhoff, whose untimely death in 1985 grieved me deeply. Her friendship with Victor Turner and her interest in his theories of ritual process (of liminality and *communitas*, of structure and antistructure) jibed well with my interest in activity patterns and resultant culture legitimation. Indeed, Turner, in his interest in the influence of brain and psychological state on human performances (1987), was converging rapidly toward the Arensberg and Kimball position at the time of his death in December 1983. The chapters on ritual and myth in this book reflect my own intellectual friendship with Victor Turner.

The premise that culture is explainable in activity itself has been much encouraged in my thought by meeting Edward T. Hall, through Paul Bohannan when he was dean with us at USC, and perusing his works, which all have to do with delineating human activities in space and, more recently, in time. Hall really is responsible for the concept of "body language." His work extends the notion that culture is implicit in action, as much as in speech and literature. I recommend Hall's works, still mostly available in paperback (1959, 1969, 1976, 1983; with Mildred R. Hall, 1987, 1990), to the instructor who seeks ways to enlarge some of the theoretical perspective of this book.

---

*A close intellectual associate of Arensberg's. The two were among the founders of the Society for Applied Anthropology.

My interest in human activity has also been greatly encouraged by several years of conversations with Arthur Iberall, an associate of Arensberg's (see Iberall, Soodak, and Arensberg, 1980) who is an engineer and systems physicist. Unlike most systems scientists and ecologists, he emphasizes momentum as much as matter and energy, hence the necessity for every living species to have an "action spectrum" that handles matter and energy through kinetic cycles (Iberall and McCulloch, 1969).

Since 1983 I have been meeting more or less regularly with an interdisciplinary group in southern California. Our group consists of Iberall, who after a lifetime as a government research and development scientist has been a visiting scholar at UCLA; Douglas White, anthropologist at UC, Irvine; Louis Goldberg, neurobiologist, UCLA; Richard Baum, political scientist, UCLA; David Wilkinson, political scientist, UCLA; Paul Wohlmuth, legal scholar, University of San Diego; and myself. Until recently it included Richard Day, economist, USC.

We have been debating our own disciplines with each other in the context of a general theoretical framework of systems science, with an emphasis on viable or self-organizing systems (Iberall, 1972; Yates, 1987). Unlike most systems scientists, we pay as much attention to physics, with its conservations of energy, mass, and momentum, and to chemistry, with its making and breaking of bonds, as we do to general "input-output" schemes. Some of us have published a variety of papers in various co-authored combinations. In Fall 1988, we even hazarded team teaching an honors colloquium at UCLA titled "Physical Foundations for a Unified Social Science," under the general direction of Richard Baum.

In the process of discussing our specific disciplines, we have also been debating the general phenomenon of *emergence*, which is one of the dimensions along which this book is structured. Chemistry emerges from physics; biology from physics and chemistry; ethology from biology, cultural anthropology from ethology, politics from anthropology; economics (here is a debate) either from politics or from anthropology; and law is a substratum conditioning all reality, while emerging consciously only late in human culture evolution.

This textbook does not pretend to do justice to the scope and detail of our group discussions, but the writing of it has been highly influenced by them. (Indeed, Chapters 5 and 6, "The Band" and "Ritual and Myth," first appeared in a reader for our colloquium, with Richard Baum as editor.)

The promise of our group effort is continuing to bear fruit in co-authored papers and symposia. Its most immediate influence on the framework of this book is in its bringing historicity to the structural functionalism implicit in the community/network idea of emerging and interdependent institutions. The idea is spelled out in more detail in the prologues and in the text itself, but suffice to say that when one regards humanity itself as an *emergent* species, one gets a view that leads to historicity, and the long cycle—millions of years—of any species' existence. Thus, between 200,000 and 50,000 years ago, armed with a new toolkit, language, kinship, and the family, and the division of labor between the sexes, our species began ranging out over its available habitat, which was *the whole world.*

Iberall maintains that humanity diffused over the world at a random walk pace, exactly as fast as it took the species to push itself out, on foot, everywhere (see Iberall and Wilkinson, 1984a, 1984b; and Iberall and White, 1988). Iberall calls this expanding phase 1 a "gas phase," meaning that people were jostling and bouncing into each other but not obliged to stay in contact with anyone other than those they were specifically bonded to. These bonds were easy to break, too. In a gas in nature, hierarchy simply does not arise among its elements and atomisms.

Later, when the whole world has filled up with hunting-and-gathering *H. sapiens*, and when in many cases certain environments, as in paleolithic North America, had been degraded by human actions—hunting big-game animals to extinction, for example—human beings could no longer jostle and flee but had to find ways to live with each other, to live with lessened resources, and to live with conflict. Eventually they had to make use of the potentials implicit in the boundary conditions, of nature and of other groups. The result was a settled, tribal society, communicating from community to community through trade and war. The changes arose through a combination of internal social pressures of more complicated institutional arrangements and external environmental pressures from habitat and neighboring groups. An advancing toolkit and self-domesticating breeds of plants and animals provided a *potential* for the new way of life but did not cause it. They had been in place for millennia before they became essential to human groups after first the mesolithic, then the neolithic transitions.

The transitions to civilized life and then to modern life were examples of the same processes: the responses of groups beset by *densification* of population, habitat challenges, internal institutional innovation, and external social-political pressures from neighboring groups. In the case of modernity we have the emergence, in historically documented times, of three new key institutions. First were price-regulated markets and legal-rational corporate bureaucracies. These two institutions made the third, industrialism, possible and were in no way caused by the Industrial Revolution, the harnessing of energy sources to power the work of machines synchronized with the activities of human beings. The rest of the book shall spell this out, however.

I might add that I view cultural anthropology as properly holistic, not only at the level of individual communities, or local ethnographies, but also at the level of civilization, culture area, and above all, modern life of expanding central civilization. I have felt that it is important that anthropologists not abandon modernity to the other social scientists. In fact, we do not. Many of us do field work and write ethnographies of modern metropolitan life. Around 50 percent of our new Ph.D.'s each year find jobs in applied settings. Yet textbooks continue to describe our discipline as if we were only students of the primitive, or at most, of peasant particularities. This book is an attempt to bring the totality of cultural anthropology to the introductory course, where it belongs.

While I believe that the interpretationist approach embodied in the later work, the collected essays, of Geertz (1973, 1983) is one understandable upshot of the community study method, now more fashionably called "ethnography," this emphasis on particularisms, on local knowledge, leads anthropologists into setting up a counter-literature to the novel, with the same intentions as novelists. Few of us are interesting writers per se, like an Ernest Hemingway or a Virginia Woolf. If we are to be writers, I prefer that we blend into our findings (as the early Geertz blends into his ethnographies of Java and Bali [1963]). What I have tried to do here is writing on an epic scale, since our whole emergence as a species is the story. Not local knowledge, but global knowledge, is the aim.

In sum, the framework on which this book hangs is an updated version of the community study method as network, discerned at the expanding "gas phase" of our species' random walk over the earth, through our settling down into trading and warring tribal societies through the mesolithic and neolithic transitions, into our densification into urban states and civilizations, and finally at our emergence as a metropolitan species of unparalleled population aggregations. The various communities have been marked by progressively elaborate toolkits, an array of domesticated plants and animals, and a series of emerging, functionally independent, yet competing, institutions. Of all these, only the process of population growth can in any way be prior; all the other parts of the equation (which I dare not spell out without the help of a sophisticated mathematician) are simultaneous and interdependent.

Acknowledgments. I am grateful to many people for helping make this book possible. First, I thank Jackie Estrada, developmental editor for Collegiate Press, for her patience, her enthusiasm, and her quiet good sense. Thomas Collins, Norman Schwartz, and Alaka Wali read the entire manuscript and made invaluable comments. Other friends and colleagues have read and commented on portions of the manuscript. These include Arthur Iberall, Paul Wohlmuth, Louis Goldberg, Richard Baum, Christopher Boehm, Robert Orlando, Joan Weibel-Orlando, Douglas White, Walter Williams, and Doris Pierce. Mae Horie, of the Department of Anthropology, USC, staff, has helped unfailingly in multiple tasks surrounding the manuscript. My dear friend Levon Mardikyan introduced me to his native Istanbul, walked me through Topkapi Palace and its harem, and explored Byzantine and Ottoman sites in Turkey with me as I researched material for Chapter 15. My students in Anthropology 201 at USC have made very helpful comments. I thank them for their patience and their advice.

Alexander Moore

PART

I

ANTHROPOLOGY: UNDERSTANDING THE HUMAN PRIMATE

CHAPTER 1

Anthropology as Encounter with Unknown Peoples

CHAPTER 2

An Overview of Cultural Anthropology:

A Succession of Cultures and Communities

CHAPTER 3

Field Work:

Accurate Data and Adequate Theory

CHAPTER 4

The Primate Homo Sapiens:

Our Place in Nature

Part I tells two stories. The first story has to do with strange encounters: encounters between explorers and strange peoples during Europe's Age of Discovery, and the encounters of today's anthropologists with strange cultures in the course of doing field work. The second story is biological: the origin of the human species and its emergence upon the world as the unique animal that could make the entire planet its habitat.

The first story is that of the discovery of culture, of human differences that we learn by virtue of membership in our groups. The second story is that of the discovery of our biological nature as a unique primate species that emerged from a line of closely related species.

The Age of Discovery found Europeans ranging out all over the globe. They were already poised to meet the Muslim, the traditional "Other" to Christian Europe. The two rival, but closely related, religions meant that Christian and Muslim were always in opposition, but they shared a common world and a common central civilization. Not so with the new peoples that Europeans encountered in Africa, India, East Asia, and above all, the New World. Explorers soon learned that other peoples were not only distinct physically from themselves, but distinct in their lifeways, customs, languages, behaviors, and beliefs as well. We now call this set of learned behaviors *culture*. Chapter 1 explores the Europeans' initial confrontation with the fact of cultural differences; Chapter 3 explores how anthropologists now study those differences in the practice of field work. In both cases a problem arises: the problem of accurate description (of writing what we now call *ethnography*) and the problem of adequate interpretation of facts described (now called *ethnology*).

Chapter 2, "An Overview of Cultural Anthropology," is meant to outline briefly what we know about the progression of human differences and social-cultural development. The chapter previews the successive community types that serve as the framework for the rest of the book. Students are well advised to read the chapter twice, first on starting the book and again on finishing it, so as to provide themselves with a convenient way to review the entire story. Chapter 4 is a review of the place of humans in nature as primates with very distinct origins.

Once we have reviewed all this background information, we can go on to the rest of the book—that is, the story previewed in Chapter 2. First, however, we venture back to the Age of Discovery. We learn the story of Hans Staden, a German captive among a cannibalistic tribal people, the Tupinambá (their warfare complex is described in Chapter 10). Then we look at the problem of a Christian scholar, Sahagún, trying to understand the rituals of human sacrifice among the urban Aztec civilization that Spain had recently conquered.

Anthropology as Encounter with Unknown Peoples

EUROPE'S AGE OF DISCOVERY AND SPONTANEOUS ETHNOGRAPHIES

INTERPRETATION OF ETHNOGRAPHIC FACTS

ETHNOCENTRISM

Human Sacrifice Among the Aztecs

Sahagún's Interpretation

CONTINUING PROBLEMS

As I was going through the forest I heard loud yells on either side of me, such as savages are accustomed to utter, and immediately a company of savages came running towards me, surrounding me on every side and shooting at me with their bows and arrows. Then I cried out: "Now may God preserve my soul." Scarcely had I uttered the words when they threw me to the ground and shot and stabbed at me. God be praised they only wounded me in the leg, but they tore my clothes from my body, one the jerkin, another the hat, a third the shirt, and so forth. Then they commenced to quarrel over me. One said he was the first to overtake me, another protested that it was he that caught me, while the rest smote me with their bows. At last two of them seized me and lifted me up, naked as I was, and taking me by the arms, some running in front and some behind, they carried me along with them through the forest at a great pace towards the sea where they had their canoes. As we approached the sea I saw the canoes about a stone's-throw away, which they had dragged out of the water and hidden behind the shrubs, and with the canoes were great multitudes of savages, all decked out with feathers according to their custom. When they saw me they rushed towards me, biting their arms and threatening me, and making gestures as if they would eat me. Then a king approached me carrying the club with which they kill their captives, who spoke saying that having captured me . . . from the Portuguese, they would now take vengeance on me for the death of their friends, and so carrying me to the canoes they beat me with their fists. Then they made haste to launch their canoes, for they feared an alarm might be raised . . .

Before launching the canoes they bound my hands together, but since they were not all from the same place and no one wanted to go home empty-handed, they began to dispute with my two captors, saying that they had all been just as near to me when I was taken and each one demanding a piece of me and clamoring to have me killed on the spot. Then I stood and prayed, expecting every moment to be struck down. But at last the king, who desired to keep me, gave orders to carry me back alive so that their women might see me and make merry with me. For they intended to kill me . . . to prepare a drink and gather together for a feast at which they would eat me. At these words they desisted, but they bound four ropes round my neck, and I was forced to climb into a canoe, while they made fast the ends of the ropes to the boats and then pushed off and commenced the homeward journey.

The capture of Hans Staden. Note Portuguese settlements in the background. (original sixteenth-century woodcut)

Hans Staden was a German who as a young man "desired to see the Indies." In the year 1547 he set off for Lisbon and its overseas empire. Seven years later, after a series of adventures that included being shipwrecked off the coast of Brazil, he fell into the hands of cannibals. His adventures during captivity, which he survived to recount in matter-of-fact detail, are a parable for cultural anthropology and modern individuals.

As a helpless captive of the Tupinambá, a Brazilian Indian tribe, Hans was obliged to watch cannibalistic execution rites and to live in constant danger of being eaten, a fate intended for him by his captors. When they first took him to their village, he was forced to announce himself to the women in their tongue: "I your food have come." His two proprietary captors presented him as a trophy gift to their mother's brother, who had recently given one of them a captive of his own. The executioner of a captive received much renown and honor. Not only did he put on the feast at which the roasted captive was the principal delicacy, but he also received a new name. This was comparable to a new rank or a medal in Western society (see Chapter 10).

But Hans was spared. His master never received that new name, for two reasons, one of which Hans understood and manipulated from the outset, the other of which he only dimly comprehended and scarcely exploited at all. First, realizing that these Indians had many blood-revenge scores to settle with the Portuguese, Hans declared that he was a German, a "friend of the French." The Indians were allied with French explorers and traders against the Portuguese colonists. Staden's claim that he was not Portuguese was supported by the fact that he had a red beard, which was uncommon for a Portuguese. The Indians were uncertain about his claim and decided to consult with a French trader. When Staden was unable to reply to him in the French language, the trader first dismissed him as an impostor; but then, months later, he claimed Hans as a German ally. The Indians ultimately ransomed Hans to a French trading vessel, but only after a fortunate series of events.

Hans praying and gazing at the moon. Note the palizaded Tupinambá village with its longhouses.

Hans had a habit of crying out for God's comfort and aid. When he was mocked and reviled in fierce celebrations, he would recite Psalms; when he was required to sing by his captors, he would sing German hymns. These were natural ritual actions for a Christian in mortal danger. At one moonlight gathering of village notables, Hans was questioned about his staring at the full moon. He idly replied that the moon "was wrath" with the Indians for planning to eat him.

Subsequently, when Hans's master and others in his family fell deathly ill (probably from a European disease to which this unexposed American Indian population had no resistance), the master and several of his friends had dreams about Hans. Because of their belief in dreams, they begged Hans to cure the sick. The amiable young German sincerely agreed to pray to God for them, laying his hands upon the heads of the sick. In addition, he insisted that if they were cured, they should spare his life. The master's mother and several of his children died, but the master survived, and in return Hans was spared. The Indians cast him in the role of a curer/prophet (medicine man or shaman) and spared him for the benefit of his "magical powers."

Forced to live up to his new role, Hans was taken along on warfare campaigns, in which many enemies were captured and eaten. He was expected to predict battles, and he did so with accuracy. Indian expectations were reinforced by a large straw cross that Hans constructed in his hut for his prayers. When a neighbor tore up the cross in order to use it to polish charms, he scolded her angrily. The Indians connected Hans's anger with heavy rains that threatened to ruin their newly planted gardens and begged Hans to cease being angry and to make the rains stop.

Hans tells us that the Indian shamans had rattles in which spirits resided that craved the blood of captives and that these rattles were used in preparing and predicting the course of battles. Yet Hans never understood that he himself was seen as a shaman who, instead of guarding a rattle, was the custodian of a powerful cross.

(Left) Hans praying for the sick. Note the dead being buried. These Indians were experiencing an epidemic of a European disease. (Right) Hans praying in front of his cross. The Indians thought this to be the action of a shaman/curer.

EUROPE'S AGE OF DISCOVERY AND SPONTANEOUS ETHNOGRAPHIES

Hans Staden's straightforward account of his captivity is one of the classic untutored ethnographies (*ethnos* is Greek for "people"). His adventures belong to Europe's **Age of Discovery** (ca. A.D. 1415–1600), during which Europeans proved beyond a doubt the global shape of the world—circumnavigating it, making maps and charts of all its islands and dry land, and cataloguing its peoples. The known world of the ancients had been limited to the land masses of Eurasia and the northern and eastern reaches of Africa. Europeans had been aware of the civilized centers of India and China, and they recounted legends of a lost Christian kingdom in Africa. And they were all too aware of the tribes of central Asia, who had often invaded Europe and whose yoke the Great Russians had only lately thrown off.

For western Europeans, the principal known "Other" was the Muslim: Arab, Berber, Turk, even Persian. Europeans shared the Mediterranean with these people and had competed with them for control of the holy places during the Crusades. The best-organized Muslim empire, the Ottoman Turks, brought down the eastern Roman Empire in 1453 by taking Constantinople, or Byzantium. Until that time, Constantinople, the second Rome, had been the center of the Christian world. For the Far East, the fabled city of Byzantium stood for all Christendom. In addition, it was through Byzantine eyes that Westerners knew of Asia. Indeed, the dual world of Christendom and Islam formed a single **central civilization** united by opposition to each other's version of monotheistic religion, rivalry over sacred sites, and trade (Wilkinson, 1987).

Beyond Europe was a curtain of foreigners the West could trade with but not pass through—Byzantines, Turks, Tartar nomads, and Muslim Arabs. But beginning in 1415, the ships of Portugal set sail along the coast of Africa, and the mariner's compass was perfected. In 1488 Bartholomeu Dias rounded the Cape of Good Hope, and in 1498 Vasco da Gama reached India by that route. Thus, the Arab world was bypassed. The coasts of black Africa were chartered, and many people whose existence had been only dimly suspected were encountered.

In 1492 Granada, the last Muslim kingdom in western Europe, fell to the Christian monarchs Ferdinand and Isabella, and Christopher Columbus discovered the New World of Nordic legend, not in the Arctic wastes of icy Greenland, but in green Caribbean lushness. When Europeans and American Indians encountered each other, the surprise was mutual.

But the participants, in the Americas and in Africa simultaneously, quickly comprehended the situation, and all had customary patterned ways for dealing with strangers. Initial communication between the literate, technologically powerful Europeans and even the most primitive natives proved quite easy. That the "savages" were true human beings and not humanlike animals was most palpably conveyed when European men readily desired and quickly courted the exotic women. In biology, mating between distant populations is taken as evidence for their belonging to a single species in spite of outward physical differences. It is probable that mixed offspring of the several continents were born almost immediately after contact.

True spoken languages, a unique property of human beings everywhere and not possessed by other animals, conform to a basic plan or structure such that they can be learned by any human being with varying effort. Adults may have difficulty reproducing the sounds of a strange tongue, but with surprising ease they can make themselves understood. Hans Staden never seemed to have any real difficulty in communicating with his fierce hosts.

Our essential humanity as a single species—capable of mating, producing offspring, and speaking languages that can be learned by everyone—was everywhere quickly established during the Age of Discovery. But the pressing diplomatic questions arose of whether there would be peace or war, trade or plunder. Trade was remarkably easy to establish because all peoples have safe ways to make exchanges, even with those who are otherwise hostile. In the course of Staden's captivity, for example, a Portuguese ship traded with his captors during a temporary truce by leaving articles untended on neutral ground for pickups and exchanges. Anthropologists call this custom "silent trade." War, with trade goods and slaves as booty, often resulted when Europeans were drawn into the feuds of the discovered peoples. Staden's captors regularly raided other Indians, although they spoke the same language, because the others had allied with the Portuguese against them.

Complex questions of colonization concerning conquest by direct or indirect rule and religious conversion were answered differently over the 500 years of Western colonialism in different climes and among different peoples. But note that in the sixteenth century, Europeans believed that they had the divine right to conquer newly discovered peoples in order to convert them to Christianity. Muslims had long the same belief in *their* divine right to conquer. Muslims would officially only tolerate the other "Peoples of the Book," Jews and Christians. (Christians would not tolerate Muslims, however. When Ferdinand and Isabella completed the reconquest of Spain in 1492, they began to expel those Muslims who would not adopt the Catholic faith.)

Later, in the eighteenth and nineteenth centuries, after decades of bloody wars of religion, Europeans found legal bases for religious toleration of Catholics and Protestants at home. They then justified their continued conquest and colonization of foreign dominions by claiming to spread "civilization," rather than the true faith. The British, Dutch, and French empires of this epoch differed, but they all produced "cultural conversion" among the educated native elite that was to arise in the colonial era. It is only now, in an age of new nations and decolonization, that the political, if not the economic, aspects of trade, plunder, conquest, colonization, and conversion are being overcome.

Back in the period of discovery and colonization, the actions of the Europeans were based on their material interests and their beliefs, but in the process the modern discipline of anthropology, the science of humanity, was born. A primary task of that discipline is to describe other peoples in a written text we call an **ethnography**. Ethnography gives us the chance to study and compare **culture,** that complex of behavior and beliefs we learn from being members of our groups.

Spontaneous ethnographies—observations and descriptions of exotic peoples done by "laypersons" such as Hans Staden—were and are a valuable source of information. To judge their accuracy, we compare the accounts against each other, against available archaeological information, and against the accounts of today's surviving peoples. The hope is that the writer's interpretations do not get in the way of reporting the facts. That is why Hans Staden's narrative is a classic: He had no theory to prove but simply wanted to tell his yarn—and he could have imagined no better tale. In his case, truth was certainly stranger than fiction.

INTERPRETATION OF ETHNOGRAPHIC FACTS

Interpreting strange facts about human beings is a scientific task. It requires an accumulation of ethnographic knowledge, careful comparisons, and a carefully constructed framework for the comparisons. How useful would it be, for example, to compare the cannibalism of the Tupinambá with the human sacrifice and cannibalism of the highly civilized Aztecs of highland Mexico? A more cogent comparison could be made with the cannibals of the tropical forest in the South Seas, whose social structure, environment, and warfare patterns resemble those of the Tupinambá.

While adventurers and travelers compiled the facts, rational philosophers pondered them. The French essayist Michel Eyquem de Montaigne kept a

Tupinambá cooking and eating victims.

simple traveler at his chateau for some time to learn of the Tupinambá, among whom the man had dwelled for ten years as a trader. Several Tupinambá had also been brought in full regalia and feathered headdress to the court of Catherine de Medici in Paris, where they were put on view in a human zoo. In 1580, Montaigne published the first edition of his essays in France. In his essay "On Cannibalism," he interpreted Tupinambá customs by close inspection of the facts and by comparison with European customs. On the specific question of cannibalism, he concluded that the custom arose, not from hunger or a need of food, but from motives of pure revenge and a desire to attain complete victory over the enemy:

They demand of their prisoners no other ransom than the confession and acknowledgement of being vanquished; but there is not one found, in a whole century, who will not rather choose death than either by word or look to abate a single point from the grandeur of an invincible courage. There is not a man among them who would not rather be killed and eaten than so much as request that he may not. They treat them with all liberality in order that their lives may be so much the dearer to them; and they commonly entertain them with menaces of their approaching death, of the torments they are to suffer, of the preparations being made for the purpose, of the cutting up of their limbs, and of the feast that is to be made at their expense. All this is done with no other aim but to extort some weak or submissive word from them or to fill them with a desire to run away, that they may obtain the advantage of having terrified them and shaken their constancy. For indeed, if rightly taken, it is in this point only that true victory consists.

Montaigne also listed the horrors of execution and torture in sixteenth-century Europe, and his second conclusion is comparative:

We may then call these people barbarians in respect to the rules of reason, but not in respect to ourselves, who surpass them in all sorts of barbarity.

As a background or general framework for these interpretations, Montaigne advanced an image of the Tupinambá as being in a state of nature comparable to the original golden age envisioned by the ancient Greeks or the Eden described in the Judeo-Christian tradition. For this image of the "noble savage," Montaigne did not recite ethnographic facts, as he did in his argument on cannibalism. Instead, he waxed rhetorical:

These nations, then, seem to me to be so far barbarous as they have received very little fashioning from human wit, and are still very near to their original simplicity. The laws of Nature govern them still, very little debased with any mixture of ours; but they are in such a state of purity that . . . it seems to me that what we now actually see in those nations does not only surpass all the pictures with which the poets have adorned the golden age . . . but even the conceptions and the very desire of philosophy. . . . This is a nation . . . wherein there is no manner of traffic, no knowledge of letters, no science of numbers, no name of magistrate or political superiority, no use of services, no riches or poverty, no contracts, no successions, no partitions of property, no employments but those of leisure, no respect of kinship save the common ties, no clothing, no agriculture, no metal, no use of corn or wine. The very words that signify lying, treachery, dissimulation, avarice, envy, detraction, pardon, never heard of. How far distant from this perfection would [Plato] find the republic of his imagination: "mortals fresh from the Gods."

ETHNOCENTRISM

There is much to admire, even today, in the interpretive essay "On Cannibalism," although our evidence concerning the Tupinambá is more extensive than Montaigne's, as are our comparative data. Montaigne's contention that Tupinambá cannibalism was only an elaboration of the expression of victory remains a plausible explanation. (We shall refer to it again in the discussion of tribal warfare in Chapter 10.) Yet, anthropologists must be much more careful concerning the acceptance of his ideas on a golden age or an Eden. We can assume that the social state of protohuman beings was indeed a state of nature. We have the authority of the archaeological record to go on now. But when we look at primitive peoples today, we can seriously question whether they lack all the achievements that Montaigne lists. If not, what substitutes do we find? What roles do these inventions—technology, kinship, laws, and government—play in human behavior? We cannot be content with an inherited image of a golden age; we must examine the evidence as we find it.

By using a concept from his Western intellectual background and applying it playfully to the Tupinambá evidence, Montaigne came close to demonstrating an **ethnocentric** bias—that is, to seeing another people in terms of one's own people and tradition. It is a bias that has by no means been overcome today. Western observers may read ethnographic facts to suit their fancy, take them out of context, fit them into preconceived schemes, or use them as propaganda for religious or political views.

Indeed, one contemporary anthropologist, W. Arens (1980), has challenged *all* spontaneous ethnographic accounts of cannibalism, putting them down to tall tales designed to denigrate the people reported. On the contrary, I find Hans Staden's account, at least, perfectly credible. Arens has challenged the facts. But his interpretive reading of the old source is based on the particular worldview of the European liberal, who thinks of human beings as inherently perfectible, and hence incapable of such barbaric acts. One has only to read the history of the twentieth century, alas, to know that as a species we are very imperfect, as evidenced in our warlike behavior toward each other.

To understand the dangers of ethnocentrism, consider the early egregious example of Friar Bernardino de Sahagún, a pioneer anthropological field worker. He compiled a magnificent document of many volumes, the Florentine Codex, during the mid-1500s in Mexico City, where the good friar ran a school for young Aztec noblemen. Sahagún collected a tremendous amount of information about the conquered Aztec civilization. At the same time, however, he was actively engaged in the conversion of the Aztecs to Christianity. His bias therefore could not have been plainer or more honestly stated.

Human Sacrifice Among the Aztecs

Sahagún learned the Aztec Nahuatl language, and he took down a tremendous amount of information in that tongue, much of it by dictation. One of the principal deities that the Aztecs worshiped was Tezcatlipoca (Smoking Mirror). Sahagún listed him in his "Book of the Gods":

> Tezcatlipoca: He was considered a true god, whose abode was everywhere—in the land of the dead, on earth, and in heaven. When he walked on the earth he brought vice and sin. He introduced anguish and affliction.

He brought discord among people, wherefore he was called "the enemy on two sides." All evils which came to men, all he created, brought down, afflicting men and dividing them.

And sometimes he bestowed riches—wealth, heroism, valor, position of dignity, rulership, nobility, honor.

Sahagún described the Aztec calendar, which divided the year into eighteen periods of twenty days, each one dedicated especially to some deity or deities. During each period, or month, a major festival took place in the Aztec capital in honor of particular deities. Sahagún describes these festivals in some detail, including the devotions of Smoking Mirror, or Tezcatlipoca, in his "Book of Ceremonies."

During a festival, it was the Aztec custom for some exemplary person from among themselves to impersonate the god. This person was considered very fortunate, for only the perfect were picked. The chosen individuals were invariably sacrificed, however, to the god they impersonated. The male who impersonated a god was conducted up the steps of a pyramid to the summit, where he was seized by five priests and held down on the high altar in full view of the multitude. The high priest then plunged an obsidian knife into the impersonator's chest, thrust his hands into the opening, tore out the beating heart, placed it on the altar, and rolled the body down the steps. The female who impersonated a goddess was slain differently. Generally, she would walk through a company of priestesses singing and throwing flowers before her while a priest-executioner would approach stealthily from behind and suddenly decapitate her. Then the victim would be flayed, the skin removed from the corpse; an aged priestess would then impersonate the impersonator by wearing the flayed skin during the rest of the festival.

Being chosen to "become" a god was rather like winning a beauty contest today. Each year's title holder, such as Miss America, is greatly honored as a perfect example of one type of femininity. We display her and parade her, and at the end of the year, we "do away" with her by having her recognize her successor. But of course we do not physically sacrifice her.

Needless to say, Sahagún, like all Western listeners, was appalled to hear of the Aztecs' sacrificial goings-on, which were very important in the order of things in Tenochtitlán, the capital. Toxcatl, the fifth period, or month, was partly devoted to the worship of Smoking Mirror. Sahagún observed that this was the "principal festival of all. It was like Easter and came very close to the Christian Easter, perhaps a few days later."

For Toxcatl, an impersonator of Smoking Mirror was chosen—a young man representing the flower of Aztec youth, a perfect physical being without blemish. The newly chosen youth-god was treated as Tezcatlipoca for one year. When he went out dressed in ceremonial robes with flowers in his hand and attended by special companions, the people would prostrate themselves at his feet. For the twenty-day period before his festival, he was given four lovely maidens as consorts; and for the last five days he was dined at banquets at the palace.

Finally, he was taken to his pyramid, and his wives left him. As he ascended each step of the pyramid, he broke one of the flutes he had played during his holy year, one for each step. At the top, he was seized and sacrificed like any other victim, and his head was later impaled on a special pole below. Immediately after, a priest wearing the victim's skin impersonated the sacrificed youth, and a new youth was selected. Although each springtime a god sacrificed himself for fertility, good crops, and the common good, a new god took his place. The god never really died.

Sahagún's Interpretation

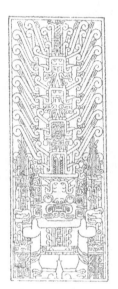

To Sahagún, as to many of us today, these rites were fascinating in themselves. But for the friar they held a peculiar appeal because of the frightful coincidence with the Christian Easter. Indeed, the rites seemed like nothing so much as a cruel parody on the Passion of Jesus Christ: the wining and dining, the being treated as a god (if not a king) by the multitude, the sacrificial death, and finally the reappearance of the god (in the person of another youth).

To explain these rites, he resorted to the wider explanation of idolatry already adopted by the church and to a particular explanation of this horrifying passion play. His "Book of the Gods," written in the Nahuatl language, is a free adaptation of the apocryphal biblical Book of Wisdom (written in Greek by Jews in Alexandria during the second and first centuries B.C. as a reaction against Greek and Egyptian paganism). Here is a passage that shows the flavor of Sahagún's refutation:

> The people here on earth who know not God, who esteem Him not, are only vain and worthless. For if men in their hearts and understanding knew God's creations, they had known God. Because they esteem and know creatures, they had known that He exists, that He is the Creator, the Creator of man—God, who is not seen.
>
> And these did not so; they took not example of God's creations. Thus they acknowledged [God's creatures] as their gods, their lords. . . .
>
> They worshipped as gods the fire, the water, the wind, the sun, the moon, the stars. These things they worshipped, saying to them:
>
> Verily, you are the creators, you guide us, you rule us. Verily, you order things, you protect things.
>
> (A) These, the blind, the mad, were idolators. Greatly they honored God's creatures.
>
> (B) As if they had wondered greatly because some of God's creatures are strong, they had considered God, their Creator, even stronger.

To Sahagún, this was the cardinal error of idolatry in Christian doctrine. Who but a devil would have instituted the worship of Tezcatlipoca as a mockery of the Passion of Jesus Christ, the true God-made man? Sahagún thundered in his refutation: "Tezcatlipoca is no god. As the word of God stateth, *Omnes dii gentium demonia*, that is to say, 'All whom the idolators worship as idols are devils, demons, evil spirits.'"

> This evil Tezcatlipoca, we know, is Lucifer himself, the great devil who there in heaven, even in the beginning, incited war, hatred, and sin. From there he was cast out, and he fell.
>
> And he walketh upon the earth deluding and misleading people. . . . He, this Tezcatlipoca [is] a great devil. The ancients adored him as a god, and they celebrated his feast Toxcatl. And they slew him who was his likeness, whom they named Titlacauan.
>
> So much were the ancients crazed.

CONTINUING PROBLEMS

The data Sahagún recorded were then only living memories. Ethnographical facts, or in Sahagún's case ethnohistorical facts, are subject to many different theoretical interpretations when they are put into an uncritical ethnocentric framework. In the examples cited, we have gone from "mortals fresh from the Gods" (Montaigne) to mortals deluded by Satan (Sahagún)—from the noble savage to the afflicted idolator. The distorted interpretations of Montaigne and Sahagún arose from Western authority, or popular belief. Montaigne relied too much on Greek philosophers, and Sahagún relied on popular medieval Christian demonology; but in neither case was there much dispute about the facts concerning the simplicity of Tupinambá social life and the festival of Toxcatl.

When Montaigne endeavored to interpret the repellent custom of cannibalism, however, he did liberate himself from his ethnocentric bias; his explanation is based on the evidence alone rather than on any traditional Western authority. In contrast, for his interpretation of the equally repellent cult of Smoking Mirror, Sahagún simply injected the Western belief in Satan.

Efforts like Montaigne's—that is, interpretations based solely on the evidence—are the central theoretical tasks of anthropology. This approach is still not universally accepted in popular Western culture, however. Demonology has been supplanted today by science fiction, and it is not Lucifer but extraterrestrial intelligence that is taken to walk abroad among exotic or past peoples to deceive them.

One popular account, which I will not mention by name so as not to give it any more unmerited publicity, has gathered widely separated archaeological facts to support an argument that extraplanetary visitors instituted the polytheistic cults of early civilizations. This is simply a latter-day ethnocentrism, a speculative scientific belief in rational life on other planets being applied to anthropological facts. The author's ethnocentrism, in contrast to that of good Friar Sahagún, is reinforced not by the desire to implement religious conversions but by the desire for commercial gain. The market has supplanted the church as a central cultural force in Western culture.

Modern anthropologists are now vastly better trained not only to gather facts but to interpret them in the light of theory and to know what facts to look for. A modern anthropologist reading Staden's account sees at once that Staden was cast in the role of a curer/prophet, yet he was scarcely aware of that. But the keen observation and faithful description he provided remain key activities in anthropology still.

All of us, not only anthropologists, have some cross-cultural experience as we travel abroad or meet fellow citizens of different cultures at home. Our cross-cultural experience also extends through the generations, which change fashions and beliefs with bewildering rapidity but predictable regularity. Educational systems teach us facts our parents never knew, facts that will be obsolete when our children go to school. Added to culture shock, which is the disorientation brought on by being plunged into the midst of new people, is future shock, the disorientation caused by the arrival of the unexpected ahead of schedule.

In the mid-1500s Staden kept his head in more ways than one. Going into the twenty-first century all of us are faced with a life, like Staden's, as a strange voyage. We, too, must keep our heads as we deal with people of other cultures and with strangers of the future, our grandchildren. And because of the contributions of both spontaneous ethnographers and their scientific successors, we may encounter all these strangers with better information and better ways to understand them. To that task, the cultivation of a greater awareness of humanity, this book is dedicated.

SUGGESTED READINGS

De Waal Malefijt, Annemarie. *Images of Man: A History of Anthropological Thought*. New York: Knopf, 1974. A clear, concise guide to the history of anthropology. Chapters 1 through 6 deal with the beginnings of anthropological thought, born in cross-cultural experiences.

Diaz Del Castillo, Bernal. *The Discovery and Conquest of Mexico, 1517-1521*. Translated by A. P. Maudsley. New York: Grove Press, 1958. The eyewitness accounts of a companion of Cortés, written years later in the 1500s. Adventures and culture shock; an epic.

Hall, Edward T. *The Hidden Dimension*. Garden City, N.Y.: Doubleday/Anchor, 1969. A lively introduction to the concept of culture as embodied in the differing human uses of space from culture to culture.

Hall, Edward T., and Mildred Reed Hall. *Understanding Cultural Differences: Germans, French and Americans*. Yarmouth, Me.: Intercultural Press, 1990. A splendid introduc-

tion to the concept of culture, using contemporary life. Also suitable for Part V of this
book.

Todorov, Tzvetan. *The Conquest of America: The Question of the Other*. Richard Howard,
trans. New York: Harper Torchbooks, 1987. A disquieting look at the first decades of
the Spanish conquest by a humanist skilled in interpreting texts—Columbus's letters,
for example.

GLOSSARY

central civilization The ever-expanding core of the known world into which diverse
cultures have been absorbed over the course of civilized history—that is, from 4000
B.C. to the present. Thus, in 1415 both European Christians and Middle Eastern
Muslims belonged to one central civilization, marked by their strong opposition to
each other. The Muslims also confined the Europeans to Europe until they began
to find the way to sail around them in 1415.

culture That complex whole of behaviors, including language, beliefs, manners, and
customs, that we learn by being born and raised in our groups or that we learn by
being incorporated into new groups in the course of a lifetime.

ethnocentrism The disposition to judge and even to perceive another culture by the
standards, values, and understandings of one's own culture.

ethnography The written description of a group, from *ethnos* or "people." Writing
ethnography is the basic activity of cultural anthropologists.

Europe's Age of Discovery The historical era dating roughly from A.D. 1415 to
1600, during which Europeans explored and discovered all the lands of the earth.
During the latter part of this era bloody wars of religion between Catholics and
Protestants also broke out in Europe.

spontaneous ethnographies Accounts of exotic groups written by untrained persons
who happen to observe them. " laypersons "

An Overview of Cultural Anthropology:

A Succession of Cultures and Communities

2

CULTURAL ANTHROPOLOGY AS NATURAL HISTORY

THE STUDY OF COMMUNITIES

THE PRIMATE TROOP: CHIMPANZEES

THE HUMAN BAND

TRIBAL COMMUNITIES

TRADITIONAL CIVILIZATIONS

MODERN METROPOLITAN CIVILIZATION

*A*s we saw in Chapter 1, anthropology originated in the encounter of Europeans, the representatives of expanding central civilization, with previously unknown peoples. The task of observing and describing other peoples accurately and interpreting observed facts scientifically grew into the discipline of anthropology. Most broadly, **anthropology** is the study of all human beings at all times and in all places. In its widest intellectual framework, anthropology is concerned with the emergence of human beings as a distinct biological species, *Homo sapiens sapiens*, and our relationship with extinct and living species.

All anthropologists look at human beings as biological creatures, a distinct species of primate with a set of "species-specific" capabilities and properties, evident from the origin of the species in bands of hunters and gatherers. The peculiar character of *Homo sapiens* has been that the major evolutionary features of our development and change so far have been biological only in the size and structure of our brains, and social and cultural, evident outside the body in our learned behavior—that is, our cultures.

As it has grown as a discipline, anthropology has differentiated into subfields, each linked with other disciplines (see Figure 2.1). The study of all human languages merged with philology of the languages of the Old World to form the science of *linguistics*. The study of our emergence as a separate primate species and of the range of our physical variations in relation to observable body types and genetics has separated into *physical anthropology*. This subdiscipline overlaps with biology and indeed with some practitioners is more human biology than anthropology. The study of human prehistory through the method of scientific excavation has given rise to *archaeology*, the "study of beginnings." **Cultural anthropology,** while drawing on the other subdisciplines, has been concerned with the discovery and description of all living peoples. Increasingly, cultural anthropology has developed its own subdiscipline of *applied anthropology*, the practice of anthropological methods brought to bear to solve some contemporary human problem. Related, developing subfields include *medical anthropology*, the study of health prac-

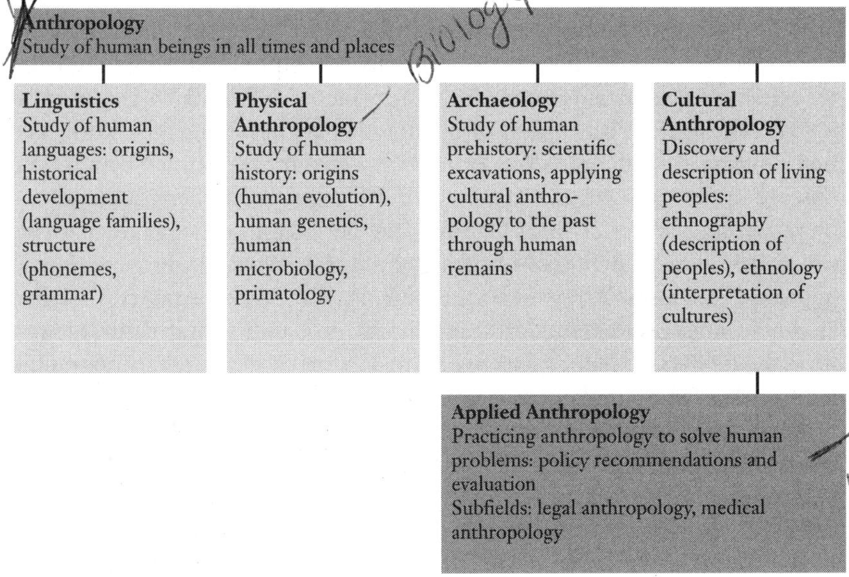

Test 2

Anthropology Study of human beings in all times and places			
Linguistics Study of human languages: origins, historical development (language families), structure (phonemes, grammar)	**Physical Anthropology** Study of human history: origins (human evolution), human genetics, human microbiology, primatology	**Archaeology** Study of human prehistory: scientific excavations, applying cultural anthropology to the past through human remains	**Cultural Anthropology** Discovery and description of living peoples: ethnography (description of peoples), ethnology (interpretation of cultures)

Biology

Applied Anthropology
Practicing anthropology to solve human problems: policy recommendations and evaluation
Subfields: legal anthropology, medical anthropology

— medical & legal anthro too.

Figure 2.1 Anthropology and its subfields.

tices in a cross-cultural perspective, and *legal anthropology*, the study of law and dispute resolution among human beings at all times and places.

Anthropology shares much of the subject matter and many of the intellectual concerns of the other social sciences, primarily because each of its sibling disciplines focuses on a single human institution—usually in modern society—while anthropologists study that same institutional behavior as part of the total complex of human behavior everywhere at all times. Moreover, since we study all human beings in all times and places, we watch each institution *emerge*, or unfold, out of earlier prototypes.

Sociology is the study of groups. *Economics* is the study of production, exchange, and consumption, based on the assumption that human beings seek to maximize profit, or "utility." Anthropologists study the same things but do not necessarily share that assumption of utility with economists. *Political science* is the study of human leadership and the allocation of scarce resources. *Psychology* is the study of the individual. Each of these disciplines is, like anthropology, represented in university social science departments. Departments of *religion*, often in schools of theology, study human rituals and beliefs, usually in the organized religions, also known as the "great world religions." Finally *jurisprudence*, the study of law and justice, is taught in professional schools of law.

Because anthropology is holistic, based on the ethnographies or descriptions of the entire way of life of particular groups, we share these areas of study with the other disciplines, but we look at each in the whole context of particular communities, as we discuss in this chapter.

CULTURAL ANTHROPOLOGY AS NATURAL HISTORY

The scientific method that most distinguishes cultural anthropology from the other social sciences is the natural history method. Essentially, this method is founded on the observation of phenomena as they occur in nature. We first isolate a field of interacting organisms—in our case, human beings. We observe their interrelations. We control and cross-check these observations by repeating them over many natural time periods. In this way, by patient, repetitive charting and cross-checking of natural events, we distinguish patterns and processes. These in turn enable us, with some certainty, to arrive at conclusions—statements of order, limits, probability, and natural law—from the field itself, seen as part of nature. Chapter 3 examines ethnographic field work as an example of the natural history method.

In philosophy natural history is an example of **induction**—that is, reasoning from a set of observations to arrive at general principles. Thus, for anthropology the facts always come first, and the principles—inferred from the facts—come second. Cultural anthropology always goes from the particular to the general. Moreover, the principles (conclusions, statements of order or "law") vary according to the framework shaping any particular set of facts. The principles, for example, that governed our emergence as a species (*Homo sapiens* as distinct from the now extinct *Homo erectus*) were primarily those of adaptive value of physical traits (speech and a larger brain case) in relation to a new ecological niche, hunting and gathering. As another example, the transition from bands to the tribal level of sociocultural organization reflected the pressures of human populations that had filled that niche over the entire world. Principles shift their level of generality as the focus or spotlight on particular sets of facts shifts.

In its widest framework, evolution proceeds from the situational ability of apparently random events, such as genetic mutations or behavioral patterns, to solve some problem, such as the movement of a group of living beings into a new habitat. The result is ever more complex biological and social "designs." Living systems exhibit, over time, population growth, escalation in scale, and increasing specialization of functional subparts. All living systems, whether a single biological organism or a larger social group, are self-regulating, responding to exterior conditions in the environment from which they must derive and transform matter, energy, and momentum in the process of reproducing both the species and the group. They also engage in a characteristic array of activities or actions to process that matter and energy, which are propelled by momentum. These activities form cycles, in the sense that they characteristically go through a "round" and start over again with the same sequence of behaviors.

Living species group themselves into "breeding populations," or **communities.** Their characteristic activities also form natural, observable divisions in their behavior, which are the basis for what we call **institutions,** or sets of more or less discrete activities that, taken together, solve some problem and perform some function for the benefit of the individual and the group. Thus, the cluster of activities that surround a chimpanzee mother's nurturing and raising of her infants and juveniles (nursing, grooming, carrying, leading, and playing on the mother's part; suckling, playing, and following on the offspring's) form a coherent social complex of activities that we call the "mother-offspring family." One way to look at human social and cultural evolution is through the successive emergence, or "factoring out," of human institutions. That is, when an institution has fully emerged, human beings have given it a name and attached names or labels to the "roles" one must play in them. Thus, the human "family" has the roles of "mother" and "son" or "daughter," as well as "husband" and "father," two roles not present in the chimpanzee family prototype.

THE STUDY OF COMMUNITIES

Anthropology differs from its sister disciplines because it includes human biology. Thus we see all human individuals as members of natural groups: living, breeding populations we call *communities*. For anthropology community is the minimum social field necessary for the survival of the group and the transmission of its culture. *Community* for us, then, is a set of human beings in contact with each other through "networks." That is, each person does not necessarily know everyone else, but each is linked to everyone else through others. Communities share space, or territory, but community populations are usually dispersed over space and come together on regular schedules, either during the solar year or during a person's typical lifetime, especially for the crises of coming of age, getting married, or death. Indeed, one of our broadest general principles is that community, so defined, exists for all stages of human cultural and social transformations.

Anthropologists have classified many community "fields" and arranged them in a typology that ranges from simple to complex. Each type is more densely populated and complexly organized, with a wider array of more fully specialized and full-time institutions. Starting with the hunting-and-gathering human band, human behaviors have differentiated themselves into successively more distinct and specialized institutions. Human bands originated out of earlier groups (the communities of *Homo erectus*), which in turn emerged out of the primate troop.

Human community fields form the sequence of band, tribe, archaic urban civilizations (open or "green" cities and closed or nucleated cities with associated peasant hamlets and villages), and the modern metropolitan region (see Figure 2.2). Starting with and including the primate troop, this sequence comprises the organization of this book. We shall take up each in turn, both for itself but also in relation to the emergence of the institutions that are the particular subject matter of the other social sciences.

In the rest of this chapter we shall briefly survey and sketch the progression of community fields not only to prepare you for the rest of the book but also to discuss these communities in relation to the emergence of the increasingly specialized human institutions, which can develop from weakly differentiated prototypes existing in each previous "stage" of social evolution. Prototypes for these institutions exist in those primates truly in a "state of nature": chimpanzees, the apes most closely related to humans.

THE PRIMATE TROOP: CHIMPANZEES

Figure 2.3 provides a summary listing of those areas of chimpanzee behavior that seem prototypical for human institutions. Presumably these behaviors were shared by our long-extinct common ancestors some 5 million years ago. Chimpanzees lack speech, yet they are highly communicative creatures. They communicate with each other by means of gesture and movement ("body language"), touch, smell, vocalizations, and richest of all perhaps, a wide array of facial expressions. Human beings find it easy to understand the communications of most other mammals—we know when our dog is threatening to bite us or is only playing at biting us, for example—but especially so with chimpanzees, since their bodies, vocal calls, and faces so closely resemble our own.

Chimpanzees are highly organized socially. Briefly, their "sociology" is as follows. They live in groups, each with its own wide range of land. Their

Figure 2.2 The progression of communities.

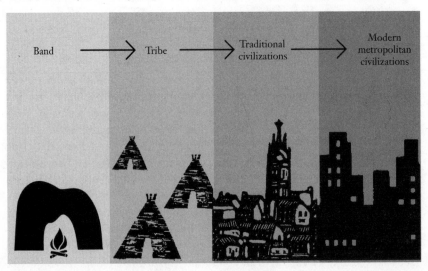

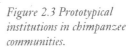

Politics
Adult males in dominance hierarchies defend against predators, patrol community boundaries; can wage "war" against neighboring groups; internally, they enforce order among juveniles.

Communication
Vocalizations, body and facial gestures. No speech.

Economics
Foraging; no systematic sharing or exchanging of food or tools ("goods"). Hunting almost a routine source of food to be shared.

Chimpanzees
Community form: "Open," wide-ranging troop. Migration of solitary young adult females from home troop to another. Troops can split into two (fission) and compete for territory.

Learning
Unable to survive unless reared in group. Without speech, collective memory resides in life experience of oldsters, who lead others to food and water sources.

Technology
Capable of making and using tools from materials at hand (except for nest building, not a routine activity).

Ritual
Dominance displays before and after critical events; mutual grooming at times of satisfaction or stress.

Sociology
Mother-offspring-sibling units, juvenile play groups, bachelor groups of adult males. Adult male dominance hierarchies; adult female dominance hierarchies.

CHIMPS have cultures— CHIMPS in Gardi & Kenya develop diff. ways of doing things (tools, etc.)

Figure 2.3 Prototypical institutions in chimpanzee communities.

27

habitat spreads across the warm tropical forests of central Africa, but that habitat is being increasingly encroached upon by human beings. The overall chimpanzee troop is a large, loosely tied group of up to fifty or more individuals, seldom if ever coming together at one place but more commonly dispersed over the landscape. Yet all animals within the group know all the others and can assume positions in relation to each other regulated by dominance whenever they meet.

Many primate species are organized by a **dominance hierarchy,** an array of adults who stand in a relations of dominance and subordination to each other in rough linear ranking. The more dominant animal displaces the less dominant one in space and has first access to a resource, such as food. Among chimpanzees there are, loosely, separate dominance hierarchies for males and females.

If an adult female is fertile and her offspring survive, she is always to be found with her infant and juvenile offspring, with whom she forms lifelong bonds. In turn these siblings form bonds with each other. Mother-offspring-sibling "families" form. When families come together, juveniles form play groups.

During the course of a day, the individuals of a troop may be scattered in diverse combinations. Solitary adults, male or female, may roam alone, as will the single mother–centered "family groups." Or several of these groups may join up and forage together. Bachelor groups of males—strictly regulated by dominance—may roam together. At times, half or more of the total community of animals may assemble around some attraction—trees of fruit fully ripened, or one or more adult females in their season, the point in the estrous cycle when they are sexually attractive and receptive. (We discuss chimpanzee sexuality in more detail in Chapter 7.)

Like all vertebrates, chimpanzees have the capacity for **ritual,** stereotyped behavior at times of change and crisis that allays anxiety and prepares the organism to act. The elaborate "display" behavior that adults use to establish dominance among themselves can also be used both individually and in a group to dispel anxiety in critical moments—by a single adult male after a tropical rainstorm, for example, or by a group of adult males returning from "patrol." Patroling consists of silent stalking through the overlap area their troop shares with a neighboring troop. Upon returning to their safe core range, the entire group can go into a splendid display directed against nature itself or against some hapless bystanding less dominant individual they may find in their way, a scapegoat for their anxiety. Likewise, chimpanzees spend much time mutually grooming each other, at times of rest and satisfaction (after a heavy meal, for example) or at times of stress and tension, to reassure each other of friendly intentions.

The "economics" of chimpanzee life is of the utmost simplicity. Chimpanzees forage, eating mostly vegetable stuff and fruits, directly off the land. They have the capacity to make tools but do not do so as a daily endeavor. They have the capacity to hunt, and do so frequently at certain seasons of the year. Adult males lead a hunting party, particularly against colubus monkeys. Once they kill their prey, more dominant males may wrest it from the leading hunter, but may then share it by handing the food to less dominant males, females, and young.

The "politics" of chimpanzee life revolves on questions of dominance, especially for the adult males. Adult males protect the others from predators and from enemy chimpanzees. Becoming an *alpha*, or most dominant (number one) male is a reward some chimpanzees spend a lifetime striving for. Dominant males also provide for "justice" and "law and order" by intervening and breaking up fights among juveniles when they get out of hand and cross the line between play and violence.

Chimpanzees grooming.

However, the most interesting thing about chimpanzees from a wider anthropological perspective is the clarity with which their nonhuman cultures have emerged. Different chimpanzee troops have different tool making and using traditions. At Gombe, chimps stick twigs and stems into termite mounds to fish out termites to eat. At another community, in contrast, chimps pound nuts with makeshift wooden tools to break them open. Mothers teach young chimps these traditions by example. Thus distinctive techniques can spread from one community to nearby ones through migrating females.

Moreover, when compared to human communities, we see that community "self-consciousness" has emerged. Troops are clearly defined units in relations of competitive expansion and contraction with neighboring troops. Jane Goodall observed the adult males of one troop make "war," systematically, against the adults of a neighboring troop, hunting each one down and killing him or her. The troop then moved into the annexed territory, only to find themselves in competition for much of it with an expanding troop from the south. We shall study that incident in greater detail in Chapter 10.

Overall, however, of the prototypical behaviors upon which human institutions later crystallize, only the community as master system of social relationships is truly present in the chimpanzee world; the rest are there only in embryo. For example, the mother-offspring unit is only the nucleus of what among human beings is the family. Husband-fathers have yet to join it on a full-time basis.

THE HUMAN BAND

Human beings, *Homo sapiens sapiens*, began to emerge as a species around 200,000 years ago. *Homo sapiens*, as opposed to its hominid predecessors, communicates by means of fully developed speech. All human beings today speak natural languages that are equally good as means of communication. All use tools that, when compared to precursors in the archaeological record, are finely manufactured. The *band* is the simplest known type of human community and presumably represents the form of group life of the earliest *Homo sapiens* (see Figure 2.4). All band peoples are hunters and gatherers. (The reverse is not true; some part-time hunters and gatherers live in tribal communities.) The archaeological evidence shows that human beings moved out in bands over all the world's surface accessible to them on foot, and by 15,000 years ago they seemed to have settled every continent and land mass except Antarctica. In short, they walked out everywhere. Part II of this book examines band cultures and the array of emergent human institutions associated with them.

A band community comprises around fifty to no more than several hundred people grouped in three "levels." The local-level camps consist of several households. These unite on a seasonal basis with other camps for sharing a food or water resource and for ritual. This makes up the second level. On some of the ritual occasions they may well play hosts to visitors from neighboring bands, forming the third and "highest" level.

Ritual among human beings has now emerged as a pattern of behavior defining both individual and group identities. Universally, human beings exhibit the same kinds of rituals. One class of rituals surround changes in the year. These *rites of intensification* get people to change behavior from one season of the year to the next. The other class, *life crisis rites*, help effect changes in individual lifetimes. Both kinds may bring the entire membership of a band together for periods of ritual observance. Such ritual assemblages in fact define the community, not only because the entire group assembles but also because claims may be made for allegiance to neighbors and kin. Many bands also have curing ceremonies, often on a seasonal basis.

Ritual then is a human universal. Band societies, rife with ritual, do not have the fully developed institution of organized religion. There are no full-time priests living from their ritual performance. Even the self-appointed religious experts, or shamans, are only part-time freelance magical curers.

All human beings have kinship and marriage (prime concerns for sociology). Band societies have families and households. They have systems of marriage, with definite ways for all persons to find spouses. The human family everywhere links adult men with adult women and invests the men with rights and duties in the women's offspring. Social paternity, something quite new from the primate prototype, has emerged.

Justice
No formal law code. Disputes decided by public talking ("palavers") or formal patterns of violence, often culminating in duels. One band may raid neighboring band in blood revenge. Violence may end in homicide or flight to another band.

Language
Fully present, true speech. Vocalizations, body and facial gestures of primates still present. No writing. Social dramas and myths recited by campfires.

Politics
"Successful" elders, both males and females, form nucleus of each band. Band membership tied to them through marriage or through offers of asylum to refugees from conflict elsewhere.

The Band
Community form: Three levels of space—local (camps); band proper (assembles at rites); foreign relations (circles of neighboring bands). Membership is "open"; males and females flow through several bands in a lifetime, clustering around influential elders.

Learning
Unable to survive unless reared in group. Must adjust to individual personality differences. Children learn from family, play group, or, if present, age grades.

Economics
Tool makers and users on a daily basis. Hunting and gathering expressed in division of labor by sex. Exchange of food, goods, and services within households, of food, goods, services, and spouses among households. These exchanges cut across bands. No explicit standard of value ("money").

Ritual
Fully developed life crisis rites (generational time) and rites of intensification (seasonal, yearly time). These may provide for assemblages giving form to the band.

Technology
Sophisticated stone points for spears and arrows in hunting; baskets for transporting food; shelters for sleeping; fire.

Sociology
Household consisting of father-husband plus mother-offspring-sibling units. Marriage; social paternity; juvenile play groups. Age grades may be present.

Figure 2.4 Emergent institutional behavior in the band.

Hunters and gatherers have a **division of labor by sex,** as have all human societies until very recent times. That is, men hunt bigger game and women hunt smaller game and gather food from the wilderness. Men and women share their food jointly at hearths. Elementary economics, then, is the sharing and giving of goods, usually within and between household groups.

All band populations are of low density, loose and scattered. Bands are permeable communities. People move from one to another, often fleeing conflict. Leaders are a few key elders who have built up kin and gift-giving ties with others in such a way as to have most of the members of the band tied to them through kinship and indebtedness. The processes of recruiting new members, by marriage or by offering asylum to refugees from conflict in other bands, and of expulsion in conflict form the basis of the elemental political system that ends up putting a few, older individuals in positions of influence and prestige, if not command.

In sum, bands are more complex and usually more populous than the primate troop. Human beings have language, toolkits, fire, regular sources of meat by hunting, and complexes of behavior that have begun to specialize and factor out of the primate repertoire of patterned behavior. At the band level the fully emerged human institutions include speech (people spend a lot of time talking to each other) and technology (people spend a lot of time making and repairing a kit of tools to extend the capacity of the human body). Especially important are the fully emerged institutions of ritual and of marriage and the family, which brings with it the increased efficiency and economic benefits of the division of labor by sex. Only in the modern era, with the rise of industrial labor and corporate bureaucracy, is that division being challenged and perhaps becoming obsolete. (See Chapter 17's discussion of the women's movement.) Indeed, in all known band societies "economy" and "politics" can be described entirely in terms of the family. That is to say, both economic and political behavior is "embedded" in the sociology of the family.

TRIBAL COMMUNITIES

The tribal community can be characterized as a "network of networks." That is, this community form is on a higher scale than that of the human band by having one more level (see Figure 2.5). Bands consist of a number of camps of around twenty individuals, grouped in households, that come together several times a year at certain centers of assemblage. Tribes are, conceptually, several band-type groupings united for common activities of ritual, feasting, and war. These groupings are usually not permanent in the sense of all members remaining in one place all the time.

Tribal societies seem to have appeared in the archaeological record with the late paleolithic in Europe and with the mesolithic thereafter. In the first

Justice
Rudimentary formal
machinery for dispute
resolution: third-party
mediators or adjudication by
tribal councils, with decisions
enforced by ritual
fraternities; blood revenge in
warfare with
neighbor-enemies.

Language
Oral literature
(consisting of
genealogies and
elaborate mythologies)
memorized and recited.
No writing.

Politics
All sorts of devices to
integrate, loosely, local
groups: short-term
feast-alliances, tribal councils,
war chiefs and peace chiefs,
feasting complexes, trading
rings. Powerful persons are
not full-time political
specialists.

Learning
Ritual initiations, age
grades, more elaborate
than in band societies.

The Tribe
Community field:
Consists of a loosely integrated
network of band-level communities.
These range from tightly organized
confederacies lasting many generations to
ephemeral warfare alliances or feasting
(exchange) complexes lasting a single
lifetime or less. At local levels
membership is less permeable than in
band societies. (It is hard to change one's
tribe.) Relations with neighboring
groups, both inside and outside the tribal
network, take place through the
activities of trade and war.

Economics
Subsistence base: hunters and
gatherers with usually rich natural
resources (e.g., bison herds), or
nomadic pastoralists with domestic
herds, or horticulturalists with garden
crops. Big emphasis on balanced
reciprocal exchanges among
allies, competitive exchanges in
feasting among neighbors.
Warfare complexes are
also exchange
systems.

Ritual
Elaborate rites of
intensification to unite group,
involving feasting and
warfare. Shamans as prophets
may lead group into war.

Technology
May be horticulturalists,
gardeners, with digging
sticks and many crops
propagated by seeds or root
cuttings. Canoes, rafts, fish
lines, and harpoons common.
So is ceramics, pottery, but
not universal. May have
domesticated fowl; may have
beasts of burden and other
herd animals.

Sociology
Lineages and clans derived
from kinship, and associations
(diversely called "fraternities"
or "sodalities") derived from
age grades, provide means to
integrate tribal networks and
unite people from different
local communities.

*Figure 2.5 Emergent
institutional behavior at
the level of the tribe.*

33

case big-game hunters were able to congregate in large settlements in Northern Europe some 15,000 years ago. Later, the inhabitable world filled up with human bands, hunters and gatherers having spread over all continents save Antarctica. Then, in the so-called mesolithic period, the combined pressures of population numbers, emerging internal institutions such as Big Men (described in Chapter 11), environmental degradation (such as the extinction of big-game animals from overhunting), and neighboring enemy groups obliged bands to congregate into larger groupings, especially near rich natural food resources, such as rivers with rich fishing located in the midst of rich vegetable resources.

In subsistence, such groups were the first to domesticate plants from among hybrid offspring of plants they gathered, sprouting up as weeds close to settled villages. Thus the great majority of tribal peoples are food producers—that is, horticulturalists who cultivate a wide variety of seed and root crops. Since they were the first people to domesticate animals beyond the hunting dog, they may also be pastoralist herders. A few, such as the tribes of North America's northwest coast, may not be food producers, since rich annual salmon runs in rivers guaranteed subsistence. Likewise, the American Plains Indians were nomadic hunters, wandering on horseback after bison herds. These groups condensed into the higher level of community form without food production. But they are the exceptions.

Collective ritual is more elaborate in tribes than in bands, uniting more people. In addition, tribes may have ritual specialists, or *shamans*—usually self-recruited religious experts who claim direct contact with divine powers and who specialize in curing the sick.

The social forms typical of tribes include the "sodality," or association, that cuts across local groupings and brings men together for purely social purposes or for feasting and war. Kinship likewise may be elaborated in tribal groups to give form to the society through grouping of people by descent into *lineages*—consisting of persons descended in a given line from a known ancestor—or *clans*—consisting of persons descended from a more distant, mythical ancestor. Villages may, for example, belong to a particular lineage.

Conflict at the band level is one mechanism for expelling some members of the community while recruiting outcasts from others. In tribal societies, because of the generally greater population numbers and density, conflict cannot be resolved by flight, by running away from trouble. Rather, conflict crystallizes into "primitive war": warfare in which the aim is not so much conquest as the "score." Warfare serves to unite the group, instilling harmony and consensus in the face of the common enemy. It also helps to space tribes out more evenly in relation to their resources. We examine warfare complexes in Chapter 10.

Tribal politics vary greatly. Leadership may be vested in "Big Men redistributors," men who recruit followers to help put on feasts in which large quantities of goods are given away. The guests at such feasts must reciprocate by giving a counterfeast. The aim of the feasting contest is to give away more than the rival can give back. In tribal politics power can flow back and forth, in Aristotle's term, among the many (the entire group assembled), the few (smaller councils representing the "tribe"), or the one (a single war leader or Big Man feastgiver who for a short time in his life is dictator). We explore competitive feasting and Big Man complexes in Chapter 11.

Politically, tribes are often united by "sodalities": associations, usually of men, drawn from all the subgroups of the community for activities of ritual and war. Tribes are often ruled collectively, by councils, which in turn are presided over by elders, called chiefs. These men often share power with war leaders. Membership in tribal councils may, in some groups such as the Iroquois, be inherited through lineages. We examine tribal politics in Chapter 12.

In sum, politics, competition, economics, play, and ritual are all embedded in a single institution, the tribal structure itself, which serves to form the "network of networks" and which gives form to the much larger and more extensive community territory.

The institution of the state, managed by full-time, specialized leaders who do nothing else and who live from the tribute of the many, has not yet appeared in tribes. Nor has trade yet factored out from family, friendship, or tribal competitive exchanges. There are no full-time merchants, living from exchange alone. Nor are there full-time priests, living from the specialized practice of religion every day of the year at a sacred place. The temple and professional priests, the state and the political elite, the marketplace and professional traders—all emerge in the next form of community: urban civilizations.

TRADITIONAL CIVILIZATIONS (State)

The same processes that obliged human beings to group themselves in semisettled, warring and trading tribal communities also obliged some of them, in historically distinct times and places, to settle down in *cities* and to develop the *state* out of their political behavior. Under pressure to reap new resources from a crowded, often degraded habitat, and reacting to a more complicated internal social structure and to competition from nearby groups, certain horticulturalists developed more intensive gardening in appropriate habitats—always river valleys. Internally, their tribal politics and competitive feasting gave way to priestly rule, followed by military rule and the rise of dynasties. We tell this dramatic story in Chapter 14.

Cities are accompanied by the greater factoring out of the array of human institutions into full-time specialization (see Figure 2.6). Rural, food-producing communities fall into satellite arrangements around urban centers. Two forms of such *traditional civilizations* are possible: one, the *green city*, has decentralized urban institutions and dispersed populations; the other, the *nucleated, walled city*, has centralized cities and aggregated populations. That is, in the one form a monarch may inhabit an isolated palace, his council may convene someplace else, his army may be scattered in barracks around the realm, and collective royal ceremonies may be performed at yet some other place—a shrine or royal tomb perhaps. The rural population of food producers is spread more or less evenly over the cultivable land (see the description of Swaziland in Chapter 14). In the other kind of city the central institutions of state, army, religion, and trade are all concentrated in a single settlement, side by side in usually distinct architecture. Moreover, the population is densely packed around the urban center, usually defended by strong walls. The food-producing population lives in villages scattered around, but there is a strong tendency, encouraged by defense in warfare, to bring the villagers inside the city and settle each one in an urban ward.

At this level of community, ritual becomes a full-time specialty of priests at shrines, which are at once the intellectual, economic, and often—especially in start-up phases of civilization—political centers of civilization. Temples and their plazas form the stage-drop for the dialogue of civilization, that communication taking place between particular local "folk" peoples and the elites—full-time leaders specializing in the emerging institutions.

Full-time craft specialization also appears. Food producers provide the crops and domesticated meats that feed full-time craftsmen and tradesmen: millers, bakers, brewers, butchers, tanners, weavers, tailors, smiths, carpenters, masons, metalworkers, jewelers, stonecutters, and so on. Crafts turn into art, as great art styles are born.

In politics, monarchs make use of kinship: Dynasties are founded by leaders who themselves rise to power from various backgrounds, some as prophets or priests, others as war leaders, seizing power by force of arms. In addition, monarchs usually employ tax collectors, district administrators, and engineers for public works. *Royal bureaucracies* appear, usually defined as an extension of the monarch's household. We shall examine these original bureaucracies in Chapter 15.

The state commissions traders to travel abroad—another type of full-time specialist. Marketplaces emerge as the places for "administered trade" between civilized royal governments and tribal peoples. Tribesmen usually exchange raw materials for fine handcrafted goods.

Yet while urban elites and high cultures of the arts, literature, religion, and philosophy may flourish in cities, folk cultures of local knowledge de-

Justice
Law codes arise to govern relations of different peoples within the same jurisdictions. Judges have powers to enforce judgments. Monarchs may be lawgivers but at same time strive to be above law themselves.

Language
Writing: calendars, sacred scriptures, accounts, law codes.

Politics
The state: full-time monarchies, conquest empires.

Learning
Specialized learning among priest-scholars, scribes. Master craftsmen train apprentices.

Traditional Civilizations
Community field: Consists of constellations of urban, commanding institutional nodes (temples, plazas, storehouses, palaces, barracks, marketplaces, etc.) and the general population of craftsmen and farmers. In one type (the "stone" or closed city) the population is tightly packed around these nodes, grouped together at the city center. In the other (the "green" or open city) the nodes are scattered, and the population is, too.

Economics
Redistributive rites effect exchanges among food producers, food processors, and craftsmen. Royal traders search for distant goods. Marketplaces allow impersonal trade among strangers.

Ritual
First cities are ceremonial centers. Calendrical rites effect redistribution (see economics). Organized religion emerges around full-time priests at shrines. Pilgrimages. Prophets and conversions.

Technology
Always food producers, with intensive gardening, irrigation; may have plow agriculture with ox teams. Fine craft traditions, metallurgy, common.

Sociology
Shamans give rise to priesthood hierarchies. Kings' lineages become royal dynasties. Kings' households grow into bureaucracies. Armies grow out of warrior age grades. Full-time craftsmen organize into fraternities, "guilds." Peasant and nomadic communities may turn inward, encapsulate own traditions, or even resist state by force of arms.

Figure 2.6 Emergent institutional behavior in traditional civilizations.

37

velop alongside them in the peasant villages of farmers and in isolated fast-nesses of herding nomads on the fringes of state domains. Peasants may turn inward and encapsulate themselves in sectarian versions of their former urban culture. Others, especially herdsmen, may resist the urban state by force of arms, sometimes even conquering the center and founding new dynasties. We take up these processes in Chapter 16.

In sum, the institutions that have now emerged inside the community form of either green or nucleated, walled cities with associated peasant hamlets and villages are

1. A state cult organized by full-time priests around shrines officially recognized by the dynastic state.

2. The extension of the fraternity–age-grade principle to recruit enormous armies for conquest and defense.

3. A variety of tradesmen and craftsmen, often organized fraternally into guilds, performing all manner of services and handcrafting all manner of goods.

4. The extension of the monarch's household to form a bureaucracy, divided into bureaus of war (army), public works, and tax collecting/local administration.

5. The extension of kinship to royal dynasties, with lineage as the ideology of legitimacy for rule.

6. The beginnings of officially organized long-distance trade and the possibility of marketplaces for moving goods locally. Most goods, however, continue to move as tribute and offerings to be redistributed by royal and priestly rituals to bureaucrats, soldiers, and ordinary citizens, who in traditional societies are better termed "subjects" and "cultists."

MODERN METROPOLITAN CIVILIZATION

The dominant community form today is the vast urban metropolitan region. This form has been well described by urban sociologists, urban geographers, and planners. In such communities, millions of people participate in the corporate institutions of trade, finance, industry, and communications (see Figure 2.7). New key institutions have emerged in modern life. The first is the market, with its potential of regulating value through the play of supply and demand in a "free" or "price-regulated" market system. That market system was instrumental in the rise of *industrialism*—the harnessing of exterior sources of power to machines, and people working together in synchronized effort. In turn, the market and industrialism made the enormous urban region, upward of 20 million or more persons living in one area, possible.

Justice
Law codes and state constitutions almost universal. International law and tribunals. Many nation-state governments unwilling to submit selves to their own or international law. In short, a gap between constitutions and "constitutionalism."

Language
Mass communications of modern media in print, film, radio, and television.

Politics
World system of nation-states regulated by balance of power and intermittent warfare. Great diversity of politics from one to another, but world-wide trend for mass participation in politics (Aristotle's "democracy") to compete with rule of the few ("oligarchy"). Protest movements of ethnic groups, labor, women, and gays and lesbians.

Learning
Mass schooling separating juvenile age grades from households. Universities and research institutes create new knowledge explosively.

Modern Metropolitan Civilization
Community field: Consists of enormous urban regions. Urban regions have specialized settlements—central business districts, industrial districts, separate residential areas by social class, and suburbs. The "unicentric" form arranges these parts concentrically around the central business district in a wheel. The other, "polycentric," form strings together many central business districts in accord with geographical features.

Economics
Price-regulated markets vie with state-regulated redistribution world-wide. The "factors of production"—land, labor, and capital, with legal restrictions—enter the market in more capitalistic countries. Economies of urban regions surpass many times that of "underdeveloped areas."

Ritual
Mass secular rituals, often extended through the media. Psychoanalysis and other schools based in psychological theories heal troubled individuals.

Technology
Industrialism—harnessing of sources of energy to machines synchronized with activities of human workers. Electronics make possible dispersal of original assembly lines and an information revolution through computers.

Sociology
Work separated from household. Huge state and private corporations. Division of labor by sex weakens. Proliferation of voluntary associations, a "bridge" between private individual and public roles. Three social classes form in relation to market and to ownership, management, and staffing of corporate bureaucracies.

Figure 2.7 Emergent institutions in modern metropolitan civilizations.

In economics, then, capitalism, working through the market, competes with state regulation, harking back to an earlier mode familiar to anthropologists from feasting complexes: redistribution. We discuss both markets and metropolises in Chapter 17.

The second key institution is the legal-rational corporate bureaucracy derived from the old dynastic bureaucracy of a monarch's household. The impersonal corporation, with careers open to talent, has spread world-wide and has been coupled with industrial organization. We shall examine its problems and human demands in Chapter 18.

In sociology, old forms are conserved while new ones overlay them. In many countries the impersonal corporation vies, still, with the dynastic principle of inherited ownership of the corporation in a single lineage. Compare General Motors with the Ford Motor Company, for example. In the latter dynastic leadership survives, if under severe challenge from professional management.

Schooling is now the corporate form of age grading in mass society. It provides for socializing large numbers of youths and giving them the skills to interact impersonally with others by role and skill in a corporate setting. The dissonance between this schooling and the cultural values that may be taught in the home is one dimension of anthropological research in the modern world.

In ritual, modern society, as in all other institutional areas, conserves everything that emerged in previous eras and adds secular rituals both of the impersonal modern state and of the local subcultures. In today's metropolises faith healers—shamans—hawk their services, while the priesthoods of the traditional religions preside over age-old liturgies. In the meantime, great secular pageants are enacted in all nation-states, alongside local community fairs. Both are secular rituals.

In addition, the corporation is balanced everywhere by voluntary associations that provide face-to-face havens for workers, managers, and professionals alike in a vast impersonal world.

In politics everywhere, mass participation is a norm. In societies where power is monopolized by the state itself, this participation is a ritual exercise in which elections reflect ritual consent of the state's choice of rulers. In other societies the participation is more nearly a reality. But in any mass society true participation is always hard to achieve.

Moreover, in most of the world old and new empires are giving way to the nation-state, a political form that tries to wed ethnic culture and identity (nationalism) with formally self-governing constitutional forms. In addition, ethnic groups, labor, youth, and—in some advanced modern countries— women and gays are everywhere forming protest movements to achieve more participation in the state and the economy.

Anthropologists see the millions of people in metropolitan societies as also participating in their private worlds of neighborhood and household. Many of these private worlds are culturally quite separate from the mainstream public world, deriving from and clustering around the themes of ethnicity and religion. In extreme sectarian forms, they are popularly called "cults."

In the world of industry, finance, and public administration, anthropology continues its mandate of looking at the view from inside and from the particular observable field of interacting behavior. Thus, anthropologists study workers on the assembly line, clients of welfare agencies, and plaintiffs' access to law, as well as native peoples on reservations.

The modern world is one community that field cultural anthropologists must share with other social scientists. Yet we concentrate on both the overview—the look at dominant urban community forms—and the local view. As always, we contribute *holism*, the search for the interdependence of all parts in a social whole. But we also document the particular: the local, regional, sectarian, or ethnic subculture that is continually reasserting itself to challenge the apparent homogenization of modern life and world culture.

Anthropologists, then, bring a rich intellectual background to the modern world. Many of us indeed are engaged in practical research and applications of anthropological knowledge to policy making and problem solving in precisely these interactions between the part and the whole. We, who know about the power of culture, of the grip of traditional personal identity formalized in ritual, can advise the impersonal professional to whom the standard majority-culture worldview is the single standard for approaching fellow human beings.

SUMMARY AND CONCLUSIONS

Cultural anthropology is concerned with the natural history description and interpretation of all the world's peoples, from the moment of contact with "central civilization" as well as from the first identifiable origins in archaeological prehistory. Rooted in biology, cultural anthropology shares the perspective of primatology about the social life of other primates. Of these, our closest biological relatives are chimpanzees; therefore, their life is relevant to ours.

Human culture and social life, based on primate prototypes, has undergone a number of transformations, starting with the earliest and most profound, the emergence of humans as a distinct species, *Homo sapiens*. Bands emerged from some lost social prototype of *H. sapiens neanderthalensis* and *H. erectus*, which in turn emerged from a prototypical troop of a lost ape ancestor.

Human communities have increased in number, population density, and specialization and complexity of institutions. These institutions correspond to the subject matter of many of the other academic disciplines: language (linguistics), learning (psychology and education), ritual (religion and theology), social organization (sociology), economics (the discipline of economics), politics (political science), and law (jurisprudence).

Cultural anthropologists study all these institutions as they emerge in community settings—which, like the institutions themselves, range from simple to complex. The progression of community forms is from bands to tribes, to archaic cities and peasant villages, to modern metropolitan regions. Each successive community form retains all the previous social patterns alongside more complex forms.

Thus anthropologists continue to study what at first might seem to be a bewildering variety of settings and problems. We still seek "unspoiled" and relatively "uncontacted" peoples. As their numbers dwindle, we look at the folk or peasant cultures within traditional civilizations. In modern societies we look at the local groupings of ethnic groups, of rural communities, or of part cultures, whether of neighborhood or institution within metropolitan regions. Bands and tribes, the so-called "native peoples," survive, and their interaction with the vast impersonal corporate bureaucracies of health, schooling, defense, and territorial administration is often mediated today by applied anthropologists—brokers between the view from the ground and that from the elite centers.

As anthropologists we leave many of the details to other social scientists. However, the peculiar mandate of anthropology is to look afresh at the modern particulars from the perspective of the whole, not only here and now but at all times and all places. Anthropology makes the familiar strange, and the strange familiar. In Chapter 3, on field work, we shall see how the Brooklyn Mohawk combine careers in high steel construction of urban skyscrapers with participation in an urban-to-rural part community that survives directly from the tribal days of the Iroquois confederacy. Such particular discoveries in the heart of the metropolis do not surprise us.

It is to the progressively more complex array of communities and institutions that this book is devoted. Like anthropology itself, this book finds order in the extreme and seemingly chaotic diversity of the human natural world.

SUGGESTED READING

Goodall, Jane. *Through a Window: My Thirty Years with the Chimpanzees of Gombe*. Boston: Houghton Mifflin, 1990. A personal account, written for a popular audience, that covers most of the major findings at Gombe, by one of the greatest living naturalists.

GLOSSARY

anthropology The study of all human beings at all times and in all places.

community A basic unit of survival and cultural transmission, derived from the "breeding populations" of other animal species. It consists of individuals linked to each other through interacting networks of individuals who inhabit a given *territorial range*, which is defined not so much by boundaries as by centers of assemblage, on some schedule, and by range of dispersal. Boundaries may be permeable and overlapping with other communities.

cultural anthropology The discovery, description, and comparison of all living peoples and their cultures. Findings are described, analyzed, and interpreted, often abstractly and comparatively, in written ethnographies.

division of labor by sex A human innovation, whereby men hunt bigger game and women hunt smaller game and gather food. Men and women share their food jointly at hearths. This was a big step toward more efficient exploitation of the habitat and indeed helped make the whole world the human habitat.

dominance hierarchy In many primate and other animal species, an array of adults who stand in a relation of dominance and subordination to each other in rough linear ranking. A more dominant animal displaces a less dominant one in space and has first access to a resource—food, for example.

induction Reasoning from a set of observations to arrive at general principles.

institution A set of more or less discrete activities to solve some problem and perform some function for the benefit of the individual and the group. A *prototype institution* has not yet come to human consciousness sufficiently to have been given a name or for names to be given to the roles involved. Leaders of bands, for example, engage in political activities, but they seldom have titles, and their authority is personal, not official. A *formal institution* is a set of functional activities that have come to human consciousness and have been formally constituted. For example, any state has permanent officials on full-time duty, all year round. They have named roles, and understood rights and obligations. This is not the case for leadership in band and tribal communities.

ritual A form of vertebrate behavior, consisting of sets of stereotyped, repetitive activities that effect transformations of state from one time phase to another. The messages of ritual are thereby catalytic, effecting changes rapidly with minimum investment of energy.

Field Work:

Accurate Data and Adequate Theory

3

PIONEER FIELD WORKER: BRONISLAW MALINOWSKI

Conditions

Methods

Scientific Aims

THE STATE OF THE ART OF FIELD WORK TODAY

Simple Practical Steps

    Selecting a Program of Study

    Selecting a Field of Specialization

    Writing a Research Proposal

    Getting the Proposal Funded

    Making Plans to Leave for the Field Site

    Developing a Strategy for Entry into the Community

    Ensuring Physical and Psychological Survival

    Combating Spy Rumors

Methodological Steps

    Specifying a Theoretical Framework

    Establishing Rapport

    Becoming a Participant-Observer

    Doing Active Research

    Becoming Socialized

    Remembering Ethics and Personal Responsibilities

    Writing Up Findings

ETHNOGRAPHIC CLOSE-UP: FREILICH AT WORK AMONG THE BROOKLYN MOHAWK

ATTEMPTING THE NATURAL HISTORY OF THE BROOKLYN MOHAWK

Step 1: Isolating a Field for Study

Step 2: Charting the Interrelationships of Phenomena Observed Within the Field

Step 3: Redefining and Validating the Interrelationships

Step 4: Making Statements of Theory (Order, Probability, Limits, Patterns, and Law)

Cultural anthropology is the field study of living human beings. Cultural anthropology's principal method is **field work,** the way we do natural history. The **field** refers to the areas in space in which cultural anthropologists find a living population to study. It is the "interacting field" for various forces propelled by human activities. The field need not have a hard boundary, it may not even be a single geographical area, but all told, a particular ethnographic field is usually some form of community.

As noted in Chapter 2, the natural history method distinguishes cultural anthropology from the other social sciences. (A minority of sociologists share this method with us, too.) This method is founded on meticulous observation. We first isolate a field of interacting people. We then observe them interact over natural time cycles (days, seasons, years, generations, a lifetime). We control and cross-check these observations by repeating them and by questioning—interviewing—our subjects for information about past activities. In this way, by patient, repetitive charting and cross-checking of human events, we distinguish patterns and processes. These in turn enable us, with some certainty, to arrive at conclusions that are *theories*—statements of order, limits, probability, and natural law—derived from the field itself, seen as part of nature.

Theories may be descriptive, relational, prescriptive, or predictive. Natural history theories are above all descriptive and relational. They are sometimes prescriptive, especially in applied anthropology: they can indicate a recommended area of conduct. But anthropologists seldom make predictions on the basis of their theories. It is important to realize that prediction is not the only test of a theory.

A **theory,** then, is a statement of the apparent relationships among observed facts. *Facts* originally referred to deeds, events observed in the past. Today **facts** refer to givens accepted as true, but they bear the connotation of deeds or events. However, emotional states or feelings can also be facts. To be accepted, both facts and theory must have been verified by repeated observations, often by several observers.

Thus, for example, we accept as a fact that each of us is the result of the union of two gamete cells, which produced a zygote with half its genetic material from each parent. This was a fact quite unknown until recent advances in the study of cells, of genetics, and of molecular biology (see Chapter 4).

Natural history proceeds by **induction**—that is, reasoning from a set of observations to arrive at general principles. Thus, for anthropology the facts come first, always, and the principles or theories—inferred from the facts—come second. This approach differs very much from the procedures in some of the natural sciences, which make use of **deduction**—reasoning from a small structure of principles to a sequence of observations, as in mathematics. The discipline of economics, for example, deduces its "laws," such as supply and demand in markets, from the a priori (beforehand) principle that human beings are rationally motivated to maximize their material goods. Essentially these sciences proceed by *two-variable analysis*. For example, economists hold that prices are the product of two variables, supply and demand.

Most social sciences—such as political science, psychology, some sociology, and economics again—also proceed by measuring statistical averages of wide runs of behavior. This is the study of *disorganized complexity*. This approach gives us, for example, broad pictures of the probability of voters voting for certain candidates (opinion polls) or of consumers buying certain products (market surveys). Conversely, when anthropologists study human peoples in the field, they are studying systems of *organized complexity*. We assume that ultimately all the behavior we observe is related to everything else, including the environment. Our job is to plot the interrelations.

This is an almost impossibly broad task. Although some anthropologists working with very small and very simple groups have maintained that they have described *everything* and have given us a completely holistic account, most anthropologists prefer to take on only limited problems, and hence sections of interrelated variables in the complex field systems they study.

This book reports on the field studies of many great field workers: Jane Goodall for chimpanzees, Richard Lee for the !Kung San bushmen, E. E. Evans-Pritchard for the Nuer tribe, and Hilda Kuper for the Kingdom of Swaziland, to name only a few. In this chapter we concentrate on the pioneer field work of Bronislaw Malinowski, who first showed us how to do it right, so to speak, and on the efforts of a then student anthropologist Morris Freilich, starting out to learn field work by doing it among the Mohawk of Brooklyn.

Jane Goodall, who has been observing the wild chimpanzees of Gombe Stream Reserve, Tanzania, is the world's greatest living naturalist.

PIONEER FIELD WORKER: BRONISLAW MALINOWSKI

Bronislaw Malinowski (1884–1942), generally considered one of the founding fathers of British social anthropology (also called structural functionalism), had tremendous influence on the practice of ethnographic field work in the United States. This first great anthropological field worker squarely faced the problem of turning experiences such as those of Hans Staden (see Chapter 1) into science.

Malinowski was a Polish gentleman and an Austro-Hungarian subject doing field work in the South Seas when World War I broke out in 1914. Austria-Hungary was at war with Great Britain, and one legend has it that he was caught as an enemy alien on the Trobriand Islands, territory controlled by Australia, and was forbidden to leave. Malinowski remained four years. He also made two expeditions to the islands from the Australian mainland during the two subsequent years. All told, his Trobriand expeditions are among the most extensive field trips ever taken. As a result, he published a number of very brilliant books from 1916 through the 1920s.

Bromislaw Malinowski.

Malinowski was only a paper enemy as far as the British were concerned. He was sponsored by a major anthropologist, C. G. Seligman, from England. He did very well socially, marrying the daughter of the governor-general of Australia and later winning a chair at the London School of Economics, certainly a prize position during the period. There, in the 1920s, he was to found the intellectual school called *functionalism.*

Our efforts today can be measured against Malinowski's methods, which have been improved only by new tools, not better strategies. Based on his extensive field work, Malinowski suggested that the productivity of field workers depends on certain conditions, special methods, and "genuine scientific aims" (1922, p. 126).

Conditions

Proper conditions include, first and always, total immersion in the field, in native society. Thus, Malinowski took up residence, not at some European house, interviewing natives on the veranda, but right in the heart of a native village, where he pitched his comfortable tent. Moreover, he believed that a proper, natural time period spent in the field is at least one solar year, with its round of seasons.

Malinowski advised field workers to stay away from their own kind, their "natural friends"—in his case Europeans—and to welcome the company of natives.

Methods

Malinowski advocated exhaustive observations, cross-checked by interviews. Observers should periodically pull their data together by compiling outlines and tables about entire institutions. He himself listed all the events he observed that had to do with launching the many *kula expeditions*, whereby fleets of native canoes visited their neighbors on either side (see Chapter 11).

As part of the observational method, Malinowski advocated recording the special effects of a people, which he quaintly termed the "imponderabilia of daily life." The daily scenes and special touches that give a culture its surface character may also convey some deeper meaning.

As for interviewing, he called for a collection of native texts: outright verbatim statements, including jokes, prayers, magical spells, speeches, and natives' explanations of their own actions. By listing these last, Malinowski most clearly distinguished himself from the American field workers of the day, who relied far too heavily on verbal statements at the expense of cross-checking observations. American anthropologists had a great sense of urgency in recording the vanishing culture of the American Indians while they could still be found. Many of the customs they investigated were only memories and no longer practices, or at least so they assumed. Thus they made rapid field trips, asking questions but not making systematic observations.

Malinowski's tent on the beach at Nu'agasi Village, Trobriand Islands. Note his dugout canoe by the tent.

Scientific Aims

Scientific aims for Malinowski meant accurate facts reflecting theory. His *working theory*, the hunches he followed in first interrelating various parts of his data, at that time was a reaction to making sense of being immersed for so long in "intensive study." This caused him to seek an "anatomy of the native culture." He expected the various compilations of data he was making to be ultimately related, as in the structure of a living organism. This point of view was quite different from the dominant habits of the previous generation of British anthropologists. "Armchair scholars," they had used the observations of travelers and missionaries to make broad statements in which they either classified peoples in terms of their evolutionary stage or identified peoples as having diffused from previous centers of innovation.

(British anthropology had two dominant schools: the evolutionists and the diffusionists. Both were concerned with classifying peoples according to an a priori scheme. The **diffusionists** theorized that all peoples partake of traits diffusing from a very few centers, such as ancient Egypt. The **evolutionists** believed, after Lewis Henry Morgan's influential book, *Ancient Society* [1877], that human beings had passed inevitably through several set stages of evolution, termed *savagery, barbarism,* and *civilization*. Neither school is accepted today in its turn-of-the-century form. But you will notice that a "neoevolutionary" theory influences the organization of this book. Our framework today differs from the original by a lack of ethnocentrism [our civilization is not necessarily "better"], by our correlation of stages with community form and institutional development rather than innate racial capacity, and by the recognition that the passage from one stage to the other is not inevitable but is in fact a difficult and chancy transition, as this book will show.)

His stress on anatomy, structure, and interconnectedness led Malinowski, when writing up his data, to formulate *functionalist* theory. In one sense, **functionalism** involves the interrelatedness of the parts of an organism—in this case, the parts of a culture. Just as the heart is related to the manufacture and circulation of the blood, so, for example, the hearth is related to the gathering, harvesting, preparation, and consumption of foodstuffs in a household. In another sense, functionalism involves adaptation for the survival of the individual and the group, a subject that Malinowski elaborated in his later work.

A classic and famous example of Malinowski's functional theory was his explanation for the prevalence of magic among the Trobrianders. Magic was adaptive, he said, because it allayed anxiety in the individual. The Trobrianders by and large were magic-ridden. They seemed to be constantly chanting spells or calling in sorcerers to chant special incantations. Much of their activity was punctuated by magic, particularly the saying of spells marked by special talismans. The Trobrianders seemed always to be uttering magical words and handling magical objects.

Going over his data, Malinowski finally realized that the amount of magic varied in proportion to the danger and uncertainty of the activity. The more dangerous and uncertain, the more magic. For example, deep-sea fishing was both unpredictable and dangerous: one might come back empty-handed or laden with a big catch, or one might not come back at all. Whereas deep-sea fishing was surrounded by magic at every step, fishing in the lagoon, which was both safe and relatively rewarding, involved very little magic. Malinowski reasoned that magic prepared the individual to act forcefully in spite of real anxieties about real difficulties. This is an example of functional theory based on ethnographic evidence of high quality.

We would still accept Malinowski's explanation today, with one qualification. We note that magic and ritual, instead of always allaying anxiety, can also actually increase it, if they are not performed "correctly" in a timely way. In short, they can become part of the problem, not necessarily a solution for anxiety at all.

Malinowski also sought to gain a reconstruction of the native mind, so that one could actually recapitulate native thought processes. Most functionalists later gave up that goal as hopeless. It has lately been revived by contemporary anthropologists who are primarily concerned with conveying an accurate representation and sensitive interpretation of another culture in their ethnographies. (This is the "interpretationist" movement in the anthropology of the 1980s and 1990s, to be discussed later in this chapter.)

THE STATE OF THE ART OF FIELD WORK TODAY

In spite of Malinowski's efforts, for many years very few anthropologists paid much attention to the methodology of field work. For most, the way to become a real anthropologist was to go out and find a people and make them one's own. The new field worker had to learn everything about the people and present it to the scientific community. Gaining access to and convincing the people to communicate with a scientific stranger was not part of an anthropologist's training. These were problems that simply had to be worked out in the field.

It was precisely because of this hit-or-miss approach that anthropologist Morris Freilich edited a book, *Marginal Natives: Anthropologists at Work* (1970), to train people for field work and to promote a movement toward making field training part of the curriculum. Freilich underwent many painful experiences in his own field work. In retrospect, he was able to see his blunders and false starts. As a result, he put together a commonsense manual for the prospective field worker, listing the most sensible and graceful ways to deal with people in a formal situation. The following discussion, based very loosely on Freilich's outline, provides a good practical guide. Figure 3.1 provides an overview of this process, characterizing it as a rite of passage.

Figure 3.1 A practical guide to field work (based on Freilich, 1970).

Simple practical steps (leading to isolating a field site)

Selecting a program of study

Selecting a field of specialization

Writing a research proposal

Getting the proposal funded

Making plans to leave for the field site

Developing a strategy for entry into the community

Ensuring physical and psychological survival

Combating spy rumors

Methodological steps (collecting data, interrelating facts, analyzing them)

Specifying a theoretical framework

Establishing rapport

Becoming a participant-observer

Doing active research

Becoming socialized

Remembering ethics and personal responsibilities

Writing up findings

Simple Practical Steps

Field work requires a great deal of advance preparation, from choosing a research topic and getting the study funded to taking steps to ensure one's physical and psychological survival in the field.

Selecting a Program of Study. It was possible in the nineteenth century for some anthropologists never to go to school at all. They might be tutored at home and otherwise be entirely self-taught.* Those days are gone. The body of knowledge is too vast; the only way to learn is from scholars who dispense diplomas. The world over, anthropology is now an academic discipline.

Thus, the prospective scholar has to select an academic program. This means more than selecting a school, since no department of anthropology covers the whole subject. Formerly, anthropology in the United States urgently attempted to record primitive peoples before they disappeared; today there are probably no unrecorded primitive people left in the world. Until the 1950s, the heartlands of unknown peoples were the interior of Brazil and the highlands of New Guinea, but now groups in both these places have largely entered into contact with the outside world. Today's students of primitive peoples must choose a program that emphasizes the culture area of Oceania or South America and some relevant intellectual problem such as social organization, human ecology, or planned acculturation.

An anthropologist today usually has a focus of interest that consists of a culture area plus one or more topical areas, such as psychology, ritual and myth, economics, cities, and so on. Graduate students are well advised to select a department where their own interests are reflected in those of the faculty.

Selecting a Field of Specialization. Usually, professional anthropologists will come up with a program that includes a cultural area, a methodological focus, and a problematic topic. One highly successful student, whom I advised during his doctoral studies, took the Caribbean as his culture area, the measurement of energy flow through systems as his methodological interest, and peasant agriculture and economic development as his topical area. He later combined these interests to great effect in his field work.

To secure their interests, students apprentice themselves to established anthropologists, their **mentors,** or intellectual sponsors. (Note that Malinowski had his Seligman.) Mentors often have many professional contacts, which are helpful when the young professional seeks a job. Training at this level is not just a question of sitting in class, taking notes, and dutifully

---

*This was the case of Frank Hamilton Cushing, born in 1857, discussed in the box on page 59. He apprenticed himself to a Cornell professor for a few months. That was the extent of his schooling.

completing reading assignments. Rather, guided individually, advanced graduate students must carve out their own body of knowledge, often by researching theoretical topics for seminars.

Writing a Research Proposal. The culmination of the previous steps is for the student to develop a proposal stating the theoretical problem, research objectives, field site and its people, previous research done among them and on similar projects, calendar or research schedule, and budget. Writing the proposal is an individual activity very much guided by the student's mentor and the other members of the supervisory committee.

The author with one of his mentors, Margaret Mead, in 1976.

My student's research proposal detailed the field site quite specifically. He was fortunate in having visited the interior of the Dominican Republic during a summer survey project conducted by a faculty member. The site was a mountain frontier area, a small valley recently pioneered by frontiersmen using time-honored slash-and-burn agricultural methods. While converting the hillsides to pasture, they were also converting the bottomland to intensively irrigated cropland that would be plowed and harvested by machines. The student's research problem was to discover the conditions of agricultural innovation. His objectives were to measure and compare energy flow between traditional and innovative cultivators. His schedule embraced an entire year's time, and his budget was reasonable: support for one person along with travel and special equipment expenses.

Getting the Proposal Funded. Obtaining funding entails tailoring the proposal to the formats required by various national and international scientific agencies and private foundations that sponsor research. It also requires meeting their deadlines for submission, usually six months or a year before the student actually plans to go into the field.

Submitting a proposal requires some special research, rather like that involved in looking for a university and an anthropology department in the first place. The student must search through brochures and annual reports to find the funding programs that most closely fit the proposal.

Making Plans to Leave for the Field Site. Although Freilich assumed that research would be done abroad, many students do their field work in the United States—Freilich himself worked among the North American Mohawk. Common problems arise in traveling to any field site, and they are simply magnified when one travels abroad. Researchers must obtain passports for themselves and dependents from the United States government, vaccinations and shots from the Public Health Service, visas from the host government, and official permits from the various agencies of the host government (the latter might well be at odds with each other). Driving permits, whether an international license or one from the particular country at hand, are routinely required. Travel might also involve a permit from the national police or permission to go into tribal, frontier, or specially administered areas.

Obtaining all the necessary paperwork can result in frustrating delays, but if such problems are anticipated at an early stage, they may be reduced to routine errands. The reason for such requirements should be understood. Wherever scientists do social research, they have a special responsibility to share their findings and expertise with the people involved. This is true at home as well as abroad. American students who journey to inner-city areas are surely obliged to share their findings with regional planning groups and local educators. Just how this should be done will vary, but the situation should certainly be explored in advance, and liaisons should be made with local agencies. Permits should indeed be safe conducts based on friendship and mutual exchange, if only of knowledge.

Developing a Strategy for Entry into the Community. Anthropologists must cooperate responsibly with local and national scientific and governmental agencies concerned with the people they study, but they must also gain the trust and acceptance of the people themselves. Although permits are tokens of sponsorship, a good rule of thumb is to always have a personal guide. Thus, a researcher can appropriately have a national or regional **sponsor,** someone at the highest level who knows the country and who has the contacts the researcher needs. A field worker can also have a *local sponsor,* someone directly connected with the locality at hand, who presents the researcher to the local authorities and to influential persons. Once the field worker is in the community, a *community sponsor* is also advisable.

In my own first field work, I had the good luck to be sponsored by a coffee planter, a man who turned out to be tremendously influential, not only economically and politically over a wide region but also among the conservative Guatemalan Indians among whom I later did most of my intensive field work. Moreover, the old gentleman was then on very amiable terms with his arch political enemy, the leader of the agrarianist Indians (who had once wanted to expropriate his estate).

The author's local sponsor in Guatemala: Don Federico Rodriguez Benito and his daughter Doña Elisa Rodriguez Paúl.

It is important to remember that if an anthropologist becomes associated with one sponsor, he or she cannot hope to be equally well associated with that person's enemies. In my case, I interviewed the agrarianist leader intensively only at the end of my field work, when I had the advantage because the wily old politician was anxious that I hear his side of the story. I would have been deceiving myself to think that he counted me as his dear friend.

The agrarianist boss who was the arch political enemy of the author's sponsor.

Years later, however, when the planter was long dead, I revisited the field and spent a week primarily in the company of the old political boss, who had been ousted from office by his own party some years before. Nostalgic and aged, he did indeed greet me as a friend that time around. Long-term field work provides ever deeper perspectives!

Ensuring Physical and Psychological Survival. Problems that ought to be originally attended to in the budget of the research proposal include what special supplies and transport must be paid for; what gear, clothing, and medical equipment must be brought into the area; whether one can expect to live on local rations; whether one must import quantities of canned goods and the like; whether one can rough it with a people living close to nature in a tropical or extreme climate; and whether a considerable amount of equipment must be imported.

Certainly it is important to go into the field in as good physical condition as possible. Freilich also noted that most experienced field workers find it advisable to live apart from others. In a separate dwelling, one can not only attend to creature comforts but can also retreat on occasion to engage in the scholarly privacy of writing up field notes (rather like being back in the library at the university) or to relax with no need to be alert to every detail of the surroundings.

It is also advisable to have an escape hatch available from time to time—to be able to go to a civilized center, get a hot shower, sleep on sheets, and converse with educated people (the proverbial "natural friends" of Malinowski). However, one must also cultivate native friends (as Malinowski says), and I advise using the hatch sparingly.

Combating Spy Rumors. It is likely that anywhere anthropologists go there will be some people who suspect them of being spies. Although government officials and city people may suspect that the researcher is working for the CIA, people in the local community are far more likely to suspect the researcher of spying for the local government. When the anthropologist's natural curiosity leads to asking questions about official boundaries, land tenure, crop yields, and the like, members of the community may believe such questions to be the national revenue service's prelude to higher taxes. An interest in health and disease might be interpreted as leading up to a vaccination campaign on the part of the authorities.

The problem is a delicate one. Although anthropologists need official permits and sponsorship, they must be careful about the impression these permits give locally. A rule of thumb is to size up the relations between local and national groups in advance. Is there a new taxation campaign? A new land survey? A public health campaign? Is the road department condemning land for a major new highway? The researcher must play the situation by ear.

Finally, of course, the anthropologist has the responsibility of not using any information against his or her informants and of not letting it fall into hands that might do so. (See the discussion about ethics below.) As trust and rapport are gained, spy rumors will recede.

So much for the practical steps that Freilich lists in his checklist. Now for the methodological ones.

Methodological Steps

The field worker, once in place, must have means for systematically collecting, interrelating, and analyzing data.

Specifying a Theoretical Framework. A **theoretical framework** sets up a relation between the collected facts and a broader theory. The aim is to discover patterns, or repetitive items and actions, and to relate them to some broader principles. Ideally, the field worker has already entered the field armed with a research proposal that specifies this framework.

However, any researcher must be aware of the importance of *serendipity*—unexpected findings as a by-product of original research. In any case, the student must keep a focus; he or she cannot expect to learn everything.

Establishing Rapport. A basic rule in field work is that you can't get something for nothing. A researcher wants strangers, the "others," to talk or to do something. In return, they must be offered something. True, first contacts may be established on the basis of introductions; the native introduced to a researcher pays off the researcher's sponsor by talking. But that social capital is quickly exhausted, and the field worker must establish **rapport,** or a fund of goodwill, on his or her own.

Fortunately, in all cultures social interaction is its own reward. Many people are willing to reveal intimate facts to a neutral stranger without fear of being embarrassed. Thus, one of the first favors the anthropologist can do for new

acquaintances is to lend an ear to their ideals, fears, old dreams, adventures, and new hopes.

A field worker can always do favors in return for good treatment. The opportunities present themselves naturally. As a rule of thumb, however, it is always better to avoid paying informants cash, except when they are hired specifically for some research task, such as administering a question-naire. Cash can quickly get in the way; for example, an informant might talk five hours to get the hourly wages, not caring about the accuracy of the information. As a researcher achieves rapport, empathy, give and take, and mutual exchange under conditions of respect, both the information and the favors flow naturally—so much so that one hardly notices the mechanics.

Becoming a Participant-Observer. Freilich noted that at the beginning of all field research, anthropologists are playing the role of "privileged stranger," which permits access only to public places and centers and to few private places. During this time, the researcher simply passively observes.

But a field worker may also become a **participant-observer,** learning the ropes of important activities while trying to be useful. As time goes on, most anthropologists help more actively in ongoing native tasks. They learn by working. They also question and interview while they work. Of course, the amount of actual effective work varies; most anthropologists are admit-tedly "along for the ride" more than to get some task done. They are ac-cepted primarily because they are good company.

Rapport and exchange in field work can deepen into lifelong friendships sealed by ritual. (Left) The author (center) stands with his Guatemalan compadres (co-parents) *after the baptism of their son, the author's godson. (Right) The author supplied his godson with his baptismal clothes and blanket and made the arrangements with the priest. He sees his godson every time he visits Guatemala, long after his field work has been completed.*

Doing Active Research. The researcher must move from passive interviewing and watching to actively pursuing particular kinds of information in a focused way. Among the easiest things to do early in **active research** are mapping—locating house types, neighborhoods, and boundaries—and relating the material to census data (and even collecting census data if they don't exist).

Field work is generally termed "qualitative research." But field workers often collect quantitative data. (*Datum* derives from the Latin word for "given." The plural is *data*, "givens." **Data** are often quantifiable or measurable facts from which further calculations can be made.) For example, in my field work in a Guatemalan community I studied the census data in some detail and extracted data on land ownership and household income, enabling me to classify all members of the community by these indices.

But I also did *qualitative* active research on the festival system of a Guatemalan community. I spent as much time as possible observing the public events of the fiestas and taking photographs for color slides, which I later invited the ranking participants in each festival to come to my house to view. They were delighted to see themselves.

After I entertained them with refreshments, I interviewed them in tape-recorded sessions, asking them quite specifically about the events we had just seen on the screen. Thus, I had my observations of the events, a photographic record, and a large corpus of native statements, some of the which were spontaneous recounts of the individuals' own speeches. On one occasion three participants became involved in a heated political discussion that shed light on one of the most important offices in the town, one that I had completely overlooked.

The ethnographic **interview** is thus a major active research technique. It is usually open-ended—that is, it may be focused around a certain topic, but the anthropologist tailors the questions to the responses received from the **informant,** or interviewee. Ideally, interviews relate to observation. The researcher questions informants about things he or she has seen. Interviews and observations are our two most important field work techniques.

Becoming Socialized. Over the long run, anthropologists are bound to become more like their subjects of study than they realize, to pick up almost unconsciously the others' point of view. In short, they become **socialized** to another culture. When anthropologists return home, they see things through different eyes; their own culture becomes strange. Anthropologists have not exactly "gone native," but they now stand in two worlds; they are bicultural. This gives them a special responsibility to speak to and for both cultures, the one they have studied and the one they themselves grew up in.

Remembering Ethics and Personal Responsibilities. Researchers can no longer expect their reports to languish in scientific journals and museum archives. Published reports are divulged widely and even get back to the people reported on. It is thus highly important for the researcher to observe professional **ethics**—to protect the privacy of informants and, more impor-

---

Did Frank Hamilton Cushing "Go Native"?

The danger of going native completely, of being socialized into the other culture, is that the whole anthropological mission will be lost. When I was an undergraduate at Harvard College, I once heard solemnly, from the lips of a tutor in social relations, that around the year 1880 Frank Hamilton Cushing was converted to Zuñi Pueblo culture and initiated into their most secret religious association; he became a high priest and never came back to write down what he knew.

I later discovered the actual facts of Cushing's experience. He had been young, adrift, and without supplies when he was taken in by the family of the Zuñi governor, adopted, and taught to dress, eat, speak, and conduct himself like a Zuñi in every way. But it is also true that he later took a job with the Bureau of Indian Affairs, married a lady from the East, and lived at Zuñi while he excavated archaeological sites. He was indeed initiated into their society of priests—but then many Americans of his class and background had been initiated into Western secret societies, such as the Masons. He did not publish much of what he learned at Zuñi, and unfortunately, he died young: he choked on a fishbone on the Phoebe Hearst archaeological expedition to Florida in 1900, where he had been excavating Indian mounds on Marco Island.

(Above) Frank Hamilton Cushing in Zuñi clothing, 1880 or 1881. (Left) Cushing in U.S. clothing, 1879.

---

tant, to protect their reputation and their legal standing. The field worker has a special responsibility not to print anything that will harm the people he or she is studying. This principle pertains to domestic field work as well and to work in urban centers anywhere in the world where anthropologists study marginal or deviant populations.

For example, anthropologists from the University of Florida once studied long-term marijuana users in South Africa and Costa Rica (Carter, 1978). It was necessary to gain each host government's promise that these persons' confidential identity would be respected. All files and data were coded and guaranteed to be immune from police inspections. A further promise was exacted that long-term users, some of whom were brought to a hospital for exhaustive physiological tests, would not be arrested or in any way interfered with. (The researchers' findings did not endorse the view that long-term, very heavy marijuana use is physically dangerous.)

Writing Up Findings. I have added this final step to Freilich's original checklist. It is the logical culmination of all the steps, and a task of which anthropologists are becoming more self-conscious. Field workers write up many kinds of reports: *term paper*s for courses in field methods, reporting on specific techniques; *masters essays* that try out a theoretical framework on a specific field situation; and *doctoral dissertations* that are supposed to be original contributions to knowledge and advance our factual and theoretical perspective. Finally, mature scholars produce *books* and *articles*. Doctoral dissertations are addressed to narrow audiences, the new Ph.D.'s doctoral supervisory committee. Books must address wider audiences.

Lately anthropological writing seems to favor one or another stylistic pole. On the one hand, field workers write as if they were objective, often quantitatively oriented, observers. They may even leave themselves out of the account completely. On the other, they write more subjectively, rendering "thick descriptions" that attempt to convey the life of **"the Other"** (a term they prefer over "native") as closely as possible to the Other's experience while still understandable to an educated, "non-Other" audience. These documents are more novelistic in their feeling; they strive to impart Malinowski's "imponderabilia of daily life." Yet they are not fiction; they "make facts out, but do not make them up." These are the products of the **interpretationist** school in anthropology, which feels that anthropologists must render native meanings as clearly as possible to a wide audience.

Interpretationists are very aware of the *self* as an instrument. Ideally, they strive for "disciplined subjectivity," trying to be aware of their own biases, their personal predilections, and the personal bases of the decisions that lead them to focus on one aspect of a culture rather than another. Frequently, they use native texts and incorporate native interview or life history material into their books. This approach is called **reflexive,** referring to the deliberate inclusion of the field worker, and his or her relation to the subjects, in ethnographic writing.

E T H N O G R A P H I C   C L O S E - U P

FREILICH AT WORK AMONG THE BROOKLYN MOHAWK

*Y*ou should now have an idea of how one does ethnography. But how, indeed, does active research lead to attaining Malinowski's proclaimed scientific aims, to the discovery of meaningful patterns in the life of a people?

Let us look at Morris Freilich's preliminary field work as both an ethnographic experience and a scientific endeavor. Bear in mind that this was not Freilich's seasoned field work but rather a stint while still in graduate school, a kind of self-conducted apprenticeship.

In 1956 many New Yorkers were aware that there were Mohawks in their midst. An article, "Mohawks in High Steel" by Joseph Mitchell, had appeared in *The New Yorker* in 1949. Feature stories continued to appear in the press from time to time. Freilich did an anthropology term paper on the group as an undergraduate at Brooklyn College. Later, as a graduate student at Columbia University, he sought to test the proposition, suggested in a scholarly paper by A. F. C. Wallace, that Mohawks lack a fear of heights.

Wallace's suggestion was by no means new; according to Mitchell, the Indians had first gone into high steel construction work back in 1886, when some Mohawks were employed in the construction of a railroad bridge across the St. Lawrence River in Quebec Province. Mitchell quoted a letter from an official of the railroad company recalling this historic event:

The records of the company for this bridge show that it was our understanding that we would employ these Indians as ordinary day laborers unloading materials . . . They were dissatisfied with this arrangement and would come out on the bridge itself every chance they got. It was quite impossible to keep them off. As the work progressed, it became

Morris Freilich in his early days, while he was researching the Brooklyn Mohawk.

apparent to all concerned that these Indians were very odd in that they did not have any fear of heights. If not watched, they would climb up into the spans and walk around up there as cool and collected as the toughest of our riveters, most of whom at that period were old sailingship men especially picked for their experience in working aloft. These Indians were as agile as goats. They would walk a narrow beam high up in the air with nothing below them but the river, which is rough there and ugly to look down on, and it wouldn't mean any more to them than walking on the solid ground. (Wilson, 1960, p. 14)

As a consequence of their agility, the Indians apprenticed themselves to the riveter, and the practice of departing in gangs to seek riveting jobs in high steel construction work soon became general among Mohawk men.

Freilich set out during the summer of 1956 to discover whether Mohawks really were unafraid of heights. He knew that several hundred Mohawks lived in a section of Brooklyn close to their trade-union hall. A Presbyterian minister, Dr. Corey, had made an effort to preach to the group, even learning Mohawk, and had some success in attracting Mohawks to his congregation. Dr. Corey invited Freilich to tea with some Mohawk ladies of the congregation. These nice, rather elderly ladies knew nothing firsthand about high steel construction, and Freilich's first attempt at entry into the Brooklyn community through a local nonnative sponsor fizzled.

It was common knowledge that most Mohawk men, when not hanging out at the union hall, spent most of their off hours at the Wigwam Bar. Originally an Irish bar, it had become the Mohawk men's social center. Unsponsored and alone, Freilich braved this preserve. Although he was told at first by the Italian bartender that strangers might easily have their "heads busted," he continued to come in for short periods, have a beer or coffee, and leave. If he came in the mornings when business was slow, any Mohawk who had decided not to go to work that day might have no one but Freilich to talk to.

During this time of passive observation, Freilich got to be known as someone who hung around the Wigwam Bar. The Indians did not regard this as unusual, because there were often non-Indians who liked Mohawks and associated with them. Convinced that they themselves are admirable people, they put up with such Mohawk fans. The turning point for Freilich was gaining a native sponsor, Joe, an aggressive, slightly built young Mohawk. Joe, who often idled at the Wigwam Bar, found Freilich a ready listener and took him under his wing. Joe's acceptance of Freilich was final after Joe impulsively invited him to visit his mother on the Indian reservation at Caughnawaga, nine miles from Montreal, Quebec. Freilich protested that he had neither documents for a trip into Canada nor money. The $10 he did have was all that proved necessary. As for documents, Mohawks, by ancient treaties, have free passage across the international boundaries at will.

Freilich, Joe, and Joe's friends piled into an old automobile and sped to the border, where they were cleared by guards in spite of the boisterously rude behavior of the Indians. At Caughnawaga Freilich met Joe's mother, Ma Joe.

From that time on, Freilich was Joe's friend, identity enough for the other Mohawks, and he was allowed to mingle and converse with them at the Wigwam Bar in perfect freedom. But his desire to do active research stumbled against the Indians' utter lack of interest in anthropology. In contrast, Mitchell had easily won active acceptance years before as a reporter. The Indians had not minded publicity in the news media at all. It was something they understood and liked. Not so an academic discipline. Unlike Mitchell, Freilich did not conduct formal interviews with a notebook and pencil. He directed

A Mohawk high steel worker at a construction site.

conversations and then retreated to the men's room or a nearby cafe to jot down notes.

Freilich's interviews and conversations soon disclosed that the Mohawks not only feared heights but sometimes confessed to that fear. In fact, when drunk, many would discuss it. One even said, "I pray every morning when I leave that I will come back alive." Sitting at the Wigwam Bar, Freilich soon noticed a display of items that we shall call a *symbolic association*. Over the bar were construction hard hats and pictures of braves in full regalia of feathers, bow, and arrows. He suddenly realized that working on high steel in a hard hat was equivalent to being a brave, a warrior decked with war honors. To be a real man one had to be a hero, and to become a hero, since one could no longer be a warrior, one walked out on high steel.

This explanation accounted for the endless reminiscences at the bar, which turned on feats of valor and the preservation of balance or cool in the heights. Freilich does not quote any of the reminiscences, but one such is recounted by journalist Edmund Wilson in his *Apologies to the Iroquois:*

In discussing the aptitude of the Iroquois for working in high steel, he [a retired Mohawk steelworker named Philip Cook] confessed that though it usually meant nothing to him to walk on these vertiginous structures, he had sometimes had seizures of fright—it was bad when it was sleeting, he said—and he told me a terrible story which almost made my hair stand on end like his. He and one of his brothers had been painting on the skeleton of a big building in Rochester. They were standing on a twenty-inch purling (a small beam laid across the rafters), ninety feet above the ground. A non-Indian, who was inexperienced but had undertaken the work on account of the high pay, looked down below and "froze." They spoke to him but he did not answer, and they knew that his situation was serious. Philip's brother, who was standing behind the man, hit him hard with his paintbrush on the back of the head, and Philip, who was standing in front of him, caught him in his arms as he fell. They had him tied with a rope and lowered, and when he found himself going down, he shrieked such a horrible shriek that Philip and his brother almost fell off their beam. On the ground, he was unconscious for a couple of hours. The Cooks were considerably shaken. (Wilson, 1960, pp. 114–115)

Not every man can maintain his bravery at great heights, and some, brave or not, die plunging from the heights. Mitchell wrote that the cemetery at Caughnawaga is dotted with the graves of steelworkers who died on the job. Each bears a cross in the form of two steel girders, a monument to fatal bravery on the heights. Yet to demonstrate bravery is the goal of all Mohawk males, even, and especially, in the face of death.

ATTEMPTING THE NATURAL HISTORY OF THE BROOKLYN MOHAWK

Freilich never issued an ethnography; his sojourn had been too short, his view too partial. His ethnological conclusion was that Mohawks do indeed fear heights and that their apparent fearlessness in high steel is a result of a complex of symbols glorifying the hero, who in turn is both the long lost brave on the warpath and the hard-hat worker in high steel. This is not a far-reaching or very profound conclusion, but there is good reason to believe that it is valid. Nothing Mitchell or Wilson, very sharp observers and meticulous journalists, have said contradicts it; rather, their evidence confirms it. But they also give additional information that allows us to place Freilich's conclusion into a wider, if more tentative, structure of Mohawk culture patterns.

Step 1: Isolating a Field for Study

For the Mohawks who worked in high steel, the appropriate field took in their natural units: the colony living in Brooklyn, consisting of a number of families residing in tenements; their gathering places at the Union Hall, the Wigwam Bar, the Presbyterian and Roman Catholic churches; and the forays of gangs of skilled workers to high steel construction sites all over the country. In addition, members of the Brooklyn colony were all participating members in the reservation at Caughnawaga. The men in particular made weekend excursions to visit parents, especially their mothers. Moreover, it is likely that most Brooklyn Mohawks, upon retiring from construction work, returned to Caughnawaga to live. One old man whom Mitchell interviewed was reluctantly preparing to do so. Such a far-flung field immediately presents problems for conducting a study. Freilich limited his activities to the Wigwam Bar for a while, but he was eventually swept up into the wild ride to Canada to meet Ma Joe.

Step 2: Charting the Interrelationships of Phenomena Observed Within the Field

Let us assume we are starting, as did Freilich, with the question of bravery. We want to relate that to everything else that seems relevant. Let us first take up the hierarchy of workers that Mitchell found in high steel. There are three kinds of work gangs: raising gangs, fitting-up gangs, and riveting gangs. One raising gang and one fitting-up gang put the steel beams and girders in place on the temporary top of the growing skeleton of a construction. Then several riveting gangs come along and weld the pieces of steel together permanently. A riveting gang has four skilled positions: a heater, a sticker-in, a bucker-up, and a riveter. The chain of workers pass the heated rivet from the heating bucket to its place in a hole joining two pieces of steel, and it is riveted into place forever. Although these jobs are interchangeable in the actual line of work and other workers sometimes relieve the riveter at his earsplitting tasks, the jobs may also reflect differences in skill, seniority, and general status. All workers have to go through an apprenticeship, however, before they are licensed for any of these jobs.

Second, let us consider the clustering of the adult men at the Wigwam Bar, mostly in the evening hours after work but also when men are unemployed and between jobs. Freilich mentions that fistfights may explode with apparent violence in the Wigwam but that the next day the two antagonists usually resume their friendship as if nothing had happened. No hard feelings are expressed; the one who has bested the other simply moves up a notch in the informal chain of status. Such dominance is called a "pecking order" in studies of barnyard fowl and a dominance hierarchy among primates, as we know. Freilich says that the lowest-ranking Mohawk at the Wigwam kept trying to pick a fight with him. He never accepted the challenge, fighting being completely foreign to his own culture. He later recognized that the Mohawk was attempting to put him at the bottom of the line and move himself up a notch.

Third, let us turn to male-female relationships in the Brooklyn colony. The Mohawks live in tenements, and Mitchell tells us that the wives of the workers in high steel often have unmarried sisters who live with them, working in local factories, perhaps taking care of the baby, and certainly keeping in touch with unmarried workers. Married sisters tend to live close together, often in the same apartment building.

Examination reveals that although the Mohawks' surnames are usually borrowed from the French or English, they also have Indian clan names inherited in the female line. Men thus belong to the clans of their mothers, maternal aunts, and grandmothers, not the clans of their fathers. Moreover, in the days before reservations, the Mohawk, like all other Iroquois, lived in longhouses inhabited by a grandmother and all her married daughters; men resided with their wives and their wives' sisters and mother. Today, sisters still tend to cluster together and to bring their husbands into contact, if not in the same house, at least as neighbors.

If we turn to the data from antiquity, we find that the men did the hunting and the fighting in gangs. Hunting parties or war parties were organized loosely but hierarchically, with older, senior, and more honored men in the lead. Honors were calculated by seniority, skill, and trophies: the amount of game bagged and the number of enemies slain or captured. Aggressive men organized both hunt and war parties around their own plans. Hunting and war were highly seasonal activities, of course, and the men spent their free time in the men's council house. Game and booty were handed over to the women for disposal. Women took care of the home and did the gardening, providing grain and vegetable produce for the hearth.

High steel construction work, like war and hunting, is seasonal, requires an expedition, and is very highly paid. Aggressive men go out, locate jobs in distant cities, and organize the work parties. One short season's work yields large amounts of cash, comparable to booty, which is handed over to the woman, minus the allowance needed to buy oneself and one's fellows beer at the Wigwam. Wives handle the household finances, as in the past they handled household subsistence. Freilich made these points in an article comparing ancient Mohawks to their descendents in high steel (1958).

Step 3: Redefining and Validating the Interrelationships

In this step, the observed phenomena should be stated in terms of measurements and comparisons so that other observers performing the same operations can come up with the same conclusions. We are not in a good position to do so for the Mohawks in high steel. Except for Freilich's observations about a pecking order at the Wigwam, we do not have many statements that can be duplicated by a trained field worker. Nobody has ever systematically observed workers in high steel; nobody knows for sure that the pecking order of the bar is transferred to the work hierarchy of the construction, as seems likely.

Moreover, we have no systematic information about contemporary tribal politics. In ancient times, honors in war, the hunt, and trading were translated into honors in the council house. Senior women in each clan nominated the clan chief from among their sons, nephews, and grandsons. This system has survived among the Six Nations of the Iroquois, of which the Mohawk are one; but in addition, individual reservations often elect councils to deal with the outside governments of the United States, Canada, New York State, and Quebec Province. How tribal politics relates to Mohawk work gangs is completely unknown.

Step 4: Making Statements of Theory
(Order, Probability, Limits, Patterns, and Law)

Despite the limitations of the data and the skimpiness of Freilich's student field project, we can make some statements pointing toward a theory of cultural persistence of social forms in modern metropolitan settings. We know much about the interrelationships of the phenomena within the field of Caughnawaga Mohawk behavior: the relationship of the Brooklyn colony to Caughnawaga; of women to their female relatives; of men to women; and, above all, of men to men, who typically shape their activity by earned rank, an expression of demonstrated bravery, both in idle social intercourse (at the Wigwam) and on the job. These patterns seem to be successful transfers of age-old hunting and warfare patterns to one of the most modern of occupations.

Thus it would seem that we have a successful retention of tribal social patterns in an urban industrial setting. Adult sisters once stayed home to do horticulture; unrelated men roamed in parties to hunt and fight. The same is true today, but the women no longer garden, and the men work in high steel, a substitute for hunting and war, permitting them to be brave men.

Tentatively, then, we can formulate a statement of **functional equivalence** or *substitutes*. Work in high steel is the functional equivalent of—the substitute for—the hunting-warfare complex of old. This idea, then, could very well serve as the framework for a new research proposal and for the focus of a more complete study. Once we had done more field work, we might feel confident about making more general statements—about the quality of fear as an inescapable component of human nature, about the division of labor between the sexes, about the extraordinary viability of a culture pattern over time. These would be statements of order, of limits, and of general human variability, perhaps even of law, especially when dealing with biological givens such as the emotion of fear. Clearly, the Mohawk community bears further field work.

SUMMARY AND CONCLUSIONS

Doing field work is the distinctive method of cultural anthropology, a method it shares with some biologists—ethologists (students of animal behavior in the wild)—and some sociologists. Field work is an inductive method that starts with the observations of facts in a natural setting and from them derives (*induces*) general principles, or theories. Field workers start with the assumption that all facts in their field are interrelated; therefore, it is wise to define a problem area for study beforehand and relate facts to each other within that framework as one goes along.

Field work in its intensive form was first publicized by Bronislaw Malinowski, with his celebrated ethnographies of the Trobriand Islanders in the 1920s.

In this chapter we have loosely followed the suggestions of Morris Freilich and outlined a checklist of practical steps for the prospective field worker. We can see from this checklist that the new ethnographer ideally goes into the field well grounded in background information about the culture area—the prehistory, previous ethnographies, and major scholarly sources on the people to be studied. Ideally, the new field worker finds sponsors at the national, regional, and local levels. Once in the field, our new field worker has adequate supplies and living arrangements and sets out to gain the confidence of the people at the field site.

Selection of the field site has to be in response to a theoretical framework to begin with. Thus we saw Morris Freilich investigating the possibility that the Brooklyn Mohawk lacked fear of heights. The new field worker achieves rapport—a sense of mutual empathy and correctness—with the subjects, observes them passively to begin with, and begins to participate in their common tasks and activities. Thus Freilich both "hung out" at the Wigwam Bar and went for wild rides back to the reservation. The field worker takes meticulous notes of observations and conducts interviews with subjects about activities observed. Interviews may simply be ongoing conversations during participant-observations, or they may be long one-on-one conversations, often tape recorded.

Once the field worker has spent at least one natural time cycle—the solar year—in the field, he or she ought to have a substantial body of data, collected in voluminous field notes. Now it is possible to start writing up the observations. This is usually done away from the field setting. Written ethnographies may be in the form of term papers, masters essays, doctoral dissertations, scholarly articles, and books. Each has its own intended audience. In each case, however, the intent is to relate data to theory and thereby to refine both. In our exploration of the efforts of a student anthropologist, we have concluded that Mohawks do indeed have a fear of heights, that bravery—overcoming fear—is both learned and valued, and that working in high steel can be the functional equivalent of a brave life of hunting and fighting in the old culture. Mohawk culture seems to have been able to preserve its values in an urban industrial world by adapting them to activities that are highly valued in that world: skilled riveting in high steel.

In the chapters that follow we shall be reporting on many other examples of facts and theories gained from field work.

SUGGESTED READINGS

Anderson, Barbara G. *First Field Work: The Misadventures of an Anthropologist.* Prospect Heights, Ill.: Waveland Press, 1991. Culture shock in a Danish Community in the North Sea.

Freilich, Morris, ed. *Marginal Natives: Anthropologists at Work.* New York: Harper & Row, 1970. A collection of retrospective essays on field work by anthropologists, plus Freilich's commentary. Freilich's account of his experiences with Brooklyn Mohawks is contrasted with field work in the Caribbean.

Kimball, Solon T., and William L. Partridge. *The Craft of Community Study: Fieldwork Dialogues.* Gainesville, Fl.: University of Florida Press, 1979. An engaging look at the field work process on the north coast of Colombia. An anthropology graduate student, Bill Partridge, writes long letters from the field to his doctoral mentor, Sol Kimball, who replies.

Lizot, Jacques. *Tales of the Yanomami: Daily Life in the Venezuelan Forest.* New York: Cambridge University Press, 1985. An interpretationist ethnography written like a novel by an anthropologist who has lived many years with his subjects.

Van Maanen, John. *Tales of the Field: On Writing Ethnography.* Chicago: University of Chicago Press, 1988. An intriguing examination of writing up findings.

Wilson, Edmund. *Apologies to the Iroquois, with a Study of the Mohawks in High Steel by Joseph Mitchell.* New York: Random House, 1960. Lively reading. Mitchell's study of the Mohawk would make good reading at the start of this book, better rereading at the end of it.

GLOSSARY

active research In field work, the formal gathering of data, as in taking measurements of any sort, administering questionnaires, or conducting formal interviews.

data Facts. Data often refer to measurable, quantifiable facts. The word derives from the Latin for "given" (singular = *datum*).

deduction Reasoning from a small structure of principles to a sequence of observations, as in mathematics. The laws of supply and demand in economics are an example.

diffusionists A school of anthropology, largely discredited today, which theorized that all human social and cultural traits diffused from a few centers of civilization, often degenerating in the process.

ethics In field work, the moral responsibility of the ethnographer not to allow information gathered to harm the subjects. On the other hand, the researcher also has a moral responsibility to report accurately. This poses a moral dilemma.

evolutionists An early school of anthropology founded by Lewis Henry Morgan, an American amateur scholar, whose famous book *Ancient Society* (1877) argued that human beings had progressed inevitably from lower stages of "barbarism" through "savagery" to "civilization." This doctrine was both ethnocentric and, in the ideas of some of its followers, racist.

facts Items or givens of information accepted as true, connoting deeds or events. For ethnographers facts are often observed events or interview statements about events.

field The areas in space occupied by a human population studied by an anthropologist. The areas may be dispersed, but they are the location of activities over natural time cycles. Thus the field for the Brooklyn Mohawk includes the Brooklyn neighborhood, the reservation at Caughnawaga, and skyscrapers all over North

America. A field's timetables are those of the year, the generation, and the lifetime, as persons travel around all these points.

field work The natural history method of study engaged in by anthropologists, in order to induce theories from facts gained by observation and interviewing.

functional equivalence The theory, tentatively advanced for the Brooklyn Mohawk, that in changed situations new complexes can substitute for old ones and fulfill the same function. High steel is thus the functional equivalent of the old hunting and warfare complex for today's Mohawks.

functionalism In cultural anthropology, the theoretical framework, first posited by Bronislaw Malinowski, which posits that all facts in a social field are interrelated so that changes in one affect all the others. A further assumption is that social facts are likely to be adaptive for the individual and the group.

induction Reasoning from a set of observations to arrive at general principles, the method typical of ethnographic field work (verb: *to induce*).

informant An ethnographic subject who regularly converses or engages in interviews with the field worker.

interpretationist ethnography A report from the field written in an attempt to represent as closely as possible the world as the subjects ("the Others") see it. Such ethnographies are often very conscious of the ethnographer as "self" and often include texts from the Others. (Also called "thick description.")

interview Along with observation, the principal technique in ethnography, whereby the field worker questions informants. This questioning can happen informally in casual conversation, or formally in response to queries thought up beforehand. Ethnographic interviews are usually open-ended, following leads in the informant's responses.

mentor A graduate student's major professor and intellectual sponsor.

the Other In interpretationist ethnographies, a term substituted for *native*. Because ethnographic subjects, such as the Brooklyn Mohawk, are often no longer strictly "natives," the term is a wise one. It also implies a gap between the "self" (the ethnographer) and the "Other."

participant observation Attempted participation in an activity that the ethnographer is also observing.

rapport In field work, a state of goodwill between the ethnographer and the subjects, manifested in easy, well-mannered interactions and exchange of information and favors.

reflexivity The self-conscious attempt to include the ethnographer (the "self"), often using informants' responses to the self, in a written ethnography.

socialization The tendency for the ethnographer to be unconsciously accustomed to and eventually absorbed into the culture of the field situation.

sponsors In field work, the influential persons at a national, regional, and local level who may help an anthropologist gain entry into the field.

theoretical framework The focus, often defined in a research proposal, whereby facts are assembled from field work in order to find interrelations among them; for example, Freilich collected facts about fear of heights among the Brooklyn Mohawk.

theory A statement of the apparent relationships among observed facts that attempts to explain and account for them.

The Primate
Homo Sapiens:
Our Place in Nature

4

*THE LIVING CELL AND HUMAN
BEINGS: THE GENETIC CODE AND
ANTHROPOLOGY*

Genetic Information in the Cell: Genes, Chromosomes, and DNA

The Nature of Genetic Variation Within a Species

*The Adult Cell as a Complete Organism, Functioning
Within a Wider System*

*HUMANITY AS A SPECIES AMONG
RELATED SPECIES*

Paleoanthropology and the Classification of the Human Species

Human Beings Versus Apes: Bipedalism, Big Brains, and Speech

*HOMINID GENUSES:
AUSTRALOPITHECUS AND HOMO*

Australopithecines: Four Species and 3 Million Years

   Australopithecus afarensis

   Australopithecus africanus and Oldowan Pebble Tools

Four Hominid Species at Once

   The Robust Australopithecines: Hominid Side Branches

   Homo habilis

   Homo erectus

   Homo sapiens

*LANGUAGE, GENETIC CODES,
HUMAN SPEECH, AND
CULTURE*

The Genetic Code as a Language

Ritual as a Language

Human Speech as a Structured Extragenetic Code

Proto-World: The Ur Language

*Speech as an Adaptive Feature Enhancing Human
Command over Resources*

O ne central issue for social science is the biological relation of human beings to other animals and its implications for human social life. Over the past thirty years views have changed drastically, and today contrary views are debated vigorously. Revolutionary discoveries at the molecular and genetic level of the basic living human cell have greatly extended our knowledge of genetics. Paleoanthropologists have made exciting discoveries of hominid fossil remains, while primatologists have made fascinating field studies of the social life of monkeys and apes in the wild. All these scientific frontiers have contributed to our knowledge of human evolution, of the behavioral potential of our prehuman ancestors and of ourselves.

In its widest framework, evolution proceeds from the situational ability of apparently random events, such as genetic mutations or behavioral patterns, to solve some problem, such as the movement of a group of living beings into a new habitat. The result is ever more complex biological and social "designs." Over time, living systems exhibit population growth, escalation in scale, and increasing specialization of functional subparts. Systems "self-organize" first into a single hierarchy, reflected by a ranked order with few parts in command and other parts in "lower" grades performing functions of maintenance and growth. These functional units become hierarchies of their own. The whole array becomes a *heterarchy*—that is, a set of hierarchies existing side by side.

All living systems, whether a single biological organism or a larger social group, are self-regulating, responding to exterior conditions in the environment from which they must derive and transform both matter and energy, in the process of reproducing both the species and the group. They are thus **factories.** Since all of us are composed of systems of living cells, let us first look at human beings from the level of the cell and its genes. Then we will look at the fossil evidence of human evolution—that is, the evidence from paleoanthropology—taking up each of the known hominid fossil species in turn. Finally, we will see how elements evident at the cellular level can also be found at the levels of the organism and of the society, using the example of language.

THE LIVING CELL AND HUMAN BEINGS: THE GENETIC CODE AND ANTHROPOLOGY

Human beings are multicelled organisms. Moreover, each of us was, at the moment of fertilization, a living organism (the *conceptus*) composed of a single cell. The nucleus of the conceptus cell, or zygote, and of each of its subsequent daughter cells, contains all the genetic material needed to provide the information to shape the development of the embryo into a fully formed organism. This is true of all zygote cells for all species that practice sexual reproduction.

The information in the nucleus, which is literally voluminous (for human beings enough, if written out, to fill 500 large printed volumes in your school library), is called the **genotype,** the potential of the individual as recorded in the genes. The actual product, or characteristics of the developed individual, is called the **phenotype.** It reflects the primary direction of the genes, modified in various ways by the organism's environment and accidental factors of growth.

Every cell in the body carries the full complement of genetic information. The zygote and a few other cells formed immediately from it can be thought of as transmitting all that information but actually using very little of it, since their purpose is to reproduce. Most cells use only the information needed to program their own structure and function. Thus, each cell uses only a fraction of the genetic information stored in its own nucleus.

Genetic Information in the Cell: Genes, Chromosomes, and DNA

The genetic information in the nucleus of a human cell is contained in forty-six ultramicroscopic helical strands called **chromosomes. Genes,** in turn, are organized sequences of molecules, or positional units, on chromosomes; genes actually transmit specific hereditary characteristics from one generation to another. Each gene on one chromosome is paired with one on a sister chromosome to produce, or not, a given observable (phenotypic) trait in an individual.

The actual mated helical structure of the chromosomes (and therefore of the genes) is at once marvelously complex yet essentially simple. The structure is complex in actual components, simple in the way it arranges them. Chromosomes are composed of two complementary long strands of **deoxyribonucleic acid,** or **DNA.** DNA molecules are chains or polymers of "polynucleotides," themselves long molecules. These chains are wrapped around each other in a nonparallel way to form a double helix, or spiral coil (see Figure 4.1).

At the time of cell division, the coils unwind in a precise fashion, and each separate strand is replicated, thus producing a new double helix or coil. Thus,

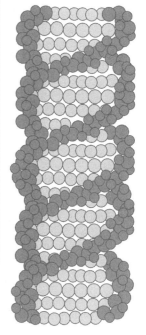

Figure 4.1 A portion of a DNA molecule, showing the double helix structure.

each independently unwinding single helix of DNA acts as a template, inducing the manufacture of its relevant partner from materials in the nucleus.

It is during this synthesis phase that "mistakes" in copying of new strands of DNA can occur. Such alterations allow for the production of **mutations,** or changes in the genetic material, and thus are a prime mechanism for the occurrence of genetic variability within any breeding population.

The Nature of Genetic Variation Within a Species

As we have seen, DNA replicates itself from cell to cell, and from one generation of multicelled organism to another. During sexual reproduction DNA is shuffled and recombined to produce daughter cells with varying combinations of genetic material. Thus, each reproductive cell has a unique genetic makeup to contribute to the zygote and subsequent organism. A species with sexual reproduction, then, has a **gene pool** from which to create new combinations of messages for the development of new individuals. The individuals born from a large gene pool show considerable variation. That is, although they are all capable of mating with one another, they vary greatly in individual appearance—or phenotypic traits. (Compare Dalmatians with Pekinese, for example; they differ in size, facial structure, hair length, and markings.)

Genetic variation within a species happens two ways: through mutations and through reshuffling of genetic materials. Mutations are "copying" errors in the replication of strands of DNA, sometimes resulting from the influence of extraneous chemical substances or of x-rays. Reshuffling happens during *mitosis*, the ordinary process of cell division. In mitosis the nucleus of the cell first divides into two, then the cell itself splits into two daughter cells, with a nucleus that has replicated its missing half. In this process chromosomes split and pull apart, and bits and pieces break off and recombine, thus forming a mutation. Reshuffling also occurs, with consequences for the entire organism, in *meiosis*, the process of producing gametes (sperm or ovum cells). These "haploid" cells each contain a nucleus with only half the genetic material of its original parent cell. In meiosis chromosome strands may be mixed as they replicate themselves and split, so that an individual does not inherit the genes in the same order as they are arrayed in the parents' chromosomes.

The Adult Cell as a Complete Organism, Functioning Within a Wider System

The new coils of DNA in a newly created cell formed from mitosis promote the production of **ribonucleic acid (RNA),** a subset of which, *messenger RNA (mRNA)*, migrates into the cytoplasm of the cell. There the mRNA provides information to organelles called ribosomes. Another kind of RNA, termed *transfer ribonucleic acid (tRNA)*, moves along the strands of ribosomal

RNA and "reads" their sequences of nucleotides. These sequences serve as instructions to link together *amino acids*, abundant in the cell's cytoplasm, to form a variety of *proteins*, such as enzymes, hormones, and antibodies, for functions both inside and outside the cell (see Figure 4.2).

In this sense every cell of our body is a tiny biochemical factory. On a daily basis, the cell receives matter and energy, stores them—thus becoming a sort of battery—and processes them, not only using energy to maintain itself but actually manufacturing complex organic substances out of the matter at hand. As an embryonic or fetal cell enlarges, it reproduces itself, by mitosis, from one generation of cells to another, to form independent organs (liver, brain, lungs, and so on) all within the body. In turn, the various body organs replicate, on a "higher" and even more complex level, the life processes and complexity of the original cell itself. However, each body cell, no matter what its function, no matter what its organ of the body—whether blood, heart, liver, muscle, or brain—must receive both matter and energy, both food and oxygen, on a daily basis to survive. Each organ is a whole suborganism within the organism.

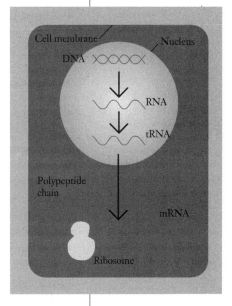

Thus the human body, as a living system, exhibits a hierarchy of cells and life processes. In the fetus the nuclei of cells are "in command." Moreover, in each cell DNA sends RNA to be read in the manufacture of the body's substance. After birth, the brain and the nervous system are "in command." The body also exhibits *heterarchy*, or the array of the various subsystems—circulation, digestion, respiration, and so on—side by side in the maintenance of life.

To summarize, the cell forms a "platform" for human life, and indeed for the lives of all multicellular plants and animals. Further, the cell is the platform for the origin, evolution, and organization of multicelled bodies. The genetic code, the language of life, tells each component cell what to do. Each knows its task in the daily process of consuming oxygen and receiving food, in the exchange of matter and energy with other cells through the various streets of the organism, such as the bloodstream and the lymph system. Disposal of waste products occurs through the same streets. Moreover, communication is going on. Some messages come from the nervous system. Other communicating is internal, as the cell in its own life cycle obeys the messages of its own genes, manifest in DNA comprising its chromosomes in the cell nucleus. We shall compare this language of the cells with human speech, our extragenetic code, later in this chapter.

We now know that all living organisms are composed of cells and that each organism and each cell is the product of its genetic code acting upon

Figure 4.2 Protein synthesis. The polypeptides produced at the ribosomes in turn make up amino acids, which combine to make up proteins.

matter and energy through characteristic actions. Organisms that share common genes are grouped into species, and it is the process of **speciation** leading to human beings that concerns us next.

HUMANITY AS A SPECIES AMONG RELATED SPECIES

A **species** is a group of living beings sharing a gene pool—a collection of genes with some considerable variation from individual to individual. Individuals in a species share that gene pool because they are capable of interbreeding. All types of human beings known today, for example, are capable of mating and producing offspring, who in turn can produce more offspring. Humanity today is a single species, although there is a wide range of variation from population to population. Such regional variations are sometimes called "races."

Paleoanthropology and the Classification of the Human Species

Paleoanthropology is the study of primate fossil remains. This study shares its field techniques with archaeology, its activities and evolutionary theory with zoology, and a good part of its interpretive theory with anthropology at large. In no area of social sciences have advances in knowledge been more rapid in the last decades and in none are the facts more likely to change over the next few than in paleoanthropology. It is an exciting scientific frontier.

One activity that paleoanthropology shares with zoology is *taxonomy*, or systematics, the classification of extinct species known only through their fossil remains. Scientific naming follows the methods of Carl von Linné. Linnaean classification was originally applied to living beings on the basis of observable structural characteristics. After the advent of Darwin's theory of evolution these classifications were understood to be the result of differential descent from common ancestors. All animals living today are assumed to be related through actual lines of descent that stretch back 600 million years ago to the first animal microbes.

We humans are first animals, second vertebrates, third mammals, and next—members of the order of primates. The biological classification of our human genealogical place among primates can be conveniently summarized as follows:

Order	Primates
Suborder	Anthropoidea
Infraorder	Catarrhini
Superfamily	Hominoidea
Family	Hominidae
Modern species	*Homo sapiens*

In zoological taxonomy, orders are divided into suborders—in the primate case, into suborders Prosimii (such as lemurs, lorises, and tarsiers) and Anthropoidea. The latter includes two infraorders, Platyrrhini (New World monkeys) and Catarrhini (Old World monkeys, apes, and humans). This last infraorder in turn is divided into two superfamilies, Old World monkeys and ours, Hominoidea, which includes three families, the Hylobatidae (lesser apes such as gibbons), the Pongidae (great apes, or chimpanzees, orangutans, and gorillas), and the Hominidae, which includes us modern hominids.

Our scientific name is *Homo sapiens sapiens*; our first name is that of our genus, the second is our species, and the third is our subspecies. There is no other living subspecies of *Homo sapiens*.

There are several things to note about the entire order of primates. First, the original species and most species thereafter were and are arboreal—that is, they live in trees. Primates thus all have hands and a grasp, obviously useful for life in trees. They likewise have eyes forward in the head with stereoscopic vision. Second, the primate diet emphasizes leaves and fruits in all species; most species eat insects as well. Moreover, the superfamily of the Hominoidea—of apes and humans—is an ancient one. Surprisingly, the Old World Monkeys, or Catarrhini, have a late genetic adaptation that gave them a great advantage over their cousins, the apes: they are able to digest raw fruit without ill effect from the toxins present in that fruit source. Like most other mammals, apes can digest only ripe fruit. Monkeys, then, for millions of years seem to have pushed the apes aside in the tropical forest as they became the more numerous, if usually smaller-sized, primates.

Human Beings Versus Apes: Bipedalism, Big Brains, and Speech

At the present time hominids are singularly closely related; human beings are one species, one genus, and one family. Unlike the family of great apes, we are not divided into various genuses, such as chimpanzees and gorillas, which in turn are divided into several species, or populations that do not interbreed.

To look at these classifications in a genealogical way leads to questions of descent. We are back to paleoanthropology, for it is certain that Pongidae, the family of apes today, are not our ancestors but merely cousins descended from similar but extinct ancestors. There are then two genealogical questions: (1) Who were the original hominoids, ancestors of both humans and apes? and (2) Who were the first hominids, ancestors of human beings alone, and not the great apes?

It is here that the evidence from the molecular biology of contemporary species is able to supplement the fossil evidence of our descent. To paleoanthropologists' astonishment, molecular biologists, working in the lab, compared the genetic material of the great apes with each other and with human beings and concluded that gorillas and chimpanzees are far more closely related to human beings and to each other than they are to orangutans, let alone to gibbons. Chimpanzees, it turns out, are especially closely related to us. Indeed, we share some 98 percent of our genetic material with ordinary chimps and some 99 percent of it with bonobos, or pygmy chimps!

As if these findings were not sensational enough (and indeed, hotly resisted for a while by those working exclusively with the fossil evidence), the molecular biologists, by measuring molecular difference within genetic material from species to species, have come up with a "molecular clock," rates by which they can calculate the time scales of species' divergence from each other. According to this molecular clock—as it is currently read—chimpanzees and human beings diverged from a common ancestor and ancestress some 5 million years ago, not the 15 million years that had been the hypothetical timeline for the paleontologists.

So those common ape ancestors, whoever they were, had traits resembling both human beings and chimpanzees. There are relevant ape fossil finds, and researchers debate whether or not they are in the human line. However, we shall not discuss them. Still, researchers have concluded—through a series of mathematical calculations on the motor habits of modern apes and human beings—that the ancestor common to both was an adept climber. It spent a lot of time in trees but was capable of walking on the ground, with the help of its knuckles ("knuckle walking"), and of standing erect or partly erect for very short periods. The ancestral forms moved around in ways similar to those of modern great apes, but they did not have the specialized ability to *brachiate*, or swing by their arms on the underside of branches, in the manner of modern gibbons.

Now if we ask ourselves what the very slight genetic difference between us and chimpanzees means in actual fact, in the real physical differences between us and them, we see that the 1 or 2 percent of our differing genetic material has produced in us an animal that is fully capable of standing and walking erect on two legs. We are the *bipedal primate*. In addition, our brains are about three times bigger than those of chimpanzees. Indeed, we have the largest brains in relation to body size of any animal in the world. We are the *brainy animal*. Finally, our vocal tract is adapted for speech, which of course originates in and is controlled by areas within our large brains. We are the *speaking animal*.

Although investigators working with chimps in laboratory settings have been able to teach them words, vocabulary, and even grammar in the form of sign language or computer signs (in place of spoken words), this has been a difficult task. Even the slowest five-year-old human child learns speech with greater facility than the brightest chimp. The intelligence is there in chimps, but a brain organized for easy speech is not.

How, then, did a bipedal, brainy, speaking primate evolve from a knuckle-walking, less-brainy, nonspeaking one? Earlier speculation centered on the relationship among brain size, grasp, and tool use. An intelligent primate would find it advantageous to stand erect and use tools, such as weapons, for hunting. In turn, the areas of the brain that govern grasp and manipulation of tools are closely related to the areas that control speech. Brain and grasp drive bipedalism, in this hypothetical arrangement. The fossil evidence has increasingly contradicted this hypothesis. It is now apparent that our earliest ancestors in the hominid line, that line diverging from the other great apes, *stood fully erect and were fully bipedal*. Stone tool use does not show up in the archaeological record for a million and a half years after the appearance of these upright hominids. Their brains were small in comparison with ours. Bipedalism, then, came first and tool manipulation and brain growth came later, and not in orderly fashion, as we shall see.

HOMINID GENUSES: AUSTRALOPITHECUS *AND* HOMO

There are approximately nine known species within the two hominid genuses, *Australopithecus* and *Homo*. All but modern human beings, *Homo sapiens sapiens*, are extinct. But for much of the period from 2 to 1 million years ago, four of them shared the tropical world, sometimes coexisting in the same places. It is likely that more hominid species shall be uncovered by paleontologists in the future. Indeed, paleontologists Niles Eldredge and Ian Tattersall (1982) estimate that up to eighteen may yet be found. In their view the hominid line is probably not a "tree" but a "bush."

Thus, when we contemplate the first divergence of hominids from apes ancestral also to chimpanzees, we must ask and seek to answer several questions: What were the physical attributes of the population making up the species? How do these features differ from those of generalized apes? What problem was being solved by the—quite accidental—appearance of these new design features?

Australopithecines:
Four Species and 3 Million Years

The earlier hominid genus is ***Australopithecus***. Raymond Dart first discovered early fossil remains of this genus in South Africa in 1925, but it took almost thirty years for the profession to accept his claim that they were in the hominid line—that is, in the line leading to modern human beings and not to the great apes as well. Because of their geographical location, Dart gave these finds the name *Australopithecus* (southern ape).

Australopithecus afarensis. Since Dart's time a great many more fossils have been found. Some hominid fossils hint of great antiquity—a molar tooth dated at over 6 million years ago, a jawbone dated to 5.5 million years ago—

but the earliest good fossil evidence dates to 4 million years ago to a species called ***Australopithecus afarensis*** after the site of Afar in east Africa. (The earlier dates contradict the calendar set by the current reading of the molecular clock; thus, some paleontologists have urged "resetting the clock" by 1 or 2 million years. The later date is squarely in line with the molecular clock. At the moment the point is moot.)

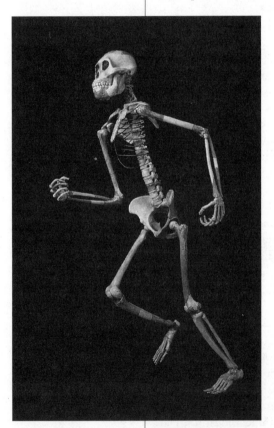

Reconstructed skeleton of A. afarensis. *This plaster cast, including parts cast from actual fossil bones, was produced by Owen Lovejoy and his students at Kent State.*

This earliest known hominid was a creature that differed from apes only in its upright posture and bipedal motion. It stood and walked fully erect. But its brain and head, perched atop an erect back, were in other respects those of an ape. Its brain, like that of all apes, was large compared to those of other primates, some 400 to 500 cubic centimeters, but small when compared to the modern human brain, at a size of 1400 cubic centimeters or so. That was still, of course, the brain of a very intelligent animal.

As a species *Australopithecus afarensis* also exhibited **sexual dimorphism;** that is, males were much larger than females. (Sexual dimorphism means that the two sexes of a species differ in size and shape.) Adult females were as short as three feet tall, weighing 50 pounds, while adult males stood as tall as four to five feet and weighed up to 100 pounds.

A. afarensis, then, was fully erect and fully bipedal. This trait reflects several genetic changes: a fairly simple change (governed by a single gene) in the tilt of the pelvis, and more complex mutations governing the shape of the foot.

Genetic changes resulting in a new species must solve some problem for an interbreeding group. Here it is clear that hominid ape populations were adapting to environments without trees, or certainly with fewer trees. Was erect posture a solution to the problem of terrestrial life for a hominid species? Chimpanzees can walk bipedally for short periods as efficiently as they "knuckle walk." Hominid bipedal walking is more efficient than the chimpanzee equivalent. Hence, of the two modes, knuckle walking or bipedal walking, the latter was the more efficient adaptation to life on the ground for an ape. Presumably these creatures were at first concerned with daily moves from one clump of trees—which provided nighttime shelter and protection—to another. Bipedal walking was the way this new species of ape did so. Erect posture further allowed a primate to use its acute vision in sighting both danger and food sources over open, treeless country.

Erect posture in a tropical climate also allows a large primate to cool its body more efficiently than quadrupedal posture does. Going on all fours exposes more of the body to the tropical sun, and, being closer to the ground, such a creature cannot avail itself of cooling breezes. Bipedal posture, then, allows a tall primate a chance to remain cool and consume less water, another advantage in a new habitat with few trees.

Thus, we have an upright, bipedal ape with sexual dimorphism originating at least 4 million years ago and dying out about 3 million years ago. There is no evidence that this animal ever used stone tools. Yet it was, among all the animals on earth at that time, perhaps the most intelligent. We assume that it foraged for a living. It was not physically adapted for exclusive predation—hunting—as are the great carnivores such as lions, tigers, wolves, wild dogs, and so on, with their speed, strong shoulders, powerful jaws, fierce canine teeth, and powerful, sharp claws. However, *A. afarensis* probably hunted small game that came its way, just as chimpanzees do today. It may have hurled objects at hand to fell that game.

In *A. afarensis*'s social organization, large males, arrayed together, probably formed a rampart for the troop, in much the way that baboons, those terrestrial and quadrupedal monkeys, also form male ramparts when the troop is threatened by a predator. If it roamed over the plains by day, it also very likely sought out trees for shelter at night.

Australopithecus africanus and Oldowan Pebble Tools. Around 3 million years ago, *A. afarensis* died out and a new species emerges in the fossil evidence, ***Australopithecus africanus*** (the same species originally identified by Dart). This species is similar to *A. afarensis*. Indeed, they differ from each other only through minor skeletal details, especially in their dentition or patterns of teeth. *A. africanus* was a brainy animal, but not much more so than the previous species. Possibly *A. africanus* also had sexual dimorphism, but some researchers find this unlikely from the fossil evidence.

We do know that during the million years of this creature's existence a stone tool kit appeared in the archaeological record, although never in association with any hominid fossil remains. We have as yet no direct evidence, then, that *A. africanus* made and used these tools. However, no other fossil hominid has been found at the same time levels, nor has any other been associated with these tools at those times. *Some* hominid was making and using them.

These tools were "pebble tools" or "Oldowan" tools, so called after the Olduvai Gorge, where they were first found (see Figure 4.3). They formed a coherent kit of tools, each with different uses: to chop meat, to scrape meat off hides, even to pierce hides. Thus, halfway through the history of *A. africanus* some hominid was butchering and processing prey, if not killing it, with stone pebble tools. This hominid did not have an efficient means of carrying its tools, so it took its game in its hands to sites where stone tools, quarried nearby, were stored or cached, for processing.

However, the hand axes and projectile points of later ages and tool traditions are lacking. If these sharpened pebbles were used as weapons for hunting, it was by hurling them at the prey, not by attaching them to spears, arrows, or other projectiles.

Because these tools were for processing fallen prey, rather than for hunting, some researchers have speculated that *A. africanus* was as much a scavenger of carrion, or dead meat, as it was a hunter of fresh meat. If so, it faced formidable competition from the original predator and from other scavengers (vultures, jackals, and so on). It is possible that early hominids did get some meat from large kills this way, however.

Thus if we speculate about the lifeways, the biograms of this second australopithecine species, we can say that hunting most likely figured in its diet, almost certainly more so than with the earlier species.

Both of these two early "southern apes" must have

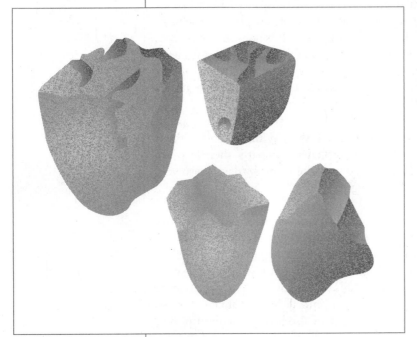

Figure 4.3 Oldowan pebble tools.

built on the potentials of their great ape background. We postulate that there is a pan-ape genetic material that allows for a variety of behaviors in the various species of apes. Australopithecine species probably ran through much of the spectrum of ape behavior. That is, australopithecine communities may have looked like those of contemporary gorillas, or of chimps.

Indeed, different species may have had either or both types of communities or even combinations at different times in their history under differing ecological conditions. As we saw in Chapter 2, chimps live in large numbers in dispersed troops. Females form mother-centered families. Males join roving bachelor groups and shake down into dominance hierarchies. Males form temporary liaisons with females when they are sexually attractive. They also form ramparts or "war parties" against predators and neighboring troops.

Younger females may move from troop to troop, thus providing for genetic variability and gene flow across geographical boundaries.

Gorillas, in contrast, have a rather different pattern. It is likely that they also form wider communities of dispersed animals who all know and recognize each other. Gorillas, however, are very large and very slow primates. For protection from predators, they rely not on speed, agility, or defensive capabilities of fangs and claws but on intimidation, especially on the part of the enormous adult, or silverback, male, who is twice as big as an adult female. These males bluff their enemies with overpowering displays. Females with young tend to associate in fairly tight groups around a single silverback, who looks as if he were herding a harem. While the silverback may tolerate other, younger, males, he monopolizes the females when they become sexually attractive. Young males, as a consequence, tend to spend much of their lives either alone or roaming in bachelor bands. Sexual dimorphism in the earlier australopithecine, *A. afarensis*, may be a clue to a similar social structure for them.

Four Hominid Species at Once

About 2 million years ago, as *A. africanus* was dying out, the hominid picture becomes quite complicated. Two new australopithecine species emerged, as did the first species classified with the genus *Homo*, *H. habilis*. Only a few hundred thousand years later, yet another species of *Homo* emerged, *H. erectus*, and for much of the million years between 2 and 1 million years ago, the four hominid species coexisted upon the earth (see Figure 4.4).

The Robust Australopithecines: Hominid Side Branches. Two large species of australopithecines diverged at this time: ***A. robustus*** and the closely related ***A. boisei,*** also known as *Zinjanthropus*. Both were quite robust—that is, big boned and heavily muscled. And both species had enormous teeth. Their large molars and jaws were perhaps adapted to grinding vegetable matter, even tender grasses, and it is probable that these forms were herbivores, vegetable eaters, even grazers on the grasslands! This is especially true of *A. boisei* (*Zinjanthropus*).

In these two species we are contemplating primates as *bipedal grazers*. No such primate species exists today, but Australian kangaroos provide some intriguing comparisons to the lifeways of such forms. Kangaroos are marsu-

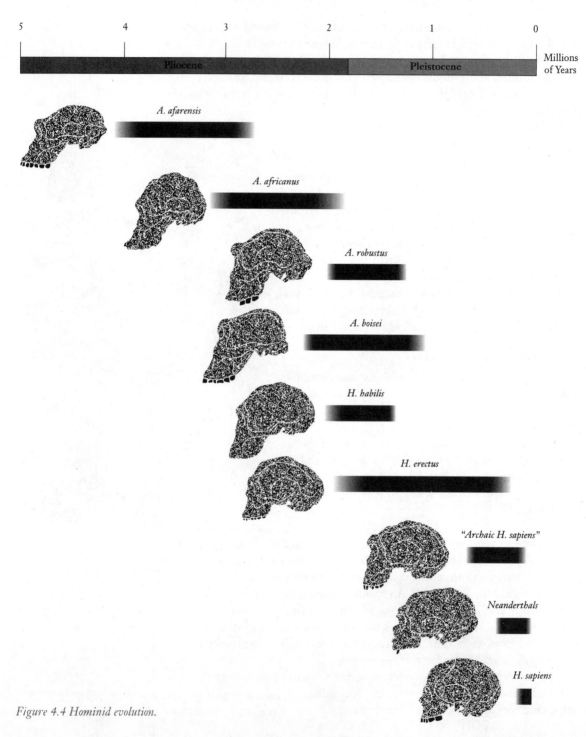

Figure 4.4 Hominid evolution.

pials, the other major class of mammals. We human beings belong to the larger class of placental mammals, who bear their young fully formed and equipped to live outside the womb. Marsupial young, in contrast, are born still fetal, although capable of breathing and crawling to their mother's pouch, where they attach their mouths to a tit and remain for a long period suckling. When they emerge, capable of unsteady locomotion on their own, marsupial infants can still take refuge in the maternal pouch, and for longer trips from one grazing spot to another, they ride in comfort.

Kangaroos, however, are bipedal, standing fully erect, their "hands" freed for grasping. They also have prehensile tails, which they use to grasp and carry straw to build their nests in the open country they inhabit. They locomote by hopping, leaping, or bounding upon their two powerful legs. They do not eat meat, and they do not use tools.

Some species, such as the giant red kangaroo, are very large. They, too, exhibit sexual dimorphism. Males form ramparts for the troop, or herd. However, each troop's females are monopolized at any one time by only one male, the "gray king," comparable to the silverback gorilla. Unlike the silverback, however, the gray king must defend his large "harem" constantly by severe fights with competitors. The fights wear him down, and his reign seldom lasts for more than a year, when he yields ground, literally, to a competitor, who then takes up his own uneasy dominion as the new gray king.

In primate societies a male recently displaced from the number one or alpha position may well form an alliance with the new alpha male. In the new leader's presence, he is number two; away from the leader, he may have some lower position. This is not the case with red kangaroos; the vanquished gray king flees to the periphery of the troop and has very low status. Often severely injured from his many fights, he usually dies within a year.

This example is simply suggestive of the potentials for the lifeways of a grazing bipedal mammal. The two robust australopithecines, however, differed in that their young could not ride conveniently in maternal pouches. Nor would the males have been able to disable each other by leaping kung fu kicks from their powerful legs adapted for bounding. The potential for alliances and social manipulation seems more extensive among primates than among any marsupials. Still, overall social organization may have been similar.

Homo habilis. A number of African fossil finds, dating from less than 2 million years ago to 1.5 million years ago, have been classified as ***Homo habilis***. As this is an intermediate form, it has also been named *Australopithecus habilis.* These are gracile—that is, small-boned—fossils. In general, these forms have brain sizes that range from 500 cubic centimeters to 775 cubic centimeters and a face that has receded considerably below the skull cap when compared to australopithecine forms. It may well be that investigators, after future discoveries, will reclassify these specimens into two or more species, but at the moment they are, in the words of paleontologists Niles Eldridge and Ian Tattersall, "a species of convenience" (1982, p. 140).

Whatever the eventual case, there is clear evidence that these specimens had a stone toolkit, hence the name "man, the tool maker." Unlike the robust australopithecines, this hominid was adapting to a treeless environment not by ponderous size and grazing but by being a lightweight runner and tool user.

Homo erectus. Not long after the emergence of *H. habilis* another species appeared and coexisted with it for a time. Its name, **Homo erectus** ("erect man"), reflects the belief that earlier forms were not fully erect, something we now know not to be true. In contrast to the disputed and relatively recent discovery of australopithecine remains, the first of this series of fossil finds was much earlier, starting in 1895. They have been known for many years in the popular literature as "Java man" and "Peking man." The most important physical characteristic of *H. erectus* was its advancing brain size over the nearly 2 million years of its existence. Its brain went from somewhat over 700 cubic centimeters to reach 1300 in some cases before the extinction of the species. These were also large-boned creatures, in contrast to *H. habilis*, thus casting doubt as to who their immediate ancestors were—*H. habilis* or some as yet undiscovered more robust form.

Some hundreds of thousands of years after the emergence of *H. erectus*, a new tool-making tradition also emerged: the Acheulian tradition. These were bifaced axes carefully flaked on all sides from a core stone (see Figure 4.5). The tradition was quite an advance over the earlier Oldowan tradition, and like the former, was to last for a million and a half years, just until the emergence of our own species, *Homo sapiens sapiens.*

Homo erectus may have been the first species to tame fire. Its remains have been associated with burnt floors but not with clear hearths, so researchers debate this point. This remarkable tool, wrested from nature, provides for warmth at night, defense against predators, and a hearth for cooking meat and vegetable foods.

About 1.75 million years ago hominids became the first primates to construct shelters in open country: rings of stones piled up and perhaps strengthened by some sort of brake of brush. Here *H. erectus* could protect a group sleeping at night and—possibly—leave mothers with infants during the day,

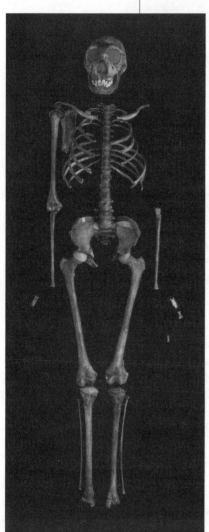

Homo erectus

provided others brought them food. Moreover, *H. erectus* was the first—and until then only—primate to spread out beyond the tropics. Whether this means that the species fashioned clothing from hides can never be known. Their spread supports the argument that they may have warmed themselves with fire.

It is likely, then, that *H. erectus* had a pattern of division of labor between the sexes, with males hunting and females gathering vegetable foods. When we speculate about their lifeways we think of the monogamous (male-female pairs) gibbons as an example of another primate potential playing itself out among hominids under the right circumstances.

Gibbons are great apes adapted to dense tropical rain forests, where they live in the highest reaches of the trees. Their "monogamy" is really male-female pair bonding and results in minimal "social investment" in the offspring. Indeed, the male does not tolerate his male offspring when they reach maturity and drives them off; the female does the same with her daughters. Each pair stakes out an area in the high forest canopy. New pairs form when wandering adolescents meet each other, bond, and stake out new territories. This is not a likely model for an ape wandering erect over open country, since a group rather than a pair provides protection from a predator by mobbing it. However, the genetic capacity to form pair bonds is probably there, latent in all apes and hominids.

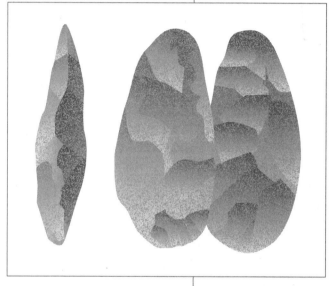

Figure 4.5 Acheulian hand axe.

What is certain about *H. erectus* is that, unlike gibbons, they lived in troops at least big enough to provide defense from predators in open country. Thus, if they began to mate monogamously it was within the context of a larger group than gibbons ever contended with, and in the context of home bases, protected by artificial barriers. Moreover, we now believe that larger group size was facilitated by advancing brain size. British psychologist and ethologist Robin Dunbar (1996) has effectively correlated the size of the neocortex—the outer thin layer of the brain where conscious thought and rational processes take place—with the size of the group among living primate species. All primates, as distinct from other animals, have large neocortexes; as the brain case grows in hominid evolution, so does the neocortex. A large group of competitive primates requires social intelligence among all its members for them to live together cooperatively. Such intelligence, in turn, requires a large neocortex. Dunbar then projected his correlation on fossil hominids to predict their population size. According to his calculations, the australopithecines lived in groups scarcely larger than the chimpanzee community, perhaps 60 individuals to the chimps' 50 or so. However, the various *H. erectus* populations went from perhaps 100 individuals early on to perhaps 120 by the time the species vanished.

Homo sapiens. Our own species began to emerge sometime before 200,000 years ago. Certain fossil finds are classified as "archaic *Homo sapiens*" and date from this period. We have brain cases still larger than those of *H. erectus*,

a face positioned more squarely under the forehead, and rather smaller bones than the previous form. Moreover, the work of molecular biologists on the composition of DNA in human cell mitochondria has produced the startling conclusion that all human beings alive today are descended from a very few female ancestors, dating from around 200,000 years ago. This discovery, popularly known as the "scientific Eve," does not mean that we descended from a single ancestral male and female pair but rather that our species emerged, as one might expect, from a small interbreeding population of several communities of up to 150 members each, not exceeding 5,000 individuals all told.

Neanderthal skull.

Indeed, when Dunbar calculated the size of the local group for *Homo sapiens* by predicting it from the size of its neocortex, he came up with 150 persons. This is more or less the upper limit for the hunting-and-gathering band we shall discuss in the next chapter!

Our species coexisted for some time with *H. erectus*, which, in comparison with the robust australopithecine forms, died out fairly rapidly. We were not alone even then, however, because of the existence of the species ***Homo neanderthalensis,*** sometimes called *Homo sapiens neanderthalensis*, thus classifying it as a subspecies of our own. Recently discovered dates put this species' origins at 300,000 years ago. Recent tests run on a sample of Neanderthal DNA put the species at a similar distance from us genealogically. That is, it split off from us long before the hypothetical common ancestress of all living human beings. The form of the Neanderthal skull, with its low forehead and beetling brow, resembles that of the earlier *H. erectus* forms.

Neanderthals, whatever their classification, were highly intelligent beings. Indeed, their brain capacity exceeded our own. It is not known for certain whether they had speech. Yet these primates were big-game hunters, well adapted for living in very cold conditions near the glaciers of the Ice Age. However, unlike the modern *Homo sapiens* who replaced them, the Neanderthals did not hunt with projectile points, nor did they have nearly as advanced a toolkit. Their sites have given us the first evidence of ritual: deliberate burials of the dead in real graves with grave ornaments in the form of red ochre paint on the remains.

We can assume that fully modern **Homo sapiens,** which emerged around 50,000 years ago, possessed speech. We do not know whether earlier or archaic members of our species were able to speak, but if so, that would help explain the relatively rapid spread of our species and the displacement and extinction of all other hominid forms. We are the most successful primate in terms of range of environmental adaptation. Let us examine the implication of speech, as a language or code we possess "above" the genetic code.

LANGUAGE, GENETIC CODES, HUMAN SPEECH, AND CULTURE

Language exists in nature, if we define language as a set of catalytic messages that govern how systems go about processing matter, energy, and action to maintain themselves, and, eventually, their species.* In other words, language governs the factory days of organisms and of their societies. A catalyst in chemistry is an agent that speeds up or even effects transformations in other matter without itself being affected. Its essence, then, is to govern and provide meaningful information that in self-organizing systems conditions adaptive behavior.

The Genetic Code as a Language

The genetic code for any living organism consists of DNA, which in the four kingdoms of life other than bacteria resides in the nucleus of each cell, and in RNA, which delivers messages inherent in the DNA. These messages are instructions about the manufacture of new materials from available nutrients in the cytoplasm. The code is a set of potential chemical messages with its own grammar, a set of rules about how the messages are produced and where they are directed. These messages govern individual biological growth and development through each cell of the body. That is, on the individual level each organism represents an unfolding of its genotype, the set of messages embodied in its genetic code. The result is its actual phenotype, which represents the interaction of messages (coming from the genotype) with matter and energy in the development of the individual, especially at the fetal stage of life. The language of the cell consists of chemical messages, sent through chemical channels and received chemically. With the evolu-

*Anthropologists will note that this is the broadest possible definition of language. I have derived it from an essay by Arthur Iberall (1983).

tion of nervous systems, electrical channels are added to the chemical ones, but the underlying chemical basis is never lost.

The collective genotype of a species, present in its gene pool, can be conceived of as a set of variable mechanistic individual characteristics that include the distinctive adaptive features marking the species off from other species. For example, the hominid lines seems to have started with *A. afarensis* in the sudden appearance of erect posture in an ape population. The genetic change was a simple one, governing the tilt of the pelvis. The adaptive value of the new message in the species' genetic code was its potential solution to the problem of life in a semi-treeless environment for a theretofore arboreal species of animal. Under those conditions, walking erect was more efficient for a particular set of apes.

Mutations are always with us in every generation. They are chemical accidents in the messages of the genes. Usually they are "noise"—that is, they are meaningless or maladaptive and are not reproduced. In rare instances, mutations provide, randomly, just the right message for changed circumstances, and they spread rapidly through the interbreeding population, as erect posture presumably did among the emergent australopithecines. What was once meaningless noise becomes highly adaptive information.

Ritual as a Language

Ritual is another set of catalytic messages, effecting transformation of state from one season of the year or one stage of the life cycle to another. *State* refers either to a social and biological stage in life—adolescence or adulthood, for example—or to social status, such as graduate student or doctor of philosophy. Many vertebrate species—especially birds but fish and mammals, too—have ritual. In these animals ritual is triggered by certain messages or symbols in response to chemical messages from the genes. For example, among the three-spined stickleback fish, the male's zigzag courtship dance, whereby he entices a prospective mate to his nest, is triggered by the sight of her red belly, which is the signal that she is biologically ready to lay eggs. We assume, further, that the form of the zigzag dance itself is genetically programmed in the male's nervous system. In any case, the ritual effects his transformation into a parent that tends the eggs in his nest.

In higher animals with more complex brains than those of fish, the triggering mechanism for ritual, and the capacity to respond to it and to modify individual behavior thereby, seems to be genetic, but the exact timing and performance of the ritual is left to learning, to individual personality development, and to particular responses to situations as they arise. Dominance displays among chimpanzees, for example, whereby individuals, especially males, make a theatrical performance out of the act of threatening others, represents a genetically programmed *capacity* for ritual acts. An animal's actual proficiency depends on learning, intelligence, and personal history. Juvenile success or failure seems to have much to do with whether an animal "likes" to put on such displays and whether it "gets good" at them.

We leave a more detailed discussion of ritual to Chapter 6. Suffice it to say that among *H. sapiens* ritual is a set of messages, defined by the culture at hand, to effect transformations of state at seasonal and life crises, or in anticipation of these crises. The "grammar" of ritual messages, however, universally consists of three phases: separation, transition, and reincorporation. At tribal and civilized levels of community, new rituals are elaborated by shamans, prophets, and priests in response to new crises, both in the individual and in the society. While the messages of any ritual are culturally given and must be learned by the participants, the actions triggered by ritual seem to reach down into emotional levels that are genetically grounded. Thus, when a set of ritual acts mark a full entrance into the middle (transitional) phase of any rite, human beings are susceptible to enter into a trance, a hypnotic state, or just a state of "spiritual awareness."

Human Speech as a Structured Extragenetic Code

In speech *H. sapiens* has acquired, through the processes of genetic evolution, a marvelous tool, built into the brain as a capability and expressed in the particular speech an individual learns through his or her culture. We now have an "extragenetic code," comparable in power to the code in our cells, and quite as voluminous. The capacity to carry this new code, human speech, seems to reside in the "higher" part of our brains, the neocortex, and to be associated with our human brains' lateralization, or "sidedness." It further has developed with assistance from our genes, in conjunction with our vocal cords or voice box in the throat.

Mechanistically, speech consists of our ability to precisely inhibit the flow of sounds we make from our throat by using our vocal cords, tongue, palate, roof of the mouth, teeth, and lips. Speech proceeds initially from our producing and distinguishing meaningless elementary units of sound, or phonemes. These vary from language to language, but each is the result of a bundle of acoustic features that distinguish it from neighboring sounds in the speech tract. In English, for example, we distinguish the *b* of *bat* from the *p* of *pat*, but the Kuna Indians of Panamá, among whom I have done field work, make no such distinction. You will note that both sounds are produced by the same position of the tongue and lips but that *b* is "voiced," that is, the vocal cords are sounded, and *p* is "voiceless," that is, the vocal cords are not sounded. Similarly, we distinguish between the *l* of *lake*, produced with our tongue in a forward position, and the *r* of *rake*, produced with our tongue relatively back in the mouth. That distinction, however, is not produced in most of the dialects of Chinese. Any given language or speech community distinguishes from thirteen to around sixty phonemes. English has over thirty. (The letters of our written alphabet are quite unequal to the task of distinguishing them.)

Phonemes in turn are combined with each other to form meaningful units, or **morphemes.** Because we distinguish the phonemes, we consequently hear the differences among the morphemes. *Form* sounds different from *dorm*, for example, because of two differing phonemes. A morpheme may be a word, or it may form a part of a word. For example, in English *form* is both a word and a morpheme, while *ing* is a morpheme that, when combined with morphemes like *form*, produces another word, *forming*.

Morphemes and words in turn are combined in speech according to the rules of *grammar* of the particular speech community to produce meaningful utterances of great variety. The most generally accepted current grammatical theory in linguistics, that of transformational grammar, stresses the relation of grammar to as yet unidentified structures in the human brain. In this view grammar is an expression of certain core conceptual relationships that are most familiar to us in the relations of noun to verb, or in being and becoming.

In what way is human speech an adaptive feature for our species, in what way might it facilitate the control of our species over resources, and how might speech have come about?

Proto-World: The Ur Language

For over two hundred years philologists have studied the historical relationships of existing languages to each other. They have grouped these languages in at least five widely accepted levels of descent. Thus, English belongs to (1) the Western Germanic family of (2) the Germanic family of (3) the Baltic-Slavic-Germanic family of (4) the Indo-European family of languages. Indo-European is grouped with Altic and Afro-Asiatic into a family called (5) the "Nostratic."

More controversially, linguists are now trying to derive a pan-world family of languages deriving from a very early speech community called "World." This speech community would in turn have derived from a single original speech called the *ur* **language.**

By comparing existing languages carefully with each other and listing the words similar enough to have been derived from a common ancestor, linguists have reconstructed the ancestral words themselves. There is now wide agreement on a word list for proto-Indo-European (the original Indo-European speech) and on the approximate phonetic form of the original words.

Pushing back even further, speculative linguists are now developing a word list for "Proto-World," or the *ur* language, our assumed original speech. Their belief is that speech arose only once, in a small group, speaking a small number—at most 300—of newly invented words based on newly distinguished phonemes. This assumption coincides with the discovery of molecular biologists that our species originated around 200,000 years ago from one small group, or breeding population/community. However, as yet we do not have any exact notion of the date for these momentous events: whether 200,000 years ago, the date for the first fossil remains of archaic *H. sapiens;* 100,000 years ago, an arbitrary date; or around 50,000 years ago, when fully modern *H. sapiens* arrives in the fossil evidence, together with magnificently executed stone points.

Some scholars are busy reconstructing these original words. They have published a short word list (Shevoroshkin, 1990) and have promised a full word list in the near future. In the meantime, two friends of mine have written a paper experimentally predicting that word list by positing what elementary nouns and verbs the original language would have needed (Wilkinson and Iberall, 1991). A portion of that list is reproduced on the right.

A Partial Postulated Word List for Proto-World

Word	Meaning
aku	eye
changa	nose
tugi	ear
tik	finger
tal	tongue
nigi/gini	tooth
matu	forehead
tari	leg
kuni	elbow/knee
pari	fingernail
nihwh/hwina	life
waru	fire
kuyan	woman
ngai	I
kuwa	rain

Speech as an Adaptive Feature Enhancing Human Command over Resources

With speech we are the first species able to communicate with each other as fast as our organs communicate within the body, at neural rates—that is, at the speed of impulses in the nervous system. This is a tremendous expansion of the capacity to communicate.

One might imagine that the immediate gain to our species from the *ur* language was to facilitate direct command over resources, as in the hunting of game animals. However, it is also apparent that wild dogs, who have no speech, are admirable team hunters and are able to coordinate the entire pack according to individual ability and specialization of task, one animal taking the lead and picking a victim, another heading it off, others chasing it, and yet another closing in for the first bite. Thus, while speech was undoubtedly used to enhance human team hunting skills, these probably already existed in admirable form.

Rather, and for this insight I am indebted to my friends David Wilkinson and Arthur Iberall, speech was probably first used to "domesticate" children and adolescents and to exact their labor in favor of the household group formed by the marriage of a man with a woman. In short, speech facilitated the command of adults over their young and the formation of the human family, in turn based on role names and the incest tabu. *Mother, father, son, daughter, brother,* and *sister* must have been in the original word list. These are, of course, the names for prohibited sexual partners (with "mother" and "father" calling each other "husband" and "wife").

Robin Dunbar (1996) theorizes that language evolved to replace the mutual grooming that occupies much of the time of monkeys and apes. Grooming sustains social alliances, soothes hurt feelings, and reconciles opponents. It happens daily. A large group of primates must invest time in grooming; the larger the group, the more time. The observed limit is 20 percent of daily time invested in grooming by gelada baboons. If early *Homo sapiens* had to groom each other to unite the group, it would have taken 40 percent of their waking time to sustain a group of 150 individuals. Clearly they could not afford that much time and still gather food and defend the group against predators. Sociable conversation, "gossip," was the answer, according to Dunbar. He guesses that true speech was preceded by sociable vocalizations, especially among *Homo erectus* populations. Talk, then, does audio-verbally what grooming does by touch.

Speech further facilitated the performance of human rituals and permitted people to tell myths about why they performed them. Marriage, birth, coming of age, bride service—all ritual activity we describe in Chapter 6—could now take form. Human beings could make use of patterns of behavior common in birds and fish but now direct them from the higher neocortex areas of the brain and enlist them to support the new social forms, household and material exchange, that were now arising.

Moreover, speech put human beings in command of a tool with many of the qualities of the genetic code itself. This "extragenetic" code put us in command of volumes of information; like the genetic code, speech stores memory from past generations. Among speechless species of primates the collective memory is only as old as the oldest individual. Among speaking *H. sapiens,* the collective memory extends back many generations. Food resources, correct hunting-and-gathering strategies, and ways of exacting obedience from the young could now be remembered far past the lifetimes of their original discoverers.

Finally, speech brought human beings to a truly higher stage in the evolution of consciousness and self-awareness. The genes of the genetic code may perform marvelous feats and may mutate and transform species in response to environmental problems with great success. But no single gene and no set of genes in a cellular nucleus is self-conscious in the same way that humans are. Genes do tap into the memory of the species, present in the gene pool, but that memory is situational and bound to particular incidents. Human beings, with speech, have a second set of memory banks, and a second code for communication, which like the first, links the generations. Unlike a gene pool, a human community can transcend the here and now and imagine other places, even gods and the supernatural.

Speech was not the last human language. Ritual is another. Literacy is yet another, expanding the spoken word and enhancing our ability to think. Moreover, in modern times language has been facilitated by electronic communication: Film, radio, sound recording, television, and computers have all expanded our ability to use language.

SUMMARY AND CONCLUSIONS

*I*n this chapter we have surveyed the biological nature of human beings seen from basic perspectives of the genetic code and of the succession of hominid species, as we know them today.

The interactions of the genes provide a platform for the emergence of multicelled organisms. Within each cell information is organized at a chemical level and by chemical means—in DNA and RNA. This information is transmitted by individual microorganisms, the *gametes* (sperm and ovum), to form a fertilized beginning cell, the *zygote*, which then develops into a fully formed representative of its species, within the limits of the genetic variation for the species as a whole. Thus, each of us started life by the social activity of a mobile sperm cell finding, penetrating, and coupling with a less-mobile ovum cell. Inside the nucleus of the resulting zygote cell, or conceptus, was a tiny pinpoint of information containing our individual genotype, the blueprint by which we developed in response to environmental conditions.

The genetic code constitutes a language, and we can conceive of it as an ongoing chemical conversation between genes, matter and energy, and the environment. Each conversation produces a life-form, basically the cell (and viruses and captured organelles within cells). The cells are the myriad factories of life.

The messages of the genes have differing time frames. Most are at the level of the split second; they occur constantly as each cell in our body engages in its cycle of growth and self-maintenance. Other messages play themselves out in embryology, the development of a fully formed fetus from a single fertilized cell. Then there is the timetable of the life cycle of any individual of a species. We all know that we are born, undergo puberty, reach adulthood, then old age, and finally death. A death from old age depends on a time limit built into the genotype. None of us expects to live much beyond a hundred years, for example, if that.

Finally there is the much longer timetable of a species, up to a million years or multiples thereof. Here, mutations, the random meaningless messages that are by-products of genetic replication and reproduction, suddenly acquire meaning in changed environmental circumstances. Mutations—changes in the arrangement of the genetic material—are constantly occurring. Most are harmful or at least not beneficial, and they do not continue in the interbreeding population in which they arise.

From time to time at crucial moments mutations occur that solve some problem for an interbreeding subgroup of a larger species. What was once "noise" becomes highly significant. The message spreads rapidly within that small interbreeding population, and a new species emerges. Species, once they have emerged, last a long time, a million years or more. There have been nine known hominid species in the group of creatures who descended from common ancestors with modern apes, especially chimpanzees and gorillas.

It is important to note that genes are only chemical messages. Each gene derives its meaning from its place among other genes. Genes are not themselves living creatures, and they certainly do not have agency or intentionality. Many current writers in sociobiology and evolutionary psychology get carried away by the effects of implied genetic patterns on behavior and speak of genes themselves as "selfish," as if they were motivated. In these cases genes are just fragments of an ongoing conversation that started with the chemical origins of life. Neither they nor their possible resulting behavior patterns are agents. The latter are cellular, both single cells and multicellular organisms.

The hominid line is from 5 to 6 million years old. It originated with *Australopithecus afarensis,* an ape that stood fully erect and walked on its two legs, just as we do, but that had a brain in all respects like that of an ape. The adult males of this species were twice as big as the females. A million years later another species, *A. africanus,* emerged, and in the midpoint of its over a million years of prehistory, it apparently began using pebble tools for processing meat.

Two million years ago, this species began to disappear, but four others replaced it at once. Two were still australopithecines, "southern apes," but two belonged to the genus *Homo: H. habilis* and *H. erectus.* The "ape" forms were exceedingly robust, and probably were grazing herd animals dominated and protected by formidably big males. The "human" forms had larger brains, and in the case of *H. erectus* a highly developed toolkit and, possibly, fire. The latter definitely had home bases or camps of piled stone or brush. Male *H. erectus* hunted game; females most likely gathered vegetable goods to bring to the common camp. This is a basic pattern for our species, as we shall see. *H. erectus* outlived its three companion species by nearly a million years. Before it disappeared *H. erectus*'s brain capacity had reached 1300 cubic centimeters (as opposed to 500 for *A. afarensis*), and its group size had reached perhaps 120 individuals as opposed to around 60 for all australopithecines. But it in turn quickly disappeared with the appearance of a new, highly successful species.

Starting sometime before 200,000 years ago, our own species, *H. sapiens*, began to appear in archaic form. By 50,000 to 40,000 years ago, fully modern human beings had appeared, displacing a still earlier, but related species, *H. neanderthalensis*. Both species exploited a new ecological niche, that of big-game hunting in cold and warm climates. *H. sapiens* is associated with a remarkable toolkit of fine projectile points and hunted big game animals by hurling spears at them. *H. sapiens sapiens* clearly was capable of speech; the Neanderthal capacity for speech remains uncertain. The way of life of this new and last hominid species, the human hunting-and-gathering band, is the subject of Chapter 5.

Primate behavior, especially ape behavior, provides a platform for the emergence of humanity. That is, we emerged from a series of highly social, highly intelligent species, all—like chimpanzees—capable of hunting and using tools. *A. africanus* is associated with Oldowan tools at its time in prehistory. *H. habilis* definitely used them, as did *H. erectus*. The latter is associated with fine Acheulian tools. In contrast, the robust australopithecines were not habitual stone tool users. The trait of tool making culminates in *H. sapiens*'s truly magnificent Solutrean tools, finely shaped projectile points (see Figure 4.6).

Figure 4.6 Solutrean tools.

H. sapiens are the bipedal, brainy, speaking primates who craft and use fine tools. At 1400 cubic centimeters, our brain is nine times larger than would be predicted when comparing us to other mammals on the basis of body size alone. Our brains are expensive; at 2 percent of body weight they consume 20 percent of our energy intake. To compensate, our species evolved a smaller gut compared to those of other living primates, which means we had to rely less on fruits and leaves and more on meat with its higher calories.

Second, our (comparatively speaking) huge brains are so large that—unlike in all other primates—their growth has not been completed at birth. The human infant's brain continues to grow for a full year after birth, thus requiring a total of twenty-one months to develop rather than only the nine months of pregnancy. The human infant is thus even more dependent than the typical primate infant on its mother.

We assume, then, with certainty that human culture is based on prehuman primate prototypes. However, at some point *H. sapiens* developed speech, a language over and above the genetic code. Speech consists of the ability to distinguish phonemes, meaningless elementary units of sound, from each other and to combine them into morphemes, the smallest meaningful units. We further combine the morphemes into words and sentences, according to the rules of grammar. Speech is genetically dependent on our large brains, especially the neocortex, and on our vocal cords.

Speech, like the genetic code and ritual, is a language, a set of catalytic messages that govern how systems go about processing matter and energy to maintain themselves and, eventually, their species. Speech probably arose only once, in a small community, and the original or *ur* language is thought to have contained no more than 300 words—which, however, served to "domesticate" the labor of the young in service of their parents and provide enough information to make sociable conversations—gossip sessions—a substitute for grooming parties. Speech replaced touch for social bonding.

The distinctive features of *H. sapiens* include not only speech but associated communicative traits "enforced" by speech. These include marriage and the family, expressed in speech through roles given names as distinct from persons, upheld by normative rules, such as the incest taboo, a universal prohibition among all human populations. These features also include rituals surrounding the transformations of yearly and lifetime schedules. These traits were first given expression in a community pattern derived from the primate troop: the human hunting-and-gathering band. We shall take up the band, ritual, and marriage and the family in Part II.

SUGGESTED READINGS

Dunbar, Robin. *Grooming, Gossip, and the Evolution of Language*. Cambridge, Mass.: Harvard Press, 1996. A lively new view of the subject with fascinating data on the relation of brain size to group size and a strong argument for human speech as a substitute for primate grooming.

Eldredge, Niles, and Ian Tattersall. *The Myths of Human Evolution*. New York: Columbia University Press, 1982. A readable synthesis by two scholars who see hominid evolution as "bushy" rather than treelike, and proceeding by jumps rather than gradually.

Lewin, Roger. *In the Age of Mankind: A Smithsonian Book of Human Evolution.* Washington, D.C.: Smithsonian Institution, 1988. A lavishly illustrated and up-to-date treatment of the subject.

GLOSSARY

Australopithecus "Southern ape," the earliest known hominid genus. Paleontologists have found four species in Africa, to date: *A. afarensis*, *A. africanus*, *A. boisei*, and *A. robustus*.

Australopithecus afarensis Dating from around 4 to 3 million years ago, this hominid stood and walked fully erect, had a brain case of about 500 cubic centimeters, and was sexually dimorphic. No stone tools date from its time period.

Australopithecus africanus Dating from around 3 million to less than 2 million years ago, this hominid perhaps did not have sexual dimorphism. The first stone tools (Oldowan) date from midway through its period.

Australopithecus boisei and *Australopithecus robustus* Dating from around 2 million to less than 1 million years ago, these were sexually dimorphic species with very heavy bones and jaws adapted for grazing. They did not use stone tools and co-existed with the first two species of *Homo*.

chromosomes Rod-shaped microscopic bodies in living cells composed of long strands of DNA. Genes are manifest as molecular sites on chromosomes.

DNA Deoxyribonucleic acid, the active ingredient, genetically, in chromosomes. Its molecules are two chains of atoms wrapped around each other in a double helix, or spiral coil. At mitosis the coils unwind, and each separate strand replicates its partner to produce a new double helix or coil.

factory In ecology, a system that extracts matter and energy from its environment, passes both from station to station, and delays their consumption in a characteristic cycle of consumption, growth, decay, and death.

gene pool The set of genes shared by members of the same species. Not all genes are present in the phenotype of every individual member of the species, since there is always variability within a species.

genes The molecular sites, or positional units, on chromosomes that actually transmit specific hereditary characteristics from parents to offspring. Chromosomes come in pairs, one from each parent. In most cases, each gene on each chromosome is paired with a gene on a sister chromosome to produce a given observable (phenotypic) trait in an individual.

genotype The potential image of the individual as recorded in the genes. Each zygote, and indeed each member cell of an individual, has all the genetic information necessary for the development of the embryo into an adult.

grammar A set of rules governing the production of messages in a language and the relationship of the classes of messages to each other. In the genetic code, grammar governs the processes of mitosis and meiosis and the relations of DNA to RNA. In speech, grammar governs the combination of morphemes into words and the relations of nouns to verbs. Spoken grammar relates being to becoming.

Homo erectus A hominid species dating from 2 to 1.75 million years ago, dying out about 100,000 years ago. These large-boned hominids had large brain cases, which got larger as their era went on. Halfway through their prehistory, they produced Acheulian tools, bifaced worked stone cores for axes and projectiles. They also built home camps.

Homo habilis A transitional species between *Australopithecus* and *Homo*. It dates from around 2 million years ago to around 1.24 million years ago. A light-boned species, it definitely used Oldowan pebble tools.

Homo neanderthalensis "Neanderthal man," a large-boned species, sometimes classed as a subspecies of *H. sapiens*, dating from 300,000 to 50,000 years ago. It had a brain case larger than our own (1400 cubic centimeters), made tools, and hunted big-game animals next to Ice Age glaciers. It lacked speech and died out rapidly after the advent of *H. sapiens sapiens*.

Homo sapiens Our own species, dating in "archaic" form from about 200,000 years ago and in "modern" form (*Homo sapiens sapiens*) from about 50,000 to 40,000 years ago. We are light boned, and highly intelligent. Modern forms made fine Solutre°an stone projectile points and blades and painted walls of caves in splendid artworks for ritual purposes.

language A set of catalytic messages, reflecting a grammar, that govern how systems go about processing matter and energy to maintain themselves and, eventually, their species. Examples include the genetic code, ritual, speech, writing, and electronic languages (film, television, computer languages, etc.).

morphemes The smallest meaningful units of speech, produced by combinations of phonemes. They may be words or parts of words that, when combined with words or other morphemes, produce another word.

mutation The biochemical process resulting in the appearance of new genes and new genetic traits in the individual. Mutations are accidents or errors in copying DNA during meiosis and mitosis. They can occur from chemical and physical stimuli, such as x-rays, or simply at random. Most traits resulting from mutations are not beneficial and do not survive. Some traits are extremely useful to a population undergoing changing conditions and thus spread rapidly. A related constellation of such changing mutations results in speciation, the appearance of a new species from an old. The constellation of new genetic traits has solved some problem for the population.

paleoanthropology The study of primate fossil remains.

phenotype The product of the genotype as influenced by external factors, such as nutrition. No individual, or phenotype, exactly replicates the genotype.

phonemes Meaningless elementary units of sound, distinguished from each other in any particular language by the differences they make when combined with other phonemes to create morphemes. *Bat* differs from *pat* in English, thus allowing us to identify two phonemes, *b* and *p*.

RNA Ribonucleic acid. The complex molecule that, in its various forms, translates the genetic code carried by DNA into the proteins that make up enzymes, hormones, antibodies, and other essential chemicals in the body.

sexual dimorphism The condition, common to many species, of extreme physical differences between males and females. The adult silverback male gorilla, for example, is twice as big as the adult female.

speciation The appearance of a new species from an old one, resulting from a related constellation of mutations that has solved some problem for a given population. Some mutations are extremely useful to a population undergoing changing conditions; hence they spread rapidly, while the population itself consequently changes.

species A population that shares a "pool" of genes in common. Individuals of the same species may mate and produce viable offspring—that is, ones capable of reproducing themselves in turn.

ur language The hypothetical first human speech community, also known as "Proto-World," reflecting the initial discovery of speech as a system of distinguishing meaningless units in the speech stream, combining them into morphemes and words, and producing utterances or sentences governed by a grammar. The *ur* language is assumed to have arisen only once and to have consisted of a very small number of words, probably no more than 300.

zygote The conceptus, fertilized egg, or single original cell beginning the embryo of sexually reproducing creatures. Each of us started life as a zygote.

PART

II

BAND COMMUNITIES AND ELEMENTAL HUMAN INSTITUTIONS

CHAPTER 5

The Band Community: Synchronizing Human Activity Cycles for Group Cooperation

CHAPTER 6

Ritual and Myth

CHAPTER 7

The Human Family:
Tn Emergent Institution in Band Communities

CHAPTER 8

Values and Exchange, The Original Economy
Moral Values, Values in Goods, and Reciprocity

Our introduction is complete. You should now have some notion of anthropology as the product of the encounter with strange peoples and stranger cultures. You should know that ethnographies are written from a process of disciplined observation and interaction called field work. You should also know that all human beings today are members of a single species, the last one to arise in a hominid line dating back 5 to 6 million years.

We will now fill in the details outlined in Chapter 2 about the earliest and elementary form of human community: the hunting-and-gathering band. After our species *H. sapiens sapiens* emerged, we spread over the face of the earth, probably in small clusters of families in camps. These camps, coming together at seasonal resources and for yearly and generational rituals, formed *bands*.

Human beings were able to spread everywhere because their tools found them food sources in hunting big-game animals, and fire and skins sheltered them from the effects of the weather. They propelled each other out as fast as they could walk, largely to avoid conflict with the persons they grew up with "back home." Moreover, land bridges formed in the Pacific and Bering Straits during the last Ice Age, when ocean water was taken up in enormous continental glaciers. These bridges allowed wandering hunters and gatherers to reach the land masses of Australia and the Americas from the original human heartlands of Africa and Eurasia. Once the world filled up, people were obliged to settle down near food resources; there was no longer a place to flee conflict at home. The result was tribal society, the subject of Part III.

Band societies survived into Europe's Age of Discovery and the present day in distinctly isolated and marginal areas. Some of those studied in the twentieth century have long had relationships of exchange and service with tribal peoples. The !Kung San bushmen, whom we discuss at length, are such a group. So are the Mbuti pygmies of the equatorial rain forests of Africa. However, the transition from one way of life to another is, contrary to our expectations, never easy. Such hunting-and-gathering bands often are able to preserve their way of life, unbeknownst to their tribal neighbors, quite intact, while they reach material accommodations with these food producers.

Chapter 5 spells out the nature of the band as a patterned system of activities based on natural time schedules (day, year, coming-of-age or generations, and a lifetime of up to ninety years) and at three territorial levels (camp, band proper, and circle of bands [foreign relations]).

Two human institutions are clearly and fully emergent in the band: the family and ritual-myth complexes. Human beings also exchange goods, and this exchange, in the context of marriage, household formation and dissolution, and ritual, provides for the economics of *reciprocity*. The question of how human beings *value* the goods they exchange is a universal one, and one still open to philosophic and political debate.

Chapter 6 looks at ritual and myth, Chapter 7 at the human family, and Chapter 8 at values and exchanges. In bands, the institutions of ritual and household have not fully run their course of variations, which are not endless but subject to logical and factual limits.

Finally, the activities of reciprocal exchange, while embedded in the family and ritual in band societies, are so much more complex and important than anything in any other animal species that it is imperative to discuss them here, at this level, even though the institutions of redistribution (offerings, tribute, taxation, and ceremonial and political "paying back") and market have not yet emerged. This part, then, is an introduction to the necessary activities and the associated cultural patterns that make us human.

The Band Community:

Synchronizing Human Activity Cycles for Group Cooperation

THE HUMAN COMMUNITY

CYCLES OF ACTIVITIES

Social and Cultural Cycles

The Daily Cycle, and Cycles of Days

The Annual Cycle

The Generational Cycle: Coming of Age and Procreating a New Generation

The Life Cycles of Elders: The Scale of Cultures

    Kinship

    Power

DAILY SPEECH EVENTS: MANAGING CULTURE

Talking Around the Campfire

Social Drama: Talking About and Managing Disruptive Activities

This chapter examines the most elementary community of human beings, *bands* of hunters and gatherers. We shall fill in the details of the outline we set forth in Chapter 2 (see Figure 5.1). The **band** is a small group, and it is autonomous—that is, relatively independent of other groups. It ranges over a known territory looking for game to hunt and vegetable foods to gather. It is composed of related families and is usually exogamous—that is, individuals marry outside the group.

THE HUMAN COMMUNITY

In biology, *community* means "breeding population," the unit of the species within which members of the two sexes come together for procreating the next generation and, if necessary, nurturing them to maturity. As biological creatures, human beings also have breeding-population communities. As in the natural world, our **community** is the unit that orchestrates individual movements in space over time. But in our cultural world, community is the setting in which, from one generation to the next, human beings learn how to be fully human. It is also the unit within which culture changes. In short, the community is the unit not only of procreation, socialization, and survival but of cultural creativity and innovation. It thus is a unit with historical depth in time.

The band is the basic unit of human social life. All other human communities derive, ultimately, from band beginnings. Thus the band contains, if only in trace forms, foreshadowings of all human future potentials. It is also built on primate antecedents. Like the primate troop, the band includes two sexes, three generations, males in leadership positions, a range over space, and functional interrelations among activities. But these elements are put together quite differently, in conjunction with others that are wholly lacking among nonhuman primates.

In contrast with apes, human beings of course have kinship systems, marriage and the family, social paternity, fully developed ritual complexes, an advanced toolkit, and the most advanced tool of all, language in the form of

Justice
No formal law code. Disputes decided by public talking ("palavers") or formal patterns of violence, often culminating in duels. One band may raid neighboring band in blood revenge. Violence may end in homicide or flight to another band.

Language
Fully present, true speech. Vocalizations, body and facial gestures of primates still present. No writing. Social dramas and myths recited by campfires.

Politics
"Successful" elders, both males and females, form nucleus of each band. Band membership tied to them through marriage or through offers of asylum to refugees from conflict elsewhere.

The Band
Community form: Three levels of space—local (camps); band proper (assembles at rites); foreign relations (circles of neighboring bands). Membership is "open"; males and females flow through several bands in a lifetime, clustering around influential elders.

Learning
Unable to survive unless reared in group. Must adjust to individual personality differences. Children learn from family, play group, or, if present, age grades.

Economics
Tool makers and users on a daily basis. Hunting and gathering expressed in division of labor by sex. Exchange of food, goods, and services within households, of food, goods, services, and spouses among households. These exchanges cut across bands. No explicit standard of value ("money").

Ritual
Fully developed life crisis rites (generational time) and rites of intensification (seasonal, yearly time). These may provide for assemblages giving form to the band.

Technology
Sophisticated stone points for spears and arrows in hunting; baskets for transporting food; shelters for sleeping; fire.

Sociology
Household consisting of father-husband plus mother-offspring-sibling units. Marriage; social paternity; juvenile play groups. Age grades may be present.

Figure 5.1 Emergent institutional behavior in the band.

109

speech, our extragenetic code. These traits, our *culture*, made our species the successful hominid, replacing earlier hominid forms.

However, apes exhibit **territoriality.** They seem genetically programmed to stake out a home area and defend it against neighboring groups. Such territoriality does not apply to bands. Human beings quarrel, but they do not fight over territory. Rather, human beings in band organization tend to flee conflict. It is flight, not fight, for them.

Bands do, like chimpanzee troops, exhibit fission and fusion, whereby the wider community splits into smaller units much of the year and comes together in larger units at given times. Unlike apes, however, human bands assemble as the *entire* community on certain occasions—the fusion process is much more complete. Moreover, again unlike chimpanzees, human beings also assemble with persons coming from other communities on certain other occasions.

Thus there are three levels of spatial organization in human bands (see Figure 5.2). First are the areas of *local residence* and day-to-day land use. These change in the course of a year as the group splits into its smallest constituent units, which then move out to the furthest reaches of its range. Second, there is the wider area of the *community proper*, usually a named "country" or band, whose population gathers at some time during the solar year. Third, there are the broad circles of overlapping and interacting bands, the areas of *foreign relations*. No band is closed; all are open to visitors and emigres from other bands.

Figure 5.2 Levels of spatial organization in bands.

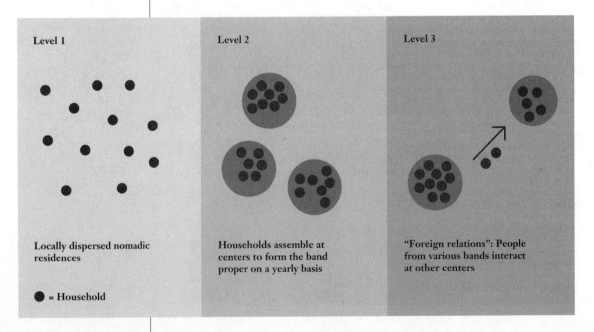

Level 1

Locally dispersed nomadic residences

● = Household

Level 2

Households assemble at centers to form the band proper on a yearly basis

Level 3

"Foreign relations": People from various bands interact at other centers

Within the band human beings bond into characteristic groupings. The elementary human bonds are first of all those of household and family, characterized by a common hearth (see Chapter 7). Several such households may camp together, forming the local group or constituent camp of the larger band at least part of the year. A circle of campfires or hearths, as we shall see, is the first major cultural architectural rendering of space.

Men form hunting parties throughout the year. The constituent hunters vary over time. These are ephemeral coalitions of convenience; hunting parties have never been observed to have hard and fast, invariable, and consequently ritualized, memberships. In large hunts women and children form auxiliary hunting groups, often as "beaters," to beat sticks and drive the game animals toward the men. Women from the same camp likewise form ephemeral hunting-and-gathering parties, in the company of their infants. These loose bonds reflect the ubiquitous and pan-human division of labor by sex.

Human juveniles, like all primate juveniles, form play groups whenever the opportunity presents itself. These cut across household and kinship identities and are the prototypical age grade from which much successively differentiated human social organization derives (such as ritual fraternities, age-graded regiments, police forces, guilds, and voluntary associations). At the end of their lives, elders, numerically far fewer than juveniles, also associate with each other, males and females together, and engage in speech rather than play. Elders talk; they reminisce, tell stories, recite myths and genealogies, and chant or sing songs.

CYCLES OF ACTIVITIES

Social life among human beings has its local *kinetics*—its characteristic motions. These form cycles of repetitive activities, processes organized in space and time. From the perspective of ecology, these activities can be seen as composing a **factory**, which moves materials from the environment to station to station. These activities occur in cycles or rounds, the **"factory day,"** after which the sequence of actions, completed, is ready to be repeated. These factory rounds were mentioned in the last chapter for the individual cell. Likewise, there are rounds of processing activities for individual human beings (most of them physiological and internal) and other rounds for human groups.

For example, food enters the mouth of every individual for biological processing, beginning with chewing. Food is transformed and expended as energy and work or is absorbed as materials to build the body, while waste and by-products are eliminated. The individual must ingest food on a daily basis. This is only one such time-delayed cycle of consumption and transformation of matter and energy.

Similarly, the group is a unit of production and consumption, gathering materials from the environment, processing them, and consuming them in the wider processes of maintaining mature adults, rearing children, and producing infant offspring. Human beings, as we shall see, are produced and passed from station to station, like material goods. As with all living creatures, we—as a group—reproduce ourselves. Finally, at death, our mortal remains must be disposed of like any waste item. (In fact, in the early paleolithic period human beings ceased to treat cadavers as mere discards and began to inter them with grave ornaments and goods. Cadavers became not waste, but products. This is one hallmark distinguishing human beings from all other animals.)

Social and Cultural Cycles

Human individuals as factories run through cycles: communication and perception cycles move neural impulses at 0.1 second and 6 seconds, cycles of ingestion and digestion occur at 3.5-hour intervals, and whole-body cycles occur over 24-hour periods (Iberall and Wilkinson, 1987). At the end of each cycle the "factory day" is over and activity starts again.

Individuals must perform their own characteristic activities and coordinate them with the activities of others on similar scales. Human beings are characteristically social. Solitary lives as hermits, typical for some primate species, are atypical of human beings. (However, hermit phases of withdrawal from the group are significant parts of the life cycle of most shamans and prophets, as we shall see in a later chapter.)

Individual cycles are *entrained*, or synchronized, with those of others. This synchronization is visible in typical solar days, in seasonal variations through the year, and in typical life cycles. Anthropologists must take into account generational maturation time (from twenty to twenty-five years) and lifetime scales (up to ninety years) for those who survive to become elders. Three to five successive cohort lifetimes form the cycles of particular cultures, at which point we can assume that the repertory of repetitive activities may have changed significantly, and—in content at least if not in form—the culture shall have changed.

Thus, culture changes by the small-scale accretion of cultural and stylistic differences invented by particular individuals. Culture also changes in response to outside pressures and instabilities: drought, flood, famine, epidemic, and the incursions of neighboring groups. The individuals with the greatest capacity to effect culture change are shamans transformed into prophets, more specifically known as "revitalization prophets" in the anthropological literature (see Chapter 13). In modern society political prophets (such as Lenin) fulfill the same general creative capability, as do—as a class—intellectuals.

Let us examine the typical cycles of activities of a hunting-and-gathering band. Our discussion relies most heavily on ethnographies of the !Kung San bushmen of the Kalahari desert (Lee, 1979, 1984) and of Australian aborigines, namely the Tiwi of Bathurst and Melville Islands (Goodale, 1971; Hart, Pilling, & Goodale, 1988). The Tiwi exhibit greater social complexity than the !Kung, based on the same spectrum of traits. Together they represent much of the range of band societies. The Eskimo, with their extreme Arctic adaptations, differ from temperate and tropical band peoples by their relatively greater dependence on hunting rather than gathering.

The Daily Cycle, and Cycles of Days

At dawn a hunting-and-gathering camp of whatever size universally wakes up from the sleeping positions of its various members around their campfires. A hearth is the station of a household, its gate for receiving uncooked food. This intimate use of fire is a universal trait of our species. The hearth is the crucible of family life, symbolically as well as energetically. The more settled dry-season villages among the !Kung San bushmen consist of circles of huts, each with its hearth directly outside and in front of it. A wide plaza for collective life is defined by the circle of campfires.

Richard Lee tells us that !Kung San villages are surrounded by a "zone of elimination" for household trash and bodily wastes. Presumably, eliminative behavior takes place privately and individually as each person wakes up and retreats behind the scenes, so to speak.

Lee does not mention breakfast, but Hart and Pilling tell us that the Tiwi have a light breakfast of leftovers from the main, evening meal of the previous day before setting off on their quest for food.

The gathering activities of women are daily and a constant source of food for hunting-and-gathering peoples. But not all women gather daily. Lee (1984) measured work effort (in terms of hours per week) against calories collected for a !Kung San rainy-season village. In the four rainy-season weeks he measured, women were less active than men, putting in only 40 work hours per week, or 5.7 hours a day. Of these, only 12.6 hours were spent on "subsistence work." Assuming that women gathered every day, their collecting activities averaged only 1.8 hours a day. But in fact neither men nor women worked at subsistence every day. Women put only about 2 days a week into gathering, while men put in 2.7 days at both gathering and hunting. Men put in longer work weeks, 44.5 hours as opposed to the feminine 40, and longer subsistence work weeks, too: 21.6 hours a week as opposed to 12.6. Even so, women contributed more calories to the !Kung diet than men did, about 55 percent as opposed to 45 percent.

Housework, which Lee defined as drawing water and gathering firewood, processing and cooking food, and washing and cleaning, occupies 22.4 of a woman's hours a week. Thus women may not necessarily gather food every day, but they certainly cook it and do other housework every day.*

What is clear is that the circle of !Kung households must synchronize their efforts with one another, just as members of a household must entrain their activities with one another as well. The result is a set of subsistence cycles forming a loose yet keenly coordinated program. Thus the solar day is a temporal unit of food preparation at all hearths. The food preparation and consumption cycle culminates each day in the evening meal around the fire. The temporal unit of subsistence activity, on the other hand, is a three-day cycle for any household, at least for food gathering. The male hunting cycle is perhaps more on the rhythm of a four- to six-day cycle. Males bring in fewer calories from hunting because, after all, hunting is a sporting proposition. Empty-handed returns are frequent, balanced by bonanzas of larger game, usually brought down by hunting teams.

The circle of camps is entrained or meshed through interhousehold kinship ties. Richer households—more populous or blessed with energetic, talented "overachievers"—share their bounty with importuning kinfolk, also at the evening meal. Such sharing back and forth is characteristic of the wider cycle of activities as a whole, and its relevant time scale—as we shall see—is also the solar year.

Other activities that must go on in some household every solar day include tool manufacture and maintenance. The !Kung have some twenty-eight "tools and devices" as well as wardrobes of animal hides. Lee's weekly averages of toolwork per individual come to 1 hour a day for men and 45 minutes for women. Once again, these tasks must be entrained differently, depending on the nature of the task and the skill of the worker, the cycle of demand and need within the household ("Wife, will you please mend our basket!"), and the cycle of such demands outside the household ("I must give that basket to your father, my father-in-law").

A typical day, then, has some individuals in a wider camp or village dispersing in the morning for the activities of gathering food, hunting, fetching firewood, and drawing water. Others remain in camp to clean up or to make and maintain tools. The day reaches its climax at the evening meal. During the day children form play groups. Individual children—like all primates—also play with older kin one at a time. Indeed, given so much leisure time for the adults of band culture, we would expect a great many recreational activities. One of these, talking at campfires in the evenings, is of prime impor-

!Kung hunter with guinea fowl.

---

*Lee's approach illustrates some of the difficulties social scientists have in reaching a dynamic approach based on the natural history of energetics, not an imposed, rigid, yet mythical, Western conceptual scheme of weeks, hours, and statistical averages. The week in this case is not an "emic" or native unit, since the !Kung San have no formal calendar, much less six days of work with a Sabbath day of rest, which is what the Western week is.

tance for synchronizing or entraining all activities. We shall discuss that at length later in this chapter.

A "typical" day would be one not marked by any events whose cycles fall on some other time scale. Thus, hunts by hunting parties are on some weekly to monthly scale. Among the !Kung the size of the hunting party must vary with the size of the seasonal settlement. The large villages of the peak rainy and dry seasons have more males available for the formation of hunting teams.

The Annual Cycle

The !Kung form different settlements over the course of the solar year based on the alternation between warming wet (spring and summer) and cooling dry (autumn, winter, early spring) seasons. From about May to October, *dry-season villages* form at waterholes (see Figure 5.3). These groupings are identified with a "country," and the core residents are said to "own" it. In other words, this grouping is the band proper. These villages range in size from eight to fifteen huts. Populations here and in all seasons fluctuate from year to year.

Rainy-season villages are more ephemeral, only three weeks rather than three months, but may be larger—from three to thirty huts—since they are located near some substantial food resource that has come into season. More-over, they may comprise people coming from several bands.

Figure 5.3 Schematic view of !Kung settlements in the annual cycle.

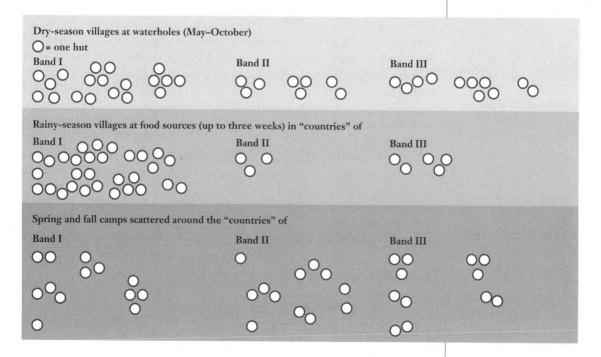

Dry-season villages at waterholes (May–October)

◯ = one hut

Band I   Band II   Band III

Rainy-season villages at food sources (up to three weeks) in "countries" of

Band I   Band II   Band III

Spring and fall camps scattered around the "countries" of

Band I   Band II   Band III

Spring and fall camps lack huts altogether and may merely indicate stopping places as one or more constituent households of the larger band move away from the waterhole village in the beginning of the wet season or toward it in the beginning of the dry season. *Overnight stops* are simply hearths constructed where "the group," which can be as small as a hunting party of a few men, spends the night while ranging around.

The Tiwi in many respects exhibit internal complexity of the same patterns found among the less complicated !Kung while retaining similar overall (or exterior) form. It is their *household structure* that is most complex. They are polygynous. A few older men have many wives, some adult men have a few wives, and no young man has any wife. Adolescent men are isolated in age grades. Yet the community is still very much the hunting-and-gathering band.

We are not told much about Tiwi teams for hunting, save in the seasonal kangaroo hunts that are organized by elders, who call up all the males of several camps. They burn off grasslands in this effort, which not only yields a bonanza of meat (everyone gorges themselves for days) but clears the land for easier tracking and hunting. Tiwi boys from age fourteen to their early twenties are segregated most of the year in age-graded initiation camps, which provide for their own subsistence. Thus they organize hunts, too.

The Tiwi likewise assemble and disperse on a yearly schedule. Late in the dry season neighboring camps unite for grassburns and kangaroo hunts, before dispersing into their constituent camps of several households with the beginning of the rains in late October. Most of the households of a given named "country" (band) assemble during the late rainy season, in January and February, for the kulama yam ceremonies, which are at once initiation rites for age-graded male youths and rites of intensification for adult males, who, like the initiates, also must perform songs and dances especially composed for the event.

At the end of the rainy season in early April, Tiwi funerals commence and continue through the dry season. Bodies are interred at death, but funeral ceremonies are delayed until the dry season, when large groups of people can be assembled from many bands by kinship ties.

Thus, band societies spend part of the year dissolved into constituent camps of several households. They assemble as sections of the band—on their way home for the !Kung, and at kangaroo hunts for the Tiwi. They assemble as the entire band, more or less, at kulama rituals for the Tiwi, and at the waterhole dry-season village for the !Kung. And finally, they assemble at gatherings that bring in kinfolk and visitors from the wider field of neighboring bands—at rainy-season food source villages for the !Kung, and at dry-season funerals of elders for the Tiwi.

The Generational Cycle: Coming of Age and Procreating a New Generation

Solar yearly time, with its changing seasons, is entrained with human generational time through ritual: Life crisis rites, called **rites of passage,** are observed on a seasonal schedule. These rituals define units of assemblage, as we saw, in the Tiwi band proper assembling for male initiation rites and in one band hosting others at a funeral.

Rites also redefine human bonds. Among the !Kung a male youth is initiated into manhood after he kills a large game animal. He is tattooed on one arm. After his second kill, he is tattooed on the other arm and is redefined as someone who can marry. He is probably given a child bride shortly thereafter, in a marriage arranged by his and her parents. He is then obliged to go live with her parents and work for them ("perform bride service"), for the next eight to ten years. He frequently marries outside his natal band. When his bride service is over, he and his wife may or may not remain with his in-laws ("affines").

Among the Tiwi, things are more complicated. Male initiation is repeated every year for six years in the seasonal kulama yam ceremonies. Ideally, the fourteen-year-old boy is carried away from his parents by a "mother's brother" contracted by his father. The youth forms a special debt to his ritual sponsor. He is also bonded to his age mates, both his own cohort and those one year above and below him.

After full initiation, the Tiwi male also starts bride service, but he is bonded to a putative "mother-in-law" at the latter's puberty ceremony. After her first menstruation, the young woman is segregated for a time in a special hut. Following appropriate cleansing ceremonies, her puberty rite reaches its climax. Her father thrusts a spear through the young girl's legs and hands it to the young man with the promise of the young woman's first daughter as his wife! The young woman herself, having been promised in marriage before her birth, has already taken up residence with her husband. (No female among the Tiwi is ever unmarried; each infant girl at birth already has a husband, who, however, does not take her to live with him until she is around nine years old.)

The point here is not to tell bizarre anecdotes of strange customs but to illustrate that life crisis rites, even those of initiation, help to move persons from station to station in the group and define the generational cycle. Age grades are a factoring out of the juvenile play group into a more pronounced spatial segregation than is the ordinary primate condition. Tiwi initiates move away from home for six years. When they are reincorporated, now as potential husbands, they may take up residence where they can perform bride service. It matters not that the bride is as yet unborn in this case, nor that the ritual bonding him to a new unit is his mother-in-law's puberty ceremony rather than his marriage. The principle is the same. He has been passed along to a new station. Moreover, female puberty, with its first menstruation, must inevitably precede marriage, pregnancy, and childbirth.

Thus one human cycle, that of coming of age and procreating the next generation, is on the order of twenty to twenty-five years, averaging for both sexes. The cycle is faster, generally, for females in band societies. They marry earlier than males and bear children early. This disparity is pronounced among the Tiwi, where females marry men much older than themselves while still little girls. Tiwi men marry after age thirty, and their first wife is usually a widow older than themselves.

This Tiwi man spent five hours painting full mourning designs at the end of a relative's funeral.

The Life Cycles of Elders: The Scale of Cultures

Funerals among the Tiwi are not only life crisis rites restoring the survivors to society but also rites of intensification defining different bands, and debts across bands. Half the kindred of the deceased are defined as "mourners"; the other half are defined as the latter's "employees." The employees come and do all the menial work of the mourners, even feeding them by hand as if they were infants. They bring fine ceremonial posts. In return, at the end of the ceremony the employees are repaid with gifts of foodstuffs and valued goods such as bricks of paint, feather balls, and ceremonial spears.

At a funeral, moreover, all the widows of a polygynous householder are remarried, bestowed upon new husbands. They, too, then, are moved from station to station at these ritual events.

Kinship. We now have the materials for seeing the ninety-year lifetime cycle. Here language comes into play again, in its subset: kinship systems, which are systems of nomenclature overlying biological relations. Human beings alone among animals have these naming systems, which are capable of extending relationships into the distant past and, by tracing common descent, of giving us "kin" among distant strangers. Kinship systems reckon descent and provide formal rules for marriage: exchange of partners, alliance of affines, who may marry whom, and who goes to live with whom. Basic to kinship systems, too, is a rule, the *incest tabu*, that everywhere among all human beings forbids persons related in the first degree to marry each other.

Kinship, then, is a mechanism to propel individuals from one camp to another and from one band to another in band societies. Universally over the course of a long lifetime in band societies, certain individuals build up kin ties within any given band. They may well come from outside bands, having married in or sought refuge. They have attracted relatives and in-laws. Eventually all the people in the in-groups are their kinpersons by blood or marriage. These key elders have attracted people to their bands and bonded them to the in-group through rituals, reinforced no doubt by campfire talks and storytelling.

Power. The sources of power, or hierarchical authority, in band society are several. Power rests first of all on consent. Those who do not consent simply leave to go to join a more congenial band. Leaders are busy recruiting dissidents from elsewhere and expelling their own dissidents. Leadership in this sense resembles the ideal type of domination Max Weber called *rational* (see Figure 5.4). Just like the alpha animals in a primate dominance hierarchy, human leaders understand where to lead their group in terms of food resources. They also understand whom to welcome and whom to reject, and with what concrete rewards they can entice others to them.

Figure 5.4 Max Weber's typology of domination. Leadership by "core elders" in band societies partakes of all types: they are grandparents, charismatic performers, and rational leaders.

Second, the very nature of their recruitment hinges most upon kinship and the giving of partners in marriage. Band leaders are invariably elders, men and women, who occupy a grandparental position among many households. This resembles Weber's *traditional* mode of domination, which he saw to reside archetypically in patriarchs. Finally, influential elders are also ritual experts. Some may be talented in these activities from the start; others may simply have to officiate at rites by default, being the most senior individuals. !Kung elders are probably expert trancers, magical curers in campfire ceremonies exorcising the ghosts of the dead. Tiwi elders are proficient at song and dance in initiation rites and at funerals. Here we have, then, Weber's *charismatic* domination—that is, power resting on claims of having charisma, "the gift of grace."

Weber's Types of Leadership

I Traditional
Power resides in family elders, especially grandfathers (patriarchs); adults respond as if still children

II Charismatic
Personal allegiance is given to those with the "gift of grace": shamans and prophets but also trancers and storytellers

III Rational
Leaders lead; in band societies, they keep the peace and lead people to sources of food and water

DAILY SPEECH EVENTS: MANAGING CULTURE

In Chapter 4 we defined **language** as a set of catalytic messages that govern how systems go about processing matter, energy, and activity to maintain themselves. Language, then, governs the factory days of organisms and of their societies. A catalyst in chemistry is an agent that speeds up or even effects transformations in other matter without itself being affected. Human speech is such a catalytic language. We theorized in the last chapter that it arose as a means of organizing the labor of children and adolescents for the benefit of that uniquely human group, the married couple, their parents.

We also joined with some highly speculative linguists to imagine an original speech community of *H. sapiens* speaking the first or *ur* language comprising at most 300 words. That remains speculation, which may or may not be better established by subsequent research. It is speculation that does seem to fit with the known facts today, however.

Talking Around the Campfire

We do know quite certainly that human speech not only surrounds all the activities of hunters and gatherers, it becomes *the* activity at one time of the day. Indeed in the typical day of hunters and gatherers the activity that most entrains—that is, synchronizes the activities of any particular day with those of the seasons, and with generational cycling of coming of age and growing old—is *talk*. Hunters and gatherers usually gather around fires at night to talk. No other primate does that. (No other has fire or speech.) Chimpanzees, for example, make individual nests in trees and go to sleep. Human beings, in contrast, always spend some time in the evening speaking to each other: going over the events of the day; telling jokes, stories, legends, and myths; and singing songs, which themselves may be stories. Thus, from our perspective such speech events are a new activity in primate evolution.

What is spoken at these campfire talks? We are told that the !Kung spin stories and recite myths. We can also assume that the kind of retrospective look at daily activity helps human beings to improve their skills. Although speech is not necessary to cooperative behavior, since other mammals are highly cooperative without speech, the fact is that speech and retrospective storytelling, by tapping into the collective memory of the group, no doubt greatly improve human cooperative skills.

Like the !Kung, the Tiwi tell stories in the evening, but we are expressly told that elder Tiwi males rail against young unmarried males at these campfire sessions, accusing them of philandering with their young wives. In a society in which most women are married polygynously to a few old men, in which no man marries before he is thirty, and then most likely to an old widow, such speech events—"gerontocratic diatribes"—are a logical means of social control.

At the level of vocabulary, speech provides human beings with words for roles. Thus, a male has names for some of his activities conducted with others. Among the !Kung he is son, then hunter, then husband, then father, then—probably—trancer (one who cures by confronting the spirits of the dead in trance) and lover, one who engages in extramarital affairs, sometimes recreational, sometimes serious enough to result in divorce and remarriage. Finally, he is grandfather and elder.

These roles become the characters for storytelling. It seems to me that the form and structure of "stories" and folk tales are likely to borrow much from the recounting of real-life "social dramas." Campfire stories, when they deal in gossip, are likely to take on the character of an ongoing soap opera.

Social Drama: Talking About and Managing Disruptive Activities

This brings us to conflict, or *agonistic behavior.* Like all other mammals, human beings often experience "the fight or flight response"—a physiological reaction to others we call "anger." The dominance competitions among chimpanzees are an example. In them, as in all vertebrates, agonistic (aggressive or conflict) sequences of behavior follow in stereotyped succession: threat, confrontation, flight, appeasement, and reassurance (see Chapter 10).

Anthropologists have worked out a similar sequence for human beings and named it **social drama,** or the conflict process (see Figure 5.5). It consists of anger or grievance, breach of the peace or encounter, confrontation, violence and/or redressive action, flight and/or reconciliation. Redressive action refers to attempts to settle the conflict without violence, whether by mediating it, talking it out, or referring it to magical judgment, such as ordeals or duels. These dramas, with their beginnings, middles, and outcomes, must be the stuff of storytelling at the campfires.

In band societies agonistic behavior is channeled according to the genetic potential inherent in us as a primate species. This genetic basis is overlaid with a cultural potential derived from speech, which stereotypes sequences and outcomes.

Among the !Kung a dispute starts as a mere verbal quarrel, goes on to "bad words," then to hand-to-hand combat, and then to spears. At that point the outcomes well may be homicide and flight, or mutual flight. Indeed, flight rather than fight is often the outcome. One party flees and takes refuge with distant friends and relatives in another band.

At any stage the dispute may pass into the court of public opinion and be talked out in a noisy **palaver** among everyone who happens by. This mechanism is not available to other primates. The wider chimpanzee community can observe a quarrel, but they cannot comment on it verbally. Frequently, the outcome of palaver is determined by some influential elder, who well may change the subject by bringing up something—even a story—about which they all can agree, thus diverting the dispute and allowing it to simmer along, perhaps unresolved psychologically, but quiescent socially.

The Tiwi elder who rails most evenings at philanderers may, if sufficiently angered, call an emergency gathering of neighboring camps and there hold a public **duel,** a redressive ritual that channels or contains conflict, not allowing it to spread beyond the two disputants. Here, decked out in full battle regalia, the elder denounces his junior "rival" in a wealth of insulting detail and then hurls his spear at the younger man. The latter's part, in turn, is to stand in silence, deny nothing, and simply dodge the spears until, when the crowd has been greatly entertained, he allows a spear to strike and draw blood. That is the end of it, the old man's honor has been vindicated, his

Figure 5.5 The conflict process, or social drama.

opponent shamed. It resembles nothing so much as a ritualization of a chimpanzee male dominance display.

SUMMARY AND CONCLUSIONS

*B*ands are the elemental human communities of hunters and gatherers. They are the prototypical community for *H. sapiens*. In them we see emerge a pattern of behavior quite different from those of other primates: the division of labor by sex. Adult men hunt for meat, gather plant foodstuffs, make and repair tools, play, sing, dance, and—at times—quarrel violently. Adult women also hunt smaller game, or help male hunting teams. Women gather plant foodstuffs, process and cook food—including meat received from men—hand out food at meals, make and maintain tools, clean house, fetch water, play, sing, dance, and—at times—quarrel, usually not violently. Like all adult primate females, they bear and nurse young as well. Old men and women tell stories. Men and women, young and old, then *cooperate* with each other, and share food as a result. These activities are synchronized in kinetic cycles.

To summarize the kinetic cycles of repetitive activities in band societies of hunters and gatherers: first, the solar day comprises a round of repetitive activities—eating, eliminating, working, playing, talking, sleeping—which come to a climax in the evening meal; second, there is a food-gathering cycle lasting approximately three solar days and a hunting cycle of four to six days.

Anthropologists had first imagined that the subsistence of hunters and gatherers was precarious, that they often verged on starvation, that they were always anxious about food, and that they had to work very hard to scrounge a living from the environment. Nothing could be further from the truth. We find hunters and gatherers working rather easy "work weeks" when we impose our measure of time upon them. They work considerably less than tribal horticulturists, for example, and have plenty of time left over for play, storytelling, and singing and dancing.

The annual round of the solar year is marked by the regular dissolution of the population into its constituent units of households and camps and their regrouping at key food and water sources according to the seasons, usually welcoming guests from other bands. These regroupings are attended by rituals that, although often life crisis rituals, tide groups over through the solar year. The generational cycle is also marked by rituals of birth, initiation, and marriage, whereupon the cycle repeats itself in the birth of a new generation. An entire life cycle, ninety years or so, flows around the life histories of strategic long-lived individuals in band societies, who use the kinship and ritual structure to recruit others to their band, often fleeing conflict (social drama) in other bands. At the death of elders, some others must emerge in their footsteps to build up the next core clientele band population.

When we look at bands, we see several uniquely human institutions fully factoring out: language and speech; kinship, marriage and the family; ritual. In contrast, politics, justice and law, and economics are only prototypically foreshadowed by actions in the other three institutions. The broader field remains the permeable band community in a field of such communities, through which the individual human actors flow with much greater ease than has ever been reported for their primate cousins. In the next chapter we take up the human practice of a trait common to all vertebrates: ritual.

SUGGESTED READINGS

Hall, Edward T. *The Dance of Life: The Other Dimension of Time*. Garden City, N.Y.: Doubleday/Anchor, 1983. A lively look at time as culture and as experience.

Hart, C. W. M., Arnold R. Pilling, and Jane C. Goodale. *The Tiwi of North Australia*, 3rd ed. New York: Holt, Rinehart & Winston, 1988. A cooperative effort reflecting many decades of field work by three ethnographers.

Lee, Richard B. *The Dobe !Kung*. New York: Holt, Rinehart & Winston, 1984. This cut-and-dried account is particularly good in its treatment of cultural ecology.

Tonkinson, Robert. *The Mardu Aborigines: Living the Dream in Australia's Desert*. Ft. Worth: Harcourt Brace Jovanovich, 1991. An accessible ethnography of yet another band culture, with a clear emphasis on ritual life and mythological belief.

Turnbull, Colin. *The Forest People*. New York: Simon & Schuster Touchstone, 1962. This classic personal, interpretationist ethnography is deservedly perennially popular. Turnbull tells an entertaining story of his life with the Mbuti pygmies of equatorial Africa, but the solid field work upon which the account rests shows through. The book remains a splendid account of a band community.

GLOSSARY

band A community consisting of a small, autonomous group that ranges over a known territory looking for game to hunt and foods to gather. It is composed of related families whose members usually marry outside the group. The band is the basic unit of human social life, and all other human communities ultimately derive from it. The band contains at least elementary aspects of all human institutions.

community Among human beings, the basic social unit of biological reproduction of the species and of cultural transmission through learning. We recognize a succession of community types: band, tribe, traditional cities (open and closed), modern metropolitan region.

duel In the theory of social drama, a ritual mechanism brought into play at the phase of "redressive actions." A duel consists of ritualized combat between the two disputants according to strict rules. In Western culture duels were historically held to be "courts of honor" in which God favored the victor and decided the outcome. All duels function to contain the conflict between the two disputants and not let it spread to involve others.

factory In ecology, a system that extracts matter and energy from its environment, passes both from station to station, and delays their consumption in a characteristic cycle of consumption, growth, decay, and death.

factory day The time scale of a factory cycle from beginning to end, when the activity then starts over again. The measure of time does not refer to the earth's day, but to the turnover of the factory cycle.

language A set of catalytic messages, reflecting a grammar, that govern how systems go about processing matter and energy to maintain themselves and, eventually, their species. Examples include the genetic code, ritual, speech, writing, and electronic languages (film, television, computer languages, etc.).

palaver Literally, "talking," a group discussion, usually noisy and agitated, that can occur in any of the sequences of social drama but is most frequent at the time the plaintiff or aggrieved party confronts the defendant or one accused of wrongdoing. Everyone is free to join in a palaver, and people often bring up quite extraneous issues. Palavers often, however, result in redressive or corrective action.

rites of passage Life crisis rites. They program individuals through generational time—coming of age and procreating the next generation—and through their lifetimes—old age and death. There are thus rites of birth, puberty, initiation into young adulthood, marriage, birth of the next generation (for grandparents), and death.

social drama A sequence of conflict between two individuals. The elemental stages are anger or grievance, encounter or breach of the peace, confrontation, violent combat and/or redressive action, flight and/or reconciliation.

territoriality In animal ethology, a group's defending a portion of its home range from others of the same species. It is assumed to be a genetically programmed trait.

Ritual and Myth

6

THE TIME DIMENSIONS OF RITUAL

*THE SPACE DIMENSIONS OF
RITUAL*

Sacred Space as Threshold: Limens and Liminality

!Kung Fire Places: The Hearth and the Bonfire

*RITES OF PASSAGE: THE
INTERSECTION OF RITUAL SPACE
AND TIME*

*ETHNOGRAPHIC CLOSE-UP: TIWI
RITES*

Tiwi Male Initiation Rites

Tiwi Funerals and Remarriages

*THE CATALYTIC POWER OF
SYMBOLS IN RITUAL*

The Nature of Symbols

Rituals as Resolution of Contradictions Through Symbols

*MYTHS: THE NARRATIVE DRAMAS
OF RITUAL AND OF LIFE ITSELF*

*ETHNOGRAPHIC CLOSE-UP: THE
MYTH OF THE MOLIMO (MBUTI
PYGMIES, ITRURI RAIN FOREST,
REPUBLIC OF THE CONGO)*

*The Molimo Ritual to Wake Up the Forest: A Male Rite of
Intensification for the Entire Community*

A Female Molimo Hearth and Ritual Fire Dance

Molimo Symbols

Social Functions of the Molimo Ritual

*The Mythic Drama of the Molimo Forest Spirit and of Men and
Women*

*R*itual exists in nature—all vertebrates perform rituals. Ethologists define ritual as stereotyped behavior that allays anxiety and prepares the organism to act. I have further defined ritual as a language, a set of catalytic messages that govern how systems go about processing matter, energy, and activity to maintain themselves. **Rituals** are thus stereotyped, repetitive activities that effect transformations in state. They speed up the biological life crises of individuals and move individuals from one stage of life to another. Rituals are catalytic in the sense of chemical **catalysis,** whereby a substance or agent can effect a chemical transformation among other substances far more rapidly than would be the case without the agent, which itself remains largely unchanged by the reaction.

Ritual serves then as a social and cultural switch. When the switch is thrown "on," changes result. Individuals emerge from rituals switched into the new "on" state or intensified in a previous state. Human rituals are more developed than those of other primates, although birds also have elaborate rituals, especially in such behaviors as courtship displays.

Human rituals differ from those of all other animals in that they are accompanied by speech, communication as fast as nerve impulses. In the animal world ritual is frequently accompanied by song, as in birds, or other vocalizations, and by rhythmic, drumming actions. Among humans the song is usually in words: the speech is sung. It is no longer, as in the rest of the animal world, simply a question of communicating by responding to another animal's action with a precise one in reply, as in any dance, but of adding speech and chants as well.

Thus, humans tell stories, **myths,** about rituals both before and during the events themselves. Myths are narratives that explain rituals, which in turn are events that enact the myths. Because rituals existed among other animals before the invention of human speech, I treat rituals as coming first. Ritual is primary, myth secondary.

Since myths explain rituals, they also explain life, which is itself only a brief transformation of matter and energy into living matter, starting, in each human case, in a single fertilized cell, which divides, develops, is born, grows to maturity, reproduces itself through sexual union, ages, and dies. A culture's myths always try to account not only for this whole process in time but for the contradiction between life and death as well. That contradiction in turn reflects the contradiction inherent in all self-organizing systems—that between organization/order and energy loss/disorder. The many other contradictions and oppositions that ritual seeks to overcome, temporarily, reflect these conditions of existence.

THE TIME DIMENSIONS OF RITUAL

Ritual behaviors are implicit regulators of the kinetic cycles outlined in Chapter 5. Indeed, they often kick energy into the cycle through joint meals and feasts and through marshaling of cooperative effort. As a set of messages, they also kick in information. They are often shorthand statements to program, and hence guide, the next kinetic cycle of activity. All human kinetic cycles follow the schedules or time scales outlined in Chapter 5: daily, seasonal, yearly, generational, long lifetime, and cultural and historical (300–500 years). There are rituals for each time scale.

Rites of intensification program groups through the changes in the season, through the yearly kinetic cycles. Participants come out programmed to do more intensely what they are supposed to do at that time of year. **Rites of passage,** or life crisis rites, program individuals through their lifetimes, carrying them through one stage of the life cycle to another, and carrying their survivors through and past death with its inevitable grief and terror.

A rite unfolds through three phases in time. These phases were first identified by Arnold van Gennep in 1909 (1960), who coined the term *rites of passage* and thought them universal phenomena that accompany transition of any kind among human beings. The phases are (1) *separation* from the old state, (2) *transition* (or liminality), and (3) *reincorporation* into the new (see Figure 6.1). Van Gennep was impressed that these rites often take

Figure 6.1 The ritual process in time, using the example of a fundamentalist Christian's being "born again."

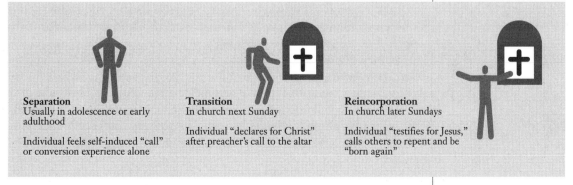

Separation
Usually in adolescence or early adulthood

Individual feels self-induced "call" or conversion experience alone

Transition
In church next Sunday

Individual "declares for Christ" after preacher's call to the altar

Reincorporation
In church later Sundays

Individual "testifies for Jesus," calls others to repent and be "born again" the metaphoric form of death and rebirth. **A neophyte**—the person in transition—may symbolically die when separated from an old identity. The individual may go down into the depths, as into a tomb; crawl through a tunnel, as if through a birth canal; and emerge reborn in the light of a new day on the other side, reincorporated. Such rites are dramas about the nature of life itself.

In this chapter we shall examine the way ritual patterns are manifest in space, time (and kinetic cycles), symbols, and myths, and how myths interact with ritual and life.

THE SPACE DIMENSIONS OF RITUAL

Some vertebrates, especially birds and hoofed animals, assemble year after year at particular places for ritualized courtship displays, dominance competitions, and—in some species—even nest building. Human beings have developed this tendency to gather at particular spots for the purpose of throwing the ritual switch "on." Special places for the transitional phase of ritual transmute the everyday, the mundane—in short, the **profane**—into the **sacred**. The places themselves become **symbols,** or shorthand (and hence catalytic) statements of the switching process itself. As symbols they become powerful reminders of the ritual and hence reinforce the transformations effected in them.

Japanese wayside shrine in the form of a portal. Travelers may pause on a freestanding threshold to purify themselves ritually.

Sacred Space as Threshold: Limens and Liminality

Space and time intersect in rituals. This is especially evident in the phase of transition, which in space always forms a kind of threshold (or *limens*, the Latin term), a stepping stone between the past and the future. For the best material illustration of this intersection of ritual space and time, we leave the world of bands and cite the occasional wayside shrines erected for travelers in the Japanese countryside in the form of a portal or freestanding open, doorless gateway. Dedicated to a particular deity, they are simply gates, seemingly to nowhere, standing above narrow thresholds. Entering the threshold, wayfarers may pause in their journey, clap their hands, pray, make an offering, and cleanse themselves from a nearby sacred fount of water. These portals are places for rest, **ablution** (ritual cleansing), contemplation of lovely natural scenic vistas, and rededication to the journey. However, they are nothing but thresholds. They thereby define and illustrate the essential nature of sacred space (see Figure 6.2).

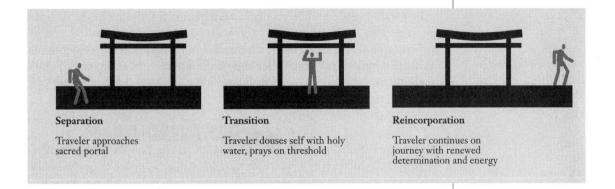

Separation

Traveler approaches
sacred portal

Transition

Traveler douses self with holy
water, prays on threshold

Reincorporation

Traveler continues on
journey with renewed
determination and energy

*Figure 6.2 The ritual
process in space, using the
example of the Japanese
wayside portal ritual.*

Sacred space is a place dedicated (perhaps only sporadically and temporarily) to the phase of transition in ritual. Once on the ritual threshold, once fully separated from the old state, one has given up all the trappings of one's old identity. In rites of initiation, especially, the individual is betwixt and between, neither what he or she once was nor what he or she shall become. Victor Turner (1964, 1969) asserts that the debasement of stripping and the loss of previous identity, effected in the separation phase, means that the transition phase is at once empty and powerful. He dignifies this quality with the term **liminality** (literally "thresholdness").

Liminality reduces participants to their lowest common denominator. Their previous identities do not count, and they have not yet assumed their new role. In cases where the role the participant is to assume on the other side is an extremely changed one, the liminality is also likely to be extreme; the neophyte may be reduced to "nothingness," or symbolic death.

Even in band societies some places are dedicated "permanently" as sacred spots, but they are activated only sporadically when people assemble at them for rituals. The European paleolithic cave sites filled with "cave art"—ritual paintings of game animals and their hunters—strike us today as places of sublime aesthetic expression, but they were only activated on some yearly, not daily, basis. In Van Gennep's term, the "circle of the sacred" (read "threshold") pivots upon those who engage in ritual, wherever they are, as the ritual itself intensifies cycles of activities.

!Kung Fire Places: The Hearth and the Bonfire

One such occasional sacred place is the ordinary human **hearth.** Fire is a tool unique to humans. We use it to light up the night, for defense against animal predators, for warmth, and to cook food. This elemental transformation of food from raw to cooked is a universal human trait. It sets us off from all other animals. Biologically speaking, cooking is not necessary for our digestive tracts. Like other primates, we can survive on raw food alone.

In bands people gather around cooking fires for the main meal in the evening. This meal is everywhere stereotyped—that is, performed according to etiquette, good manners. This etiquette involves not only not offending others but not offending the animals and plants that one eats! **Tabus,** symbolic prohibitions on certain behaviors—and prescriptions to perform other behaviors—are common at meals. Eskimos, for example, may not eat seal meat at a meal in which caribou meat is served. To do so would offend the Spirit of the Caribou. Meal taking is the basic human daily ritual.

On a seasonal rhythm we observe that the !Kung San, for example, leave their household hearths to make one grand bonfire in order to perform curing rituals, to drive away sickness. They dance when one or more members of the residential group are actually sick. They also dance when different households, of both friends and strangers, camp together and when tempers, as a consequence, are short; sickness—in the form of threatening ghosts—is thought to be imminent.

In a dry-season village the bonfire is at the center of the circle of hearths and huts. Generally, the women sit around it in a circle and clap and sing. The men in turn circle the women and dance to their beat. The dancers sometimes impersonate the actions of game animals. During the dance one or more of the men—and at times some of the women, too—fall into trance.

Trance is an altered state of consciousness brought on first by ritual separation, then by drumming, rhythmic singing and dancing, and even drugs. Everywhere it is marked by dissociation, sensory distancing, seeming unawareness of one's physical surroundings, and an intense concentration on the interior mental experience. A human being in trance evidently experiences it as being in a waking dream.

Different cultures interpret the experience of trance differently, thus influencing the interior state of mind of the person in trance. The !Kung San, for example, believe that in trance one's spirit is free to see and communicate with the spirits of the dead. Sickness, they believe, is the result of a ghost's attempting to kidnap or capture the soul of a sick person. Ghosts usually only want their own loved ones to come live with them in the land of the dead. The man or woman in trance must persuade or frighten the dead into giving up their hold on the ailing person, who is thus restored to health.

This belief is transmitted through myths interpreting the trance experience. When a new !Kung initiate goes into trance, he or she already knows what to expect from the myths. The recently dead are readily "seen," as in a dream. When the trancer comes back to consciousness and recites adventures wresting the souls of the ill from the dead, a new specific myth on an old theme is being recited.

This, then, is a place, the central bonfire in a plaza doing heavy duty in a special event. Instead of many household hearths, a single sacred bonfire is the focus of the entire group. The group assembled around it is attempting to flip a switch and effect a transformation of sick persons into healthy ones, or to maintain good health by warding off ghosts. An unintended side effect is to foster fellowship and good feeling among people often at odds with each other.

RITES OF PASSAGE: THE INTERSECTION OF RITUAL SPACE AND TIME

Humans share with other primates similar stages of the life cycle marked off by similar biological crises—birth, puberty, procreation, old age, and death. In most societies rites of passage are linked in some way to these biological crises. This is most clear for birth, female puberty, and death.

To begin with, the stages of the life cycle have been given names by human beings and have become categories of partial social roles to be learned and enacted. The infant, a helpless, unweaned babe, is sexually neuter; children are boys or girls; adults are men or women. Old men and old women are elders. Adolescents may or may not be recognized as having a distinct age role. But there usually is a stage, however brief, in which the young person is recognized as marriageable and hence ready to become an adult.

However, the kinetic cycle propelling a human being from birth to procreation to death in any one lifetime is never solitary. Every life cycle has to be synchronized with other life cycles. Indeed, some rites of passage, especially those of initiation, are collective. Others bear double duty. For example, to my knowledge no ethnographer has ever described any rites for menopause, celebrating the cessation of the female's menstrual flow, although that is definitely a biological life crisis. Instead, the birth of grandchildren, especially a first grandchild, is a much more pleasant way to change the status of adult women and men to that of elder. Grandparents may welcome a new generation while not explicitly acknowledging their own loss of physical power.

For an example of the particular named stages (or age and sex categories) of the life cycle see Figure 6.3, which lists those of the Tiwi (Goodale, 1971, p. 22).

Figure 6.3 Age and sex categories among the Tiwi.

The Unborn

pitapitui (sexless spirits; they are summoned in dreams by their fathers to be born)

The Living

Female

kitjinga	small girl
alinga	young girl
muringaleta	puberty
murukubara	young woman
poperinganta	pregnant
pernamberdi	mother of girl
awri-awri	mother of boy
badamoringa	barren woman
parimaringa	menopause
intula	old woman

Male

kitjini	small boy
tajinati	young boy
malikanini	youth
imbalinapa	father of girl
awri-apa	father of boy
arakulani	big man
irula	old man

The Dead

mobuditi (men and women)

133

E T H N O G R A P H I C   C L O S E - U P

TIWI RITES

Now that we have a notion of the space
and time dimensions of ritual, let us take up some
examples from a band society: the Tiwi. We shall not
attempt to give examples of all kinds of rites known
to anthropology. This chapter is not a catalogue. But
male initiation and funeral rituals of the Tiwi are
interesting because they are very much synchronized
with other rituals and because they reflect the particular emphases and priorities of this band culture.

Tiwi Male Initiation Rites

Biologically speaking, a male initiation would be a
puberty rite. But, in fact, puberty among males is
hard to pinpoint exactly. Thus in most societies male
initiation has little to do with physical changes in any
one male but rather more to do with chronological
age.

Traditionally among the Tiwi, a young man is
initiated around age fourteen. A household with a
fourteen-year-old boy is also likely to be a household
with many wives. That is, besides the boy's mother,
his father (or stepfather, if she has remarried after his
father's death) may have as many as twenty additional
wives living in camp. Such a father is likely to be
much older than his son or stepson, perhaps in his
sixties. Some of these wives are twelve and thirteen
years old, some even younger.

Clearly there is social tension in such a situation.
Here is a pubescent boy; here are all these women,
some of them his own age or close to it. These
women are keeping their husband rich in food—
going out and hunting small game, gathering roots
and berries, and collecting all manner of edible
things. Consequently, the successful polygynous
householder can devote himself to the finer things.
He can carve fine spears, prepare fine graveposts for
funerals, and compose songs for dances at the

funerals. He hasn't time to police his son's activities
all day long when his young wives are scattered
around in the bush.

The solution to this social tension presents itself
in the boy's initiation rites. These rites are greatly
prolonged. A father sends his son away to make a
man of him, and it takes six years of transition and
isolation to do it. The father calls upon an adult
kinsman of the boy, usually a cousin engaged to be
married to the boy's sister and therefore in the
father's debt for the promised wife. Father and
cousin agree upon a day for the initiation. The
cousin gets together a war party of adult men. One
fine day, when everyone is in camp, the war party
suddenly descends. The father looks on in horrified
surprise as his young son, a mere boy, is carried off
to the bush by ferocious warriors in full battle paint.
The women scream and run for cover. It is all a
sham, and the only one who is in the dark is the boy.
It is always a surprise for him.

The new initiate is not alone in his transition, for
he is going to find a bunch of other miserable
fourteen- to twenty-year-olds in the bush under the
supervision of men all age twenty-four or older.
Here the adolescents are trained in hunting and
gathering. The group more or less supports itself off
the land. Their fathers give up the meat of the boys'
hunting during the long period of their isolation and
transition.

The capture of the fourteen-year-old boy is a rite
of separation, the beginning ritual of a long ritual
transition. For the next year the boy lives in his
transitional, liminal state with the other neophytes in
their camp. Once a year the whole sequence of
separation, transition, and reincorporation is
repeated in the kulama yam ceremony, in which each
grade of initiates separates from the bush, passes
through the ritual, and reincorporates one grade

ahead at the end of the rites. At the end of six years, the young man is fully initiated and graduates to the status of marriageable young adult. He no longer has to return to the bush, except in the role of teacher-guardian for some young cousin whose sister he expects to make his wife.

The kulama yam ceremony occurs at the beginning of the dry season and is a rite of intensification or seasonal rite for the wider Tiwi band. It is also an annual rite of ongoing initiation for the young men, in which each of six age grades is advanced one step up the ladder.

Tiwi females also have age grades, corresponding to those of the young men (Goodale, 1971):

Men	Women
1. *Marakamani*	*Marakumaringa*
2. *Kulpaniati*	*Kulaminatinga*
3. *Wadjineti*	*Wadjinetinga*
4. *Mikinatringa*	*Mikinatinga*
5. *Mikidara*	*Mikidaringa*
6. *Mikiaterima*	*Mikiateramunga*
7. *Mikigula*	*Mikigulinga*

(The alert reader will note that there are seven age grades but that it takes only *six* years to get through them. That is so because Grade 2 is a very short one before the initiate's second kulama ceremony.)

Female age mates of the boys are promoted with them, but unlike the boys, the girls have not been isolated in the bush. Rather, each has been married and living in her husband's household since about age nine.

During the three days of the ceremony, the initiates leave the bush and assemble in a special camp at the kulama ground. Nearby, the home-camp groups of the entire band are assembled for the ceremony (see Figure 6.4). Each Tiwi band has special ceremonial grounds where the various neighborhoods within the band come together. This, then, is the one time of year when the entire band may assemble as one body. At the kulama ground there are sleeping places for the initiated men and the various grades of initiates, separate from the household camps of women and uninitiated children, the spectators.

The rites are extremely detailed and are conducted by the fully initiated men in a dramatic pantomime treating the yams as their symbolic enemy. Women gather the yams beforehand. The men gather them again and soak them overnight in a swamp reached by a special passageway. They battle the yams as if they were animals, defeat them, bury them, and discover them "reborn" at the foot of a nearby hardwood tree the next day. Then they roast them in the center, or "navel," of their own sacred circle they have traced at the kulama grounds. Finally, the yams are consumed by the men, who have instructed the male and female initiates in "yam ways" as they go along. Once the yams are eaten the rites are over.

During the ceremony, within their sacred arena men dance and sing songs of battle for the women and

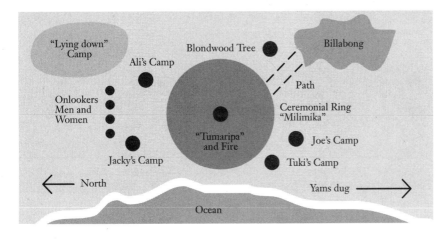

Figure 6.4 Kulama grounds diagrammed by anthropologist Jane Goodale for a particular band.

children. For each male initiate the most important event is his debut during his induction into the third age grade, when he is obliged to sing his own songs solo in the sacred circle before the onlookers. It is desirable to have a good voice and to shine theatrically in songs and dances. All Tiwi men have opportunities to show off their song and dance routines after their debuts—every year for the rest of their lives in fact. Figure 6.5 summarizes the series of events in the Tiwi male initiation.

Tiwi Funerals and Remarriages

The Tiwi place great importance on funerals. The ritual transformation of all funerals is for the survivors to assuage their grief and go on with their lives without the lost social tie. Thus, each widow receives a new husband at a funeral. Her new ties, in remarriage, completely redefine the survivor. She goes from widow to wife. Strictly speaking, the Tiwi do not celebrate marriage by a rite of passage. (A girl's first daughter is promised in marriage at her puberty rite. That is as close as they come to a marriage ceremony.)

Funerals are not band events but kinship events. They pull people together from several Tiwi bands and thus operate in the arena of "foreign relations." Because kin ties extend across many bands, relatives from many places attend a funeral. Close relatives are obliged to attend, but others may come for profit.

Funerals always take place in the dry season; therefore, they may be held months after the actual

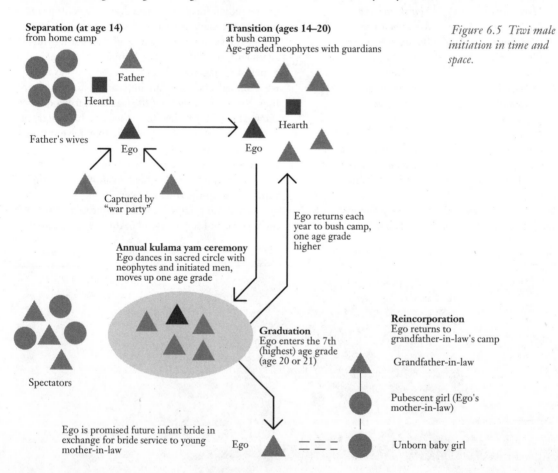

Separation (at age 14)
from home camp

Father

Hearth

Father's wives

Ego

Captured by
"war party"

Transition (ages 14–20)
at bush camp
Age-graded neophytes with guardians

Hearth

Ego

Ego returns each
year to bush camp,
one age grade
higher

Annual kulama yam ceremony
Ego dances in sacred circle with
neophytes and initiated men,
moves up one age grade

Spectators

Graduation
Ego enters the 7th
(highest) age grade
(age 20 or 21)

Reincorporation
Ego returns to
grandfather-in-law's camp

Grandfather-in-law

Pubescent girl (Ego's
mother-in-law)

Ego is promised future infant bride in
exchange for bride service to young
mother-in-law

Ego

Unborn baby girl

Figure 6.5 Tiwi male initiation in time and space.

death and burial and they usually encompass several deaths. People are always given ample time to get ready for them. At the start, the close family of the deceased enters a state of severe mourning. Mourners include siblings, parents, children, and spouses of the deceased, as well as any great-grandparents and great-grandchildren. The bereaved paint themselves in special designs, wear special armbands, and, most important, refrain from any work.

Daily needs and work of the funeral must be taken care of by funeral servants, who are related to the deceased through a relative of opposite sex. They include a man's mother's father and above all his male **cross-cousins** (specifically, father's sister's son and mother's brother's son; a cross-cousin is related to you through a parent of opposite sex from your parent). In effect, these are persons from whom one can expect to receive a spouse. They are the class of *affines,* or "in-laws." Funeral servants throng to be attentive at the funeral of an important person.

The actual festivities may last several days, during which all participants, men and women, perform special songs and dances. There are also ritual combats, generally between the mourners and servants and between cross-cousins (potential spouses). Moreover, there are quite likely to be many loud quarrels, especially between parties from different bands who are sometimes just spectators and who are not tied to each other through the annual kulama ceremonies.

The grand finale of the last day is the erection of posts on the grave. This ceremony is accompanied by many special dances and ends with rich payment of the servants by the mourners for all their services, including the posts. Payment is made with food, carved spears, and other valuables. Once it is done, the mourners are released from their mourning and the widows are released from widowhood. They take new husbands immediately and move off from the funeral grounds to new homes (see Chapter 8).

A big Tiwi funeral—one for a polygynous householder, an elder with many wives—is an exchange event of the greatest magnitude. Widows leave the burial ground to live as wives of their deceased husband's brothers or other men decided upon according to the debts of their own kin—sons, brothers, brothers' sons. In addition, this is the only event at which large quantities of handcrafted objects change hands—since there are no marketplaces in band societies.

Tiwi father with his daughter. His face paint and feather ball are symbols of mourning.

THE CATALYTIC POWER OF SYMBOLS IN RITUAL

Both rites of passage (lifetime rites) and rites of intensification (yearly rites) teach and induct and compel some persons into new roles while confirming others in old ones. There may be slow instruction going on, as in the isolation of the bush camp, and fast—liminal—instruction going on, the content of which is largely symbolic. Transformation into something new and intensification of something old are the twin effects of throwing on the ritual switch.

In each case, sacred ground marks the inner, or transitional, stage of the rite of passage. This is, literally, the spatial threshold of liminal time. In Tiwi male initiation, it is the initiate's secret camp in the bush. Later, in the kulama ceremony, it is the sacred navel at the center of the circle, where the adult men roast the yams in a sacred hearth. At funerals, it is the burial grounds with their stern bristling array of fine hardwood graveposts, which can be sighted at a distance. The posts, which endure longer than personal memories of the deceased, are monuments to the human past, symbols to the descendants that they belong to the band's country because these dead ancestors once summoned their unborn spirits to be born.

Part of the Kulama yam ritual is for the men to be painted with an elaborate white, yellow, and red design that must always be the same. Other rituals are accompanied by their own distinctive painted design.

The Nature of Symbols

Symbols are shorthand statements, which are thereby catalytic. They are particular items that stand for objects, events, or relationships. A symbol may have some association with what it represents, or it may be entirely arbitrary. However, symbols usually draw upon the ordinary, transmuting the profane into the sacred in the ritual context. Thus the !Kung bonfire stands for all hearth and cooking fires. It signifies warmth, protection, nurture, and safety.

Water, which is necessary to all life itself on earth, is also a nearly universal sacred symbol. It figures prominently in female puberty rites, where it is used to wash away menstrual blood, commonly feared as dangerous, if not polluted. Blood is another symbol, commonly associated with danger, pollution, and death; it appears symbolically in sacrifices, especially of offerings to appease the spirits of game animals.

The acts of separation and assembling frequently define ordinary space as sacred. The construction of a sacred bonfire in the midst of their camp by the !Kung illustrates this.

Staple foods, the meat of prized game animals, and feared but desired plant products are also often sacred symbols figuring in rituals. Take the kulama yams, for example. They have come to stand for all yams. Kulama

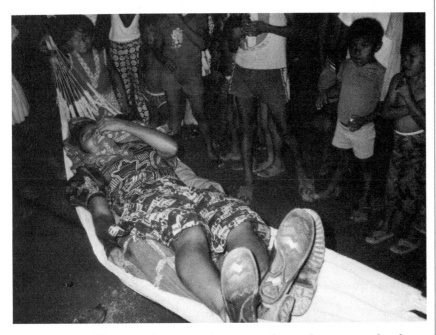

Flame is a nearly human sacred symbol. Whether the burning of incense, candles, or offerings, flame is a symbol in all the major world religions today. Eternal flames are key symbols in the secular ritual of modern war memorials. Making a hearth can symbolize a marriage. For example, among the San Blas Kuna Indians whom I studied in Panama, burning brands are thrust under a hammock into which a (ideally suddenly and unannounced) betrothed couple have been bodily placed. Three days later the bridegroom seals the match by going with his father-in-law to fetch two stout logs that, placed in a cross, form, at their center, the hearth symbolizing the new couple. The flame devouring itself at a cross's center is a common symbol of a gateway to the divine.

yams are special because they are poisonous and must be processed to have their poison removed before they are eaten. They are thus feared, yet desired, objects. In their shape, yams are somewhat phallic, and their straggly beards of roots resemble the facial hair of men. They are thus a masculine symbol, although they are gathered by women.

The kulama yam ceremony attempts to resolve a number of symbolic contradictions. A symbol of masculinity is ordinarily gathered by women. The ritual reclaims the yams for men, who get rid of the poison. (Symbolically, yams become "enemies.") Basically, this part of the drama revolves around the inescapable biological opposition between male and female.

Rituals as Resolution of Contradictions Through Symbols

The kulama yam ritual tries to resolve the contradiction between poison and food, between sickness and health. A desired food is poisonous. The rite dramatizes the driving out of poison but is also said to drive away—exorcise—sickness in general. The most basic opposition here is that between life and death. It touches on the inevitable fact that living creatures, save for the most primitive single-celled organisms, must eat other living creatures—or their organic products—to survive. Life feeds life. Or, put another way, life lives on death.

That is the cosmic drama. The more mundane drama has to do with ordinary social life. By subduing the yams, adult men are symbolically subduing women, who gather them. But yams are also symbols of the masculinity of the youths, the initiates whom the adult men put in their proper place as subordinates.

Likewise, the drama of a Tiwi funeral has to do not only with the opposition between life and death but with the conflict between affines, or "in-laws"—people related through marriage or the promise of marriage. Life's greatest anxiety for any Tiwi male concerns getting a wife. He is, from his early twenties, in a state of tension with his future father-in-law, an older man who has promised him an infant daughter in the future. At a funeral, actual and potential fathers-in-law, brothers-in-law, and "in-laws" in general are pitted against one another in ritual opposition. The mourners may do no work; their "servants" (actual or potential in-laws) must even put the food they eat into their mouths. At the end of the funeral the mourners must repay their servants with large quantities of valuables. Thus, the opposition between groups of people who marry each other is, temporarily, canceled.

MYTHS: THE NARRATIVE DRAMAS OF RITUAL AND OF LIFE ITSELF

We saw in Chapter 5 that evening storytelling around the fire is a universal human characteristic. We also saw that many of the stories concern *social dramas*, the real-life conflicts between real people. Many other stories are *myths*, narratives of cosmic conflicts, about the inescapable contradictions and oppositions of human existence. Myths are dramatized in ritual. Their form, however, is similar to that of social dramas.

In social drama we have a protagonist (hero or heroine) who feels a grievance (or, in myth, is subject to a contradiction), confronts an opponent, engages in conflict or gains ritual redress, and is either victorious or flees. Myths employ these same dramatic sequences, but whatever the outcomes for the protagonists—redress, flight, or victory—the mythic drama is never finally resolved. The oppositions that mythic protagonists represent keep cropping up again and again. That is so because myths, like symbols, mediate between oppositions drawn from our knowledge of the world and from our immediate social structures. These oppositions can never be fully overcome.

Myths are myriad. Anthropologists have recorded thousands of them. Here, however, we shall examine one short myth to illustrate the relation of myth to the ritual that enacts it, to the unconscious mind, to the symbols it employs, to the social relations of the people who tell the myth, and to human existence.

E T H N O G R A P H I C   C L O S E - U P

THE MYTH OF THE MOLIMO (MBUTI PYGMIES, ITRURI RAIN FOREST, REPUBLIC OF THE CONGO)

Band peoples recite many myths. We have mentioned that !Kung trancers recite specific versions of the myth that recently deceased ghosts are seeking to take a loved one with them to the land of the death, thus causing the illness in the patient the trancer has been "fighting over with the ghost." The !Kung myth explaining curing ceremonies is thus both open-ended and variable. In general, at the band level people do not tell particularly rigid myths, which then seem to bind human beings, very specifically, to a way of action. Peoples living in bands have a high degree of personal freedom, including freedom from myth.

We shall here examine one typically sketchy band-level myth because it illustrates the interrelation between myth and behavior. Myth always explains why people perform ritual. In this case the ritual is thought of as necessary for an entire way of life.

The Mbuti Pygmies are a group of hunters and gatherers in the Itruri rain forest of the Republic of the Congo, studied by anthropologist Colin Turnbull. Only in passing, Turnbull recounts their myth of the forest spirit, the *molimo*, whom they revere and personify in giant, "secret" flutes. Another myth connects the molimo with the origin of fire:

> There is an old legend that once it was the women who "owned" the molimo, but the men stole it from them and ever since the women have been forbidden to see it. . . . There is another old legend which tells that it was a woman who stole fire from the chimpanzees or, in yet another version, from the great forest spirit. (1961, p. 154)

Earlier in his ethnography Turnbull, after describing male youths dancing, performing a tug-of-war on the flutes during molimo ritual, says

perhaps this represented the original struggle for possession of the molimo [the sacred flutes], a struggle which some say was between Pygmies and animals, or others say was between men and women. (ibid., p. 86)

The myth (or "old legends") explains why Mbuti men own the molimo flutes, but not why they play the flutes in the ritual. One Mbuti man explained that:

> Normally everything goes well in our world. But at night when we are sleeping, sometimes things go wrong, because we are not awake to stop them from going wrong. Army ants invade the camp; leopards may come in and steal a hunting dog or even a child. If we were awake these things would not happen. So when something big goes wrong, like illness or bad hunting or death, it must be because the forest

A Mbuti Pygmie camp.

141

is sleeping and not looking after its children. So what do we do? We wake it up. We wake it up by singing to it, and we do this because we want it to awaken happy. Then everything will be well and good again. So when our world is going well then also we sing to the forest because we want it to share our happiness. (ibid., p. 92)

This text is also a myth, because the informant is telling a story: the ritual wakes up the benevolent spirit of the forest and causes it to protect its people from danger, or simply to rejoice with them.

The Molimo Ritual to Wake Up the Forest: A Male Rite of Intensification for the Entire Community

Mbuti men undertake the ritual at any time during the year, whenever the community has been upset by a death, illness, simple misfortune, or even good fortune. When a band decides to hold the molimo ceremony, they usually make a camp deep in the forest. Between ceremonies the owners of the sacred flutes store them high in specially selected trees. During the month or longer they play the flutes, they must take them down and hide them in a nearby stream. Much to Turnbull's surprise, the flutes in use during his field trip were not made from traditional bamboo; one was fifteen feet of metal drainpipe retrieved from a highway, and another was a shorter piece of such a pipe. These would not rot, and they had a beautiful sound when played.

Each evening several unmarried youths went from household to household collecting food for the molimo basket, which they hung up at the molimo hearth site. Men then gathered there, leaving the women and children shut up in their dwellings. The men sang, then danced, then ate, and then listened to the sound of the molimo flutes that approached from the forest, circling the village. Their songs were songs of praise and devotion, the instrumental response from the flutes, pure music. Some nights there were two adjacent hearths, one for grandfathers and fathers ("elders and hunters") and one for unmarried youths, who might spend the hours before

dawn in a raucous race through the village, bearing and playing the flutes, and striking the huts of anyone who had committed any transgression the day before. For a month or more the men and youths sang, danced, and ate by night and hunted by day.

A Female Molimo Hearth and Ritual Fire Dance

Women and children supposedly believed the molimo to be an "animal" forest spirit rather than flutes played by men. Thus, they could not come out at night, and the flutes were tabu to their sight and touch. In fact, the women knew better. Indeed, to Turnbull's astonishment, on one occasion they even participated in a special molimo ceremony, focusing on a very old woman from another band, visiting especially for the purpose, and accompanied by a local young wife who after two years of marriage was still childless.

This "special" molimo came the evening the old woman arrived. The first night the men clustered in age-graded groups—the elders, the hunters, and the youths—and danced and sang competitively. However, the women joined them early in the evening and danced and sang songs of their own before retiring.

The second night the girls and women, who had gathered in the childless woman's hut, came out with their bodies painted black and their hair done up with twine made from a vine. Alongside the men's hearth they made a fire of their own where they danced and sang. Suddenly they were singing the molimo songs that, as women, they were not supposed to know. The old woman, accompanied by the childless wife, led the dancing. Before dawn, at the climax of the event, the old woman charged into the women's fire and kicked and stamped the coals with her bare feet. The men cast the coals back into the hearth, and she kicked and stamped the revived fire twice more before ending her dance and the event.

Molimo Symbols

The most obvious symbols are the molimo flutes, the "voice" of the animal forest spirit. With adolescence, Mbuti males all know for a fact that the flutes are material objects, possessions of older men. Young men may play them to deceive women and children. Nonetheless, according to Turnbull, they clearly believe that the spirit of the forest *does* somehow speak through the flutes when men play them.

Second, there is the fire and the hearth, primarily the special molimo hearths where men gather. Women, however, "own" fire that they have at their own hearths. When the women, rallying around an old grandmother, try to cure a barren young wife, they do so by invoking the molimo around their own molimo hearth, which the old female ritualist dominates by dancing on the embers.

Social Functions of the Molimo Ritual

The male gathering at the molimo fire—staying up all night for as long as a month to wake up the forest while hunting by day to have meat to eat each night—on the face of it seems irrational behavior. One thing they surely are doing, however, is scaring away predators. No leopard is going to come near those noisy nighttime camps. Another thing they are doing is focusing communal effort on the daytime hunts. Yet another thing they are doing is disciplining camp members who misbehave by thrashing their huts when the molimo flutes rush by. Finally, by singing collective songs of praise and joy, they are orchestrating fellowship and good feeling. The female ritual is clearly a fertility ritual, aimed at bringing children to a barren woman.

The Mythic Drama of the Molimo Forest Spirit and of Men and Women

By allowing the women an occasional molimo fire and female fire dance, the Mbuti are dramatizing the opposition between the sexes while conceding that both have their "spheres of influence": the forest for the men, the hearth fires for the women. The very sketchy myth simply says that men fought the forest animals for possession of the molimo flutes and that women fought chimpanzees for possession of fire. Or, in other versions, men fought

women for possession of the flutes and women fought men for possession of fire. There are two basic oppositions here: the opposition of men and women against animals and of men and women against each other. Remember, however, that in daily life it is men who hunt and kill the forest animals, and women who cook the animal meat on the home fires.

Note, however, that the myth—the narrative explaining this opposition—is extremely sketchy. The molimo forest spirit is not represented as a person with a personality and whims and desires, such as a god or a heroic figure might have. It is simply a spirit. The late-nineteenth-century anthropologist Edmund Tyler posited a belief in **animism**—the imputation of spiritual force to the elements of nature, such as the forest, the sky, the sun, rain, fire, and so on—as the original religious belief. Our studies of band-level people supports his conclusion.

Thus, powerful mythological texts featuring contests—social dramas—between gods and heroic figures only appear with tribal peoples and their own constant warfare and complicated social allegiances. Such mythologies then may become as important as the rituals that enact them, in some cases, letter perfect, especially after sacred texts are written down, with the invention of writing in early civilizations. If you are a Jewish reader, reflect on how the Seder dinner ritual at Passover must invoke the story of Moses and the exodus of the Jews from Egypt. If you are a Christian reader, reflect on how the Lord's Supper or communion service of the Eucharist reflects the events of the Passion and Crucifixion of Christ.

With the Mbuti Pygmies, however, the story of the struggles between men and animals and between men and women for the possession of the molimo flutes and fire need not be recited in any letter-perfect way. In contrast, an explanatory text, what we today would call a *sermon*, is recited in the passage quoted above in which an elder explains why the Mbuti must wake up the forest. A sermon or homily may recite a myth, but it always does so while exhorting to good conduct.

Thus the ritual and mythic drama is never done. It needs to be constantly repeated. Both myth and ritual constantly deal with and pretend to resolve conflicts—latent or open—that can never be resolved. All of human life is a struggle with these conflicts and tensions, some defined by the particular cultural situation (as with the Tiwi opposition between affines, or in-laws), others inherent in the human situation, as in the !Kung fears of the dead, or the Tiwi fears of poisonous yams. The catalytic effect of myth and ritual is to transform human beings, if only temporarily, into beings whose fears have been conquered and who are poised to act as the rituals and their myths have told them to do.

SUMMARY AND CONCLUSIONS

Rituals are a form of language, already present in nature, whereby vertebrates send messages to each other to synchronize their efforts to command matter and energy, thus managing activities from one kinetic cycle of activity to another. Rituals are stereotyped, repetitive activities that allay anxiety and prepare men and women for new actions required by any crisis—that is, by the necessity to shift from one stage to another. Ritual action, displaying symbols and explained verbally in myth, is catalytic. Ritual (with associated symbols and myths) is an agent to effect swift transformations without itself being changed.

Ritual operates, then, at every human time scale that needs intensification and transformation: daily—as in the !Kung nightly meal at the hearth; yearly—as in the Tiwi ceremonies taming the kulama yams; and generationally—as in the Tiwi funerals sending the ghost safely away. We generally call daily and yearly rituals *rites of intensification*, since they function to intensify people in existing roles. Generational rituals are usually called *rites of passage*, since they induct people into new roles. The two Tiwi examples, however, are both yearly and generational, both rites of intensification and rites of passage. That is not unusual; many rites of passage for the initiates are rites of intensification for the other participants and spectators, especially when they are scheduled every year.

Rituals have characteristic form in space and time. They have three phases: separation, transition, and reincorporation. This is true even for solitary ritual acts, such as saying a prayer before sleeping or observing a tabu while hunting. Each phase has, analytically at least, its counterpart in space. The transitional phase can also be termed the *limens*, or threshold, and the catalytic nature of the symbols presented there and the myths enacted there is called liminal. Sacred places may be well defined architecturally, or they may be anywhere that a ritual is celebrated. They then become *liminal*. Like a giant spotlight, the "circle of the sacred" encompasses the ritual and transfigures the place it is held.

Symbols are elements or items used in rituals to stand for other things. For example, flame is a nearly universal symbol of warmth, protection, safety, and connection with the other world. (In the Christian tradition lighted candles on an altar are said to symbolize prayers; the light and heat waft upward.)

Myths are narratives, usually resembling real-life social dramas in plot, that explain rituals. Indeed, rituals usually reenact myths. Myths address in speech the same fundamental problems of all existence that rituals address in actions.

Mythologically, the transitional or liminal phase-place is often conceived of as a threshold or gateway to the divine. It is certainly a psychological gateway to the unconscious life of the mind, an avenue for tapping into the world we experience in dreams. This access is achieved, after separation, by altered states of consciousness such as trance, the use of hallucinogenic drugs, or simply "losing oneself" in ritual drama.

It is here that ritual taps into the genetic heritage of the species, by touching the limbic system in the brain and the autonomic nervous system. The frequent trance and semihypnotic states of liminal periods put the individual in touch with a "deep self," embedded in the nervous system, but also in touch with his or her extragenetic language, speech, through myth and the poetic expression of myth in song and verse.

This interior, dreamlike world is at once interpreted in terms of prior myths, which in turn are reinterpreted in the light of each ritual interior journey or trip. Ritual, then, can be paradoxically a force for change by fostering the invention of new myths.

The creative, innovative role of ritual systems is not fully developed at bands. *Shamans* are self-appointed ritual experts who proclaim personal supernatural powers and the ability to heal—that is, solve the crisis of illness. Shamans can be potent sources of piecemeal changes in ritual because of their personal gateway to the inner, dreamlike mythological experience. Shamans undergo their own personal "conversion experiences," called "rites of salvation." In these private rituals the catalytic agent itself is changed and hence ready to effect different transformations afterward.

However, shamans are seldom important in bands. The !Kung trancers foreshadow the shaman, but their powers are always collectively learned and performed. Exceptions are the Eskimo shamans, who are busy placating angry spirits of their game animals, especially the seal. The Eskimo, however, are only minimally gatherers. Hunters above all, they rely almost exclusively on two sources of food: seals and caribou. They feel, consequently, very dependent on those who claim ritual powers over their prey. Few band societies are as anxious as the Eskimo; most are indeed rather free and open in their collective ritual and myth.

Prophets, like shamans, claim supernatural powers and the ritual ability to lead mass followings. Their revitalization movements effect catalytic ritual change at the time scale of culture itself, on 300- to 500-year cycles. The transformation of one culture into another is thus aided by a certain type of ritual. (We examine both shamans and prophets in Chapter 13.)

However, the ritual, symbol, and myth complex does unquestionably uphold the status quo most of the time in most societies. This is especially true of bands. Ritual instructs members how to behave in each stage of the life cycle and dramatizes valued behavior. Tiwi males, for example, are expected to be good singers and dancers, who dramatize bravery and boldness. As such, not only can they send the spirits of the dead off properly at a funeral, they can also attract unborn spirits of babies to enter their wives. The Tiwi do not admit the physical role of sexual intercourse in pregnancy. Their myth amounts to a doctrine of virgin birth for everyone!

Moreover, all rites of intensification deflect social tensions among competitors and potential rivals, as when !Kung households begin to cluster together, coming out of the rainy-season desert in their annual rounds. They quickly put on a curing dance when tempers mount. In fact, the shared experience of liminality is a powerful one, uniting erstwhile potential enemies and helping to do the ritual work of overcoming social oppositions. So powerful is this feeling of fellowship that anthropologist Victor Turner dignified it with a special term, **communitas**. The liminal period thus taps powerful social energies that are then bound up in symbolic ties among human beings.

But rituals, symbols, and myths do much more than merely foster good fellowship and cooperation. They speak to and explain the fundamental conditions of human existence. They dress up these conditions in dreamlike mythological dramas, which address both the fundamentally human and the particulars of their own culture.

Thus, ritual survives and adapts itself even when the social oppositions it mediates change their form. For example, Tiwi initiation, described above as it was in the 1920s, in the 1950s had shifted from adolescent men and women to adults! Boys had gone off to the Australian school, making the opposition between married men and unmarried youths no longer in urgent need of ritual redress. Today the adult male initiates spend little time in the bush camps, but the kulama ceremony flourishes as before. The opposition between men and women endures, and so does the ceremony expressing and reconciling it. The initiates are now men and women in their thirties.

The fundamental human conditions reflect oppositions and contradictions in our very being. We have the contradiction between birth and death—elders die yet grandchildren are born—and between killing and living—hunters kill game animals that human beings may live. Similarly, we have the opposition between health and sickness. The !Kung identify this with the opposition between life and death. For them, sickness represents the mythological deceased trying to claim the patient to come live with them, just as real-life relatives try to induce one to come live next to their camp. On an equally fundamental plane is the opposition between oneness and duality. We all start off life as a fertilized egg, a single cell; yet to reproduce ourselves we must join with another multicelled organism of the opposite sex. This, then, is the opposition of male and female. It is also the opposition between self and other.

Myth and ritual try to reconcile these oppositions. For a brief liminal moment they may succeed, but the task is never done; the conditions endure.

Rituals, symbols, and myths, then, form a powerful complex regulating human existence. Among human hunters and gatherers living in bands this complex is fully developed. That helps explain how these societies can live without fully emergent and developed political systems. Ritual carries much of the order and coherence that these societies exhibit, despite the lack of a formal institution of politics. When we study the emergence of tribal societies, we shall see that ritual is an important framework for feasting and warfare complexes, both important ways that tribal regions are integrated. Later, we will see that feasting and royal rituals are important ways to order early bureaucracies as well.

Indeed, at all stages of human cultures and communities, the oppositions of life and death, male and female, self and other are all handled by rituals, symbols, and myths. This ambitious human attempt to master the world by means of an age-old vertebrate mechanism—ritual—is still very much with us today. Here, however, we have seen that ritual systems are the most im-

A Kulama ritual participant performing his inherited "shark dance."

portant informational steering mechanism for band societies, which lack formal government but not fully developed ritual systems.

SUGGESTED READINGS

Campbell, Joseph (with Bill Moyers). *The Power of Myth*. Betty Sue Flowers, ed. New York: Doubleday, 1988. Based on a televised series of interviews between Moyers and Campbell, a succinct overview of the life work of this great student of mythology.

Lansing, J. Stephen. *Priests and Programmers: Technologies of Power in the Engineered Landscape of Bali*. Princeton, N.J.: Princeton University Press, 1991. An engaging look at the complex irrigation works of the island of Bali, which turn out to be "programmed" by age-old ritual calendars administered by priests. A very complex system moves water without modern engineers, bureaucracies, or formal government intervention.

Lessa, William A., and Evon Z. Vogt. *Reader in Comparative Religion: An Anthropological Approach*, 3rd ed. New York: Harper & Row, 1972. A magnificent compendium of articles, some of which are too technical for a general audience, others of which are all-time classics.

Turnbull, Colin M. *The Forest People: A Study of the Pygmies of the Congo*. New York: Simon & Schuster Touchstone, 1961. A timeless classic of popular ethnography, recounting the author's personal quest to discover, guided by local informants on their own rhythms in their own time, the flutes producing the molimo music he had heard on an earlier field trip.

Turner, Victor. *The Ritual Process: Structure and Anti-Structure*. Chicago: Aldine, 1969. A collection of breathtaking essays, relevant for all the chapters in this book that treat ritual.

van Gennep, Arnold. *The Rites of Passage*. Monika B. Vizedom and Gabrielle L. Chaffee, trans. Chicago: University of Chicago Press, 1960. There is nothing like the real thing. This 1909 masterpiece is surprisingly fresh and interesting.

GLOSSARY

ablution Ritual cleansing, usually involving "holy" water. A notable example is the Christian rite of baptism, which washes away "original sin" (the mythical sin of Adam and Eve, who disobeyed God, accepted forbidden fruit from the serpent, and were expelled from Paradise; they also thereby became sexual beings).

animism From the Latin *anima* or soul. The belief that the visible, audible, and tactile elements of nature, such as the forest, the sky, the sun, the wind, rain, fire, and so on, each has its own spirit. Edmund Tyler classified animism as the first human religious belief.

catalysis In chemistry, a chemical reaction whereby a catalytic substance or agent can effect a chemical transformation—often a bonding of atoms into molecules—among other substances far more rapidly than would be the case without the agent, which itself remains largely unchanged by the reaction.

communitas Ritual fellowship fostered by the liminal period in ritual. It at once overcomes previous oppositions and tensions and bonds human beings together, ready for the next task.

cross-cousins Specifically, a father's sister's child and mother's brother's child. A cross-cousin is related to you through a parent of opposite sex from your parent. In many societies, the Tiwi included, cross-cousins are the preferred marriage partners.

hearth A sacred space in daily time among all band-level peoples. Cooking itself is a ritual activity symbolizing "we are not animals." Families gather at hearths for meals, signaling the close of the day and a time for storytelling before sleeping. Especially in the evening, meals with their dietary tabus are themselves rituals.

liminality Literally "thresholdness," from the Latin word for threshold, *limens*. A term applied to the transitional period in rites. It may be characterized by extreme stripping away of old identities prior to assuming new ones.

myths Narratives that explain rituals, which often reenact the myths. Myths thereby account for the origins of human beings, the universe, and nature. They often are distantly based in the actual histories of prophets and culture heroes.

neophyte A person undergoing a rite of passage for the first time.

profane The ordinary, the mundane—that which has not been sanctified by the focused energy of a rite. Often the most profane becomes the most sacred in a rite. For example, the sacred elements of Christian ritual derive from the ordinary food and drink of Mediterranean agricultural peoples: bread, wine, oil, and water.

rites of intensification Rituals that program groups through the changes in the day and in the season; they intensify, even speed up, daily and yearly kinetic cycles. Participants come out programmed to do more intensely what they are supposed to do at that time of year.

rites of passage Life crisis rites. They program individuals through generational time (coming of age and procreating the next generation) and through their lifetimes (old age and death). There are thus rites of birth, puberty, initiation into young adulthood, marriage, birth of the next generation, and death.

ritual A form of language embedded in behavior, consisting of sets of stereotyped, repetitive activities that effect transformations of state from one time phase of life to another. The messages of ritual activities are thereby catalytic, effecting changes rapidly with minimum investment of energy.

sacred Those items, elements, and narratives that are set apart and venerated in any ritual.

symbols Particular items used in rituals that stand for objects, events, or relationships. They are shorthand statements. A symbol may have some association with what it represents, or it may be entirely arbitrary. However, symbols usually draw on the ordinary, transmuting the profane into the sacred in the ritual context. They become powerful reminders of the ritual and hence reinforce the transformations effected in them.

tabus Symbolic prohibitions on certain behaviors—and prescriptions to perform other behaviors. Tabus may be quite minor (one must not spill salt at the dinner table, for example), or major (one must not have sexual relations with one's mother, father, sister, or brother—the incest tabu that is universal in human societies).

trance An altered state of consciousness frequently induced in the liminal phase of rituals, first by elemental separation, then by other devices, such as drumming, rhythmic singing and dancing, hypnosis, and even drugs. Everywhere it is experienced as if being in a waking dream.

The Human Family:

An Emergent Institution in Band Communities

THE HUMAN FAMILY AND CULTURE

The Incest Tabu, Culture, and the Marriage Tie

Gibbons: Monogamy Without Lifelong Parenthood

THE HEARTH AND THE HOUSEHOLD

The Hearth

Household Personnel

THE NUCLEUS OF HUMAN FAMILIES

Nuclear Families

The Nuclear Family and Divorce

The Nuclear Family and Levels of Sociocultural Development

ETHNOGRAPHIC CLOSE-UP: THE MARITAL CAREER OF NISA, A !KUNG SAN WOMAN

Trial Marriages and Bride Service

Romantic Adolescent Newlyweds

Adulthood: Bearing and Rearing Children

Widowhood and Later Marriages

Synchronization of Life Crises, Rites of Passage, and the Family

GROWTH AND DEVELOPMENT OF AN INSTITUTION: POLYGONOUS EXTENDED HOUSEHOLDS

HUMAN SEXUALITY, GENDER ROLES, CULTURE, AND THE FAMILY

The Nature of Sexuality

> Chimpanzee Sexuality

> Human Sexuality

Marriage and Sexual Behavior

Male and Female Roles and Gender

CONSCIOUSNESS, NORMS, TABUS, LAWS, AND THE HUMAN FAMILY

*W*e now have a sense of elemental human communities—the bands of hunters and gatherers—and the symbolic events that hold them together, the rites of passage and intensification. *Ritual as a human institution has fully emerged at the band level of society.* We must now turn our attention to the internal social life of the community, first to one institution that, like ritual, is built on primate prototypes but that is at the same time so distinctively human as to be the hallmark, quite literally, of our species. That institution is the **family.** Families as social organizations are **households,** actual units of relatives living together in identifiable spaces. The family as an idea exists in speech, in kin terms. We shall examine this terminology in Chapter 9.

THE HUMAN FAMILY AND CULTURE

The family is so much a part of human nature that we surmise that its distinctive features arose with our species and must have been fully in place between 50,000 and 30,000 years ago. Perhaps they arose with "archaic *Homo sapiens*" some 200,000 years ago.

Human family life is so distinctively different from that of apes that we consider it, for all its variations, to be species-specific behavior. But, paradoxically, we also believe this behavior to be learned, not innate. That is, it does not replay a code programmed into the genes, but rather it *does* replay a code programmed into human *culture.* Remember that culture refers to the traits that human beings *learn* and that they possess by being members of the group. Culture is thus also an *epigenetic potential*—that is, it exists above the level of the genes. (It is our particular genes as *H. sapiens*, however, that allow us to be culture bearers.)

The Incest Tabu, Culture, and the Marriage Tie

Culture seems almost infinitely variable—consider the babel of human languages around the world. But in fact there are limits to cultural variation. This book explores those limits.

The most universal culture trait is an expression of an implicit human law code: the *incest tabu*. The **incest tabu** is a symbolic, inhibitory feature of all human groups. Basically, all human societies everywhere prohibit sexual relations (and by extension, marriage) between brothers and sisters, mothers and sons, and fathers and daughters.*

Human societies possess two things quite lacking in nature: incest prohibitions and the *marriage tie*, a bond linking an adult male not only with an adult female but with her children as well. In fact, the human family *must* find spouses for the children. That is, logically, a corollary of the incest tabu. Otherwise we have the hypothetical prospect of brothers marrying sisters in an unbroken line. Apart for the loss of the beneficial effect of drawing upon a large breeding population with some variation in its gene pool, such a society would lack the basis of cooperation and exchange across households. One of the first such exchanges is that of young people given in marriage by their parents to the parents of the new bride or groom.

Gibbons: Monogamy Without Lifelong Parenthood

In general, all primates can be grouped into four broad social structures. Many species are *solitary*. Adult males and females live apart, but a female, of course, lives with her young until they reach adulthood. Other species form *parental pairs* that range together but tolerate the young only as juveniles. Yet other species form *single-male groups*, in which the dominant male has a harem of sorts and tolerates no other adult males. The fourth social structure, that of chimpanzees, most baboons, and many others, is *multimale groups*, in which the males form a dominance hierarchy and work out a means of sharing the sexually desirable females among them.

The one species of ape that forms parental pairs is the gibbon, which has a *monogamous* mating pattern. Male and female adult gibbons pair off in the high forest canopy, living together and staking out their own territory against other gibbons. Together they nurture the female's young, which are born one at a time. When the young grow up, the adult male drives off his sons, and the adult female her daughters. The offspring wander off in solitary fashion, each to find his or her own mate, repeating the process of pairing off and staking out a territory.

In gibbons, then, we have the bond between an adult male and an adult female. For a while she forms a mother-offspring unit. But when the offspring

---

*The only exceptions to this general prohibition are three cases of "royal incest": The ancient Egyptians, the Incas of Peru, and the Hawaiians all had monarchs, considered divine, who married their sisters. In fact, this custom provided a clear rule of succession to the throne, since the monarchs had many wives and many sons. Only the son of the highest-ranking wife could inherit. The king's sister, herself a king's daughter, outranked all the other wives.

matures, the unit is broken. *Each adult male-female pair of gibbons forms a community of its own.* It is a shallow and small community. Shallow, in that it is only one generation deep; it never outlives its original pair. Small, in that it never contains more than three individuals at any one time. The mother-offspring units are ephemeral. The adult pair bonding is the tie that lasts.

In great contrast, human communities combine the parental pair pattern with the multimale community. Moreover, we have both male-female and female-offspring bonds at once, and consequently we bond the adult male to the female's offspring. Thus, we have a *marriage tie* and a *kinship tie*. That is another way of saying we recognize kinship through "blood" and through marriage. The male is bound to his children beyond their adolescence. He has an obligation to help raise them and has rights in their future. The most obvious right is a say in their wedding plans, as we shall see.

Kuna Indian hearth, Panamá. This woman is cooking a rice porridge.

THE HEARTH AND THE HOUSEHOLD

Family bonds are played out in space. Many animals have nests, including primates; chimpanzees construct nests in trees to sleep in, usually anew each night. Chimp mothers share their nests with infant and juvenile offspring. The human nest is the place where the family happens, where its members come together as a unit. It is intimately connected with technology and the toolkit. One unique architectural feature proclaims a place to be human and domestic: the *hearth*. Fire is the first and universal symbol of the family and its household.

The Hearth

Although it is possible that *Homo erectus* first tamed fire, *H. sapiens* definitely had it from the start. Fire, then, ranks with speech and the incest tabu as a distinctively human cultural trait. Hearth fires are a means of defense against predators. They are also a distinctively cultural means of food preparation. Cooking, perhaps the most domestic activity and usually but not always performed by women, adds something important to the primate nest. It makes the hearth not only a place for sleeping, like the nest, but also a place for gathering to eat meals on a daily schedule, as we saw in Chapter 5. The individual social units within the human band are bonded at hearths.

The hearth gives men a claim on the women's children and their labor and a right to help decide their future residences. The hearth is a spatial focus of human activities with its own subunit of personnel arising out of the wider community. Just like band communities themselves, households are subject to cycles; they recruit personnel, grow, and perpetuate themselves, and they are very likely to be dispersed into other groupings when old hearth fires are extinguished on the death of old dowagers.

Household Personnel

To understand the cycles of personnel changes in human households, we must reiterate that the natural family unit is the mother-offspring unit and that the cultural family unit links that mother to a man. Human beings link a man with that mother; usually he is her husband and the father of her children. The elemental personnel of the human household are given names in human languages. One role, that of husband-father, does not exist among other primates, where males take no responsibility for their mate's offspring.* Instead, human males *do* assume responsibilities for their wife's children, even into adulthood (see Figure 7.1).

We can conceive of families and households as a series of thermodynamic engine processes, run like computers by their own internal "programs" of norms, values, tabus, and laws. As engines, they are busy taking in and processing matter and energy from nature, as we saw in Chapter 5, while producing their own distinctive "product": adult human beings, from the "raw materials" of babies. In some households these adults leave when they are married off. In others it is their business to bring new partners into the family. The variations in types of households are first of all a question of how many mother-offspring units are linked with one man—that is, the question of *polygyny*. Second, they are a question of the inclusion or exclusion of the personnel produced—that is, whether sons or daughters stay home after maturity and bring new spouses in. This is the question of the formation of patrilocal or matrilocal extended family households, which we examine in Chapter 9.

THE NUCLEUS OF HUMAN FAMILIES

Personnel can be arranged in a limited number of formal patterns that make up the kinds of families and households that the human species exhibits.

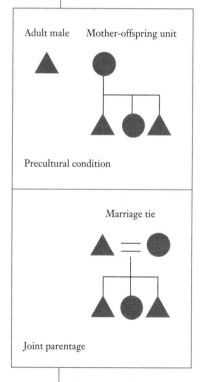

Figure 7.1 *Precultural hominid males were not linked to mother-offspring units. Human males today, with culture, are so linked through marriage. Triangles signify males, circles are for females.*

The figure contains the following labels: Adult male, Mother-offspring unit, Precultural condition, Marriage tie, Joint parentage.

*British social anthropologists sometimes make a distinction between a woman's mate as *genitor*, who begets her biological children, and as *pater*, who assumes social responsibility for raising them as their father.

Later we shall examine these forms as basic permutations on the "nucleus" formed by the union of a man with a woman and their joint assumption of the nurture of the children. This is called the "nuclear family."

Nuclear Families

Perhaps better called the *small family*, the **nuclear family** consists of a single mother-offspring unit and an adult male, her husband. To understand the nuclear family we must chart its phases in time. We are dealing, of course, with generational, or life cycle time. That developmental cycle is simply diagrammed in Figure 7.2.

The developmental phases of the nuclear family begin with a pair of newlyweds. They settle down together as man and wife and, in due course, enter the *childrearing*, or second, phase of the cycle. The system requires that the children grow up and set up their own independent homes, their "family of procreation." When this happens, the original "family of orientation" enters its third and last phase, becoming an "empty nest" with the old couple alone together again. The sequence is thus (1) the newlywed phase, (2) the childrearing phase, and (3) the "empty nest," or final, phase.

We associate the status of newlyweds as coming after a phase of *courtship*. Free and open courtship is a mechanism for setting up new small families in many cultures at all levels of sociocultural development (band, tribal, civilized, and contemporary). The system is open and competitive. Young people must go out and compete with each other for marriage partners during the courtship period. They may also compete with siblings for gifts and favors from their parents (hope chests, trousseaus, and the like) to help establish their new home. No new householder is favored by free shelter of the parental roof for a new spouse and family.

Figure 7.2 Developmental cycle of the nuclear (small) family. Horizontal straight lines indicate a collateral tie, as between brother and sister. Vertical lines represent a generational tie, as between parents and offspring.

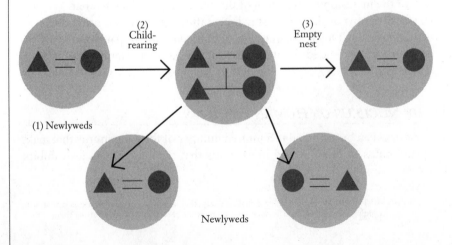

(2) Child-rearing

(3) Empty nest

(1) Newlyweds

Newlyweds

The elements of free courtship are, of course, sexual attraction and, perhaps, romantic attachments. The courtship period, as we all know, may be a time for transferring the young person's strong affections from the parents to some outside partner, found almost at random.

On the other hand, it is also perfectly possible that parents may take such an important task as finding a spouse for their child upon themselves and arrange the match with other parents. This is equally common, and the custom exists again at all levels of culture and community. It is the preferred way to get married in modern, metropolitan Japan today.

The Nuclear Family and Divorce

It is possible that the nuclear family is a brittle structure by its very nature. It depends on the alliance of a man and a woman. Once parental or grandparental pressures on the couple cease, the pair may split up. Divorce, moreover, is a feature of the nuclear family in several societies, such as that of the Eskimo (Burch, 1970) and of the Javanese peasantry, in which most people have not one but two or more spouses in a lifetime (Geertz, 1989). In the United States, where the nuclear family has been the dominant form, the escalating divorce rate concerns many observers.

Modern nuclear family.

The Nuclear Family and Levels of Sociocultural Development

Some observers have supposed that the nuclear family is the family of modernization, and one that has been strengthened by the industrial system. However, it is also the family form of many band societies, including the Eskimo. In fact it was also the dominant family form of many European peasants, those who lived in closed corporate communities, which were imported almost intact in the Puritan villages of New England (Homans, 1941). (See Chapter 16.) Therefore, we cannot suppose that there is anything essentially "modern" about the nuclear family. It is a basic invention of *H. sapiens*. What is also clear is that the various extensions of human households are far more frequent and well developed in the tribal and traditional civilized societies than in the band. Thus band societies and modern ones notably share, by and large, the same family forms.

THE MARITAL CAREER OF NISA, A !KUNG SAN WOMAN

Anthropologist Marjorie Shostak (1983) has published a life history of Nisa, a !Kung San woman. She taped Nisa's own words in open-ended interviews. The !Kung are a hunting-and-gathering band people who do not allow young people to court each other; rather, parents arrange marriages. A young man of fourteen or fifteen completes his rite of initiation into adolescence by hunting and killing two large game animals, one male and one female, one at a time. After each kill, he is tattooed, first on one arm then the other (see Chapter 5). Then it is very likely that the parents of a girl will ask for him to marry their daughter, a girl as young as eight or nine or as old as fourteen. This was the case with Nisa.

Trial Marriages and Bride Service

Still a very young girl, Nisa went through a marriage ceremony, a *rite of passage*. Like all !Kung San brides, she was enclosed in a ceremonial hut. Attended by her mother, the !Kung San bride is painted and wears special clothes. Her feet cannot touch the ground; she is carried on the backs of adults. Her new husband comes to spend the night with her in the bridal hut, a liminal space for a liminal period, the wedding night—in which, however, he cannot enjoy his immature bride sexually. After the ceremony, Nisa's groom slept next to her.

For the next few years the !Kung husband must perform bride service for his parents-in-law by hunting game for their hearth. During these years a !Kung groom may attempt to have sexual relations with his child bride, but she invariably rejects his advances. Indeed, he has no recognized sexual claim to her until after her first menses and female puberty rite, which among the !Kung San is likely to come *after* a girl's marriage!

This rite involves enclosing the young girl in yet another ceremonial hut, surrounded by all the adult women of the band, who sing bawdy songs and remain with her until the menstrual blood stops flowing. When she emerges, the girl is now considered a young adult ready for sexual intercourse with her husband. Adults now press her to accept him.

In Nisa's case she rejected her first "husband" emphatically, and not only in sex, so the adolescent

A !Kung nuclear family.

gave up and left her. The same thing happened with the second husband her parents found for her. It was only on the third attempt, with a boy named Tashay, that the match "took." However, like most !Kung San brides, even after Nisa had sexually matured she continued to reject her husband, even to the point of having affairs with other men. It was only slowly that he won her affections and her sexual favors.

Romantic Adolescent Newlyweds

Nisa, like other !Kung San women, reports having experienced several years of intense sexual and romantic attachment to her young husband. This third trial marriage was successful. When she gave birth to their first child, Tashay's bride service period for the in-laws had been fulfilled, and the young couple set up their own hearth. An independent childrearing couple may choose to stay near the girl's parents, or they may favor the boy's. Remember that among the !Kung the "core elders" of each band are always trying to attract young couples to their territory. Couples may indeed live in several different bands in their lifetime and migrate to the territory of other bands during the course of any given year.*

Adulthood: Bearing and Rearing Children

In Nisa's case the couple went to live near his parents and had three children over the next ten years. A !Kung San woman typically gives birth alone, unattended in the bush. A juvenile daughter of five or six may accompany her. Indeed, Nisa starts her life history by recalling the birth of her younger sibling. When the infant arrived, Nisa's mother made her decide to keep it—rather than bury it alive—perhaps because the mother hoped to avoid jealousy (sibling rivalry) in the older child. Births are spaced from three to five years apart among the !Kung San. Apparently lactation and breastfeeding inhibit the

!Kung mother's fertility. Weaning and initiation of the infant into childhood occurs with the birth of a younger sibling. Weaning is thus a life crisis for the older child.

Widowhood and Later Marriages

This happy period in Nisa's life was cut short by the sudden and untimely death of Tashay after about ten years of marriage.

As a young mother and widow, the grief-stricken Nisa slowly began to entertain lovers. She had affairs with three men before marrying an adult man, Besa, who, however, left her after she became pregnant. The child was stillborn, and Besa later tried to remarry her, but she refused him.

For a short while Nisa was married to a man named Twi, who left her because Besa, her former husband, was pestering her to take him back.

Nisa then married yet a fourth adult husband (not counting the two adolescent trial husbands) whom she does not name. He died, leaving her a widow for a second time.

Finally, when Nisa was around 36 years old, she married for the fifth and last time, a man named Bo. By this time she was, evidently, past her childbearing years. Tragically, her three children all died, including a young daughter whose trial husband, enraged at being refused sexually after his bride's puberty ceremony, attacked her and accidentally broke her neck. Nisa was consumed with rage and grief.

Synchronization of Life Crises, Rites of Passage, and the Family

Let us look at !Kung San male and female life cycles to see how they are synchronized—coordinated through time—with each other as males and females move through their nuclear families at different rhythms (see Figure 7.3).

Synchronization takes place by marrying the adolescent boy to the prepubescent girl and obliging him to do bride service for her on the promise of her sexual favors after her puberty. The girl invariably rejects his advances anyway, and these trial marriages often fail. Her puberty becomes a life crisis for him,

---

*N!ai: The Story of a !Kung Woman, a film by John Marshall, documents the process of setting up an independent nuclear family household. N!ai, a grandmother, laughs at footage of herself, a child bride, rejecting her husband of many years.

Figure 7.3 The rhythms of the !Kung San female and male life cycles.

!Kung San Female Life Cycle

	Biological Crisis	Life Stage
	Birth	Infancy
Death at	Weaning/birth of sibling	Childhood
any stage	Trial marriage	Child bride
	Puberty	Adolescence/romantic phase
	Motherhood	Adulthood
	Birth of grandchildren	Old age
	Death	Death

!Kung San Male Life Cycle

	Biological Crisis	Life Stage
	Birth	Infancy
Death at	Weaning/birth of sibling	Childhood
any stage	Puberty	Adolescence
	Trial marriage	Bride Service
	Wife's puberty	Romantic phase
	Fatherhood	Adulthood
	Birth of grandchildren	Old age
	Death	Death

too. The !Kung San synchronize male adolescent sexuality with female late-childhood in an effort to harness the hunting activity of young males (shaky and unmotivated otherwise) to the promise of sexual satisfaction later. After a trial marriage, couples often report a phase of high sexual activity and marital bliss.

In the normal course of events, the life crises of others *entrain* or synchronize with one's own to help move one along and to produce one's own stages in life. For example, one's children marry and have children, which moves grandparents along into old age. Nisa was denied that pleasant way to enter into old age. Remember that adult grandchildren among the !Kung San are tickets to influence and high status. The leaders of any band are influential grandparents who can entice descendants and their relatives to come live near them.

Moreover, in any life cycle death may occur at any time and change the course of events. Nisa was widowed twice. Her life would have been very different had Tashay, her first adult husband, been as long-lived as she.

Marjorie Shostak ran through a number of possible informants before settling on Nisa for intensive interviews. Shostak wanted an informant who would relate to her with affection, as a friend, not as a source of material goods. Nisa came close, but not entirely, to being that. In any case, Nisa proved very good at telling her story.

Perhaps this was so because Nisa needed the therapy that telling her story might have provided. Deaths of husbands and children had robbed her of the ideal course of life. She was facing an old age with no grandchildren and no influence. Perhaps she would have told many of these stories to grandchildren, had she been fortunate enough to have had any.

In any case, we can conclude that at the band level of culture and community there is an unconscious self-organization operating through rites of passage that orchestrates and synchronizes many life cycles at once. That is one reason why bands can do without formal political leadership, much less written law codes.

GROWTH AND DEVELOPMENT OF AN INSTITUTION: POLYGYNOUS EXTENDED HOUSEHOLDS

While it is probable that the nuclear family is the original family form invented by *H. sapiens* or its immediate precursor, human beings have extended household personnel beyond the mother-father pair and their offspring. Various household arrangements are effected by adding spouses to the basic, nuclear household along some dimension: horizontally on one generation or vertically up and down two or more generations. A household that has more than one mother-offspring unit is an **extended family household.**

As we said, most bands have the ordinary nuclear family; they seldom extend the household beyond it on any dimension. But in the Tiwi case, most households are very large, with many women being married to one man. Each adult wife has her own campfire, or cooking hearth. However, not only are the hearths very close to each other, but the household head makes decisions for the entire group as a unit and disposes of the goods gathered by the women as he pleases. It is thus a **polygynous extended family household.** This is the only extended household type we are likely to find, and then rarely, in bands.

In this type of household, personnel are added through the marriage tie on a single generation. The household grows along that single dimension only, the dimension of multiple marriages. Two types of households, polygynous (many wives) and polyandrous (many husbands), are both subtypes of *polygamous* households, those having many spouses for a single partner. (Polyandrous households are discussed later.)

Polygynous households consist of a man and many wives. They are fairly common in tribal societies and traditional civilizations. They are logically neat and look quite simple to achieve, even in band societies, but in fact they are quite difficult to form and maintain. All the energy that goes into making a single marriage must be repeated many times over, with additional time and energy going into the relations between co-wives. In the case of the !Kung San, for example, grown men often attempt to effect a second marriage in addition to their first, which was invariably arranged by their parents. They attempt to bring some younger woman to their home and do bride service for her parents. Unless the new wife happens to be the previous wife's younger sister, this arrangement is often vigorously resisted by the established wife, who might very well divorce her husband if she is unsuccessful in fending off her rival. Tension between co-wives is a fact of life for polygynous households.

The Tiwi example is much more extreme and complicated than the !Kung one. Here the majority of households are polygynous, wives being concentrated in the households of a few old men. Polygyny is the accepted cultural ideal for men, and the practical norm for women. That is, few men have many wives, but most women live in a polygynous household for much of their life.

The Tiwi system is built up by elders who essentially trade daughters, or the promise of them as yet unborn, as wives in exchange for wives for themselves. In many societies fathers trade daughters for wives not for themselves, but for their sons. Tiwi society, as we saw in Chapter 6, can only pull off this inequitable distribution of women by exiling youths into all-male initiation camps for six years and then promising each initiated young man a future bride, in the form of an unborn daughter of a pubescent girl! The promise has to be made, or the system would not work.

From the wife's point of view, the important thing about the Tiwi "harem," or group of co-wives, is that it is age graded. A wife joins a household as a young girl of nine or so and reacts to the other co-wives as she would to a group of mothers, aunts, and older sisters. Senior wives, often quite a bit older than the husband-householder himself, direct the junior ones. A large harem, if it is to be successful, must work out some mechanisms of ranking and cooperation among the wives.

The Tiwi polygynous household is also an economic and political institution. An elder with many wives is thereby a rich and powerful man. He has lots of food, and he has several prospective sons-in-law working for him and promising him their sisters in exchange for the future bestowal of infant daughters. As we shall see in Chapter 15's discussion of archaic kingdoms, a harem can be a powerful political device for chiefs and monarchs. The Tiwi, then, exhibit an institution that comes into its own at the intermediate (tribal, traditional civilized) levels of human sociocultural revolution.

HUMAN SEXUALITY, GENDER ROLES, CULTURE, AND THE FAMILY

Anthropologist G. P. Murdock (1949) assumed the nuclear family to be the universal human social building block. He noted that the family fulfills the functions of sex, reproduction, education, and economics. However, these functions are really performed by the wider community, since none of them is exclusive to any domestic group. Still, we might say that these functions are focused on the hearth and that the family, manifest in the group that comes together to share food on a daily basis, is a distinctive subunit of human communities.

In short, the family is not what it seems. It is not a natural unit of reproduction, but a cultural one. It is not the natural arena for sexual activity, but a cultural one. Let us consider what we mean by that, by taking up the nature of human sexuality and of human gender.

The Nature of Sexuality

What is sex? Sex is a mechanism in nature, found among eukaryotic single-celled living organisms, of reproducing by exchanging DNA. Prokaryotes, the more primitive single-celled form (typified by bacteria), may occasionally come together and unite, exchanging stray chromosomes across their membrane walls, and then rush off, refreshed. With eukaryotes, however, there is the process of meiosis, as mentioned in Chapter 4, in which the cell first divides in half, by mitosis, then into half again, producing cells that contain only half the DNA of the original nucleus. These cells, called gametes, in turn join together in the process of sexual union to form cells called zygotes, which as fertilized eggs are the ancestral cells to the future adult organism.

Among higher plants and animals, gametes tend to be either male—that is, relatively mobile—or female, much slower in motion (in flowering plants even fixed in place). For the sexual union to take place, the gametes must meet, and that involves movement.

Clearly, then, at the cellular level sexuality involves differences in behavior. At the level of the fully formed adult multicellular organism, sexuality also involves differences of behavior. Every species has its modal behaviors for bringing the two kinds of gametes together.

Once a zygote is formed, its relation to it parents varies from species to species. In some species adults may be very much involved in nurturing immature offspring and bringing them to maturity, and the social life of the species may revolve around the production of adult offspring. This can be accomplished in many different ways. We think of the basic parental actions as being those of nurture and defense, which can involve such behaviors as food getting and nest building.

Parents of young animals are necessarily of two sexes. But the various tasks or activities needed to bring a youngster to adulthood may be differentially proportioned by sex among the adult members of the species. Indeed, it may be all the adults of the local population or community who bring up the young, rather than merely its two biological parents.

In species for whom the two parents assume the major responsibilities for bringing the young to some stage of independence, the various parental tasks may be shared jointly, as among many species of birds, or each parent may take different tasks, depending on sex. In the first instance, many birds form monogamous male-female mated pairs and then assume joint responsibility for constructing a nest, incubating the eggs, and feeding the offspring, as well as defending them from predators. Among some species of fish, however, it may well be the male alone who assumes the parental functions of constructing a nest, fertilizing the eggs, and then caring for them and for the newly hatched fry.

163

Among mammals, obviously, females have more responsibility for the young than do animals that lay eggs. Because of the suckling function, nurture is inherent in mammalian maternal behavior, although "paternal" roles of defense, nest building, and even food getting and nurturing after weaning may well fall on males of the species (as in wild dogs, for example, all of whose adults, male and female, defend the pups and bring home food for them by regurgitating meat devoured at kills).

Chimpanzee Sexuality. As noted in Chapter 4, chimpanzees share some 98 percent of their genes with human beings. Their sexuality is the basis of much of their social behavior, as you can imagine. There are several key differences in sexual behavior between our two species. For one thing, chimpanzee females are generally sexually attractive only during their periods of estrus, when they exhibit sexual swelling of their exterior sexual organs, which also give off an alluring odor.

Adolescent chimpanzee females are sterile for the first few years after they come into estrus. They are sexually attractive for about ten days out of every thirty-six, the length of their menstrual cycle. Once a female becomes pregnant, however, and for the three years or so after the birth of her infant when she is lactating (producing milk), she does not go into estrus and is therefore not sexually attractive.

When a chimpanzee female is fully sexually swollen, adult males seek her out, and the full dominance hierarchy is often in attendance. Access to her is regulated by dominance; the males taking turns, with the more dominant male having first turn, and so on. It is possible for the alpha, or most dominant male, to monopolize her for a day or two when she is at the height of her estrus. Copulation occurs between chimpanzees with no foreplay and is consummated in a matter of minutes, so taking turns is easily effected.

Not all females are equally attractive. Some older females cause the most excitement. Some younger females are preferred over other younger females, apparently for social reasons. They are more relaxed and friendly with adult males, although generally females are equally receptive to male advances.

A male may also seek to get around the dominance hierarchy by monopolizing a female in a period of **consortship,** during which he literally herds her to some remote part of the range and copulates with her repeatedly for days on end. To do so he must detach her from the group during the early days of her swelling, before others have begun to notice her. (During this time she is also quite likely to be mounted by juveniles, who are not yet part of the dominance hierarchy.) Thus some males are able to satisfy themselves sexually without entering into the aggressive behavior that establishes a dominance hierarchy over time. We must note, however, that this male has no subsequent relations with his erstwhile consort's offspring.

Human Sexuality. Clearly the sexuality of *H. sapiens* differs from that of chimpanzees. As a species we lack the clearly defined estrous cycle for females, with its flaming sexual swelling. Human males are capable of finding human females sexually attractive at any time of day or year, and vice versa. This capacity is present, undeveloped, among chimpanzees, where some small percentage of sexual activity takes place when the female is "flat." Moreover, for a consortship to be carried out effectively, the male must claim the female when her swelling is still unpronounced. Interestingly, male *pygmy* chimpanzees or bonobos (a distinct species of chimps) seem to easily find "flat" females attractive, a trait resembling our own behavior.

Finally, sexual behavior is *learned* in both chimps and humans. It might seem that chimpanzees, with their free and open community form, are only doing what comes naturally. But captive chimps who have been raised in zoos and laboratories away from adult examples literally do not know how to copulate with adults of the opposite sex when presented with arousing circumstances. They experience sexual arousal but have no idea of what to do. Chimpanzees in the wild, therefore, have learned from example many times over.

Human beings likewise learn about sex from others, not so much from observation as from conversation. It is true that some brides in some cultures are supposed to go to their wedding beds not only as virgins but sexually ignorant as well. Yet at least one partner is supposed to have some experience or knowledge to guide the pair.

Marriage and Sexual Behavior

Sex is not sufficient reason for marriage. This assertion may appear to contradict common sense. But consider that chimpanzees, a closely related species, satisfy their sexual needs without marriage. Presumably, early hominids such as the australopithecines did so as well.

Sexual behavior is rarely limited to marriage in any given society. We have seen that the !Kung are given to extramarital affairs. The Tiwi repeatedly contend with a man's sons seducing his father's young wives. Elders rail against young men and periodically challenge them to ritual duels, but the philandering goes on. Tiwi boys segregated in initiation camps engage in a great deal of casual homosexuality as well. The Eskimo, ever the extreme in band societies, practice spouse sharing, whereby a couple from one band, when visiting another band, exchanges sexual favors with both partners of their host couple. That is, the guest woman sleeps with her host, and her husband with the hostess. This relationship is formalized and well recognized in Eskimo culture, so that the children of spouse-sharing couples have a special quasi-sibling relationship with each other.

Marriage, then, is not a device for exclusive sexual activity. On the contrary, it is a device to link men not only with women but with children as well! Marriage harnesses men to the next generation and enlists their help in providing food for specific hearths. Both partners exchange food with each other and harness their young to the wider household by exacting labor from them, too. One thing both partners ideally get from a marriage, however, is an assured sexual outlet.

Male and Female Roles and Gender

It should be obvious from our discussions thus far that male and female behavior is typically different among human beings at the band level of society. As noted earlier, this is called the *division of labor by sex*. That is, women typically gather and men typically hunt, although these occupations are not exclusive to each sex. Human mothers, like chimpanzee mothers, usually take major responsibility for suckling infants and for nurturing small children. They tend to have infants and children in their charge most of the time, although children do, when presented with the opportunity, form age-graded play groups in all societies. Moreover, males and females, young and old, in the human household are bound to share with each other the products of their separate roles. Fathers protect children and in return have a hand in domesticating their labor and exchanging them, as we shall see in the next chapter, for marriage partners.

Gender is the grammatical classification of words in a language according to some set of distinctive features. In many Indo-European languages, gender distinguishes between masculine, feminine, and neuter (*he*, *she*, *it*). In many other languages, gender concerns such distinctions as animate versus inanimate, for example. Gender distinctions by sex and age, however, are basic to the patterning human beings have given their family in all the many languages we speak.

CONSCIOUSNESS, NORMS, TABUS, LAWS, AND THE HUMAN FAMILY

We are back where we started. We must assert that the human family is qualitatively different from many of its predecessor forms in other primates. It resembles the consortship of chimpanzees and, even more, the adult life-long monogamous pair bonding of gibbons. But the human family represents a step forward in *consciousness*, which in turn has been enabled by our extragenetic code, our spoken language.

The first qualitative difference is the awareness of paternity and the giving of a name to the father-begetter role. True, the Tiwi, among others, do not equate social fatherhood with biological paternity, since they believe spirit babies choose to enter the future mother on their own. Nonetheless, they do have *social* paternity.

Second is the awareness of **norms**—the common, statistically normal modes of behavior for a group. Next, using speech, early human beings formed from these norms, first *tabus* (that is to say, *morals*) and then, however ill defined, *laws*. Thus, the basic tabu of the human condition, in the sense of a normative prohibition for all groups known to anthropology, is the incest tabu. This tabu is a matter of both morals and law.

Mother-son incest avoidance is already normative behavior among chimpanzees. That is to say, mother-son incest avoidance is the statistical norm among these animals. Copulation between mother and son, although it occurs, is extremely rare. Brother-sister avoidance is *almost* the norm. It happens rather more often, with certain individuals, but other adult brothers are quite likely to ignore their sisters who go into estrus and are trailed by all the other males of the troop. Since many, if not most, chimpanzee females transfer into adjacent troops before becoming full adults and mothers, they end up avoiding their brothers in any case. What is lacking among chimpanzees, of course, is father-daughter incest avoidance, since these animals do not recognize paternity, social or biological.

What must have happened in the hominid evolutionary trajectory, then, was the emergence of consortship as normative behavior. Only then would we have the possibility of the recognition of paternity and the emergence of the father-daughter incest prohibition. This prohibition is the one most likely to be violated in all societies known to anthropologists. Consortship must have emerged in the context of the emerging division of labor as hominids became more fully hunting-and-gathering societies. That, coupled with the emergence of language and the recognition of gender differences in speech labels, led to the full-blown complex of incest tabus, the marriage tie, social paternity, and the family. *All of these traits seem to have been present from the start among* H. sapiens. *They are the behavior accompanying the emergence of the species.*

The incest tabu is thus more than just a set of prohibitions. By forcing individuals to seek sexual, and hence marriage, partners outside the nuclear family of origin, it is a kind of kinetic force propelling individuals into marriage alliances in the wider group and beyond. All human households depend on the incest tabu to keep their developmental cycles in motion.

SUMMARY AND CONCLUSIONS

The human household with its personnel of family members is based on primate propensities. Essentially, early human beings successfully com-

bined the early primate pattern of parental pairs within the context of a multimale community. This combination is entirely new among primates. Furthermore, the family and its households represent leaps forward beyond the other primates in consciousness, notions of morality, and ideas of legal rights and obligations. The topic "family" excites emotions, even passions. That is because it is the arena of human bonding through generational time. It is based first on the mammalian mother-offspring tie. An infant's initial dependency and self-identification with its mother is a powerful image in all human cultures known to anthropologists. Father-offspring ties are also formed. Every human household attempts to enact a set of values embedded in its culture's worldview.

Then there is the marriage tie, which usually moves new partners into and out of households and bonds man and wife together, whatever their emotions for each other. Households may extend the marriage tie by bringing in many wives for the same man. But in that case there must also be ties among the co-wives, something difficult to achieve unless they are sisters already—or represent a range of ages and experience, as among the Tiwi.

Every family and household system has its ritual and mythologies that uphold it. The marriage ceremony is the most obvious one (although the Tiwi lack marriage rituals; they have only the ritual promise of an unborn daughter at a girl's puberty ceremony). A rite of marriage attempts to bond a man and a woman together and also dramatizes the assent to it of all the interested parties—their two families of orientation from which they come. When children are born to a couple, that too is ritualized, and children are claimed by their households and their kinsmen.

When there is conflict, the morality of the family is turned into law, as third parties, the court of public opinion or respected mediators, seek to render judgments that uphold a system's form and give it legal validity. The !Kung divorce frequently, as a wife leaves a husband who has taken a younger rival as a co-wife. She may take her children and rejoin her parents in another band. Tiwi elders challenge sons and stepsons to ritual duels to uphold the elder's marriage ties to young wives.

The !Kung San manage to make their nuclear family system work by "marrying" newly initiated adolescent male hunters to prepubescent girls, who always reject them, thus creating a phase of serial brittle trial marriages while the young man performs bride service and hunts for her parents. A girl's marriage ceremony comes *before* her puberty rite among the !Kung. After puberty, wives are supposed to consent to their husband's sexual advances. When a young husband and wife awaken to each other sexually, they may have several years of intense romantic bonding before having children and entering into the independent childrearing phase of their marital careers. As in the story of Nisa, death may break up a marriage at any time. Death may rob parents of children, too, and thereby also of grandchildren, tickets to respected elder status as grandparents. Nisa, for example, faced a lonely old age without children, grandchildren, or influence.

No family system ever works exactly as it is ideally described. For example, among the !Kung San a girl enters a trial marriage with a youth before her puberty. One might expect, first, that her marriage to that same youth will be consummated at puberty; and, second, that she then bears children to that same marriage and lives out her life with only one husband. But ethnographers tell us that early trial marriages are easily broken, that divorce among adults is not unusual, and that death breaks up marriages. Both men and women may have extramarital affairs. Thus, Nisa had two trial marriages before her long-term marriage to Tashay. All told, she had five adult marriages, two of which ended in death, and two in divorce. In addition, she had three lovers between marriages. However, two of her adult marriages were long term and enduring. Thus people obviously find their way through a family system as best they can.

Polygynous householders find ways to bring more than one wife into their households, not uncommonly by the expedient of trading their daughters for other men's daughters.

If we examine the peculiar polygynous household of the Tiwi, we see that many factors allow it to work: six years of segregated male age grades; bestowal of infant daughters to young men, to delay their actual dates of marriage; mutual exchange of daughters, thus favoring men who are already married; very early marriage of girls, who enter an age-graded group of cowives; mandatory widow remarriage at funerals; and finally a system of ritual duels, which lets off tension between old men with many wives and adulterous young men with none or few.

Ecologically speaking, the old men can not only direct collective kangaroo hunts but can also manufacture fine goods to help interband exchanges at funerals. But it is certain that this system could only arise in relative isolation, on two islands off the Australian subcontinent. On the mainland the pressure for wives from the multitude of other bands would never have allowed the elders of a mere small group of bands to monopolize so many women.

Each family and household system has its own morality, values, committed practitioners, rewards, costs, rebels, and troubles. The Tiwi value oratory and skilled performance in song and dance. Polygynous elders have the leisure to cultivate these skills. They have worked hard over a lifetime to accumulate many wives. They paid the cost of delayed marriages and must put up with the impatience of their sons and stepsons. These, in turn, are paying the same costs. Some may never have the skills to get many wives, or they may die before they have the chance. Some may engage in adultery with their father's or stepfather's younger wives—acts of rebellion, rendered less costly by the Tiwi indifference to biological paternity. Some of these acts erupt into conflict, resulting in duels that are ritual punishments of the young troublemakers, whatever the merits of their case, and ritual shoring up of the system.

In tribal and civilized societies polygynous households—harems—are far more common than they are among bands. Some societies also extend households along the dimension of one generation by bringing in spouses to marry the sons and daughters already there. We shall study these in Chapter 9.

In modern society, as we shall see in Part V, the family is under pressure to change. The prevalence of divorce is turning the experience many of us have of the nuclear family into "binuclear" families, whereby divorced parents remarry, have children with new spouses, and children find themselves with two sets of parents. Or, in contrast, children may find themselves in the increasingly common single-parent household. Gay and lesbian couples are forming same-sex parent households, in which two individuals of the same sex, committed to a sexual and companionship union, also rear the children of either or both of them (see Chapter 19). These forms do not mean that the family is "dead"; rather, it, like all social forms, is changing in response to new circumstances.

All family and household systems are based on exchange relations between the sexes and between the generations. They also reflect cultural values. We turn to value and exchange systems in the next chapter.

SUGGESTED READINGS

Bohannan, Paul. *All the Happy Families*. New York: McGraw-Hill, 1984. A study of divorce in the United States today and the subsequent changes in the nuclear family. The book ends with a call for divorced parents to work out ways of caring for their children.

Geertz, Hildred. *The Javanese Family: A Study of Kinship and Socialization*. Prospect Heights, Ill.: Waveland Press, 1989. Beautifully written account of nuclear families in a culture quite different from that of North America but with a tremendously high divorce rate.

Kephart, William M. *Extraordinary Groups: The Sociology of Unconventional Life-Styles*. New York: St. Martin's, 1982. A lively exploration of intentional experiments with cultural form and household structure, including the polygynous nineteenth-century Mormons, the "free love" Oneida Community, and the celibate Shakers.

Shostak, Marjorie. *Nisa: The Life and Words of a !Kung Woman*. New York: Vintage, 1983. A life-history document as narrated by a !Kung woman to the anthropologist. It is both a fascinating account of !Kung life and a full picture of the family system through a life cycle.

GLOSSARY

consortship Among chimpanzees, a pattern of behavior in which a male pounces on a female who is first entering her estrous cycle, herds her to a far corner of the range, and monopolizes her sexually during her estrus, beyond the notice of the other males in the dominance hierarchy.

extended family household A family unit living together "extended" beyond a single childrearing pair, either on the plane of one generation by multiple marriages of one man to many women, or along several generations by importing marriage partners for persons born to the household.

family A unit of human beings bonded to each other through marriage or kin ties, engaged in the production and raising of children.

household The spatial dimensions of a given family; the gathering of personnel around a common hearth, for food preparation and eating, and around a common sleeping area.

incest tabu A symbolic, inhibitory feature of all human groups, prohibiting sexual relations (and by extension, marriage) between brothers and sisters, mothers and sons, and fathers and daughters.

norms Statistically common ways of behaving, which are considered morally desirable by those behaving in this way.

nuclear family A family formed by the union of one man and one woman, raising children together, but without other relatives. It goes through three phases: the newlywed phase, childrearing phase, and "empty nest."

polygynous extended family household A household formed by a man's marrying additional wives after his first wife. Such households must solve the problem of relating the co-wives to each other peacefully.

Values and Exchange: Bands and the Original Economy

8

VALUES

Values as Guides for Action

Worldview: The Universal Plan of Values

Values and Exchange

ETHNOGRAPHIC CLOSE-UP: THE TIWI FUNERAL

VALUES IN EXCHANGE: SYSTEMS OF GIVING AND GIVING BACK AT VARIOUS LIFE STAGES

Values in Exchange on a Generational Scale: Spouses, Songs, and Dances

Goods Exchanged on a Yearly Timetable

Perishable Goods Exchanged on a Daily Basis

SORTING OUT THE VALUE OF GOODS

RECIPROCITY

Generalized Reciprocity

The Dynamics of Reciprocity

Negative Reciprocity

OTHER MODES OF EXCHANGE: REDISTRIBUTION AND THE MARKET

Redistribution

Market

BAND COMMUNITIES AND EMERGENT INSTITUTIONS: THE CONCEPT OF CULTURE RECONSIDERED

The Domesticated Dog

Race and Culture

Adequacy of Band-Level Cultures

Culture Is the Organization of Diversity, Not the Replication of Uniformity

*H*uman beings differ markedly from other primates, and indeed from all other living creatures, in our habit of *mutually sharing* goods. True, chimpanzees have the capacity to share game from a kill, but they do not do so on a daily basis. Chimpanzee mothers have the capacity to gather food and pass it on to their young, but generally they cease to do so as soon as the young animal has learned to gather on its own. The common primate pattern is for mother and offspring to forage separately, side by side.

In Chapter 7 we discussed the division of labor by sex. We saw that human males and females share not only sexual favors but foodstuffs as well. Men share game with women, who share plant foods in return. **Exchange,** then, is the mutual sharing of goods. It is the gift of one good in the expectation of another gift in return. Exchange is a characteristic of *H. sapiens* as a species.

However, anthropology, unlike its sister discipline of economics, does not regard exchange as some sort of logical machine inherent in human society, only waiting to find expression according to the rules of individual self-interest or "utility." Rather, anthropologists view exchange as a series of actions, which it is their duty to plot and then make sense of. Because anthropologists start with elemental societies, in this case the human hunting-and-gathering band, the discussion you will encounter in this chapter is very different from the exposition you'll find in an introductory textbook in economics. That discipline's views are only appropriate for the system of exchange called *markets*.

VALUES

Foods are differently valued. Oddly enough, many common staple foods are valued highly. The Eskimos prize seal and caribou meat, for example, while the !Kung San prize mongongo nuts, a plentiful foodstuff, and giraffe or wildebeest meat. More scarce foods may be valued if they are also delicious.

Foodstuffs are also valued for their symbolic role in contributing to the value or worth of the man or woman who wrests them from nature. Thus, to become a man, a !Kung San boy must hunt and slay two large game animals. Only then can he claim a wife, whose parents bestow her only in return for several years of steady hunting of game animals. His masculinity depends upon his slaying these valued animals. He wears his initiation into manhood in the form of tattoos on each arm, *trophies* of the initial game animals he slew. They are also symbols of his right to have a wife.

Values, then, have to do with the way human beings perceive and conceive of their world. On the one hand, anthropologists talk about **values** as referring to priorities among possible actions in life. But they also talk about values when analyzing material transactions, as in the exchange of goods. Values as guides for action seem to deal with both morals and worldview; **values as goods** seems to deal with crass materialism and rational self-interest in the sharing of goods back and forth. In fact, the two anthropological discourses (ways of talking) about values are not so far apart.

!Kung San bushman finding ostrich eggs, a valued foodstuff.

Values as Guides for Action

The !Kung San man values *hunting;* he wants to be a good hunter in life. He admires other men who are accomplished hunters. He also values *women;* he enjoys sexual activity and woos his young child bride very hard. He is happy to have clandestine affairs with other women as well. He values a wife who is a good gatherer and nurturing mother. She in turn values a *man* who is a good lover, a good hunter, and a playful father. They both value *old people* and offer allegiance to the "core elders," two pairs of married siblings who are grandparents and who are the leaders of every band. They also value *children* and are happy to spend hours playing with their offspring. They fear *the dead,* since ghosts bring sickness and death. They admire men who go into trance, for these men are able to persuade ghosts to leave the living alone, thus restoring the sick to health.

We thus have a statement about a !Kung San person's relations to nature (a man desires to be a good tracker and aggressive hunter); about the relations between men and women (both desire to be good lovers and generous providers); about their relation to children (they desire to be nurturing, playful, indulgent parents); about their relation to elders (they desire to be loyal, respectful, and generous to parents and parents-in-law); and about their relation to the supernatural (they desire to obey tabus and be persuasive in trance to keep ghosts at their distance). We see that these values define ideal relations of men and women to nature and animals, to each other, to children, to elders, and to supernaturals.

As for a man's relation to other men, he desires to be a cooperative hunter, willing to share his skills and teach them to younger men. Yet he is also in competition with his age mates, for game and for women as wives and lovers. The skills of hunting, including spearsmanship, can be used in anger against other men. These angry social dramas of !Kung society often send young men as fugitives to join other bands, where they are under the protection of elders. Thus, masculine values are in conflict. Cooperation does not always harmonize with combativeness; both are necessary values in a hunting party. Combativeness can also be used against male peers, leading to the most serious trouble.

Worldview: The Universal Plan of Values

Anthropologists generally conceive of human values as differing in content from culture to culture but as having an overall similarity in form—a **worldview**. Universally, values must answer key questions about the nature of human interactions and existence: What is the relation of human beings to nature (including to plants and animals)? What is the relation of human beings to each other? What is the relation of human beings to the supernatural? Implicit in these questions is also an orientation toward time and space.

To illustrate, let us think again about the !Kung San. For them, men and women must reap from nature without offending it. Tabus are observed to keep the game and gathered foods bountiful. Human beings are generally considered to be equal, but age is respected, as is prowess in hunting. The important supernatural beings include a distant, paternal creator God, who needs little placation, and feared ghosts of the recent dead, who must be kept at a distance. The time orientation is toward the present, rather than the past or future, and the space orientation is broad ranging: from waterhole to waterhole, through the territories of many overlapping bands. The key values, then, are harmony; equality; play, singing, and dancing; and skilled work, which is only a 40-hour work week for women and a 44-hour work week for men. The !Kung San are not workaholics. Work yields the rewards of prized foods and tools. Thus, the egalitarian !Kung value friendships among peers, work skills for adults, respect for elders, and play for children and adults.

American anthropologists have tended to see the "universal plan" of values orientations as a result of the social circumstances of our species. But there are also theories that see such universals as an expression of innate structures in the human brain in relation to other organs. After all, consciousness is one of the main results of our larger brains. Perhaps the developing brain, through consciousness, the extensive use of abstractions, and the development of speech (our extragenetic code), assisted in its own programming as we differentiated ourselves from hominid forbears.

Values and Exchange

Ideal and moral images have much to do with exchange, and hence with material values. Chimps have values, if we judge by their behavior. They value the dominant male and his traits of aggressiveness and reassurance. They value similar traits in the more dominant females. Male chimps value females in estrus, although they value more those sexually receptive females with social skills. Yet chimpanzees do not systematically exchange goods with each other. Once a hominid species starts exchanging goods systematically, ideal values immediately come into play, and then the exchange can never stop.

Consider: A !Kung youth undertakes to marry. He must perform bride service for his child bride's parents. That is, he must provision them with game. Game is itself a highly valued good. By the time his years of bride service are over, he is engaging in regular, even very intense, sexual intercourse with his newly matured wife. He is now proud to bring her game, and she soon is to bear him a child, so his material obligations increase.

There will be no end to the exchanges set in motion. When the couple's own daughter is past nine years old, they, too, will betroth her to an initiated youth and expect to receive game. Likewise, they will be losing the hunting services of their own teenaged son, for the same reasons.

When they enter the empty-nest phase of their cycle, they still expect occasional gifts of food from their adult children and sons- and daughters-in-law. If they survive into the grandparental years, they may very well be one of the couples of "core elders" who "own" the band territory and especially its waterholes. They will have a voice in settling disputes, exiling troublemakers, and welcoming fugitives from other groups. All will give them gifts.

Moreover, an elder is likely to be one of those who manufacture the poisoned arrows that younger hunters use to bring down large game animals. In that case the "owner of the arrow" gets the first portion of the meat that the hunter then bestows on his friends and relatives. In the case of a very large kill, such as a giraffe (as one might see in the celebrated ethnographic film *The Hunters*), in which a team of hunters cooperate, the first claim as always goes to the owner

!Kung San elders at a gathering of the band.

of the arrow. Then the hunters each take equal shares to be divided up and smoked on the spot, then distributed, first to each man's wife and children at her hearth, then to parents and parents-in-law, and then to adult siblings and their families. The food is quickly shared throughout the immediate group, through ties of kinship. However, the hunters who give away their game expect the recipients to reciprocate at some future date.

Thus, with ideal values and social honors goes *credit*. Parents in effect bestow their daughter's hand on credit and enjoy collecting the debt for several years. An elder gives out the poisoned arrow and collects on the debt later. Hunters share game, knowing others will share in return.

ETHNOGRAPHIC CLOSE-UP

THE TIWI FUNERAL

In many rites of passage we may observe the coming together of values as moral guides to actions and as guides for the exchange of material goods. The Tiwi funeral is both an expression of the relative renown or moral standing of the deceased (that is, the deceased's success in embodying moral values in his or her lifetime) and an event in which a great many goods of different value are exchanged. (The Tiwi funeral ritual was described in Chapter 6; here we shall emphasize the exchanges taking place during the ritual.)

When a Tiwi dies, the body is buried almost immediately, but the large gathering at the grave to erect gravepoles occurs only during the dry season, which can be shortly after or months later. In any case, close relatives of the deceased (the spouse and others) go into a state of ritual tabu, which lasts until the gravepoles are up and the ghost of the deceased has been sent away to join the world of the dead. In this state they cover their bodies in paint and weave pandanus leaf bracelets, which eventually cover their arms. Aside from that, they do no work, not even putting food or drink in their mouths, and they must be fed by their friends and neighbors. For this service they incur considerable debt. During this time they

may hunt, however—even Tiwi women hunt small game—but their catch is tabu to them: They must give it away.

The relatives of the deceased divide themselves into several categories. One group consists of persons in the generations directly above and below the deceased: his or her parents and their siblings, and his or her siblings' children (blood nieces and nephews). Another group consists of persons of the deceased's own generation and grandparents' generation, as well as the sons and daughters of the deceased's siblings' daughters. When more distant relatives gather for the big ceremonies, they are assigned roles according to one or another of these categories. From these several categories two groups, roughly translatable as the "employers" and the "servants" (as we first described in Chapter 6) appear. The deceased's children do not belong to either group but maintain tabu mourning throughout.

The employers, who direct proceedings, consist of *ego*'s (the deceased's) parents and his or her siblings' children, plus selected members of the two higher and lower generations (see Figure 8.1). The servants consist of ego's spouses and their siblings and of his or her mother's father and father's sister's sons (see Figure 8.2). They must serve the others: they dig the grave, ritually cleanse the deceased's possessions with smoke, help the employers in their songs and dances, and make and paint fine baskets as offerings left on the gravepoles. Most important, they carve and erect the gravepoles, of which there may be as many as fourteen for the grave of an important elder.

During the days leading up to the funeral itself, guests gather from several bands and make camp by the burial grounds, band by band. As in the kulama ceremony, they engage in a great deal of song and dance. There are also mock battles between spouses. Widows or widowers sing special songs commemorating the deceased's life. The climax of the ceremony is the raising of the gravepoles, which ensures the final departure of the ghost to dwell with the dead.

Something else of utmost importance goes on at the funeral of a male householder. His widows are bestowed in marriage on new husbands. No woman is ever without a husband among the Tiwi, except during her short mourning period of widowhood. Then her male kinsmen—father, brothers, brothers'

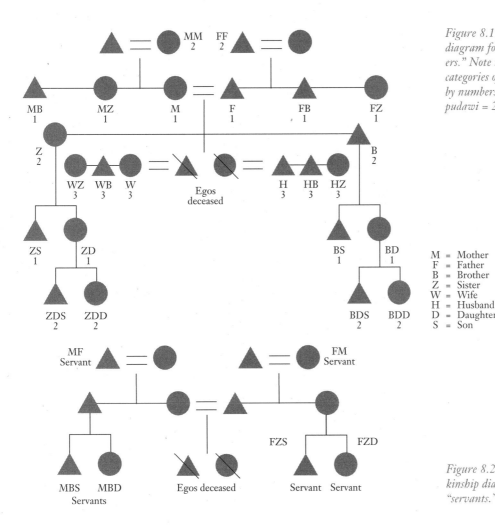

Figure 8.1 Tiwi kinship diagram for the "employers." Note the several categories of kin, indicated by numbers: unandawi = 1; pudawi = 2; ambarui = 3.

M = Mother
F = Father
B = Brother
Z = Sister
W = Wife
H = Husband
D = Daughter
S = Son

Figure 8.2 Tiwi kinship diagram for the "servants."

sons, and her own sons—all vie in having a hand in giving her away again. In return, the new husband promises future wives to her kinsmen.

Sometimes men swap widows. Hart, Pilling, and Goodale (1985) report two young men whose elderly mothers became widowed around the same time. Since these were older women, their fathers were dead and they were not valuable enough (in terms of women they might be exchanged for) to excite the interest of their brothers. Their sons started their own marital careers by trading them. Each thus

started a household to which he was eventually able to bring much younger brides.

If we look, too, at the servants who are doing the work and about to receive payment, we see that they are a man's in-laws. If a dead man leaves many widows, then he has many servants at his funeral. His servants are also his mother's father and father's sisters' sons, all men whom the kinship system define as spouse-givers, in-laws by definition. (See the discussion of Iroquoian kinship and cross-cousin marriage in Chapter 9 to understand this better.)

The Tiwi value human life. They conceive of life as a period between two spirit existences, first as an unborn baby spirit, and afterward as a person spirit in the world of the dead. They value a man who is a good performer: an expert singer, dancer, song composer, and carver of fine objects. They

value a woman for performance skills as well, and for her prowess in getting food and game. Neither sex values the dead, but men court unborn baby spirits in their songs and dances, hoping to attract them into their wives.

The highest value is placed on a successful, renowned life. To that end mourners gather and servants erect gravepoles, monuments to human worth. Second, women are valued as spouses.

We therefore have two values on human life in play: first is the deceased's life story, second is widows as betrothed wives. The glory of the deceased is symbolized by a good: the painted gravepole. The more prestigious the dead person, the more gravepoles. A gravepole, then, is the highest-ranking good or

The gravepole is the highest-ranking valuable among the Tiwi.

valuable object among the Tiwi. It constitutes a *symbol* of the good life. Poles are paid for with assorted goods. (We shall discuss that later in this chapter.) A wife, however, is paid for by another wife and by a series of services, including the obligation of becoming a servant at her in-laws' funerals.

Let us take up the questions of the relative values of goods, and their relations to values on a human life.

VALUES IN EXCHANGE: SYSTEMS OF GIVING AND GIVING BACK AT VARIOUS LIFE STAGES

Returning to the Tiwi funeral, we are now in a position to sort out the many different exchanges, of both persons and goods, in time and space. There is the time scale of a lifetime, which can last up to ninety years or so for elders, people who have seen four generations come and go. Funerals of elders, then, dramatize values surrounding a life, ideally filled with honors and renown. These in turn are memorialized by the erection of gravepoles, a good that can never be circulated again but that the kin group of the elder must pay for, acquiring each pole from in-laws, some of whom may have come from other bands.

A great lifetime, once it is lost, can never be regained, and energy is lost to the environment on the occasion as old bonds with the deceased are broken and as survivors forge new bonds with the living. Tiwi widows are bestowed again upon new husbands, for example.

Values in Exchange on a Generational Scale: Spouses, Songs, and Dances

This leads us to **marriage exchanges,** which happen on a generational time scale. That is, people grow up and get married roughly on a time scale of twenty years. The Tiwi of course complicate this time scale by delaying marriage for men to age thirty and speeding it up for women to about age fifteen. (Recall from Chapter 6 that all girls are already married at birth in the sense that they have been promised to some young man, but they are not actually handed over until years later.) Tiwi women are likely to be married several times in a lifetime, however, and Tiwi men, once they start getting married, are likely to wed several wives of different ages.

At the level of lifetime values, we also have the performances in song and dance. Annual performances are part of a man's coming of age. Subsequent performances build a lifetime career. Composing good songs, dancing well while singing them, and shining theatrically are highly valued in Tiwi culture. Title to songs is a kind of good, comparable to at least the prestige of holding copyright to highly valued music and choreography in our culture. As we saw in Chapter 6, boys must first perform theatrically in the annual kulama ceremonies, leading to generational coming of age. Afterward, men have a chance to perform as an "employer" in a funeral, once again perhaps every year. Men attract unborn baby spirits with their performances; one imagines they also attract prospective fathers-in-law as well.

Goods Exchanged on a Yearly Timetable

While a funeral memorializes a lifetime, funerals happen every year, and the goods that are exchanged for the once-in-a-lifetime gravepoles can circulate from year to year. Some of them, such as finely carved spears, will last a generation, although they may be exchanged many times. Others, the more consumable items such as bricks of paint or bark baskets, will be consumed in a few years' time. At the level of yearly exchanges, however, the survivors enter into transactions with a set of people whom they seldom see otherwise and exchange a great many goods.

Thus the lifetime memorial brings together people from several bands spread across space. The distant in-laws must be repaid for their services during the funeral itself. There is no extending of credit over time here. But one may pay out fine goods, such as carved spears, received oneself from other funerals in the past.

Perishable Goods Exchanged on a Daily Basis

Finally, there are the foodstuffs fed to the mourners from day to day. We all must eat on a daily basis. This is the sort of exchange that goes on at the level of the household, at its hearth every day, and among circles of kin living in neighborhood camps. In contrast, the gifts of foodstuffs at a funeral form a collective exchange on a nearly yearly basis, as one kin group must feast and entertain another, from more distant camps and even bands.

SORTING OUT THE VALUE OF GOODS

If we look at the comparable worth of the things the Tiwi actually exchange, we see that the highest value is a renowned human lifetime, memorialized in a set of grave monuments. The gravepoles, symbols of a life, are not thought of as an exchange for a life (but they do induce the ghost, gratified, to leave the land of the living). The next highest value is placed on a spouse in exchange, another lifetime value. A wife is worth another wife, and a considerable amount of bride service as well. But a bride is never "purchased" with other goods.

Not so gravepoles. They cannot be exchanged for each other but are exchanged for an assemblage of goods. These goods are implicitly ranked in value. Here is that rank order: stone axes, fine "semipermanent" body ornaments, carved spears—all goods that can last several generations. Next are baskets, which can last perhaps half a lifetime. Then come goods that can last a few years: bricks of paint and perishable body ornaments. Finally come foodstuffs, which last at most a few days. Theoretically, it should be possible to work out strict equivalences, so that so many spears would equal one gravepole, so many baskets a spear, so many paint bricks a basket, and so on. But the Tiwi are not reported to do that. Instead, they work out an assortment of all these goods and hand them over in exchange for each gravepost. Exchange, then, starts out in human societies not as a strict quantitative system, but as a qualitative system ordering values and reflecting the timescale of exchange. Strict calculations of equivalences amount to the notion of a just, or fixed price, given by custom and later by law. **"Just" prices** *are* common in the tribal world and in traditional civilizations, as we shall discuss in Chapters 11 and 17.

RECIPROCITY

Reciprocity is a technical term used by anthropologists for exchanges governed first by social relations and only secondarily by a desire for the goods themselves. It usually is a kind of barter; primitive money (of shells and other valuables) is often involved.

Balanced reciprocity is an exchange that is usually immediate. Credit is not left open, and the goods traded are considered of equivalent value. It usually characterizes exchange between distant kin, or near-strangers, as in the case of the Tiwi funeral, and happens on a yearly timetable.

Generalized Reciprocity

In ongoing systems of mutual support, as in a household or neighborhood camp, partners give each other things freely and share without keeping a careful tally of the transactions or expecting them to be repaid according to any definite timetable. In such **generalized reciprocity,** repayment takes care of itself according to the timetable of daily and seasonal activities. These exchanges involve the perishable items of food, and some tools as well, but no ceremonial objects.

!Kung women gathering mongongo nuts, contributing to the household economy.

One attribute of the household economy of band peoples is *pooling*. All members generally gather some foodstuffs from nature and contribute it to the cook at the hearth, who doles it out to the others at meals.

Contributions within the household vary with age, sex, and the daily tasks appropriate to the seasons. In hunting-and-gathering societies, women and children gather food on a constant and steady schedule, usually daily. Although there are spectacular gathering bonanzas, as when a fruit crop matures, the yields are usually small but dependable.

Male hunting activities may be much more fitful and sporadic, reflecting rests and lulls that often follow successful hunts, and even unsuccessful ones. In some cases, the hunt is quite arduous, and the yield, while sometimes a bonanza, is not always so. Hunting has always been something of a sporting proposition; it needs to be complemented with sure sources of food.

Thus, in primitive societies the labors of all household members sustain each other, and everyone helps according to age, ability, training, and sexually defined tasks. There are variations in individual productivity and in license for laziness. The young unmarried hunter, for example, gets his share of the regular family meal whether or not he has contributed to it. He is not expected to contribute meat every day, nor is his share of the daily meal calculated against the amount of meat he bags over any period of time; but he is expected to hunt according to some reasonable pace. In a household with a compulsive hunter who bags far more than most, a youth need not exert himself terribly much. Of course, if he grows scandalously lazy and never hunts at all, he could be threatened with long-term retribution. His parents might warn him of failure in courtship, as no girl will have a poor hunter.

Generalized reciprocity also operates in exchanges between two related households. Say that two sisters who live in separate households and keep separate hearths have husbands who hunt. Because a hunter's catch may vary substantially at any given moment, one sister might well send a portion of a good catch to the other, expecting that the other will reciprocate. But the reciprocity is not strictly calculated, and no deadlines are set.

Just as some individuals are more or less productive than others, so households vary in productivity. Some do not produce enough food to keep their members alive during the year, while those composed of energetic go-getters may produce far more than they can consume. Precisely because of reciprocal relations between households, underproductive households can survive through handouts from productive ones. But they lose out in relative prestige, as all band societies value skilled food production.

In the West, ceremonial gift giving, such as at weddings and Christmas, reflects the age, wealth, and status of the partners, and exchanges are not expected to be of articles of equal market value. Generalized exchange, like all systems of reciprocity, survives in modern societies that allocate goods through redistribution and the market.

The Dynamics of Reciprocity

With reciprocity, goods are exchanged between two partners who are already linked in some social relationship other than gift giving. That is, gifts are not exchanged out of a pure desire for the articles themselves but because the two partners have some social reasons for giving each other something.

The same holds true for exchanges among strangers. Typically, when strangers from two different bands meet, they will exchange whatever goods they have on hand. This event is not primarily an economic one. Rather, it is a crude diplomatic exchange whose meaning is friendship and peace rather than enmity or war. Although it is extremely useful for the parties involved to acquire some articles that they do not make themselves, such utility is not the precondition of the exchange but rather its by-product. The end of the exchange is to assure peace.

To cite a hypothetical case from the reciprocal gift-giving complexes of our own society, say that your sister's mother-in-law, with whom you do not exchange gifts, gave your sister an anniversary gift that was something you had long wanted for yourself. You cannot go to your sister's mother-in-law and give her a gift in the hope of acquiring the desired item, too, because you two customarily do not exchange gifts. However, you could give your sister, with suitable hints, a particularly nice gift when an appropriate occasion arises (her birthday, her graduation, her housewarming, whatever) in the hope that on the next occasion, such as your birthday, she will hand over the article wanted from the mother-in-law.

Reciprocity may be simply represented. If we use a capital letter to represent each person and a slash for each reciprocal relationship, we can observe the qualities of a small reciprocal system: A/B B/C C/D D/E E/F F/A. The point of this abstract example is that the partners represented are not free to alter the order of the exchange as they see fit. B may not trade with D if D has something B wants. Rather, B must trade with established partners. Thus, B can acquire a good produced by D only through C, or wait for it to circulate the other way and eventually arrive at A, with whom B trades or exchanges gifts (a more accurate way of putting it).

This may sound like a tiresome procedure, but bear in mind that among most band peoples it is the only one. They cannot simply go down to the marketplace and purchase the items they desire; they must wait for the items to reach them through some social network. Thus, Tiwi funerals are very important events for the circulation of the various goods exchanged for gravepoles. There is no other easy way to acquire them from others.

Reciprocity in redistribution. Here Kuna men who have contributed cash to a community feast line up alongside a dugout canoe filled with chica, *an alcoholic beverage, in preparation for a toast. Playon Chico, San Blas, Panama.*

Negative Reciprocity

Negative reciprocity occurs when one partner gets something for nothing or, if articles are exchanged, when one partner receives something he values more highly than that which he gave in return. Thus, if a particular Tiwi funeral "servant" for whatever reason had coveted a fine spear and managed to get it in a funeral exchange, it would be more valuable to him (probably for sentimental reasons) than to those who gave it to him. The most blatant negative exchanges are the spoils of war—booty. This topic is covered at greater length in Chapter 10, "Tribal Warfare Complexes." But the spoils of war tend to be evened out, as counterraid follows raid. The forcible exchange of booty between enemies tends to become balanced reciprocity. Negative reciprocity is characteristic of dealings between a home community and strangers and enemies far beyond its boundaries.

OTHER MODES OF EXCHANGE: REDISTRIBUTION AND THE MARKET

The great economic historian Karl Polanyi, in his work with anthropologists, identified reciprocity and two other modes of exchange (Polanyi, Arensberg, and Pearson, 1957): *redistribution*, and *the market*. These modes are very different in their formal characteristics. We examine redistribution in great detail in Chapter 11 and markets in Chapter 17. Here it is convenient simply to introduce the abstract nature of these two modes.

Redistribution

A special form of reciprocity, **redistribution** indicates that a single person is the center for reciprocal relations with a great many others. Goods flow in to the individual, often one at a time, and the individual then gives the goods back, often all at once in a great feast. This flow of gifts to a central person and their mass return can also be quite simply represented. Let us say that E is the central figure and that A, B, C, D, and F all give goods to E: A/E B/E C/E D/E F/E. E then returns them at once to many friends: E/ABCDF.

Redistribution always involves the pooling of goods at a central place before giving them out again. Here two Kuna women cook cauldrons of plantains and game meat in coconut milk in preparation for feeding the entire community, whose members have all contributed to a female initiation ceremony. Playon Chico, San Blas, Panama.

Market

Market exchange differs from reciprocity and redistribution in that anyone may trade anything with anyone else quite impersonally. The exchange is free of domestic, kin, ritual, or political relationships and depends instead entirely on the desire of the two partners for each other's goods. A market system can be represented abstractly as A/B A/C A/D A/E; B/C B/D B/E B/A; C/D C/E C/A C/B . . . all may trade, and all combinations of trading partners appear.

The famous laws of supply and demand, formulated by Western economists, operate only in the market system. The relative proportions of the goods exchanged depend on their quantity (the supply) and on the desire or demand for them. If I have pots to exchange and you have fish, the fish will be worth so many pots, depending on how plentiful your catch is, how desirable the fish are for eating, how many pots I have on hand, how easily I made them, and how great your desire is for them. Other factors operative in supply and demand would be competitors also offering fish and pots. We shall examine both of these types of exchange in later chapters.

BAND COMMUNITIES AND EMERGENT INSTITUTIONS: THE CONCEPT OF CULTURE RECONSIDERED

In Chapter 1 we defined culture as "that complex whole of behaviors, including language, belief, manners, and customs, that we learn by being born or raised in our groups or that we learn by being incorporated into new groups in the course of a lifetime." Let us examine that concept in the light of what we have learned from band societies.

We have studied the patterned ways of life of hunters and gatherers as they move each year through space, from nomadic seasonal camps, to larger settlements of the band proper, to occasional gatherings of people across bands. We have seen that their lives are orchestrated by rites of passage and intensification that regulate their movements through the solar year and that synchronize their various lifetime schedules with each other.

We have also seen that band peoples have speech, which permits them to tell myths: stories invoking the spirit world that explain their rituals. Speech also permits them to define each other by the names they give to family roles, such as husband and wife, son and daughter. Through speech they define a system of moral values that stand as guides to action. Once they map these values on the material world, they have the means of expressing priorities among foods wrested from nature, and among goods manufactured by themselves, always in relation to the standard of value of a human life well lived, and always exchanged according to the demands for reciprocity among family, community, and neighbor community members.

Hunters and gatherers have sophisticated tools: spear and arrow points of stone, sometimes exquisitely struck; stone axes of high quality; baskets—sometimes with such fine designs in the weave that collectors and museums vie to possess them today; and shelters, huts made from plant materials at hand such as boughs, grasses, and leaves, or igloos of Arctic snow. They clothe themselves in animal hides. For ritual they may ornament their bodies with paint, feathers, and belts.

The Domesticated Dog

Most reported hunters and gatherers today have hunting dogs. Indeed the Arctic Inuit or Eskimos rely on dogs for transport, pulling sleds. Recent biomolecular studies on the genetic relationship between contemporary domesticated dogs and wild wolves puts the origin of the domesticated dog—

splitting off as a species from wolves—at roughly 200,000 years ago, about the time of the emergence of *Homo sapiens*. This is much earlier than previously suspected. Archaeologists had not reported dog remains from Stone Age sites. The biologists said this was so because, first, archaeologists were not looking for them, and, second, because they confused dog remains with those of wolves. It was only with the Mesolithic transition that human beings began to breed dogs with sizes and shapes quite distinct from wolves. We may infer, then, that dogs were with us from the start, along—perhaps—with speech and the nuclear family.

The point is important because this human-dog relationship is the first of its kind in the natural world of vertebrates, let alone primates. Generalized reciprocity arose between the two species: Dogs helped in the hunt in return for a share in the food and protection against predators. We assume that the

The domestication of wolves occurred much earlier than previously thought.

pact originated in the adoption of orphaned wolf pups by human families. Wolves in the wild live in packs, regulated entirely by a single dominance hierarchy. The adult dog simply applies that hierarchy to human society and accepts his master or mistress as his alpha animal. Wild wolves coordinate their activities in the hunt and the rest of life, with leadership activities of the *alpha* (who can be male or female).

The importance of this original domestication—whose evidence is entirely from genetic molecular material and is yet to be confirmed by archaeology—for explanatory theory is the idea that human culture also meant the domestication of our own species! Parents domesticated the labor of their own children, and by controlling their marriage partners, also the labor of their grandchildren. Along with dogs, we are the original domesticated mammals.

Essentially dogs granted their lives in trust to human beings, since they do not have speech to exact their rights. Many, indeed, have been mistreated and starved over the years, but the reciprocal benefits of the domestication "pact" are such that most if not all human groups have dogs of some breed today. Individual dogs, in turn, may have suffered, but the species has prospered. Dogs today are incapable of sustaining themselves over time when they run wild; newly feral dog packs do not perpetuate themselves into a second generation. Dogs need human beings to survive.

Race and Culture

Human beings today possess many varieties or breeds of domesticated dogs, all the product of fairly short-term artificial selection whereby breeders have sought to bring forward some trait that caught their fancy. The Dalmatian, for example, is famous for black and white spots (a minority are brown and white), a purely aesthetic attribute that accompanies these dogs bred for physical endurance. Dalmatians are "coach dogs," capable of running long distances alongside stagecoaches to fend other dogs away from the horses. Dalmatians today love to run, but they also are extremely aggressive with other dogs.

To discuss breeds of dogs with the "races" of human beings is not far-fetched. The breeds of dog differ widely among themselves, yet all domesticated dogs form a single species capable of interbreeding and producing viable "mixed" offspring without difficulty. Geneticists tell us that their varietal differences are, genetically speaking, superficial.

Geneticists tell us the same thing about ourselves. All the "races" of humanity can interbreed at will and produce perfectly viable human offspring. Genetically speaking, human "racial" variations in skin color, hair texture, nose outline, eyelid folds, and—to some extent—stature are insignificant, even less important than the differences among breeds of dogs. Human races, then, are breeds of human beings reflecting variations that are in some measure adaptations to changed habitat, or are simply random, reflecting the "drift" of some neutral characteristic across an interbreeding population. The pale skin, blue eyes, and blond hair of Scandinavians reflect an adaptation to a climate with little sunshine through the solar year. The presence of tawny hair among Australian aboriginal peoples, on the other hand, is a reflection of genetic drift.

If we turn to the theory of the single origin of *Homo sapiens* and the notion of the **mitochondrial Eve,** we find confirmation of the view that human "racial" differences are unimportant. This book adheres to the theory of a unitary origin of our species, rather than several "crossovers" from *Homo erectus* to *Homo sapiens* in different times and places, thus possibly giving rise to racial variations based on differences in the *Homo erectus* prototypes. When choosing among two alternative theories in science, I prefer the simpler one, with the least complications—provided, of course, that it is supported by good evidence from several sources. This is the case with the "mitochondrial Eve" theory. It is far simpler than the alternative, and it is supported by increasingly good evidence. Its implications for a theory of race are also simple. Race does not matter genetically. All human beings are extremely closely related through a relatively short family tree of only 200,000 years.

These implications also are in line with what cultural anthropologists have been saying for over one hundred years. Race and culture are separate. One's culture does not reflect one's race or its physical characteristics. Culture belongs to the species; we are all equally good at supporting culture. We all have speech, marriage and the family with its incest tabu, ritual and myths, fine tools, and at least the domesticated dog. As a species our capacity for culture depends directly on the size and structure of our brains. But the brains of all human beings ever reported supports speech and the rest of the list of cultural traits above. Since the work of Franz Boas, founder of American anthropology at the turn of the twentieth century, anthropologists have assumed that intelligence is an individual attribute distributed in about the same proportions among the members of all human populations.

After Boas, then, anthropology has rejected **racism,** the unscientific belief in the innate *cultural* superiority or inferiority of one or another of the various breeds of human beings. People have been likely to believe that their own phenotype—and the associated spectrum of physical traits in their group's collective genotype—is not only superior physically, but indicative of superior cultural capacity as well. Sometimes certain groups are targeted— even scapegoated—as inferior. Racism is a regrettable characteristic of civilized peoples, rather than band or tribal ones.

In sum, culture is made possible by the large and peculiarly structured brain of *Homo sapiens*. All human groups today share equally in that brainpower potential. Other hominid species and subspecies that did not have that brainpower were left behind and rapidly became extinct after our species emerged. We no longer have either *Homo erectus* or *Homo neandertalensis* with us in the flesh for us to make—with the speech that they probably lacked—distinctions between ourselves and other species with a lesser physical capacity to support culture. Those rival species disappeared long ago.

Adequacy of Band-Level Cultures

Under the influence of Franz Boas, American anthropologists have often embraced **cultural relativism,** the assumption that all autonomous human cultures fulfill human needs and provide satisfying lives for those who bear them. That is not to say that all cultures are "equal," only that all do their job. The peoples we have studied at the band level of sociocultural organization are fully human. They are able to get through their lives and provide for their offspring through the self-organizing synchronization of many lives at once provided by the ritual process. Thus, they are able to do without the dominance hierarchies of the apes, or the political command structures of tribes and civilizations.

Indeed, in some ways life at the band level provides an image of a "primitive paradise." Men and women do not have to work terribly many hours to provide for themselves and their families. Conflict sometimes leads to homicide, but more likely it ends in flight. Moreover, many of the institutions we shall study for "more advanced" peoples seem of dubious worth in comparison to the hunting-and-gathering lifestyle. Both tribal peoples and civilized peasants have to labor many hours in their gardens and fields. Tribal peoples engage in constant warfare, civilized ones in wars of conquest. Tribal peoples sacrifice war captives, and civilized peoples enslaved them in great numbers. In the twentieth century civilized peoples have attempted to exterminate entire groups of people on racial, ethnic, or social class criteria. This, the crime of genocide, is made possible by modern technology.

However, while band-level peoples, like all human beings, can rely on speech to learn from the accumulated knowledge and wisdom of elders, they lack writing and the even more voluminous cultural memory that it brings. True, tribal peoples commit to memory vast oral literatures, but the effort put into learning such genealogies and mythological sagas is far greater, and for less knowledge, than you are expending in reading this book.

Yet circumstances allow band-level lifestyles to be simple. Hunting-and-gathering life reflect the demands of people living at low levels of population density. They are not forced into proximity with their enemies and they do not have to find food sources for large numbers of persons.

Culture Is the Organization of Diversity, Not the Replication of Uniformity

Culture, then, is indeed that complex whole that we learn as members of our groups. Even at the band level, however, culture is not unitary. For example, men and women learn different skills and go through separate rites of passage, especially at coming of age. The is true of the !Kung San, but even more true of the Tiwi, who exile their male youths to bush camps for six years to live off their own hunting and to compose and learn their own songs and dances. Even at very simple levels of sociocultural organization there are different bodies of knowledge within the group for people of different sexes and ages. We shall see that these differences only grow and become stronger at the tribal level of societies. Even very simple cultures are not monolithic.

SUMMARY AND CONCLUSIONS

*A*ll cultures known to anthropologists have a set of values as moral guides to action, setting priorities in life. Values as *worldview* define the desired relations between men and women, among men, among the generations, and between human beings and nature. They also orient us in time and space: toward the past, present, and future and toward the natural world, as well as toward a supernatural cosmology.

Separate values may well be in conflict with each other. The !Kung San value both cooperation among men and combativeness toward game animals. Combativeness may be turned against their fellow man. As we shall see in later chapters on the tribal world, a culture may well value one mode of behavior for young men and quite another for elders.

Values provide us with a measure whereby we evaluate human lives. No one fulfills his or her culture's values to any degree of perfection. For one thing, in the primitive world few live long enough (past forty years) to even begin to fulfill them all. Those who do, earn respect and even a degree of fame. Those renowned persons who wish to do so may convert prestige quite easily to power over others. People in all cultures are eager to have reciprocal transactions with renowned persons.

Thus, a key human value and symbol in all cultures is a long life fulfilled according to that culture's life goals. Persons who achieve this value are celebrated in song, poetry, and dance at the end of their life. Monuments may be raised for them and grave goods donated to their final resting places. Some truly exceptional persons are also heroes, and their exploits mix with those of the gods. We shall discuss them in Chapter 13, "Shamans and Prophets."

Human beings are also valued as spouses—marriage partners. Marriage is an exchange, first of the two partners who give each other themselves and second for their two families of orientation that exchange two offspring. Marriage exchange often brings with it the exchange of services, as in !Kung bride service, and hence a supply of valued foodstuffs, such as game. In more settled societies the bride may bring a dowry as an advance on her inheritance. In all cases, people generally reject the notion that a spouse is being "purchased"; rather, they are concerned that a balanced, fair exchange of values exists between the partners and between the kin groups from which they come.

Moral values are played out on the time scale of a human lifetime, up to ninety years, give or take a decade. The transactions of marriage exchange are played out on a generational time scale of twenty years or so. Other transactions take place on a yearly schedule for collective exchanges among social groups, and on a seasonal and daily basis for exchanges between related households and within the household.

At band and tribal levels of society, human beings are constrained to exchange goods in the mode of reciprocity—that is, according to their social relationships with each other—and not by their mutual desire for the goods exchanged. That may sound strange to us, but it is only when the market emerges fully as an institution in civilized society that the goods, through the so-called laws of supply and demand, can come into play as if on their own account.

Goods in human societies are evaluated according to moral values, and they are ranked vis-à-vis each other. Some goods are symbols of moral values. Relative rankings of goods reflect this symbolism as well as objective factors, such as their durability and their place in the time scales of exchange. Gravepoles are the most valuable symbolic good in Tiwi society, but they do not circulate. Their construction, however, sets into motion the circulation of a range of ranked goods, some of which, such as fine ornaments and carved spears, will circulate many times over the course of a generation. Indeed, value is stored in such ceremonial objects as fine body ornaments and carved spears. Their owners possess the means of credit. They can commission gravepoles for their deceased relatives from their in-laws with ease.

Thus, some goods are worth more than others. Tiwi ceremonial spears are worth more than bricks of paint, for example. Theoretically, one spear ought to be worth a certain number of bricks, but the Tiwi are not reported to have worked out their commodity values that explicitly.

Tiwi carved spears, like gravepoles, fall into the category of a **valuable,** a good worth an array of lower-ranked goods in return. Valuables are used in ritual (as in the funeral) and bear symbolic weight. They commonly carry the name and fame of past owners with them and are thus symbolic of the good life. Tiwi polygynous elders, with ample leisure, carve the spears. Elders hurl them at junior rivals in ritual duels. They are symbols of power and prestige, fitting items to exchange for enduring gravepoles.

Mass ritual exchanges among distant kin and near strangers, of the sort that happen almost annually at a Tiwi funeral, constitute *balanced reciprocity.* Balanced exchanges are supposed to represent equal values. In the Tiwi case the entire hierarchy of differently valued goods, from stone axes to foodstuffs, changes hands. But an assortment of goods pays off the entire debt for each gravepole during the funeral. The exchange is completed then and there.

At the level of daily exchanges of perishable goods and utilitarian tools, generalized reciprocity prevails within a household and among related households in a community. That means that exchanges are open and not expected to be repaid immediately with exact equivalent values. In popular expectation they shall balance out in the long run.

As one gets further from home, exchanges are more likely to be balanced. With distance, exchanges are more carefully calculated, and repayment is expected more promptly and is more likely to be demanded from a stranger. However, with neighboring but separate communities, where acquaintances are not friends, exchanges tend to be ambiguous, falling somewhere between generalized and balanced reciprocity. If strangers are less strange, transactions are left a little more open and are not quite finished.

Is there a universal objective standard of value? Much scientific effort has been spent in Western society trying to find a universal, objective standard of value for all human goods. Karl Marx thought the scientific measure of the value of a good was the labor that went into producing it (a day's labor ought to bring a basket of foodstuffs and goods sufficient to feed and otherwise maintain the worker and his family for that day). Non-Marxist economists believe the correct value of an item is its "price"—whatever people will pay for it in an impersonal market. In the primitive world such measures are meaningless, since the goods are all related in some symbolic way, played out in ritual, to the moral goals of the culture. The ultimate standards of value are first of all a good life and second of all a good spouse. Goods are related to these standards in a variety of ways, dramatized, as in a Tiwi funeral, in ritual. Hence the ambiguous but dynamic relationship of gravepoles to a packet of goods in Tiwi culture. The Tiwi have moral values and they have values in exchanges of goods, ranked according to moral values. But they have not yet hit upon *price*. We shall find price later, in tribal societies.

The human family, then, can only work through systems of generalized reciprocity. Today certain radical feminists proclaim that the marriage tie is always and everywhere exploitive of women, who become thus subordinate to men. The evidence at least from band societies does not support this view, not even for the Tiwi, where even a very young wife receives gifts of meat from one or more young prospective sons-in-law, hoping for the hands of her infant or even unborn daughters. In the nuclear family in particular, a man and a woman come together in patterned reciprocal exchanges. They also maintain those exchanges with the generation of children they procreate, and with those children's marriage partners.

Band societies earn adequate livings for their members as hunters and gatherers, not food producers, with a fine toolkit. In terms of institutional emergence, they have the family, found in space in nuclear or—more rarely—polygynous households. They often have divorce, and marriages end for some partners by death in any case. Rites of passage and of intensification orchestrate people's movement through space and households over the course of the solar year and an individual's lifetime. Although bands have leaders, their activity is informal; institutionalized politics have not emerged. Family ties and ritual activities provide means for hunters and gatherers to exchange goods, and at the same time project a relative ranking of values on these goods, reflecting the worth of a fully lived human lifetime.

The anthropological doctrine of cultural relativism holds that band societies and their cultures are adequate answers to the human problems of living together. Clearly band cultures are limited examples of total human knowledge, since societies without writing cannot store more information than can be learned by individual human brains. Nor are band societies called to orchestrate vast numbers of persons engaged in mass food producing (agriculture) or manufacture. Instead they present an alluring picture of a primitive paradise. In the continuing vitality of voluntary associations in all societies "beyond" the band, perhaps we are seeing the constant attempt of human beings to return to face-to-face communities, an attribute that hunters and gatherers have by the nature of their societies.

In the tribal world, households and kinship are subject to the pressures of large numbers of people having to organize themselves in much closer proximity. The next chapter will concern this more complicated organization: Manifest in more types of extended households, kinship terminologies, and systems of marriage exchanges, we see that human beings are objects of value.

SUGGESTED READINGS

Hart, C. W. M., Arnold Pilling, and Jane C. Goodale. *The Tiwi of North Australia*, 3rd ed. Ft. Worth: Harcourt Brace Jovanovich, 1988. Considerably updated, this is perhaps the most intriguing descriptions of a band society.

Holmberg, Allan R. *Nomads of the Long Bow: The Siriono of Eastern Bolivia*. Prospect Heights, Ill.: Waveland Press, 1990 (1950). A classic ethnography, first written in 1950 by a man who went on to pioneer applied anthropology. Holmberg characterizes the hunting-and-gathering Siriono as the world's "most technologically handicapped" people.

Kearney, Michael. *World View*. Novato, Calif.: Chandler & Sharp, 1984. A lively cross-cultural synthesis.

Sahlins, Marshall. *Stone Age Economics*. New York and Chicago: Aldine-Atherton, 1972. A collection of essays, some of which are highly technical. Still timely and interesting.

GLOSSARY

balanced reciprocity Reciprocal exchange in which an attempt is made to immediately give back goods of equivalent value to that of the original gift; characteristic of exchanges between persons distant in space and, possibly, kin ties. It happens on a generational or annual schedule.

cultural relativism The anthropological doctrine that all cultures are adequate attempts to solve universal human problems that at least succeed in getting most people through their lives in a satisfactory manner. The doctrine does not address questions of more or less complex social organization, nor the relative amount of knowledge, which in nonliterate cultures is limited by the memory capacity of individual human brains.

exchange The mutual sharing of goods. It is the gift of one good in the expectation of another gift in return. Exchange is a characteristic of *H. sapiens* as a species.

generalized reciprocity Reciprocal daily or seasonal exchange between persons closely related in both space (sharing the same households or neighborhoods) and kinship or friendship, in which return gifts, or paybacks, are delayed and not expected to be of equal value immediately, but to balance out in the long run.

"just" price The setting of value for goods in terms of other goods in some fixed and immutable quantities, conceived of as divinely bestowed, and upheld by custom. Just prices arise in tribal societies and are firmly held in traditional civilizations.

market exchange Impersonal exchange of goods among persons who may be strangers. Anyone can trade anything with anyone else. Market exchange is difficult to achieve and very rare at band levels of society, where strangers are by definition dangerous, potential enemies.

mitochondrial Eve Also known as the "scientific Eve," the discovery made through examining the DNA (genetic material) in the mitochondria—the organelles in every human cell that enable us to breathe by burning oxygen—of widely scattered human populations. Molecular biologists concluded that all human beings today descended from one of several females living in a single population around 200,000 years ago.

negative reciprocity Reciprocal exchange (which at first seems nonreciprocal) in which one party does not reciprocate with goods for goods received. This is first of all goods seized or destroyed by force, as in warfare. The counter-"gift" is then also forcible: reparation or indemnity. In a looser sense, negative reciprocity refers to exchanges in which the partners evaluate the goods exchanged differently, so that one believes he or she has received "something for nothing."

racism The unscientific belief in the innate *cultural* superiority or inferiority of one or another of the physical breeds of human beings. One's own phenotype—and its collective genotype—is taken to be superior physically and is linked—mistakenly—to a superior culture as well. Likewise, other groups may be targeted as physically and culturally inferior.

reciprocity A mode of exchanging goods that is bound to the social relationships of the partners to each other, rather than to their desire for particular goods; for example, the "employers" and "servants" at a Tiwi funeral stand in the relation of in-laws ("spouse-givers") to each other.

redistribution A specialized kind of reciprocity in which many partners each give goods to a single partner, who in turn then gives back the goods, usually received individually, in a collective ritual event.

valuables In band and tribal societies, certain durable ceremonial objects used in ritual exchanges on a yearly schedule for generational events. They usually can only be exchanged for each other or for large quantities of less valuable goods.

values The moral priorities in life considered desirable in particular cultures, reflecting a particular worldview.

values as goods The principle that any good can be converted into another by some standard of value. All cultures rank goods in accord with moral values. More durable goods can be exchanged for greater quantities of less durable ones.

worldview The entire set of a culture's moral values, defining the relations of men and women, of the three generations, and of human beings to the supernatural and to the natural world, including a people's priorities in time and space.

PART

III

TRIBES AND EMERGENT INSTITUTIONS

CHAPTER 9

*Extending the Human Family and Forming Tribal Communities:
Households and Descent Groups Among Tribal Peoples*

CHAPTER 10

*Tribal Warfare Complexes:
Aggressive Sequences and Balanced Negative Exchanges*

CHAPTER 11

*Feasting and Trading Systems:
The Economics of Redistribution and Trading Rings*

CHAPTER 12

*Tribal Politics:
Leadership and Its Rewards*

CHAPTER 13

*Shamans and Prophets:
Catalysts for Therapy and Cultural Change*

The theoretical view of human social evolution in this book is first of all that it results from restless human wandering. As a species we are mobile walkers; every human being needs to move about every day. From about 30,000 years ago, physically fully modern (as opposed to archaic) *H. sapiens sapiens* began a relatively rapid diffusion, walking out over the face of the earth. In the Old World that diffusion was completed by about 15,000 years ago, and thenceforth as people moved—exiled men, or whole families fleeing anger in their home bands—they ran into neighbors. A species that had been expanding out over peopleless frontiers suddenly found its members jostling up against each other.

Although some hunting-and-gathering band communities and their cultures have survived to this day in relatively inhospitable spaces—such as deserts and the Arctic—elsewhere human beings began to cluster into tribal communities at the location of richer resources. The northwest coast of North America, for example, is surely one of the world's most abundant natural habitats. Here people found rich supplies of all sorts of fish, especially salmon, and plentiful forests full of acorns and game animals.

In the archaeological record this process of settling down close to rich natural resources is called the *mesolithic* transition. It happened in many places around the world, after the globe had filled up with humans, and in many cases after certain wider environments, as in paleolithic North America, had been degraded by human actions—hunting biggame animals to extinction, for example.

Inevitably the domestication of plants followed, if by many thousands of years. Women gathering seeds and berries dropped some near camp. In settled campsites the seeds cross-fertilized, and new varieties of interesting grasses appeared spontaneously near human settlements. This gave rise eventually to the Old World domesticated grains around 10,000 years ago. Because the process was spontaneous, we might say that grains domesticated themselves. In tropical forest regions this same process took place with root crops, such as yams and manioc. In the New World the process gave rise first to gourds, then to maize, or Indian corn. The appearance of villages of horticulturalists—deliberate gardeners of domesticated staple crops—is called the *neolithic* transition. (Archaeologist A. Moore has effectively presented this picture of both mesolithic and neolithic transitions in the Middle East [1987].)

Thus, after the world had filled with hunting-and-gathering *H. sapiens*, human beings had to live with conflict with their neighbors (often former friends), and to live with lessened overall resources. Eventually they had to make use of the potentials implicit in the boundary conditions of nature and of other groups. To tap into a potential in a boundary condition in nature is to start deliberately planting the grains from self-domesticating plants around one's campsite. To tap into potentials in social boundary conditions is to form alliances with other groups, to expand the region of one's community, and to create formal rivalries with still other groups, who then belong to one's community through that very enmity. The result was a settled, tribal society, communicating from community to community through trade and war.

These changes arose through a combination of (1) *internal* social pressures of increased numbers of persons (population growth) and of more complicated institutional arrangements, and (2) *external* environmental pressures from habitat and neighboring groups. An advancing toolkit and self-domesticating breeds

of plants and animals provided a *potential* for the new way of life but did not cause it. They had been in place for millennia before they became essential to human groups after first the mesolithic, then the neolithic transitions.

In sum, the transition to tribal life was a result of several processes operating at once: densification of population, habitat challenges, internal institutional innovation and complexity, and external social-political (conflict and warfare) pressures from neighboring groups.

It is important to understand exactly how the term *tribal community* is being used in this book. There are a number of loose and imprecise usages of the word *tribe*. It may be synonymous with *nation* or *people*, or it may mean simply the people who speak a common language in a given territory and who perhaps even claim common descent. These are all indications that a *tribal community* is at hand but not enough to make us sure we actually have one.

At the tribal level we are looking for a *kind of community organization* characterized first of all by the union of several local communities—each composed of three "levels" as in a band—into some sort of integrated *alliance* capable of unified action, at least from time to time. *Common leadership*, then, is an essential feature. That alliance, in turn, is part of a *network* of such alliances, arrayed against each other.

The tribal community, then, from the point of view of any individual member, includes friends and enemies. It stretches out on the individual's horizons in space to include friends of friends, who are also enemies of enemies. In these communities, warfare and raiding is an act of communication *within* the wider community. Friends and enemies belong to the same wider community, communicating with each other through war and trade. The closest image of this in the contemporary world has been the city of Beirut, Lebanon, which somehow survived for over twenty years as a city of trade and industry while its separate ethnic subcommunities fought pitched battles in city streets with each other in shifting patterns of alliance and revenge.

Tribal boundaries and alliances are always shifting. The schedule for these changes, which might be thought of as relatively regular oscillations, varies from one region to another. Among the Nuer, discussed in Chapter 9, regular alliances are called up on kinship dimensions every year; the variation depends on how widespread an alliance is activated each year. Elsewhere, as among the Dani discussed in Chapter 11, alliances may be activated, broken, and realigned on a schedule ranging from once every six to ten years to once every twenty to thirty years. Still other alliances, such as the North American Cheyenne, discussed in Chapter 12, or the League of the Iroquois, in Chapter 13, are semipermanent, lasting for 200 to 300 years or more.

Remember that a tribal community is a *system* that provides for the survival of a people and their culture from one generation to another. As a system it has many component parts: individuals, households, settlements of households, ritual assemblages, political gatherings, feasts, war parties, and trading expeditions. Only certain tribal communities—the tightly knit tribal confederacies with annual warfare complexes—maintain all of these parts in a closely integrated fashion. In any case, *denser populations and more intense communication* among local communities than among bands are also essential.

Part III examines the variations of tribal community organization as they appear through the dimensions of particular institutions that emerge and develop in the tribal world. Our discussion shall draw on classic ethnographic case studies: the Nuer of the Sudan for segmentary lineage organizations and elaboration of kinship; the Tupinambá of Brazil for primitive warfare complexes; the Siuai of the Solomon Islands for political-economic organization around "Big Men redistributors," who turn feasting into a way of life; the Cheyenne of the North American Great Plains, for political organization; and the Iroquois for a revitalization movement.

We shall see tribal communities as they coalesce along several emerging institutional dimensions: *kinship* and its extensions through lineages; *conflict* through social dramas escalating into blood feuds and *warfare*, in which redressive action is nearly impossible to come by; *economics* and incipient dictatorship in the Big Man *feasting* complexes; *politics* and its practice through ritual fraternities and councils of chiefs in a tribal republic; and *ritual* as prophets emerge to revitalize cultures after defeat or collapse.

Extending the Human Family and Forming Tribal Communities:

Households and Descent Groups Among Tribal People

9

EXTENDING HOUSEHOLDS

Residence Decisions

Patrilocal Extended Households

The Matrilocal Navajo

Matrilocal Extended Households

DESCENT GROUPS

Ambilineal, Omnilineal, or Nonunilineal Descent Groups

Unilineal Descent Groups

A PROBLEM IN ETHNOLOGY: KIN TERMINOLOGIES AND MARRIAGE EXCHANGE

Marriage as Exchange

Terminologies

    Eskimoan Cousin Terminology

    Iroquoian Cousin Terminology

Iroquoian Terminology and Cross-Cousin Marriage

KINSHIP AND COMMUNITY AMONG THE NUER

Nuer Kinship Terminology

Nuer Descent Groups: Segmentary Lineages

Nuer Community Forms

Nuer Alliances and Complementary Opposition

Nuer Marriages and Bridewealth

Village Residential Composition and Bridewealth

Justice Through Bloodwealth

Nuer Counterbalances

*T*he family, the household, descent groups, and the language of kinship terminologies provide the first notable dimension of institutional development in the emerging tribal world. Tribal peoples cluster in ever more dense populations; they settle down semipermanently, or, if they follow herd animals in a nomadic pattern, they do so in greater numbers with greater organizational demands than band peoples. In coping with organizing greater numbers of people with more complicated resources—usually horticulture and domesticated animals— tribals make use of an institution already available (the family) to define their way of life, before developing ritual, political, and economic institutions.

Kinship is also a key dimension along which tribal cultures attempt to develop larger communities. The essence of **tribe** is alliance and opposition. A **tribal community** consists of a grouping in space very much like that of a band—households in neighborhoods that gather together on some yearly schedule, or even live together tightly. This group in turn is allied with others like itself for purposes of exchange (such as marriages) and war against a common enemy. A tribal community consists of an alliance of such local groups *and* their common enemies, who form a similar alliance (see Figure 9.1). Kinship is a convenient way for people to begin to sort all this out.

EXTENDING HOUSEHOLDS

Tribal peoples organize themselves on the dimension of kinship in two ways: They extend their households patrilocally or matrilocally on the level of a single generation, and they also extend their larger communities in the same manner in the formation of descent groups—lineages, clans, or kindreds. Kinship is also a highly technical subject, and this chapter, while grounded in ethnographic description, is therefore the most technical chapter in this book.

Justice
Rudimentary formal machinery for dispute resolution: third-party mediators or adjudication by tribal councils, with decisions enforced by ritual fraternities; blood revenge in warfare with neighbor-enemies.

Language
Oral literature (consisting of genealogies and elaborate mythologies) memorized and recited. No writing.

Politics
All sorts of devices to integrate, loosely, local groups: short-term feast-alliances, tribal councils, war chiefs and peace chiefs, feasting complexes, trading rings. Powerful persons are not full-time political specialists.

The Tribe
Community field:
Consists of a loosely integrated network of band-level communities. These range from tightly organized confederacies lasting many generations to ephemeral warfare alliances or feasting (exchange) complexes lasting a single lifetime or less. At local levels membership is less permeable than in band societies. (It is hard to change one's tribe.) Relations with neighboring groups, both inside and outside the tribal network, take place through the activities of trade and war.

Learning
Ritual initiations, age grades, more elaborate than in band societies.

Economics
Subsistence base: hunters and gatherers with usually rich natural resources (e.g., bison herds), or nomadic pastoralists with domestic herds, or horticulturalists with garden crops. Big emphasis on balanced reciprocal exchanges among allies, competitive exchanges in feasting among neighbors. Warfare complexes are also exchange systems.

Ritual
Elaborate rites of intensification to unite group, involving feasting and warfare. Shamans as prophets may lead group into war.

Technology
May be horticulturalists, gardeners, with digging sticks and many crops propagated by seeds or root cuttings. Canoes, rafts, fish lines, and harpoons common. So is ceramics, pottery, but not universal. May have domesticated fowl; may have beasts of burden and other herd animals.

Sociology
Lineages and clans derived from kinship, and associations (diversely called "fraternities" or "sodalities") derived from age grades, provide means to integrate tribal networks and unite people from different local communities.

Figure 9.1 Emergent institutional behavior in the tribe.

Residence Decisions

Returning to band societies, while most have only the nuclear family household, some may also have an ideal preference toward newlyweds coming to live near their parents. We have a terminology for the kinds of residences newlywed couples can take up. In the "pure type" of nuclear family, the residence of the newlywed couple may be *neolocal*—in a new location altogether. *Matrilocal* residence occurs when a newly married man goes to reside with his bride at her mother's home. Other newly adult householders choose a *patrilocal* location—in the neighborhood of the father of the male householder. Yet another possibility is *avunculocal* residence, in the vicinity of an uncle, usually a mother's brother's. This is found among tribal horticulturists. New nuclear family households may also be *bilocal*—in a matrilocal or patrilocal vicinity, depending on personal choice.

Why should there be any variation in the first place? Some experts have theorized a correlation between residence decisions and cultural ecology. Thus hunter-and-gatherers were thought to favor patrilocal bands composed of married sons living near their fathers, who would better be able to direct the hunting party. Similarly, the invention of horticulture at the tribal level was thought to favor matrilocal families, whereby adult married sisters lived near their mother and gardened together.

But bands are seldom patrilocal. Tribal horticulturists are, more often than not, matrilocal. But there is no one-to-one correlation. Rather, it would seem that the pressures of internal social life, coupled with those of the environment, induce people to make choices leading to a certain pattern. Once a pattern takes hold, it becomes the norm and is difficult to change. There are different kinds of households, then, because at different times and places different forms solve different problems. But the number of forms is quite limited.

Patrilocal Extended Households

In the previous chapter we discussed polygynous households that add wives to the original nuclear couple. Another way to "extend" a household beyond the nuclear unit is to do so along the dimension of generation. These households retain members from the childrearing phase and have them bring in spouses. Such households link newlyweds together with the grandparental couple in one residence, usually with one hearth. In such forms, then, the "empty nest" ideally does not exist.

Mobility and flexibility are highly functional in band societies, so this form is not as common as the nuclear family with them. However, extended households are common among tribal peoples, who often settle semipermanently near their gardens, and it is also common among permanently settled rural or urban civilized peoples.

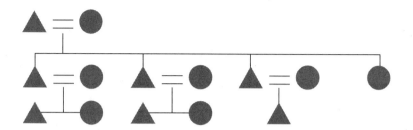

Figure 9.2 Patrilocal extended household, three generations. Equal signs indicate marriage ties.

In the **patrilocal extended family household,** each son, upon marrying, brings his bride home to live with his father and mother. In such a household the head of a house is often a grandfather, living with his wife and their married sons and their offspring. Any adult daughters living at home are as yet unmarried, for in this system the bride goes to live in the home of her groom, usually under the command of his parents. Instead of helping her own mother in the kitchen, this bride is obliged to work for her mother-in-law at the side of her sisters-in-law. If she is fortunate, these are her own sisters as well. As you can imagine, there are many tensions and difficulties for this young woman as she learns to adjust to living with women who are not of her own blood kin.

The case may be diagrammed simply, as shown in Figure 9.2. The developmental cycle of the patrilocal extended household reaches its climax when the household is three generations deep, as in the diagram. When the grandfather-patriarch dies, each married son is likely to set up his own household, which for a while resembles the nuclear family at the childrearing phase. Then grown sons bring in their wives and extend the household by forming additional mother-offspring units under their father's roof.

We can see this household in incipient form among the Algonkian-speaking Chippewa (also known as the Ojibwa) of the Great Lakes region of Canada and the United States. These northern hunters are also settled horticulturists at least part of the year. Young men prefer to bring their brides to new homes near their father's home. Some few households, however, are fully extended, and the Chippewa construct longhouses to hold all the sons and their brides under one patrilocal roof. Among civilized peoples, the patrilocal extended family is preferred by Maya peasants of Guatemala and Mexico, so much so that archaeologists assume that it was preferred by precivilized tribal Maya at the dawn of their high civilization 4,000 years ago. Patrilocal extended households were also the ideal for the Chinese gentry, as well as for upper classes of the Middle East, to name only a few.*

---

*Another form of extended family household is the stem-family household, including its most unusual variant, the polyandrous household, where one wife has many husbands. These forms are adaptations to keep property in a single family line and are found only in rural civilized societies (see Chapter 16).

The Matrilocal Navajo

Residence decisions obviously are important for the settlement pattern of any community from one generation to another. Such decisions can lead to the formation of a number of households under a single direction, a form sometimes called the *joint family*. The traditional Navajo once lived in circumstances roughly comparable to the Tiwi with the addition of a pastoral economy. That is to say, the Navajo were originally a hunting-and-gathering band people. Over two centuries ago they took up herds of sheep and mounted and bred horses. Like the Tiwi, they live scattered over desert country and have local residential units composed of a collection of households. These units are entirely matrilocal.

Such local residential groupings, *outfits*, were built up during a strong man's lifetime and dispersed after his death. In the case of Natani Tsani, his outfit included some seventy people:

> [They] included the old man . . . who lived with his granddaughter and her husband and children, a son and his family, and five married daughters with their families of husband and children. The dwellings and herds of the "outfit" were scattered over a territory of about thirty-six square miles. (Arensberg and Kimball, 1965, p. 57)

In the Navajo system young men usually moved to the outfit of their brides. In this case some five sons-in-law had done so, as well as one grandson-in-law. One son had not done so but had brought his bride into the group.

When the old man died, the unit broke into its constituent households. The son, who was out of place, very likely moved to the territory of his wife's sisters. Slowly, in the second generation, one of the erstwhile sons-in-law was expected to grow to command an outfit of his own. His prosperity was such that his daughters had no trouble enticing husbands to come there to help with his herds. Such a big man, it turns out, is also a widely respected ritual leader; he presides at sings for curing and for rain that are attended by Navajo from a wide area.

Matrilocal Extended Households

It is one short step from a local community of matrilocal households to their enclosure under a single roof as one household. The Kuna Indians of San Blas District, Panama, whom I studied, have classic **matrilocal extended households.** In this form, the climax of the developmental cycle consists of a grandparental couple and their grown daughters with their husbands and children, all living under one roof and sharing one hearth (see Figure 9.3). The men have all married in. Most likely, they are unrelated to each other yet must learn to cooperate under the direction of their father-in-law. The

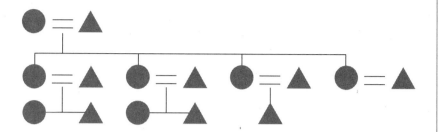

*Figure 9.3 Matrilocal
extended family household.
Note that husbands have
all married in.*

women in the kitchen are a relatively smoothly interacting team of sisters
under the direction of their mother.

On the death of the grandparental couple, this household usually breaks
up into its constituent units. One daughter and her husband have been named
by the grandparents as heirs to the homestead. Other married daughters
must build their own houses, either on close-by inherited maternal land or
on land claimed from the forest (for mainland villages) or land filled in on
the shoreline (for island villages). Although the Kuna pass homes and
houseplots down in the maternal line, their garden plots and coconut palm
plantations are passed down in both lines—men and women inherit these
from both their father and their mother. Eventually, large corporate groups
of cousins form to manage these resources. (See the discussion of kindreds
in the next section.)

DESCENT GROUPS

In the tribal world, kinship can be a way of forging alliances among communities, thus linking them into macrocommunities. Kinship can become extremely useful in such a world—so much so that anthropologists seemed to
have spent an inordinate amount of time studying and describing kinship
almost as if it were an end in itself, rather than a means to an end. That end
is community definition and survival.

In this section we shall survey the various ways people from many different households can group together according to calculations of common
descent. After considering how kin terminologies can influence marriage
exchange between descent groups, we shall look at an ethnographic case,
the Nuer, to see how descent groups can form the basis of complex tribal
communities.

Kinship systems of preferential marriage rules, incest tabus, kin terminology, and residence decisions are a kind of *language*. They provide us with
codes to regulate our extraction of matter and energy from the environment, in terms of how we relate ourselves to *relatives*, persons connected to
us through marriage or descent. We shall see that as a language, a set of

symbolic catalysts, kinship systems can likewise be the basis for membership groups defined through common descent. Kinship provides a code to govern group membership (in or out, yes or no). The groups generated by this code are variously classified as *kindreds*, *lineages*, and *clans*.

We are, in biological fact, each the descendants of many individual human beings. We have two parents, four grandparents, eight great-grandparents, sixteen great-great-grandparents, and so on in expanding progression indefinitely. There are more ancestors in each generation as we step backward.

Human beings early became aware of this web of descent and have categorized it in relation to living generations in different ways. Some systems, our own included, come close to recognizing the potential infinitely branching tree in *bilateral kinship*, described a bit later. But in point of fact, we are not the descendants of all the potential persons in potential places in that genealogical tree. All human beings, like other animals, descend from particular breeding populations, which limit the branches of the tree. Every few generations crossover ancestors add branches from other groups.

A breeding population is in fact almost synonymous with *community* as we use the term in this book. Human beings have attempted to shape those breeding populations by classifying people in living generations into relations with one another by defining who their ancestors are and by identifying certain family lines as more important than others. These classifications can be the basis for organizing tribal communities.

Ambilineal, Omnilineal, or Nonunilineal Descent Groups

It is possible to recognize kinfolk in every direction and to calculate kinship equally according to descent from the same ancestors in whatever line. Such a system is called **bilateral descent**. In our own society the heirs to great family fortunes calculate descent in all lines from the founding ancestor, the tycoon who made the family fortune. Because they share corporate interests in inherited wealth, we can call such collections of descendants *ancestor-oriented kindreds* (see Lomnitz and Perez-Lizaur, 1988). These crop up much more commonly in family reunions of persons descended, again in all lines, from certain **apical ancestors** whom some of their descendants have chosen to honor in this way (see Neville, 1987).

Bilateral descent inevitably comes up with kinfolk in concentric circles from any given individual, *ego*, with each exterior circle being a degree of kinship. This is the way descent is reckoned among the band-level Eskimo, among the tribal Anglo-Saxons of antiquity, and today in Western Europe and North America. You might try to chart all relatives known to you; you should come up with a circular format. Such circles of kinfolk make up a

kindred; when calculated from a single living individual, this is called an *ego-oriented kindred*. Such kindreds are overlapping and dispersed. If you are a North American reader, the only persons with whom you share your kindred equally are your full siblings—brothers and sisters—by the same two parents. Your father does not share your mother's kin with you, nor vice versa. Similarly you do not share half the kin of your first cousin, since they are those of his or her parent who "married in."

Such an "ego-oriented kindred" is seldom required to act as a group, and then only in relation to ego. In the Anglo-Saxon tradition, such a group was called a *sib* and was calculated within seven degrees of kinship to ego. The sib was activated in cases of blood feud and revenge. If, for example, ego had killed an enemy, all his "siblings" were obliged to contribute *bloodwealth* to all the siblings of the victim to avoid a revenge killing in return. This was a way, then, to activate a tribal community in the distant past of our own cultural tradition.

Affiliation with a descent group that reckons from the founding ancestor in both male and female lines—**ambilineal, omnilineal,** or **nonunilineal descent**—is very important among some peoples for determining residence and property rights. In many Polynesian societies, a newly married couple chooses one particular descent group from among the kin lines of both sets of parents and then goes to reside there. The choice depends on the congeniality of the relatives and the availability of lands.

Unilineal Descent Groups

One way people may become organized is by sorting themselves into *descent groups*—that is, by classing people together through common ancestors. The ancestor-oriented kindreds mentioned above are descent groups. Descent groups are found among some band societies and are also important in such civilized societies as the traditional Hindus or Chinese. As dynasties, descent groups provide for succession to kingship in many civilized monarchies. Descent groups obviously have much to do with residence, ownership of territory, inheritance of property, and symbols of personal, household, and community membership.

Descent groups are especially important at the tribal level of sociocultural evolution. Indeed, some anthropologists guess that such groupings originated from the clustering of households in neighborhoods by residence decisions. This implies, of course, the settling down into denser communities, something that did begin to happen in ancient times in the **mesolithic period** as human beings began to be concentrated at rich natural food sources. This settlement intensified later as human beings congregated near domesticated plants and animals in gardens and fields after the **neolithic transition.**

Households often cluster on land inherited from a common ancestor. It thus becomes important to remember all the links between the living and the founding ancestor, however many generations back. When the genealogy linking the living with the original (*apical*) ancestor can be demonstrated in some fashion, anthropologists call the group a **lineage.** In the Kuna case, any household forms a lineage descended from the deceased mother of the senior female. If there are other households founded by sisters of that senior female, they, too, are part of that lineage, being descended from the same known, apical ancestor—the deceased mother of all the senior females. In such a case we might call each household a *sublineage*. Many groups that lack writing commit quite elaborate genealogies to memory and chant them on occasion. (Such genealogies may be partially fictitious, but people believe them.)

When the exact genealogical relations are forgotten and persons claim common descent from an ancestor whose genealogical relation to them is unknown and perhaps even mythical, anthropologists prefer to call the descent group a **clan.** A clan is usually but not always composed of constituent lineages. However, it may not have such lineages and may simply identify a collection of households.

Lineages and clans may be **matrilineal,** as among the Navajo. That is, they may trace descent through the female line. Men in such a society belong to the lineages and clans of their mothers; a man's son belongs to the man's wife's group. Or they may be **patrilineal,** tracing descent through the male line. A man then belongs to his father's lineage and clan, as does the man's own son.

Groups that calculate descent in a single line from an apical ancestor are **unilineal.** In a few cases "double descent" involves both a patrilineage and a matrilineage and is thus doubly unilineal. Although most people recognize kin in lineages other than their own, with unilineal descent the only "real relatives" are those related to an individual through the preferred line. For example, if a bride in traditional China married out and moved into her husband's patrilocal extended household, she was lost to her unilineal descent group and was no longer considered their kinsperson. She and her children had no inheritance claims on her father's property at his death. (Her dowry at marriage had settled that in any case.)

A PROBLEM IN ETHNOLOGY: KIN TERMINOLOGIES AND MARRIAGE EXCHANGE

Tribal societies have long perplexed ethnographers because of their frequent rules preferring one or another kind of cousin as a marriage partner. Let us examine this preference more closely.

Marriage as Exchange

We can understand marriage as an exchange from two points of view: from that of the partners and from that of their original families. The partners give themselves to each other. Consider the Western mutual wedding vow, "I take thee . . ." But their two sets of parents may also view this marriage as an exchange between their families. Especially in systems with extended matrilocal or patrilocal households, one child is being given up to another household. The donor household wants a partner back for one of their stay-at-home offspring. A spouse for a spouse, in this morality.

We noted in Chapter 7 that the incest tabu prevents individuals from marrying within the nuclear family. Its effect is kinetic, to force people to seek marriage partners beyond their family of procreation. In some kinship systems they do not have to look far: They are expected to prefer to marry certain kinds of cousins.

Terminologies

Kinship terminology is the linguistic recognition of ties with other human beings by descent, marriage, or adoption. All languages have a subsystem of terms to describe their living kin, to divide up the biological universes of kinpersons in some way. However, no language has terms for all biological relatives—for a cousin to the eighth degree, for example.

In the English language, we speak of brothers and sisters, but when social scientists needed a term to apply to brothers and sisters combined, they resurrected the Anglo-Saxon term *sibling*, which originally meant one's kinfolk within seven degrees of relation. Other kin of the same generation besides brothers and sisters are referred to as *cousins*. If you want to signify sex, you have to specify girl cousin, and so on, and if you want to specify side of the family, you say cousin on my mother's side, and so on. The terms *father* and *mother* recognize sex; for every other individual on that generation, we recognize the sex but not the side of the family; your father's brother and your mother's brother are both uncle. For in-laws, or affines, in that generation, the man who married your mother's sister is just as much your uncle as your father's brother is.

Eskimoan Cousin Terminology. Languages in general, and English very much so, single out some individuals for particular terms (for example, the English *mother*) and lump many others under a single term (for example, the English *cousin*). One kind of nomenclature that differentiates siblings from cousins and parents from aunts and uncles is called **Eskimoan.** It is diagrammed in Figure 9.4, where the same numbers signify the same term. This nomenclature is associated with the nuclear family and with kinship calculated bilaterally or omnilaterally (through all lines) and infrequently

Royal Incest

In traditional civilizations, urban elites may rely on marrying relatives to sustain their wealth and power. Members of European royalty today often marry cousins, although seldom first cousins. The closest thing to "royal incest" in European history is the marital career of Philip II of Spain, who ruled from 1555 to 1598. He practiced serial monogamy as his wives died. His first wife was his double first cousin, Catherine of Braganza, daughter of his father's sister and his mother's brother. His second wife was Queen Mary Tudor ("Bloody Mary"), daughter of his father's mother's sister, Catherine of Aragon, and Henry VIII of England. His third wife was the exception; Elizabeth of Valois was unrelated. Finally, he wed his niece, Anne of Hapsburg, his sister's daughter

Phillip II of Spain.

by their first cousin, Maximilian II of Austria. His heir, Philip III, in turn wed his own Hapsburg first cousin, Margaret of Austria. These marriages all represented political alliances and were exercises in imperial diplomacy as well as in kinship.

---

with extended households. Thus, kinship terminologies seem to have some relation to behavior and to institutions such as the household; kinship terms are at least indicative of ideal norms, although in changing circumstances they may not really reflect behavior.

In Eskimoan terminology the question of the extension of incest tabus to first cousins is moot, since siblings are not called by the same term as some cousins (as they are in the next two kinds of terminology we discuss). That question varies from culture to culture with Eskimoan systems. While frowned on in the United States, and in fact outlawed in some states, marriage between first cousins is a common device among Latin American upper-class people in order to keep inheritances "in the family."

Iroquoian Cousin Terminology. The **Iroquoian terminology** is of interest because it appears to foster marriage exchange between households of

Figure 9.4 Eskimoan kinship: (1) brother, (2) sister, (3) cousin, (4) father, (5) mother, (6) uncle, (7) aunt.

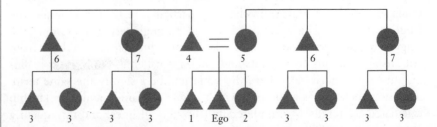

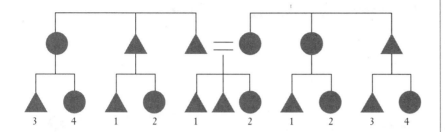

Figure 9.5 Iroquoian kinship. Ego's generation: (1) brother, father's brother's son, and mother's sister's son (parallel cousins); (2) sister, father's brother's daughter, and mother's sister's daughter (parallel cousins); (3) father's sister's son and mother's brother's son (cross-cousins); (4) father's sister's daughter and mother's brother's daughter (cross-cousins).

orientation. Iroquoian is also called Dakotan, or Dravidian, from the other languages that use this terminology. Iroquoian terms (along with some other kinds of terminologies) differentiate between *parallel cousins* and *cross-cousins*. A **parallel cousin** is related to you through a parent of the same sex as your parent. That is, he or she is your father's brother's child or your mother's sister's child. A **cross-cousin** is related through a parent of the opposite sex from your parent. That is, he or she is your father's sister's child or your mother's brother's child. This distinction is totally absent in English, but a moment's reflection should assure you that these are, in biological fact, different kinds of relatives. Iroquoian terms lump your parallel cousins with your siblings, and they are called by the same terms as brothers or sisters. Cross-cousins have other terms. The four terms are diagrammed in Figure 9.5.

In the parental generation, fathers and their brothers and mothers and their sisters (the parents of the parallel cousins) are called by two separate terms. Father's sisters and mother's brothers (parents of the cross-cousins) are called by two separate terms. The technical term for this is *bifurcate merging* (see Figure 9.6).

Iroquoian Terminology and Cross-Cousin Marriage

Kinship terms relate to behavior—the actual exchanges of marriage partners within household developmental cycles. Iroquoian cousin terminologies are logically compatible with the practice of preferring cross-cousins as marriage partners, and marrying others only if there is no cross-cousin.

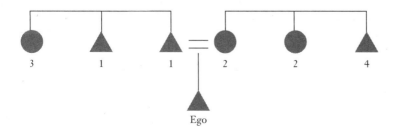

Figure 9.6 Iroquoian kinship. Ascending generation: (1) father, father's brother; (2) mother, mother's sister; (3) father's sister; (4) mother's brother.

Preferential cross-cousin marriage has in fact been widely reported among many primitive groups. It is much more common than that of parallel cousins.

Iroquoian kinship, when fully understood, looks like a linguistic charter for marrying one's cross-cousin. It is a kind of morality for action encoded in the language. If you examine the diagram for Iroquoian cousin terms (Figure 9.6) again, you will note that parallel cousins are lumped with brothers and sisters under the same term and thus, in name at least, are included under the incest tabu. They will therefore be avoided as marriage partners, just like brothers and sisters. Of course, this does not explain fully why cross-cousins should be preferred. A few explanations of native meanings, or glosses, can be added.

In Iroquoian terminologies where cross-cousin marriage is practiced, the terms for *cross-cousin* also mean *spouse*. Thus, the term for the daughter of a mother's brother and the daughter of a father's sister (number 4) is also the term for wife. And the term for a father's sister's son and a mother's brother's son (number 3) is also the term for husband.

Furthermore, in such a system a mother's brother's daughter and a father's sister's daughter, both called *wife*, are going to be one and the same person, for mother's brother and father's sister are logically going to be cross-cousins and married to each other. This is so much the case that in Iroquoian systems the term for mother's brother's wife is the same as the term for father's sister. And the term for father's brother's wife is the same as the term for mother's sister.

The nomenclature of this system embodies a logical structure: two "lines" (lineages or descent groups) of men exchange women in perfect harmony in every generation and produce offspring for such exchanges in each future generation. The system is quite elegant and can be expressed mathematically in both geometric and algebraic form (Arensberg, 1972). In geometry the system forms a cube, as shown in Figure 9.7. In algebra, the system forms a permutation matrix where A and B represent two males exchanging sisters, a and b, and have two offspring, a male and a female, in each generation who continue to exchange (see Figure 9.8). The matrix can go on forever.

If you examine this matrix carefully, looking at the marriage partners after the first generation, you will soon see that they must be each other's cross-cousins and that the other terminological identities are true here, too. Thus, when cross-cousin marriage is practiced with an Iroquoian terminology, we can see the articulation of the marriage practices with the linguistic terms in the lumping of the terms *cross-cousin* and *spouse*; marriage rules and kinship terminologies coincide at precisely this point. These relationships constitute a linguistic syntax, not only for speech but for action.

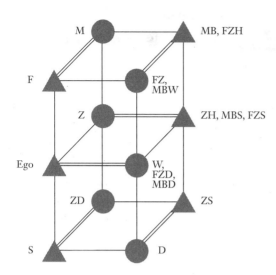

Figure 9.7 Geometric form. (Z = sister)

Bear in mind, however, that even though the two subsystems seem to coincide so perfectly, reality does not always conform to logical and moral structures. In such societies, spouses are not always born at the appropriate times to the right persons. Spouses are found somehow, perhaps from outsiders. All that is needed is enough conformity enough of the time to give a sense of actuality to the nomenclature.

By taking the whole complex of Iroquoian kinship terms and looking at them over several generations at once, we come up with a mathematical system that groups human beings into two lines of descent that practice *exogamy*, or marrying out, with each other. Iroquoian kinship terminologies are in fact associated with unilineal descent groups more frequently than they are with preferential cross-cousin marriage.

Anthropologists have paid much attention to preferential cross-cousin marriage ever since the publication of French anthropologist Claude Lévi-Strauss's work on elementary forms of kinship in 1949. Lévi-Strauss is one of the most famous anthropologists in the world. He did field work in Matto Grosso state in Brazil, where he spent some months with the Nambicuara, whose speech happens to include Iroquoian kinship terms. The French admire his capacity to synthesize a great deal of strange information into elegant, rational systems built on elementary parts. This is the fashion of linguistic analysis and is termed *structural analysis*.

Lévi-Strauss decided that cross-cousin marriage is a necessary prerequisite for the incest tabu among human beings and that it had everything to do with the emergence of human kinship systems and human marriage.

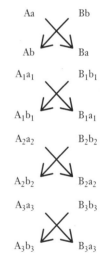

Figure 9.8 Algebraic permutation matrix.

First, he reasoned that the incest tabu, by being universally human, is "natural" and therefore is a link between nature and culture, between our animal past and our cultural present. Second, phrasing the prohibition from the male point of view, Lévi-Strauss thought of incest as obliging males to give up the females to whom they have a "natural" claim—that is, their sisters, mothers, and daughters. (Lévi-Strauss's reasoning here is purely logical. The primate evidence, as we know, does not support him, although a hominid group practicing extensive consortship may have laid the groundwork for such conditions.)

Third, following Lévi-Strauss's reasoning, it is unnatural for men to give up something for nothing. They must get something in return. The solution is cross-cousin marriage, which allows two sets of men to observe the incest prohibition while at the same time assuring them of wives. The solution means men give up their sisters to their male cross-cousins in return for their female cross-cousins.

Claude Lévi-Strauss.

Lévi-Strauss claimed, to astonished audiences, that the elementary forms of human kinship, Iroquoian, were the consequence of the sudden elaboration of unilineal descent groups exchanging women over the generations, so that marriage, the incest tabu, and preferential cross-cousins all arose at once.

Dazzling as the theory that marriage exchange actually created the incest tabu is, it is not widely accepted by American and British anthropologists, and it has sparked considerable controversy. Scholars have debated the problem of the frequency and nature of the three kinds of cross-cousin marriage (matrilateral, patrilateral, and both) as well as the mathematical description of what happens when *three* unilineal descent groups exchange women.

I would prefer to view cross-cousin marriage as having much more to do with the emergence of unilineal descent groups than with the emergence of marriage and the family. Thus, I would see Iroquoian terminology and cross-cousin marriage as probably arising well after the emergence of *H. sapiens*, as human beings began to settle down and coalesce into tribal communities. But the discussion does make us aware of marriage as an exchange. When two people marry, those in their original households of orientation might well feel that they are owed a partner "back" for a sibling left behind.

But if we look at marriage as an exercise in individualism, as a mutual exchange of two selves, we see that all that one needs in morality and law is the basic incest tabu that obliges people to look for partners outside their family of orientation. Spouses then circulate in a *generalized marriage exchange* among all the households of a community. This is exactly the situation in cultures (such as ours) that have Eskimoan kinship terminologies. Here individuals are not concerned with getting a spouse "back" from the family they marry their son or daughter to. A spouse will turn up naturally in the general flow of marriage partners.

This section has examined the problem of the flow of linguistic symbols, kin terms, and spouse terms. Let us return to kinship and descent groups as a dimension for developing tribal communities.

KINSHIP AND COMMUNITY AMONG THE NUER

Many tribal communities organize themselves on the basis of lineages. In the remainder of this chapter we examine all the kinship relations of the Nuer in Northern Africa. We will see how kinship and descent groups can become the basis for organizing two mutually interacting tribal cultures, which together form sets of shifting, warring communities.

Nuer village: homesteads and cattle on a mound.

The Nuer were studied by the great British social anthropologist E. E. Evans-Pritchard (1940, 1951) in the 1930s, just after they had been pacified by the British administration of the then Anglo-Egyptian Sudan. Most of their territory is subject to flooding half the year. Yet the Nuer go to great lengths to herd cattle under inhospitable conditions of floods and insect plagues. The people of their "nation" inhabit the low savannahs of the Nile headwaters, speak the same language, and have no central government whatsoever. Indeed, we would be hard pressed to find any government at all among them. But leadership they do have, as we shall see.

Let us examine the kinship system of the Nuer, and then their community forms.

Nuer Kinship Terminology

The Nuer kinship terminology, **Sudanese,** is a most rare type, of which there are seven known examples. Unlike all other kinship terminologies, it does not lump any kind of cousin with any other kind. On the ascending generation, distinct terms are used for each kind of relative. Thus, there are sixteen separate terms for each relative in these two generations. Figure 9.9 should make this clear. Each number signifies a separate term; you might supply the corresponding English glosses for your own amusement (e.g., father's brother).

Nuer Descent Groups: Segmentary Lineages

The Nuer nation conceives of itself as a giant patriclan descended from the Original Nuer, the ancestor of all the living. Their genealogy is conceived of

Figure 9.9 Sudanese kin terms.

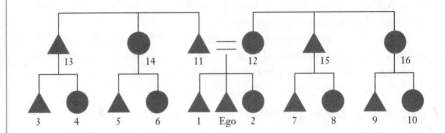

as a system of symmetrical segments, as if every great ancestor had begotten two sons, who in turn begot two sons, each patriline then dividing in two each generation. This is called **segmentary lineage.** Of course, these divisions are not actual and may represent the outcome of several generations. What is important is that a sense of balance or complementariness is preserved in the calculation of segments.

Any individual Nuer man belongs to a minimal lineage that calculates descent three to five generations back to a known ancestor. This lineage in turn is linked with several others in a minor lineage, which in turn is linked with yet others in a major lineage, all linked with others in a clan descended from a distant, and perhaps mythical, ancestor.

Theoretically, clans belong to one of the *moieties*, or halves, and indeed Nuerland is split territorially into Eastern and Western Nuerland. However, clans as such are never called up to make war together as a moiety. Still, the Nuer believe that the ancestors of all the clans were descended from the Original Nuer in symmetrical fashion. Thus, every Nuer man knows to what lineages he belongs, in what order, and to what clan these lineages belong (see Figure 9.10). But it is important that residence among the Nuer is not particularly patrilocal. It is not obligatory for a man to reside with his patrikin. Thus, in any given community there are householders from several lineages.

Figure 9.10 The structure of Nuer segmentary lineages.

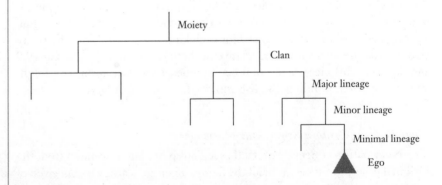

Nuer Community Forms

Although each territorial division must belong to a lineage segment, each is in fact inhabited by members of other lineages as well. The levels of Nuer communities are as follows. First, there is the neighborhood unit, the village, a cluster of households on high ground above the flood line. Second, several villages make up the community proper, which Evans-Pritchard calls the *section*. The section is easily recognized as a unit because its members gather every four years or so around a **man of cattle,** who has the ritual duty of initiating adolescent boys into their age grade. The man of cattle always belongs to an outside lineage, not to the one that owns the section.

The Nuer think of their sections as expressions of the segmentary lineage system. Each section, then, "belongs" to a lineage. Most section/communities belong to minimal lineages. Evans-Pritchard calls them *tertiary sections* (see Figure 9.11). It is possible that a section/community, one holding its ritual initiations together, might make up the next level of the genealogy; that is, a *secondary section* might be such a community.

The genealogical identification has a certain "legal" validity that is manifest in conflict. When one section/community quarrels with another, the men gather around one or more of the section's **men of the spear,** those resident householders who belong to the owning lineage and accompany any war party. Finally, within each section there is a resident **leopard-skin**

Figure 9.11 The relationship between descent groups and territorial groups in Nuer segmentary organization.

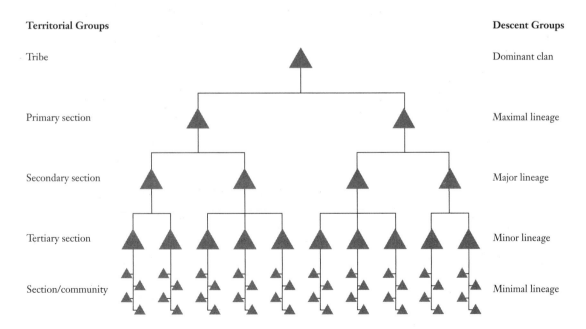

Territorial Groups   **Descent Groups**

Tribe   Dominant clan

Primary section   Maximal lineage

Secondary section   Major lineage

Tertiary section   Minor lineage

Section/community   Minimal lineage

Two Nuer youths from different clans. They are still undergoing scarification of their foreheads every four years during their communities' initiation rites.

chief, an outsider with sacred powers for keeping peace within the villages that make up the section.

At the level of foreign relations, each section conceives of itself as belonging within a larger territorial division of either a secondary section, identified with a major lineage, or a primary section, which belongs to the maximal lineage of its own resident men of the spear. This territorial division is in turn part of a *tribe*—that is, the territory, comprising many sections, that is identified with the clan to which all their men of the spear belong. The actual members of that clan and its subsidiary lineages may be a distinct numerical minority within its titular territory. Still, they are thought to be essential to it; they hold its title. Evans-Pritchard translates the term for them as *aristocrats*. There has to be at least one adult aristocrat, the man of the spear, residing in each section, or community proper, since this circle of villages wages war together, and an aristocrat with his sacred spear must company every war party.

Nuer Alliances and Complementary Opposition

All tribal communities are organized around alliance and warfare. When it is a question of making warlike alliances, the Nuer treat their fellows as if they were kinsmen, rallying to those closer and against those more distant, and rallying to all Nuer fighting against outsiders. Anthropologists tend to identify Nuer tribal disputes and the Nuer segmentary lineage system as if they were one and the same thing. In fact, both are structured by the same principle—balanced segmentation. This principle of **complementary opposition,** which shapes warlike alliances for solving disputes, comes into play most often at the level of the tribal section.

The Nuer are individualistic, proud, and very quarrelsome. They roam herding their cattle and are very prone to argue with their neighbors, especially those belonging to sections of another tribe—that is, communities whose title is vested in the aristocratic clan of the tribal territory. The helpful diagram in Figure 9.12, developed by Evans-Pritchard, can be translated into behavior. Let us say that two men from neighboring but different communities, sections Z1 and Z2, quarrel. Both belong to a larger primary section, Y2, and are equally close. They can look for no allies in this particular quarrel and must either fight it out or find a leopard-skin chief to resolve their case.

But let us say that a man from Z1 is involved in a dispute with a neighbor in one of the sections of Y1, the next other higher primary section in the territory belonging to their clan. Immediately, his erstwhile enemies in Z2 drop their quarrel and rally to him, as a member of tribal section Y2, against members of the more distant section Y1, whose constituent sections in turn rally against them. So we have all the communities of Y1 arrayed against those of Y2. But not for long. Let us say someone in Y1 is involved in a

Moiety A	Moiety B	
	Tribe X	Tribe Y
	X1	Y1
	X2	Y2
		Z1 / Z2

Figure 9.12 Nuer alliances.
Z = Section/communities
Y2 = Secondary section to which Z1 and Z2 belong
Y1 = Primary section, identified with a maximal lineage
Y = Entire tribe, identified with lineages all derived from the same "aristocratic" clan, holding the spear for all its territory
X = A rival tribe, identified with another aristocratic clan

dispute with someone in another tribe, in the territory of another clan altogether—someone in primary section X1 of the X tribe. Immediately his former opponents in Y2 rally to him as fellows of the Y tribe. Their opponents in X1 lose no time in calling upon their fellows of X2, however, to form a united X.

But this quarrel can also be dropped if any party to it is threatened by anyone in the opposite moiety, A. Then immediately tribes X and Y coalesce as the other moiety, B. Both moieties, however, could conceivably unite against outsiders, such as the Dinka. Thus, the system can array sections against sections, tribes against tribes, moiety against moiety, and Nuerland against the foreigner.

Often this hypothetical case is presented by means of the segmentary branching diagram used to portray a Nuer lineage system. But that is misleading, for the sections are not lineages, and the tribes are not clans, although each is symbolically identified with lineage and clan. Thus, the segmentary lineage structure has been grafted upon territory in Nuerland to provide an ideal framework for ordering disputes.

While busily fighting their enemies, the Nuer are also marrying their friends (sometimes erstwhile enemies).

Nuer Marriages and Bridewealth

Marriage alliances involving the exchange of marriage partners and women build up the local Nuer villages. The inhabitants of any particular Nuer section, or circle of villages, belong to several lineages. All Nuer are required to obey a rule of complete exogamy and marry outside the minimal lineages on both sides. Remember their Sudanese kinship terminology: all cousins are different from any other cousin, and none is a permissible marriage partner. Thus, no young Nuer man or woman may marry a cousin on either side. They must look beyond them. This means that there is a great emphasis placed on courtship. Like so many things among the Nuer, courtship is individually initiated and collectively controlled. All the young men are on the prowl for prospective brides in other villages. A good place to meet them is at the wedding dance of some other couple. Because all the relatives of the bride and groom are invited to the wedding, many people from many villages are brought together.

Nuer sweethearts. They are not any kind of cousin to each other.

A young man and a maiden court each other in perfect freedom—much as in the West. This is to be expected, for most households among the Nuer are of the nuclear family type, although some are polygynous. But when a couple seeks to establish itself as a wedded pair, it must get the consent of the members of four lineages. The paternal and maternal lineages of the young man must agree to provide the bridewealth, which is to be distributed among the paternal and maternal kin of the young woman.

Figure 9.13 shows how forty head of cattle are distributed among the kinfolk of the bride: twenty go to the immediate family—her father, her mother, her father's oldest son, and her mother's son (two are dedicated to the ghosts of her father's ancestors and two to her mother's, and these cattle are kept in a place of honor in the family corral); ten are distributed to more distant kin on her father's side: her father's mother, father, sons by another wife, and full brothers and sisters; and ten are distributed to her mother's side: her mother's parents, sons, and full brothers and sisters.

The actual distribution of these cattle is the subject of lengthy negotiations on both sides. The young man has to get his own kin to stake him in

Figure 9.13 Nuer bridewealth distribution among the bride's kin.

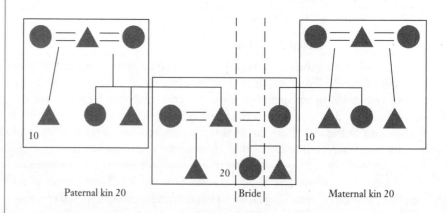

Paternal kin 20 | Bride | Maternal kin 20

approximately the same proportions as they would receive cattle for his full sister. This means he has to visit each individual personally and beg his or her favor. On the bride's side, the actual distribution has to be agreed upon. If any rightful recipient is deceased, the next of kin has a claim.

The betrothal and the bestowal of cattle take place at a big feast with much dancing. At this ceremony, about half the cattle are actually handed over to the bride's kin in order of seniority. These cattle have to be given or the couple is not allowed to consummate the marriage. Afterward, the young man and his bride sleep in a nuptial hut, but the bride remains in the household of her father and is not transferred to her husband's home until after she has had a child and the rest of the bridewealth has been paid. She is under tremendous pressure to have a child, for if within a year or two she does not, the marriage is dissolved and the cattle have to be returned. Shamans (medicine men) make great reputations for themselves in Nuerland for curing cases of barrenness.

Village Residential Composition and Bridewealth

Through the Nuer marriage system, brides ideally move from their home villages to new ones, while cattle are dispersed into their fathers' villages and those of their mothers' kin, and wives with new babies move to their husband's villages. That is the ideal picture, but from the perspective of the adult householders, it is advantageous to keep as many brides and cattle as possible in the village. The mark of a skilled marriage broker in Nuerland—someone who negotiates his own marriages and those of his grown offspring, nieces, and nephews—is that he is able to parlay these marriages into the nucleus of a village settlement whose residents are in his debt.

Such a man becomes the informal leader, the **"bull" of the Nuer village;** he need not belong to the aristocratic lineage that holds title to the section, nor, of course, to that lineage's clan, which holds title to the tribe's (clan's) territory. A "bull" must make sure, however, that an aristocratic householder continues to reside in the district, since all rely on his sacred spear in battle. For example, an analysis of the composition of Konye village in Figure 9.14 reveals that every household is linked with that of one elder, Rue (number 8).

To the right of the chart you may see that two senior householders (numbers 9 and 3) are the sons of Rue's mother's brother. They thus had a claim on the bridewealth paid for Rue's sisters. Then there are a cluster of Rue's in-laws, some of whom must have received bridewealth for Rue's two wives. Thus householder number 11 is Rue's second wife's maternal half-brother, a man with a legal stake in her bridewealth. Householder number 10 is her grandfather's sister's son, a man who might well have claimed a share of that

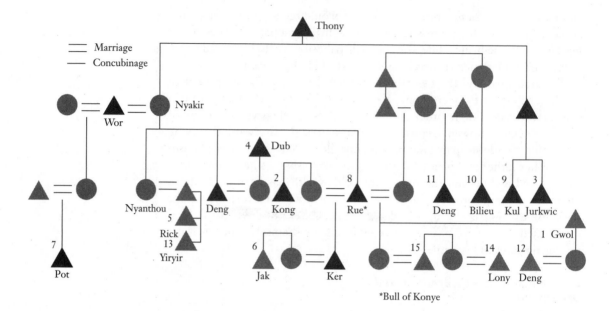

*Bull of Konye

*Figure 9.14 Chart of
Konye Village kinship.*

bridewealth. Householder number 2 is Rue's first wife's brother, a beneficiary of his first bridewealth distribution.

Householder number 4 is Rue's brother's father-in-law, and Rue helped
pay for this man's daughter. Householders numbers 5 and 13 are the brothers
of Rue's sister's husband and helped pay Rue bridewealth for her in the past.

In the descending generation, householder number 7 is Rue's paternal
half-sister's son, and Rue was obliged to help him marry his several wives.
(He is the most polygamous householder in the village.) Rue has one married
son living in his household. The brother of this son's wife has his own household, number 6. He was a prime claimant of his sister's bridewealth. Finally,
there is the household of Rue's one son-in-law, a man who received Rue's
daughter, gave cattle for her, and still came to live near his father-in-law.

In sum, all the households of the village are related to Rue through marriage and bridewealth payments. Rue has had a hand in all the negotiations
and residence decisions as well.

Marriage exchange thus can provide the means for populating villages
in apparent disregard of the principles mapping segmentary lineages on
settlements.

Justice Through Bloodwealth

A mechanism borrowed from marriage exchange, wealth, in the form of
bloodwealth, is the means for keeping the peace among those Nuer who cannot rally allies, those belonging to adjacent sections. Likewise those in the

larger tribal territory who would rather not fight a fellow clansman or unrelated neighbor by force of arms have this same means of resolving disputes within a tribe and the territory of its clan. Nuer justice works by a simple mechanism: levying bloodwealth upon the kinsmen of offenders and then converting this bloodwealth into bridewealth to marry a woman to the ghost of the homicide victim.

As mentioned earlier, within each circle of villages that gets up a war party together, the lower-level section/community has a householder known as the leopard-skin chief, named after the leopard skin he is entitled to wear. He is not a member of the aristocratic lineage that owns the community and is usually an outsider with no kin in the district.

The Nuer quarrel frequently, and their quarrels sometimes end in murder. Evans-Pritchard did not do a criminological survey, but he leaves the impression that most homicides involve young unmarried men, usually from neighboring villages. These are footloose individuals, roaming in search of women to court. They are also cattle herders.

A leopard-skin chief.

Let us say that two such youths meet and quarrel over a cow or a woman or both, that tempers flare, and that one suddenly runs the other through with his spear. The murderer flees at once to the homestead of a leopard-skin chief and takes asylum there. No avengers may violate this sanctuary, although certainly they shall soon lay wait outside and keep their enemy penned in his new lodgings. The chief first lets blood from the murderer's arm, in a rite of purification. Next, the murderer presents his host with a steer, a ram, or a he-goat for sacrifice, and the chief slays the male animal, a symbol of the recent murder.

The chief waits for the aggrieved parties' tempers to subside, usually until after the funeral. In the meantime, he visits the kinfolk of the refugee to sound them out on how to make a blood payment. Sometime later, he pays a formal call on the parents of the deceased to discuss the possibility of compensation. These first efforts are usually rudely rejected out of hand by the victim's kin, who haughtily (and with some reason) say that no herd of cattle will ever bring their son back to life, nor can cattle ever be the equivalent of a man.

If the aggrieved delay too long, the chief can threaten them with his curse. At the same time, he cultivates their more distant kin; not having any claim on the blood payment, they do not have to swallow their pride by accepting it and can assume a more reasonable view. Finally, the amount of bloodwealth is set: from forty to fifty head of cattle.

These cattle are not handed over all at once, but an initial payment of some twenty is made. When that is done, the slayer can emerge from his asylum, although it is best for him to lie low and avoid his enemies for some time to come. It is prudent to remain out of their sight until the last of the bloodwealth has been transferred. Even then, the slayer still risks attack until after a child has been born to his victim. What has happened is a repetition of the pattern of marriage exchange, but in a very different context.

The family of the victim immediately puts their new wealth to use to pay for a bride to marry the deceased in a Nuer "ghost marriage." A young woman goes through a marriage by proxy to the symbols of the deceased; but since no one can really marry a ghost, the brother of the deceased takes the bride to bed. While the leopard-skin chief negotiates, it is the victim's brother who stands most to gain from the affair, for the payment can stake him to bridewealth free and clear from any debt to his own relatives. Just as clearly, his lack of interest in revenge can be misinterpreted as cowardice, so it has to be distant relatives and not the leopard-skin chief who persuade him to accept. It is true that the new wife and her children are in name the wife and children of the dead man; but over the years that title can be of little inconvenience to the dead man's beneficiary, his brother.

As for justice, we obviously have come a distance from the "safety valve" duels of the Tiwi. With the Nuer, a third party, the leopard-skin chief, serves as mediator. He also has the power to put a curse on recalcitrants. One could argue that the murderer is not punished. True, he is not executed and does not serve time in prison, the punishments we are accustomed to. But consider that he has to languish for months in confinement in the leopard-skin chief's asylum and that the blood payment is roughly the same amount of cattle that he might have counted on for his own bridal payments, thereby diminishing or at least delaying his chances of marrying. From the point of view of the relatives of the victim, by using the bloodwealth as bridewealth, they have been compensated in the only meaningful way—an opportunity to replace the deceased, not with a herd of cattle, but with a child raised in his memory. Among the Nuer, justice is totally phrased in the idiom of kinship.

Nuer Counterbalances

The Nuer system illustrates the limits to which a culture can push kinship. Warfare and alliances are shaped by the segmentary lineage system and are only secondarily political. The Nuer kinship terminology and marital exchange system are highly individualistic. Couples may court each other freely, provided they avoid their individually named cousins on either side. When the marriage is consummated, four lineages must agree to it, so that all the kin in the couple's maternal and paternal lines are parties to the transfer of bridewealth. Terminology and practice here coincide; heads of cattle are turned over with precision to specified relatives.

The segmentary lineage system also appears to be very individualistic. It seems to spawn individual lineages from every male descendant of the original Nuer. But such an ideal system could begin to work only if residence were patrilocal, and we have seen that it is not. Residence patterns are often neolocal as people respond to the manipulations of a prominent marriage broker, the bull, and move to his attractive village. Thus, the segmentary lineage system and the residence system do *not* coincide in a perfect fit.

The Nuer overtly model their territorial divisions on an ideal statement of somebody's genealogy, and therein lies the synchronization of the tribal system and the descent system. The segmentary lineage system does shape community form in Nuerland by providing for the symbolic identity of the community proper, which is recognizable in the group of villages that unite in a war party. In order to do so, they must have at least one aristocrat of the clan who owns the clan territory identified with the tribe and who wields his sacred spear. The genealogy of the tribe and, in a sense, its political charter are that of the aristocrat and his clan.

The kinship system, through segmentary lineages and complementary opposition, gives the Nuer a clear language for effectively uniting and acting upon their environment.

SUMMARY AND CONCLUSIONS

Tribal cultures have taken the institution of kinship and used it to model their communities while developing family and kinship ties in the process. They have used residence rules to recruit people to local communities and, often, to settle them around one hearth in an extended family household, either matrilocal or patrilocal. They do so in the first place to respond to the pressures of increased population, of the necessity of dealing with neighboring groups, and with the need to organize themselves in response to more intense exploitation of natural resources, usually in horticulture and animal husbandry.

Each of the household forms we have considered is a set of individuals bonded and interacting together in an enterprise that has as its object the production and bringing to maturity of new human beings. At maturity new young people must be affiliated with their kin, and they must seek marriage partners as they join a household of procreation.

Marriage is an exchange—first, of the two partners who give each other themselves, and second, for their two families of orientation who exchange two offspring. Marriage exchange often brings with it the exchange of services. Among the Nuer, marriage requires an exchange of bridewealth, at least forty head of cattle staked by the young husband's paternal and maternal kin groups, and not fully delivered until after the bride has given birth to a child. In all cases, people generally reject the notion that a spouse is being "purchased"; rather, they are concerned that a balanced, fair exchange of values exist between the partners and between the kin groups from which they come.

The puzzle of preferential cousin marriage can be explained as an attempt to provide for regular marriage exchange between two descent groups in perpetuity through the generations.

Descent groups represent attempts to classify people according to a conceptual order that human beings have imposed on the potentially wide-branching trees of ancestry that each person might have. Societies and cultures with a bilateral kinship, such as our own and the Eskimo, conceive of that ancestral tree in the broadest terms and delineate overlapping and not hard-and-fast groupings, *kindreds*, by classifying all the persons who might have descended from a given ancestor, or all the persons who are related to ego.

Other descent groups specify particular ancestral lines and classify the living by only these ancestors. One may belong, then, to a matrilineal or patrilineal lineage, whose founding ancestor is said to be a known historical person, or to a matrilineal or patrilineal clan, whose founding ancestor is a dim legendary figure.

The rules for household and descent group membership form one feature of *kinship systems*. These are codes, present in each human culture, formed by the interrelations of incest tabus, kin terminology, marriage rules, and residence decisions, as well as rules for descent groups. They are a special form of language, regulating our extraction of matter and energy from the environment, in terms of how we relate ourselves to *relatives*, persons connected to us through marriage or descent.

Classifying people into descent groups can be a convenient way for a tribal society to begin to handle alliances, warfare, and, to a lesser extent, settlement. Segmentary lineages can classify people, in native theory, over wide areas according to their place in a branching system of lineages, all related in lines that lead to a single ancestor.

In a sense, the segmentary lineage system is like a legal framework, a constitution, and complementary opposition, like elections and majority rule, is an ideal process that makes the system work. That is to say that when societies develop, human beings bring to conscious awareness the conditions of their own existence. We, sophisticated and literate heirs to almost 5,000 years of civilization, have such a model in our constitutions and law codes. But law and law codes only emerge slowly; a code of conduct and organization based on kinship emerges first. Kinship, like law, is a special form of language. But all language can only provide a blueprint. Like genotype, the ideal blueprint of the genetic code implicit in our genes, and phenotype, the actual manifestation of that code in our persons, any blueprint is never the equivalent of its product. Genetic codes, kinship systems, and ultimately law codes remain only a framework. The reality is an outcome of the blueprint interacting with matter, energy, and activities to produce genotypes in the case of the biological individual, and specific cultures in the case of the Nuer system we have examined here.

We may also conclude that when a society as large as the Nuer, composed of so many people and so many settlements, attempts to model itself on a descent system, the effort must end up as an **ideology,** a system of belief that explains the status quo and justifies it, while obscuring or even hiding some of its real features.

Thus, the individualism inherent in the Sudanese kinship systems and the complementary opposition inherent in the segmentary lineage system provide an ideological framework for Nuer culture and community. The kinship terminology, the marriage exchange, the shifting residence patterns, and the justice through ghost marriage all reflect these principles.

Descent groups provide the framework for the territories and for allegiances. Yet the broader framework of Nuer culture is the community, which can never be completely assimilated under the kinship model. That is so, basically, because Nuer kinship is exogamous—Nuer are required to marry beyond both their father's and their mother's kin. The blueprint itself is contradictory.

The individualism that pervades the Nuer kinship terminology, marriage system, and distribution of bridewealth is channeled by the segmentary lineage system and its mechanisms of complementary opposition. These, in turn, also operate within the section/community, by explicitly political means. This individualism also contradicts the ideal segmentary lineage blueprint. Every aristocratic man of the spear is countered, balanced, or complementarily opposed by a number of other men from other lineages: The bull's marriage exchange influence puts him on a par with the owner of the spear. The man of cattle conducts the male initiation rites. The leopard-skin chief resolves disputes between lineages within the section and the tribal territory of the aristocratic clan, using the same skills that a marriage negotiator does, since the resolution of a homicide requires a repetition of the exchange pattern of marriage.

The community framework reflects the three levels of human territoriality: local villages, built up by marriage exchanges in disregard of the segmentary principle; the community proper or section, which assembles in a war party and declares itself in collective male initiations every four years; and foreign relations with other communities, which is completely regulated by segmentary allegiances and complementary opposition.

But in some ways the Nuer have it right. The broader community *is* much more than the section. At times the primary section—alliances of several sections—is activated for warfare; at other times it is the entire tribe, all the sections inhabiting the territory vested in its aristocratic clan. Occasionally all Nuerland may be swept into war against an outsider under the leadership of a prophet. The view from the section, then, sees all outsider Nuer as potential friends, but they are just as likely to be enemies. Nuerland divides at any one time, then, into circles of friends and enemies. The latter are also part of the wider community.

One's enemies include other Nuer, but complementary opposition and bloodwealth payments (and subsequent marriage feasts) provide a means to transform former Nuer enemies into friends and allies—rather quickly when a common enemy is perceived.

Few cultures push kinship as far as the Nuer, but then few have found their kinship system to have been so terribly advantageous in the constant warfare with neighbors that is a characteristic of all tribal societies. Let us take up that warfare itself in the next chapter.

SUGGESTED READINGS

Beidelman, T. O. *The Kaguru: A Matrilineal People of East Africa*. Prospect Heights, Ill.: Waveland Press, 1983. A general ethnography, with careful attention to the kinship system.

Deng, Francis Mading. *The Dinka of the Sudan*. Prospect Heights, Ill.: Waveland Press, 1984. A readable account of his people written by a Dinka anthropologist.

Evans-Pritchard, E. E. *The Nuer*. Oxford: Clarendon Press, 1940. Written with a stiff upper lip, this book makes better sense if read along with Evans-Pritchard's *Kinship and Marriage Among the Nuer*, but still a classic.

Fox, Robin. *Kinship and Marriage: An Anthropological Perspective*. Baltimore: Penguin Books, 1967. Readable and thorough.

Kelly, Raymond C. *The Nuer Conquest: The Structure and Development of an Expansionist System*. Ann Arbor: University of Michigan Press, 1985. Despite turgid academic prose, the author's argument remains fascinating. This reading might be appropriate for researching a term paper.

Lomnitz, Larissa, and Marisol A. Perez-Lizaur. *A Mexican Elite Family, 1820–1980: Kinship, Class, and Culture*. Princeton, N.J.: Princeton University Press, 1988. A splendid ethnography of an ancestor-oriented kindred in an upper-class Western setting.

Neville, Gwen Kennedy. *Pilgrimage and Kinship: Rituals of Reunion in American Protestant Culture*. New York: Oxford University Press, 1987. A fascinating account of the symbols and rituals of the kinship system among Protestant Americans.

GLOSSARY

ambilineal, omnilineal, or nonunilineal descent Reckoning descent from the founding ancestor in *both* male and female lines. Such a descent group, if it forms itself to hold property or even celebrate family reunions honoring the founding ancestors, is called an *ancestor-oriented kindred.*

apical ancestor The ancestor "at the apex" from whom descent is calculated. Apical ancestors may be known, historical individuals (in the case of lineages) or mythical (in the case of clans).

bilateral descent The recognition of descent in both maternal and paternal lines and, by extension, in the maternal and paternal lines of *every ancestor.* Ego's ancestry is seen as a giant tree branching in all directions.

"bull" of the Nuer village A skilled marriage broker who negotiates his own marriages and those of his grown offspring, nieces, and nephews into the nucleus of a village settlement whose residents are in his debt. The informal leader of the community.

clan A group of persons who claim to have descended from an apical ancestor whose exact genealogical relation to them is unknown.

complementary opposition The principle whereby shifting alliances are formed in a segmentary lineage system such as the Nuer's. One allies with closer kinsmen against more distant ones. For example, if a first cousin (father's brother's son) is attacked by a second cousin (grandfather's brother's grandson), ego rallies to the first cousin. But if the enemy second cousin is attacked by a third cousin, yet more distant kin, then first and second cousins rally to the former enemy's defense.

cross-cousin A father's sister's child or mother's brother's child—that is, a cousin related to you through a parent of the opposite sex from your parent. This distinction is important in many kinship terminologies, a subset of every language.

Eskimoan terminologies Systems of linguistic classification of kinpersons in which cousins are differentiated from siblings but cross-cousins and parallel cousins are not distinguished; associated with generalized marriage exchange.

ideology A system of belief that explains the status quo and justifies it, while obscuring or even hiding some of its real features. The Nuer segmentary lineage system explains their pattern of warfare but hides the fact that most people in particular communities may not belong to the lineage that "owns" that community.

Iroquoian terminologies Systems of linguistic classification of kinpersons in which parallel cousins are lumped with siblings and the word for cross-cousin also means spouse; associated with cross-cousin marriage.

kindred Groups potentially present in systems with bilateral descent. *Ancestor-oriented* kindreds unite people descended from an ancestor in all lines, usually because they share in a common property inheritance. *Ego-oriented* kindreds may unite people on both sides around a living person, often to help against some external challenge.

kinship systems Codes, present in each human culture, formed by the interrelations of marriage rules, incest tabus, kin terminology, residence decisions, and rules for household and descent group membership. They are a special form of language, regulating our extraction of matter and energy from the environment, in terms of how we relate ourselves to *relatives*, persons connected to us through marriage or descent.

kinship terminology A set of words in all human spoken languages naming specific kin relations through descent, marriage, or adoption. No spoken language recognizes all possible terms. Anthropologists classify specific types of kinship terminologies according to how each recognizes cousins. In our own, Eskimoan type, all cousins on both sides are lumped in the same term.

leopard-skin chief Among the Nuer, an outsider householder who gives a local murderer asylum in his house and negotiates a bloodwealth payment from the culprit's kin to the victim's kin. He stands as a ritual mediator between plaintiff (the victim's kinfolk) and defendant (the culprit).

lineage A group of persons calculating descent in a single line from a known apical ancestor.

"man of cattle" Among the Nuer, the ritual expert who has the duty of initiating adolescent boys into their age grade. The man of cattle always belongs to an outside lineage, not the one that owns the section. He is one of several essential, informal leaders at the level of the local community.

"man of the spear" Among the Nuer, the aristocrat of the clan who "owns" the clan-territory and displays the sacred spear of the clan. The genealogy of the clan-territory and, in a sense, its political charter are that of the aristocrat and his kinsmen.

marriage exchange For the partners, the mutual gift of themselves to each other. For their households of orientation, possibly the exchange of one of their offspring as a spouse for another of their offspring. *Generalized* marriage exchange is the condition of marriage partners selecting each other at will, without the obligation of paying back partners to particular households of orientation, associated with Eskimoan kinship.

matrilineal descent Tracing descent through the female line from an apical ancestress. Men in a matrilineal society belong to the lineages and clans of their mothers; a man's son belongs to the man's wife's group.

matrilocal extended family household A family unit extended by importing, usually, husbands for the daughters of the family; the sons marry out.

mesolithic period The settling down of human beings into villages and fairly dense populations near a natural food resource, which happened around 15,000 to 8,000 years ago in widely different places around the world.

neolithic transition The appearance of domesticated plants and animals, cultivated and kept carefully by horticulturalists and herders in settled communities. This first occurred around 10,000 to 4,000 years ago in different places in the world. The tribal level of culture and community could be, more or less correctly, referred to as neolithic.

parallel cousin A father's brother's child or mother's sister's child; a cousin related to you through a parent of the same sex as your parent. This distinction is important in many kinship terminologies, a subset of every language.

patrilineal descent Tracing descent through the male line. A man then belongs to his father's lineage and clan, as does the man's own son.

patrilocal extended family household A family unit extended along the lower generation by importing brides to the sons of the household. Daughters marry out and leave home.

preferential cross-cousin marriage The moral expectation that one shall marry a cross-cousin; associated with Iroquoian terminologies in which parallel cousins are lumped with siblings and the word for cross-cousin also means spouse.

segmentary lineage A system of descent found among some tribal peoples. The Nuer are an example. A segmentary genealogy is a system of symmetrical segments, as if every great ancestor had begotten two sons, who in turn begot two sons, each patriline then dividing in two each generation.

Sudanese kinship A rare type of kinship terminology. It does not lump any kind of cousin with any other kind. On the ascending generation, distinct terms are used for each kind of relative. Thus, there are sixteen separate terms for each relative in these two generations. The Nuer are one of seven known examples, as are the Bedawin.

tribal community A kind of organization that revolves around local communities, themselves composed of households, camps, neighborhoods, or other divisions in settlements. These units in turn make alliances with other units for purposes of trade and war. The alliances are often highly volatile and shifting.

tribe In common speech, a tribe refers to a people who assume common descent, speak the same language, and share a common culture. In anthropology, tribal peoples are above the evolutionary level of the band and below that of civilization. They have denser populations and richer food resources than band hunters and gatherers, but lack the urban settlements and state politics of civilizations.

unilineal descent The practice of calculating descent in a single line from an apical ancestor, characteristic of lineages and clans.

Tribal Warfare Complexes:

Aggressive Sequences and Balanced Negative Exchanges

*AGGRESSIVE SEQUENCES AND
HUMAN ACTIVITY CYCLES*

*CHIMPANZEE AGGRESSIVE
SEQUENCES AND CHIMPANZEE
WARFARE*

Chimpanzee Aggressive Sequences

Chimpanzee Warfare

*SOCIAL DRAMA: AGGRESSIVE
SEQUENCES IN BAND SOCIETY*

TRIBAL WARFARE

The Phases of Conflict Theory

The Problem of the Score in Tribal Warfare: Losses and Trophies

*ETHNOGRAPHIC CLOSE-UP: THE
TUPINAMBÁ AND THEIR WARFARE*

Phase One: Mobilizing for a Campaign

Phase Two: An Allied War Party Seeks to Attack

Phase Three: The Raid—Armed Struggle

Phase Four: Symbolic Victory: The Treatment of Captives

Climax of This Round: A Cannibalistic Feast

The Executioner's Own Rite of Passage

The Meaning of the Executioner's Rite

*THE WARFARE COMPLEX AS BLOOD
FEUD: NO TRUE REDRESS AND NO
TRUE OUTCOME OR RESOLUTION*

Conflict as a Bonding Mechanism

Conflict as Repulsion: A Spacing Mechanism

*WARFARE AS POSITIVE EXCHANGE:
ALLIANCE FEASTING*

*I*n the previous chapter we saw that among the Nuer regional integration occurs through the activation of macrocommunities as circles of alliances and counteralliances. This process occurs because a principal result of the condensation of the human species in place—that is, of the transition to tribal communities—is that flight from anger and quarrels is much less easy. Consequently, human bonding—alliances—is intensified.

The tribal world tends, then, toward coalescences of **macrocommunities,** which comprise clusters of separate communities that unite to mount specific expeditions for warfare (or for trade and feasting, as we shall see in the next chapter) *and* their rival cluster of opposing communities. The two rivals are thrown into competition for a time. Each has peripheral allies and rivals not involved in this particular combat, but the activated circle of warfare is what I call the macrocommunity.

The most important characteristic of macrocommunities is not so much their internal organization as their external poise, their constant striving toward balanced reciprocity with their neighbors. Thus, the model of complementary opposition discussed for the Nuer warfare patterns is really a model for deadlock. As soon as one contender or community has a chance of winning (that is, overpowering or even annihilating the opponent), some more distant ally enters on the side of its opponent. Allies are found, sides are balanced, and old enemies are enlisted against some more distant and common enemy (and forgiven their old offenses, through the payment of bloodwealth, in the new common cause). The upshot is that no particular warring Nuer community ever wins very much from other Nuer communities.

Before examining the sequences of a particular tribal warfare complex, let us discuss some of the theoretical bases for analyzing and understanding primitive warfare.

AGGRESSIVE SEQUENCES AND HUMAN ACTIVITY CYCLES

In Chapter 5 we emphasized that human beings, like all living creatures, engage in a characteristic array of activities or actions to process matter and energy, propelled by momentum. These activities form cycles; they go through a "round," then start the same sequence of activities over again. We commonly think of daily rounds of sleeping, eating, working, playing, and so on, but what of competing, potentially escalating into fighting? Is *that* a necessary part of kinetic cycles processing matter and energy, propelled by momentum? The answer is an emphatic *yes*.

Any interacting, breeding population of living beings needs mechanisms to space itself out in relation to its resources. Among primates, for example, an individual of a solitary species typically defends its range against other individuals, except during the mating season, when necessarily couples of opposite sex come together. Primate species with multimale groups, which include human beings, likewise have to find ways to internally space the group out in relation to its resources, as well as to lay claim to a given territory for the entire group against the claims of other groups. (Remember that *H. sapiens* combines the multimale group with male-female bonded pairs and is thus unique among primates.)

The mechanism for ensuring this spacing of the group in relation to its resources is *dominance-status competition*, which follows a regular sequence of activities, learned in juvenile play groups and then applied with deadly seriousness in adult life. The sequence is one that is genetically programmed as a potential. Animals feel a response that very much resembles anger when they are impeded by another animal from getting something they want. The ability of animals to then go on and confront their rival and compete to get what they want is at least partly learned, and is constantly reinforced by success in the life histories of the more dominant individuals.

In this chapter we shall examine the nature of aggressive sequences as evidenced in primate ethology. Then we shall see how quite similar activities, with a much greater emphasis on coalition and third-party mediation, are built up among tribal communities. In all these cases, the activity cycle of agonistic, or aggressive, behavior differs from the usual activity cycles of food extraction, while it is linked with those of play, leisure, and storytelling. Sequences of aggressive behavior function *internally*, to space individuals out in relation to each other and to their resources. Let us see how this occurs among chimpanzees.

CHIMPANZEE AGGRESSIVE SEQUENCES AND CHIMPANZEE WARFARE

Recall from Chapter 2 that chimpanzee communities or troops are characterized by dominance hierarchies of adult males. These hierarchies are stable over seasonal and yearly rounds and are the outcome of many weekly or even daily "dominance competitions" among adult males, especially young subadult males coming of age, who are vying to take their place in the hierarchy. The dominance competitions most often occur in the presence of a sexually attractive female and hence regulate access to her among the males.

Chimpanzee Aggressive Sequences

These dominance competitions take the form of a sequence of aggressive behavior between two males. However, a male may enter a competition with one or more males allied at his side in a *coalition* against his rival. The **aggressive sequence** consists of the following actions: *threat, attack, defense, escape, appeasement,* and *reassurance.* (I have changed the order of Jane Goodall's [1986] sequence, putting threat first, rather than attack.) To threaten is to "display," that is, to put on a show of one's strength and potential fighting ability. Similarly, attack and defense may largely be "displays" rather than actual physical combat. But they may also be violent encounters using hands, feet, teeth, and body weight.

Two or more male chimpanzees, especially brothers who have grown up together in the company of their mother, may bond into a tight coalition. As

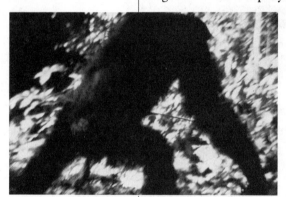

a pair they always either challenge others together or defend themselves from others as a pair (or, possibly, a triad). They may achieve higher dominance than they would otherwise. One of them, however, is usually the more dominant partner.

More-dominant males will sometimes take on the role of a third party in dominance competitions and break them up. This is especially true of the *alpha* or number one male of a troop. He will intervene in a dispute by charging or threatening the disputants, driving them away from the scene of their confrontation. This intervention may be

A chimpanzee in display mode.

"even-handed," or it may favor the side of one or another of the combatants (Boehm, 1992).

According to Goodall (1986), a stable dominance hierarchy has obvious benefits for both more and less dominant males, because over the short run it works to suppress "serious fighting" but not "aggressive interactions and displaying" as adult males vie for access to a scarce resource—females in heat—or simply for higher dominance status.

If we examine chimpanzee dominance competitions with their sequential phases, we can come to realize that they, paradoxically, are *bonding mechanisms* within the group, while representing mechanisms of repulsion outside it. This aggressive sequence, then, both repels and attracts. Attraction is confirmed in the final actions of *appeasement* and *reassurance.* Thus, a vanquished animal may present his hindquarters as if for mounting, in a gesture of appeasement. The victor may then embrace the former rival in a gesture of reassurance. Immediately thereafter the loser is likely to groom the victor, who may respond by grooming his subordinate, but for shorter intervals than the former grooms him.

Chimpanzee Warfare

When chimpanzee adult males venture into territory overlapping with the range of a neighboring community, and especially if they venture into the core range of another troop, they go on *patrol*. That is, these noisy animals suddenly fall totally silent and proceed with stealth, taking care not to make noise as they tread over vegetation. If they encounter a young stranger female, they may recruit her back into their core territory (where, however, she may well be attacked by the resident adult females). If they encounter adult male strangers, they threaten them, and if these males are alone, they may attack them.

In 1972, during Jane Goodall's extended research at Gombe stream reserve, it became evident that the chimpanzee community she was studying was splitting into two. That is, a group of adult males were spending more and more of their time in the southern part of the wider community range, accompanied by numbers of adult females and their offspring. Similarly, another group of adult males were spending most of their time in the northern part of that range. By the end of the year the process was complete. Individuals from the two groups now avoided each other.

Chimpanzee males on patrol.

Early in 1974, Goodall's research team observed the first of a series of attacks by patrols from the northern or *Kasakela community* against individuals of the southern or *Kahama community*. (Since the chimpanzees lack speech, these names are of course the invention of the human researchers.) By November 1977 these northern patrols had caused the deaths of *all the adult males* of the southern community, and in early 1978 the victorious Kasakela males began to sleep in the former home range of their defunct enemies. Shortly thereafter, they retreated, yielding half the territory gained to yet a third troop, the more southerly *Kalande community*.

Goodall's descriptions of the attacks make depressing reading. In brief, when a northern patrol would come upon a solitary southerner, the group would attack, with the most dominant animal in the lead. They would pin the animal on the ground, sometimes lifting him up and throwing him down again with great fury. One attacker would often hold the victim down while other attackers would run about and display furiously, then rush forward to bite, stamp on, and wrest and twist the limbs of the victim, who at this point never offered any resistance, but lay limp and inert to a painful fate. The attackers would tear off strips of flesh, break bones, and inflict severe wounds. The victims survived the attacks, but most died soon after.

This astonishing warfare episode was carried out with systematic thoroughness. One young adult female of the defunct community transferred into the victorious one. Other young females may have transferred to the community further south. With these exceptions, the entire Kahama community was annihilated and its range taken over, in a series of attacks that certainly seemed intentional. Lacking speech, the attacking community somehow communicated an awareness of its purpose among its members. What is extraordinary to human observers, however, is that the victim community never retaliated. The Kahama males never joined forces to fight back. Perhaps what was needed was for them to have formed patrols. They were always encountered alone, or, if in the company of others, they were taken by surprise before they could form a counterpatrol.

If we analyze this aggressive episode, we see that in the sequence of threat, attack, defense, escape, appeasement, and reassurance, *threat* and *attack* were carried out. Moreover, the victims invariably tried to *appease* their foes, who paid no attention to their submissive postures but continued the attack. We should substitute *injuries causing death* for *escape*.

To summarize for chimpanzees, then, they space themselves out within the troop by means of dominance-status competitions, which may be mediated by a more dominant third party, often the *alpha* male, in the interest of containing conflict. These same animals, arrayed as a patrol, then act as a coalition to defend the group's territory against other groups and, in some cases, to take territory from others. Aggressive sequences are thus a kinetic cycle that works on the social order, as well as directly on the environment in the case of competition for community territory.

SOCIAL DRAMA: AGGRESSIVE SEQUENCES IN BAND SOCIETY

We saw in Chapter 5 that **social drama** is a model for agonistic or aggressive sequences among human beings at the band level. The sequences are clearly based on primate potentials and include the following steps: anger or grievance, breach of the peace or encounter, confrontation, violence and/or redressive action, flight and/or reconciliation (see Figure 10.1).

Because humans use speech freely, the encounter and confrontation stages can themselves be sequenced in particular cultural patterns. For example, among the !Kung San a quarrel between two men starts with angry verbal accusations and threats. This then escalates to "bad words," insults, usually graphically sexual in nature, that cannot be ignored and require some retaliation—if only verbal—from their target. "Bad words" can lead to hand-to-hand physical combat with blows, which can, finally, escalate to hurling spears at each other. The last phase may end in homicide, or in flight by one or both combatants. At any time during this potential escalation, the "court of public opinion" can intervene as bystanders noisily discuss the merits of the dispute in a palaver.

Third-party intervention, then, is a mechanism to restore order by invoking outsiders to a dispute, on either one or the other side, or as neutral mediators. It is the basis on which judges and courts arise—remember the leopard-skin chief in Chapter 9.

In tribal society the model of aggressive sequences becomes rather more complicated, because it is generated by alliances or coalitions, rather than merely individual activity—although individuals may activate the coalitions. This situation produces yet another model of aggression, if closely related to the previous ones. That is to say, instead of social dramas, contained and worked out by the immediate network of actors, in tribal society we have *conflict* escalating and drawing in whole groups against other groups.

TRIBAL WARFARE

Tribal communities define themselves through a pattern of shifting alliances among local groups. Any given local group is always allied with others in order to make war against a similar alliance. We can understand the nature of this pattern, which not only shifts in space but has variable rhythms in time, through a theory of the phases of conflict.

The Phases of Conflict Theory

The phase model of conflict and competition, devised by Swartz, Turner, and Tuden (1966), is very relevant to the macrocommunities of tribal societies. It closely resembles the sequences of chimpanzee aggression and of band-level social drama but differs in that the principal units of action are *coalitions*—alliances of pairs or groups of persons (see Figure 10.2).

In the first stage of the model, a political contender (presumably a leader or would-be leader) *mobilizes political capital;* that is, he rallies his followers and supporters and seeks new ones, often by suborning the followers of an unwary opponent. Such a competitor has some end in view—the control of an office or territory or simply the desire to score.

The second stage is the **encounter** or **showdown:** the competitor precipitates a crisis with his opponent by a breach of the peace, a challenge that

Chimpanzee aggressive sequence (with gestures, no speech)	Human social drama (with gestures and speech)
	1. Encounter/ breach of peace
1. Threat	2. Anger/grievance
2. Attack	3. Confrontation
3. Defense	4. Violence
Intervention of more-dominant third party (at any stage)	Redressive action: palaver (at any stage)
4. Escape	5. Flight
5. Appeasement	6. Reconciliation
6. Reassurance	

Figure 10.1 Chimpanzee aggressive sequence compared to human social drama.

Chimpanzee aggressive sequence	Conflict phases
	Phase 1: Mobilization of political capital *Example:* A wants to move against B A mobilizes his allies: A\CDEF
1. Threat	Phase 2: Encounter or showdown *Example:* A challenges B, and lets him know his strength
2. Attack	Phase 3: Crisis
3. Defense	*Example:*
4. Escape	The two rivals and their allies square off: A\CDEF vs. B\GHIJ and do battle One side may judge it hopeless, and flee Phase 4: Countervailing tendencies *Example:* The rival mobilizes his allies: B\GHIJ
5. Appeasement	Phase 5: Redressive mechanisms *Example:* A\CDEF vs. B\GHIJ AB\X (X is the neutral third party)
6. Reassurance	Phase 6: Restoration of the peace Either escape and permanent flight *Example:* A\CDEF (B\GHIJ has fled) *or* Victory and dominance of one side *Example:* A\CDEFBGHIJ (the rank order may be shuffled in the outcome) *or* A\CDEF B \GHIJ (hierarchy of hierarchies)

Figure 10.2 Chimpanzee aggressive sequence compared to the phases of human conflict.

throws opposing forces into relief. Obviously, timing and secrecy are important here, so as to catch the competitor off guard and gain some early advantage.

The third stage is the period of **crisis** itself in which opposing forces are marshaled. This stage may be fought out on the battlefield, as with the Nuer, or it may find expression in angry discussion in public places.

The fourth stage involves **countervailing tendencies,** such as tacit "sizing up" of each other's forces. That is to say, the rival rallies his own allies, which may enter the conflict on his side. So, too, among the Nuer do erstwhile enemies rally to sections threatened by more-distant common enemies. Here and elsewhere cross-cutting ties mean that allegiances are diffused and are not held exclusively or for very long.

The encounter may escalate into full-scale *warfare.* However, the next period can follow or precede the battle. It is the period of **redress,** or *deployment of redressive mechanisms,* such as outright negotiation in the tribal confederacy's council house or use of the good offices of a mediator such as the leopard-skin chief, who acts to restrain both parties within the Nuer section.

Finally, there is the stage of **resolution,** or *restoration of the peace.* The crisis has been resolved. This can mean the defeat and routing of one contender, in the form of death or exile. However, because of countervailing tendencies and the ability to garner ever more allies, this outcome is probably less usual than the balanced award of resources or honors to both competitors.

The Problem of the Score in Tribal Warfare: Losses and Trophies

This brings us to the very nature of the "score" in tribal warfare. The **score** may be merely a balancing out of losses. When the other side loses, the rival "wins" in this philosophy. It is evident that tribal societies inflict all sorts of losses on each other in warfare. Booty is taken. But in the absence of effective means of transport and food preservation, actual staple goods are not as important as we might imagine as spoils in primitive war. Moreover, the conquest of territory is seldom done explicitly. One group expands against the other when it flees, but victors seldom occupy abandoned village sites or gardens immediately.

Loss of human life is the most evident score in this kind of warfare. Patterns vary widely in how human life is ranked in calculating scores. Some groups count *any* loss on the other side as evening the score on their side. Thus, the slaying of a small child or an old woman would cancel out the loss of an adult warrior on one's own side. This is unusual, however. Most groups rank children, killed or captive, as having lesser value than adults. Young adult women are usually of greater value than children and are more likely to be captured and kept as wives than killed. Again, one's loss of a woman is balanced by inflicting the loss of a woman on the other side. Most valued of all, usually, are adult men, as kills or as captives. Captive men are quite likely to be killed eventually, as we shall see, in an attempt to inflict symbolic losses on the other side.

In addition, most tribal societies place high value on war **trophies.** Trophies stand for losses inflicted and thus symbolize the score. For the individual trophy taker they are points or statistics in a calculation of prestige. Thus, the Cheyenne Indian warrior of our Great Plains took scalps from the enemy. The Cheyenne also counted *coups,* the feats of touching the enemy in battle with the bare hands, and each warrior tallied his coups on his tally stick, a clear but nonmaterial way of keeping score.

Trophies of all sorts have been recorded: skulls, shrunken heads, leg bones, dried male genitals, and above all captives. An adult male in the prime of life is often considered the best trophy—symbol of a winning score—of all. This was true of North American Iroquoian groups (Trigger, 1969) as well as of the Tupinambá, hosts of Hans Staden. Let us take a closer look at what is known of the latter case.

E T H N O G R A P H I C   C L O S E - U P

THE TUPINAMBÁ AND THEIR WARFARE

We started this book with the plight of Hans Staden among the Tupinambá. Hans had fallen into a full-fledged primitive warfare complex as a captive victim. He extricated himself only after his captors recruited him to the role of shaman.

The environment of the Tupinambá was an extensive habitat of tropical forest. The Portuguese found them spread along the narrow coastal shelf of Brazil, a ledge of tropical forest seldom more than 20 miles deep from the shore to cliffs with mountains rising up to the central plateau. There were Tupinambá at the mouth of the Amazon extending in a continuous belt down past the port of Sao Paulo—some 2,000 miles of the same people speaking closely related dialects and practicing common customs.

The Tupinambá were congregated in large palisaded villages, some of which were populated in the thousands. Inside the stockade were longhouses, residences for their matrilocal extended families. Their descent groups were patrilineal. Men married women of other descent groups and went to live among strangers. Villages were grouped in loose alliances and known by separate tribal names. They were constantly at war with villages from other alliances, some of which were sworn enemies.

Each village chief was honored in war, had many local relatives, and evidently was a great feastgiver. Each longhouse had a headman. In certain tribes, some village chiefs presided over as many as four other villages. Even without the hegemony of a single chief, friendly villages feasted each other and made war together against common enemies.

The Tupinambá sustained their rich cultural life by a tropical forest gardening complex. Their staple was manioc, a starchy root crop, but every garden was replete with many other crops. Up to eighty have been recorded for the South American tropical forest tribes. The Tupinambá went naked and plucked out their facial hair. They covered themselves with body paint in rich designs, wore stone ornaments in their ears and lips, and adorned themselves with feathers.

The Tupinambá had shamans, self-appointed ritual experts, who officiated at a cult of sacred rattles. Each man had a rattle that was inhabited by a guardian spirit that craved the blood of captives. Tabu to women, the rattles were kept in a house where men gathered for shamanistic rites, at which time the shaman's rattle spoke to the others. Ventriloquism is widely reported as shamanistic stock-in-trade. The performance that Hans Staden watched must have been technically poor: "I went away marveling at the simplicity of the people and the ease with which they were beguiled."

Let us discuss Tupinambá warfare sequentially from the point of view of an individual village.

Phase One: Mobilizing for a Campaign

All villages had old scores to settle with enemies. They needed no pretext to campaign against them every year, deciding to do so and choosing their target, among many possible enemies, and the date of the expedition in a war council composed of the elders and honored warriors. The council consulted the leading shaman about their plans, and he asked them for their dreams. If they dreamed of their own flesh in the pot, he might advise against an expedition. Otherwise they held a war ritual in the rattle house, each warrior dancing with his sacred rattle and calling on its spirit for aid in capturing a victim.

Phase Two: An Allied War Party Seeks to Attack

A war party, perhaps composed of warriors from several neighboring and allied villages, then departed for the village of some distant enemy group. The day before the attack, they repeated the dream divination and the rattle dance to prepare themselves for battle.

Phase Three: The Raid— Armed Struggle

They fell upon the enemy village in a surprise attack before dawn, shooting flaming arrows into the roofs of the enemy longhouses and somehow scaling the stockade. They attempted to drive off and kill the enemy, but this was strictly to facilitate their real aim—the capture of adult men.

Capture was effected by seizing and disarming a man, overpowering him by force, and tying him up with a special lasso each warrior brought into battle with him. Although several warriors might cooperate in capturing one man, the first to touch him with his bare hands was the captor. (In the capture of Hans Staden, they disputed about this.)

A raid ended quickly, usually as soon as some captives were secured, and the war party beat a hasty retreat before the enemy could rally and secure allied reinforcements.

The Tupinambá returning home with captives.

Phase Four:
Symbolic Victory:
The Treatment of Captives

The war party made a triumphant tour of their allied villages to display their captives. The return of the war party was festive. Runners went ahead to inform the people, and before they entered the village, a captive was set free and run off, to afford some friend of the captor the pleasure and privilege of recapturing him and sharing in the glory of the capture.

On entering the village, the captive was reviled, spat upon, and beaten by the women, especially those who had lost their own men in battle. Then the captor gave the prisoner to one of the war widows as her temporary husband, no different from other citizens save for the symbolic rope around his neck. He lived in his avenging wife's house, kept for an execution feast to be held at a later date when the village leaders decided on it. From time to time during his captivity, the prisoner was invited to a drinking bout by his captors, who, when drunk, told him about his terrible fate. In reply, he calmly reminded them of the revenge his own people were going to visit upon them.

Climax of This Round:
A Cannibalistic Feast

The execution feast itself was the major rite of intensification among the Tupinambá. A village invited the populations of several allied villages to share in the feasting and spent days preparing manioc pudding in huge pots. The festivities lasted from three to five days, depending upon the quantities of food available and the number of guests invited. On the first day, a special ceremonial death rope was plaited and tied to the victim. The death club, about 6 feet long and phallic in shape, was made and adorned, according to Staden,

> with a sticky mess, after which they take the eggs of a bird called Mackukawa (Macao), which they break up to powder and spread over the club. Then a woman sits down and scratches figures in the powder. When the club Iwera Peme is ready, decked with tassels and other things, they hang it in an empty hut upon a pole and sing in front of it all night.

The women painted the victim black, pasted green eggshells on his face, and glued red feathers to his body. They spent the first night with the victim, singing him songs about his horrible death to come.

The night before the execution, the prisoner was confined under close guard in a hut built specially for the occasion and torn down and demolished the next day, after he left it. The climax of the feast was the execution on the third or fifth day. The victim was led to the execution spot by old women who tied the death cord around him in full view of the assembled villagers and guests. The victim was taunted with the death club, to which he calmly replied with renewed predictions of bloody revenge.

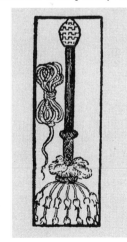

The death club.

247

[Left to right] The death club on display all night. The execution. Cannibalistic barbecue.

Then the executioner, who had been painting his body gray with ashes, approached and was invested with the death club by the village chief. Some European observers noted that the only regret voiced by the victim concerned those times the executioner was "a young man who had never been on the battlefield" rather than a seasoned warrior (Metraux, 1944, p. 124). As Staden renders the scene:

> The slayer seizes [the club] and thus addresses the victim: "I am he that will kill you, since you and yours have slain and eaten many of my friends." To which the prisoner replies: "When I am dead I shall still have many to avenge my death." Then the slayer strikes from behind and beats out his brains.

When this happened the old women painted green rushed forward with gourds to catch the blood, screaming and yelling. The body was dragged off, the limbs were cut off and the women, clutching them, rushed around the village to display the severed members. The trunk was divided and roasted on a great barbecue bonfire. All joined in the feast, with the captor presiding as feastgiver, apportioning the choice morsels. The most choice delicacies were the heart and the liver, and the grease surrounding them, which went to honored allied guests.

The Executioner's Own Rite of Passage

Meanwhile, the executioner, who had fled as the victim fell dead, was taking refuge in his own hut. His sisters and female cousins now ran through the village shouting his new name. According to Metraux (1944):

> [I]ndoors (the executioner) continued running to and fro as if escaping from his victim's ghost. . . . The members of the community then rushed into the killer's hut and looted all his goods, while the killer himself stood on wooden pestles, where the eye of his victim was shown to him and rubbed against his wrist. The lips of the dead man were sometimes given to him to wear as a bracelet. However, his flesh was strictly tabu to the killer. After this the executioner had to recline in a hammock until the hair on his shaved forehead had grown again. For 3 days he might not walk but was carried whenever he needed to leave the hut. . . . His return to normal life was celebrated by a big drinking bout, at which the killer tattooed himself by slashing his body in different patterns . . . the more tattooing marks a man could exhibit, the higher was his prestige. (pp. 125–126)

The Meaning of the Executioner's Rite

Why was the executioner secluded? Why was his name changed? Alfred Metraux, the ethnologist who wrote the report on the Tupinambá for the *Handbook of South American Indians,* used many European eyewitness accounts, including Hans Staden's. Metraux's report follows a standard outline for the Handbook. Under "Life Cycle" he lists only "Girls' puberty." One is left to infer that the Tupinambá lacked male puberty rites.

The female rites were quite elaborate. After a girl's first menstruation, her head was shaved and a design was carved into her back with a rodent tooth, leaving a lasting scarification. She was secluded in a hammock, was made to fast for three days, and was not allowed to touch the ground until her second menstruation. After the third menstruation period, she was allowed to resume life as a young woman, receive suitors, and engage in sexual relations with those who pleased her. But the young woman newly of age could receive only the suit of a warrior, meaning a man who had killed one or two enemies.

If you recall the execution, the slayer received a new name. In addition, he also took to his hammock, where his feet could not touch the ground for three days; he had to remain in the hammock until the hair of his shaven head grew again; and his body was scarified to commemorate his new name, which he was allowed to assume only after several months in this liminal period.

So although the Tupinambá may not have had puberty rites for men, they did have constant rites of initiation into higher status as a warrior. Moreover, most young men were given a captive to slay by their fathers or uncles before going on their first war party. Thus, the execution and its rites served as the functional equivalent of a male puberty rite, and this partly accounts for their great similarity in form to the female puberty rite.

Thus, for a Tupinambá adolescent male to serve as executioner of his father's captive was, in effect, to be initiated into manhood. Thereafter, he was free to court and receive the sexual favors of Tupinambá maidens.

The warfare complex had become integrated into the ritual complex of these people. The execution often served as the male initiation rite as well. Moreover, it was the funerary rite of the victim, and each executioner who wielded the death club had an excellent chance of perishing by the same means in some distant village. His initiation rite might well be repeated in his own captive death feast!

The execution also served as the major rite of intensification. It was the annual ritual that expressed alliances among villages. It gave partial form to the macrocommunity—that is, one such feast had to be reciprocated at a later date, this year or later, by each allied guest village.

Consuming the victim.

THE WARFARE COMPLEX AS BLOOD FEUD: NO TRUE REDRESS AND NO TRUE OUTCOME OR RESOLUTION

If we now analyze the Tupinambá example according to our theory of the phases of conflict, we shall discern something true of *all* tribal warfare complexes: *They oscillate forever in the phases of crisis and countervailing forces.* The ritual slaying of the Tupinambá captive looks like a redressive ritual action—it *is* intended to right a wrong suffered at the hands of the enemy group. But it does no such thing. It simply feeds another wrong into the system of endless revenge killings. There is no way out. This treadmill is called the **blood feud.**

Conflict as a Bonding Mechanism

It has often been observed that external warfare promotes internal cohesion and social solidarity (Murphy, 1957). Warfare is thus functional to any society that has notable cleavages. The Tupinambá village contained internal social tension that warfare could alleviate—the tension caused by the calculation of descent in patrilineages and residence in matrilocal extended family longhouses. Many men from different lineages lived in the same house with women from at least two different lineages. Because the women belonged to the lineages of their fathers, the grandmother of the house belonged to one lineage, and her daughters belonged to the lineage of her husband (their father). If her married granddaughters resided there as well, they belonged to the lineages of their fathers.

The counterbalance to this arrangement was the house of the war cult, the men's house, tabu to women and filled with masculine rattles whose spirits craved the blood of captives. This house of warriors cut across both households and descent groups and formed a counterweight to internal divisiveness and tensions. External conflict often focuses energy and intensifies effort as little else can. Because the very rites of intensification among the Tupinambá were warlike, all their efforts revolved around the warfare complex in some way. It seems only just that so many of them died by the enemy's death club.

Note, too, that captive men married *into* this system, however briefly, like any other man. All men married into stranger households. This may help explain the bundle of contradictory and ambivalent symbols that all find expression in the captive. The captive represents the loss of his war widow's dead husband, slain like himself in a cannibalistic feast. He represents, also, attraction and desire, for his new wife has sexual relations with him. Yet she must give him up, too, and even participate in his demise. He becomes a scapegoat for all ambivalent feelings toward men among women.

Conflict as Repulsion: A Spacing Mechanism

Primitive warfare spaces groups out in some sort of optimum relationship to material resources, and this spacing often functions to maintain area-wide populations at levels well below the maximum possible. This is particularly likely in forested areas, which seem prone to warfare complexes. Such an ecological argument for the external environmental adaptive advantages of primitive warfare is quite plausible.

The Tupinambá were spread fairly evenly over 2,000 miles of territory, and it is thought that the spread was accomplished in a comparatively short time, perhaps only a few hundred years. Excessive losses of adult males might have induced some villages either to fuse with stronger villages or to flee to the frontiers of Tupinambá settlements, far away from their more blood-thirsty avenging enemies.

The flight to frontier areas, which would have given the refugees a temporary respite from warfare and a chance to rebuild their male population, would also have afforded an ecological advantage to enemy populations left behind. The typical way for tropical forest people to garden is by slash-and-burn methods. Plots, or *swiddens*, have to be abandoned every few years and left fallow for periods lasting up to twenty years. Fallow swiddens revert to jungle that is dense second growth, which is much easier to clear by slash-and-burn methods than are vast stands of tall virgin forests. Thus, an unintended result of such a warfare complex would be to allow the dispersed population to make even less intensive use of land resources, leaving much of it in unfelled stands (Vayda, 1968).

WARFARE AS POSITIVE EXCHANGE: ALLIANCE FEASTING

The Tupinambá warfare complex united allies: in the war party, in the raid, and at the execution feasts. Thus, a great deal of *balanced trade* was going on here. For every feast your ally gives you, you must respond with one of equal value. Thus, when your ally shares the meat of a captive with you, you owe him a captive! The flesh of the captive is merely symbolic of the great quantity of other food that is being exchanged here. The Tupinambá captor offers the choicest cannibalistic morsels to the allied chief.

There have been attempts to explain cannibalism in the Americas as a response to a "protein deficit" in forested land masses, which lacked the large sources of animal protein, especially domesticated animals, found in the Old World. That may have certainly influenced the prevalence of the custom. In other regards, the complex functioned exactly as did other complexes that lacked cannibalism. In Melanesia, for example, the desired food for an alliance feast was pork, as we shall see in Chapter 11. There pigs, not captives, were sacrificed to cement an alliance. The ally in all such systems was recruited by positive scores—gains, not losses.

SUMMARY AND CONCLUSIONS

*P*rimitive warfare builds on agonistic sequences that are part of our primate biosocial potential. Social dramas, narratives of a social disturbance and their resolution, are adaptations to these aggressive sequences in band societies. In the tribal world, denser populations and more organized social life mean that these aggressive sequences become, as they are with chimpanzees, a *bonding mechanism.* Groups of men from neighboring settlements ally themselves against common enemies.

Chimpanzee aggressive sequences, when combined with the behavior of going on patrol, can become mechanisms of repulsion and even of extermination of competing chimpanzee communities. While coalitions among individual chimpanzee males may build up within the community, they have not been observed to occur between communities. One chimpanzee community does not ally with patrols of another community to go against a third.

The agonistic sequences of chimpanzee life are kinetic cycles that operate not only on the material environment but also on the social one. They act to space the animals out in relation to their resources. Paradoxically, they also act to bind animals to each other. The bonding occurs first through relations of dominance and submission, sealed through acts of appeasement and reassurance (and maintained by mutual grooming sessions). Second, animals bond in coalitions to support each other in dominance-status competitions. The entire dominance hierarchy of a troop, when engaged in the silent activity of a patrol, forms such a single coalition. In short, aggressive sequences both repel and bind individuals socially.

This is exactly what happens in human social life, most elaborately at the tribal level of social and cultural evolution. Warfare becomes a system of alliances, which in turn form half of a macrocommunity that meets, always, at feasts. The trade of food, and often marriage partners as well, is a positive exchange of goods, the cement of the alliance.

The other cement is, alas, always negative. It binds alliances, however temporary, together against the other half of the macrocommunity, the enemies, who always owe the alliance a human life, usually many lives.

We have seen how in the Tupinambá case that bloody debt is built up into an elaborate ritual complex, which combines the positive exchanges of alliance feasting with the symbolic payment of the blood debt score. It is thus a ritual switch, a rite of intensification, that intensifies alliances and warlike behavior. It is also, for the executioner, a rite of passage into warrior status, or advanced warrior status, as his tattoos tally up his victims.

The aggressive sequences of human conflict, based on primate originals, in tribal warfare always depends upon the *mobilization of allies* as the initial stage. Allies can be suborned, however, and suddenly make common cause with one's enemies, new allies of one's erstwhile friends. Such "betrayals" can lead to ever more vindictive and vengeful fighting.

Thus tribal warfare, unlike the social drama of band societies, is never ultimately resolved. Someone is always fighting someone else. There is no true redress, nor righting of any wrong, only the illusion that, through revenge killings, old wrongs have been righted. Such killings only lead to more killings, and the system perpetuates itself forever in a treadmill of focused, and generally limited, violence.

The attempts at peaceful resolution of disputes generally take place within the community that makes war together, as we have seen with the leopard-skin chief of the Nuer section.

The tribal world involves the two closely related institutions of warfare and trade. In this chapter, we have seen that area-wide warfare systems integrate many communities in a precarious, fragile balance that oscillates between the negative exchanges of war and the ideally equal trade exchanges of peace. The latter involves the concept of compensation or reparations and leads us into the subject of the emergence of feasting as a redressive mechanism in warring tribal societies. Trade through feasting becomes the mode of alliance integration, a matter we turn to in the next chapter.

SUGGESTED READINGS

Boehm, Christopher. *Blood Revenge: The Enactment and Management of Conflict in Montenegro and Other Tribal Societies.* Philadelphia: University of Pennsylvania Press, 1986. Although this book deals primarily with "civilized tribes," and therefore is just as apt for Chapter 16, it is the best accounts of blood feud in the literature.

Chagnon, Napoleon. *The Fierce People*, 5th ed. Ft. Worth: Harcourt Brace Jovanovich, 1997. An account of the Yanomamo of the Venezuelan rainforest. Their warfare complex is extremely volatile, and they do not practice cannibalism. Otherwise theirs is a classic example.

Heider, Karl. *Grand Valley Dani: Peaceful Warriors*, 2nd ed. Ft. Worth: Harcourt Brace Jovanovich, 1991. A clear, thoughtful ethnography by a man who was on the expedition that made the film *Dead Birds* in the 1960s.

Trigger, Bruce G. *The Huron: Farmers of the North.* Ft. Worth: Harcourt Brace Jovanovich, 1969. Details a warfare complex in North America whose similarities with that of the Tupinambá are quite remarkable.

SUGGESTED FILMS

Ax Fight. Timothy Asch. Cambridge, Mass.: DER, 1975. The sudden eruption of an aggressive sequence in a densely populated Yanomamo village, filmed live, and superbly analyzed.

Dead Birds. Robert Gardner. Cambridge, Mass.: Independent production, 1962. Graphic illustration of a warfare complex in the New Guinea highlands, showing the round of revenge killings and almost ritualized combat.

The Feast. Timothy Asch. Cambridge, Mass.: DER, 1969. A dramatic depiction of a feast allying two formerly enemy Yanomamo villages in order to raid a common rival.

Magical Death. Napoleon Chagnon and Timothy Asch. Cambridge, Mass.: DER, 1970. Yanomamo shamans attempt to kill enemies by sorcery, as a rite of intensification before two allied villages are to take to the warpath.

GLOSSARY

aggressive sequences Among chimpanzees, a competition between two males for a place in the dominance hierarchy. The sequence consists of the following actions: *threat, attack, defense, escape, appeasement,* and *reassurance.* Human social dramas as well as the phases of conflict (coalition) theory follow similar sequences. All are kinetic cycles acting to space individuals and groups out in relation to their material resources.

blood feud The endless crises versus counterveiling forces in primitive warfare. Every killing on one side requires survivors to kill someone on the other side in revenge, and so on.

countervailing tendencies A phase in the model of human conflict during which opponents "size up" each other's forces and rally additional allies to potentially enter the conflict on their side.

crisis A phase in the model of human conflict, after the encounter, in which opposing forces are marshaled. This stage may be fought out on the battlefield, or it may find expression in angry discussion in public places.

encounter or **showdown** A phase in conflict during which the competitor precipitates a crisis with his opponent by a breach of the peace, a challenge that throws opposing forces into relief.

macrocommunities Clusters comprising separate tribal communities that unite to mount specific expeditions for warfare *and* their rival cluster of opposing communities. The two rivals are thrown into competition for a time. Each has peripheral allies and rivals not involved in this particular combat. The activated circle of warfare is the macrocommunity.

redress A phase in the conflict model, after the encounter; it may follow or precede physical combat. It involves the attempt to right the wrong. Mechanisms can vary from outright face-to-face negotiation, to invoking a third party to mediate, to invoking ritual—such as an oracle or an ordeal—to decide the conflict.

resolution Restoration of the peace, the last phase in the conflict sequence. The crisis has been resolved. This can take the form of defeat and routing of one contender, or the balanced award of resources or honors to both competitors.

score In tribal warfare a balancing out of losses. When the other side loses, the rival "wins" in this philosophy. The specific losses most often tallied are human lives, but booty—stolen goods—may be tallied as well.

social drama A model for agonistic or aggressive sequences among human beings, based on primate potentials. They sequence includes anger or grievance, breach of the peace or encounter, confrontation, violence and/or redressive action, and flight and/or reconciliation.

third-party intervention A mechanism to restore order by invoking outsiders to a dispute, on either one or the other side, or as neutral mediators. It is the basis on which judges and courts arise, starting in human evolution with the intervention of everyone expressing a noisy opinion in a palaver at any phase of a social drama. It can also refer to countervailing tendencies in conflict phases, in which more-distant allies rally to one or another of the contestants.

trophies In tribal warfare, items symbolizing losses inflicted on the enemy. To amass them is to add up points or statistics in a calculation of prestige. Trophies are most often graphic symbols of enemy deaths, such as shrunken heads and the like. They can include live captives.

Feasting and Trading Systems:

The Economics of Redistribution and Trading Rings

11

THE BIG MAN: FEASTGIVER AND REDISTRIBUTOR

Redistribution

Alliance Feasting

The Competitive Feast

ETHNOGRAPHIC CLOSE-UP: THE SIUAI OF BOUGAINVILLE ISLAND

Generalized and Balanced Reciprocity

Siuai Men's Houses

The Chief: Big Man

Big Men and Feastgiving

A Feastgiving Career: The Rise of Big Man Songi

ANALYSIS OF THE SIUAI COMPETITIVE FEAST

A Ritual of Reversal: Winning by Losing

The Siuai Competitive Feast as Politics

The Siuai Competitive Feast as Economics

TRIBAL TRADING RINGS

ETHNOGRAPHIC CLOSE-UP: THE TROBRIAND ISLANDERS

Kula Expeditions

The Kula Exchange of Gifts and Countergifts

Receiving Expeditions and the Countergift

The Kula and the Life Cycle

BRIEF ANALYSIS: THE COMPETITIVE FEAST AND THE KULA EXPEDITION COMPARED

*I*n the previous chapter we were, in effect, discussing values and reciprocal, if negative, exchange. Groups locked in warfare complexes value bravery; they exalt the warrior's life and revere the warrior's sacrificial death. Their most poignant exchange is to cancel the blood debt of one warrior's life for another. We have seen that revenge cycles in blood feuds only breed more deaths. They are constantly negative.

We have also noted that **feasting** is a way to cement alliances. It is a way to focus the attention of two groups against a common enemy. It is also a positive, ideally balanced, exchange of goods. Feasting can also be a way to mend differences, even to end a feud, and to cancel or at least to suspend a blood debt, usually in favor of some common revenge campaign. In terms of conflict theory, feasting is thus a redressive mechanism. It can turn enemies into partners, building coalitions where before there was conflict.

Feasting is a ritual event. And as with all ritual, it attempts to overcome contradictions, to make friends and allies out of what were at best neutral acquaintances. It invokes a myth, usually of the common enemy, perhaps of past alliances.

Feasting further glorifies the feastgiver. Feastgiving offers a route to honor and fame more sure than war. To give a great feast may be quite as glorious as to die a sacrificial death, and the great advantage is that the feastgiver, unlike the fallen war hero, lives on to enjoy the fame. Thus, the career of a great feastgiver can become its own myth: Past feasts and exploits are boasted of and remembered.

In the more densely settled populations of the tribal world, especially those that grow their own food, exchange with outsiders is by means of the raid or the feast, and leadership emerges around figures of the warrior and the feastgiver.

Apart from sealing warfare alliances, feasting systems can also become *competitive systems* of their own, positive substitutes for warfare that even more than war compel a wide variety of goods into circulation and keep many hundreds of people and many separate communities busy producing and exchanging goods.

In competitive feasting the object is for one feastgiver, the Big Man, to give his guest and rival more goods than the rival can give back later at a greater value. At the end of such a feast the host goes hungry, but he wins by giving more than he can receive!

In short, feasting systems are great thermodynamic engines, throwing all sorts of goods into circulation, just as we saw in the Tiwi funeral. It is here more than anywhere else that we can speak of "primitive economics." We are now concerned with the production and circulation of goods on a wide scale, far wider than is usually the case in band-level societies.

This circulation of goods proceeds, as we shall see, by the combined mechanisms of generalized and balanced reciprocity, redistribution, and competitive negative reciprocity. To call such a system "economics" does not imply that it is a *rational* system for maximizing useful material benefits. In fact, most anthropologists would say that primitive economics is not a set of rational behaviors, whereby men and women produce foods, material goods, and services and exchange them for maximum material value. Rather, anthropologists say that all human beings are busy trying to live up to the values-as-goals of their culture. Certain goods may symbolize these values (such as the Tiwi gravepole). Under conditions of constraint, the more settled nature of tribal life than band life, and the absence of places to escape to, people maximize values that crystallize around the figures of the warrior or the feastgiver. The warrior's own life is such a good, when sacrificed. The items given away at a feast are other such goods.

Some groups, moreover, allow leadership to crystallize fully in the figure of the Big Man or feastgiver, who overshadows the figure of the warrior.

Feasting, then, is a ritual system to convert rivals into allies, a means for strong single leaders to lead hierarchies of men and women, a substitute for war, and a means to circulate certain kinds of valuable goods. It is also a means to make peace—a redressive action—within the alliance, and thus a way out of blood feuds.

THE BIG MAN: FEASTGIVER AND REDISTRIBUTOR

A **Big Man** is a kind of leader frequently observed by anthropologists in tribal societies; he organizes feasts and induces his followers to give him large quantities of goods. These goods he then gives away, sometimes back to his followers. Sometimes, however, he gives the goods to strangers, rival guests at the feast. In those cases, he and his followers must wait, sometimes years, for the guests to reciprocate with a feast of their own in order to get any material return on their original "investment." A Big Man is self-made; he does not inherit his position, and the "office" is not distinct from the man.

Redistribution

Redistribution is the giving of gifts by many partners to one person, who then returns them in mass feasts and rituals. As a special form of reciprocity, redistribution indicates that a single person is the center for reciprocal relations with a great many others. Goods flow in to the individual, often one at a time, and the individual then gives the goods back, often all at once in a great feast. This flow of gifts to a central person and their mass return can also be quite simply represented (see Figure 11.1). Let us say that F is the central figure and that A, B, C, D, and E all give goods to F: A/F B/F C/F D/F E/F. F then returns them at once to many friends: F/ABCDE. But in competitive feasting F does not return the goods to his followers. Instead, he gives them to a rival Big Man, G: F/G. G in turn redistributes the goods to his followers: G/HIJKL. These will now have the obligation to help G host F and his followers for a similar, ideally richer, feast.

Alliance Feasting

Alliance feasting, the "inside" half of any competitive feasting, is easy to comprehend as political economy, as we saw with the Tupinambá in Chapter 10. At **alliance feasts** the Big Man orchestrates relatives, neighbors, and allies as they come together and actually share goods under his direction. Sitting down and eating together is usual. While the political motive of the feasts is clear, they are often the occasion of rites of passage, especially collective male initiation rites.

For example, the Grand Valley Dani of West New Guinea or Irian have such feasts that are extremely complex. They are at once initiation rites for small boys, weddings (and hence initiation rites for young girls and "graduation" initiation rites for the young men who marry them, thereby attaining young adulthood), and funerary feasts in which all the dead of the years elapsed since the previous feast are commemorated by exchanges between the two paired and opposing sets of exogamous lineages (called "moieties" or halves), those of the deceased and the opposite set of lineages. (Valuables, in this case ornamental *je* stones, have previously been given as symbols of the deceased, at their individual funerals.) Women wear hot and dripping cooked pigskins on their backs to commemorate their deceased. The event ends with an enormous redistribution of pork (Heider, 1991).

In the Dani feasts two dynamics are at work. One is the sealing of new alliances, after neighborhood confederacies have abruptly broken with erstwhile allies and realigned with components of old alliances to form new ones.

Phase 1 Gift giving

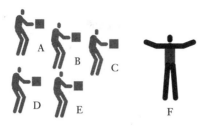

Figure 11.1 Redistribution.

Phase 2 Focal figure has goods

F (Redistributor)

Phase 3 Redistributor gives goods out

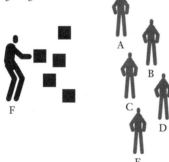

Such alliances last on schedules of around thirty years, while the time scale for calling the feasts is from six to ten years or so. Feasts affirm and legitimize the new alliances among erstwhile enemies.

The other dynamic is the rise of the Big Man who orchestrates the feasts. Alliances take the name of their Big Man; he is at once redistributor and battlefield marshal. When communities break with their old enemies, usually in a bitter war with much loss of life, burning of fields, and reshuffling of territories, they respond to the strategies of newly rising Big Men. Big Men arise among the Dani, then, by tying their feastgiving and war-making schedules to those of the life crises—initiations, weddings, and funerary commemorations—of their constituents and clients.

The Competitive Feast

Alliance feasting often is complemented by **competitive feasting.** In this odd cultural complex, one *wins by losing.* That is, the Big Man strives to get his followers to accumulate such a store of goods that those who receive them are not able to reciprocate with a bigger feast at a later date (see Figure 11.2). The host Big Man has won, and his rival may be rendered "near death," and ethnographers have been told that some defeated Big Men indeed *have* died of shame.

Phase 1 Gift giving

Phase 2 Redistributor (Big Man) has store of goods

Phase 3 Big Man gives *all* the goods to his rival

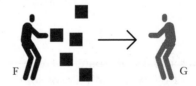

Phase 4 Rival bestows goods on his followers

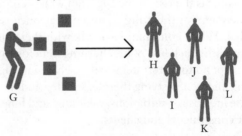

Figure 11.2 Competitive feasting.

Utility or maximizing theorists might easily claim to explain away the anomalies of this situation. The host Big Man and his followers are in fact expecting a handsome return on their investment in some years' time. The defeat of the rival Big Man, putting him out of business so that he cannot reciprocate, like the downswing of a business cycle, is simply a risk he must take; so-called winners merely rationalize their material loss by claiming a higher score and prestige. I believe that, on the contrary, the score *is* made higher by material losses. The rival's unpayable debt is a symbol of one's own victory.

In the following ethnographic close-up we shall examine the career of a competitive Big Man among the Siuai of the Solomon Islands to see how this may be so.

ETHNOGRAPHIC CLOSE-UP

THE SIUAI OF BOUGAINVILLE ISLAND

There are many known cases of fully developed redistributive economies, but none is more interesting than that of the Siuai. Douglas Oliver, who studied them in the late 1930s, made an incomparably detailed report (1955). Redistribution among the Siuai is based on numerous reciprocal transactions and is built anew with great political and ritual skill during each leader's lifetime.

The Siuai inhabit the jungled south shore of Bougainville, one of the Solomon Islands to the southeast of New Guinea. A handsome people, speaking a Papuan language, they numbered close to 5,000 when Oliver lived among them. In spite of Australian attempts to relocate them in nucleated villages, the Siuai maintained their single-family huts scattered in the jungle, close to their cultivated plots of taro, the staple produce.

Generalized and Balanced Reciprocity

The basic social unit is the household, usually composed of the nuclear family, although the biggest leaders have as many as fifteen wives if they can manage it. The Siuai calculate descent in matrilineages, but matrilineages are dispersed through the jungle as the households are. The households are the basic productive units; within households and between closely related households, **generalized reciprocity** prevails.

Every household has several plots of taro gardened by women. Taro, known to us as the ornamental elephant ears of some Southern gardens, is a starchy tropical crop that provides rich yields all year. It cannot be stored, however. In addition, families grow coconuts and almonds, valuing both highly. Many Siuai men, especially leaders, manufacture pots from local clays. They also manufacture wooden utensils and weapons, nets, and baskets. But their most prized product of all is pigs. One or two pigs may be conveniently raised by one woman and her children as household pets and may grow fat on the leftovers of the family taro plots. But a man who wants many pigs raised at home must have many wives.

Pork is the principal source of protein among the Siuai. Because one pig is too much for a single nuclear family household to consume at one sitting, and because even when smoked, pork will not last long in the tropics, it is always shared by many households. However, it is only consumed at a feast, when circles of related households practice generalized reciprocity, and redistribution as well, by consuming pork together.

One important basic event in Siuai culture is the birth feast, whereby members of all households related to the baby on either side gather at its homestead. They bring pigs to the child's father and contribute almonds and coconuts as well. In return, the parents give a tremendous feast in which all the pork is consumed. It is a fine meal replete with taro pudding spiced with almonds. This is the basic and spontaneous redistributive event among the Siuai, but it pales in comparison with others, as we shall see.

Most Siuai men practice a form of **balanced reciprocity** with men from other districts who are their **trading partners.** This is a man, usually not kin, with whom one has entered a trading relationship by sealing it with a special ritual. A man can usually obtain a large hog from a trading partner when he needs it for a feast. In about a year's time, transactions with a trading partner are supposed to be balanced, but full payment for such goods as a tusker can be delayed. Trading negotiations are started with a small overture that Oliver calls a "coercive gift." By accepting it, the recipient obligates himself to give his partner the really big item he wants later—at a price, of course.

To expedite balanced reciprocity, the Siuai have shell **money**—spans of shells imported from the north. Though they seem cumbersome to us, the

Spans of shell money carefully laid out prior to being given away to the viewers at Big Man Songi's great redistributive feast.

spans serve as both a standard of value and a means of exchange. All goods are valued in terms of spans of shells. Using them, natives can purchase most things based on well-known local standards of equivalence, or price. Prices are long term and set by custom, not by day-to-day market fluctuations of supply and demand.

One span of shell money will pay for the entire yield of a plot of taro. The value of the plots themselves is far from precisely standardized, however. One span will also buy one measure of almonds or twenty coconuts or a hunting spear or a medium-sized pot. Pigs, the most valued stock of all, can also be bought with shells (see Figure 11.3). A piglet costs 10 spans, an adult sow 50 spans, and a large tusker 100 spans (100 times as much as a plot's yield of taro). In general, shell money seems to have expedited trade among the Siuai. Although marketplaces do not exist, neighbors not related to one another commonly purchase small goods and services from each other by means of spans of shell money. These transactions are balanced, however, payment being immediate and in full.

Siuai Men's Houses

The most important place for Siuai social activity, aside from the single-family homestead, is the men's house. These houses are quite numerous and are scattered around through the jungle near the crossroads where trails come together. Tabu to women, any clubhouse has some twenty to forty men in its membership. They spend most of their free

1 span of shells	=	Harvest of 1 plot of taro
	=	1 measure of almonds
	=	20 coconuts
	=	1 hunting spear
	=	1 medium pot
10 spans of shells	=	1 piglet
50 spans of shells	=	1 adult sow
100 spans of shells	=	1 tusker hog

Figure 11.3 Siuai values in goods.

time there—idling in the company of friends, working on some craft such as spear making, or preparing for a feast by obeying the commands of the clubhouse leader, the chief (Siuai: *mumi*).

A clubhouse is of spacious open construction for viewing the performance on the large cleared ceremonial plaza in front. A complete clubhouse has at least nine slit-gongs, made from hollowed logs and arranged around the sides of the building. The small central one is the leader's and is used for beating announcements to his men. The gongs are all named and are used in specific combinations at specific sequences in the unfolding of a feast.

In addition, a small stake is driven into the front house pole, where small offerings of pork are left for the house's patron and resident demon, a hobgoblin who craves the blood of pigs. This supernatural being is believed to reside either on the largest gong or on the ridgepole.

The Chief: Big Man

Every clubhouse belongs to a leader, or Big Man, and takes his name. Big Men are the native chiefs among the Siuai, and together with their followers, who are recruited from kinsmen and neighbors, each forms a feastgiving association. Big Men do not inherit their positions, although they are often the sons or nephews of Big Men. They do not order the wives of their followers around (although they do call on any child in the neighborhood to run an errand).

The team or following in the men's house is ranked. The Big Man spends most of his time in the inner circle of his top followers, who surround him and advise him directly. These in turn have followers of their own, whom they direct when undertaking tasks. These then transmit commands to yet a fourth and lowest echelon of men, young bachelors who are on the outskirts of the group.

The Siuai believe their Big Men are the embodiment of human values. These men are deemed outstanding—ambitious, industrious, skilled at many tasks, and good, meaning generous, cooperative, genial, and decent. A Big Man's authority is largely the natural result of his being able to run a successful enterprise. His sanctions are largely positive and unnoticed, and his commendation is the sweetest of

all rewards. However, the Big Man also wields negative sanctions. Some informants say his disparagement could lead directly to suicide. Less drastically, he can levy a fine against a follower for quarreling with another in the clubhouse or for having failed in some task. His most drastic sanction is expulsion from the group.

The Big Man also has certain mythical, even supernatural, attributes. He is the custodian of the guardian goblin, who has attached himself to the Big Man precisely because it craves the blood of pigs. If the Big Man is a poor feastgiver, the goblin withers away and dies, but not without first killing his unsatisfactory human host! Because of the patron goblin, the Big Man has the power to tabu his followers' groves of coconut and almond trees, symbolically dedicating them to the goblin. When he lifts the tabu, however, he does so in time for a feast.

Big Men are almost always shaman/curers in their own right. But since one out of every four adult Siuai men is one, too, this is not a special trait. Rather it is another means for the Big Man to raise shell money, which he constantly needs. For the same reason, a Big Man is usually a skilled craftsman, manufacturing and selling pots, for example. In general, Big Men work very hard all the time. More than any private citizen, they have many trading partners in other neighborhoods with whom they are always involved in transactions concerning pigs.

Big Men and Feastgiving

The object of a clubhouse is to put on ever bigger and better feasts. Most feasts are directly redistributive. But Big Men aim to give competitive feasts against rival Big Men as well. The pattern of the feast is taken directly from the birth festivities, in which the new baby's relatives all contribute pork, coconuts, and almonds for their joint consumption. A Big Man gives the feasts and distributes similar foods. He gives them frequently—each time the clubhouse is rebuilt or enlarged, each time a gong is installed, each time a new song is composed and rehearsed. Because of the tropical climate, building materials rot rapidly, so clubhouse members are involved in a fairly steady schedule of small feasts for themselves alone.

A Siuai men's house belonging to the chief, Songi, with his own followers and those of allied chiefs massed in front, waiting for "guest attackers" at a feast.

Because there are no pronounced seasons in the tropical year, rites of intensification are not seasonal. Siuai rites of intensification depend on cycles of effort by the chief feastgivers. These cycles are long term and competitive, and they depend on the careers of the Big Men. The small internal feasts and some of the feasts Big Men give for each other are friendly and cooperative. For example, one neighboring leader might be asked to build a gong for the clubhouse and another to transport it. The host Big Man and his followers will put on a feast for their friends, regaling them handsomely with pork and puddings, which they consume together at the clubhouse.

But the *competitive feast* is more keenly relished. Its object is to humiliate a rival Big Man by feasting him so lavishly that he is unable to stage a better feast in return. A defeated Big Man is rendered "near death." It seems that some do die of a broken heart; others quietly retire from feastgiving or accept defeat gracefully by allying themselves with the victor and joining him as a helper in competitive feasts against new rivals.

Big Men are always trying to get their hands on pigs, since a feast requires a suitable redistribution of pork. It is the most prized good of all, but you will remember that it is consumed only at feasts. A Big Man can raise his own pigs, but he can raise enough only if he has many wives to help, as only two pigs are raised per wife. Although some chiefs acquire as many as fifteen wives, most do not. Their efforts are limited by two factors: preferential cross-cousin marriage (every suitable wife is a cross-cousin) and the competitive nature of courtship, which requires an investment of time.

A Big Man can acquire pigs from neighbors who are not his followers by outright purchase with shell money earned from the sale of crafts and from curing payments. Ordinarily only piglets are for sale; adult sows and giant tuskers are not for sale at any price to people who are not trading partners or kinfolk. So a Big Man resorts to many means to acquire adult pigs. For one, he can buy a piglet with shell money and give it to a follower, who, at the time of his feast, returns it full grown. In token return, the Big Man gives the follower 10 spans of shell money (some 90 spans less than the proper worth of the pig!).

The Big Man can also dun his trading partners for pigs. Often he will force a partner to go get a pig from a relative for the occasion. Such negotiations are started well in advance of a feast by sending the partner a coercive gift good enough to force him to come through with a tusker. If the pig is destined for an important feast, the partner usually lets the chief have it at less than the proper rate "to share in the glory of the feast." The Big Man's highest-placed followers repeat the same activities with their relatives and trading partners as they, too, attempt to acquire as many pigs as possible for the feast. In short, acquiring pigs for a feast becomes a central pastime for the Siuai population.

A Feastgiving Career: The Rise of Big Man Songi

Oliver lived in the northern section of Siuai territory and made friends with Songi, the biggest man of the region. Songi's career typifies the process and drama of feastgiving and leadership. He was born in 1893, and his career started around age fifteen, when his mother's brother staked him to a small clubhouse. This uncle and other relatives evidently believed that Songi was a natural-born chief, so they became his principal followers and advisers. To launch the first clubhouse feast, all the relatives got busy making pots that they sold for shell money. They converted the shell money into piglets and pigs and gave the feast, which did not differ very much from an ordinary birth feast in scale.

Songi rebuilt and enlarged his clubhouse twice, filled it full of gongs, and never stopped giving feasts. After a few years, he entered competitive feasting with nearby chiefs, and his career was a succession of victories. He defeated some rivals totally, rendering them near death. Some few reciprocated with feasts of equal value but let it be known that they did not care to compete further (translating defeat into simple balanced reciprocity). Eventually, he had no peer in the northern half of Siuai territory.

Over one year's time, from 1938 to 1939, Oliver had the opportunity to observe Songi, then forty-six years old, prepare one of the most renowned feasts ever given among the Siuai. In one way or another the feast touched on the activities of every individual Siuai during the year. In February 1938, Songi started preparation by sacrificing a pig to his hobgoblin and tying strips of pork around his followers' coconut and almond trees, thereby tabuing the groves and symbolically dedicating them to getting pigs for his hungry demon.

Next Songi reminded all his followers who had received piglets from him in the past year to pen up the growing pigs in preparation for the feast. He extracted one fine pig from a follower by promising him a place of honor in the feast. Then he gave the pig to another man in honor of the man's child's birth. This was a coercive gift to shame the man into giving Songi his fine tusker, which he did. All Songi's followers became busy calling in debts from their relatives and trading partners. Songi sent messengers to his own trading partners far and wide, negotiating for pigs; sometimes the partners themselves went off in search of pigs from others.

Negotiations to acquire a fine tusker from one young partner in another village fell through; so on the eve of the actual feast, Songi humiliated him by inviting him to come to the feast as if he were the rival chief, the guest of honor. The man was deeply shamed by the invitation since he could not possibly reciprocate, and he had to send the tusker itself as repayment for the invitation gifts.

In late November 1938, Songi appointed an important neighboring Big Man as his resident defender to attend the feast and to dance at the side of Songi's followers. He also commissioned a musician to compose the theme song for the feast and gathered his followers and those of the resident defender to practice it. The song referred to a sore on Songi's foot. Here is a translation:

You sore! Demon!
If you were a man
I would rise, and slay you
And place your skull in the clubhouse.
But, alas, you are only a sore,
And I can only look at you
And weep from pain.

According to Oliver's interpretation, the meaning is as follows: "I am a powerful warrior and a clubhouse owner and can work my will against mortal men but against a little sore I am powerless" (1955, pp. 432–433).

In mid-December 1938, Songi held a small feast, butchering seven small pigs and eating them with his followers, the resident defender, and his company as they rehearsed the song. Officially, the feast was to

of his own, as did the other friendly chief. Speculation was rife about the identity of the guest of honor. Preparations began in earnest. One of Songi's top followers began to organize workers for six days of cooking puddings.

Then Songi's "war party" departed for the "surprise attack"—the invitation to the rival to attend the feast. All Siuai were tense; they suspected the identity of the guest, and they were right: the most influential Big Man in the southern region, the only chief whose accomplishments were on a par with Songi's. The war party brought him insultingly fine gifts, so that to have refused the challenge (or invitation) would have been very shameful. The invitation was accepted.

Finally, the grand day came on January 10, 1939, almost a full year after preparations had formally begun. The rival Big Man was on his way with his own co-defenders, lesser chiefs whom he had invited. The affair now involved all the Siuai and a few chiefs from other tribes invited by Songi's allies.

Ritual separation began before dawn as several hundred supporters massed around Songi's clubhouse for the pig counting. Each pig to be given away was taken from its pen and exhibited, to the proper banging of the gongs. Bang the gong! Count the pig! And so it went. One high-placed follower claimed that he saw the hobgoblin himself "dancing along the ridgepole, vastly pleased with all the noise and the smell of food."

Songi's guest defenders practice singing and dancing for his forthcoming feast.

Songi, at left, supervises preparation of puddings for his great feast.

The hundreds of defenders spent hours getting their persons ready. They painted themselves, oiled their weapons, and turned themselves out in full and elaborate battle regalia. By noon, the defenders with their spears had massed in front of the clubhouse in battle formation. They heard the shouts and battle yells of the attackers, the guests. Songi sat inside on his great gong next to the site believed to be the seat of the goblin. All was ready.

Then a single spearman shot into the clearing, threatened the men lined up in front of the clubhouse, and retired, followed by others in quick succession until scores had rushed in shouting, brandishing spears and axes, and twanging arrows against bow-strings. More men ran in carrying pigs, gifts from the guest reciprocating the invitation pigs given him.

celebrate lifting a tabu against sounding Songi's gongs, silenced briefly in mourning for the death of one of Songi's three wives. In late December, Songi lifted the tabu against almonds and coconuts, and his followers busily harvested them for preparing puddings of taro, sago palm flour, and almonds. But soon it became apparent that they needed more labor for food production and cooking, so Songi sent pigs and a "war party" to invite yet another neighboring Big Man to join as a second allied Big Man.

Excitement was mounting among the Siuai. The resident defender invited some lesser chiefs as allies

The vanguard of attackers ceremonially "attacking" Songi's clubhouse.

The two groups massed at opposite ends of the dance plaza and danced, piped, and sang. The object was to drown the other group out. In the excitement, Songi's group quite forgot the song about his sore and sang another, more spirited tune. After an hour or so the pace of dancing and singing slackened. The attackers massed together and pressed toward the clubhouse center in an effort to glimpse their host. The defenders made way; Songi stood up in full view of the multitude and gave a signal. The defenders rushed to the pigpens, brought out the pigs, and lined them up. Others brought out the baskets of food and puddings.

Songi signaled his rival. The attackers stampeded to seize puddings and coconuts, while their chief recorded on a tally stick the value of the pigs and

then distributed them among his allies and followers. Pig there, food here. Pig to so and so. And so on. The pigs were strangled on the spot and tied to poles for transport. As soon as all the loot had been gathered up, the attackers and the allied nonresident defenders moved off, the latter carrying gifts from Songi, too. The gift distribution lasted only two hours. What had taken a year to bring together was suddenly and totally dispersed:

> Some 1100 natives attended the feast and received 32 pigs, distributed as follows: 17 pigs worth a total of 1070 spans of [shell money] to Kope (the rival, guest of honor); 7 pigs worth a total of 450 spans to Kaopa (the principal resident defender); 4 pigs worth a total of 220 spans to those (local) leaders who were directly invited; 3 pigs worth 160 spans given directly to Songi's principal (trading) partners; and one pig worth 20 spans given to the Australian Patrol Officer, whom Songi invited in order to show him "how Siuai leaders act." (Oliver, p. 439)

As you can imagine, the members of Songi's immediate clubhouse experienced a tremendous letdown. No one had had a bite to eat. They all went home dejected and hungry to rest and find leftovers after all their hard work. But the next morning, they were all startled by Songi's gongs booming from the clubhouse and the leader himself storming out:

> Hiding in your houses again; copulating day and night while there is work to be done! Why, if it were left up to you, you would spend the rest of your lives smelling yesterday's pig. But I tell you, yesterday's feast was nothing. The next one will be really big. Siham, I want you to arrange with Konnu for his largest pig; and you, Maimoi, go to Makakaru and find a pig for Uremu . . .

ANALYSIS OF THE SIUAI COMPETITIVE FEAST

Each redistributive feast is a ritual event, a freely scheduled rite of intensification. *Separation* starts with the pig counting before dawn and the ritual making up of the defenders. *Transition* or *liminality* consists of the mock battle between the two sides, with dancing instead of fighting going on, but

Guests viewing some of the pigs awaiting presentation at Songi's feast.

Leaders of guest attackers view cooked food presented to them by Songi.

making full use of the symbols of battle in weaponry and warrior dress. The songs and dances have to do with manliness and leadership. The culmination of the ritual is the strangling of the pigs, which symbolically represent human warriors. Before the British imposed internal peace and outlawed headhunting, each clubhouse had the human skull of an enemy enshrined in the rafters. Today they put the jawbones of the pigs of enemies in their place.

The patron hobgoblin with his insatiable craving for pig's blood is a mythological creature. The past exploits of all chiefs also form a mythology, and the feasts thus reenact famous events of the past.

Reincorporation is effected with the departure of the guests. Enemies and allies suddenly and precipitously leave, as in an actual warlike raid, carrying off their gifts, the symbolic booty. In a local noncompetitive feast for the clubhouse alone or in cooperation with a friendly chief, the feast would have been prolonged and a ritual meal would have been partaken of by all in the plaza. This is not the case in the competitive feast; each departing "war party" consumes the goods in a separate feast safe on its home ground. For them, reincorporation takes place only after they eat at their own leader's suddenly lavish hospitality.

For the host, however, the ritual ends as the last guests disappear into the jungle. He is left alone, reincorporated into his ordinary existence, with no feast to prepare for. He wonders whether his rival will be able to compete and invite him to a better feast in a year's time or more.

A Ritual of Reversal: Winning by Losing

Curiously, the feast reverses the usual dealings between strangers in **negative reciprocity.** Instead of the winner carrying off the booty, as in ordinary warfare, it is the loser who does so. Reversing the usual order of events often happens in the symbolism of liminal periods. It is one mechanism, perhaps, to overcome contradictions. It is true, of course, that if the rival Big Man accepts the challenge, he must put on a better feast. If he does, Songi and his followers, instead of going hungry, will make haste taking the booty to their clubhouse for the pork eating of their lives. But if the rival does not do so, he is *defeated*. Instead of growing fat, he is supposed to waste away. By reversing the fortunes of war, the feast has undertaken one of the functions of diplomacy: dealing with strangers and making them safe for exchange. To do so, a Big Man loses materially but wins in prestige.

The Siuai Competitive Feast as Politics

The Siuai feasting complex is not only ritual, it is political. A leader, the Big Man, directs teams of followers that lead the activities of all others, and he represents the community that is formed around his leadership to outsiders.

The successful Big Man becomes the apex of several other teams. Each time a vanquished Big Man becomes his ally, a true hierarchy is formed, with one leader ordering around another, who conserves his own team intact. In Songi's case, as a result of his many victories and his great renown, he had several such Big Men subordinate to himself at the feast, and they in turn had their own subordinate Big Men in attendance on them (see Figure 11.4). Songi thus stood at the apex of a chain of command three ranks deep.

Not only is the single team complexly formed, but the Siuai system can array several teams together in a chain of command down from a single leader. This kind of pyramid is very different from the circles of notables with overlapping and conflicting followings of primitive republics. Among the Siuai such formations are short term and last for the conduct of a feast and no longer. When mobilized for longer periods, however, such formations are the basis for the development of chieftaincies and primitive monarchies.

Figure 11.4 Hierarchy of Big Men and their subordinates.

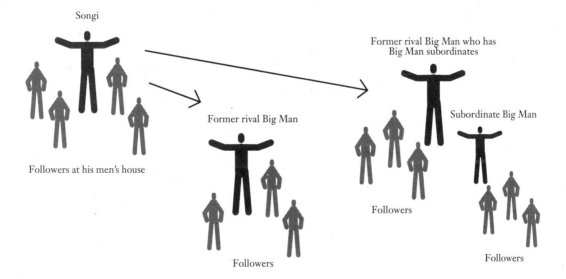

Songi

Followers at his men's house

Former rival Big Man

Followers

Former rival Big Man who has Big Man subordinates

Subordinate Big Man

Followers

Followers

The Siuai Competitive Feast as Economics

Feastgiving among the Siuai is clearly a way to allocate goods. It is the way to consume pork, for example. Feastgiving directly stimulates production of all sorts, from raising taro to the manufacture of pots and baskets, and above all to the breeding, distribution, and fattening of pigs.

It may be said that the system has its beneficial effects. First, like any ritual system, it marshals efforts and coordinates people within the time cycles they cannot escape: the cycle of planting and harvesting taro, for example, or of breeding and raising pigs. Long term, it has the effect of *minimizing famine and risks,* as people can always go to someone else's feast in a lean season—subject, of course, to eventual reciprocity or to humiliation and loss of prestige in the case of continued lean conditions.

Now let us see what happens when an exchange system is institutionalized, around the existence of **valuables,** sufficient to integrate large areas.

TRIBAL TRADING RINGS

We have seen that a competitive feasting system can integrate wide areas; in the case of Songi's feast it integrated an entire linguistic nation, the Siuai. This was possible only because the Australian colonial government had stamped out warfare. Before then, warfare and feasting had been the two ways the area was integrated. We can hypothesize that competitive feasting grew out of alliance feasting as an attractive alternative to warfare.

Competitive exchange, with rather less feasting, can also grow out of the formalization of distant trading partner alliances. This, too, can become a ritual of reversal, a substitute for warfare, and a lifelong ladder to gain prestige among competitive men. When this happens, wide areas can be integrated into a formal, rigid, ritualized pattern of regional exchange, the **trading ring.**

The best known of these is the **kula ring** of the western Pacific, studied by Malinowski and portrayed in his justly famous book, *Argonauts of the Western Pacific* (1922). Networks of trading partners have been reported for many tribal peoples and worked out with some precision for Melanesia. Sahlins (1972) reports in detail on three of them in an essay titled "Exchange Value and the Diplomacy of Primitive Trade." These networks vary from a direct chain in Northern Queensland, Australia, to rings in Melanesia (Vitiaz Straits and Huon Gulf).

It is this level of foreign relations, the formation of macrocommunities and regional systems of warfare and trade, that is the least understood aspect of the tribal world, simply because most anthropologists have concentrated on single cultures and not their regional integration. Such regional integration among tribes revolves around warfare or around competitive feasting or trading rings, two institutions that have been widely reported but not understood as images of each other. The kula ring is a like a formalized competitive feasting system, recast into a widespread ongoing minuet of peoples.

The kula ring is often cited as an example of reciprocal economies. It is true that the kula consists of trading partners arranged over distant islands in a grand circle encompassing hundreds of miles. It is also true that trading partnerships are fixed and that the valued items are not exchanged freely in any direction according to supply and demand but follow prescribed routes. Still, the kula is much more than that. Kula trading involves thousands of individuals from many communities and constitutes their most complex rites of intensification.

Like the Siuai competitive feast, a kula expedition is a ritual and symbolic statement of opposition between strangers and potential enemies. They are rendered friends and safe by the exchange of gifts—not ordinary gifts, nor even prized consumables like Siuai pork, but *trophies*, symbols of the exchange itself that are counted up and tallied for each partner, added to his score, and then passed on in a competitive game with rivals in either direction. They resemble the trophy captives of warfare complexes. One does not store the trophies; one cherishes them just long enough to add one's name and the circumstances of one's acquiring them to the lore of the treasured article. Then one bestows it upon a rival in the expectation of receiving at least an equivalent treasure. Let us look at how the system works.

E T H N O G R A P H I C   C L O S E - U P

THE TROBRIAND ISLANDERS

Malinowski studied the kula from the perspective of the Trobriand Islanders, with whom he lived. He accompanied them on their sailing expeditions and watched them receive foreign sailing expeditions on their shores. Because the kula unites many people of diverse cultures, not all the particulars of Trobriand behavior are equally applicable to all members of the ring. The Trobrianders, for example, have chiefs, but groups that do not aren't at all deterred from avidly participating in the kula.

Trobriand chiefs, like Siuai chiefs, are Big Men in feasting complexes. But unlike the Siuai they are chosen and groomed for their positions from among each chief's sisters' sons. Trobrianders practice matrilineal descent and avunculocal residence. That is, men go to live with their wives in the villages of their mother's brothers, the seat of their matriclans. A chief's son, therefore, never inherits a chieftainship; one of the chief's nephews does.

Chiefs are also the centers of redistributive feasting. They take many wives, which automatically brings a flow of food into their households from the wives' brothers. A Trobriander man works hard for his sisters, so that his sisters' husbands receive the major yield of his tropical garden. In addition, a chief receives regular tribute gifts from all the households in his village. In turn he regularly gives feasts for his in-laws and his "subjects."

The food distributed at this feast is called **sagali,** the term also applied to the provisions distributed at a funeral feast from the contributions brought by the surviving members of the matriclan. We have met the foods before: taro puddings, yams, and above all, pork. The village chiefs are in charge of village horticulture. They set times for planting and harvesting and give feasts accordingly. In short, they are the masters of ceremonies for the village rites of intensification.

Kula Expeditions

Chiefs are the masters of the huge seagoing outrigger canoes that sail on the kula. Chiefs commission skilled craftsmen to manufacture the canoes and call up communal laboring parties for felling the giant hardwood tree, moving the log to the beach, and launching the finished canoe. Launching is the occasion of a grand feast. The chief then sails the new canoe for a ceremonial visit to all his local allies, and together they then hold a race, which is more like a review, since the boat of the ranking chief always wins. This is the occasion of a great feast uniting the several local communities that go on to the kula together.

Trobriander villages are grouped into coalitions that Malinowski says are "one community for purposes of war and of the kula." He calls these alliances kula communities. (In our terminology, of course, the wider or macrocommunity at any one time includes not only the coalition but also the group they are raiding or are engaging in kula exchanges.)

A kula expedition takes off for overseas every two to three years, going in either a clockwise or a counterclockwise direction (see Figure 11.5). All the seagoing canoes of all the villages of a kula community are gathered, and each is captained by a chief (a village or subsidiary headman). The crew consists of four to six adult householders, each of whom, like the chief, has kula partners abroad. Two apprentices who do not trade in the kula work for them as sailors; in addition, each crew includes a small boy, usually the chief's son. The chief, the captain of a canoe, always feasts his crew royally upon their return with a pork banquet.

The natives assemble at the launching beach and say their farewells to the crews from all the villages. Relatives load each canoe with gifts, especially taro and other foodstuffs. Then, after much incantation of magic and spells, the expedition departs. To Malinowski's surprise, the enterprise sails only a short distance to a nearby island and beaches itself. There—out of sight of their homes—they make camp and prepare for a great feast, an enormous distribution of vegetables and pork. The entire fleet is presided over by one village chief, sort of the expedition admiral, who coordinates its movements abroad. He presides as master of ceremonies at the feast. After much feasting, they set sail the next day for foreign shores.

They first head for the nearest friendly landing, skirting an island belonging to dangerous enemy cannibals with whom they do not kula but whom they have raided in revenge expeditions. When a fleet arrives at its destination, the greetings on both sides vary depending on the distance and strangeness of the guests and hosts. In the expedition Malinowski studied, the first stop was at a village in the Amphlett Islands. The Trobrianders were on exceptionally good terms with these nearby friends, so there was no formal mass introduction upon landing. The arrivals beached their fleet, and with no ceremony they dispersed themselves, each going to the house of his trading partner.

Canoe under sail.

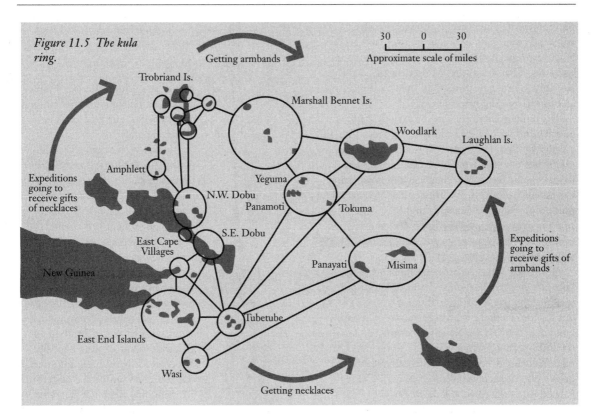

Figure 11.5 The kula ring.

Getting armbands

30 0 30
Approximate scale of miles

Trobriand Is.

Marshall Bennet Is.

Woodlark

Laughlan Is.

Expeditions going to receive gifts of necklaces

Amphlett

Yeguma

N.W. Dobu
Panamoti

Tokuma

Expeditions going to receive gifts of armbands

East Cape Villages

S.E. Dobu

New Guinea

Panayati

Misima

East End Islands

Tubetube

Wasi

Getting necklaces

The final destination of the same expedition was the distant Dobu, whose inhabitants are a fierce and warlike lot. The Trobrianders see them only on the occasions of big kula expeditions. Before approaching the Dobuans, the Trobrianders paused to work "beauty magic" on their persons to make themselves irresistibly attractive. Then they worked more magic on their conch shell trumpets, whose blasts announced the news each time a kula valuable changed hands during the trading.

The Kula Exchange of Gifts and Countergifts

The kula exchange always consists of a round: a gift and its countergift. When a member of a kula expedition arrives in a foreign village, he either is in the *middle* of a round, having given a gift the last time his partner visited him, or expects another round to begin, having given a countergift on his

A canoe fully loaded with a crew of men, just about to arrive in the Amphletts.

275

partner's visit. The object is to maintain strict balanced reciprocity between the two partners, even when the reputation and worth of their treasures escalates. They are always ready to argue that they have given better trophies than they have received. Let us see how the game works.

If a ranking chief goes on the kula to visit his partner and start a new round, he expects a fine gift, a valuable, from his partner. If the trading community is but one stop from home, he may already know the name and history of some valuable his partner has recently received; at a greater distance he would not know. Etiquette demands that the visitor give a small opening gift, **pari,** before the kula exchange takes place—some less valuable item such as a lime pot, a lime stick, or a comb.

If our man wants a particular fine and valuable kula gift, he gives pari plus a handsome gift of food, **pokala** (the same term for tribute given to a chief); but for pokala there is no expectation of an equivalent countergift; it simply enhances the reputation of the kula gift our partner is hoping to receive. Our man may also give solicitory gifts of lesser value, prized objects such as polished axes, which are valuables not classified as kula treasure.

When our man arrives in the Amphletts, he goes to the house of his partner, presents him with a small opening gift, chews betel nuts with his host, and talks about the sea voyage. Nothing happens. Then our man gives his partner a rich tribute of taro, followed by a number of small but valuable hard goods. Finally, the host brings out a shell necklace, the gift always received from partners one visits in a counterclockwise direction. (The Amphletts lie counterclockwise from the Trobriands and from Dobu, their last stop farther west and south.)

When the host bestows the necklace, the first act of the round is complete. A conch shell is blown to announce to the entire gathering that a kula valuable has changed hands. The guest receives the valuable indifferently, hiding his excitement and pleasure behind a cool facade. The host gives the gift with belligerence and hostility, talking angrily about the history of the necklace. He tells from whom he received it and in exchange for what armband, and he gives all the details of the last round, an important

A kula valuable, a necklace made of red spondylus shells.

part of the value and lore of the necklace. The host impresses upon all listeners that a true treasure has changed hands.

Necklaces are conceived of as *male*. The countergift is a *female* shell armband, which is always received from the partners one visits going in a clockwise direction. The exchange or round is conceived of as a marriage. Our Trobriander would be obligated to provide a shell armband countergift when the Amphlett partner pays a visit to him during the next year. The Trobriander would have acquired such an armband on an expedition going in the opposite direction. The round in question is not complete until the countergift armband has made the marriage.

The Trobrianders have the most cordial relations with these nearby people, although the Amphlett villages are constantly at war with each other. After a friendly sojourn, the expedition pushes on to Dobu. The Trobrianders are not great friends with the fierce Dobuans, who are practitioners of black magic. They visit the Dobuans only for purposes of the kula exchange. Because the voyage to Dobu is much more uncertain, problematic, and dangerous, the encoun-

Men wearing armbands. These kula valuables are usually adorned with beads, pendants, and ribbons, but it is unusual, according to Malinowski, to see them worn.

ter with the Dobuans is the focus of much lore and nervous excitement.

Upon arriving at Dobu, after the appropriate magical prelude, the Trobriand fleet draws up opposite the Dobuan village and the "admiral" orates from the bow of his canoe, declaiming eloquently toward the Dobuan chief. Some Dobuan partners approach the canoes to offer (low-ranking) necklaces to their Trobriand partners. The Trobrianders then land, giving "landing gifts" to those who have greeted them, and seek out their partners. Here they do not solicit particular valuables, since they do not know what their partners have acquired in the last year or so. Our man goes to the house of his Dobuan partner, presents him with a small opening gift, and then hands over the other soliciting gifts—the food tribute and the lesser valuables.

His Dobuan partner then gives him a necklace. Because the Dobuan received the necklace on an expedition further counterclockwise in a region where Trobrianders never venture, our man is greatly interested in discovering its identity and hearing how the Dobuan acquired it. The necklace is recognized. The Trobrianders remember that it last passed through the Trobriands some years ago, and for this part of the story they know exactly who acquired it, from whom, under what conditions, and to whom it was passed. Such is the lore of the kula—which the Dobuan now expounds upon with great hostility of manner; meanwhile, the conch shell blasts the news. The Trobriander receives the treasure with studied indifference.

During the next few days, our man dedicates himself to other business. During the course of an expedition, all members are free to engage in haggling barter with anyone other than their kula partners. In the Amphletts they have purchased many fine local pots in exchange for Trobriand-grown foodstuffs and other goods. In addition, they have received many parting gifts from hosts at both stops. Their partners in the Amphletts loaded them down with fine pots as they set sail. In Dobu they receive farewell gifts of betel nut and other useful items.

The Trobrianders do not eat meals with their Dobuan hosts (or have sexual relations with their women). Rather, they take meals on their canoes, eating food they have brought with them.

The fleet heads for home, stopping on the way to fish and dive for shells. They arrive heavily laden with valuables and other wares and are met at home with great excitement. Their imports (other than the necklaces) are quickly dispersed among their relatives and friends in return for the many parting gifts bestowed on them when the expedition set out. After the master of each canoe has feasted his crew, the expedition is over. Plans turn toward the next one.

Receiving Expeditions and the Countergift

Our Trobriander may next journey in the opposite, or clockwise, direction and enter new rounds with other partners who give him shell armbands. When Dobuan and Amphlett partners visit him in the next year or so, he is expected to make a countergift of shell armbands to complete the round of exchange. If he does not have an armband worthy of the necklace gift he got from his Dobuan partner, he may give a lesser armband as a promissory gift, a token of his good faith and his intention to complete the round with a real countergift eventually. The token keeps the round open, but it may be received with harsh words and recriminations by the Dobuan in an attempt to shame the partner into giving a worthy countergift.

If our Trobriander has a fine shell armband to give in final exchange for the necklace received in Dobu the year before, the "marriage" is complete. The

Dobuan canoes pulled up on a Trobriand beach on an expedition of their own.

initial gift is called the bite, the countergift is called the tooth, and the exchange is called a biting. If the Dobuan is not satisfied, he may complain that the tooth is not equal to the bite, and bad blood may follow. The Dobuan may hire a sorcerer to work witchcraft on his trading partner in revenge for the unequal exchange (negative reciprocity) he claims was worked upon him. An important part of the lore of the kula valuables is the list of the names of those "who died for them" from illness brought by the witchcraft of dissatisfied givers. Therefore, when a countergift is handed over, the host orates in a flowery speech about the value of the piece.

The Kula and the Life Cycle

Most adult Trobriander men practice the kula; chiefs have as many as ninety trading partners, commoners far fewer. Lists of partners and valuables acquired are comparable to Tupinambá lists of captives slain, as shown by the body scars of warriors.

A young Trobriander past adolescence is initiated into the kula by his father. Because his father belongs to another clan, and because the young man goes to live with his maternal uncle, his father is a "friend" living in another place, an ideal person to start the round with. A father teaches his son the magic necessary for departing on an expedition and then

Dobuan kula visitors with their hosts in the Trobriands.

gives him a valuable. He takes the boy with him on the next expedition and sees to it that one of his trading partners gives a gift not to him, but to his son.

The boy thus acquires two kinds of valuables and two trading partners, one of them being his father—all one needs to launch a kula career. Upon his return home, he presents his father with the valuable he received on the expedition or he waits and gives it to yet a third partner, someone who visits him. The rest of his life will be planned around the acquisition and bestowal of treasure. And a time-consuming occupation it shall be.

BRIEF ANALYSIS: THE COMPETITIVE FEAST AND THE KULA EXPEDITION COMPARED

In their formal characteristics these two institutions are much alike. Trobrianders go on an expedition, much as guests do to a competitive feast. At the event both sides are on guard, apart, and give each other gifts formally. There is in fact no feasting in the sense of eating together at the competitive feast, and no such feasting occurs during the kula interchanges. Both sides eat apart. Both sets of guests receive gifts and take them back home for consumption. In the kula, however, the guests do bring many gifts with them, and there is much trading at the event, something that does not happen at a competitive feast, in which the giving is entirely one way. The guests, however, trade only lower-ranking goods as tokens for the sought after valuables.

In both alliance and competitive feasting the guests are rivals, even enemies who owe blood scores. In the kula, the guests are merely strangers, distant trading partners—potential enemies, but not necessarily so in deed. But it, too, is a ritual of reversal of warfare. The prized valuables are brought home as if they were booty. Because the valuables are traded widely, yet always come back to those who once held them, the system can consciously integrate wider areas than any feasting system does.

SUMMARY AND CONCLUSIONS

A redistributive system such as that of the Siuai is built on many reciprocal transactions, both generalized and balanced, that culminate in the climactic acts of competitive feastgiving, which in turn are examples of negative reciprocity. Big Men and their followers start from the model of a group of households related by kinship and practice *generalized exchange* whereby all contribute to the leader just as they do to the parents at a birth feast. Each Big Man has many trading partners in distant communities with whom he practices *balanced reciprocity*. Any two Big Men engaged in a feasting contest are practicing *negative reciprocity*, in which one side seems to get something for nothing. The side that does, *loses* prestige.

Similarly, the kula exchange is conceived of as ideally balanced, but it is also competitive, and the man who gives his partner a better gift than the last round *wins* momentarily while demanding a better gift next time, and so on.

It is the nature of the score that concerns us. Scores are, after all, expressions of value. Both alliance and competitive feastgivers and hosts to trading expeditions typically give away an array of ranked goods. At the low-ranking end of the sorting are, typically, subsistence goods such as starchy puddings, branches of bananas, and so on. Consumable goods come next, followed by prize foods such as pork, in great quantities. Primitive money, items that may be standards of value but not necessarily means of payment or of exchange (they are not "all purpose" money like our currencies), come next. In Melanesia money is typically strands of shells. Finely worked valuables come last, at the other end of the ladder of ranked goods. These are symbols standing for the entire feast or trading event, but they cannot be purchased outright by a feast or by low-ranking goods; they must be purchased—usually—by other valuables. They are thought of as being without price. (In Papua New Guinea, Ongka, a Big Man immortalized in a film and two books by

Andrew Strathern [1971, 1979], wore a tally necklace, each slat in the necklace standing for a feast he had presided over.)

Thus, some valuables, such as those of the kula, take on the fame of the events in which they are exchanged and bear the name of the chiefs who owned them. It is as if the Tiwi gravepoles had been put into circulation. Kula valuables, like gravepoles, are monuments to past lives and past achievements. When a man possesses one, he shares momentarily in the great exploits of the past.

The closest analogy to tribal valuables in the contemporary world is in the art market. When wealthy private collectors or museums acquire a work of art today, they invoke the story (myth) of the artist who created it and recite a litany of past owners. They may tell stories that the object was not appreciated for years or was even hidden, and they exalt their current superior appreciation of the object. Thus, the dollar value of works of art skyrockets, because, like kula valuables, they are held to be without price, but of the deepest human values.

The similarities among a tribal warfare complex, a competitive feasting system, and a reciprocal trading ring are astonishingly close. Each consists of expeditions formed hierarchically and blessed by many parting and returning rituals. Each ranges far into foreign territory and settlements of known strangers. The object of each is to return laden with goods, whether booty or trade goods, and with coveted trophies, whether human captives or kula treasure. The object of each is to even or better the score between the two sides. Moreover, the traffic in each serves to validate male status and initiate a young man into adulthood. In each system, internal energies are focused outward, collective efforts are marshaled, and internal tensions, as between in-laws, are dispersed.

In the competitive feast the same pattern of actions applies, only now the guests are bidden openly to come to the home of their rivals. Instead of stealing, they receive gifts, which, however, they treat in exactly the same manner they treat booty. *And, while booty is a token of winning, gifts are a token of losing.* The hosts defy loss by giving away their goods. They also transmute the bloody exchange of war into the peaceful exchanges of feasting. *They are triumphing over war.*

Acts of war are attempts to balance negative exchanges, and in feasting and trading rings these warlike acts are transmuted symbolically into the safe acts of gift giving. However, partners are always potential enemies who sometimes engage in witchcraft and avenge a negative exchange by a magical murder. War does break out, and in the midst of the kula, some groups may be at war with others, usually peripheral to the system.

The kula ring is unusually systematic; it has been worked out quite precisely over hundreds of miles and has assimilated all foreign communication to two flowing currents: female armbands going clockwise and their husband necklaces going counterclockwise. Because both trophies are awarded to expeditions that come to fetch them, they exactly resemble war trophies in their movement. That is, no one takes them and bestows them on the stranger at his home; rather, one goes and wrests them from the stranger, just as in warlike systems one seizes the trophies abroad.

It is clear that it is difficult for us to talk about the behaviors we have examined here as *economic* in the sense of rational human choices maximizing material gains. Certainly the natives do not think of them that way. But feasting, trading, and warfare do provide for the circulation of values and for the production and circulation of goods.

Competitive feasts and trading rings also provide beneficial unintended side effects. For one, they minimize risks of famine and want by setting up credit with feastgivers and kula traders. One can get food from outsiders in lean years. Feasts and ritual trade, too, are rational choices when contrasted with their ever-present close alternative, which they in fact imitate so closely in form, warfare. In sum, it is better to give than to kill.

Another potential outcome of any competitive feast is the transmutation of competition into alliance. A "defeated" guest Big Man may chose to give a noncompetitive feast in return, either trying to end his career honorably and retire from the field (especially if he is an old man) or signaling an alliance as a follower of the victorious host Big Man. By this means hierarchies may appear. Thus we have a victorious Big Man who commands former Big Men he vanquished early in his career. These men continue to give feasts in their home districts but do not command other Big Men to attend them. When our Big Man has bested renowned Big Men, he commands them and, through them, their subsidiary Big Men.

One way to define the score, then, is by the number and ranking of the lesser Big Men in a leaders' hierarchy. The score, then, is a function of political economy and is measured by human lives and allegiances, not by other material goods. It is to explicit tribal political systems that we turn in the next chapter.

SUGGESTED READINGS

Codere, Helen. *Fighting with Property.* Locust Valley, N.Y.: Augustin, 1950. (Monographs of the American Ethnological Society, No. 18.) A dramatic study of potlatching on the northwest coast, showing that Big Men and redistribution are by no means confined to Melanesia.

Heider, Karl. *Grand Valley Dani: Peaceful Warriors,* 2nd ed. Ft. Worth: Harcourt Brace Jovanovich, 1991. A good account of alliance feasting in relation to Big Men, who however do not engage in competitive feasting.

Malinowski, Bronislaw. *Argonauts of the Western Pacific.* New York: Dutton, 1961. (Reprint of 1922 book.) Incomparably solid and detailed; the long sections on mythology may be skipped by the casual reader.

Oliver, Douglas L. *A Solomon Island Society: Kinship and Leadership Among the Siuai of Bougainville.* Cambridge, Mass.: Harvard University Press, 1955 (Beacon Press paperback, 1967). Long and detailed; the author seems to use many theories to organize his data, but the descriptions of competitive feasting are unmatched.

Strathern, Andrew. *Ongka: A Self-account by a New Guinea Big-man.* New York: St. Martin's Press, 1979. A life history of a Big Man as told to anthropologist Strathern. It contains a fascinating account of a particularly bitter warfare episode with erstwhile allies and of the alliance feasting that restored the alliance.

Strathern, Andrew. *The Rope of Moka: Big-Men and Ceremonial Exchange in Mount Hagen, New Guinea.* New York: Cambridge University Press, 1971. Another account of a Big Man, whose gifts include motorcycles and a Toyota pickup truck.

Weiner, Annette B. *The Trobrianders of Papua New Guinea.* Ft. Worth: Harcourt Brace Jovanovich, 1988. An ethnography that emphasizes the many complex ritual exchanges between men and women within the Trobriands. It sets the context within which the kula happens.

SUGGESTED FILMS

The Feast. Timothy Asch and Napoleon Chagnon. Cambridge, Mass: DER Associates, 1974. An alliance feast among two former enemy villages of the Yanomamo Indians of the tropical forest of Venezuela.

Ongka's Big Moka. C. Nairn. London: Grenada Television, Disappearing World Series, 1974. A look at a Big Man marshaling festivities for the climactic feast of his career.

GLOSSARY

alliance feast A ritual event staged to transform two sets of enemies into allies. It is thus a redressive mechanism in an ongoing conflict process and aims to cancel old scores in warfare.

balanced reciprocity Reciprocal exchange in which an attempt is made immediately to give back goods of equivalent value to those of the original gift.

Big Man A leader who builds a career of feastgiving, first from generalized, redistributive, family events and later by competitive feasts against other Big Men, whom he defeats by negative reciprocity, giving them more than the other can repay. Defeated Big Men may become followers of their victors. Big Men do not inherit their positions.

competitive feast A ritual event staged by a Big Man, the object of which is to defeat the guest/rival by bestowing so many gifts on him and his followers that they will be unable to stage a more generous feast in the future.

feasting A ritual system featuring the symbolic redistribution of goods, in order to convert rivals into allies, thereby making peace within the new alliance. Feasting is a means for strong single leaders to lead hierarchies of men and women, a substitute for war, and a means to circulate certain kinds of valuable goods.

generalized reciprocity Reciprocal daily or seasonal exchange between persons closely related in both space (sharing the same households or neighborhoods) and kinship or friendship, in which return gifts, or paybacks, are delayed and not expected to be of equal value immediately but to balance out in the long run.

kula ring In Melanesia, a far-flung trading ring in which expeditions go to receive gifts of one class of valuables (necklaces) in a counterclockwise direction, and another class (armbands) in a clockwise direction over hundreds of miles.

money Arbitrary symbolic objects that serve as standards of value (other objects can be evaluated in their terms), as means of exchange (one can trade them for anything else), and as means of payment (as when one pays a fine).

negative reciprocity Reciprocal exchange (which at first seems nonreciprocal) in which one party does not reciprocate with goods for goods received, as in warfare. The counter-"gift" is revenge or indemnity. In competitive feasting, to receive a gift one cannot repay in greater value is to lose prestige, and hence the game.

pari In the kula ring, small opening gifts presented by the guest to the host prior to the host's giving the guest a valuable.

pokala Among the Trobrianders, the "tribute" or contributions followers make to their chiefs, who are usually their brothers-in-law. Also, the large gifts of food and consumables a guest on a kula expedition may make to his trading partner prior to receiving a valuable. Such gifts enhance the prestige of the valuable but do not pay for it.

redistribution A specialized kind of reciprocity in which many partners each give goods to a single partner, who in turn then gives back the goods, usually received individually, in a collective ritual event.

sagali Among the Trobrianders, the name for the consumable goods that a chief gives to his followers at a feast. It is the payback form of tribute, *pokala*.

trading partner A former stranger with whom one enters a trading relationship by means of a special ritual, which transforms the stranger into a safe partner. In the tribal world, lacking markets, it is otherwise both difficult and dangerous to trade with strangers.

trading ring The trading of certain valuable goods with ritual trading partners in specified directions from group to group.

valuables Goods, usually finely made, durable, and possibly ornamental, that are ranked more highly than lesser, consumable goods exchanged for them, usually in large quantities. Valuables become trophies commemorating their past owners and the exchanges they have passed through.

Tribal Politics:
Leadership and Its Rewards

12

POLITICAL LEADERSHIP

Aristotle's Political Terminology

Unspoken Constitutions and Social Organization

Natural Leadership and Coalitions

*ETHNOGRAPHIC CLOSE-UP:
AN ELEMENTARY LEADERSHIP
PATTERN: NAMBICUARA LEADERS
AND THEIR FOLLOWERS*

The Chief's Duties

The Chief's Reward

The Chief's Role in Foreign Relations

*THE LEADER-FOLLOWER UNIT: THE
NAMBICUARA CASE*

Leader-Follower Ties and Exchange Transactions

Values and Legitimacy

Sanctions, Negative and Positive

Political Time Scales and Tensions over Payoffs

TRIBAL REPUBLICS

*ETHNOGRAPHIC CLOSE-UP:
THE CHEYENNE TRIBAL REPUBLIC*

Cheyenne Bands, War Parties, and Leaders

Associations: Military Societies for Ritual and Police

Peace Chiefs

*OVERVIEW OF THE CHEYENNE
POLITICAL SYSTEM:
RULE BY THE FEW IN
CONSULTATION WITH THE MANY*

*I*n band societies leadership is embedded in the institutions of family and ritual. Leaders seldom stand out among band peoples. But in tribal societies there emerges much more clearly the institution of **politics,** a set of activities in which leaders and followers together strive to keep the community in balance with its resources, maintain internal order, and represent the community to outsiders, while verbally and dramatically attempting to uphold the dominant worldview and values of that community's culture.

POLITICAL LEADERSHIP

Leadership, like so much human behavior, is based on primate capacities. All primate communities classified as multimale troops form male dominance hierarchies. Adult males are constantly competing with each other for rank in the hierarchy. In many species the most dominant, or alpha, male, leads the troop on its daily rounds in search of food. Dominance regulates access to sexually attractive females and keeps order among juveniles, whose play spills over into fighting. The dominant males represent the troop to other troops and predators and form a rampart to protect it.

Dominance hierarchies perform functions of maintaining the equilibrium of the group and its material resources and of controlling pressures welling up within the group, such as sexual desires or the increasing strength and assertiveness of maturing adult males. Male chimpanzees, for example, form coalitions, especially if they are brothers, to compete together for higher dominance status. More-dominant males intervene in status competitions to keep the level of violence down within the troop. Meanwhile, the erstwhile competitors make a common coalition for the whole troop when they go on patrol. Leadership, expressed through dominance, regulates the activities of the troop on a daily and seasonal timetable and, over generational time, maintains the troop in equilibrium with other troops. In short, there is such a thing as primate politics, and we human beings are heirs to it.

In human bands leadership is much less clearly patterned. The invention of the family and kinship seems to have dissolved the dominance hierarchy in band-level human beings. Leadership is exerted in much less clearly formed coalitions of elders. We saw this in the "core elders" of the !Kung San band and in the circles of polygynous elders of the Tiwi.

In the tribal world, leadership begins to appear, like the dominance hierarchy, for its own sake and in forms, such as the war party, that are similar to it. Across the many competing tribal communities leadership is always multiple and competitive and is often but variably connected to ritual, warfare, and exchange. In Chapter 11 we studied leaders, Big Men, who arise from exchange (and ritual). In Chapter 13 we shall study leaders—shamans and prophets—who derive their power from rituals and myths of their own devising. In this chapter we shall examine leaders whose power is simply a function of their leadership. In short, we shall look at *political leaders*.

Aristotle's Political Terminology

The Greek philosopher Aristotle, in his treatise titled *Politics*, asserted that peoples regularly oscillate back and forth among rule by the one, by the few, and by the many. Each kind of governance can be for the common good or for the selfish interest of the leaders (see Figure 12.1). Rule of the one can take the form of **monarchy,** in the common interest, or **tyranny,** self-interested. Rule by the few is **aristocracy,** in the common interest, or **oligarchy,** self-interested. Rule by the many is **polity,** in the common interest, or **democracy,** self-interested. (You can see that current usage differs from Aristotle's; we use *polity* to mean a political system, and use *democracy* in a good sense. *Demagoguery*—mob rule in response to inflammatory leaders—is the closest word we have for "self-interested" democracy.)

Many anthropologists, when thinking about human evolution, have, perhaps unwittingly, implied that human societies evolve in the direction from rule by the many to rule by the few to, finally, rule by one person. That is,

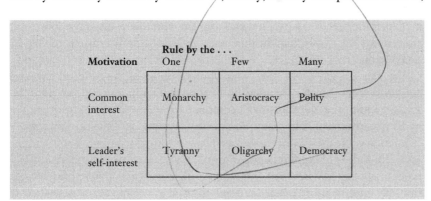

Motivation	Rule by the . . .		
	One	Few	Many
Common interest	Monarchy	Aristocracy	Polity
Leader's self-interest	Tyranny	Oligarchy	Democracy

Figure 12.1 Aristotle's terminology for types of political systems.

tribes are thought to be democratic, while chiefdoms (a posited stage lead-ing to civilization, which I feel is unnecessary) are thought to be oligarchic or aristocratic. In this view, civilization emerges only with monarchy and the creation of ancient cities and empires.

This view is too simple. In tribal societies the three variations seem in-stead to be in constant play, back and forth, in kaleidoscopic variety. Over the long term, the political formations of tribes are constantly changing. The same is true for civilizations. It is not the presence of monarchy that tells us we have civilization, but rather the existence of a *full-time state*, which commands permanent settlements, monumental architecture, stores of wealth, and literate records; coordinates many ethnic groups; and conducts an aggressive foreign policy, if sometimes only in defense. A civilized state, however, can be monarchy or tyranny, aristocracy or oligarchy, democracy or demagoguery.

The **state** usually emerges only out of informal polities at the level of civilizations. It consists of a formal, explicit, publicly constituted set of offi-cials (as opposed to persons) with full-time duties and coercive police pow-ers that can be used against the members of the community. Tribal leaders often hold power personally, rather than through an office, and they are almost never full time.

Unspoken Constitutions and Social Organization

In any given tribal society, leadership patterns crystallize and remain stable for time scales ranging from one generation to perhaps 300 to 500 years. The oligarchic/aristocratic/anarchic Nuer, for example, for generations have followed four kinds of local leaders, each with different functions: the "bull," who serves as marriage broker and village patriarch; the "man of cattle," who initiates the village boys; the "man of the spear," whose lineage "owns" the community and who must go on every war party; and the leopard-skin chief, who acts as mediator. This multiple leadership is shaped by the overall framework of complementary opposition. Occasionally, however, a shaman may turn himself into a prophet and lead the Nuer nation against some out-side enemy on a holy war. In this case the Nuer briefly consent to rule by one person.

We can say, then, that the Nuer observe, most of the time, an *unspoken constitution* that can be summed up in the leadership patterns we have de-scribed and in the mechanisms of complementary opposition as worked out by Evans-Pritchard. The Nuer do not have writing, and their mythology of segmentary lineages is not recited as if it were one document. Yet it and the associated ideas of conflict, cooperation, and internal mediation all amount to an unspoken constitution, which gives shape to their public life. We can thus say that in most tribal societies the social organization described in

Civilized Constitutions

In civilized societies constitutions need not be written down; the British constitution is an example of an unwritten constitution embodied in understandings, common practices, and various key laws. The United States's written constitution gives us an illusion of immutable stability, but in fact the Constitution has been formally amended many times, and amended informally by historic circumstances—the Civil War, for example. In practice we perform many constitutional acts, such as presidential nominating conventions, that were never in the original image of the body politic.

Civilized constitutions can change quite rapidly and violently. France since 1789 has had many constitutions, embodying differing principles of governance. France has had five republics, two monarchies, and two empires. One constitution, that of the Third Republic, lasted for three generations, but on the average, France has rewritten its constitution every twenty years over the last two centuries.

U.S. Constitution.

ethnographies by anthropologists amounts to at least short-term **constitutions,** understandings of how the society ought to operate in public affairs and of how leadership is properly conducted. Such images change over time, but the time scale for change is from twenty to several hundreds of years.

Leadership can also crystallize around kinship and descent. In Chapter 11 we saw that the Trobriand Island chiefs inherit their positions from their mother's brother, who picks a nephew to succeed to the office. Once in office, a Trobriand chief takes many wives and has many brothers-in-law raising yams for him. This gives him the material resources to contract as many as ninety partners in the kula trading ring.

Politics, then, refers to the patterns of leadership that couple a community to its material resources and maintain it, often through warfare, in equilibrium with its neighbors over cycles of from a few years, to many generations, to 300 to 500 years in a stably patterned polity.

In this chapter we are interested in analyzing leadership on its own terms, as *politics*, rather than in terms of family, feasting, or ritual, and in analyzing it as abstractly as we can find it in the ethnographic record.

Natural Leadership and Coalitions

The potential for *leadership* is a genetic potential distributed among individuals in any human group. We can assume that from the primate evidence, but there is good evidence from among humans as well. Some people take the lead, assert themselves. Like primate alpha animals, they take the initiative in aggressive episodes, displace others for access to some resource, and rush forward to attack when the group is threatened by outside dangers. Dominant personalities no doubt come into their own when given the opportunity to lead others, as in hunting expeditions, and then later in warlike raids.

However, for such a personality to rise to a position of influence in human groups he or she must take into account human values. Most groups value harmony and sharing. The dominant human personality must be able to invoke these values. More than the aggressive nonverbal displays of chimpanzees, human leaders must develop skills in oratory and persuasion. They must be able to argue, by words or by deeds, that their own life is exemplary of the values of the group.

In elementary form, then, human politics at the tribal level is the formation of coalitions of followers around a leader, who literally leads them through territory in activities often aggressive and competitive. Like the primate alpha male, he represents the group to other communities. The human leader is the spokesman, or diplomat, standing in front of and speaking for his group.

As societies grow more complicated, several political teams, or coalitions around separate leaders, compete within the wider community as well as with others outside it (Bailey, 1969). As politics emerges more fully toward the state, the teams become activated more constantly and formally and together use some team as police—rather like war parties turned inward on the community.

Although some tribal societies are chiefdoms in which the tendency for one-man rule has prevailed, many others are **tribal republics,** ruled by a number of leaders, assembled in councils, usually with all the adult men. Republics sort their leaders out by order of rank and rules of rotation through terms in office, a tendency we shall examine among the Cheyenne.

Natural leadership, the elementary principle of politics, consists of a leader attracting followers by his own performance (or vice versa), and not necessarily through kinship ties or ritual services. (Some leaders do use such ties and are both patriarch and shaman. Others, and these are the ones we expressly *do not mean*, are simply thrust into office by inheritance or divination, regardless of whether they have any aptitude for the task. Inept heirs bring unstable politics.)

AN ELEMENTARY LEADERSHIP PATTERN:
NAMBICUARA LEADERS AND THEIR FOLLOWERS

One superb example of natural leadership is found in Claude Lévi-Strauss's study of the Nambicuara chieftainship in Matto Grosso state in Brazil (1944). Lévi-Strauss encountered these Indians during the dry season, the time of the year when a chief is always in command. They spend the wet season along rivers where they plant their gardens, but in the dry season the river village splits into two or three groups, each following its chief across the savannahs in a nomadic search for food. Half the year the Nambicuara are gardeners, the other half hunters and gatherers.

During the dry season, the activities of the Nambicuara chief are much like those of the dominant male in a nomadic primate troop. The chief decides when the group shall move and paces its journey across the savannah; he forges ahead himself and finds sources of food; he starts the group moving in the morning and picks its camping ground in the evening. And, when the group is threatened, he represents it to outsiders.

The Chief's Duties

Lévi-Strauss investigated chieftainship at length. Is the chief's position hereditary? He was told that sons of chiefs are preferred, but only if they are suitable. If not, someone else is picked, with no apologies to the hereditary candidate. What privileges does the chief have? "His privilege is to go ahead on the path." It turns out that the chief's duties are many, however. He must work all the time, far harder than anyone else. Not only does he go ahead looking for game and food, he also collects it. At night, he tells jokes and stories to his people and sings them lullabies as they go to sleep. Often, he is good at games as well.

Nambicuara playing panpipes.

Yet the leader does not seem materially rewarded. He does not eat better and he has less material wealth than the others. Lévi-Strauss had brought many trinkets to give his Indian hosts—baubles, beads, scissors, mirrors, and the like. He gave them to the chief, who, within the day, had turned them over to his male followers. Within a few days, the goods had trickled to the outskirts of the group and become the playthings of the children.

When Lévi-Strauss wanted to get back to the river village to contact other groups of the Nambicuara, he convinced the chief to interrupt usual nomadic routines and lead him back. Because Lévi-Strauss's draft animals were laden with supplies, the chief did not take his usual route through the dense forest but rather took a more open one. After several days, the food was exhausted, the destination had not been reached, and it was evident that they were lost. In short, the Indians saw that their leader was not leading them properly.

When the chief sought to make camp, the bunch of sullen Indians lay down on the ground and refused to light fires or speak to him. The next morning they stayed in bed (on the ground) and did not stir. Quietly, the chief disappeared into the bush with one companion. He returned at the end of the day with huge baskets filled with grasshoppers. Everyone got up, lit a fire, roasted the grasshoppers, and consumed them. The next morning, the group, its good humor restored, got up and went out to gather grasshoppers. On the following day, they set out again toward the river village.

The Chief's Reward

Lévi-Strauss was perplexed. Why would anyone accept a chief's position? He leads, scouts, hunts, collects food, entertains his following, and keeps them happy. Yet he seems to get no reward for harder work, and he has fewer material possessions. There is, however, one reward for the chief: he alone among the Nambicuara has an extra wife, sometimes two. Usually they are his first wife's nieces and considerably younger than he. Such wives are called "tomboy wantons" in the South American tropical forest region. The tomboy, usually teenaged, tags along after the chief and helps in all his work, instead of staying at home by the fire and cooking as his first wife does; she is a valuable help on the leader's path.

According to Lévi-Strauss, granting the chief an extra wife represents a real sacrifice for the group, because in a small population the sex ratios are nearly even, and if the chief gets extra wives, some young men must do without. Consequently, some young men engage in temporary homosexual unions, quite openly calling each other "spouse."

The Chief's Role in Foreign Relations

Within the wider Nambicuara community of the river village, two or three chiefs live together peacefully, recognizing one of themselves as village headman and allowing him to pick the garden sites and to decree the days for planting. But out in the savannah, each separate chief is responsible for foreign relations. Events in this connection are quite dramatic.

Lévi-Strauss observed what happens in such an encounter with outsiders. He described a group wandering out at evening on the high savannah, with its vast views, and suddenly seeing the fires of another group on the horizon, perhaps as far as 50 miles away. They nervously discuss the identity of the strangers, and if they believe them to be a

Nambicuara family shelter.

party from their own village, they approach in the next day or so to have a pleasant encounter and to exchange news and food. But if they are uncertain, they cautiously circle the area for the next few days, each night the campfires glowing closer, until finally they are within meeting distance.

That morning women and children are sent into hiding. The men of the two sides draw near, the leaders approaching each other at the head of their groups. One takes the initiative and acts aggrieved, shouting in a stylized manner with a nasalized whine at the end of each word: "We are very annoyed! You are our enemies!" The other chief exclaims in the same manner, "We are not annoyed! We are your friends! Your friends! True friends! We can understand each other!" (Lévi-Strauss, 1948, p. 92; my translation.)

Finally, the two sides retreat about 20 yards, light separate campfires, and dance, each one entertaining and applauding the other. After the dancing, individual men from one side make stylized assaults on others on the opposite side, approaching the opponent with menacing gestures and seizing his G-string tassel. Sometimes the exchange becomes so heated that others fall on the pair and separate them, but they only return to their pantomimed fray. After this prelude has dragged on quite some time, with the same hostility of manner, the two men begin to inspect each other's personal adornment and to demand gifts: "Give me, give me, see, see, it's pretty!" One will seize some ornament such as an armband.

The articles demanded are handed over, and then each adversary partner brings out other articles and simply gives them to the other. Each exchanges whatever he has on hand. In no case do they stop to calculate value or equivalency of goods exchanged. Lévi-Strauss observed that most groups have possessions that other groups lack and want. A more distant section of the tribe that does not manufacture pottery depends on these encounters to get some. All manner of goods change hands: cotton thread, cotton balls, beeswax, resin, vegetal insect repellents, tobacco, seeds, shells, earrings, bracelets, necklaces, feathers, bamboo slivers for making arrows, porcupine quills, gourds, and pottery vessels.

The exchange goes on all day without any sort of haggling or taking stock of the gifts. When they are done, the two groups beat a retreat into the bush, collect their women, and retreat further to a campfire. Here they stop and take stock. Then come the calculations. Some men may indeed be discontented with the goods acquired from the strangers and think

regretfully of the articles they have given away. Some may covet the strangers' women.

The dissatisfied group may then decide to mount a war party and a raid, with the object of taking booty, especially captive women. If so, they find a shaman to perform a war ritual over them. In some cases, says Lévi-Strauss, they get themselves all painted up, perform the powwow, rush off, and then give up the next day without having found the enemy. If they do raid, their object is to surprise the strangers at night and to carry off as much booty and as many women as possible. Although Lévi-Strauss observed the peaceful form of encounter and its exchange, he never observed the warlike one; presumably it would be under the direction of the day-to-day chief, who goes ahead in all things, including the warpath.

THE LEADER-FOLLOWER UNIT: THE NAMBICUARA CASE

The Nambicuara provide a pure example of leadership politics because the tie between the leader and his followers is not formed by kinship, ritual, or even feasting but rather simply depends on the attractiveness of the chief and the insistence of the followers that he lead. They form a mutually dependent foraging team, which also competes sporadically with the teams of strangers.

The Nambicuara political coalition does not reach deeply into society. It is composed only of the chief, his male adult householder companions, and his own polygynous household; this group responds directly to his commands. The chief's household does not participate when the coalition faces strangers together. The chief never orders around the wife of one of his followers. Rather, the follower himself transmits the chief's instructions by

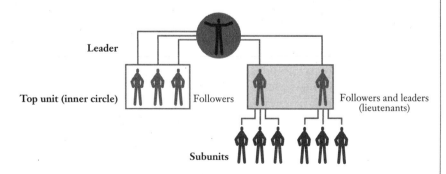

Leader

Top unit (inner circle)   Followers   Followers and leaders (lieutenants)

Subunits

Figure 12.2 Hierarchical leader-follower units.

issuing his own commands to wife and children. Political life stops, then, at the boundary of domestic life.

In more complex societies, leader-follower units are often more hierarchically formed and extend more deeply into society. In such cases, top followers have followers of their own. A flowchart of coalition activity (Figure 12.2) shows several lines of influence going out from the leader to his followers. Some stop at a follower and some lead out in a chain from the follower to others. This is the case with Songi and his subsidiary Big Men, as we saw in the last chapter.

Leader-Follower Ties and Exchange Transactions

What is the nature of the tie between leader and followers? Lévi-Strauss says it is an exchange relationship in which the leader does extraordinary feats in return for helpful labor and sexual favors. In material terms, the leader goes ahead to find food and to collect much of it; in return, the group yields him tomboy helper wives. But there is more to the transaction than that. In purely social terms, the followers gain the assurance that their next steps will be taken care of. They do not have to worry about the details of the range or what awaits them tomorrow. The chief, who does have to worry about these details, has the dramatic reward of being center stage and having all eyes focused on him and has the pleasure of dominance and prestige.

Lévi-Strauss believes that some persons are born with the temperament to enjoy these things but that in the absence of born leaders, the group will find someone and force him into the role anyway. Because leadership is a dramatic transaction, it is no accident that leaders are often competent performers in activities valued by the group. They need not be brilliant, but they can carry off most tasks with skill. The Nambicuara chief, for example, is expert in many things—craft manufacture, for one. With a competent chief, followers have the satisfaction of seeing necessary acts done right and of associating with a person who provides a pleasant model.

F. G. Bailey (1969) says that some leader-follower units are based on moral *transactions* in which there are no material payoffs to the followers, only moral ones. Vicarious satisfaction is such a payoff. In many cases, such rewards are expressed through ritual. Chiefs are often the leaders in rites of intensification. When Songi completed his greatest feast, as we saw in Chapter 11, the only immediate payoff to his followers was a moral victory. They might have to wait years, if ever, for a material reward from the shamed guest of honor. When shamans are transformed into prophets, the moral claims between leader and followers are quite clear; the followers, or fanatics, are quite content to await their reward in the next life and to exact a spiritual one on earth.

Values and Legitimacy

Moral transactions must of course reflect the worldview and values of the culture of the leaders and followers. Leaders, therefore, are well advised to seem to embody the values of the culture. They must be able to perform valued activities well, and not just those of leading, but of entertaining, as we saw in the Nambicuara case. (Esteemed Tiwi elders are all good at performing their song and dance routines, for example.)

As we noted in Chapter 8, values can be contradictory. The !Kung value harmony, but they also value the combative skills of the hunter, who can use those skills against his fellows. In tribal societies such aggressive values can be focused on the outsider. Prophets, as we shall see in the next chapter, can actively formulate new values and codify their application to behavior. They can remake unspoken constitutions and verbalize them (and in civilized societies, put them in writing).

By and large, however, leaders must appeal to cultural values, uphold them in their actions, and reinforce them in their speeches. They must seem to have **legitimacy**—that is, they must seem to express that which is valued, good, and clearly lawful. In tribal society, lawfulness is not fully brought to consciousness; much law is not spoken, let alone written. But people know when some action violates their sense of rights and obligations.*

Sanctions, Negative and Positive

Leaders and followers also exercise **sanctions** on each other and on society at large. Social scientists tend to think in terms of physical sanctions or punishments, reflecting European laws and customs that define a legitimate leader as one who may use physical force to coerce and punish others. Among the coalitions of tribal societies, however, it is apparent that most leaders have slight recourse to punishment, or negative sanctions. Most such leaders rely on a single form of punishment, which varies from silently ignoring or boycotting an offender to outright expulsion from the group, the most drastic punishment.

The more important sanctions in a primitive coalition are positive. The rewards or payoffs for participating in a going concern go quite unnoticed as long as things are faring well. Things that go as they should are their own reward. But the moment things go wrong, followers may apply their own negative sanctions on the leader, as the Nambicuara did by their sitdown strike when their leader led them somewhat astray.

---

*For example, in the English-speaking countries there has usually been no need to pass laws or ordinances against killing a dog for meat and eating it. Such an action is so deeply tabued in the Anglo-Saxon cultural tradition that people are not even aware of its possibility. But for over a century in the former British Crown Colony of Hong Kong, and recently in San Francisco, lawmakers have found it necessary to outlaw the consumption of canine flesh, which is not tabued in Chinese culture and is even considered a delicacy.

Political Time Scales and Tensions over Payoffs

Leader-follower units are activated with varying frequencies, by daily, seasonal, and generational rhythms. The Nambicuara coalition is activated every day during half the year and then falls dormant after the group returns to the river village, at which time subsidiary chiefs group themselves around the village chief, quite informally. The group goes from rule by the one to loose rule by the few.

In Chapter 11 we saw Songi the Big Man rise to almost dictatorial prominence for half the Siuai nation. He could channel their energies into putting on a great feast. His rise was on a generational time scale. This performance was only possible, however, because the Australian administration had stamped out warfare, so no war chiefs were diverting energies every few years from Songi's lifetime goals.

In politics in general, as Aristotle observed, a dynamic tension is maintained between the payoff for the group and the payoff for the leader, between the common good and the leader's advantage. You are no doubt familiar with the phenomenon of cult leaders who live in extreme luxury from the offerings of their followers, who in turn live in extreme self-inflicted penury, making sacrifices for their leader. All leaders, whether they know it or not, are engaged in a sort of tug-of-war with their followers, to see how much of a material reward they can get and how much they have to reward their close followers or henchmen by depriving others of goods. Generally, extreme inequities occur only in civilizations, for reasons we shall examine in another chapter.

TRIBAL REPUBLICS

As I have said, many anthropological discussions of political evolution unwittingly sound as if a unilineal course from rule by the many to the few to the one were the progressive path of human social evolution. But in fact all societies at tribal and civilized levels grapple with all three forms, at least on scales of 300 years or more, since unspoken constitutions over five or six lifetimes must grapple with new generations, changes in natural habitat, and ideas and alliances from outside. Therefore, I wish to discuss at some length a tribal republic that mixes rule of the few with consultations with the many and that keeps the one, the successful war leader, hemmed in by many fellow leaders.

In a tribal republic, many chiefs preside in councils over the body politic, and several mechanisms exist to sort them and their followers out and keep the peace. The first and primary mechanism is to sort people out through rank and precedence order according to prestige earned from fulfilling the culture's values in the course of their lifetime. The second is to rotate ranking persons in office; no one has a monopoly on high status for very long.

The Cheyenne Indians of the Great Plains, in common with many North American Indians, had a republican political system. Some of their many chiefs were war chiefs specializing in foreign relations, and others were peace chiefs specializing in keeping peace within the tribe (Hoebel, 1960).

E T H N O G R A P H I C   C L O S E - U P

THE CHEYENNE TRIBAL REPUBLIC

The Cheyenne were seminomadic hunters roaming across their territorial portion of the plains. During their heyday, they mounted horses, herds of which they owned and greatly valued. Their main source of livelihood was hunting the bounteous herds of buffalo, best done en masse and after the midsummer solstice celebrations.

Half the year, however, the Cheyenne were sedentary. In the late fall and through the winter they resided in secure winter camps waiting out the snows and relying on stores of dried meat to see them through the lean season. Winter camps were dispersed along the foothills of the Rockies, and each was inhabited by a separate Cheyenne band, of which

there were ten, each composed of bilateral kindreds (see Figure 12.3). The Cheyenne had no lineage or clan system and, unlike the Nuer, did not disguise their political system with a kinship ideology.

Cheyenne Bands, War Parties, and Leaders

Each of the ten bands had a headman, once renowned as a war leader but now, as an older man, transformed into a peace chief within the forty-four–member tribal council. The band chief acted much as did the Nambicuara chief, leading his band to their winter camp and keeping the peace there. During the summer he went into eclipse, save as a possible

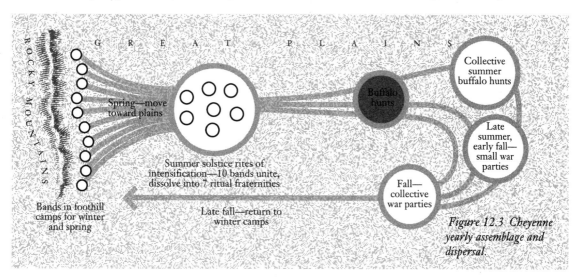

Bands in foothill camps for winter and spring

Spring—move toward plains

Summer solstice rites of intensification—10 bands unite, dissolve into 7 ritual fraternities

Late fall—return to winter camps

Fall—collective war parties

Buffalo hunts

Collective summer buffalo hunts

Late summer, early fall—small war parties

Figure 12.3 Cheyenne yearly assemblage and dispersal.

297

*Figure 12.4 The
Cheyenne war party; it
lasts for only one raid.*

Adolescent
youth—
observer/initiate

War leader
recruits
followers

Followers are ranked
by seniority and
previous war honors

member of the tribal council. Thus, during the
winter, the tribe was split into the basic units of
bands, and within each band there was a political
coalition, composed of selected adult men under the
kinsman chief.

Another coalition, recruited separately from the
band, was the war party (see Figure 12.4). All
Cheyenne men had to be warriors (except those who
chose to be *berdaches*, transvestites who lived as
women and wore women's clothing). Starting around
age fourteen, a boy requested that a war leader let
him join his war party. At first the neophyte mainly
observed and did menial tasks on the campaign. Full
participation in the acts of war came in subsequent
expeditions.

A recognized warrior organized war parties with
the consent and blessing of the council of forty-four
members. A war leader had already earned many
honors based on *coups* (the symbolic feat of having
touched the enemy in battle with his bare hands), on
bringing in scalps of slain enemies, and on capturing
a certain number of horses. Such a warrior would
organize a war party to avenge a slain kinsman or
comrade or to obtain booty, horses, and honors. He
recruited his own followers. As a group they were
properly doctored by a shaman beforehand in a rite
of separation from the peaceful life of the tribe.

The war season fell in late summer and early fall,
after the collective buffalo hunts and before the tribe
dispersed by bands to winter camps. On one historic
occasion, after particularly grievous loss of life to
enemies, the whole tribe was whipped up to mount a
tribal revenge expedition, but an early snowfall
caused them to wait until the next year. The pace of
war could rapidly escalate during the short war

season, and so could the size of the war parties. A
great, fierce, bloodthirsty, and successful war leader
clearly could become a powerful man in Cheyenne
society. Many different men would be tied to him
through their successes under his direction in many
campaigns. He might rally them to attempt to make
himself dictator, if not tyrant, over the tribe.*

Associations: Military Societies
for Ritual and Police

Oddly enough, it was another set of coalitions, the
military societies, that actually served as a check to
the influence of such men. All Cheyenne men joined
one of seven military fraternities after having been
initiated in war and the hunt. But members of a
military society did not necessarily make war
together. Occasionally, a military society did
organize a large war party in revenge for the loss of a
prominent member in battle, but this was a minor
part of its activity.

These **associations** were larger than and quite
independent of the ordinary war parties. Moreover,
they were composed of men who came from different
bands, and their membership thus cut across kinship
and residential ties (only one fraternity was composed
exclusively of men from one band). The military

---

*This is not such a far-fetched possibility. Renowned war leaders
are always potential tyrants in times of foreign stress. Under pretext of rallying people against the enemy, or as a reward for victory, they may attempt to monopolize leadership for themselves.
This happens in tribal republics as well as in the republican city-
states of antiquity. Gearing's (1962) account of the eighteenth-
century Cherokee shows how under pressure from the British
and Americans the tribe literally fell apart, half under the traditional "beloved men" (peace chiefs/elders) and half under the dictatorship of a warrior, who set up a police force and a jail.

societies were each under the control of four war chiefs, who had been renowned and successful war leaders but who had also gained ritual honor within the fraternity (see Figure 12.5). Ritual honor was gained through the conduct of the summer solstice rites of intensification, which marked the coming together of the ten bands and their preparation for the great communal buffalo hunts of summer.

Any of several dramatic ceremonies could be performed for the whole tribe at this time. Each had to be sponsored by a "pledger," an adult householder from one of the fraternities, and conducted by his fraternity. Thus the ritual responsibilities were rotated through the various societies and were an alternative means of earning fame within them. In addition, while one society put on the great feast, the others were busy performing the particular dances that belonged to each, numbering in the hundreds.

As the tribe assembled as a group and camped together by band, at the center of their semicircular formation were the giant tepees, or tent lodges, of the fraternities (see Figure 12.6). During the most sacred moments of the rites of intensification, members of the sponsoring lodge policed the entire encampment to enforce ritual silence. No living creature in the gathering could utter a sound, not even babes in arms or dogs. The punishment for noise was drastic: a skull crushed by a fraternity club. Somehow even puppies were successfully hushed by their Cheyenne mistresses.

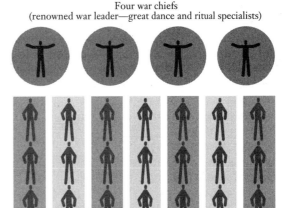

Four war chiefs
(renowned war leader—great dance and ritual specialists)

Fraternities (members rank ordered by
age, war honors, ritual honors)

Figure 12.5 Cheyenne ritual military fraternities (associations).

Immediately following the rite of intensification, which lasted many days, the entire tribe moved out for the collective buffalo hunt. The animals, which were gathering in large herds, had to be hunted carefully, for one false sound or move could stampede them too soon, and all would be lost. It might be days before another herd was sighted.

The military society that had sponsored that year's ceremony also served as police on the collec-

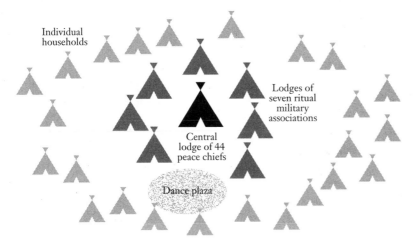

Individual households

Lodges of seven ritual military associations

Central lodge of 44 peace chiefs

Dance plaza

Figure 12.6 Cheyenne summer solstice rites of intensification. The ten bands have gathered and dissolved.

tive hunt. The object of the hunt was to surprise the herd and stampede it into a giant V-shaped formation so that lines of hunters could ride up close and spear or shoot each beast with an arrow. The buffalo police could arrest and severely punish any hunter who broke formation or moved before the word had been given by the fraternity chiefs. The military societies thus provide one of the rare examples of police power known in the primitive world. *Negative sanctions* could be suddenly and severely applied to any member of the nation, whether babe in arms or jumpy young hunter.

The military societies undercut the power of the successful war leaders because the latter's war followers were dispersed throughout the fraternities and had to be rallied separately for each expedition. The power of the band peace chiefs was also undercut, because the men of all but one band were dispersed among the societies and could not be easily rallied as a war party.

Peace Chiefs

At the central and most sacred giant lodge, the council of forty-four peace chiefs was custodian of the sacred arrow bundle, symbol of Cheyenne identity. Peace chiefs, elders all—past their late forties—served ten-year terms, each retiring chief picking his successor from his band. There were four peace chiefs for each band, plus four sacred chiefs who presided over the council and who had always served previous terms as ordinary peace chiefs (see Figure 12.7). Peace chiefs were famous former war leaders; some had been military fraternity chiefs. But on joining the council, they had to renounce war and warlike office and live in complete harmony with their tribal fellows. They could not even exact compensation from others for adultery with their wives, ordinarily a heinous offense. Unlike all other Cheyenne, they had to turn the other cheek.

The peace chiefs were in charge of the most sacred ceremony, the *arrow renewal*. Whenever one Cheyenne murdered another, this ceremony symbolically cleansed the sacred tribal arrows of Cheyenne blood. The peace chiefs formed a court of justice in such homicide cases. The murderer was shunned by his own family and banished by the

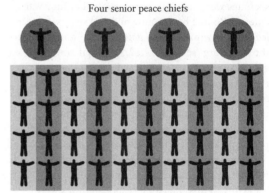

Four senior peace chiefs

Four elders from each band (former war leaders and chiefs of military societies)

Figure 12.7 Schematic diagram of the Cheyenne's council of forty-four peace chiefs.

council. The sentence was enforced by that year's buffalo police fraternity.

After some years, the wrongdoer might return to the tribe and offer blood payment, which went to the council and not to the victim's kin. In addition, the murderer was required to perform the sun dance

Sun dance participants.

300

through his fraternity, including a spectacular form of self-torture as penance. The sun dancer was suspended from ropes attached to skewers burrowed under his chest muscles, and in this state he spun around for all to see as he was offered up to the burning sun.

In general, the council of peace chiefs made overall policy for the tribe as a whole. They decided which fraternity and which sponsor would undertake each season's rite of intensification. They decided with which tribes the Cheyenne were at peace (with whom they traded) and with which at war (whom they raided). They passed on all proposals for large-scale tribal campaigns, always for revenge, and assigned the direction of these campaigns to particular military societies.

OVERVIEW OF THE CHEYENNE POLITICAL SYSTEM: RULE BY THE FEW IN CONSULTATION WITH THE MANY

Of the many leaders and coalitions drawn from the wider Cheyenne society, the most dangerous for internal peace were the short-term war parties around a renowned war leader. Such a man could cherish ambitions of becoming dictator, if not tyrant. Yet war leaders could never count on their followers for long, because men in each war party always belonged to longer-term coalitions in other contexts. In addition, most Cheyenne warriors were anxious to organize war parties of their own. In the peculiar yearly schedule of Cheyenne politics, coalitions were not activated on a daily basis.

In the sedentary winter season, only the band headmen were in office: elders, peace chiefs or potential peace chiefs, attended by the company of their male household heads. In the late spring and early summer, the military societies were activated in preparation for the coming together of the tribe and the performance of the annual collective ceremonies. One military society served as yearly sponsor and police of the entire nation during the rituals and the collective hunt.

In the late summer, the private war parties went off in search of glory, to be welcomed back into camp by purification rituals, conducted by the berdaches, in which all the unmarried young men and women had to dance, a kind of courtship ritual. (Having bilateral kinship and the nuclear family, the Cheyenne needed opportunities to get free courtship going.)

The individual war parties could escalate into larger revenge expeditions conducted by one of the military societies, and then into vast campaigns, decided on by the council and conducted by one military society with the participation of all the others. This was by no means an annual event, however. Not only was leadership exercised by many men in different contexts, it was age graded as well. Men were expected to start earning honors early in the war and the hunt and to validate them in the prime of life by sponsoring collective rituals. By the time they reached their late forties, such men could be acclaimed for positions as war chiefs in their military lodges, but such men were within the next few years quite likely to be promoted to peace chief and required henceforth to leave bloodthirsty ways behind.

Thus, one mechanism of sorting out Cheyenne men was rank order; most knew where they stood in terms of relative age and relative possession of honors. The other mechanism of sorting them out was rotation. The top leadership was recruited into the council for ten-year terms that could not be renewed immediately. Thus, all men who achieved renown were assured of sitting on the council if they lived long enough. The rotation principle was also observed in the turns that the military societies took in sponsoring the rites of intensification and as police.

Material rewards in such a system were also widely distributed. Basic rewards were those of the hunt and war. In the hunt, meat and hides were quickly distributed among the households of the hunters. The warriors shared in their booty of horses, but when each individual counted coups on a tally stick and displayed his captured scalps, symbolic honors quickly displaced material ones. Further honor came from success in the songs and dances owned by one's military fraternity, and from sponsoring the yearly festivals. In short, the Cheyenne were prosperous, but they did not store great amounts of wealth, which could only have been a burden to their nomadic existence.

Overall, then, Cheyenne politics were characterized by their own sort of formal internal complementary opposition. The two basic units were the band and the private war party, which cut across the bands. Next were the military societies, counterweights to the other two groupings; they, in turn, were countered by the tribal council of peace chiefs, which formally represented the bands since membership was recruited by band. But in fact, the peace chief elders were former war chiefs from the military societies. Formal opposition and individual interconnections, balance and cross-cutting ties, were characteristics of the Cheyenne system. Moreover, the forty-four peace chiefs, through their sacred arrows, saw to it that there was no opportunity within the tribe for any man to organize a revenge expedition against a fellow Cheyenne.

This brings us to the limited nature of the reward in tribal politics and the emphasis on honors rather than on more tangible spoils. The Cheyenne took horses from enemy tribes, but they also took trophies—scalps—and counted coups.

The wealth of Cheyenne society and the spoils of its competitions were invested in dramatic ritual performances and were portable and artistic. Ritual paraphernalia, magnificent buffalo-hide lodges, the richness of the dances, songs, and folklore, and mythological knowledge of the old chiefs constituted the true tribal treasure of the republic. Such wealth could not be stolen; it had to be earned.

A Cheyenne mother, daughter, and granddaughter, ca. 1902.

Peace chiefs were not only former war chiefs, men who had gained honor on the warpath and who had followers to attest to their bravery and successes; they had also gained ritual honor. They were good performers; as individuals, they had sponsored the tribal rites of summer at some time in their lives. But as peace chiefs they had become something more: mediators, third parties, perpetually upholding the peace among the fierce braves (which they once had been themselves), and calling, if need be, on a party of such braves to police and punish any offender of the tribal peace and its sacred arrows.

The peace chiefs still had the memory of their war honors, but they gained another reward at the end of their lives. That reward was the applause, however it was delivered, of the tribal multitude.

SUMMARY AND CONCLUSIONS

*P*olitics consists of leading-and-following behaviors that enable a human community to maintain itself in accord with some ideal, lawful image of itself in relation to its worldview and values, its resources, its internal social pressures for those resources, and the diverse needs of individuals of two sexes, maturing and aging over three generations within the group. Moreover, politics maintains the group, always uneasily, in balance with outside groups.

That ideal, lawful image of a group and its leadership is its *unspoken constitution*. It may barely be in a group's consciousness, or it may be so taken for granted that it need seldom be stated. In tribal societies an unspoken constitution corresponds to the social organization (at least for twenty-year cycles), as described by ethnographers. Just as written constitutions in the civilized world are often amended or even overthrown, so, too, are unspoken ones changed. For example, the probable union of an independent band with the Cheyenne nation, by which all the men of the band entered the tribe as members of a separate ritual "military" society, was certainly a constitutional change in that body politic.

Paradoxically, politics as behavior is much more explicit in the dominance patterns of multimale nonhuman primate groups than it is among band-level human beings. The invention of the family and of kinship dissolved the dominance hierarchy among bands. At that level, leadership is fulfilled by people in key family and kinship positions.

At the tribal level, when the world has filled up with human beings and groups jostle against each other in response to population growth, politics emerges again in units of leaders and followers that look very much like a dominance hierarchy, save that they are based more explicitly on individual leader-follower alliances. These alliances imply transactions, in which the leader performs many services for the group in return for some advantages in prestige and material rewards.

Leadership crystallizes around family and kinship transactions, around warfare, and around feasting. It further crystallizes around ritual, especially in the figure of the prophet, whom we shall examine in the next chapter. In short, the tribal world contains many leaders of different sorts available to follow. How any given set of tribal communities, always in alliance and warfare in any case, sorts them out is extremely variable.

In the tribal world leadership is almost never full time, instead responding to the diverse schedules of seminomadic and horticultural peoples and to their relations with their neighbors. Thus, the Nambicuara literally follow the leader for half the year in foraging migrations. In the settled, horticultural wet season, they respond to a village leader, and dry-season leaders retire from leading.

Little Wolf, a Cheyenne chief.

Leaders, especially in the tribal world, make more use of *positive sanctions* than of *negative sanctions*. That is, their authority tends to derive from their very success in leading and from the payoffs to the group. Their only effective negative sanction, or punishment, is ostracism or exile. Effective negative sanctions need police to enforce them; such policing generally arises full time only in the *state*.

Anthropologists, like all Westerners, are prone to read more authority into chiefly positions than is usually there, and more long-term permanence than is ever the case. They tend to classify many tribal groups as "chiefdoms." Take the Trobriand example. There are many Trobriand chiefs, each tending to be paramount in a given area. Chiefs inherit their positions by the will of their mother's brothers, and they consolidate their status by marrying many wives, thus making alliances with many brothers-in-law. A chief is obliged to forge many kula trading partnerships, and he is busy in long-distance trading expeditions. Note, however, that there are many chiefs, and all are too busy with their marriage and kula alliances to be able to move against each other. The Trobrianders are in no danger of coming under the rule of one man.

When tribal groups do arrange their leadership patterns in symmetrical, balanced coexistence with each other, they may make use of the *association*, such as the Cheyenne military societies. Associations are derived from pan-primate juvenile play groups. In them, people from different households or even communities come together for purely social and ritual activities. Associations are a common mechanism for holding a tribal community together.

A *tribal republic* sorts its chiefs out by rank and precedence order, depending on seniority and the statistics of the honors—war and ritual—each has received. This is the case among the Cheyenne. In Aristotle's terms, the

Cheyenne are ruled by a nonhereditary *aristocracy* of meritorious warriors, ritualists, and elders, who operate in consultation with the people (Aristotle's *polity*, our *democracy*) for major decisions of peace and war.

Essentially, political behavior can be gauged by asking who responds to a would-be leader when he cries, "Follow me!" The Nambicuara follow the leader to forage and to confront strangers. The Cheyenne follow leaders to war, to dance ritual dances in the associations, to enforce silence in ritual and the buffalo hunt, to hunt buffalo, and to make peace within the group through the council of forty-four peace chiefs.

Leaders and followers improvise their own implicit exchange contracts, whereby the leader receives some rewards—if only in prestige—in exchange for services performed. Close followers or henchmen of a leader expect their own rewards, while the general population expects some payoffs for following a leader and his men. There is, inevitably, a dynamic tension between the rewards afforded the leader and his inner circle and the payoffs for the population. Aristotle expressed this tension as being between the ruler's self-interest and the common good and classified all governments according to the number of leaders (one, few, or many) and the nature of their rewards (self-interested or interested in the common good). All leaders must balance their desire for rewards with the need for achieving the common good and with the values that a people will grant to them, or tolerate of them.

The state consists of a set of full-time officials with police powers—strong negative sanctions—to enforce their decisions on the group. Much social science theory sees the state as an instrument to uphold the self-interest of some elite group and imputes the origin of the state to the predatory actions of small groups, as if a gang of bandits had either taken over a society by force from the inside or conquered it from the outside. We shall debate such theories in a later chapter. However, it is clear that in the much more diffuse set of leaders of tribal societies, no one of them, or single group of them, can corner a society to rule in their own interest for very long.

Thus Songi, as we saw in the last chapter, could persuade his followers to give away large amounts of property with little immediate expectation of a return. His followers well might have argued that they had become destitute just to satisfy the leader's vanity. But in this Big Man institution, Songi would eventually die, and no one would inherit his position, since it was not a formal office. Other up-and-coming Big Men would take his place for a while. The size of Songi's "achievement" was possible only because the colonial government had stamped out warfare. In the previous course of events no Big Man could have pulled off quite such a big feast as Songi's, because war parties would have diverted resources long before that.

Similarly, in the kula ring Trobriand chiefs extract wealth from their villagers and from brothers-in-law, but they are obliged to give it away in two directions at once, to many partners, so that the kula game never builds up to be seen as tyrannical by the common Trobrianders who participate in it.

There is one further leadership "game" that we have not considered, that of shamans and prophets, self-appointed ritual experts who claim supernatural sanctions for their leadership. They are the subject of the next chapter.

SUGGESTED READINGS

Gearing, Fred. *Priests and Warriors: Social Structures for Cherokee Politics in the 18th Century*. Menasha, Ill.: American Anthropological Association, 1962. One of the best studies of a tribal republic, showing the transition from a republic to tyranny.

Hoebel, E. Adamson. *The Cheyennes: Indians of the Great Plains*, 2nd ed. Ft. Worth: Harcourt Brace Jovanovich, 1977. Provides a great deal of information in a few pages.

Vogt, Evon Z. *The Zinacantecos of Mexico: A Modern Maya Way of Life*, 2nd ed. Ft. Worth: Harcourt Brace Jovanovich, 1990. Describes peasant community whose culture, encapsulated in the wider Hispanic society, maintains the legitimacy of a pure, local, tribal republic.

Whyte, William Foote. *Street Corner Society*. Chicago: University of Chicago Press, 1955. A social science classic describing leadership, coalitions, and direct social interaction leading from adolescent gangs to political elections in 1930s Boston.

GLOSSARY

aristocracy In Aristotle's terminology, rule by the few ("the best"), in the common interest. In modern usage, rule or influence by a hereditary nobility ("aristocrats") whose elite status derives from birth, not from individual merit.

association A social group, emerging as an institution out of the juvenile play groups of all primates, that forms a "bridge" between the individual's family and the wider group, or between the local residential unit and the wider group. Associations have been called a substitute for rites of passage, or "institutional shock absorbers." For example, the Cheyenne military societies integrated people from the constituent bands to the wider tribe. Their manifest function was to perform rites of intensification for the whole tribe, and, in turn, to police it. The one military society that drew its members from one band was thereby a potential source of division, even secession, in the tribe. (*Synonyms:* fraternity, sodality, ritual society)

constitution A set of ideal images of how leadership and public affairs ought to be conducted in any given community. Tribal societies have *unspoken constitutions*, which are embodied in their general social organization and their ideas of right and wrong. Political leaders, especially prophets, may make changes in these ideas.

democracy In Aristotle's terminology, rule by the many in their own interest (as in mob rule). In modern usage, rule by the people in the common interest.

leadership A set of behaviors, probably derived from primate dominance patterns, in which one individual rushes forward to confront group crises. Leaders recruit followers, usually by an implicit contract, exchanging services for a reward. Leadership may crystallize around kinship, around feasting exchange, around ritual, around war, or purely for its own sake—that is, around *politics*.

legitimacy The belief that a leader-follower set of interactions are valued, good, and clearly lawful.

monarchy In Aristotle's terminology, rule of the one in the common interest. In modern usage, rule by a hereditary ruler, regardless of in whose interest.

oligarchy In Aristotle's terminology, rule by the few in their own self-interest. The term has retained this negative connotation today, although it often refers simply to rule by the few.

politics Leadership patterns in which leaders and followers strive to keep the community in balance with its resources, maintain internal order, and represent the community to outsiders. It thus comprises an internal, supervisory set of behaviors and an external, foreign relations set. The dynamic movement of politics derives from the acts of "following" and also from the tension between the value of the reward to the leader (and to his followers) versus the payoff to the group as a whole. Aristotle expressed this as the tension between the ruler's self-interest and the common good.

polity In Aristotle's terminology, rule by the many in the common interest. In modern usage, this meaning has come to be expressed in the term *democracy* (quite the contrary of Aristotle's usage). *Polity* today means the political system or the political institution of a society, insofar as one can detect one. The Nambicuara chief and his coalition of followers is a shallow, intermittent polity, active half the year. The Cheyenne council of forty-four and the seven military fraternities form a deep, tightly controlled polity with police sanctions, but again for only half the year. The state is a full-time polity with police powers enforceable on everyone (except, perhaps, the tyrant).

sanctions Social forces upholding a leader-follower tie. They are expressed negatively as punishment (usually exile in the tribal world) or rewards, which may only be praise, or can be material. Successful leadership, maintaining group balance with its resources and its foreign relations, may be positive sanction enough in many cases.

state Formal, explicit, publicly constituted leadership patterns of a community, manifest in a set of offices (as opposed to persons), full-time official duties, and coercive police powers that can be used against the members of the community. The state usually emerges only out of informal polities at the level of civilizations. Thus, the Cheyenne were not quite a state; they had formal offices and internal police powers, but these were activated only half the year.

tribal republic A form of intermittent tribal polity in which many leaders are sorted out by rank or precedence order, and by rotation in office. The Cheyenne are an example. In form it is oligarchic-democratic, without the connotation of self-interested rule.

tyranny In Aristotle's terminology, rule by one person in his own self-interest. This is pretty much the usage today, although we also use the term *dictator* as synonymous with *tyrant*.

Shamans and Prophets:

Catalysts for Therapy and Cultural Change

ETHNOGRAPHIC CLOSE-UP:
SOCORRO MARROQUÍN, HIGHLAND
MAYAN SHAMAN

Socorro's Salvation

Socorro at Work: Self-cure

THE DYNAMICS OF SHAMANISM

Shamanistic Conversion, Salvation, and Curing

The Therapeutic Process of Ritual

FROM SHAMANS TO PROPHETS

PROPHETS AND REVITALIZATION
MOVEMENTS

Phase 1: The Old Steady State

Phase 2: Individual Stress

Phase 3: Cultural Distortion

Phase 4: Revitalization

   A Prophet Formulates a Code

   The Prophet Communicates the Code

   The Prophet Organizes the Followers

   The Prophet and Followers Adapt the Code to
   Objective Conditions

   The Prophetic Movement Transforms the Culture

   The Movement Routinizes the New Culture

Phase 5: A New Steady State

ETHNOGRAPHIC CLOSE-UP:
THE REVITALIZATION MOVEMENT
OF THE SENECA PROPHET
HANDSOME LAKE

The Old Steady State of the Iroquois

Collapse of the Iroquois

Prophecies of Handsome Lake

Preaching the New Gospel

The New Steady State: Formation of the Handsome Lake Church

*I*n the tribal world institutions emerge more visibly than in the world of band cultures and communities. In some cases kinship organizes settlements and alliances around lineages and corporate bilateral kindreds. Everywhere warfare plays out in endless cycles of revenge. Feasting and trading rings may transmute warfare into peaceful competitions. Political leaders lead more clearly and frequently than in bands, if still only intermittently. Associations (adult play groups) may unite people from various local communities within the wider tribe for socializing and ritual. Finally, ritual experts, **shamans**—curers and mythgivers—are universally present, rather than spottily so as in bands. They are also more numerous.

Every few hundred years, in times of crisis individuals of shamanic type—**prophets**—arise and convince whole peoples not only to change their collective rites, or *cults*, but also their *culture*. Prophets preach mythical versions of new worldviews; they also give new codes of conduct. They are mythmakers and lawgivers.

Shamans and prophets both are individuals who claim powers directly—either by contact with the supernatural or by some authoritative but mystical revelation of worldview, of the nature of the universe. They are likely to have suffered interpersonal difficulties themselves and at some point in their lives to have undergone solitary journeys or vigils. Although other shamans often officiate at a new shaman's rite of initiation into shaman status, the conversion process is self-generated and unique; we call it a **rite of salvation.**

Prophets undergo similar self-generated rites of salvation. They then attempt to apply these rites not simply to cure the ills of individual clients, as do shamans, but to cure those of entire societies. Sometimes the society is listening. It has undergone recent shocks and ills and feels the need to be saved from its troubles.

Shamans, then, are once-troubled individuals who have found their own myths and rituals to restore themselves to sanity and society, where they specialize in treating the ills of individuals. Rarely do shamans lead a group of clients to some therapeutic goal. Prophets, in contrast, are not interested in individual clients. They attempt to cure the ills of a troubled society. The processes whereby shamans cure individuals and prophets revitalize peoples are quite similar; both processes follow similar phases and center on similar rites of salvation for both kinds of leaders.

Not all peoples have shamans. In many band cultures, the ongoing and regularly scheduled rites of intensification are enough to safeguard public health; the Tiwi kulama yam ceremony, for example, "drives away sickness." But where shamans do practice, they add two ritual complexes to the ritual life of their people. First are the rites of salvation, the rituals converting ordinary people into shamans. In them, says A. F. C. Wallace (1966), an individual changes an old identity for a new one. Second, there are the rituals of *curing*, of leading people from sickness into health. These, of course, follow very different schedules than rites of the yearly and generational cycles.

Shamans are mentioned frequently in the ethnographic literature. There are many accounts of the cures they effect, fewer of their becoming shamans. The story of one shaman I knew in my own field work illustrates both sides of the shamanistic complex: the conversion and the curing.*

ETHNOGRAPHIC CLOSE-UP

SOCORRO MARROQUÍN, HIGHLAND MAYAN SHAMAN

The shaman was a woman, Socorro Marroquín, the mother of my cook-housekeeper where I was doing field work in Guatemala. I came to know her as a friend and not simply as an informant. She was one of the leading curers of her peasant community, Alotenango. Like most of its peasants, she was an Indian who once spoke only Cakchiquel, a Mayan language, but who came to speak mainly Spanish.

For the better part of her life, Socorro was a Mayan wife and mother much like most women in her community, but she suffered many social handicaps and was widely regarded as unfortunate. Born around 1900, Socorro had bright prospects. Her father was easily the wealthiest Indian of the region, owning extensive lands and over a hundred ox teams, which he used to transport the regional coffee harvest for the nearby plantations.

Socorro fell in love with a poor Indian peasant. In Alotenango, newlyweds are expected to live in a patrilocal extended household until several children have been born. If the girl's father is unusually wealthy, her husband may come to live matrilocally. In either case, the parents of both must agree to the

---

*This case study derives from a civilized, peasant society, not a tribal one. There is no difference in the shamanistic process at either level of culture and community, although witchcraft (antitherapy, negative ritual) may be more important among tribal peoples. I put this account here because I personally studied it.

match. Not so here. Socorro's husband, Vicente Chabac, alienated her father by his surly manners. The couple eloped, and Socorro was disowned by her parents.

Luck continued bad, for Vicente was not a good husband. He drank heavily, spent his earnings on other women, and neglected his wife and family. Socorro could only make ends meet by working full time weaving the traditional costumes of the community. Even after her parents died and her older brother allowed her the use of the ample family lands, and even after Vicente inherited a fair landholding himself, the bad situation continued. Vicente simply spent more generously on other women. Moreover, he conspicuously shunned sponsoring the fiestas, local rites of intensification, that would have brought prestige to the couple and furthered cooperation between them as they entertained the entire community.*

As Socorro entered her fifties—a mother of five children, one still small and many others lost in infancy—she became increasingly bitter. Finally, she had an experience that we might call a nervous breakdown but that was quite differently interpreted by a local shaman.

Socorro's Salvation

One morning Socorro was left with no food in the house. Her husband had marketed the choicest sweet potatoes from the harvest, keeping the money for himself, and had left those fit only for feeding pigs. She gathered them up, took her young son by the hand, and walked three miles uphill in the hot sun to the next town, where she went from door to door trying to sell the leftovers. Sales went well, and eventually she got together 70 cents, a good sum in those days.

Showing her son the coins, Socorro told him the things they would buy: sweets for him, some meat, tortillas for the family. They had stopped to buy the

Socorro Marroquín, prosperous and contented as a respected shaman.

sweets and were headed toward the meat shop when the boy cried out, "Look, Mother, there is your luck." He did not dare pick it up, but he urged her to do so. It was a bronze lady's brooch, set with a large crystal engraved with four roses. Socorro seized it and thrust it into her blouse next to her breast. They returned home, only to find her husband sitting contemptuously at the door.

That night Socorro fell into a fit, became rigid, and so frightened her son that he ran outside saying that his mother was dying. They called an old man who was a licensed practical nurse and bonesetter and an acknowledged shaman as well. He knew the family, and they told him what had happened that day and showed him the brooch. When Socorro regained consciousness, the old man explained that the brooch, her "luck," was a sign of great power. She must give in to it, accept it, and struggle against the evil that wanted to possess her. Otherwise she would die. He would show her the way.

The old man worked with Socorro for some time, praying with her, lighting candles, and discussing her symptoms. For a long time she remained ill. The evil spirit that was besieging her came upon her at night—a great round cold *thing*. It would cover her, after which it would become quite hot, slide off, and stare at her in the darkness with great wicked eyes. The old shaman taught Socorro to see into the brooch and to invoke its powers. The central rose engraved there was no rose, he said, it was a sign of *Señor Padre Sacramento* (Our Lord Father Sacrament)

---

*See Chapter 16 for a discussion of Alotenango and its ritual life as a mechanism to close the community in upon itself. In my previous publications I used a pseudonym, Atchalán, instead of Alotenango, and referred to Socorro as "Amparo" to protect her and others' privacy. But now that many years have passed since my initial field work and many of my principal informants, including Socorro, have died, I am using real names.

and Jesus of Nazareth. The three roses that surrounded it were signs of three guardian angels.

The old man showed her the general techniques of curing; he also discussed the root of all curing powers and read to her from several spiritualist books. Finally, the *thing* rolled off Socorro one night; it never returned. By then, Socorro had given in to her charm, or luck, and was obliged to honor its powers.

Socorro's first patient and first cure was her own infant granddaughter. When the baby fell ill and Socorro's daughter brought her to the old curer, he was annoyed and insisted that she take the child to its own grandmother. Socorro cured the baby. The news spread, and soon Socorro had built up an excellent clientele, not only in her own community but around the region as well. Once poverty stricken and miserable, Socorro grew prosperous from her practice. She took more initiative in the management of her family lands. She separated from her husband, moving into a rented place of her own. When I knew her, she lived with her daughter, my employee, and was a busy and respected curing practitioner.

Socorro at Work: Self-cure

I had one occasion to observe Socorro practicing her curing. It was an unusual cure because the patient was Socorro herself. From my point of view that was an advantage, since I did not have to learn the background of some strange patient. It was some

Vicente Chabac, Socorro's estranged husband, reunited with her late in life after her shamanistic practice had made her prosperous.

years after my principal field work in Guatemala. I had returned for a visit, and I called on my old friends.

I found Socorro reunited with her husband, Vicente. He had been gravely ill, and the old woman had cured him. In addition, Socorro had drawn close to her husband because of a dispute with her brother, who had suddenly deprived her of the land inherited from their father, which he had allowed her to use while retaining title in his own name. Socorro had invested quite a bit of cash for coffee seedlings, had hired hands to plant them, and had carefully tended the plantation. After three years, when it was just beginning to bear fruit, her brother swooped down and chased her and the two hired laborers off with his machete. She had taken the matter to court, but the affair was still tied up.

In the meantime Socorro had fallen ill. When I called on her, her head was bound in kerchiefs, and she was bundled in sweaters. She complained of symptoms like those of flu and of not having slept the night before. It was not an ordinary cold, she assured me. Her brother was having a witch cast a spell on her. She accused a well-known shaman, an old friend of her brother, of accepting a large sum of money for this mischief. She knew it was not an ordinary sickness; the fever did not come and go the way an ordinary fever does, and her headache was deep down and constant and could only be the result of supernatural practices. She was planning to cure herself in the morning, and she invited me to the cure.

I arrived at 7:05 the next morning and found Socorro warmly dressed against the morning chill. Her braids had been pulled up over a blue wool kerchief that covered her head. She wore a heavy wool sweater over her handwoven huipil (native blouse), beads, and a checkered apron over her tie-dyed native skirt. She was waiting for a friend and companion to come help in the ritual. She needed an unrelated person to be the "servant." While we waited, I inspected the household altar, which had been prepared for the occasion. It was a small high table against the rear wall of Socorro's formal receiving hut.

Propped up in the center of the altar was a commercial lithograph showing Jesus Christ over clouds and above him God the Father. To the left of the print were a small crucifix and a bunch of pink carnations in a tin container. In front of the print and centered exactly on the altar was Socorro's charm, her luck, the engraved brooch. To one side of the charm was a box of pine incense and a spoon; in front of it was a stack of small white candles, four inches long. At the table's edge were a blackened clay candle holder, a pint bottle of holy water two-thirds full, a small bottle of commercial rose water, and a plastic cup. Above the altar and to the viewer's right, four thick yellow candles hung on the maize-stalk cane wall.

When the "servant" came, Socorro sat on a small chair in front of the altar. Her daughter, Lucía, sat facing her to one side. Socorro started a formal prayer-speech, an oration, addressed to God the Father and Jesus of Nazareth, saying that if this were an ordinary illness and God's will, then she was resigned. As her message grew more personal, her tone less formal, she said that if this illness had been sent by others, God and Jesus must save her. She wept as she pressed the parts of her body, especially her head, that hurt her. God the Father must save her; Jesus of Nazareth must save her.

After this formal opening, Socorro stood up and invoked her charm. The Lord Father Sacrament (*Señor Padre Sacramento*) and Jesus of Nazareth must save her. Then she leaned over and sorted the small white candles into pairs, addressing each one individually. She named each with the name of an ancestor, starting with her parents and working back through her genealogy. First, she named her father and mother, one pair. Then she sorted out their parents, two pairs. Then she took up three pairs on the next generation (omitting her mother's mother's parents); six pairs or twelve ancestors in all.

In a low, almost inaudible voice she addressed the candle-ancestors, telling them that she had dreamed that an out-of-town witch had recently gone down into the crypt in the ruins of the cathedral in Antigua to work a spell against her. She begged them to counteract it. She then sat back and relaxed, catching her breath before the next sequence in the ritual. She loosened her kerchief, and then grasped her twelve candles, one bunch in each hand. Lucía stood up, removed her kerchief, and let her braids fall loose

down her back. She folded back her mother's sweater to reveal her neck, laden with beads.

Socorro rubbed her head all over with the bunched candles, weeping and sniffling plaintively, pressing all the points that pained her and invoking God the Father, Jesus of Nazareth, and her ancestors to save her from the pain. This done, Lucía lifted her mother's braids. Socorro pressed hard on each sore spot with the candles, and removing the candles quickly, let Lucía blow hard at each spot. Then both women relaxed and paused a minute.

They gathered up the twelve candles, wrapped them in newspaper, and called for the *señora*, the "servant" who had been sitting outside, to come and take them to the house of the custodian of the statue of the Virgin of the Conception and to leave them lighted there on the altar. They would have to wait for the woman to return. In this relaxed atmosphere, Socorro took the holy water from the pint bottle and mixed it with rose water in the plastic cup on the altar. This she poured onto her hands and rubbed on her face, her head, her neck, even her blouse. The effect was bracing and astringent on her wrinkled skin.

The servant returned to report that her mission had been accomplished; she was thanked, and left. Socorro smiled and told me confidently that on the morrow she would be well and that in the meantime

The statue of the Virgin of the Conception, to which Socorro sent candles via a "servant."

her headache was lifting. Tomorrow she would take the four fine candles, one of which she lit as she spoke, to the house of St. Michael Archangel, where his statue stands with sword uplifted, and leave them. The cure would be over.

Distractedly, the old woman leaned and looked into her charm by the light of the votive candle. She called excitedly for me to look. "There, there," she cried, pointing into the brooch. "There is God the Father, right there, right at this moment." The old woman may have been hallucinating. She grew more excited and clutched my arm. "Right there, there He is." And she sighed and smiled as I had never seen her smile.

THE DYNAMICS OF SHAMANISM

To analyze the story of Socorro Marroquín we must refer to the three phases, the symbols, and the myths of ritual. Shamanistic personnel are different from those of ordinary communal rites of passage and intensification because shamans are experts with individualistic followings of their own. Socorro's illness and her salvation by becoming a shaman involved more than an ordinary cure. The cure required taking on a whole new profession, a changed identity. She underwent a rite of passage of a particular kind.

Shamanistic Conversion, Salvation, and Curing

Objectively, Socorro's illness was described as a fit with body stiffness. A modern physician might have diagnosed hysteria and referred the case to a mental health specialist, or he or she might have diagnosed heat prostration, malnutrition, or any number of maladies that might have been appropriate. Not so the old shaman. He diagnosed the trouble in terms of the accidental discovery of the brooch, which he took to be a sign of and a charm for supernatural powers.

In effect, the old man told Socorro a *myth* fabricated on the spot that explained her particular situation: She was the object of a struggle between good and evil forces. To cure herself, she must give in to the good powers and master their secrets. Otherwise, she would fall victim to the evil spirit that preyed on her, and she would die. The shaman's diagnosis was a myth; the cure was worked with *symbols*.

The shaman taught Socorro to interpret the central rose in the brooch as twin attributes of the Godhead. The first, God the Father as a Sacrament, refers to the Roman Catholic custom of enshrining the consecrated communion wafer in a crystal vessel in the shape of a sunburst and placing it on the high altar as the Body of Christ; this is also known as the Most Holy Sacrament. The second attribute, that of Jesus of Nazareth, refers to Jesus bearing the cross to Calvary; a statue of this is paraded with great penitence during Holy Week. In addition, the three other roses were angels. The old shaman was known to control the secrets of twenty angels who were rain bearers. I do not know whether Socorro had already hallucinated upon looking into the brooch, but the specific images of the Godhead were undoubtedly induced in her mentality by the shaman who was teaching her.

There are *three phases* to the rite of salvation, the transformation into a new identity (see Figure 13.1). Before her illness, Socorro had been suffering. Her married life was miserable. She was ending her childbearing years and entering the stage of life that is supposed to bring the greatest prestige and reward for Indian peasants of her culture. Instead, she faced poverty, bitterness, and public scorn. Immediately prior to falling ill, she had undergone the degradation of going from door to door selling pig fodder. Small

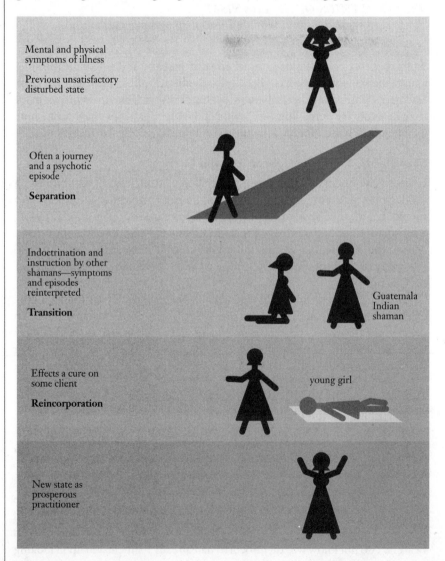

Mental and physical symptoms of illness

Previous unsatisfactory disturbed state

Often a journey and a psychotic episode

Separation

Indoctrination and instruction by other shamans—symptoms and episodes reinterpreted

Transition

Guatemala Indian shaman

Effects a cure on some client

Reincorporation

young girl

New state as prosperous practitioner

Figure 13.1 The process of becoming a shaman, the rite of salvation, a kind of rite of passage.

wonder that, after the discovery of the brooch, a superstitious belief in luck and signs triggered a hysterical collapse.

Socorro's physical and mental collapse *separated* her from her previous identity as an embittered wife (phase one). The old shaman kept her in a *transitional* or *liminal* state by instructing her during the cure (phase two). Her full *reincorporation* as a shaman was effected when she cured someone else, the granddaughter (phase three). Prosperity, prestige, and separation from her no-good husband all followed. Socorro had assumed a new identity that was fully recognized and rewarded by her community.

It has often been observed that shamans are misfits, psychologically disturbed persons for whom shamanism is a socially acceptable form of deviance. On the other hand, Lévi-Strauss (1963) argues that in the absence of such deviant personalities, would-be clients of shamans can thrust the role on unwilling recruits by dreaming of their curative powers (remember Hans Staden in Chapter 1).

In Socorro's case, one could argue that her troubles were socially caused and put the blame on her husband. But it is perfectly possible that the outcome of her collapse might have been stark raving madness. Alotenango did have an unkempt madman, Pablo Peludo (Hairy Paul), who wandered about laden with layers of rags, begged, and slept in the ravines. Perhaps a shaman never got to him in time. To be separated from her husband and live alone was extremely deviant in Socorro's culture. But hers was a deviance well rewarded.

Socorro later used myth in curing her own sickness. She fabricated a particular myth on the spot that explained her flu symptoms: Her brother was engaging a witch to cast a spell on her. She dreamed the event exactly: a known witch went down into the crypt to do his evil work. She said that witches, unlike curers, do not have charms like hers. Rather, they work their evil in the cemetery or in the gaping tombs of ruined churches with the real remains of the dead. A skull is perfect. (A **witch** is a shaman engaged in antitherapy or negative ritual—"black magic.")

In the ritual Socorro performed, she specifically conjured up the myth of God the Father and Jesus of Nazareth in company with twelve guardian ancestral spirits. They were to engage in battle, with the help of the Virgin of the Conception and Saint Michael Archangel with his avenging sword. This was another male and female pair, like the ancestors, and mystically they were to undo the spell, probably by subduing evil forces.

The *symbols* that Socorro used were those of her power, taught to her during her conversion into shamanism; others appropriate to the illness were also used. God the Father and Jesus of Nazareth were symbolized explicitly in the lithograph and mystically in the charm. The votive candles, the symbols of prayer and communication with the supernatural, in the sacred number of twelve (for the twelve apostles, servants of Jesus of Nazareth) were identified with Socorro's ancestors, whom she called on to judge their other descendant, her brother. These candles were massaged against the site of her pains, which were then blown away. Presumably, if Socorro had been working on someone else, she would have performed this therapeutic technique of blowing herself.

As for the three phases, Socorro expected the ritual to effect her *passage from sickness to health*. The ritual *separated* her from her symptoms. Already her headache had lifted after the first part of the rite. The *transitional* or *liminal* phase consisted of the prayers to the deities and ancestors, the manipulation of charms and candles symbolizing them, and the therapeutic pressing and blowing on painful spots. It further consisted of lighting candles that day and the next, before the images of a female and a male saint. She expected that, on the next day, after the four fine candles had been offered to the avenging angel, that she would be well. In short, her symptoms were dispelled by this process, and one day later she was *reincorporated* into daily life—*cured*.

The Therapeutic Process of Ritual

Students have often asked how shamans, with all their hocus pocus, are so widely regarded as effective by their clients, who keep coming back for more cures. Lévi-Strauss (1963) has proposed that what makes shamanism so effective is a psychological process induced in the patient by the shaman whereby the patient listens to, believes, and symbolically acts out, or **abreacts**, the shaman's diagnostic myth. The mental process of sympathy for their abreaction dispels old tensions and rallies bodily forces. If the symptoms are psychosomatic, they are dispelled. If they are organic, at least they are not aggravated.

In Socorro's conversion and in her self-cure, it is obvious that the cure had in some sense acted out a myth in each case. In the first case, the total effect of the ritual was to change Socorro's self-definition. Abreaction of a dramatic sort was going on here. In the second case, the acting out of a myth was similarly effective, for the time being. But no restructuring of the social context was effected, and we have no assurance that the brother would not continue with his mischief. After all, it is objectively quite possible that this man *was* hiring a witch to cast a spell on his sister. But if, as is likely, Socorro's symptoms sooner or later reappeared, the same explanation was readily available and the same cure just as easily practiced.

The conversion changed the social context and Socorro's identity, while the self-cure merely alleviated symptoms. It is likely that the ailment was indeed psychosomatic, brought on by nervous tension and stress incurred during the ongoing dispute with the brother. But what of shamanistic treatment of disorders that are not psychosomatic but are caused by injuries or by disease-bearing microorganisms? Shamans are often credited with curing diseases with such objective causes.

The answer lies in four things. First, because most human populations are in a state of dynamic equilibrium with the microorganisms that they harbor, most such illness, if left alone, will run its course. Second, shamans are usually the repositories of a great deal of herbal lore and know of other home remedies. During my field work, for instance, Socorro's herb teas never failed to relieve my colds.

Third, aside from objectively commanding folk medicine, shamans can provide a process of psychological support for patients suffering a disease caused by a microorganism; if the rituals do not cure the patient, they may at least allay anxiety and prepare the patient to marshal bodily forces against the illness. What such "cures" do, then, is often to conjure up and reveal old social tensions and deal with them symbolically. A patient suffering from some physical malady may well have nervous tensions dispelled, which can only be beneficial for his or her recovery.

Finally, shamans, like physicians in our society, do not need to achieve 100 percent cures to keep their clientele. They need only achieve enough cures to maintain their credibility. "The operation was a success, but the patient died" holds true for shamans just as much as for surgeons. Neither profession is in any danger of going out of business.

The sun dance is a therapeutic ritual practiced by the Cheyenne.

FROM SHAMANS TO PROPHETS

Occasionally in the ethnographic record we find shamans who lead their clients collectively. For example, the Naskapi, caribou hunters of the Canadian arctic, will prevail on a shaman to perform a divination, using a caribou scapula, or shoulder bone. The shaman thrusts the bone into a fire, then reads the cracks as if it were a map. All the men of the group gather around the shaman, beseeching him to find game, which has inexplicably disappeared. Then all the men follow the shaman's directions in their magical search for game.

The Nuer, whom you recall from Chapter 9, sometimes rallied around shamans and rose as one body to repel invaders. Nuer shamans are specialists in curing barrenness in women, possibly caused by the tremendous pressure relatives put on brides to bear a child so they don't have to return her bridal wealth. A trip to the shaman often allays anxiety, thus facilitating conception. Consequently, many Nuer shamans grow rich from fees in cattle, and their fame grows throughout Nuerland. When such shamans preach that direct messages from the sky god have called on the Nuer to rally around them and repel a foreigner, they become *prophets*. Prophetic campaigns are effective, but the power of the prophet as military commander lasts only as long as the campaign and dissolves with the foreign threat, at which time the Nuer relapse into their customary state of internal complementary opposition.

St. Francis of Assisi, an exemplary prophet.

The great German sociologist Max Weber labeled such prophets "emissary"—that is, bearing a message from the gods. **Emissary prophets** are often quite specific about the sins of society that require redressing and frequently propose concrete steps of penance, expiation, and moral reform. Weber thought that prophets are former shamans ("magicians") who attempt to cure the collective ills of society, which they prophetically diagnose as being brought on by the sins of the people. To shamans, one's sins are often the causes of one's disease.

Other prophets, such as Hindu gurus and St. Francis of Assisi, may be leaders of great magnetism who teach by example. Weber called such men **exemplary prophets.** Exemplary prophets such as gurus concentrate on ailments of the soul and total fellowship with the prophet. The relationships of both kinds of prophets with their immediate disciples is characteristically liminal, or like that of the transitional period in a rite of passage. Exemplary prophets are still with us. Hinduism always has new gurus, and Christianity new saints. Emissary prophets with their divine messages also appear continually; they are not so easy to contain, however.

PROPHETS AND REVITALIZATION MOVEMENTS

Tribal peoples have repeatedly had prophets, some of which have simply repelled invaders without establishing a lasting movement, as with the Nuer prophets and Joan of Arc in medieval France. In times of cultural crises, prophets have repeatedly arisen to set things right. We now have such a backlog of recorded cases that anthropologist A. F. C. Wallace (1956) has given us a comprehensive theory of prophetic action. Here we examine prophets and their **revitalization movements,** a model for the successful conversion of a people to a new way of life under the self-appointed leadership of a prophet.

Wallace's developmental framework for analyzing revitalization movements consists of a number of logical phases or steps. Figure 13.2 provides an overview of the steps. Not all revitalization movements successfully complete all the steps; many of them miscarry, for reasons we shall discuss later. Examine this model carefully and compare it to the curing process of a shaman working on a single patient.

Phase 1: The Old Steady State

A culture and society in a steady state are more or less in balance with their environment. Change goes on at a rate that is easily contained, without disruption or great individual stress. Even traits we think of as pathological, such as a primitive warfare and cannibalism complex, are fit into the ongoing steady state in terms of regular, customary behavior. The community, then, is comparable to an individual in a state of good health.

Phase 2: Individual Stress

Wallace is a psychological anthropologist who thinks in terms of individuals as much as societies. When a society is under stress, Wallace looks to the individual, whom he sees as being prevented from successfully engaging in customarily rewarding behaviors. This happens when a society is subjected to shocks that cannot be routinely accommodated into the ongoing steady state: the natural disasters of earthquakes, floods, droughts, and famines; foreign invasion, causing flight and migration; devastating defeat, often without outright conquest; and simple contacts with a technologically superior (usually Western) outsider.

One of the first reactions to stress is for individuals to cling rigidly to old ways, even if they are no longer appropriate. If the old ways are unproductive or blocked, the individual is obliged to doubt and question the nature of the old life and to consider alternatives, even repugnant foreign ones.

Phase 3: Cultural Distortion

In the third phase, old ways break down completely. There is a high incidence of individual pathological behaviors that are not contained within the ongoing processes of the society—gambling, alcoholism, unpatterned or random sexual promiscuity in defiance of old mores, and actual or suspected witchcraft. I might add that civil, legal, and ritual authority may break down and that household structure may be severely threatened—indications that things have fallen apart at the seams.

Phase 1: The old steady state
Phase 2: Individual stress
Phase 3: Cultural distortion
Phase 4: Revitalization
    A prophet formulates a code
    The prophet communicates the code
    The prophet organizes the followers
    The prophet and followers adapt the code
       to objective conditions
    The prophetic movement transforms the culture
    The movement routinizes the new culture
Phase 5: A new steady state

Figure 13.2 The phases of revitalization.

Phase 4: Revitalization

Wallace divides this stage into several periods.

A Prophet Formulates a Code. In the midst of cultural distortion and social breakdown, an individual withdraws from society and formulates a code of theory and action. Prophets formulate such codes in periods of ritual transition, even if solitary and self-induced. In short, the would-be prophet undergoes a conversion experience, or ritual of salvation, just as does the ordinary shaman. Indeed, the dynamics of the prophetic and shamanistic conversion experiences are exactly the same. They combine old myths and symbolisms in new ways so as to produce a revelation that solves the plight of the prophet and of the people as well. The prophetic revelation, however, is always much more sweeping than the shamanistic ones.*

The Prophet Communicates the Code. When prophets offer their diagnosis of the ills of society and their prescriptions for a cure, they must, like shamans, find a clientele—in this case, listeners. They preach and convert followers to their message. The format varies. It is likely that almost all prophets use the political assembly, as the war prophets of the Israelite confederacy used the war assembly to go into ecstatic trances and inspire the multitude to follow them into battle. Prophets may also appear in the midst of traditional rites of intensification to preach their new word.

The Prophet Organizes the Followers. Prophets may or may not have an organization blueprint. Some, such as St. Francis of Assisi and most Hindu gurus, expect to live in complete liminal otherworldliness with their following. Such emissary prophets may confront problems concerning how to organize thousands of holy beggars, how to define entry into the movement, and how to regulate the relationships between men and women. Emissary prophets may have an explicit organizational blueprint, especially when their visions and goals are political. As disciples appear around the prophet, the movement may be divided into inner and outer circles of followers (something we saw happening with feastgiving Big Men, too).

Inner-circle persons have usually experienced at the hand of the prophet a conversion experience so thorough and genuine that their entire personal-

---

*Some revitalization leaders in modern times see themselves not as prophets but as modern, rational revolutionaries. Such leaders often formulate their plans in scholarly retreats and claim no divine inspiration nor any of its symptoms, such as trances and hallucinations. Still, the psychodynamics of such revolutionists are similar to those of prophets in general. Moreover, they often claim infallible authority, if based on "scientific law" rather than supernatural revelation. They invoke an authority derived from a revised worldview. There is no question that great revolutionary figures such as Lenin and Mao were seen by their followers as inspired and possessing charisma.

ity is altered for life. These are the true believers, the fanatics, and they may number in the thousands. Often in the outer circles are the more numerous hysterical converts, those who adopt the slogans and behaviors of the movement in the heat of rallies or other mass rituals. They follow the crowd, but their basic personalities and identities are unchanged; given the chance, they are prone to relapses and backsliding.

The Prophet and Followers Adapt the Code to Objective Conditions. All revitalization movements must face reality, including the sources of the original stress. Many movements abort when they have to pass such a reality test. Prophets whose short-term predictions have not come to pass must do some fast talking, often putting off such false prophecies into the distant future. So-called doomsday prophets who predict the end of the world, the arrival of the ancestors, or other such millenarian events for a certain date have to produce quick explanations when the predicted day comes and goes. To the amazement of outsiders, such doomsday groups are often able to weather the unfulfilled moment and prepare themselves for some other more distant or unspecified date.

The Prophetic Movement Transforms the Culture. According to Wallace, the long-range goals of the prophet become the goal culture, and leaders and followers together devise a program aimed at producing the desired long-range effects, or "transfer culture." As the program starts, changes go into effect and old ills are remedied. Some groups embark enthusiastically on the new program. Whether a movement fails or succeeds at this point depends in large measure on the wisdom of the policies formulated in the inner circle.

In this stage and the previous one, the inventive capacities of the followers may be just as decisive as the inspirational capacities of the prophet. St. Francis's movement, for example, received its organizational form more from his successor as head of the order, Elias, who formulated the rule governing the Franciscans approved by the Pope. St. Francis had relinquished control of his movement by this time; he died young, in the woods, while others carried on his message.

Ryuho Okawa, a modern-day would-be prophet who claims to be the reincarnation of Buddha, is said to have 5 million followers in Japan. His Institute for Human Happiness runs 250 "Angel Schools" where Japanese can study his teachings.

The Movement Routinizes the New Culture. Once substantial reforms have been effected, they are taken for granted and no longer need the day-to-day policing of the movement. A new generation grows up to whom they are a matter of course.

Phase 5: A New Steady State

After a revitalization movement has spent itself and its impetus is over, it can be considered successful if its society and culture have weathered the crisis that sparked the movement. Utopian visions of founders have never been totally achieved. Many temporary expedients and compromises and the accidental results of policies are incorporated as standard practice. As life goes on, rituals commemorating the movement, now part of the official culture, are no longer lived day to day with sectarian enthusiasm by members of the revitalized and eventually quite humdrum society.

E T H N O G R A P H I C   C L O S E - U P

THE REVITALIZATION MOVEMENT OF THE SENECA PROPHET HANDSOME LAKE

The case study from which Wallace (1969) derived his general theory is the story of Handsome Lake, a visionary who revitalized Iroquois Indian culture in the United States in the early nineteenth century. Let us see how the five phases apply in this instance.

The Old Steady State of the Iroquois

The Iroquois were a tribal confederacy, a primitive republic, composed of six tribes (Seneca, Mohawk, Onondaga, Cayuga, Oneida, and, in affiliated but not full status, Tuscarora) in what are now the states of New York and Pennsylvania. The entire confederacy was regulated by a great council of forty-nine peace chiefs, *sachems*, who met at the council house of the Onondaga tribe. Sachems were representatives of their clans, not their tribes. Each was nominated by the senior matron of his matrilineal clan; each adopted a new name, which came with the office, and a set of sacred wampum belts upon investiture. The death of an old sachem and the installation of a new one were the great rites of intensification for the entire Iroquois confederacy.

The Iroquois waged war every year during the fall. War parties were drawn from the entire league, never from one village alone. Their alliance, a macro-community, engaged in highly successful raids against enemies in a pattern reminiscent of the Tupinambá. Their aim was to capture able-bodied adult men, whom they brought back to Iroquois villages and gave to war widows. Captives finally met their death following an all-night torture, after which their bodies were cooked and devoured in a grim feast.

In their villages, the Iroquois had a full calendar of rites of intensification that were conducted in the communal assembly, the longhouse. Some were joyful festivals of gathering and gardening involving women and children. In June, groups of women went on picnics in the woods to gather strawberries. There was a planting festival in May or June, the high point

of which was the women's dance in which they carried ears of corn. At the green-corn ceremony in August or September, which celebrated the growing corn, all the babies born in the village since midwinter were named. The harvest festival in October ended in a fierce sacrifice of a white dog, symbolic of the men's thanksgiving for past victories.

In January, after the hunting and war seasons had ended, the village gathered for its greatest ceremony, Midwinter, in which the false-face societies drove out illness, cured the sick who had dreamed of them, and allowed their members to act out all sorts of repressed fears and desires.

Collapse of the Iroquois

The Iroquois had become a buffer state between French Canada and the British colonies, useful to both French and English as a shield against other Indians, whom they fought with firearms supplied by the Europeans. In spite of the escalation of their warfare complex under European encouragement, the Iroquois did not suffer unmanageable stress from European contact. In fact, they thrived on diplomacy. They grew rich in firearms and trade goods, and their territories continued to be ample as colonial settlers skirted them. However, all this changed after the Revolutionary War.

Instead of remaining neutral or playing both sides against each other, the Iroquois made the mistake of allying themselves with the British. The eight years of the war were a disaster—when Cornwallis surrendered at Yorktown, nothing was salvaged for his Indian allies save begrudging asylum for those who sought refuge in Canada. Over the next thirteen years, the United States proved vindictive. Enormous tracts of Iroquois territory were annexed to New York and Pennsylvania states. The Iroquois confederacy fell apart as a political entity as tribes were confined to separate and scattered reservations.

In 1793, the Seneca sold most of their remaining lands; they were finally confined, like the other five tribes, to a fraction of their former territory. Moreover, from the start of hostilities in 1776, the Iroquois population had declined by about half. Thus confined to reservations—with insufficient land for successful hunting parties, no opportunity to form war parties against any enemies at all, and increasing dependence on annual federal handouts for subsistence—the Iroquois, especially the men, had nothing to do except brood on their losses and drink.

Once the proud and fierce buffer people of the frontier, the Iroquois had become a fragmented and engulfed minority inside the boundary of white American settlement. In response, they lost themselves in drunkenness, in accusations of witchcraft, and in petty squabbles. Abortion was rife, lowering the population further. The Iroquois and especially the Seneca faced the possibility of extinction.

Prophecies of Handsome Lake

Handsome Lake, a peace chief of the shattered league, lay ill throughout the spring of 1799 at Cold Spring, the village of his brother, Cornplanter, on the Allegheny reservation in New York State. He was in a deep depression over the death of his niece, which he attributed to witchcraft. During the day he drank to excess. On June 15, at the time of joyous strawberry picking, Handsome Lake fell into a deep coma and at first was taken for dead.

As plans were made for his funeral, Handsome Lake showed signs of life, and he slowly revived. Coming out of his coma, he hinted at the impending destruction of the world and announced that he had spoken with three angels who had commanded him to pronounce "four evil words"—four new tabus for

An Iroquois mask.

the Iroquois people: whiskey, witchcraft, love magic, and abortion. The angels also commanded the Iroquois to hold the strawberry festival.

Handsome Lake had two more visions, each one accomplished in deep trance. In August he went on a "sky journey" accompanied by a supernatural guide. On the way, he spoke with Jesus Christ and with George Washington, who commended his intentions of bringing the Iroquois back to their true way. He also visited a hell for the damned, including some Iroquois of his own acquaintance, and the Creator's heaven for the just. His third and final vision took place some six months later. The three angels reappeared and told him to preach unity to all the towns of the old league and to adhere to the old forms of worship.

Preaching the New Gospel

Handsome Lake's announcement of his visions received great attention from all the Iroquois; after all, he was a respected peace chief. He went from longhouse to longhouse in the villages, preaching his revelations at political meetings. In June 1801, the Iroquois of the six nations formally gave him dictatorial powers, making him "High Priest and principal Sachem in all things Civil and Religious," according to a contemporary account (Wallace, 1969). He continued to preach, attempting to get his program implemented and emphasizing the negative commandments of the tabus on whiskey, witchcraft, love magic, and abortion.

Because of his prophetic visions, the Iroquois insisted that Handsome Lake act as shaman and cure their illness. Never having been a shaman before, Handsome Lake reluctantly consented, going into trance to diagnose illness. He often accused others, especially old women, of witchcraft against the patient and called on the accused to confess, repent, and cure the patient; if the accused witches refused, Handsome Lake passed sentence of death and called on young warriors to execute it.

The issue of witchcraft eventually led to Handsome Lake's political defeat. He actually had an old woman executed in 1809, much to the dismay of her family and New York State. As a result, the state

authorities joined his nephew Red Jacket, always his political opponent, in ousting him from the dictatorship, forcing him to flee his longhouse at Coldspring.

With only six more years to live, he still traveled from village to village, preaching his gospel in longhouses. Over the years, his message was expanded beyond the original tabus to include ritual and social gospel.

Handsome Lake called Indians to public confession and repentance of their sins before the faithkeepers, customary officials of each village council. To this ceremony he added the collective drinking of strawberry juice, in joyous invocation of the spring picnics of old. He called for the maintenance of the old agricultural rituals. Naturally the old war cult was out of the question. He disliked the elaborate funeral ceremonies for the league sachems and unsuccessfully sought to do away with the false-face medicine societies.

Handsome Lake's social gospel was learned in part from Quaker missionaries who discretely set up a model farm near his reservation. Rather than opposing Handsome Lake, they sought to influence him and especially to educate the Indians in European farming techniques. Handsome Lake came to agree wholeheartedly with these ends. He called for the Indians to hang onto what was left of their lands, to farm them in the European manner, and, while abstaining completely from alcohol, to live in peace and unity with each other and their American neighbors.

He also called for a restructuring of household relationships. Formerly, the Iroquois had lived in matrilineal and matrilocal extended families. Handsome Lake deemphasized the role of grandmothers and matrons and emphasized that of the husband-father, whom he enjoined to take up the plow in the fields, displacing the women with their digging sticks. He enjoined sons to obey their fathers and called for husband and wife to treat each other with respect and fidelity.

The New Steady State: Formation of the Handsome Lake Church

A **cult** is a set of rituals and the beliefs that uphold them. (In modern societies "cult" also means a separatist community founded by a fanatical prophet.) Handsome Lake made no distinction between *cult* and *culture*. He worked within the old communal framework of Iroquois culture, in which politics and ritual were closely intertwined and in which the village rites of intensification were organized and led by faithkeepers. In his view, all Iroquois properly belonged to his movement, which he simply saw as the six tribes revitalized by divine revelation. However, his ouster from political control and the competition of Christian missionaries meant that not all village longhouses practiced the prophet's teachings.

In the ordinary course of events in indigenous North America, indeed among all tribal peoples, movements such as Handsome Lake's must have happened many times. (Wallace is certain of it.) If a prophet encounters resistance in such conditions, he can simply withdraw with his followers from the previous tribal alliance and form a schismatic community by carving out its own territory. This course of action was denied Handsome Lake and his followers. Instead, they formed a separate *religious institution* within the Iroquois peoples, especially the Seneca.

Handsome Lake died in 1815 while on one of his preaching journeys. After his death, his teachings

The New Coldspring Longhouse, a Handsome Lake congregation, near Steamburg, New York, in 1968. Each longhouse is host in turn to the six-nations meeting of all the longhouses, the central ritual of the Handsome Lake Church.

continued to be preached in many village longhouses. Several of the close followers of the prophet composed his gospel, *Gaiwiio* (literally, "Good Word"), which consists of a verbatim oral rendering of his visions plus an account of his life. There are several recognized versions. By 1850, however, the preaching meetings separated from the purely communal or civic meetings. Another religious denomination, non-Christian, had been born in North America.

The founder of the new religion was Jimmy Johnson, Handsome Lake's grandson, who knew the Good Word by heart. He called delegates to the longhouse at Tonowaga, where the prophet's wampum belts, now the most sacred relics of the movement, are kept. The central new ritual of the church are the six-nations meetings, modeled on the old council meetings of the league. They last for four days, and during the mornings the Handsome Lake gospel is recited in its entirety. In the after-noons, individuals are called to confess sins before the longhouse faithkeepers, and all drink strawberry juice in a kind of communion.

Six-nations meetings are rotated among the Handsome Lake congregations, or longhouses, of which there were ten in 1951 when Wallace studied

A "cargo cult" in the New Hebrides. Members of this tribe worship a cross in belief that it will bring a return of Americans who were there in World War II.

them. Congregations are governed by headmen and headwomen, two for each moiety of the Iroquois, and a committee of faithkeepers, a man and a woman for each clan. Each longhouse has a preacher whose only responsibility is to recite the Good Word. This gospel is learned by heart from another preacher, since the tradition is passed on orally. Only a preacher found letter perfect by the others and allowed to chant the word at the Tonowaga longhouse is allowed to preach at other longhouses.

The Handsome Lake church, although modeled on the old political ritual organization of the Iroquois confederacy, does not claim every Iroquois today. Handsome Lake's revitalization movement ended up turning itself into a religious *cult*, not a culture. The prophetic cult in turn became the basis for a **sect**, a religious organization splitting off from and pulling people out of the wider culture for ritual. Sociologists, always talking about civilized society, classify such religious organizations by the extent of the allegiance and separation they demand from the rest of the society; cults are full time and all inclusive, sects are less so, and denominations usually are only activated for their membership on special days. One does not live the denomination as a whole culture.

SUMMARY AND CONCLUSIONS

Ordinary rites of intensification on annual calendars and rites of passage on generational cycles provide for catalytic reactions that are programmed in accordance with the worldview and values of the particular culture. Recall from Chapter 6 that a catalyst in chemistry is an agent that in the presence of certain substances effects a chemical reaction, transforming the substances without itself being affected. The catalyst provides for much swifter reactions than would otherwise happen and touches off expenditures of energy without itself expending very much, if any, energy.

Ordinary rites do just this. They transform persons and elicit appropriate behavior in accord with changes in the seasons or in the person's own aging. They effect these changes through the three phases in time and space, the manipulation of symbols, and the invocation of myths. But though they effect changes in the individual from one state of life to another, and in the group from one stage of the year to another, they function more to maintain the status quo than to change the overall culture of a community.

Shamanistic and prophetic rituals are also highly catalytic. *But they are not necessarily in accord with preprogramming set by the culture's prior values and world-view.* Ordinary ritual is in response to regular events; shamanism and prophetic movements are in response to irregular ones.

All societies have ritual experts, usually elders or other influential persons who have the requisite knowledge to conduct the relevant rite of intensification or of passage. Such persons do not claim any *personal* ritual powers. Not so with shamans.

Shamans come to their callings by highly personal rites of initiation, called *rites of salvation*. Such individuals have usually suffered stress, misfortune, even mental illness. Although they often call on some other shaman to oversee this rite of salvation, *they themselves are the objects of their own catalysis.* Objects and events from their own experiences form the symbols and myths through which shamans reinterpret their misfortunes, positing some direct relationship with supernatural power and the source of their culture's values. They come out of the experience transformed, having "submitted" to their power, and ready to practice it on others.

Shamans perform therapeutic rituals upon clients. The circumstances and timing of these rituals are extremely variable, unlike those of the regularly scheduled rites of a culture. Rather, shamans respond to the illness and misfortunes of the persons who seek them out, demanding cures. This means a slow revision or elaboration of the official myths and symbols of the culture. Individual patients are helped, but the official communal view is interpreted from an individual perspective, that of the shaman interpreting the condition of the patient. Shamans themselves are usually former patients. They have "been there" and they know the way back.

In terms of the efficacy of both rites of salvation and rites of shamanistic therapy, the shaman presents the patient with a *myth*, which the patient in turn "acts out" mentally, or *abreacts*, responding to the symbols that accompany the verbal suggestions of the shaman. Shamans commonly call on patients to confess sins, faults, and transgressions against kinspersons. The latter, in turn, are commonly called on to rally to the patient and act as "servants" in the ritual curing. Thus, at the very least shamanistic therapy allays anxiety and allows the patient to rally bodily strength to fight the illness. In the case of psychosomatic illness, shamanistic rites may be highly effective. Interpersonal conflicts are sometimes redressed in this way.

Shamans also perform *antitherapy:* witchcraft. We have not examined it much in this chapter, partly because anthropologists seldom observe it firsthand, save in cases of warfare complexes where magical weapons are hurled by the shamans of one side against the other. Much shamanistic diagnosis points out the presence of evil spells; the patient is said to be bewitched. The curing rite must then undo the spell. This is just the rite we witnessed in Socorro Marroquín's self-cure. Most shamans openly profess only the best intentions and deny that they ever could engage in witchcraft. Clients, on the other hand, may press them to practice witchcraft in their behalf, especially when the client's enemy is too powerful to be assaulted openly by physical means. Witchcraft thus may deflect anger, sending social dramas down detours on hidden paths. But suspicion thus crops up, and accusations of witchcraft may cause as much public trouble as the quiet practice of witchcraft dispels troubles from public attention. The two factors probably cancel each other out in the long run.

Shamanism, like every other human institution, is variably expressed in the ethnographic record. It is likely that tribal and civilized groups have run through every possible variation in its frequency and use. At the band level, the trancing of !Kung San men foreshadows shamanism, but these men are not markedly changed from their pretrancing days, and the powers they assume—to talk with ghosts and dissuade them from pulling the sick to the land of the dead—are not remarkable, personal myths.

Some tribal groups, such as the Yanomamo Indians of the jungles of Venezuela, make shamanism almost the norm. Many men are initiated into shamanism by taking hallucinogenic drugs and calling visions of spirits, under the tutelage of senior shamans. They then form shamanistic clubs or groups and work black magic in public, often in alliance with shamans from an allied village, against the enemy.*

However, shamanism is more likely to arise in response to the random experiences of particular individuals, those whose body chemistry predisposes them to the inward life, the life of the mind and its images.

Whereas shamans are common—ethnographers expect to find them—prophets are rare. Shamans can always find individual clients to heal and minister to, but societies are much less certain clients.

Prophets are individuals of shamanic type. Like shamans they go through an individually generated rite of salvation. They come out of it preaching a myth, of their own personal powers and revelations of the nature of the universe, and of right conduct. They formulate these revelations into a code of conduct. Their attempts to preach to society, to gain followers, and to reform behavior is analogous to the piecemeal ministrations of shamans to troubled persons. The difference is that prophets do it collectively.

Some prophets are of *exemplary* type. They do not preach, they simply act, and they attract people by their extremely holy (that is, in anthropological terms *liminal* or *transitional*) actions. Most prophets are of *emissary* type: they bear messages from the supernatural or from the universe.

The efforts involved in founding a prophetic movement and carrying a community through the various phases of revitalization, from cultural distress to a new steady state, are ultimately political. Thus, while shamans can confine their efforts to the arena of therapeutic (or antitherapeutic) ritual, prophets must also be leaders and recruit followers. They must incite people to follow their lead.

Revitalization prophets effect changes in the worldview and values as well as the behavior of an entire community. They do so in part by instituting

---

*You can see this society vividly portrayed in the astonishing ethnographic film *Magical Death*, by Napoleon Chagnon and Timothy Asch (1970).

new rites of intensification, and perhaps by banning old ones. Handsome Lake banned some Iroquois rites, while redesigning the strawberry festival. His followers now have a special new ritual, the six-nations meeting, modeled on the old collective tribal republic's meeting, that specifically recites the myth of Handsome Lake's life and teachings.

A prophet claims gifts and powers beyond those of ordinary experience. Max Weber calls this claim *charisma*, or the "gift of grace." As we saw in Chapter 5, Weber thought charisma to be one of three kinds of legitimate political authority, which he termed *charismatic domination*, and he held it to be the origin of many traditional states. We shall examine this claim in the next chapter, on the nature of traditional urban civilized communities.

Weber thought the other kind of legitimate authority among precivilized peoples was *traditional domination*. By this he meant domination by patriarchs through kin ties. We now know, nearly a century later, that such domination is also effected through warfare, feasting, and voluntary leadership and followership, as we said in Chapter 12.

None of these other traditional leaders, however, is likely to meet the challenge of great external crises for a community, crises as acute as those of severe illness or disturbance for the individual. Only prophets, forging charismatic domination out of their own minds, can produce the new cultural syntheses, and the ritual catalytic actions necessary, to effect the desired change.

There have probably been far more would-be prophets than successful ones. Not only do their movements have to pass crucial "reality tests" once they get going, but conditions have to be ripe to begin with. The society has to be in sufficient distress for its members to be ready to listen to a prophet. (In civilized societies, where large areas are integrated under single civil governments, it is quite possible for prophets to appeal to only one sector—the unemployed, the uprooted, and so on—and hence to found a sect, not a new culture.) Revitalization prophets probably arise in the tribal world among any group every 300 to 500 years or so. Wallace asserts that the League of the Iroquois was founded by such a prophet several centuries before Handsome Lake.

Shamans change myths and symbols slowly and incrementally, rather like slow, random genetic mutations. Prophets effect change all at once, in "jumps," to new steady states. Shamans invent new myths from old elements to explain particular individual circumstances. Prophets change entire worldviews, also from familiar materials, in order to revitalize a distressed culture. The one effects individual therapy; the other, if the society is distressed enough and ready to listen, effects culture change—provided, of course, that the new doctrines can pass a reality test.

SUGGESTED READINGS

Connor, Linda, Patsy Asch, and Timothy Asch. *Jero Tapakan, Balinese Healer: An Ethnographic Film Monograph*. New York: Cambridge University Press, 1986. This book and the film listed below document a shaman's rite of salvation and curing practices in details quite astonishingly similar to Socorro Marroquín's.

Kehoe, A. *The Ghost Dance Religion: Ethnohistory and Revitalization*. Ft. Worth: Harcourt Brace Jovanovich, 1989. The classic story of the 1890 failed Ghost Dance revitalization movement among the Indians of the Great Plains—with comparative chapters on Black Elk and his Sioux religion, Handsome Lake, and Navajo peyotism.

Kendall, Laurel. *The Life and Hard Times of a Korean Shaman: Of Tales and the Telling of Tales*. Honolulu: University of Hawaii Press, 1988. A shaman tells her life story to the anthropologist. The dynamics are completely parallel to those of Socorro's case history.

Lawrence, Peter. *Road Belong Cargo: A Study of the Cargo Movement in the Southern Madang District, New Guinea*. Prospect Heights, Ill.: Waveland Press, 1988. A study of five unsuccessful revitalization movements.

Lessa, William A., and Evon Z. Vogt. *Reader in Comparative Religion: An Anthropological Approach*, 4th ed. New York: Harper & Row, 1979. A magnificent compendium of articles, some of which are too technical for a general audience, others of which are all-time classics. Additional classics, including Gillin's "Magical Fright," can be found in the second edition, 1965.

Wallace, Anthony F. C. *Religion: An Anthropological View*. New York: Random House, 1966. An exhaustive catalog of rituals by type, followed by a discussion of their functions. A breakthrough; parts are brilliant.

SUGGESTED FILMS

Jero Tapakan: Stories from the Life of a Balinese Healer. Timothy Asch, Patsy Asch, and Linda Connor. Cambridge, Mass.: DER, 1983. The life history of a shaman presented on film.

Magical Death. Napoleon Chagnon and Timothy Asch. Cambridge, Mass.: DER, 1970. A group of Yanomamo shamans, in company with those of an allied village, seek to slay their enemies in a distant village by magical means.

GLOSSARY

abreact To "act out." In the theory of the efficacy of shamanistic curing, the patient mentally abreacts the diagnostic myth the shaman suggests during the curing ritual. The shaman's myth explains and justifies the illness and provides a way out. At the very least the ritual dispels tension and rallies body forces in the patient.

cult A socially organized rite. Every community and every institution within it has its cult, in the sense of its rites of the daily round (for families) and the yearly and generational rounds (for communities). Shamans add a therapeutic or antitherapeutic cult to societies. Prophets may found a *religious* cult, one with its own personnel as distinct from the rest of society.

emissary prophet A prophet who claims to have *messages* from the supernatural to preach to followers, often with specific diagnoses of the sins and failings of society, and who offers detailed prescriptions, the prophetic code, to remedy them.

exemplary prophet A prophet who claims divine inspiration but teaches above all by example, concentrating on the ailments of the soul and on total fellowship, *communitas*, with followers in small groups. Examples include most Hindu gurus and St. Francis of Assisi. If, in the future, Mother Teresa of Calcutta is canonized by the Roman Catholic Church as a saint, she would also be termed an exemplary prophet.

prophet A leader, resembling a shaman in personality and life experience, who attempts to minister to the ills of a society rather than to cure the ills of individuals.

revitalization movement A social and political movement, founded by a prophet, that seeks to provide a new code, and hence culture, to a society deemed in desperate circumstances. In effect it tries to do for societies what a shaman's curing rite does for a sick patient. In Wallace's model, a revitalization movement has five phases.

rite of salvation The rite of passage into shamanism. Although often assisted by another shaman, the experience is frequently self-generated. The shaman is separated from an old, unsatisfactory identity and abreacts a myth—derived from the subject's own interior mental life—during the transitional period, which is one of recovery from some disturbance. Finally, the shaman emerges, ready to practice new powers. The same process is true of prophets.

sect A religious organization derived from a cult or set of ritual practices established by a prophet, which does not include the whole population of a community or region; typical of civilizations rather than tribal communities.

shaman A ritual expert, claiming direct powers and contact with the supernatural, who conducts rites of therapy or antitherapy for individuals.

witch A shaman who conducts his or her rites as *antitherapy*, seeking to damage or cause injury to his or her own enemies or the enemies of his or her clients, rather than to cure the clients.

CHAPTER 14

Urban Cultures and Communities:
The Nature of Early Civilization

CHAPTER 15

The Original Bureaucracies

CHAPTER 16

Folk Cultures and Communities:
Civilized "Insolents" and Peasants

T ribal cultures and communities are in constant flux. By now you should have some notion of the extreme variability of these cultures, and their flow back and forth among different forms, of which the Seneca revitilization under Handsome Lake, discussed in Chapter 13, is an example.

In the long course of human sociocultural evolution, relatively more integrated territories, united under single full-time political authorities (states) in seemingly more stable patterns of culture and community, emerged out of this flux. These community forms are called urban or rural, their culture, "civilized." In Part IV we examine these new community patterns and the array of developing and flowering institutions that come with them. We look at urban culture and community, the archaic state, and peasant communities. We reserve one developing institution, the market, for Part V and modern life.

The new patterns of life emerged in five or six "hearths" of civilization around the world at different times. This development occurred after most of the world had gone from band to tribal peoples. The transition to civiliza- tion seems to have happened in similar habitats—river valleys—which at the time were relatively marginal to the richer tribal lands nearby. We shall discuss the dynamics of the transition in Chapter 14.

In civilization, at the "state" level the distinctive community forms are urban centers. These centers may be either nucleated, enclosed (walled) cities or dispersed "green" cities, whose urban nodes are scattered at some distance from each other. However, there is little completely new in what we have to learn here; all the institutions we have met before are here but are basically trans- formed by an escalation in size, by the gaining of new functions, and by the context of denser populations, more extensive communications, and greater energy invested in human relations. Thus, prophets, whom we have met before, give rise to both priesthoods and monarchies. *Priests* are full-time ritual specialists, gathered around a fixed holy place, a *shrine*. They often supervise the large-scale redistribution of goods flowing into them as ritual offerings.

Monarchs (and some tyrants), who may descend from prophets or even priests, are rulers who expand their households to rule large areas and thereby invent (over and over again in many times and places) the "patrimonial" bureaucracies of archaic states. Monarchs' royal lineages become *dynasties*, thereby fixing the state in the hands of an elite claiming high status from kinship.

Thus we have full-time ritual and political specialists, *elites*, who usually live off tribute (or offerings) and do not themselves labor to produce food. Society has become more hierarchical or stratified. The hierarchy of bureaucracy eventually must be understood in its own terms. But for now we have the tools to see how hierarchies have arisen from what came before.

In Chapter 14 we shall look at the problem of the emergence of civilization in human social and cultural evolution. We shall examine, too, an archaic civilization grouped around a monarchy, Swaziland, that rules a large territory and complex polity entirely through the kinship system.

For archaeologists the traditional, dynastic, state is the final diagnostic feature of civilization. When a monarch asserts that his lineage is a royal dynasty with a divine right to rule, and when his subjects comply with these claims, then we have a state. Monarchs also improvised the invention of a major new institution, bureaucracy, out of their households. The original bureaucracy entailed a small organization of persons who, standing for the monarch, administered large territories. This is obviously a new and major *political* function grafted on to an institution that was originally, as we saw in Chapter 7, a device to domesticate children to work for their parents. When an institution gets such a major new function, it may well change its method of recruiting personnel. Eventually its origin becomes quite remote, and it bears scant resemblance to the institution from which it grew. For that reason we examine the dynastic state and its variations, especially the half-rational imperial bureaucracy of the Ottoman Turks, in Chapter 15.

Finally, in Chapter 16, we survey the cultures of the rural component of civilized realms, the peasants and their more militant neighbors, the often nomadic "insolents" on the borders of civilized dominions. That done, we can take up modern culture in Part V.

Urban Cultures and Communities:

The Nature of Early Civilization

*THE PROCESSES OF SOCIAL AND
CULTURAL EVOLUTION*

Time Scales for Cultural Flux

*The Transition from One Level of Culture and
Community to Another*

*THE URBAN, CIVILIZED PATTERN:
POLITICAL AND ECONOMIC ORGANIZATIONS*

*MESOPOTAMIA: THE RISE OF THE
NUCLEATED, WALLED CITY*

Growth and Differentiation of Urban Institutions

    Specializations by Labor

    Clustering of Villages/Wards Around a Central Shrine

    Guild/Regiments, Cross-Cutting Ties, and Republican
    Politics

    Internal Hierarchies at the Temples: The Appearance of
    Elites

    Palaces Emerge from Temples

    New Kings: Arbiters of Internal Struggles, Leaders in
    External Wars

    Warfare as Conquest

    Writing, Law Codes, and Judges

Overview of the Evolution of Mesopotamian Civilization

    Irrigation Was Not Sufficient to Cause Civilization

    Warfare Likewise Was Not a Cause of Civilization

*THE NUCLEATED, WALLED CITY:
AN IDEAL FORM*

THE GREEN CITY: ANCIENT EGYPT

*ETHNOGRAPHIC CLOSE-UP:
UNDERSTANDING AND
EXPLAINING SWAZILAND*

Swazi Settlement Pattern

Movement in the Swazi System

*The Annual Ceremony of Kingship: Ritual of Rebellion and
National Rite of Intensification*

*SWAZI URBANISM IN
PERSPECTIVE: CIVILIZATION OR
CHIEFDOM?*

*B*eginning some 6,000 to 7,000 years ago in the Old World, and some 4,000 years ago in the New World, some tribal cultures condensed into **civilizations.** There is nothing inevitable about the transition into civilization; it happened irreversibly in antiquity only in six places, the **hearths of civilization:** Mesopotamia, Egypt,* the Indus Valley, North (Shang period) China, Mesoamerica (Mexico, Guatemala, and Belize), and Coastal Peru.

In several cases, notably ancient Jericho in Palestine and the Hopewellian cultures of North America, monumental quasi-civilizations appeared before horticulture, on an intensified food-gathering base. In other, horticultural, cases, notably the Chaco cultures of our Southwest, they flourished briefly, only to collapse before sustaining "takeoff." However, once a civilized pattern has crystallized, and it did so in trading and warlike interactions with neighboring tribal societies in each case, that pattern may spread to neighbors by conquest, diffusion, or imitation (stimulus diffusion). Civilizations expanded, coalesced, and took over the world, so much so that both band and tribal ways of life are today in retreat, coming to terms in all cases with encroaching urban civilization.

Civilizations first emerged, then, in a context of a world filled up with tribal societies, of a coalescing of local communities responding to particular social and environmental challenges. *River valleys* present habitat challenges to such tribal settlers. River deltas are often boggy and swampy, which makes them ideal refuges for groups fleeing warfare. Their high ground favors certain places for settlement and assemblage. The economics of redistribution and the technology of drainage canals are both essential here. Eventually some groups realized the potentially rich horticultural resources of such river valleys, with their drained fertile bottomlands and waterways for

---

*There is some disagreement as to whether Egypt was a "pristine" or spontaneous hearth of civilization or was simply reacting to the stimulus of Mesopotamia. In any case, civilization here was of great antiquity, and its beginnings needed very little stimulus, if any, from neighbors.

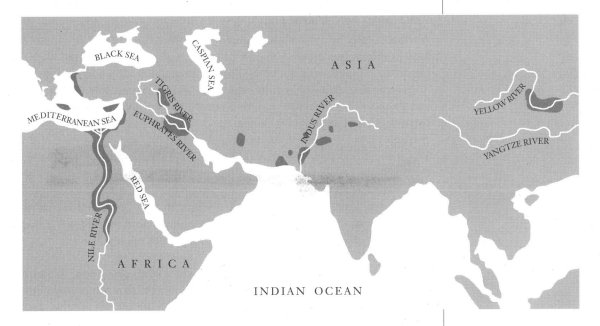

long-distance communication. They did so in the context of warfare with local competitors and defense and trade with seminomadic tribal neighbors.

The earliest civilizations in the Old World could be found in the fertile river valleys (darker areas).

THE PROCESSES OF SOCIAL AND CULTURAL EVOLUTION

The emergence of our species, *H. sapiens sapiens*, from another species, *H. erectus*, was an event in physical evolution that reflected significant genetic changes in the composition of the genes of the newly emerging species. *This has not been true of subsequent human evolution.* That evolution has occurred instead in the social institutions of our species and in the organization and amount of cultural knowledge transmitted, by speech, from generation to generation. Furthermore, social and cultural evolution is not significantly correlated with subspecies physical variation, or *races*. All human races today may enjoy the full accumulation of cultural and scientific achievements, all stored outside the genes—nowadays mainly by written speech, or literature. Human evolution, since about 100,000 to 50,000 years ago, has taken place not at the level of the genes, but at the level of culture.

That evolution builds on what has gone before. In Part III we saw band communities *condense*, or coalesce, bringing local communities into tribal alliances, variously dominated by councils of leaders, Big Men, and chiefs. This condensation resulted from a process of *population growth and slow spatial diffusion*. The livable world became filled with human beings, and they have been exerting pressure on each other ever since.

341

Time Scales for Cultural Flux

A tribal society and its shared cultures are formed of shifting coalitions of local communities arrayed against others in incessant but shifting warfare patterns, mingled with countervailing patterns of trade and competition. Their spatial scale is on the order of 300 kilometers (about 150 miles) across, and the population density ranges around 3 persons per square kilometer, versus 0.03 for band-level societies.

The Human Lifetime Scale: 70–90 Years. Tribal societies tend to realign themselves in space over cycles of 70 to 90 years, which would reflect the lifetimes of great leaders: Big Men and prophets. During this time, gardens may become exhausted in some soil systems; houses decay and fall down; tools wear out. New leaders arise. Ethnic groups move, often fleeing their enemies, or expanding at the expense of weaker opponents.*

Constitutional–Cultural Patterns Time Scale: 200-1,200 Years. Cultures tend to be reformulated, often by prophets in revitalization movements. Shadow constitutions are amended, polities oscillate among all the forms we have mentioned: rule by the one, the few, or the many. Cultural actions and beliefs "mutate," as when the proto-Nuer invented segmentary lineages and complementary opposition, thus giving themselves a clear legal framework for forging alliances quickly. Technologies change, but much more slowly.

The Transition from One Level of Culture and Community to Another

When we plot these changes against population growth and clustering, and long-term accretions in technology and subsistence, the following picture emerges. Bands turn into tribal alliances, first without food production in the mesolithic transition, and second with food production in the neolithic transition (see Chapter 9). Tribes, in turn, under certain circumstances that mirror exactly in principle those of the transition to tribal life, turn into civilizations.

Overall, the transition to first tribal and then civilized life is a result of several processes operating at once: the responses of groups beset by densification of population, habitat challenges and technological responses to them, internal institutional innovation and complexity, and external social-political (conflict and warfare) pressures from neighboring groups. The up-

---

*This discussion of time scales, and the notion of civilization's reflecting a further condensation of human beings in place, draws heavily on pieces by Iberall and White (1988) and Iberall and Wilkinson (1985).

shot has been the appearance of both tribal and—thousands of years later—urban and rural civilized communities (see Figure 14.1). Let us look at this transition in more detail.

THE URBAN, CIVILIZED PATTERN: POLITICAL AND ECONOMIC ORGANIZATIONS

Urban centers and a state are the primary attributes of civilization. A civilized urban settlement pattern is distinctive. At least one settlement is an urban **node,** tying many lesser settlements to itself and thereby linking them. All civilized societies have some version of the **state,** a political system with a set of leaders occupying formally named full-time offices. State offices are continuous over the generations; the death of a ruler does not occasion the collapse of his political apparatus, as the death of a Melanesian Big Man most assuredly does.

Moreover, dependent communities tend to be food producers (peasants) for the urban center. They supply its needs through tribute, offerings, and ritual redistribution. In return, the center provides managerial, ritual, and defense command services, as well as an array of manufactured goods. Full-time craft experts appear at the centers, manufacturing all sorts of fine tools and luxury goods. The center also manages long-distance trade for goods and supplies not produced locally but rather extracted from tribal neighbors (barbarians) through enticing them to come visit as pilgrims or through trading fine manufactured goods with them in return for basic raw materials.

The elemental constituents of an archaic civilization are urban centers and their satellite communities and a set of full-time urban leaders (ritual, political, and military). Shrines become urban nodes, where villagers come to worship and leave offerings and where elites and masses alike are rewarded in redistributive rituals. Such centers do not appear overnight; they grow from one distinctive elemental form—a place of assemblage for redistributive rituals—in a challenging, relatively deprived habitat, around which, in differing sequences, ritual leaders, craft specialists, and military and political leaders arise. These leaders and specialists, through processes of both internal and external competition, eventually organize their communities into new settlement patterns with full-time states. Let us look at one case and then attempt to account for it theoretically.

MESOPOTAMIA: THE RISE OF THE NUCLEATED, WALLED CITY

Mesopotamia is *one* of the several independent hearths of "start-up" civilizations. It is the region where our knowledge of the self-sustained appear-

Justice
Law codes arise to govern relations of different peoples within the same jurisdictions. Judges have powers to enforce judgments. Monarchs may be lawgivers but at same time strive to be above law themselves.

Language
Writing: calendars, sacred scriptures, accounts, law codes.

Politics
The state: full-time monarchies, conquest empires.

Learning
Specialized learning among priest-scholars, scribes. Master craftsmen train apprentices.

Traditional Civilizations
Community field: Consists of constellations of urban, commanding institutional nodes (temples, plazas, storehouses, palaces, barracks, marketplaces, etc.) and the general population of craftsmen and farmers. In one type (the "stone" or closed city) the population is tightly packed around these nodes, grouped together at the city center. In the other (the "green" or open city) the nodes are scattered, and the population is, too.

Economics
Redistributive rites effect exchanges among food producers, food processors, and craftsmen. Royal traders search for distant goods. Marketplaces allow impersonal trade among strangers.

Ritual
First cities are ceremonial centers. Calendrical rites effect redistribution (see economics). Organized religion emerges around full-time priests at shrines. Pilgrimages. Prophets and conversions.

Technology
Always food producers, with intensive gardening, irrigation; may have plow agriculture with ox teams. Fine craft traditions, metallurgy, common.

Sociology
Shamans give rise to priesthood hierarchies. Kings' lineages become royal dynasties. Kings' households grow into bureaucracies. Armies grow out of warrior age grades. Full-time craftsmen organize into fraternities, "guilds." Peasant and nomadic communities may turn inward, encapsulate own traditions, or even resist state by force of arms.

Figure 14.1 Emergent institutional behavior in traditional civilizations.

ance of civilization is perhaps the most complete. The archaeological record is very thorough and includes some of the most spectacular finds in the world, and the Mesopotamians themselves left written records in the form of indestructible clay tablets. Mesopotamia is between the Tigris and Euphrates rivers, the land of the biblical Ur of the Chaldees, and today comprises much of Iraq and something of Syria as well.*

From 5000 to 3800 B.C., in the marshes between the rivers, small villages grew gradually into imposing city-states. They became so monumental and enduring in form that even today this type of settlement, the **nucleated, walled city,** is still conceived of as the true urban form in much of the world.

The original settlers had moved out of the hills where agriculture had been developed. They found that higher ground in the marshes—ground that they drained—could be especially productive, being renewed each year by silt deposits. They also found rich fishing and even herding possibilities. They plowed with oxen. It is probable they were fleeing warfare in the hills when they entered what looked like unpromising habitats.

The earliest communities surrounded a shrine dedicated to a deity, who was thought of as the owner of the village and its lands. The shrine at the original village level excavated at Eridu, dating from 5000 B.C., was a one-room structure of mud brick measuring 12 by 15 feet, simply furnished with a central altar and a side niche for the statue of the deity. Perhaps 500 people lived in Eridu at that time. Such shrines were rebuilt many times, as were the dwellings around them; but the temple mounds rose even higher than the general mound on which the city stood. As the cities grew, the number of shrines increased as well.

View of the archaeological site of the Mesopotamian city of Uruk, looking southwest from the ziggurat, or temple tower.

Around the year 3000 B.C., this piling up of settlement mounds and temple mountains reached a cultural climax. Some twenty city-states had emerged in Mesopotamia, eclipsing the simple villages and their shrines. The city of Uruk had not one but several temple mountains rising above the habitation mound of the city, 60 feet high (Mallowan, 1965).

At the center of this complex was an immense square, fringed on three sides by the monumental walls of temple platforms. To the northeast bulked a giant platform, measuring 245 by 100 feet, dedicated to the Goddess

---

*This discussion draws on Childe (1954) and Adams (1966). It is heavily influenced by Flannery's (1972) attempt to recast the discussion, especially Adams's "multivariant factors approach," in terms of general systems theory, while avoiding Flannery's technical jargon.

E-Anna (see Figure 14.2). This was the oldest sanctuary in the city, many times rebuilt. Archaeologists excavating at the summit marveled at its magnificence, and down in the square they could catch a glimpse of the buttresses and recessed walls of the shrine at the top.

Opposite this structure there loomed across the square the great bulk of the temple of Anu. Its asphalted summit formed the ceremonial assembly area for a comparatively small shrine, the White Temple, set upon its own artificial mountain 35 feet high. Its small dimensions, 75 feet by 57 feet 6 inches, contrasted with the plaza below and made its long, narrow sanctuary almost a private place. The multitude could not fit in there, only priests and their initiates.

To get some idea of this monumental temple-building enterprise, imagine a large university campus that did not repair its buildings but instead tore them down when they became old and damaged and used them as the foundation for new and better ones. The best and symbolically most impor-

Figure 14.2 A plan of the walled city of Uruk, one of the most important centers of early Mesopotamian civilization. Note the positions of the White Temple and the E-Anna Temple.

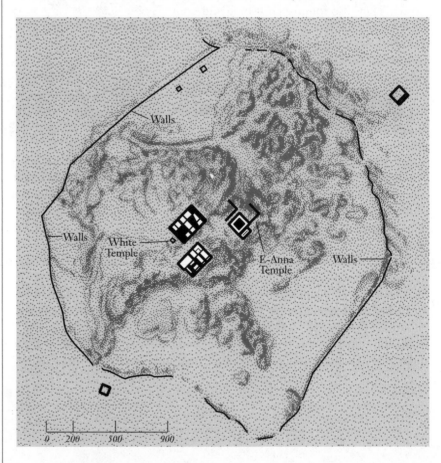

tant ones—the school stadium, for example—would be buried in order to form a base for another stadium on top. Such a university would become quite an incredible mound in a few centuries.

Growth and Differentiation of Urban Institutions

Cities grew out of villages on the same sites. In the original pattern, the early shrine village may be thought of as the nucleus of a cell that included diverse populations. The first settlers were farmers, herders, fishers, harvesters, and workers in reed. However, all were members of the temple household, which belonged to the god. In the god's name, all shared the common produce of the others. Thus, the temples were redistributive centers from the start.

Specializations by Labor. Full-time craft specialists soon joined the temples. The first were brewers and bakers, who changed the village grain into beer and bread, which were distributed to temple ritual participants along with fish and meat. Temple servants also shared at the sacred board. Redistribution for the first time supported full-time specialists who were once removed from primary food production. The possibility was opened to support others—elites—as well.

Clustering of Villages/Wards Around a Central Shrine. The clustering tendency continued into protodynastic times, of which there are written histories. Some villages simply moved into the more important centers, enlarging the settlement and acknowledging the seniority of the earliest shrine on the site but retaining their own shrine. We need more information about the exact history of these mergers, but it is reasonable to speculate that they were linked somehow to the redistributive economy, and perhaps to warfare with nomadic herdsmen in the hills.

Richer communities, able to sustain more elaborate and generous feasts, may well have attracted and perhaps even symbolically vanquished lesser villages, rather in the manner that a Siuai Big Man is able to defeat another chief by staging a feast he is unable to equal.

Populations of united villages within one set of walls provided increased numbers for maintaining defense and constructing temples, levees, canals, and fortifications. Other dispersed villages became satellites dependent on the clustering centers. The cities resembled congeries of cells, with the former villages forming separate wards around their small temples.

Guild/Regiments, Cross-Cutting Ties, and Republican Politics. In many ways, politics in the cities before the protodynastic phase was like a complicated version of the Cheyenne political system. The various wards (composed of kindreds) with their temples were analogous to the Cheyenne bands. In addition, there were military societies that, like those of the Cheyenne, cut across kin and temple groupings. The military societies or regiments were the guilds of the various craft specialties, the list of which for one important temple included bakers, brewers, spinners, weavers, a smith, other artisans, scribes, and accountants.

These guild regiments could repel raids for booty from mounted barbarians from the hills, as well as more dangerous attacks from neighboring cities with whom they competed for lands and water rights. Moreover, the device of having warfare in the hands of guilds had the effect of undercutting the power of the priests of any particular temple. There was also some sort of council of elders, analogous to the Cheyenne council of forty-four peace chiefs, who set policy for the entire city.

Internal Hierarchies at the Temples: The Appearance of Elites. In the development of the temples and their economics of craft specialists, the simple republican cross-cutting devices were lost. The major temples grew and differentiated themselves into **hierarchies.** The temple accounts of the Goddess Bau of the city of Lagash give a detailed idea of this complexity. First, there was the ward congregation of the goddess (probably a clan or a kindred). These charter members of the temple community worked three-fourths of the 17 square miles of agricultural land that belonged to the divine household. Wage earners or tenants not belonging to the temple kindred worked the rest. In addition, there were the craft specialists who lived off the temple board. These men and women were assisted by a number of slaves (perhaps war captives).

At the apex of the household, the **priests** directed its multiple activities and reaped the greatest material reward. While the land allotment for a common household member was from 0.8 to 2.5 acres, a priest held 35.5 acres for his own use, which were worked by his own retainers (Childe, 1954). Moreover, these priests could purchase land formerly belonging to the temples and their corporate kin groups.

This stratification process was intensified in early dynastic time when royal favorites bought up land. Priests, princes, palace officials, and merchants chartered by the palace became land owners quite independent of divine households, military societies, and guilds. Robert Adams (1966), who uncovered the evidence for this social stratification, asserts that the landowning group became an endogamous **elite.** There does seem to have been a tendency for them to intermarry.

Palaces Emerge from Temples. A new kind of building emerged in the protodynastic phase that immediately followed this florescence of

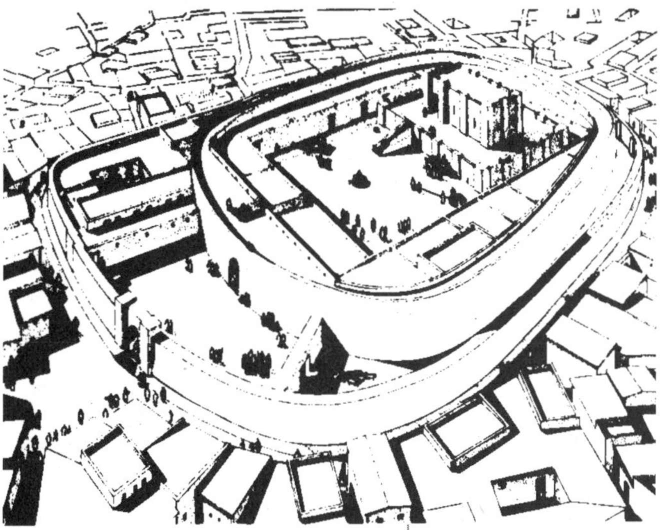

Mesopotamian city-states. These were palaces; they were not devised from the architecture of private dwellings but rather grew out of the temples.

Sometimes temples contained fortified residences for priests within the temple walls, usually next to the sanctuary (see Figure 14.3). Priests who officiated at these shrines were also war leaders, and the chief priest was the "steward" of a particular god. Eventually the quarters of the chief priest and his servants got bigger and bigger; his audience and banquet halls grew, and the sanctuary shrank to the size of a mere chapel. What had been a shrine became the household of a king, who still retained his title as priest and steward. But architecture gave him the lie. Soon, city after city got its king, each with his palace, and something very important had been added to the sacred mountain.

Figure 14.3 This reconstructed drawing of the Temple Oval at Khafajah shows the sanctuary set on an elevated platform with the priests' house located between the inner and outer perimeter walls.

New Kings: Arbiters of Internal Struggles, Leaders in External Wars. The palace and the new king suddenly replaced the republic and those in power—temple priests, military societies, councils of elders, and the growing elite of priestly and merchant land owners. Adams argues that the kings were created by the new landowning elite, although it is possible that the converse was just as true. The first kings did not call themselves kings. They had such titles as steward or tenant farmer of the god.

These men were priests of particular temples and at the same time war leaders, probably claiming divine war powers. Because they were privately wealthy persons, they could also claim support from the newly emerging elite of land owners. In short, they were dictators who could more easily resolve the new tensions and demands of Mesopotamian urban societies than could the old council of elders. They could do so for two reasons: (1) They could focus energies outside in war, and (2) they still controlled the traditional source of ritual sanction and redistributive economics—their temple. Although it was slowly being converted into a palace, it never gave up its redistributive and ritual functions (see Figure 14.4). New rituals appeared that surrounded the person of the king as much as the statue of the deity.

Warfare as Conquest. Warfare among these city-states was quite different from the tribal warfare discussed in Chapter 10. At first, it surely had much

Figure 14.4 The early dynastic palace at the Mesopotamian city-state Kish is comparable to the temple shown for Khafajah (Figure 14.3) and is one of the earliest examples known of a palace set apart for the king as distinct from the temple, the god's residence.

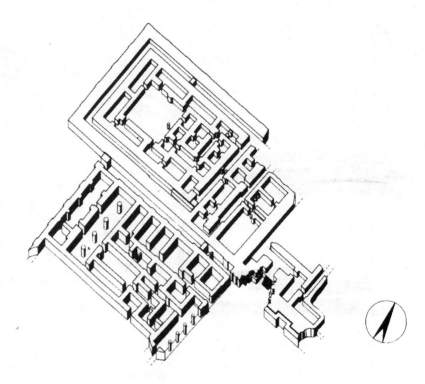

to do with competition for lands, with the ingathering of villages into the city precincts, and with the struggle over the control of water supplies for irrigation, as well as with raids by mounted tribal barbarians. When the various city-states reached the natural limits of their territorial expansion, they attempted to assert hegemony, control over others.

At first this hegemony consisted of defeating the rival and obliging the defeated king to pay tribute to the victor. With Sargon of Akkad (ca. 2300 B.C.), however, this situation changed. Sargon was a self-made king who seized power in one city-state. He founded his own city, and his palace took over the peak of the artificial sacred mountain. His was the first empire, for he replaced the kings of defeated cities with his own appointed governors and installed their principal idols as hostages in his own shrines in Akkad (Service, 1975).

Writing, Law Codes, and Judges. Writing is generally thought of as a diagnostic trait of civilization. This is true only if we include as writing the knotted ropes used to keep accounts by the Inca of pre-Columbian Peru, as they had no script but were highly civilized. Writing in Mesopotamia evolved from accounts at shrine redistribution centers. The first known texts are lists, made with crude pictures of the items to be stored, imprinted on clay tablets, first appearing around 3100 B.C. By 1800 B.C. these crude pictographs had evolved into cuneiform script, symbols with phonetic meanings, derived from the sound of the items represented in the original pictographs.

Priests soon used writing for more than accounts. They wrote down myths. Kings desired written chronicles to make their own exploits and dynastic origins mythological; they even rewrote myths. After a victorious king conquered a rival city and installed the idol of that city's paramount god in his own shrine, he sought to have the myths changed as well, making his deity more important than those of the conquered foes.

Finally, kings wrote down laws. The earliest known example of this is the so-called law code of Hammurabi (1792–1750 B.C.), who turned his city, Babylon (*Babilani*, "The Gate of the Gods"), into the capital of an empire uniting most of Mesopotamia. The "code" was a basalt monument inscribed in forty-nine vertical columns and seems to have been an offering to the gods, testifying to the king's virtue, rather than a text to be consulted in actual law cases (Oates, 1986). However, the notion of a king as lawgiver, delivering laws written in stone, was to remain part of the legacy of central world civilization. Some theorists believe that written law codes were useful when different peoples, such as the subject peoples of Hammurabi's empire, came together, making it necessary to reconcile differences among them in their customary law.

Judges had also appeared. They were groups of wise men sitting at the entrances of temples, appointed perhaps at first by priests, later by kings or their officials. They heard disputes brought before them. Their judgments were then enforced by royal officials, backed by armed constables.

A bronze head of a Mesopotamian ruler, c. 2300 B.C.

Overview of the Evolution of Mesopotamian Civilization

Mesopotamian urbanization germinated from the appearance of redistributional places at shrines. Instead of being a union of loose confederacies like the kula communities, dense populations were formed by clustering some shrines around other, more important ones. Single cities, formed of many former villages and shrines clustered together, ruled still other villages scattered in a hinterland, whose borders were disputed with neighboring growing city-states. This amalgamation may have been related to the redistributional rivalry of competitive temple feasts.

Within each city, however, the temple households composed originally of descent groups became more complicated as priests, slaves, tenants, and artisans were all added to the temple personnel. To undercut the competition among temple communities within a city, military guilds were formed by occupational specialty, cutting across the temple memberships. This balance was upset by the appearance of wealthy land owners, mainly priests.

The final arbiter of this complicated system emerged as king in the person of a combined commander-in-chief and high priest.

All the institutions we have met before are here, but they have been transformed. They have escalated in size and scale and have gained new functions. For example, **redistribution,** no longer a mechanism for competitive feasting, has become the synchronizing mechanism to keep the primary kinetic cycle going: divvying up the annual harvest and storing it for later redistribution. Now full-time nonfood producers could be supported by the producers. Large, dense populations could be successfully regulated in ways that made for ever greater populations, as cities grew by in-gathering of villages.

With the invention of writing and full-time messengers, language took a step forward—not as revolutionary a step as the invention of speech, but communication did become more extensive. Accounts could be kept exactly over many years, future resources could be estimated, and monarchs could send written directives to govern distant conquered cities. As a consequence, life became more regimented, and greater energy was invested in human relations.

Each escalation of scale—the appearance of competing temple communities in one place, for example—brought yet more energy investment in human relations (the appearance of cross-cutting military fraternities in this case). The final arbiters, kings, invested even more human energy in their campaigns of conquest.

Irrigation Was Not Sufficient to Cause Civilization. In this account I have mentioned irrigation, especially drainage of marshes, only in passing. In contrast, some theorists, following Karl Wittfogel (1957), would assign it primary importance in the evolution of civilization, asserting that social change arises only and always from technological change. My view is that technological change, once it happens, provides a *potential* for social advance, but not an inevitable one. There are tribal societies with extensive and complicated irrigated systems (for example, the rice terraces of North Luzon, Philippines, which are shared by several warring tribal groups). In the Mesopotamian case, and apparently also in the cases of the river hearths of the other five original civilizations, primary importance rests with a redistributive economy, centering on relatively permanent *shrines*—that is, centers that last much longer than one lifetime, unlike the centers focusing on the ephemeral careers of single tribal Big Men.

Irrigation does provide for richer crop yields, hence even denser populations, and hence also the managerial features of water flow control, construction of public works, and above all, storage of excess crops at central storehouses in order to support specialized craftsmen, to support standing armies, and to allow trade with barbarians for raw materials lacking in the wet river valleys. However, the mechanism of redistribution is needed first, as well as the semipermanent shrines.

Warfare Likewise Was Not a Cause of Civilization. Yet another theorist, Robert Carneiro (1970), following earlier thinkers, assigns warfare the status of prime mover in the origin of civilization. We have seen that warfare is one constant attribute of tribal cultures. What is unique with early civilization, however, is the use of warfare to conquer rather than to merely compete or to even some score. This new trait, however, arose well after the urban pattern was fully in place in the Mesopotamian case, and cannot be considered to have caused it. Moreover, in at least one original civilization, that of the classic Maya, conquest warfare never fully evolved, but instead the new dynasties of the many city-states used warfare as a means of validating their claims to individual thrones by capturing princely captives from rival realms to sacrifice in their royal accession (coronation) rites (Schele and Miller, 1986; Schele and Friedel, 1990).

THE NUCLEATED, WALLED CITY: AN IDEAL FORM

Mesopotamia gave us the enduring image of the **city,** that of a densely populated settlement with control over every major institution and many smaller food-producing villages. This ideal type was derived from the first Mesopotamian prototype, which was quite precise in form by late dynastic times and persisted unchanged right down to 1911, when the last emperor of China was stripped of his imperial power.

Old Peking (today's Beijing) in 1911 was an excellent example of the prototype. All that had been added to the basic Mesopotamian pattern were the marketplaces. The city was divided into adjacent walled square precincts, the Manchu city to the north and the Chinese city to the south. Centered in the south of the Manchu city was the "sacred mountain"—a palace surrounded by a moat. This was the Forbidden City—tabu to ordinary people—and from its gates the emperor would emerge on state ceremonial occasions. He would move along a causeway from the great square to the spacious parks of the Altar of Heaven and the Altar of Agriculture on either side of the principal city gates to the south (see Figure 14.5). These were great temples, one for

A massive gilded gateway in Old Peking with the wall of the Forbidden City in the background.

Figure 14.5 Schematic map of Old Peking.

1. *Imperial palace (Forbidden City)*
3. *Agricultural temple*
4. *Temple of Heaven*
5. *Altar of Agriculture*
6. *Lake*
7. *Scenery Hill*
8. *Literary (Confucian) temple*
10. *Palaces of imperial relatives*
11. *Administrative offices (yamen)*
12. *Imperial warehouses (tribute goods to be redistributed)*
13. *Temple*
14. *Temple*
15. *Temple*
16. *Bell tower*

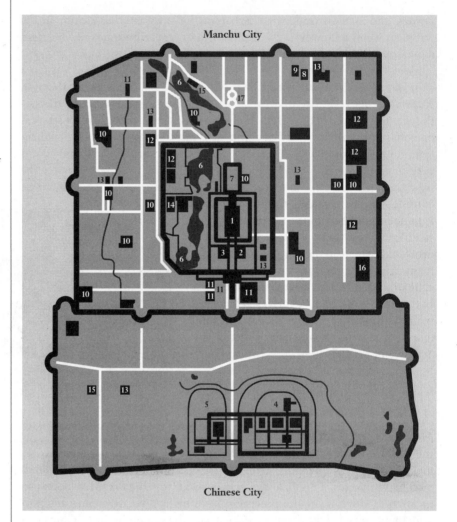

each half of the Chinese (southern) city, where the emperor made the annual sacrifices for the commonwealth and demonstrated for all that his was the mandate of heaven.

Peking's four-square pattern was further divided into wards, occupied by different ethnic groups. Manchus and Mongols lived in the northern half, with a separate ward in their midst for Muslims and their mosque. Other wards were for artisans and farmers who plowed fields outside the city walls. Peasant villages survived, encapsulated within the stone city (Arlington and Lewisohn, 1935).

All traditional Middle Eastern cities are of this type, although few are as geometrically perfect as Peking. All have a central palace, a garrison, a great square, and a central mosque or shrine for the city. All are divided into units called quarters (there may be more than four), each with its great mosques. Quarters in turn are divided into wards, each with its houses of worship (synagogues, churches, mosques, or saints' tombs) and its public baths. If you go to Timbuctoo, this is exactly what you will find, as a book by anthropologist Horace Miner (1965) can tell you.

THE GREEN CITY: ANCIENT EGYPT

The walled, nucleated city with its dense population and its concentration of state, ritual, economic, and military institutions in one central place has been the dominant image of the city. The capital city of a state with its hinterland is likewise the dominant image of civilization. The other major form, the **green city**, is an *open* one that does not concentrate populations densely in one place and that disperses the commanding functions among several centers. Thus, the food-producing population is scattered among the fields, and the elites likewise reside in the countryside at their "command centers," such as temples, garrisons, or administrative headquarters. Such a form is still urban and still civilized.

In ancient Egypt there was no single imperial city. In fact, there was never a nucleated city in Egypt until Alexander the Great founded Alexandria, a Greek city. Rather, there were many diverse control centers. First, there were the palaces of the pharaohs. Each new king usually built himself a palace. Retainers often had quite fine homes near the palace, but that was all. There was no city in any other sense at a palace center. Second, there were the royal tombs, especially the pyramids, which were population centers during seasonal construction.

Third, there were major temples scattered over the land. These were cult centers, but bear in mind that the pharaohs were divine and that the palace was a political cult center as well. Finally, there were the provincial administrative centers around the residence of the royal governor, the nomarch. Associated with this was a garrison stationed to keep order in the province.

Marble bridges across an artificial canal lead to the main audience hall of the Forbidden City, center of the "sacred mountain" where emperors once ruled.

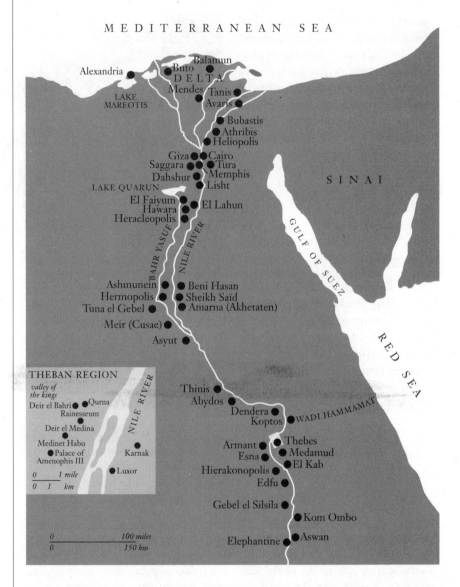

Ancient Egypt and the principal sites in the reign of a single Pharaoh, Akhenaten (reigned 1358–1346 B.C.).

Such dispersed cities have been reported for the ancient Maya of Yucatan and Guatemala, for Southeast Asia, especially among the Khmer and their famous ceremonial center at Angkor Wat in Cambodia, and for Japan before the eighteenth century. In examining the essentials of the green city form, its contrast with the nucleated city, and its implication for urban living today, I use Swaziland as an example—the closest thing to ancient Egypt still in existence.

E T H N O G R A P H I C   C L O S E - U P

UNDERSTANDING AND EXPLAINING SWAZILAND

Swaziland is an independent nation in southern Africa, between the Republic of South Africa and Mozambique. About the size of the state of Oregon, it was once a British protectorate (Kuper, 1947; Marwick, 1940).* Lobamba, the capital of Swaziland, is a type of city called a royal village by the British. The king does not live at the capital but within a day's walking distance at his own village. Instead, Lobamba is the residence of the female monarch, usually the king's mother. The British called her the queen mother, but her title is Ndlovukazi—literally Lady Elephant.

---

*This discussion portrays Swaziland mainly as it was in the 1930s. For an exposition of how this system has survived and adapted to modernity, see Kuper's third ethnography (1986).

Each of the other royal villages is occupied by a prince, an uncle or a brother of the king, and each is the seat of the prince's mother, a widow of a deceased king. In addition, certain villages are ruled by hereditary chiefs linked directly to the capital and the king's village. Linked to these royal and chiefly villages are the scattered homesteads of the commoners, each of whom owes allegiance to some local prince or chief.

Swazi Settlement Pattern

The capital and all royal and chiefly villages represent an expansion and elaboration of the design or town plan of a commoner's homestead. As shown in Figure 14.6, the basic pattern is an enclosure of huts for sleeping and cooking, facing onto a large cattle

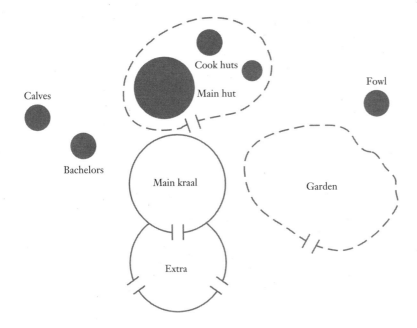

Figure 14.6 Pattern of a commoner homestead, Swaziland.

357

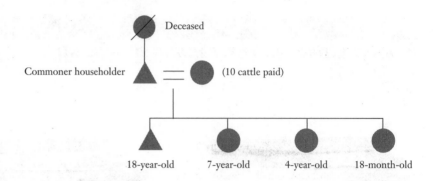

Figure 14.7 Personnel of a commoner homestead.

Deceased

Commoner householder   (10 cattle paid)

18-year-old   7-year-old   4-year-old   18-month-old

kraal (corral). If the commoner's mother, the lady of the house, is alive, the main hut is hers; the houses of the commoner's wife are to the right. If the sons remain at home rather than going off to the barracks at a royal center, they build bachelor huts at the edges of the settlement, forming the horns of the crescent around the cattle kraal. Possible inhabitants are shown in Figure 14.7.

A chief's village (Figure 14.8) is actually his homestead, filled with the enclosures of his wives. The chief's mother (M) has the central hut; as the senior female, she is the lady or mistress of the establishment. Households of chief's wives (W) are distributed according to rank on either side of the lady's house. Some wives have clan sisters living with them as servants (MS). The chief (CH) whose village

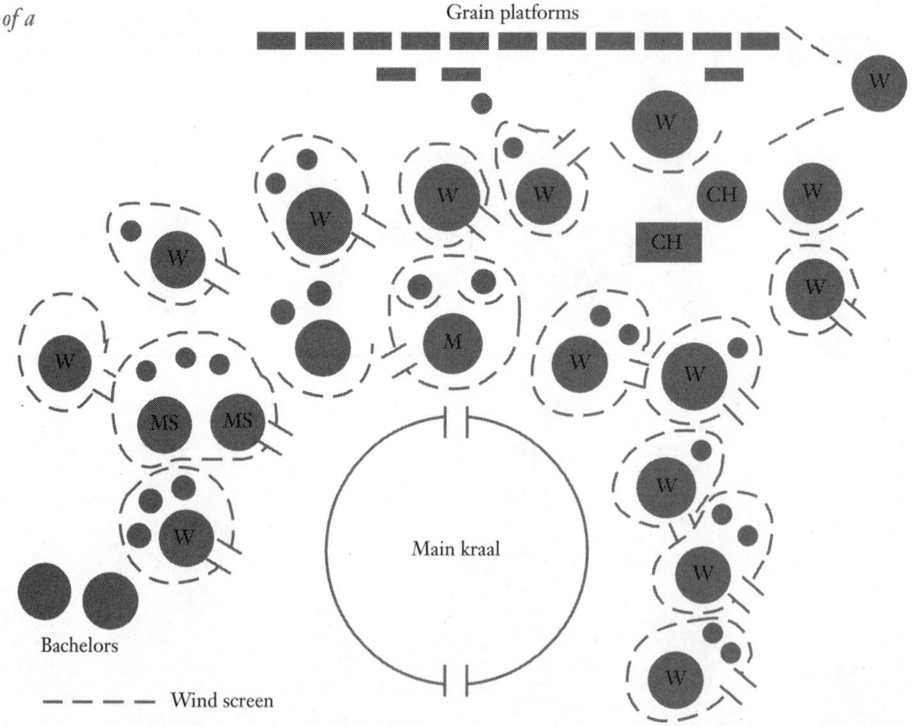

Figure 14.8 Village of a chief in Swaziland.

Grain platforms

W
W   W   W
CH   W
CH
W

W
W
M   W
W

MS   MS

W   W

Main kraal

W

W

Bachelors

- - - - - Wind screen

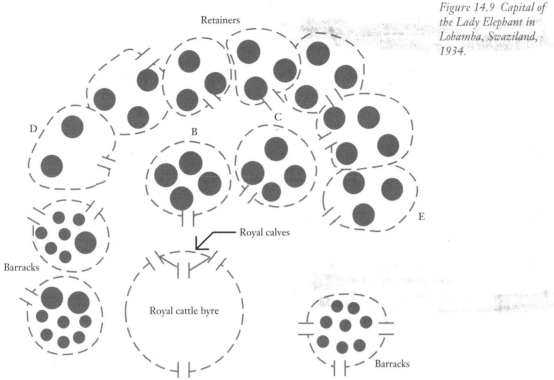

Retainers

Figure 14.9 Capital of the Lady Elephant in Lobamba, Swaziland, 1934.

is diagrammed here had twenty-eight wives; not all of them lived at his village. Only one of his several bachelor sons chose to reside at home; the barracks and the mines were more attractive to the rest.

At the capital of the Lady Elephant, where the mistress of the nation presides over her own enclosure and her own village, elements from the commoner homestead level are magnified (see Figure 14.9). Homesteads of the chief councilor of the realm (D), the commander-in-chief of the army (E), and other retainers surround the queen mother's residence (B). Her capital is a cluster similar to the cluster of wives' enclosures at a chief's village. Near her are the other wives of the king (C).

The royal cattle kraal at Lobamba, where the king's herds are kept, is a combination parliament grounds and stadium. The Great Council of the realm, composed of all ruling princes, chiefs, leading councilors, and headmen, meets at the kraal. The Council of Princes convenes there on the death of a

king to invest his heir. Once a year, the entire military manhood of the Swazi nation, as many as 40,000 strong, assembles there with the princesses and the royal wives for the ceremony of kingship, the rite of intensification for the Swazi nation and its entire religious observance.

Movement in the Swazi System

All Swazi settlements are moved on a generational rhythm. When a commoner householder dies, for example, his homestead is abandoned. If he had only one wife, he has only one heir, one of her sons, who moves to a new site and sets his mother up there as the lady of the house. He tries to accumulate the cattle necessary for bridal payments for at least one wife. If he has a sister, he has a much better chance, for he collects her bridewealth (Kuper, 1947). Other brothers have claims, in sequence, in the bridewealth paid for any other sisters (some are likely to remain bachelors for life).

359

The same pattern holds true for a chief. When a chief dies, his designated heir, the son of his highest-ranking wife, moves with the lady mother to a new site. Other high-ranking wives of the chief may have already been installed in villages with their adult sons in charge. The pattern after the chief's death is thus one of dispersion: One son of each wife is allowed to set her up in a household, now as a commoner (save for the chief's heir). Many chiefs' sons, those who do not inherit a mother and a claim in a sister's bride-wealth, never marry. However, their brother, the new chief, like their father before them, marries many women. Not only does he have a claim on the bridewealth of many sisters, but he pays slightly fewer cattle than the going rate for his wives, and he distributes his daughters to ambitious commoners for more cattle than the ordinary bridal payments.

When a king dies, the pattern is slightly more complicated. A king marries his highest-ranking wife only late in life; she is the woman he expects to be the next queen mother. She bears him one son and no more. At his death, the little son is invested with the kingship by the Council of Princes. At the same time, his mother becomes the new Lady Elephant and shares her powers with the elderly Lady El-ephant at the old capital. (As long as a king lives, a queen mother has to preside at the capital; if she dies before him, a clan sister is appointed in her place.) The new queen mother moves with her son to found a new capital, which assumes full status once the dowager grandmother queen has died and once the young king, who comes of age at sixteen, has taken a wife and moved to his own royal village.

As you can see, the selection of a queen mother is of great importance politically in Swaziland. Not only does she share monarchical power with her son during his adult life, she is the major power during his childhood, sharing power only with an aging queen who is expected to die shortly.

The selection of the queen mother is a republican feature in Swazi governance. There are only a limited number of queen-giving clans, and these are mostly those of chiefs. Most chiefs represent old tribal groups who were conquered by the first Swazi kings in the sixteenth century. Some speak different

The queen mother or Lady Elephant of Swaziland today, Ndlovukazi Ntombi.

languages from the Swazi proper. The queen mother is drawn from one of these groups and represents it at court. Chiefly clans quite literally have a chance to share in the monarchy.

But the system works the other way, too. The monarchy reaches into each chiefly domain by bestowing princesses on ranking chiefs. Each new chief who inherits his father's title is the son of his highest-ranking wife, usually married late in life. No woman ranks higher than a daughter of a king, and most mothers of chiefs are also kings' daughters. Chiefs are thus often grandsons of the king, as well as—eventually—the king's son-in-law. Therefore, it is quite likely that a queen mother is related to the royal line through her mother or grandmother.

These were the constitutional arrangements as Kuper described them for the 1930s. When King Sobhuza II in fact died in 1982, he had not desig-nated a future queen mother or heir from among his many wives, although he had taken many "queens" from queen-giving clans. A Council of Princes (excluding the late king's sons), including a senior princess (sister of the deceased king) and the queen mother (by now a clan sister of the king's deceased mother appointed to her place), met to select a junior queen mother and a boy king. They chose a young royal wife from a high-ranking clan, but not one of those supposedly entitled to be a "bearer of kings." The lady had one minor son, designated to become king.

The choice was well received by the public. However, the council soon clashed with the senior queen mother and removed her from office. The new queen mother, Ntombi, was made sole ruler while her son, Prince Makhosetive, the king-to-be, remained under age. Indeed, the boy was sent to school in England. The old constitutional forms were upheld but were bent by political power plays (Kuper 1986). The prince was invested as King Mswati III in April 1986. A few months later the 18-year-old king took his first wife.

The Swazi Economy. The king's own village is the nexus or relay point for the Swazi redistributional economy, which works in several ways. First, the marriage system ties all the settlements together, women moving to weight the chiefly and royal villages with their numbers. A king, unlike everyone else, pays no bridewealth at all; in contrast, his daughters and sisters fetch quite high payments in cattle. Thus, hundreds of women and thousands of head of cattle flow in to the king, and his daughters and sisters flow out.

Second, the queen mother performs a service several times a year at the royal tombs for commoners who come in numbers to ask for it: She makes rain magic. Finally, there is the great ceremony of kingship that takes place at the capital once a year and in which the bachelor age grade does labor service for the queen and is feasted in return. This happens just before the harvest, at a lean time in most commoner homesteads.

The Life of Bachelors. One must also understand the circulation of men each generation in the system. Recall that a commoner lucky enough to inherit his mother and acquire a wife maintains a bachelor hut for the teenaged son. Most sons in Swaziland are urged to leave home and join the age-graded regiments. The bachelor's age grade is roughly ages eighteen to twenty-eight. No man may marry at all until the king has lifted the marriage prohibition of

his age grade. The regiments fill the barracks at the royal villages and particularly the capital.

Before the British imposed peace on the region in the late 1800s, the Swazi were frequently at war. This gave the bachelors much to occupy themselves with. Moreover, the king was generous, rewarding those who did well in battle with gifts of booty and eventually even captive wives. Thus, the age-graded regiments were a device that very much expressed the power of the monarchy while also being quite functional for the marriage system. The regiment simply removed most young men from their fathers' harems and kept them occupied during their bachelor years. The army also provided a haven for those of them, about one-third, who never married.

Now, after the imposition of the British peace, the bachelors, instead of going on campaigns, spend years as laborers in the mines at Johannesburg in the Republic of South Africa. The King of Swaziland and the Republic of South Africa have a labor agreement whereby a large number of Swazi laborers go to the mines each year and live in barracks there. They earn

Swazi money (a five emalangeni note) features King Mswati III on the front and a scene from the Incwala on the back.

money that can be sent home, and some of it is later applied to buy cattle for bridal payments. The king, princes, and chiefs, especially, benefit from the arrangement, since they monopolize the greater share of the women and find it convenient to have large numbers of men away from home who are still contributing to the home economy. The South African mines have in some ways replaced the old regimental barracks. Nonetheless, the most pressing question of statescraft that weighs over today's Swazi monarchy is to create an economic and diplomatic position of strength in dealing with their neighbor, South Africa, so much more powerful than Swaziland.

The Annual Ceremony of Kingship: Ritual of Rebellion and National Rite of Intensification

Lobamba is the center for a great gathering of men each year for the ceremony of kingship, the **Incwala.** This lengthy ceremony culminates on the night of the new moon closest to the summer solstice— December 21 in the southern hemisphere. The high point is thus on the moonless night of one of the longest days of the year.

The ceremony is too complex to discuss in detail, but some essential features are of interest. It is started by the old men of the regiment from the king's deceased grandmother's capital. But it is taken up and maintained thereafter by the bachelor age grade of warriors. No one but a virgin may participate; otherwise the ceremony is ruined.

Most of the fifteen days of the ceremony proper are spent in a curious ritual of rebellion, in which the sexually starved young men confront their much-married king, who unlike them was never part of a virgin group. The king stays inside the enclosure of the royal calves in the cattle kraal. Outside, the bachelors regularly sing him songs of hate. At one point early in the proceedings, the shamans who surround the king in his enclosure let loose a black bull that has been secretly stolen from a commoner's herd. As the bull goes through the crowd of bachelors, they kill it with their bare fists. They tear it apart, and the badly bruised meat is then given to uninitiated boys and little children to eat.

The next day the king emerges triumphantly riding another black bull, this one from the royal herd. The king also emerges from time to time covered with medicines made from the slain bull's entrails. When the king confronts the regiments, the royal princes are banished from the kraal, and the warriors keep up their song of hate.

At the high point of the ceremony, the king walks naked through the crowd (minus royal princes), past the assembled royal wives and princesses, who are weeping, through the regiments singing songs of hate, to the enclosure of his wives at the capital. He enters the hut where he took his first wife to bed. From there he throws a magic green gourd containing symbols of fertility to the multitude. They catch it and rejoice. Hate gives way to joy. The next day there is a great first-fruits feast. On the final day they burn all the paraphernalia of the ceremony.

In this way the men of the Swazi nation ritually express loyalty to the king and their tension and frustrations as bachelors. The confrontation is a cleansing. It dispels tensions while confirming ordinary ties and thus fulfills the functions of any rite of intensification. In addition, there is the redistributional feasting and labor exchange, as all the gardens of the queen mother are weeded and tended by the incomers during their stay.

SWAZI URBANISM IN PERSPECTIVE: CIVILIZATION OR CHIEFDOM?

Swazi civilization is exceedingly simple in structure. It consists of the dual monarchy and the state, composed of the princes and chiefs who rule many commoners in the king's name; the military age-graded regiments, which can be used as police against recalcitrant subjects; the redistributional economy, which centers on a marriage system; the ritual system; and the national shrine in the royal cattle kraal.

There are no craftsmen, aside from a few smiths, and there is no priest-hood other than a few hereditary custodians of royal relics. The elite is gen-erated from the marriage and clan systems, and war gives an alternative form for recruiting bright young men into the elite. The commander-in-chief, for instance, always has to be a commoner.

What makes Swazi urbanism so strange to us is its dispersion of urban nodes. Political, redistributional, judiciary, military, and administrative func-tions are dispersed between the capital and the king's village, not to mention the royal and chiefly villages. Only in ritual does Lobamba have the monopoly, and the king, the focus of this ritual attention, has to jour-ney to the political shrine for the rites.

Moreover, the Swazi population is dispersed over the countryside. At the urban nodes there are women in harems and men in barracks, two institutions that are functionally dependent on each other. All others live alone on their farms.

The Swazi are by no means primitives; but are they a civilization? Some anthropologists might argue that their correct classification is a "chiefdom." **Chief-doms** are sometimes conceived of as intermediate forms between tribes and civilizations, in which a hereditary elite control a region but the other traits of civilization are absent. I argue that the Swazi are more correctly consid-ered an *archaic civilization*. Not all the urban institutional attributes are fully developed—there are no craft guilds, no temples with priests. What makes the system urban are its nodes, its commanding centers. These are not long lived—they last on schedules of chiefly and royal lifetimes—but that seems long enough. (Ancient Egyptian royal seats often moved upon the death of a pharaoh, too.) In addition, the dual monarchy with its standing army of age-graded regiments is definitely a state. It rests on kinship: the royal lineage and the lineages of the chiefs, all dynamically interrelated by the circulation of wives, and on the differential inheritance of princes and chiefs each gen-eration. There are many ways to run a state, and this one uses lineage, mar-riage and bridewealth, and age grades to make itself work.

How are we to account for Swaziland theoretically? We may say that it and many other native states arising in tribal areas do so in part by the *stimu-lus diffusion* of the example of nearby states and in part by a response to greater social pressures on the tribal region emanating from encroaching civilization. Swaziland arose along with a number of other Bantu monar-chies in southern Africa in response to the encroachments of both Arabs and

Sobhuza II, King of Swaziland, with British diplomat in 1968.

Europeans. As a constitutional form, it was fixed under British colonial administration and now survives in a period of independence.

SUMMARY AND CONCLUSIONS

*A*ll cultures, tribal and civilized, are in flux on time scales of 70 to 90 years (the human lifetime) and 200 to 1,200 years (that of an enduring whole culture). Such fluxes led to the independent emergence of civilizations in six different hearths of ancient civilization. Once human beings had passed this watershed, by 4,000 years ago in Eurasia and 2,700 years ago in the Americas, civilizations expanded into tribal territories, and many tribal societies, often semi-independently, adopted a civilized pattern of settlement and governance. This is the case for Swaziland; it was also the case for ancient Greece.

Swaziland and ancient Mesopotamia illustrate the nature of civilization and urbanism, a pattern fundamentally different from that of the primitive world. Settlements are the urban nodes, the capitals. They do not need to be densely populated, although that is one form they may take, and overall the regional population is always relatively dense. Urban nodes need only be in command. The essential nodal institutions are shrines for rituals of control, mass rites of intensification, a redistributive economy, a military apparatus, and a state. Those who command these nodes of control constitute an elite and usually live off the labor of others, even enjoying great luxuries. A tradition of fine craft specialists is usually thought of as an ingredient of civilization, but the Swazi, for one, do not have them, let alone their social organization in guilds.

To cross from tribal organization to an urban, civilized, state-run way of life was not something that came easily to human beings. They did it spontaneously only six times. To do so they made use of technological potentials, such as irrigation, but also communication potentials, such as systems of runner messengers. Ancient Mesopotamia's course toward nucleated settlement differed considerably from ancient Egypt's adoption, under Mesopotamian stimuli, of a sacred monarchy. Once civilization has been invented it can spread, but people adapt the basic dynamic forms to their own ways of life, as was the case with the Swazi, who evolved a complex kingdom from the simple mechanisms of marriage and inheritance on a regional scale.

In Part III we saw how in advanced tribal regions, communities coalesce into macrocommunities for trade or warfare. The civilized pattern is very different. Foreign relations of single communities give way to supervision and control from urban centers. Trophies and valuables give way to tribute and state rituals such as the Swazi ceremony of kingship. Warfare is turned outward against other urban centers, and the aim is not balance but conquest. This is no less true of the Swazi kingdom with its green city of royal villages as it was of dynastic Mesopotamia.

Yet civilization always rests on previous institutions. Thus shamans give rise to priests, who in turn give rise to state cults around official shrines. Fraternity age grades give rise to immense armies, like the age regiments of Swaziland. Tool manufacture, once the activity of everybody, is now relegated to specialists, craftsmen organized in guilds, who, in turn, live off the redistributive economy, revolving not around Big Men but around shrines and priests, kings and palaces. Kings use the kinship institution of the lineage to create **dynasties.** They use the family institution of the household to turn their personal staff of kinsmen and servants into bureaucracies.

In sum, the dynamic nature of civilization lies in a pattern of settlement that has a center and periphery and a pattern of control that has elites and masses. Let us turn next to control, the nature of the civilized state, and the emergence of bureaucracy.

SUGGESTED READINGS

Hamblin, Dora Jane, and the editors of Life. *The First Cities.* Waltham, Mass.: Little, Brown, 1973. Interesting and beautifully illustrated.

Kuper, Hilda. *The Swazi: A South African Kingdom*, 2nd ed. Ft. Worth: Harcourt Brace Jovanovich, 1986. A condensed account from the 1930s; the curious student might want to consult Kuper's longer book of 1947 or Marwick's of 1940. But the original book has been doubled with an update about the Swazi grappling with modernity and independence.

Mallowan, M. E. L. *Early Mesopotamia and Iran*. Library of Early Civilizations. New York: McGraw-Hill, 1965. Beautifully produced, a true archaeological volume.

Mumford, Lewis. *The City in History: Its Origins, Its Transformations, and Its Prospects*. New York: Harcourt Brace Jovanovich, 1961. Chapters 1 to 4 are especially relevant to a theory of urbanism.

Sabloff, Jeremy A. *Cities of Ancient Mexico: Reconstructing a Lost World*. London: Thames & Hudson, 1987. Contains splendid literary portraits of what the ancient cities may have been like when people actually lived in them.

GLOSSARY

chiefdom A community form posited by some anthropologists as a "level" between tribes and civilizations, in which some hereditary rulers are set off from the common population and together they control large regions. By this definition Swaziland is a chiefdom.

city A community form in which a number of central commanding institutional nodes regularly receive goods, especially foodstuffs, and services from outlying food-producing settlements, in return for ritual, political, redistributional, and military functions.

civilization A form of culture whose dominant communities are urban, even if the major part of the population may be rural; cultures that have cities.

dynasty The name given to a royal lineage, whereby succession to the monarchy may be kept in one family line. Dynasties, like lineages, may be patrilineal or matri-lineal, and succession may be determined by election among and by the princes (Saudi Arabia today), by the will of the previous monarch (the Aga Khan), by the rank of the candidates' mothers (ancient Egypt, Swaziland), by primogeniture (the U.K.), or simply by warfare among rival princes, even among brothers (numerous cases).

elites In civilization, classes of individuals who perform executive functions in ritual, political, military, economic, and judicial institutions and who thereby are sup-ported from redistribution (tributes) rather than themselves being engaged in food production or craft manufacture. Elites may be open to new talent each generation or may be relatively closed, hereditary groupings.

green city A dispersed form of urban community in which the commanding nodes are dispersed in the countryside among the hamlets of the food-producing peasants, often at some distance from each other. Typical of ancient Egypt, Bali, and Swaziland, and partially true of the ancient Maya, most of whose population lived relatively dispersed around many large and small ceremonial centers.

hearths of civilization At least six areas in the world in which archaeologists have concluded that civilization, defined as urban centers surrounded by peasant settlements, arose spontaneously and independently in prehistory. These are Mesopotamia, Egypt, the Indus Valley, North China, Mesoamerica (Mexico, Guatemala, and Belize), and coastal Peru. Since then civilization has appeared, usually in relation to foreign urban centers, among many tribal peoples, sometimes in quite autonomous forms. Civilizations are always in flux, rising and falling and reforming on 200- to 1,200-year time scales.

hierarchy The arrangement of human beings in linear rankings, whereby those higher on the ladder command those down the line. The distinctive thing about human hierarchies, as opposed to the dominance hierarchies of apes, is that at each rank there can be many persons, each one commanding a whole rank below themselves. Instead of a straight line, human hierarchies form a "tree."

Incwala The annual rite of intensification of kingship for Swaziland, held each summer solstice at the capital of the queen mother. The warrior age grades assemble and engage in a ritual of rebellion against the monarchy, after which they are abundantly feasted and renew their allegiance to their king.

judges Third parties to conflicts and disputes among plaintiffs and defendants. They differ from the mediators of band societies and the arbitrators of tribes in having police powers to enforce their decisions. When they levy fines, payments may go to the state rather than to the plaintiffs.

nodes Centers in space where commanding institutions are located and to which masses of people must go with tribute and to receive directions. They include shrines, palaces, religious or government storerooms, courts of law, and military posts.

nucleated, walled city The ideal image of the city as it evolved in southern Eurasia. The commanding nodes of palace, temples, barracks, storerooms, and manufacturing workshops are all concentrated in one densely populated central settlement, surrounded by walls. Although food producers may live within the walls, most live in surrounding peasant villages.

priests Permanent, full-time ritual experts. Unlike shamans they do not necessarily claim direct supernatural powers. They are usually trained for the job and in most civilizations are highly literate, having access to a great deal of esoteric information of which the masses are largely ignorant.

redistribution A kind of reciprocity in which many persons each give goods (gifts, offerings, tribute) to a single central person or institution, such as a shrine or a king, who in turn then gives back some of the goods. In civilized societies such goods are usually called tribute, and kings and priests support themselves, as well as many retainers, on this income. Craftsmen are also often supported from state or temple revenues.

state A formal, explicit, publicly constituted leadership pattern, manifest in a set of offices (as opposed to persons), full-time official duties, and coercive police powers that can be used against the members of the community. All civilizations have the state.

The Original Bureaucracies

*ROYAL KINSHIP AND
HOUSEHOLDS*

The Swazi Royal Family as a Bureaucracy

Harems: Bureaus Emerging Within Royal Households

    Lovedu: A Queen's Wives as House of Representatives

    Dahomey's Three Harem Bureaus

*EXPANDING AND DIFFERENTIATING
THE ORIGINAL BUREAUCRACIES*

*THE OTTOMAN TURKS: A DYNASTY
AND ITS SLAVE BUREAUCRACY*

The Ottoman Dynasty: The House of Osman

Gate Slaves

    Foreign Boys: Soldiers in the Janissaries

    Pages: Servants and Schoolboys in the Palace

*The Harem of the House of Osman: Slave Brides,
Slave Mothers, and Lady Sultans*

Rewards of Office

The House of the Pen: The Muslim Clergy/Judiciary

Turkish Prebendaries: Sepoys

Form of the Ottoman Imperial Bureaucracy

Maintaining Dynastic Imperial Power

Decline of the Ottomans

    Abolition of the Gate Slave System

    The Attempt to Convert to a Legal-Rational Bureaucracy

*THE ORIGINAL BUREAUCRACY AS
A DYNAMIC INSTITUTION*

*T*he state consists of full-time officials on duty, day and night, to listen, adjudicate, receive tribute, spend it, consult, decide, command, and lead. A state is a universal characteristic of civilization. While some small-scale civilized states, especially those of the classic Greeks, closely resemble tribal republics like those of the Cheyenne, differing only in their full-time, year-round nature, some early empires created *bureaucracies*, one of humanity's most important social inventions. *A* **bureaucracy** *is a social device enabling the one or the few to rule not just the many, but multitudes.*

Technically, a bureaucracy is a government apparatus divided up into bureaus, or agencies, with special functions. As conceived by the great German social scientist Max Weber (1946, 1951; Bendix, 1960), bureaucracy maximizes efficiency in administration.

The original bureaucracies make use of two simple principles—royal household membership and redistribution (in the form of *tax farming*)—for their organization. First, they expand and extend the monarch's household to rule large areas. They are thus **patrimonial;** the realm is considered the *patrimony* of the royal dynasty. Palace revenues—redistributional tribute—support central officials. Often officials receive no salaries, only maintenance at the palace board and occasional gifts of luxuries and valuables from the monarch.

Second, monarchs often give less central royal servants (kinsmen, slaves, or friends ["clients"]) rights in the tribute to certain villages or districts. These districts are "tax farms," called fiefs, benefices, or **prebends;** the officials are **prebendaries,** tax farmers. The official collects taxes or tribute himself, keeps as much as he needs for his own support, and sends the rest to his royal master.

Thus, the original bureaucracies do not recruit their personnel impersonally by talent and training but primarily through what modern civil servants consider irrelevant criteria: membership in the royal household or personal friendship with the monarch. The institution of the household expands, and its resemblance to a childbearing prototype is largely lost, but it remains the matrix of government. Thus, a qualitatively new institution has emerged in human affairs, out of social material (the household) already at hand.

Such original bureaucracies develop specialized officials, who in turn are able to command mass followers. Just as priests at shrines are able to mobilize masses of followers, bringing offerings for great ceremonies, so the early monarchs mobilized masses of laborers for public works and masses of warriors for war (armies). Both public labor and military services are a kind of offering: tribute service. These early states are tribute states.

Early armies are usually age grades. Whole masculine generations can be called up for military service (labor tribute) ranging from a few years to a decade or more. Other soldiers, indeed whole legions, may be recruited from the homeless and the uprooted among the devastated populations on an empire's warring frontiers.

Such bureaucracies always exist in uneasy union with a state cult. Monarchies are often founded by prophets; their descendants may claim to be divine or may simply, as in Mesopotamia, head the state cult. A royal lineage, a **dynasty,** always seeks to bolster itself with supernatural symbols. Charisma, the "gift of grace," must be mythologically attributed to royal blood and upheld by royal rites. But priests at state-supported shrines are not usually members of the royal household and are often recruited by independent criteria. Monarchs everywhere strive to control these priests and to identify themselves with their symbols. Such state cults remain a potential challenge to the monarch and a counterweight to despotic power.

Politics, the problem of leadership, is now transformed. Leaders in state societies still strive to keep the community (now vastly escalated in scale) in balance with its resources. They maintain internal order and represent the state to foreign states, often through warfare and attempts at conquest. Leaders now recruit followers by the mechanisms of kinship or of nonkinship ("clientage" or servitude, and age-graded drafts). The problem remains of the value of the reward to the leadership, now the entire state apparatus, as opposed to the followers, now often vast populations of subjects, many of them conquered. In whose interests do the bureaucrats rule—their own or those of their subjects?

All original bureaucracies are subject to the same dynamics. All royal dynasties undergo a cycle of growth, florescence, decay, and collapse, which in turn regenerates into a new dynastic cycle. They all are beset by foreign enemies, many of them insolent "barbarian" tribes on their frontiers, eager to swoop down and seize the center. They also attempt, always imperfectly, to

The Empress Dowager Tzu Hsi, with a princess and a eunuch, part of the last dynasty of China, the Manchu. She ruled in the late nineteenth century.

solve the problem of responsiveness and legitimacy. That is, they strive to make their followers loyal and willing subjects. But their instruments for responsiveness are often imperfect, and they therefore rely more on terror and coercion than need be.

Reason and Law in Bureaucracy: Legal-Rational Bureaucracy as an Ideal Type

The great German sociologist Max Weber (1864–1920), who originated the concept of bureaucracy, thought that all earlier forms were imperfect, less-rational precursors of the "modern" form, an ideal type, **legal-rational bureaucracy,** which we discuss at length in Chapter 19. Here we must stress the role of reason and law in the form. An ideal bureaucracy is founded in a *legal charter*, which sets out to fulfill a clear, reasonable ("rational") mandate. Its job is some public function: defense, public works, treasury, education, foreign affairs, internal administration, and so on, as one can list all the essential cabinet ministries of the government of any contemporary nation-state. Each bureau fulfills its function impersonally and logically.

Officials—bureaucrats—are *trained* for their specialized jobs. Military officers have graduated from a military academy, for example. Recruit- ment to office—and to the special schools leading to office—is open to all citizens by ability and merit, as demonstrated in written aptitude and achievement examinations. Once in office, officials are promoted by seniority—that is, by age grades.

Moreover, all actions are followed and supervised from above by *paperwork and files*. Last but not least, finance is handled by a *central treasury*, which takes in all revenues and disperses them according to law. It keeps central *accounts* and knows exactly who pays taxes and who is spending what. No officials support themselves from the "take," the customary way for "prerational" patrimonial bureaucracy to finance local administration through tax farming.

What is lacking in Weber's concept is some explicit idea of **responsiveness.** That is, a bureaucracy must not only have a rational purpose, it must also be accountable to a constituency, its clients.

ROYAL KINSHIP AND HOUSEHOLDS

Royal kinship serves as the basis for bureaucracy in a number of interesting societies.

The Swazi Royal Family as a Bureaucracy

Swaziland, discussed in Chapter 14, is one of the few polities left in the world today that resolutely use the king's kinsmen and household for governance. No son of a prince inherits his royal village. As these princes die, their sons become little different from commoners, and the king sends one of his sons to "awaken" the deceased prince's village near its former site, abandoned at his death. Administration is kept in the hands of the princes immediately related to each king: uncles, brothers, and sons, but not cousins, nephews, or grandsons. This is an important constitutional provision, because it keeps the legions of royal princes more responsive by limiting their ability to perpetuate themselves into the next generation. Only the king can perpetuate the legion of royal princes.

Each king accumulates wives who fulfill several functions. They provide sons to administer the realm; they do the gardening that provisions the king and his sons; and they produce the daughters whose marrying-off brings in great numbers of cattle to swell the royal herds. This royal marriage system constitutes much of the royal redistributive economy.

The leading ritualists in the realm are the queen mother, who makes rain magic at the royal tombs, and the king, who is the object of the annual Incwala ceremony of kingship. The only exceptions to patrimonial rule, seemingly, are the capitals of the chiefs and regiments of the army. But even these are controlled in part by members of the king's lineage. The lady-mother who presides at each chief's village is likely to be a royal princess, a daughter of a king; and each regiment is headed by a prince. However, a commoner heads the entire army, which in turn rests on the principle of age grading, not kinship. In sum, Swaziland is permeated and controlled by immediate kin-folk of the monarch, whose military power rests on drafting the age grade of men from eighteen to thirty-two or so, who are forbidden to marry.

Harems: Bureaus Emerging Within Royal Households

When monarchs set out to govern large realms, they begin to divide tasks among their servants. The tendency for subunits to appear within palaces is quite apparent in harems. Harem inmates—hostages or representatives of their kin groups and communities—may form labor corps (as among the Swazi), may serve as hunters, and may become soldiers or public prostitutes. Some are expected to breed a legion of royal sons to be used as administrative personnel.

Lovedu: A Queen's Wives as House of Representatives. The harem can be a device for political integration and control. One of the best examples occurs in Lovedu, a small native state within the Republic of South Africa (Krige and Krige, 1943). Its monarch is a queen; there is no king. The queen has at least a hundred of her own wives residing with her at her palace, strange as it seems. Every year, one or another of the many village headmen of Lovedu gives a daughter to the queen in marriage. The queen goes through a marriage ceremony with the young woman and keeps her at court with her for a few years.

The Lovedu capital consists of a central hut for the queen surrounded by many smaller beehive huts for her wives. These women provide the main source of labor at the capital; they garden busily for their consort and keep her well supplied with foodstuffs. Eventually, the queen redistributes her human goods: she gives each wife to some other headman in marriage. Thus, all the headmen give daughters to the queen and get wives back (see Figure 15.1).

If a headman impregnates his wife, he incurs a double obligation. He must send one of her daughters back in marriage to the queen, and one back to his wife's father (Krige, 1964). The queen's harem knits the realm with crisscrossing marriage ties among all the headmen and the court. To seal these ties, the sacred queen makes rain rituals for her own subjects and neighboring peoples.

Although the queen is legally and ritually married to her wives, she does not claim them for her sexual pleasure. While they are celibate in her harem, she has one male consort who is her adviser and who impregnates her. Her sons are highly placed servants at the palace, but none of them inherits; one of her daughters does. Thus, a sojourn at court for a Lovedu maiden is to belong to a female age grade, a sort of royal sorority. They serve and wait on the queen while learning something of the world.

Figure 15.1 The dynamics of the queen's harem in Lovedu.

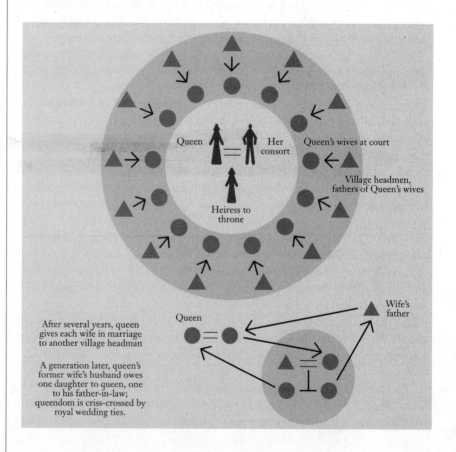

Dahomey's Three Harem Bureaus. This tendency to specialize was carried even further in the kingdom of Dahomey on the Guinea coast in West Africa, where the royal women were divided into three bureaus. In the first were those who shared the king's bedchamber and bore his children. In the second were the Amazons, an elite fighting corps of 5,000 women under their own female commander that waged war in the king's campaigns every year.

The Amazons had their origin in a palace company of female elephant hunters whom the king called onto the battlefield at a desperate point in a campaign. Their victory won them a place of honor in the Annual Customs, the redistributive ceremony held at one of the royal villages.

A mass army was also raised by drafting a portion of all the able-bodied men of the kingdom; however, the Amazons were the only full-time soldiery, defending the king's person and providing him with a ready police force on constant call (Polanyi, 1966). They struck terror in the king's enemies, including the French, who did not subdue Dahomey until 1892. The Amazons' booty belonged entirely to the king. Volunteers from the population at large, they remained virgins for life, and they were rewarded with pensions on retirement from battle. They never gave up their role as royal elephant hunters, adding meat, hides, and ivory to the royal provisions.

In the third harem-derived bureau, the king appointed public women to take up residence at marketplaces throughout Dahomey "to safeguard the peace of private families" (Polanyi, quoting a source

The head of the royal lineage of Dahomey and his favorite wives in the 1930s.

of 1793, 1966, p. 51). Thus, these royal women were redistributed to the bachelor population as royal prostitutes, readily available at a set low price that went toward their maintenance; the king contributed the rest. Dahomey, like Swaziland, shifted most women to the harems of ranking men. By sharing some of his women with the bachelors, the king provided his realm with a sexual safety valve.

EXPANDING AND DIFFERENTIATING THE ORIGINAL BUREAUCRACIES

One way to expand the royal household is to breed a tremendous number of royal offspring at the harems. This was done in ancient Egypt and in Inca Peru, where the heir to the monarchy was the son of the divine monarch by his sister. These cases and a similar example from Hawaii are the only known exceptions to the brother-sister incest tabu. Like the pharaohs, the Incas needed thousands of officials for their army, civil administration, and state priesthood. The first place to recruit them was the royal lineages.

The other way to expand bureaucracy is to recruit nonkinsmen, or *clients*. Such men usually do not belong to the king's household. They are often rewarded with prebends (grants in tax rights over villages or districts) and thus given a share in the redistributive economy. They are therefore likely to be prebendaries. Royal relatives might engage in struggles over the succession, so many monarchs, including those of the Incas, used them as a counterweight to the princes. The Incas often picked clients at whim from the populace, making them favorites, calling them adopted orphans (*yanaconas*), trusting them with secret missions, and sometimes rewarding them with grants in the tribute rights of whole villages.

The dilemma of patrimonial monarchs is that royal kinsmen are potential rivals to the throne, while nonkin servant prebendaries are potential rebels, ready to secede with their villages and turn them into petty princedoms. Both dangers have come to pass among the many African examples of patrimonial bureaucracies. Successful archaic empires find some mix of princes and other servants. They also find some way to fix the loyalty of both through training, ideology, and ritual. Even so, such empires are still subject to dynastic decline, the growth in power of provincial prebendary officials, the revolt of these officials, and the eventual dissolution of the empire.

THE OTTOMAN TURKS: A DYNASTY AND ITS SLAVE BUREAUCRACY

Anthropologists have studied several surviving archaic patrimonial bureaucracies. It is instructive to turn to a climax form, the empire of the Ottoman Turks, who passed into history in the early part of the twentieth century. As befitting a climax form, the bureaucracy made ingenious adaptations to problems of personnel, legitimacy, justice, and control.*

The Ottoman Dynasty: The House of Osman

Somewhere around A.D. 1250, a small band of pagan Turks, nomads from central Asia, led by a chieftain, Ertaghul, appeared in the troubled area of northwestern Anatolia (today's Turkey) on the boundary between the Muslim Seljuk Turks and the Christian Byzantine or Eastern Roman Empire. It is probable that the Seljuk sultan bought Ertaghul off with a grant of a prebend, or tax-farming district in the region. The origin myth of the dynasty, which asserts its divine right to rule, tells that the chieftain's son, Osman,

---

*Information in this section on the Ottomans has greatly relied on Coon (1958), Kinross (1977), and Davis (1986).

had a dream vision of the city of Constantinople and of a tree. A Muslim clergyman prophesied that Osman would found a dynasty that would rule from that city, but he would first have to convert to Islam. The holy man would give him his daughter in marriage. From this union of the son of a nomad chief and an Anatolian Muslim woman sprang a dynasty known as the *House of Osman*.

Recruiting a brotherhood of mystic Muslim warriors, or *Ghazis*, to help him, Osman set out to build his principality, fighting both Byzantines and Seljuks. Just before his death in 1326, he and his son Orkhan conquered the Christian mountain stronghold of Bursa and made it the capital of the Ottoman (Turkish: *Osmanli*) Turks.

A series of brilliant sultans succeeded Osman. The third, Murad I (1359–1389), introduced an important innovation. He decreed that, as the price of

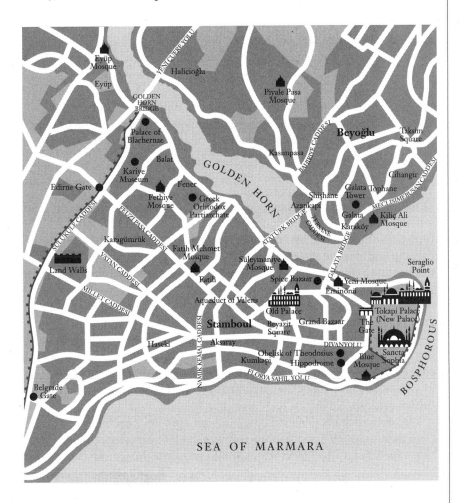

Ottoman Constantinople.

religious toleration, Christian villages he conquered would pay a special human tribute. They were obliged every seven years or so to yield up a gift of nine-year-old boys, who where promptly recruited, under the tutelage of the holy Muslim warriors or dervishes, into the Ottoman army, now given the name of **Janissaries** (*Yeni çeri*, new warriors). Other such slave boys were recruited directly into the palace as royal servants, as we shall see.

Thenceforth the sultans had a fierce, cruel, loyal, and *professional* fighting force at their disposal. They went on to conquer the Balkans—all Greece, Albania, Yugoslavia, Bulgaria, Rumania, and most of Hungary—and the Arab world—Syria, Lebanon, Palestine, Iraq, Arabia, Egypt, Libya, Algeria, and Tunisia, excepting only Morocco. The Ottomans were orthodox Sunni Muslims. To the south and east, their expansion was limited by the Persians and Azeri Turks, who both belonged to the other great branch of the Muslim faith, the Shiites.

The seventh sultan, Mehmet the Conqueror, took the city of Constantinople in 1453 and made it the Ottoman capital. His grandson, Selim I, after conquering Egypt, became the Caliph of Islam in 1517. A descendant, Mehmet VI, the thirty-fourth of his line, lost his throne in 1922, when the dynasty was abolished by the great Turkish revitalization leader Kemal Atatürk, who instituted a secular and nationalistic democracy (and changed the name of Constantinople [Turkish: *Konstantiniye*] to Istanbul). The House of Osman had ruled much of a vast realm for 600 years. Let us see how they did it.

Gate Slaves

Ottoman civil administration, the military, and the supply corps were all staffed by members of the sultan's household. The Turks developed the patrimonial principle not by breeding thousands of royal kinsmen but by recruiting and training slaves. Slaves have many advantages over royal kinsmen from a monarch's point of view. They have no claim by blood or descent on the monarchy, and hence they seldom pretend to the throne. Bereft of any other identity, they cannot be more loyal to a family, ethnic group, or religion than to their master.

The Ottoman Turks drafted prepubescent Christian boys into imperial service at the sultan's Gate (see Figure 15.2). This entrance to the sultan's palace (literally meaning High Door and called by Europeans *Sublime Porte*) was the office building of the grand vizier—a sort of prime minister, head of the bureaucracy.

Boys arrived at the Gate and entered a vast, complex establishment, henceforth their only real home. Comparisons in modern experience include army career men and novices in Roman Catholic monastic orders who devote their lives to obedience to superiors and the pope. All **gate slaves** (pages and

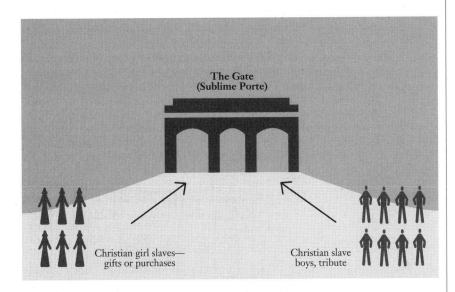

The Gate
(Sublime Porte)

Christian girl slaves—
gifts or purchases

Christian slave
boys, tribute

"foreign boys") belonged to the imperial household. The pages were sent directly a few blocks away to the Old Palace, early abandoned as a residence by the sultan, who had converted its men's quarters into a slave school. (Today it is the site of Istanbul University.) The New Palace (today's Topkapi Palace Museum) was the residence of the sultan. Here also was the imperial harem.

Outside the harem was the *inner court*, where the sultan was waited on by a company of European **eunuchs** and their servants, an age grade of pages (gate slaves). From this page school, the inside service, the highest officials of the empire graduated.

Next, and much closer to the outside world, was the *outer court*. The sultan's audience chamber, where he received officials, high clergymen, and foreign ambassadors, lay just inside the entrance of the inner court. The council chambers of the Divan, the cabinet of highest officials and provincial governors, was in the outer court, which was staffed by companies of slaves as laborers and guards under the command of seventeen *stirrup aghas*, or lords of the stirrup.

The little boys who arrived as tribute at the Sublime Porte entered an organization made up of others like themselves. The grand vizier himself was also a gate slave. The terrified stripling, not even a Turk, arrived at the Gate with the chance of someday ruling it as grand vizier.

The gate slave bureaucracy, including the army or Janissaries, was composed of thousands of men at all ranks. The greatest numbers were at the bottom ranks, the infantry. These in turn were commanded by deputy officers, comparable to our army sergeants. Above the soldiers, laborers, and clerks

Ground plan of Topkapi
Palace Museum, Istanbul

1. Gate of Salutations
2. Stables
3. Divan
4. Inner treasury
5. Kitchen
6. Gate of Felicity
7. Arz Odasi (audience chamber)
12–15. Page school quarters
16. Pavilion of the Sacred Mantle
17. Library of Ahmet III
21. Hekimbaşi Odasi (doctors' room)
22. Pool
25. Siinnet Odasi (circumsicion hall—princes)
26. Iftariye Kşkü (Ramadam feast pavilion)
Harem:
28. Carriage gate (to leave the harem)
30. Guardroom
31. Black eunuchs' mosque
32. Black eunuchs' courtyard
33. Black eunuchs' barracks
34. Princes' school (upstairs)
35. Chief black eunuch's apartment (upstairs)
37. Courtyard of the cariyeler (concubines)
38. Rooms of the three senior women
39. Apartments of the valide sultan
40. Courtyard of the valide sultan
44. Sultan's hamam
47. Salon of Murat III
48. Library of Ahmet I
51 Consultation Hall of the Djinns
52. Courtyard of the Favorites
53. Golden Road
54. Kusshane Kapisi (saucepan gate)

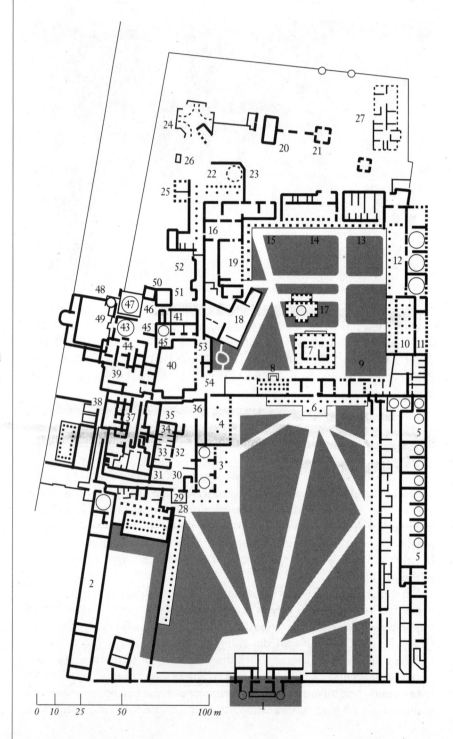

How to Read the Ground Plan of Topkapi Palace Museum, Istanbul

This plan omits the much larger exterior court of the palace complex, used for parades and very large ceremonies, and bordered by the barracks of the Janissaries. It contains the Byzantine church of Haghia Irene, now a museum, used for centuries by the Janissaries as an armory. This court precedes the entrance to the palace (1) shown here. The plan also omits the garden and park complex, connected to the palace through the exterior court, whose outside entrance was the Gate (High Door or Sublime Porte), whose many buildings housed the grand vizier and the outside service. Overall, the palace complex was *green*, raising much of its own foodstuffs on the extensive grounds, which would be to your left viewing this plan.

While the exterior court was used for vast parades and was open to the public, the second, or outer court, was used for redistributional court ceremonies. Here the Janissaries received their pay and were feasted by the sultan—hence the enormous kitchen complex to one side. At the Gate of Felicity between outer and inner courts the funeral of each deceased sultan started with the display of the coffin prior to burial, and here on the same day his successor was invested with the imperial turban, symbol of office.

In one corner of the inner court is the Pavilion of the Sacred Mantle. As caliphs of Islam, the Ottoman sultans claimed to be successors to the Prophet Mohammed, "Shadows of God on Earth." This building is a shrine displaying many relics of the Prophet. Here the House of Osman enshrined its divine right to represent the Muslim faith and rule in its name. Pilgrims were allowed to visit this shrine.

The pages were housed and schooled in the buildings dividing the inner court from the furthest section of gardens and pavilions where the sultans resided when they were not in the harem.

The harem ("forbidden section") is much more condensed and crowded, although it once had extensive private gardens. There are no open courts for public ceremonies, but smaller ones for "family" entertainments. There were two corps of eunuchs: black eunuchs lived in the harem, European or white eunuchs in the inner court. The harem was entered through the "Saucepan Gate," where servants brought dishes of cooked food from the kitchens and left them on side benches for serving girls to pick up. The imperial women did no cooking.

Note that the figure of the sultan is the most central and sacred object in this architectural plan. Ritually, he stands in front of the Gate of Felicity between inner and outer courts at the life crises of death and accession. He gives audiences in the throne room of the inner court.

Only the sultan and his male heirs were permanent, native-born, lifelong residents of this palace. Only the sultan moved freely between the harem and the men's side of the palace. In some reigns adult princes did likewise; in others, they were confined to apartments ("the cage") in the harem until one of them inherited the throne. Sultans frequently, but not always, killed their brothers upon their accession.

Everyone else in this complex came from somewhere else or left it for other places. For pages, it was a college prior to joining the bureaucracy of the empire. For girls, who like the pages were always born Christians and who often came from outside the empire, the harem was a cloistered school, from which many were graduated as wives of officials. Others became wives of the sultan. One of their number became the *valide sultan*, empress, upon her son's accession. Widows of sultans and elderly serving women were retired to the Old Palace's harem. Daughters and sisters of sultans—princesses of the House of Osman— left the harem to marry high officials in grand ceremonies celebrated, among other places, in the exterior and outer courts. Only the sultan and, less happily, the other males of the dynasty were born into the earthly house of Osman, never to leave it.

Exterior of the New Palace.

were the gate slave officials, who were ranked in five grades. These grades, somewhat age graded, also reflected achievement and the rank of the post to which the official was assigned. The five ranks were symbolized by horse tails attached to a standard. Flying horse tails had once denoted war honors when the Turks were a tribal nomadic people. An ordinary bey at the lowest level had a single horse tail carried before him; the grand vizier had five, the sultan nine.

Gate slaves had two paths of advancement: one was as a page, the other was up through the ranks of the military. These two paths reflected the division of the tribute boys into two groups upon arrival: a smaller group chosen for intelligence and a larger one, the "foreign boys," for physical strength. (Presumably those who were both intelligent and strong went to the elite pages.)

Foreign Boys: Soldiers in the Janissaries. The foreign boys were sent to the barracks at one side of the exterior court in the New Palace for training in military arts and later were formally inducted into companies in the army, navy, and supply corps (armorers, woodcutters, and so on). Some were selected by their superiors for promotion into official ranks, but the great majority remained common soldiers. Higher positions were few, ranks of soldiers numerous.

The Ottoman infantry, the Janissaries, formed the elite standing army of the empire. In battle they were joined by the far more numerous but less disciplined cavalry, raised and commanded by rural Turkish tax-collectors or prebends (sepoys) for each campaign. The Janissaries had 169 battle companies, each composed of one hundred men, six deputy officers (sergeants), a clerk, a Muslim chaplain, and only one company commander at the lowest official rank. The companies were grouped into three subcorps, two of them commanded by officers of the third highest rank, assisted by a number of staff officers of the second rank. The commander of the entire corps and central subcorps of 16,900 Janissaries was an agha with four horse tails and a seat on the imperial Divan, the policy-making council presided over by the grand vizier.

Foreign boys promoted into official positions and rising to places in the imperial Divan were few indeed compared to the thousands of their fellows they left behind in the ranks. Their chances were diminished even more by the practice of training pages in military tactics and giving them battle commands. On the other hand, boys put into the much smaller group of the pages had an excellent chance of achieving high official rank in the empire.

The Gate today, now the entrance to the Istanbul zoo. The central door is the Sublime Porte.

Pages: Servants and Schoolboys in the Palace. From the start, pages were placed in the imperial palace while foreign boys went to the barracks (see Figure 15.3). After graduation from the slave school at the Old Palace, pages

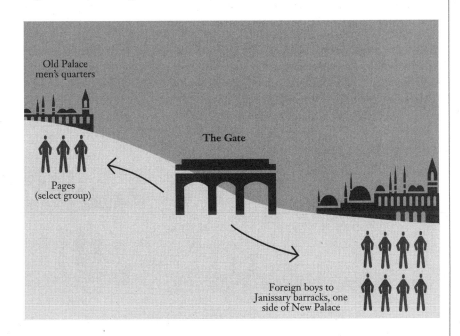

Old Palace
men's quarters

The Gate

Pages
(select group)

Foreign boys to
Janissary barracks, one
side of New Palace

Figure 15.3 Ottoman gate slave careers, phase two: early schooling.

went to a secondary school nearby and then finally to the inner court at the New Palace, where they did menial service in the sultan's residential quarters under the tutelage of eunuchs. Thus, pages occupied the bottom rung of the inside service. But unlike most of the soldiers in the infantry, no page remained at this low level for life; for them it was merely an *apprenticeship* (see Figure 15.4).

The inside service was divided into departments headed by eunuch officials responsible for the daily life of the sultan when he was not in the harem, including the larder for his meals and his privy chamber for dressing and bathing. Pages coveted the job of barber. There was no better way of coming to the attention of the sultan than by shaving his face; former barbers often got good posts in later life.

After graduation from the inside service at age twenty-four, a page might work as a clerk for the grand vizier in the Gate. The grand vizier's staff included a number of high officials, who were assisted by hundreds of clerks. High officials who needed scribes to help them included the chief treasurer; the herald of imperial decrees; the chief secretary, who recorded the imperial decrees and checked their legality with the grand **mufti** (head Islamic judge); and the chief usher, who was attorney for the grand vizier when he heard cases at the supreme court of appeals (he was also bailiff for the court).

Some clerks served officials in the provincial administration. There were thirty-six provinces at the empire's height. The most important were governed by a slave with four horse tails and the title of vizier. Some of his eight subordinate officials, such as the treasurer, were former pages. It was crucial for former pages to be promoted out of the ranks of clerks and be given

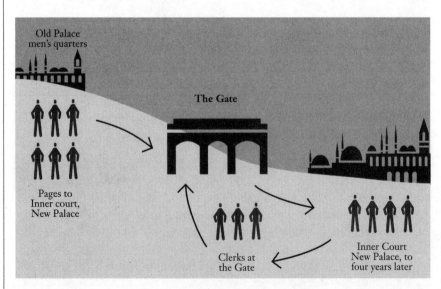

Figure 15.4 Ottoman gate slave careers, phase three: young adulthood.

Old Palace men's quarters

The Gate

Pages to Inner court, New Palace

Clerks at the Gate

Inner Court New Palace, to four years later

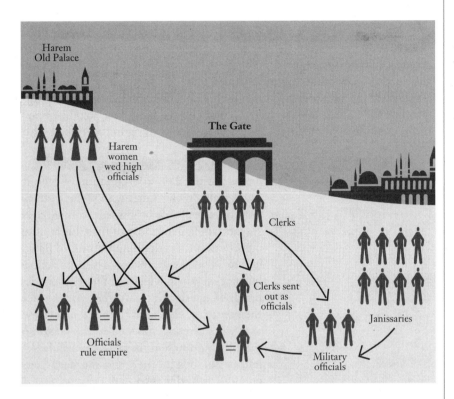

Figure 15.5 Ottoman gate slave careers, phase four: high office and marriage.

official posts. Once this was done, they were likely to have a varied career (see Figure 15.5). Officials were rotated frequently; the term of provincial governors, originally for life, was eventually reduced to one year.

Many posts were available to gate slaves within the imperial household in the outside service, where former pages and Janissaries mingled in a welter of offices whose titles did not necessarily match their job descriptions. For example, one stirrup agha was called the Gardener; he commanded some 2,000 Janissaries who were not only gardeners but also served as an imperial bodyguard, as oarsmen on the sultan's barge, and as a secret police force in charge of tortures and executions at the personal command of the sultan.

The grand vizier, as the sultan's prime minister, presided over the outside service and the king's slaves outside the palace, who made up the standing army, the navy, and the civil administration.

THE HAREM OF THE HOUSE OF OSMAN: SLAVE BRIDES, SLAVE MOTHERS, AND LADY SULTANS

There was a constant flow of European girls into the seraglio (as Europeans called the harem), similar to the flow of Christian boys to the Gate. Harem women were either slaves purchased in the market or gifts from provincial officials (especially from the bey of Algiers, who ruled the famous Barbary pirates). Even after the abolition of the tribute of Christian boys to the Gate, slave girls of Christian origin continued to be received into the harem right down until the end of the dynasty in 1922. In the nineteenth century they were mostly Circassian girls from Georgia on the Black Sea, sold by impoverished families "in the hope of a better life," according to the official Ottoman view.

Although crowded and confined, the harem was the female mirror image of the slave school for pages. There was parallel differentiation of recruits into career tracks. Girls who seemed strong but not beautiful or bright were trained to be servants and spent most of their life waiting on others, until retirement to the Old Palace harem. These women could rise in rank to become stewards in charge of harem services: hairdressing, the infirmary, the coffee service, the pantry, or the baths. Other female stewards were directly attached to the person of the two high harem officials: the valide sultan, or sultan's mother, and the head black eunuch, or Kizler agha.

The head black eunuch, the Kizler agha, was the third ranking official of the empire and enjoyed the income from vast prebends. He was the official Keeper of the Holy Shrines at Mecca and Medina and therefore a man of great prestige as well as wealth and power.

The black eunuchs were the only males other than princes to live in the harem. They were slaves recruited, and physically emasculated, through Egypt from the Sudan, and were highly schooled, even learned. They in turn instructed the young girls. Most new harem inmates spent their time learning the arts of a courtly gentlewoman. They learned to speak the sultan's Turkish, were converted and schooled in Islam by a black eunuch Muslim clergyman, and learned reading, writing, dance, music, sewing, and embroidery.

Most of the young women so instructed and cultivated were given as wives to ranking officials of the empire. The harem was, in effect, more of a school

Courtyard of the harem. Each window or door opened to a cell for a harem inmate.

Mannequins of the Kizler agha with servant eunuchs, Topkapi Palace.

for officials' wives than a residence for the sultan's consorts. Moreover, former harem ladies had the privilege of visiting inmates and could become propagandists promoting their husbands' careers.

Other inmates reached the sultan's eye and bed and hence never left the harem. They fell into three ranks: four recognized consorts, or "women" (Turkish: *kadinlar*) who had borne imperial children; "favorites," usually also mothers of children; and concubines with whom the sultan had slept. Adult sons of the sultans also had their consorts, favorites, and concubines.

The woman who presided over the harem, jointly with the Kizler agha, was the valide sultan, the sultan's mother. A naturalized Ottoman Turk and converted Muslim, upon the accession of her son she became a woman of great wealth, with many prebends supplying her with income. She could hold audiences with state officials, travel around the city (properly veiled from sight), endow mosques and support charities, meddle in politics, and even—if she were talented—engage in statecraft. But she was always in origin a slave.

The princesses of the House of Osman—daughters and sisters of sultans—also bore the title of *sultan* (usually translated *sultane* in French or *sultana* in English; the Turkish language distinguishes no gender classes—all pronouns are "it"). These lady sultans were of-

Mannequin of a valide sultan in the harem, Topkapi Palace.

ten given in marriage to the highest officials—governors of provinces or the grand vizier himself. At that time the sultan would build them a palace. They also received the largest prebends, huge tax farms, to support themselves and their households. They were often leading figures in endowing charities. Although the sultan practiced polygyny, the lady sultans practiced monogamy. Their husbands had to divorce any other wives upon marrying them. Moreover, in the wedding rites themselves, which usually lasted more than a week, the bridegrooms, career imperial servants usually in their forties or fifties, had to go through a special ceremony in which they swore obeisance to the bride as her "slave." In the early centuries of the empire, they were indeed gate slaves.

These great ladies, for all their high degree, were forbidden their sons, who were strangled at birth. Their daughters, however, also bore the rank of *sultan* and continued to enjoy their mothers' incomes. The great families of today's Turkish aristocracy are descended from these ladies and their high-ranking bureaucrat husbands. Figure 15.6 diagrams the roles of women in the Ottoman Empire.

Rewards of Office

All gate slaves, including the common foot soldier, were paid from imperial stores and lived well for the times. However, the Janissary infantrymen were, like the serving girls in the harem, supposed to remain celibate through life. Janissary devotion to a dervish mystical order no doubt helped some of them sublimate their sexual urges. In contrast, officers were richly rewarded. Most lived lavishly and were further rewarded with brides schooled in the harem. Both were of foreign origin, but both had become paragons of Turkish official culture.

Certain high posts carried large prebends (tax rights) in villages. However, the gate slave did not keep this prebend for life, but relinquished it to his successor in the post. Indeed, there was danger in a gate slave's amassing too much wealth. He might be denounced for stealing state funds, his property confiscated, and his body beheaded suddenly by the sultan's swift justice.

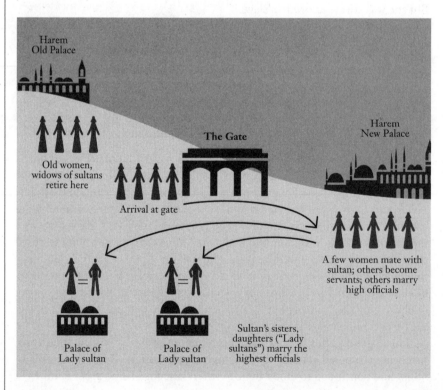

Figure 15.6 Women in the Ottoman imperial family.

388

The House of the Pen:
The Muslim Clergy/Judiciary

The slave bureaucracy we have described was officially known as the House of the Sword. In addition there was a judicial-religious arm of the government, known as the House of the Pen.

The Ottoman sultans replaced the Arab **caliphs,** divinely appointed rulers in succession from Mohammed, and delegated religious administration to a scholar known as the sheik of Islam or the grand mufti of Constantinople. This man was in charge of the judges of the empire, the **qadis,** appointed for all the principal cities and towns and the provincial capitals.

The grand mufti was responsible for university administration, which was financed, like the qadis, out of religious endowments—prebends from villages whose taxes were dedicated to the income of a shrine, mosque, or school. Sultan/caliphs were expected to give gifts to qadis and scholars on great Muslim feast days. University faculties were learned men divided into five ranks. A student became a scholar or mufti when his university teacher decided he had learned enough, got other professors to agree to it, and wrote out a certificate that had to be recognized by the qadi of the city. The House of the Pen could then appoint him university professor or judge.

Most muftis remained humble scholars at village shrines or mosques, where they instructed children in the faith, taught some of them to read and write, lead the faithful in their prayers, and served as village scribes. Qadis, on the other hand, were respected and wise men, renowned for their justice. They tried disputes between Muslims according to one or another of the Islamic law codes. With the help of the provincial governor, they also tried cases between Muslims and Christians, Muslims and Jews, and Jews and Christians.

Christians who quarreled with each other took their disputes to their priest. Their high courts were the various bishops, including the Greek Orthodox patriarch of Constantinople, who was in charge of internal justice for the entire Greek Orthodox community. His counterpart for Jews was the grand rabbi of Constantinople.

The scholarly judicial apparatus of the House of the Pen was exceedingly simple. Few scribes or servants were at the bottom level, since the qadis did not keep elaborate records. Legal clerking, in fact, was concentrated in a section of the palace administration.

Turkish Prebendaries: Sepoys

In the provinces, the conquering sultans made grants of tax rights in villages to Turkish cavalry leaders, or **sepoys** (Turkish: *sipahis*), who in return had to raise and lead a company of mounted troops on demand. They thus made up a militia or reserve that was rotated up frequently, two large companies of sepoy cavalry being on imperial duty at all times.

The sultan's throne and entertainment salon in the harem, Topkapi Palace.

Sepoys were true prebendaries, imperial servants supported by a separate piece of the redistributive economy. They did not own their prebends, and they could not sell or buy them. Each sepoy heir had to be confirmed in his grant by the sultan and had to be able to meet his military obligations; otherwise the prebend was reassigned to somebody else. Sepoys could not rise far in the imperial army, and there were only two official ranks for them, although in the provinces they formed a Turkish corps of "Kentucky colonels." They elected one of their number as provincial commander and put him and his cavalry at the disposal of the provincial qadi to serve as police to back up that judge's decisions.

Form of the Ottoman Imperial Bureaucracy

Ottoman administration was a climax form, but it contained the elements of a classic patrimonial bureaucracy. First, there was the *dynasty*. This lineage of males claimed the right to rule as the representatives of Islam, first as the conquerors of eastern Christendom—including the Second Rome, Constantinople—and later as *caliphs*, direct successors of the Prophet.

Second, there were the *gate slaves*, members of the monarch's household, directly financed by his patrimony. The gate slaves were organized in vast numbers according to the principles of age grading and training. Although they were differentiated into functional bureaus—army, navy, supply corps, clerking, accounting—at the higher reaches and within the New Palace itself these functions were not so distinct, but rather overlapped.

Third, there were the *prebendaries*, Turkish sepoys who controlled land grants in return for staffing the militia. At their height, they commanded some 200,000 potential men in arms for the imperial forces. However, provincial civil administration, justice, and the standing army were *not* in their hands.

Fourth, the sultan as caliph headed the *state cult*, the House of the Pen staffed by a body of learned wise men who served as judges. Although all patrimonial bureaucracies include a state cult, the Muslim example is unusual in that justice is also a function of the clergy.

Finally, the whole apparatus was financed by *tribute*, a form of redistribution, including the farming out of tribute rights in *prebends* to dynastic princesses, imperial officials, sepoys, and religious endowments.

Maintaining Dynastic Imperial Power

The Ottoman empire was based on military conquest. It dealt with internal rebellion severely, with swift and cruel repression. Its military posture was also external and defensive. It posed as the defender of Sunni Muslim areas against their Shiite enemies. Likewise, for centuries the Ottomans posed as defenders of subjected Eastern Orthodox Christian populations against their traditional Roman Catholic enemies.

In addition, in common with most early empires, the Ottomans left local administration in the hands of traditional village and neighborhood notables and elders. Ethnic and religious groups were left to their own devices. Nevertheless, to regulate conflict and trouble, a learned judge was always available to pronounce judgment and levy fines and punishments, which were enforced speedily.

Gate slaves also served as a check on possible abuses by judges and local sepoy constabularies. Indeed, the three main branches of administration served as checks or counterweights on each other. The courts of the religious judges in particular were arenas for denouncing both sepoys and gate slaves and so helped keep them in line by calling down swift and drastic punishment from the center. Thus, Murad IV (1623-1640) (who abolished the slave tribute system) brought rebellious and corrupt Janissaries and sepoys alike to heel by instituting *terror* in the form of bloody purges, with the backing of the qadis. Literally thousands of imperial servants were summarily executed by the sultan's special execution squads.

In common with most early empires and with all modern ones, the Turks rotated their officials in their posts, especially in the provinces, thus preventing them from building up personal power bases in any one region.

Finally, the Muslim law code in the provinces, and Christian canon law in the Christian communities, gave the Ottomans an advanced tool for civil administration and keeping the peace. Muslim belief differs from the pagan practices of many patrimonial bureaucracies in its simple written scripture and practices that are readily available to every believer. It further differs in containing a rational body of civil law readily applied to any personal dispute.

The Ottoman Turks thus had the means of resolving conflict on the local level. The man who remained malcontent could always flee his enemies and join the Ottoman army, deflecting his aggression against the enemies of the sultan!

Although the sultan delegated the state cult almost completely to the grand mufti, the sultan/caliph did make public appearances at the mosques on the

Muslim feast days, some of which were the occasions for palace officials to slaughter great numbers of sacrificial beasts for public feasting. More important, the doctrines of Sunni Islam gave the sultans the divine right to rule not only Muslims, but Christians and Jews ("Peoples of the Book") in God's name as well.

Decline of the Ottomans

In the Ottoman case, as in all original bureaucracies, the imperial household and military were under the personal command of the monarch. (Monarchs who rule above the law are called *despots*.) Sultans regularly had their brothers murdered upon their accession, justifying this violation of the law of Islam with a decree of Mehmet the Conqueror to that effect. Mehmet was simply trying to avoid a struggle for succession. (New sultans were picked from among the eligible princes by the valide sultan, meeting with the Divan, or imperial cabinet.) Mehmet III (d. 1603) held the funeral of his nineteen murdered brothers jointly with the funeral of his father, bidding farewell to all those coffins at once from the Gate of Felicity upon his accession. Beside this "legal" fratricide, Ottoman history is stained with incidents of filicide, when sultans had bright and promising adult sons murdered, sometimes at the behest of jealous wives, who wanted their own sons to succeed. There are also several incidents of patricide-regicide, in which young princes slew their fathers in order to obtain the throne.

Starting with the basic question of the right to succession, there was a large arena open to personal politicking and intrigue. The sultan's decisions could be entirely capricious and personal, rather than based on the merits of any policy-making decision, or on any law case. Injustices and injudiciously adopted policies might easily be put into place.

Abolition of the Gate Slave System. In its heyday, the gate slave bureaucracy worked admirably. The empire was administered by talented and highly trained officials, totally loyal to the sultan and his imperial household. All that began to change in the reign of Selim the Sot (1566–1574), when the Old Palace school for pages was opened up to a quota for the sons of ranking Turks. Murad IV (1623–1640) finally abolished the gate slave tribute, and the schools became exclusively for free Muslims. The word for gate slave (*kapikulu*) is henceforth best translated as "gate servant."

Paradoxically, opening the page schools represented a victory for the incumbent gate slaves as well as the Turkish sepoys. The one major complaint the gate slaves might have had about the system was that there was no place in it for their own sons. Some could join the sepoys' troops as common soldiers, and others could train to become Muslim judges, but none could become gate slaves and follow in their fathers' footsteps to fame and fortune.

The sons of gate slaves were free men, Turkish Muslims. The son of a grand vizier could never hope to become grand vizier himself. That changed after the abolition of the slave tribute; indeed, for four generations (1648–1703) the grand viziers were one man (a Muslim Albanian palace kitchen scullion who went from cook to prime minister) and his descendants, some of whom married lady sultans.

The Attempt to Convert to a Legal-Rational Bureaucracy. In 1826 Mahmud II The Reformer (1808–1839) went further and bloodily abolished the Janissaries and palace schools altogether, replacing them with a new bureaucracy modeled directly on that put in place in France by Napoleon I.* He instituted ministries, and a series of military and professional schools to train upper-class Turks for them. However, the Ottoman bureaucracy had lost the vitality of its first centuries. Whatever was gained in modernization did not make up for old strengths.

The new civil and military servants all came from the conservative, ethnic Turkish landlord class, from the sepoys and the families founded by gate slaves. They were drawn from a more restricted population base and were simply not as talented and inventive as their forebears. Moreover, the system had long lost its latent integration through the slave system with subject Christian populations. That system had tapped into the energies, however cruelly, of half the empire.

The Ottoman empire began to grope for another basis of legitimacy, first through secular administrative law, then consultative councils, and finally a brief attempt at constitutional, representative monarchy. Still, the new bureaucracy was never able to become completely *responsive* to its constituents, the Ottoman subjects, who never entirely made the transition to becoming Ottoman citizens. The new bureaucracy stumbled against the nationalities questions, first of the Christian minorities, which rejected such a state and one by one broke away with the help of European powers to form the explosive nation-states of the Balkans, and finally of the Muslim Arab nationalists. Turkey became the "sick man of Europe," only to be revitalized on a true European model as a single nation-state of ethnic Turks in their homeland of Anatolia. This was brought about by Mustafa Kemal Atatürk, a revolutionary secular revitalization leader, in response to the defeat of the Otto-

---

*Mahmud II's mother, Valide Sultan Naksidil, was in origin a Frenchwoman, probably born in the West Indies and captured as a girl by Barbary pirates from a ship on its way to France. Legend has it that she was Aimée duBec de Rivery, first cousin of Josephine Bonaparte, born like Aimée on the French island of Martinique, who, as the wife of Napoleon I, became empress of France. It is romantic to believe that the two cousins both became empresses in very different realms. But there are those who say Aimée duBec died in France in a convent in 1820 and not in the imperial harem in Constantinople. At least two recent novels have been written about this valide sultan that impute the more romantic identity to her (Chase-Ribaud, 1986; Prince Michael of Greece, 1983).

mans in World War I. The subject nationalities, the dynasty, the religious judiciary, and the empire were gone. A very new Turkey, a nation-state rather than a multinational dynastic empire, has emerged today.

THE ORIGINAL BUREAUCRACY AS A DYNAMIC INSTITUTION

The Ottoman Turks, while originally patrimonial and certainly prebendary, were in many ways legal-rational even before 1826 and the Reforms. They based their legal right to rule on Islamic law, and their judges were Islamic

Chinese Dynastic Cycles

*I*n traditional Chinese history many dynasties succeeded each other, each after a 60-year interregnum or "time of troubles," in which China was divided up by rival warlords, one of which, upon conquering the others, would assume the "Mandate of Heaven" and found a new dynasty. These could last 350 years or more, but they inevitably dissolved.

Each new dynasty would reinstate the imperial Confucian examination system, run annually from Confucian temples, to recruit scholar/officials, *mandarins*, all trained in philosophy and letters. Inevitably, these new officials would enrich themselves from their prebends and found gentry families, entrenching themselves locally over several generations. They also came to dominate the examinations system by presenting their own sons as candidates.

As these families grew locally dominant, they engaged in disputes with governing families in neighboring regions. Flood control works fell into disrepair at provincial boundaries. Rivers broke through dikes. Flood, famine, and natural disaster were seen as the withdrawal of the "Mandate of Heaven" from the reigning dynasty. Thus, the **dynastic cycle** started over again with a new "time of troubles."

The Chinese dynasties, far more than the long-lived House of Osman, exemplify some of the fatal weaknesses of patrimonial bureaucracies.

The Empress Dowager of China, a powerful, long-lived, but incompetent ruler, weakened the Manchu dynasty. It fell in 1911, a few years after her death.

clergymen/scholars. They *trained* some of the imperial servants, the gate slaves. In the one case the servants were recruited by an irrational criterion, membership in the king's household, and in the second, by the assumption of a divine right to rule, not the consent of the governed.

But a government based on dynasty can never last in the long run. Dynasties always fall, *unless* they become merely ceremonial, like the long-lived Japanese house, in whose name de facto dynasties, those of the military commanders or shoguns, ruled, or unless, as in Great Britain, the monarchy becomes constitutional, presiding as figureheads over a legislature and a bureaucracy *legally responsive* to its citizens.

Accidents of biology are the first weakness of dynasties. In the original bureaucracies monarchs sought to use the principle of *lineage* to justify the concentration of enormous power in the hands of one person. This principle is not rationally linked to the demands of administration. Single lines of descent do not guarantee a source of talented individuals every generation. Thus, the dull-witted, the mad, or the merely incompetent may inherit. Under-age heirs may cause a crisis on ascending the throne, too.

Furthermore, attempts to recruit nonkinsmen rationally are only partially successful. Some original bureaucracies sought to recruit *rationally*, that is by merit and training. But such attempts were either limited partially to particular tasks, such as the state cult, or by class or ethnic considerations in recruitment.

Finally, officials at the periphery grow strong at the expense of the center. Those who rule provinces, supporting themselves by a "take" of the revenue, invariably seek to keep as much as they can for themselves. Sooner or later they may marry into local elites and come to feel they represent the region and not the empire. When their rise in local power coincides with a "downswing" in the biological vitality of the central dynasty (that is, when a minor or a madman inherits the throne), the empire begins to divide up into realms ruled by warlords. If the realm is reconstituted at all, it is by one warlord conquering the others.

SUMMARY AND CONCLUSIONS

*I*n the original bureaucracies we see a more complex system emerging from less complex ones. The original bureaucracies were able to organize dense populations, sometimes over vast distances, on a scale many times more numerous and far-flung than any tribal community can organize. But to do so, human beings made use of the institutions at hand, just as some species in the hominid line—our own or *Homo erectus*—created human marriage and the family by putting together two primate patterns: male-female consortship and lifelong mother-offspring ties, investing male parental rights and duties in the newly created role of father.

The original bureaucracies were invented as improvisations. In them, monarchs took lineages and made them dynasties. They took royal households and made them bureaucracies. They took a redistributive economy and financed huge enterprises with tribute, although in many cases they farmed out local pieces of it to their servants. They legitimated their effort by orchestrating annual ritual in state cults, often taking over the teachings of a revitalization prophet and claiming to rule by his divine inspiration. Finally, they called up age grades and made them armies and labor battalions. They further age-graded the ranks of their servants and rewarded them by seniority.

In sum, the institutional components of such bureaucracies, universal in the primitive world, are transformed into something unique. To repeat, these institutional components are (1) lineage, (2) household, (3) redistributive economy, (4) state cults from which that economy originated, and (5) age grades for the military and labor draft organization. (For a discussion of growth and development of subsystem components within a larger natural system, see Boulding, 1956; Buckley, 1968; and Katz and Kahn, 1966.)

The cultures of the original bureaucracies reflect different emphases, often quite improvised to begin with, on the various components listed above. The Ottomans emphasized the sultan's slave household. The Incas emphasized the imperial lineage, and its sublineages, which provided servants equivalent to the Ottoman gate slaves. Such decisions reflect values already present in the culture. The Ottomans did not value kinship and cared not at all who the mother of a prince was. Today, the Kingdom of Saudi Arabia, also a Muslim monarchy, is structured by Arab, not Turkish, values. Among Arabs it matters a lot who one's mother is. The ruling House of Saud is descended from King Abdul Aziz, who unified much of the Arabian peninsula in the 1920s after the downfall of the Ottomans. Abdul Aziz (also known as Ibn Saud) married many women, mostly the daughters of Bedouin tribal chiefs from all over the peninsula. Like the Lovedu harem, his became a kind of house of representatives. Today every Saudi royal prince is identified by the tribal affiliation of his mother or grandmother. The branches of the royal house stand for the Bedouin tribes, their maternal cousins, with whom they maintain close relations. The result is a regime strikingly different from the Ottoman one.

Only after bureaucracy had been invented, put into place, and made to work in many empires, over thousands of years, did it begin to emerge as something more explicit: "legal-rational" bureaucracy. Such bureaucracies, as Weber conceived them, function to maximize efficiency in administration by recruiting and training the best people specifically for separate functions and tasks. They promote and reward their servants impersonally by seniority, keep track of everything by writing, and administer the tribute from a central treasury. Finally, they are chartered by law with a rationally (logically) mandated mission. What Weber never satisfactorily explored was that dependence of the legal charter not merely on functional efficiency, but upon responsiveness, upon direct accountability to the citizens served by the bureaucracy. We shall explore that modern form and its dynamics in a later chapter.

But we are not to believe that these imperial institutions we have examined were thereby less meaningful or were culturally lacking to those who embraced them. Each was a way of life that for all its imperfections managed to channel human energies, for the most part constructively, over the centuries of any particular dynastic cycle.

Thus, the Ottomans provided for local peace and justice in many regions, while maintaining that the sultan, for all his fratricidal ways, embodied traditional authoritarian patriarchal values and demonstrably revered and respected his mother. Furthermore, he was the successor to the Prophet Mohammed and was thus divinely appointed to rule. This must have seemed divinely proper to that council of slave officials, the Divan, that met at the death of a sultan with his imperial slave mother to pick a new sultan from among the male heirs to the dynasty, whose fortunes had become so closely identified with those of their servants.

This chapter has considered the urban, controlling side of the civilized world. We turn next to the other half, the rural society of peasants.

SUGGESTED READINGS

Bendix, Reinhard. *Max Weber: An Intellectual Portrait*. Garden City, N.Y.: Doubleday/Anchor, 1960. Chapter 11, "Traditional Domination," is particularly germane to this chapter. Chapter 1, a brief biography of Weber, is interesting for this and later chapters of this book.

Chase-Ribaud, Barbara. *Valide: A Novel of the Harem*. New York: Morrow, 1986. A serious biographical novel about Aimée duBec de Rivery as Naksidil, mother of Mahmud II.

Coon, Carleton. *Caravan: The Story of the Middle East*, rev. ed. New York: Holt, Rinehart and Winston, 1958. This remains the best single ethnology of an entire culture area. For patrimonial bureaucracy, see especially Chapters , 7, 14, and 15.

Fei, Hsiao-t'ung. *China's Gentry: Essays in Rural-Urban Relations*. Chicago: University of Chicago Press, 1953. Fascinating portraits of mandarins and land owners.

Lewis, Herbert S. *A Galla Monarchy: Jimma Abba Jifar, Ethiopia, 1830-1932*. University of Wisconsin Press, 1965. Lively account of a recent archaic bureaucracy.

Prince Michael of Greece. *Sultana*. Alexis Ullman, trans. New York: Harper & Row, 1983. Yet another romantic novel about Naksidil, mother of Mahmud II.

GLOSSARY

bureaucracy A social device enabling the one or the few to rule not just the many, but multitudes. Technically, a government apparatus divided into bureaus, or agencies, with special functions.

caliph In Sunni Islam, the divinely appointed successor to the Prophet Mohammed who was both a religious and a civil leader, with the right to rule Muslims, Christians, and Jews in God's name. The caliphate was abolished by Atatürk in 1923.

dynastic cycle A process whereby a dynasty, founded by an energetic, inventive warrior (or war-prophet), goes through an initial phase of florescence, followed by a phase of slow disintegration as local governors, living on prebends, become entrenched and challenge each other and the dynastic center. When this phase coincides with incompetent or underage dynastic rulers, the dynasty collapses and local warlords struggle to found a new one.

dynasty A royal lineage that assumes the right to rule according to some mythological justification, enacted in rituals surrounding the throne. A dynasty seldom rules more than 350–500 years, unless its monarchs become ceremonial figureheads, leaving the business of government to someone else.

eunuch A castrated male, whose duties are to guard harem women, usually in a royal palace. In the Ottoman New Palace there were the black eunuchs in the harem, who had been completely emasculated, their entire genitals removed—they had to urinate with the aid of a silver tube. In the inner court were the white eunuchs, who were less drastically altered.

gate slaves Ottoman imperial servants, both military and civil, drawn from a tribute of slaves exacted from Christian villages for the first 300 years of the dynasty. Thereafter the palace slave schools were open to free Muslims, and they became, in effect, "gate servants" until the palace schools were abolished in 1826.

Janissaries Slave troops of the Ottomans drawn from a tribute of preadolescent boys taken from Christian villages. They formed a fierce and professional fighting force. After 1640 they were free Turkish Muslim recruits. The Janissaries were abolished in 1826.

legal-rational bureaucracy According to Weber, a set of government bureaus defined by a legal charter according to specialized, logical function. Careers are open to talent, by training, and are rewarded by seniority. Activities are supervised by paperwork and records, revenues are budgeted from a central treasury bureau, and the whole enterprise justifies itself by efficiency.

mufti A high-ranking Islamic official and judge.

patrimonial Referring to the real property of an empire or commonwealth as belonging to the monarch, whose produce properly flowed to him as tribute, and dispensed by him personally as part of his household income to reward his servants and kinsmen.

prebendary An official, religious or civil, who enjoys the income (tax-farming rights) from a prebend.

prebends Tax farms or benefices; districts or villages whose taxes or tributes have been granted (farmed out) to a royal official, to support that official and his establishment in exchange for military or governmental activities for the monarch. Also refers to similar endowments for church or religious offices or foundations.

qadi An Islamic scholar licensed to act as a judge.

responsiveness For a bureaucracy, the quality of answering to the people it serves. For original bureaucracies, Aristotle's question of whether they ruled in their own interest or the common interest. More concretely, the mechanisms of communication whereby a bureaucracy learns what its followers want.

sepoys Turkish warriors who were granted prebends in exchange for raising and leading troops for the Ottoman sultan. In the nineteenth century many of them became, in effect, local landlords.

Folk Cultures and Communities:

Civilized "Insolents" and Peasants

16

INSOLENT CIVILIZED TRIBES

*ETHNOGRAPHIC CLOSE-UP: THE
CRUZOB MAYA: RESISTANCE,
CULTURAL REVITALIZATION, AND
THE BIRTH OF A FOLK TRIBE*

*OPEN PEASANTRIES AND THE STEM
FAMILY HOUSEHOLD*

Stem Family Households

The Irish Countryfolk

*CLOSED CORPORATE PEASANT
COMMUNITIES*

The Original Communes: European Wheat Villages

Valdemora: Long-Term Balance Through Competitive Courtship

*ETHNOGRAPHIC CLOSE-UP:
ALOTENANGO, A MAYA
CLOSED CORPORATE COMMUNITY*

The Patriarchal Family: A Model for Community Organization

The Civil-Religious Hierarchy

Rotating the Cargos

*The Cult of Judas: Resistance and Ambivalence Toward Urban
Hispanic Culture*

*TOWN- AND CITY-DWELLING PEASANTS:
URBAN AGRARIAN PLEBEIANS*

*I*n civilized societies, **peasants** and **pastoralists** are food producers who live and work on the land and share, somehow, in the wider urban culture. They are the **folk,** as opposed to the **elite,** to whom they are linked through redistributive economics, especially tribute. They also rely on cities for finely crafted goods. These they obtain, usually, through exchanges in marketplaces. They also supply cities with people, sending their excess sons and daughters to settle there (as we saw Christian peasants supplying the Ottomans with gate slaves). They are bound to urban centers through ritual pilgrimages or simply by subscribing to the official religion of their rulers. They provide the labor for public works, and the conscripts for armies. They are linked with urban upper classes through many mutually dependent ties, as when they work the land for great estates, pay tribute to individual tax farmers, or go to fight for "their" feudal lord. Sometimes they actually live in cities.

But some of the folk, the **"insolents,"** are linked with the urban world through armed resistance. Instead of paying tribute, they resist the state: they fight, or retreat to remote areas to preserve their local rule. Alternatively, they strive to exact the opposite of tribute from the state: a subsidy. In either case, the concern for local autonomy is so strong as to produce a rebellious warrior society that fiercely resists external interference.

Some states provide insolent civilized tribesmen with money and weapons simply to embarrass or fend off a rival state. Pastoral nomads with wide-open ranges and with herds of horses and camels, in particular, are often perennial rebels, maintaining a loose autonomy as civilized tribes. At times they even swoop down and conquer the state. For the urban state they are both sources of power and potential sources of resistance and rebellion.

All told, the folk—pastoralists and peasants, rebels and serfs—represent an array of local communities, many of them linguistically and ethnically diverse. Complexity on a regional scale is the norm. In that, they are little different from the tribal world we have examined. Yet they are different in that they have access to the great urban centers and share in urban culture, although they refract it and change it in each locale, culture, and community.

Folk cultures form a continuum from insolent, autonomous "civilized tribes" in deserts, mountains, and jungles—in short, in inaccessible regions—to urban elites in cities (see Figure 16.1). Civilized tribesmen are often nomadic pastoralists. Next come settled peasants. These may be *open* or *closed* to urban cultures and their elites. Next come the elites themselves, who can generally be found at urban nodes. These nodes range from isolated manor houses on noble estates, through isolated temples, monasteries, and garrisons, to towns with their marketplaces, shopkeepers, and officials, to, finally, nucleated cities with concentrated urban functions.

Traditional open peasantries have always been integrated into the wider society—through exogamous marriage systems, direct ties to elite overlords, or fervent participation in urban cults. Rather than turning inward toward local shrines and elders, they have enthusiastically looked outward for marriage and for political, economic, and ritual ties with elites.

On the other hand, closed corporate peasant communities hold outsiders in fear and contempt. They do not marry outsiders, they watch vigilantly over village lands, and they form single religious congregations that may be quite different from the state cult. Politically, they are corporate republics that deal with outsiders through a single headman. Economically, however, such villages *cannot be completely closed*. They often participate in marketplaces, and they *must* yield tribute, rent, and **corvée labor** (drafted gangs paid at set low wages) in response to imperial demands. They are too much under outside control to be "insolent." They never have military autonomy, for example. When they do, they are transforming themselves into "insolents."

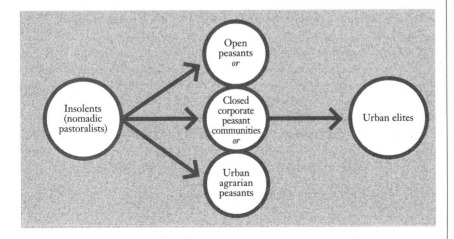

Figure 16.1 The rural folk to urban elite continuum.

INSOLENT CIVILIZED TRIBES

The insolents are **civilized tribes** (not to be confused with uncivilized tribes) who live on the margins of state domains. In the Middle East they live in the mountains and deserts. Others have extended across central Asia, where they gave rise to the nomad hordes that at various times conquered the dynastic states of China, Islam, and Eastern and Central Europe. These insolent fighters of Eurasia have repeatedly swept down from their strongholds in times of trouble to seize cities and found new royal dynasties. They are all mounted, whether on horses or camels, and have access to metal weapons, often manufactured in cities. Some of them live in nucleated fortified villages. Their social organization is based on segmentary lineages, but they obey lords (aghas or khans) with whom they calculate kin ties and with whom they intermarry. These aghas are comparable to the chiefs of the Scottish clans of old (Coon, 1958).

Afghan rebels are modern-day examples of civilized insolents.

The tribes of Berbers of North Africa live scattered in fortified single-family households along mountain valleys.* Each small hollow forms a canton, or miniature republic. Each is ruled by a council of elders split into two moieties that (like U.S. Republicans and Democrats) cut across all communities and keep everyone in perpetual feud but also in perpetual stalemate. Marketplaces at shrines at the borders of cantons provide the Berbers with regional integration and yet another joint body of elders to enforce the market peace (Coon, 1958).

The common civilized tribesman is linked with, or open to, his tribal chief through kinship; in republican tribes, he participates openly in tribal assemblies. It has always been difficult for shahs and sultans to rule these mountaineers; they do so only during exceptionally vigorous reigns, and then either by exacting tribute from the tribal lord or by appointing their own lords at the marketplaces. More often than not the monarch pays off these fierce fighters with a state subsidy, thus buying peace on his—often internal—frontiers.

Civilized tribes are not considered peasants. They are food producers, but they live in their own realms, linked to each other through politics and endemic warfare (after all, a kind of communications system). In some

---

*The Berber lands were known traditionally in Morocco literally as *Bled el Siba*, "the Land of Insolence," while the lands governed by the sultan were known as *Bled el Makhzen*, the land of the storehouse ("magazine"), referring to the sultan's stores of food and goods for redistribution (Benet, 1957).

areas, the marketplace is the central communication device. These tribes are open social systems, ever ready to rally in holy war and to conquer the people of the plains. Unlike peasants, then, they have local political autonomy upheld by a fierce military posture. Each community is a miniature standing army.

Let us look at the rise and fall of an insolent civilized tribal folk culture out of a peasant one using the example of the Cruzob Maya.

ETHNOGRAPHIC CLOSE-UP

THE CRUZOB MAYA: RESISTANCE, CULTURAL REVITALIZATION, AND THE BIRTH OF A FOLK TRIBE

After 1546 the ancient civilization of the Maya of the Yucatán peninsula was subjugated by the Spanish conquest, causing a radical cultural transformation. The intolerant Crown of Castile declared war through the Inquisition against the "followers of Satan," which is what all the native religions were termed. Bishop Landa burned the Maya books. The Maya became, officially, Roman Catholics. The friars reorganized them into closed corporate parish communities around enormous churches. They remained ostensibly obedient Roman Catholics and Spanish subjects for the next three centuries.

After independence from Spain in 1821, Mexico underwent both economic development and political turmoil. In Yucatán, the two cities of Merida and Campeche were rivals in the development of the henequen industry, and the great Spanish land owners converted their large cattle estates to labor-intensive haciendas, recruiting Indians from the closed communities as debt serfs ("peons"). Many other Indians fled to the jungle frontier to live in semi-independence. In 1847 the two rival cities were fighting each other with their militia troops, recruited from Indian peasants. Led by *mestizos* (persons of Hispanic culture and mixed Indian-Spanish race), the Indian troops rebelled against

their urban officers, massacred Spanish Creole towns and garrisons, and were about to take the city of Merida in 1848 when they melted away in order to plant their crops.

The urban militias counterattacked and drove huge numbers of Indians into the bush. Over 200,000 men, women, and children died. But in 1850, they rallied. A Talking Cross, and its ventriloquist prophet, had appeared! By 1855 several independent Maya groups had established themselves in the south of the peninsula. The largest, most warlike, and most feared were the Cruzob, the People of the Talking Cross.

From 1856 to 1901 the capital of this independent realm of perhaps 30,000 rebel Mayas was Chan Santa Cruz, today's city of Carrillo Puerto, in the state of Quintana Roo (established as a territory after the 1901 reconquest). A *tatich*, or prophet, ruled the Cruzob in the name of the resident deity, the Talking Cross, which originally spoke through a ventriloquist and later contented itself with leaving written messages on its altar in the church.

The church itself was built by the Cruzob to house their deity. This urban ceremonial center was laid out like a proper Spanish town, on the grid plan around a central plaza (see Figure 16.2). Four crosses guarded the entrances in the cardinal directions.

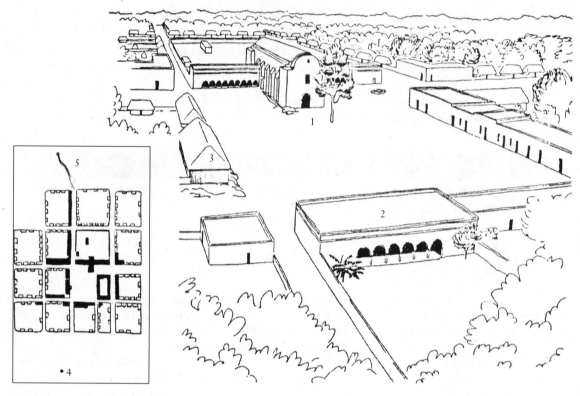

Figure 16.2 Ground plan of Chan Santa Cruz.

Key:

1. Church of the Talking Cross
2. Palace of the tatich
3. Headquarters of military commander
4. Original settlement
5. Sacred waterhole and crosses

Three crosses were enshrined at the natural well to the north. The palace of the prophet stood across the plaza from the church. Other buildings were the palace of the military commander, the barracks for the companies, and a council house.

The villages of the Cruzob each belonged to one of seven militia companies. Only one company of the seven did duty at the capital, a fortnight at a time. Otherwise the center held only the rulers and their captive mestizo slaves (and Chinese laborers,

runaways from Belize) and concubines. On fiesta days all seven companies were called up.

The Cruzob were able to purchase or get grants of firearms from the British in nearby Belize, who were happy to have a buffer group between themselves and the Mexican army.

Culturally the Cruzob spoke the ancient Maya language. Although they worshiped their own cult object, product of a revitalization movement born from despair in defeat, they called themselves

Christians, and their priests recited the Latin mass in their church. A few scribes were literate in Latin and Spanish, but their old Mayan hieroglyphics had been lost for centuries. They were thus culturally an example of **syncretism,** the combination of several different cultural elements into a new synthesis.

The Cruzob were conquered by General Ignacio Bravo in 1901, after the British withdrew their arms supply. They fled Chan Santa Cruz and lived underground as an autonomous tribe of "wild Indians" in the bush until the 1930s, when the Mexican government extended land rights and services to them. Today the Cruzob survive as a highly distinct folk culture of peasants, no longer rebels, in a group of five villages of thatched huts north of their former capital. One sacred village houses the Talking Cross and the tatich (the office has survived). The "military" companies, now ritual fraternities, still do guard duty for the cross.

The cross inside the church of the former Chan Santa Cruz as it is today. Of course, the Catholic priests who say mass here do not maintain that this cross can talk!

OPEN PEASANTRIES AND THE STEM FAMILY HOUSEHOLD

Eric Wolf (1955) defined Latin American peasants selling more than 50 percent of their produce on a cash market as "open peasantries." I prefer to measure openness along not just the market but all the institutional dimensions: migration, kinship, religion, and local political organization—whether or not the local community is a *corporation* controlling resources.

Open peasants usually do not form a corporate body. *They are not communes.* They do not hide behind a hard shell of symbols and practices that exclude outsiders. Moreover, they participate fully in several of the institutions of their civilization.

Stem Family Households

One particular peasant adaptation of the family is the **stem family household,** in which additional childbearing units are added in a single line down the generations by allowing only one heir to marry and bring in a spouse to join the parents, who otherwise would have an empty nest. The emphasis is on inheritance, and the form is common only in civilized societies, where immobile goods can be handed from one generation to another.

This form is common in western Europe. Here the buildings and lands of the homestead are of the greatest symbolic significance, for they are inherited intact with each successive marriage.

A variation of the stem family occurred in China and Japan, where only the senior homestead was kept in the hands of a single line. Lands were carved into new homesteads for younger sons. The form was thus often a transitional one between the great fortunes of an extended family of the gentry and the many little farms of their peasant descendants.

To describe the natural history of a western European stem family, let us start with a man, his wife, and their children living on the homestead. When the parents are old, at least old enough to feel feeble at farm work, they choose one child as heir, such as the youngest son. By choosing the youngest, the old couple can hang on to the property as long as possible.

The chosen heir inherits at the time of his marriage; he and his wife are expected to bear children for the next generation. His siblings may stay on at the homestead as unpaid help as long as they do not marry. When they marry, the household head is expected to give them a dowry comparable to the one his own wife brought with her. But they inherit no real estate from the family holdings. This system can be simply diagrammed, as shown in Figure 16.3.

One of the best described examples of the stem family is that of the peasantry of western Ireland (Arensberg and Kimball, 1968; Arensberg, 1937). When an old couple decide to retire, they find a spouse for their selected heir. If they have picked a daughter to inherit, they find her a husband. The match is made with parents from another homestead, and the dowry of the spouse who marries in, man or woman, reflects the worth of both families' farms. At the time the dowry is handed over, the old couple sign a marriage contract deeding the farm to the new couple. The farmhouse is a cottage with two rooms: to the east the kitchen with hearth and sleeping loft; to the west the formal parlor (see Figure 16.4). The old couple retain residence rights in the west room of the cottage, where they remain until their death and passage to the land of the dead—the West, in Irish folklore.

While the Irish case is a rural one, stem family systems extend to shopkeepers, nobility, and royal lines in western Europe. As practiced by the aristocracy, however, the system differs. The inheritance rule is not left to pragmatic choice but is explicitly that of *primogeniture*, whereby the eldest

Figure 16.3 Stem family.

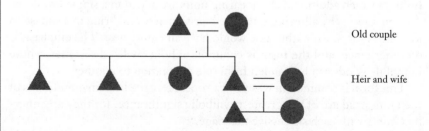

Old couple

Heir and wife

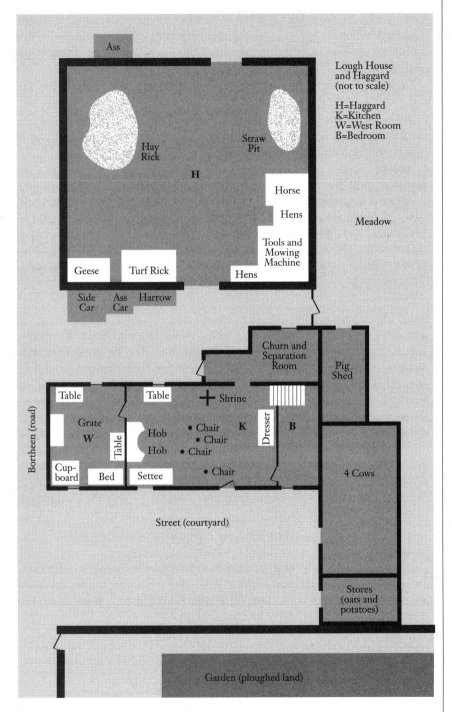

Figure 16.4 Schematic plan of an Irish peasant stem family homestead. Note the west room to which the old couple retires.

Lough House and Haggard (not to scale)

H=Haggard
K=Kitchen
W=West Room
B=Bedroom

Ass

Hay Rick

Straw Pit

H

Horse

Hens

Tools and Mowing Machine

Hens

Geese

Turf Rick

Meadow

Side Car

Ass Car

Harrow

Churn and Separation Room

Pig Shed

Table

Table

Shrine

Grate

W

Hob

Hob

Chair

Chair

Chair

K

Dresser

B

Table

Chair

Cup-board

Bed

Settee

Chair

4 Cows

Bortheen (road)

Street (courtyard)

Stores (oats and potatoes)

Garden (ploughed land)

son inherits. National laws differ as to whether they allow a female to inherit a title when there is no male heir. Under Salic law, females could not inherit the throne of France; disputes regarding this law led to wars of succession over the throne of Spain.

Stem family forms emphasize the symbols of the unbroken lineage and its indivisible property. Among the nobility, the property was protected by *laws of entail*, which specified which holdings must pass along with the title. But the family line was symbolized by the family seat, often a castle or manor house, and by the coat of arms and family crest.

Among Basque peasants, such symbolism is very highly developed. The surname of the family is the place name of the homestead. If a woman brings a husband into the homestead as her spouse, their children still bear the name of the house, although this custom contradicts Spanish national law. In addition, each homestead has its own burial plot on the floor of the parish church. Here the mistress of the house stands every Sunday during mass with a lighted taper, commemorating all the dead of the homestead in an unbroken line through the past (Douglass, 1969).*

The Irish Countryfolk

The Irish countryfolk studied by Conrad Arensberg and Solon Kimball in the 1930s are also a good example of open peasantry. The small farm families they studied in County Clare in western Ireland are scattered around the countryside in small homesteads, clustering in small groups on either side of a road. Each holds title to scattered fields; each grows a variety of livestock, from chickens and goats in the farmyard to cattle and horses in more distant pastures.

These country people are well integrated into national culture through several institutions. First, they are fervent Roman Catholics, participating in the mass, communion, and confession as dispensed by their parish priests (Arensberg and Kimball, 1968; Arensberg, 1937). Second, they participate in urban marketplaces, buying many of their foodstuffs and clothing from shopkeepers and selling their produce, especially calves, to acquire the necessary cash.

However, country people attempt to close their land resources from the open market. They limit purchases of land as far as possible to persons whose ancestry entitles them to it. That is, if there is no heir for a homestead, first rights to purchase go to relatives of the previous owners.

---

*One extreme variation of the stem family household is polyandrous households—found notably among Tibetan peasants where *all* the brothers of a single land-holding homestead expect to share the same wife while inheriting the household equally. For an excellent study see Levine (1988). This form—like all stem families—is an adaptation to perceived scarce resources but is less open to the wider civilization than the usual varieties.

It is the Irish stem family system, however, that is their most intense link to the national culture. The Irish countryman not only keeps a single heir on the family homestead each generation, he also exports other offspring to the towns by marrying his daughters "up" (hypergamy) and by apprenticing his

sons to shopkeepers. The Irish stem family household consists of the retired grandparents, one chosen heir and his or her spouse, and other siblings with no claim whatever on the real estate of the homestead. A farmer arranges his children's future, finding a spouse from another farm family. He "walks the farm" of the girl's parents, negotiates the dowry, and draws up a wedding contract that deeds the farm to the new couple upon their marriage.

If any daughters marry shopkeepers from the towns, the amount of the dowry reflects not only the worth of her farm but the worth of the shop

An Irish farm community.

into which she is marrying. Her relatives become customers at her shop, and in return she and her husband are lenient in extending credit and flexible about collecting debts.

Sons are sent to the towns in a similar manner and are apprenticed to shopkeepers and artisans. The process of placing a boy in a shop as an apprentice closely resembles matchmaking. The farmer inspects the shop and its premises; the shopkeeper and his family live upstairs and the boy is to board there. Then the two sit down with an attorney and draw up an indenture agreement by which the master agrees to take the boy for two or three years, train him, and provide room and board. In return, the boy's father makes an indenture payment, comparable to a dowry.

Several years later, the apprentice becomes a salaried journeyman, an accredited shopkeeper's assistant. He saves money, and with the last of his "dowry" from his father, he sets up his own shop. At that point, he goes and "walks the land" of a farm girl, marries, gets her dowry, and brings in her relatives as customers. The system is open-ended, for in the next generation there is a tendency for the sons of successful shopkeepers to go to the university, enter the professions, leave town, and sell their shops to aspiring new shopkeepers, formerly farm-boy apprentices.

CLOSED CORPORATE PEASANT COMMUNITIES

Closed peasant communities have been studied so often that anthropologists are in danger of confusing them with peasantries in general. Such communities are easy to recognize because of their stubborn adherence to local ways. They tend to form corporations with legal title to land or other resources, are endogamous (refusing to marry outsiders), form one civil body dealing with the state through a single headman, and form one ritual congregation. They further tend to make a cult of their own hard-shell borders, which however are not totally impermeable. They send labor (either temporary or permanent, in migrating offspring), tribute, and produce for sale across their local borders at the behest of urban elites. I shall not discuss all varieties but rather only two examples that are close to the North American experience.

The Original Communes: European Wheat Villages

The closed corporate peasant villages found throughout Europe are closely related to similar forms in the Middle East and India (Arensberg, 1963; Moore, 1984). The European wheat village is the origin of New England Puritan villagers. Territorially, the wheat village is recognized by a precise ecological pattern: an open expanse of wheat fields, usually on level ground or plains, stretching around and away from a tight cluster of houses.

Inside the settlement, there is a church or shrine; an open space, for threshing wheat and for assemblies; and common fountains for watering people and animals (see Figure 16.5). The basic foods of these villagers are breads made from their grains and the products of cattle: cheeses, yogurts, butter, and beef. (It is these foods, beef and milk especially, that give Europeans

Figure 16.5 Ecology and settlement of a wheat village.

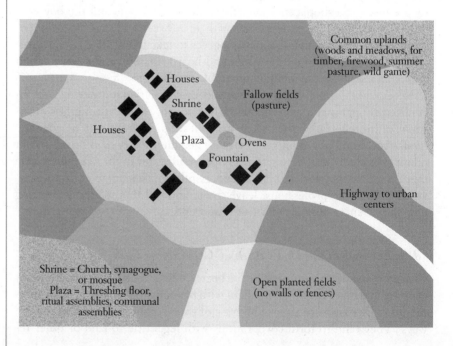

Common uplands (woods and meadows, for timber, firewood, summer pasture, wild game)

Houses

Shrine

Fallow fields (pasture)

Houses

Plaza

Ovens

Fountain

Highway to urban centers

Shrine = Church, synagogue, or mosque
Plaza = Threshing floor, ritual assemblies, communal assemblies

Open planted fields (no walls or fences)

their distinctive "stink" to the nostrils of Chinese, for example, who consume no milk.)

The fields of such a village are unfenced and are usually plowed in common, often by an ox team belonging to the village. Because the best way to grow wheat is in broad unbroken fields, the internal economy of such a village is redistributional. Originally (and even now in eastern Europe and the Israeli kibbutzim), village lands were held in common. In some cases, the land was worked by age-graded work teams. In other cases, as in the Middle East, the harvest was redistributed from a common grain pile in harvest ceremonies. In medieval Europe it was more common to assign individual households separate plots, but to rotate them each planting season so that each family harvested a different section each year.

Israeli Kibbutzim are among current forms of communal villages.

Such communal activities and redistributional devices require common consent and strong leadership, usually in the form of an assembly of adult male householders. An executive council of elders, rather like the Cheyenne peace chiefs, presides over the assembly, sets the dates for agricultural tasks, and apportions activities among the various workers.

The social life of such a community is unusually coherent. The English word **commune** applies fully to it. The village is a ritual unit as well as a small republic; the congregation assembles around the shrine (church, mosque, or synagogue). Elders of the congregation and executives of the village council are drawn from the same age grade. The same men take turns in both offices when they are not in fact one and the same body.

In Europe and the Middle East, wheat villages are endogamous. The Middle East and the Balkans tend toward patrilocal extended family households, the rest of Europe toward the stem family, or especially the small nuclear family.

The wheat village has always been linked politically and economically to the wider society. In medieval Europe, this was accomplished through feudal institutions. A fief or manor was held by a nobleman to whom villagers owed an oath of loyalty. Their lord relied on them for men in arms and for provisions, his "dues." In Europe, feudal military obligations were entirely abolished. In France, Great Britain, and much of Germany, feudal dues were translated into property rights in land. The lord became landlord, something he never was in the Middle Ages. In Great Britain, as a consequence, the peasants either were expelled from the villages (in the enclosure movement) or remained as tenants paying rents. In tsarist Russia, they remained serfs on the land until the 1860s; after emancipation the nobility retained title to the land. Peasants still met their obligations to noblemen by share-cropping and contributing labor to farm the lord's private fields.

Valdemora: Long-Term Balance Through Competitive Courtship

In much of Europe the communal wheat village lingers in some form. A study by Susan Tax Freeman (1970) describes such a village, Valdemora, in a mountain valley in Old Castile. Here a hamlet of seventeen households forms a civil and ritual corporation that holds much land in common and survives through an open and competitive marriage and inheritance system.

The houses are clustered around its church and an open threshing floor. The unfenced, irrigated wheat fields stretch outward on the valley floor. Higher on the hillsides are pastures and woodlands held in common by the village corporation through an ancient feudal grant from the Duke of Medinaceli, to whom the commune still pays collective dues.

The Spanish land reforms of the 1840s abolished communal title in wheat fields, which are now held by individual households. However, the village council regulates their use. Half the wheat fields lie fallow, unplanted, each year, and all villagers may graze their cattle there. The council also regulates the use of public irrigation waters. Communal tasks of cowherd and baker are rotated by the council, and each year a different household takes its turn.

A town assembly of all the male married heads of households makes the decisions necessary to regulate the open fields and the communal pastures. Today the national government appoints a slate of officers to head the assembly (the commune), but in the past these offices were probably occupied by seniority. The assembly is a Roman Catholic congregation—officially, as a parish, and also as a grassroots ritual brotherhood devoted to the Castilian saint San Isidro Labrador, a peasant.

Another ritual brotherhood is a burial society for the funerals of all villagers. Brotherhoods are officially distinct from the commune, although the membership of all three is exactly the same. Office in ritual brotherhoods is held by seniority. New brothers of San Isidro are newly married householders; they are obliged to sponsor the fiesta of the saint and feast the entire village with bread, wine, and sweets.

Life is highly age graded. At age seventeen, every male youth enters the company of bachelors by staking them all to a round of drinks—after which, he can spend evenings with his buddies and court a girl. As in all Spanish villages, courtship takes place in full view of the public in the streets. Coming of age and getting married are crucial to the whole system.

Marriage and inheritance are free, open, and competitive, but the number of farming households in the village has remained constant at seventeen for centuries. Of each generation, no more than seventeen married couples actually remain in the village. To get married, a young man and woman must pool resources and must have a house and sufficient plots in the wheat fields to support a family. Moreover, newly married householders must pay an entrance fee to the commune—in addition to staking the village to the fiesta of San Isidro—and not all are able to do so. Thus, some never marry, and others seek their fortunes in the cities, where they usually marry spouses from the village.

Because the process of courtship entails saving and pooling resources, savings start early. A boy at age fourteen works for his father for wages, which he saves to buy land. He also must win his parents' favor. Although inheritance is legally equal among all siblings, it is possible for parents during their lifetimes to give away some of their holdings. Parents also may rent a house for newlyweds.

A girl sews, stitches, and amasses a hope chest of clothing, enough to last for years to come, helped by gifts from her parents. Couples are likely to be engaged ten years or more, and they manipulate their parents jointly. The culmination of this laborious engagement is a house and "estate" of wheat fields in all sections of the plain, and an expensive wedding ceremony followed by the feast of San Isidro. The couple then truly belongs to the commune as they set up housekeeping and at last prepare to have children.

E T H N O G R A P H I C   C L O S E - U P

ALOTENANGO, A MAYA CLOSED CORPORATE COMMUNITY

The wheat village is of great antiquity. Indeed, Conrad Arensberg (1963), who defined the type, believes that it originated in the Mesopotamian villages surrounding the nucleated, walled city. It is so much a part of Old World culture that Spaniards exported it to the New World. Thus, American Indians, who had never planted wheat or plowed but rather cultivated maize with digging sticks and hoes, were forced into communal communities. (In the

Peru of the Incas, Indian communities had long been communal.)

Some Indians successfully resisted populating the settlements laid out for them in four squares around a church and plaza, and they stayed scattered over the countryside. But even without nucleated settlement, and even without wheat and plows, Spanish Empire Indians everywhere came to practice the social forms of a closed community with a fervor that surpassed the European original.

I studied such a community, Alotenango,* in Guatemala—four wards around a Franciscan friary and a monumental church that could hold thousands of worshipers (Moore, 1973). The nearby courthouse

---

*As mentioned in Chapter 13 in the portrait of the shaman from Alotenango, Socorro Marroquín, all my previous publications refer to the community as "Atchalán." With the passage of time that pseudonym is no longer necessary.

was originally just a large thatched hut. The sandy expanse of the plaza accommodates assemblies of householders and a Sunday market as well.

Mesoamerican Indian communities are more intensely closed than European wheat villages. Since the fifteenth century, the population of Europe has increased tremendously, putting great pressure on the land. Yet in the Spanish New World, the population remained low for centuries, the land nearly empty. The pressure that native villages first experienced was more a Spanish effort to capture their labor than a need to exploit their land. In many countries a truce was worked out between Indian villages, protected by both church and crown, and Spanish Creole cities. Indians kept their communal lands in return for yielding up their labor, often in the form of corvées. The effect, however, was to turn the Indians fiercely inward toward their communities.

In Spanish Indian communities, there was little competition for lands until recently; all men were likely to establish households. Today all men participate in civil and religious offices. Energies are focused not so much on households and courtship as on "bearing a cargo"—that is, achieving the higher offices of civil and religious organizations, which unlike their Spanish originals are hierarchies of many linear ranks divided into groups of officers, sergeants, and unranked fellows. All achieve sergeant ranking, but perhaps only a third achieve officer status, and of these only a fraction take the highest posts to become elders ("ancients"), something like living ancestors.

The Patriarchal Family: A Model for Community Organization

Civil and religious organizations are built on the model of a three-generational patrilocal extended family household living under the authority of a grandfather/patriarch. Unlike the Spaniards, these Indians do not exalt the nuclear family; rather, they tend to cluster in extended family compounds. By applying this model to their organizational life, they are relentlessly repeating one message: "We are one great family strictly ordered by seniority." Not all, however, achieve grandfather status.

A grandfather/patriarch, respected elder of Alotenango, stands with his wife and great-grandchildren at the doorway of his ceremonial hut. Note the couple's clothing, traditional and distinctive of Alotenango.

Such residential extended family compounds consist of many huts surrounding the grand ceremonial hut of the patriarch. Some of his adult sons may also have such grand huts; in their shadow are the sleeping huts of their own married sons. When such a family group appears in public, which it might do on a Sunday, the grandfather goes first, his sons follow by order of birth, and his young adult or adolescent grandsons bring up the rear or the sides in an unranked grouping. The movement can be simply diagrammed as shown in Figure 16.6.

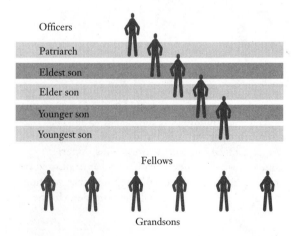

Figure 16.6 Alotenango three-generational extended family grouping in public.

416

The Civil-Religious Hierarchy

This formation is repeated in the civil government organization. Instead of the simple assembly and council of Valdemora, there is a rigid rank order. The senior official, the mayor, comes first, assisted by his staff of five aldermen ranked two through six. Under them is a large company of village guards or constables (*ministriles*), an age grade of youths (analogous to the warrior age grades of many societies). The company is composed of six patrols of eighteen youths. Each patrol consists of three senior cadet officers, or sergeants ranked one, two, three, and fourteen fellows who are unranked peers, although some may be doing a repeated year of service and are therefore implicitly senior to neophytes. The civil hierarchy is simply diagrammed in Figure 16.7.

The ritual organization of Alotenango, the congregation, consists not of two simple brotherhoods, as in Valdemora, but of seven rigidly rank-ordered brotherhoods, each dedicated to the cult of a saint; the saints are themselves ranked in serial order from senior to junior. Each brotherhood is directed by its mayor, or chief steward, and his four assistant stewards, ranked two through five. At ritual meals they are served by five pasados, younger men doing their third service for a brotherhood, who in turn direct five deputies, a still more junior set of ranked brothers. Assisting them are some fifteen to twenty unranked young men, newlyweds for the most part, who have served their first year as unmarried village constables (see Figure 16.8).

Rotating the Cargos

Each office in the **civil/religious hierarchy** in Middle American villages is known as a **cargo** ("burden"). Cargos are conceived of as sacrificial offerings to the deities (saints) they honor, or to the community's ancestors.

In Alotenango, advancement in the ranks of the civil and religious hierarchies—that is, in the rank and prestige of the cargo assumed—is not assured to all men. Men who achieve the rank of alderman or steward form a village elite from whom are drawn the elders who direct the whole system. However, all men pass through the lowest age grade in both civil and religious organizations, get married, and discharge their public obligations by achieving at least the sergeant level in both hierarchies. Once they have done that, they have carried the minimum cargo. Thus, they have publicly validated their claim to manhood and their right to raise families in their households.

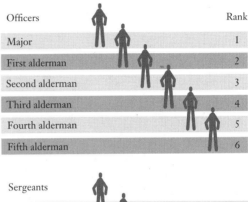

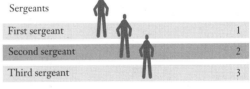

There are six patrols, each with three sergeants and fifteen constables.

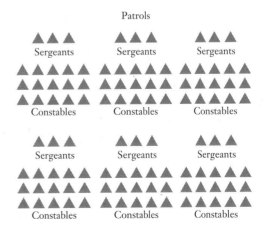

Figure 16.7 Alotenango civil hierarchy.

Figure 16.8 The religious hierarchy of a brotherhood in Alotenango.

Officers

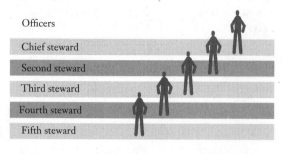

Chief steward
Second steward
Third steward
Fourth steward
Fifth steward

Sergeants

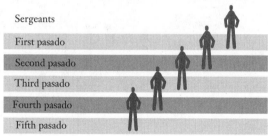

First pasado
Second pasado
Third pasado
Fourth pasado
Fifth pasado

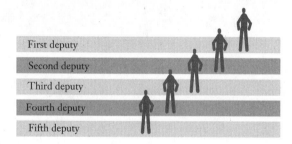

First deputy
Second deputy
Third deputy
Fourth deputy
Fifth deputy

Fellows

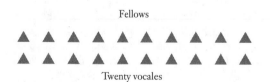

Twenty vocales

In terms of a male life cycle, all boys are drafted as constables on the New Year's Day following their eighteenth birthday. After their year of service (in which they take a one-week turn out of every six), they are free to marry. Then they might serve as a ritual servant for a brotherhood. Theoretically, they owe the civil government every third year as constables until their fortieth birthday. But the years they serve brotherhoods are excused. Moreover, once they serve as sergeant, they "graduate" from civil office and never have to serve again. A term as alderman is strictly voluntary. Likewise, on the religious side, the man who serves as a pasado in his third brotherhood graduates from religious service. He could decline when the elders ask him to become a steward, but he would be shamed.

A mere one-third of those eligible become officers (aldermen or stewards). Of these, fewer still graduate from the entire system to become elders, men who used to recruit the civil officers and still recruit the religious ones today. Before the national government took over the civil offices in 1935, the two sides were closely coordinated. The man who agreed to the elders' request to serve as mayor was also obligated to serve as steward for the patron and ranking saint, San Juan, on the following year. Because he had already sponsored a lesser fiesta, the ranking one would cost him the rest of his life savings. In return, however, he would be welcomed to the status of elder, titular great-grandfather, waiting for death while directing all junior officers.

The fellows of the brotherhood of San Francisco in Alotenango push and shove as they enter the compound of their chief steward, bearing the sacred case to house the saint's statue during its sojourn there for the next two years.

Elder is the highest status Alotenango can offer its citizens. It is rife with symbolic honors. The elder and his wife take the senior places at any gathering. When they die, they lie alone in state in the church. An old and priceless crucifix rests upon their bier. In the same spot, on All Soul's Day, another bier is covered with little yellow flowers (*flores de muerto*); on this bier is a primitive carving of a male and female pair, All Souls, ancient ancestors of all Alotecos. To die an elder is to achieve a certain immortality in Alotenango.

By identifying the graduates of the civil and religious hierarchy with All Souls and with the ancestors of all the living, Alotecos reward these great-grandfather figures with their greatest local honors. This is only one manifestation of the richness of their folk cults. Such cults tend to focus the careers of individual men inward toward local dramas and local honors.

The Cult of Judas: Resistance and Ambivalence Toward Urban Hispanic Culture

In contrast to the cult of the official saints and their cargos, the cult of Judas involves symbols of danger, ambivalence, and outsiders. On Tuesday of Holy Week, the constables at the courthouse set up a life-size figure of Judas behind a table, light a candle in his honor, and place a collection plate for offerings in front of him. While other saints' images are finely carved statues, that of Judas is a tied-up bundle of clothes with a mask like that worn by Spaniards in dance dramas portraying the Conquest of Guatemala. During Holy Week, the constables stuff this life-size doll with fresh leaves. A cigarette is kept burning between his lips, and he is dressed in a soft hat, shopkeeper's vest, white shirt, large tie, khaki trousers, leather belt, and good shoes. In short, his attire is identical to that of the Ladino (non-Indian) plantation managers and shopkeepers of the region.

Judas's day is Easter Saturday, when God is dead and in the tomb. The constables take Judas on a lengthy procession around town, stopping with a marimba at the compounds of many adult men, who give them cash offerings and ceremonial toasts of liquor in honor of Judas. The hosts dance with the doll to the strains of the holiday marimba. This goes on all day. A raucous evening finale occurs at the courthouse, where the youths hold open house, repeating the music and dancing with Judas for all comers. Before nightfall they carefully unstuff Judas and hide the bundle away for the coming year.

Judas, Alotecos told me, looks after the man who gives him cash offerings, who toasts his health, and who dances with him by protecting him from any misfortune in drunkenness and revelry during the coming year. One Aloteco told me that Judas had been good to him—he had never in his life been arrested for drunken brawling or had any misfortune whatever while drunk!

The cult of Judas only shadowily reflects the Passion of Jesus Christ, but that, too, is told in Alotenango. On Good Friday, devotees nail a statue

Two stuffed Judas figures hang from the wall of the provincial barracks in Antigua, Guatemala, near Alotenango. Indian peasant conscript soldiers put them there. Note the soccer ball tied between the legs of one. Its maker wants good luck in sports in the coming year.

of Christ to a cross in the church; that evening they take another one, a huge statue of Christ bearing the cross, and carry it in a glass coffin in a lengthy funeral procession. The next day, however, Judas takes over. Like the mayor, he sits behind a desk at the courthouse and collects money. (The mayor collects fines in punishment for public brawling; by giving Judas offerings, his devotees hope to avoid paying fines later.)

Judas, after all, as an elder of Alotenango assured me, "is both sainted and accursed." He represents authority figures higher than the mayor—judge, governor, president—all Ladinos. Judas's face is that of the Spanish conquistador. He is thus the hated outsider who paradoxically brought Christianity and made the Indians "people."

Alotecos have had a long and tense relationship with Spaniards and Ladinos. During centuries of colonial rule, they paid tribute to the crown and sent corvées to work for officials and aristocrats. From the 1870s until 1920, corvées were revived with great intensity, and many Alotecos sought relief by becoming indentured peons on coffee plantations that had taken over some of the former communal lands. Today, although peonage or debt servitude has long been abolished, the population has increased so greatly that most young Indians must work as day laborers on the plantations. Land hunger has assured the aristocrats of a cheap labor force. Aloteco Indians are also important producers of maize on the regional market, and they traffic daily with Ladino merchants now living in their midst. Economically, Ladino plantation managers and shopkeepers are a necessary evil, like Judas who wears their clothing exactly.

It is no accident that the cult of Judas is conducted by the village guards, Indian youths who quell internal quarrels (usually drunken) and protect the community. They are armed with machetes only, however, and have never been allowed to bear firearms, mount horses, or take action against Ladino city folk. These youthful police, in whose company every boy must serve to become a man, appease the symbolic outsider, the accursed saint, collecting cash offerings for him, drinking his toasts, dancing with him, and then surreptitiously dismembering him and hiding the bundle away until the next year.

In Alotenango, as in all Mesoamerican closed corporate peasant communities, forms inherited from the European wheat village have been elaborated and intensified. It is one of the most intense social forms, revived in the Western experience as a morally exalted one. The continuing appeal of the commune is demonstrated by such old intentional communities as the New England Puritans and the Hutterites and such twentieth-century ones as the Bruderhof (described in an excellent study by Zablocki, 1971), the Israeli kibbutz, and other collectives. For its encapsulated citizen, the commune is a fortress of strength amidst the tumultuous dangers of civilized powers.

TOWN- AND CITY-DWELLING PEASANTS: URBAN AGRARIAN PLEBEIANS

Finally, there are the peasant food producers, who, in the Mediterranean world at least, often live in face-to-face contact with their lords, the local patrician land owners. The two-class patrician-plebeian distinction goes back to the rise of the Greek city-state. **Patricians** tend to be literate, and full participants in the urban culture. **Plebeians** tend to be the opposite, rooted in place.

In central Spain, for example, Belmonte de los Caballeros, studied by Lisón-Tolosana (1966), is an example. It is nothing so much as a larger Valdemora dominated by an upper-class elite. In the first place, there are unfenced fields in a rich irrigated valley floor belonging largely to the sixty-one patrician households. Forty-nine households of yeoman own enough land to support themselves without seeking outside work. The patricians prefer to live along the main street, a highway lined with three-story homes.

A Spanish agrotown.

The yeomen and newly wed patricians live on the other central streets in two-story homes. Most of the plebeians, some 225 households who do the hard agricultural labor for wages, live in caves on the hillside overlooking the town.

The patricians practice the same patterns of marriage, estate formation, and inheritance as the Valdemorans. They dominate the local council, which through its festival committee is also the community's religious body.

Belmonte has been stratified for at last 400 years. The distinctive feature of the Mediterranean culture area is its combination of the open-field, nucleated settlement pattern with a large class of town-dwelling agrarian laborers and a smaller class of aristocrats. Dating from antiquity, Mediterranean urbanity encompasses a pervasive worldview, the enclosed urban settlement pattern, and class stratification.

The next example, Estepa, studied by Gregory (1972), is much further down the road to urbanity. Estepa is an Andalusian **agrotown** of great antiquity, whose population of 9,000 live close together against a hilly slope. Estepa has, foremost, a powerful group of noble and gentry families, who live close to the castle in their own ward in town; second, a larger agrarian proletarian population (80 percent of the total) living within the town; third, nine satellite villages comprising a total of some 35,000 persons, all agrarian laborers, under Estepa's municipal jurisdiction; and fourth, the *cortijos*, or great estates of the aristocrats, on the plain below the town.

One further example finds plebeian peasants right inside a small city. Trujillo is a preindustrial city in the western Spanish province of Extremadura (Schwarz, 1972). Like Estepa, it is densely populated (there were 12,500 people in Trujillo at the time of the study). The bulk of the residents are agrarian laborers, settled in a total of thirteen barrios or wards around the ancient center of the city, which is graced by the castle and the palaces of the gentry. The numerous palaces and churches particularly interest students of architecture, but of special symbolic importance is their association with many families holding the rank of grandee of Spain. Further, these buildings are of international importance because of their association with the Pizarro family, conquerors of Peru. The grandest achievements of Spain's aristocracy are enshrined around the plaza of Trujillo.

Unlike Estepa, Trujillo also has its center of artisanry. In this quarter, each craft and guild has its own street, bearing its name. Nearby are the shopkeepers' retail establishments. Both artisans and shopkeepers often live over their shops. Trujillo also has a Thursday market and four yearly fairs.

Trujillo's artisans, retailers, market, and fairs give it its "cityness." These are the nodes that draw countrymen to the city. But alongside the rural peasants who come to town from elsewhere, the bulk of Trujillo's "urban" population work the fields belonging to the great families whose palaces dominate the city. These urban agrarian peasants are seemingly the most powerless of any of the folk we have considered. They do not own the resources necessary for their livelihood but must depend on the patricians for access to land. Far from being demoralized, however, they use the moral claims of friendship to exact favors from their patrons. As inevitable clients, they learn to manipulate patronage by personal appeals to their traditional lords. Theirs is a hard life, but they can temper their lot by the implicit threat of rioting or causing a civil disturbance if things go very wrong.

States have generally given patricians the obligation to raise troops and lead them, so urban agrarian plebeians have been a prime source of manpower for armies as well.

SUMMARY AND CONCLUSIONS

The two previous chapters stressed the urban, commanding heights of civilized cultures and communities; this chapter has stressed the agrarian or pastoralist, folk side of civilizations. All cultures, whether tribal or urban civilized, are in flux on long cycles. These cycles range from the fluxes caused by heroic or prophetic human lifetimes, on the scale of around 90 years, to dynastic cycles of 350 to 550 years, to even longer-scale dissolutions and reformulations of civilizations on scales of 500 to 1,200 years. These last cycles are influenced by events such as epidemics, natural disasters, and the migrations of whole peoples. These events in turn have much to do with local ecological balance between resources and populations.

Alongside most traditional civilized areas have always been marginal regions inhabited by *insolents*, who refuse to pay tribute and are ever eager to exact a subsidy from the state by force of arms. These communities flourish or decline according to the strength of the state and according to their ability to play rival states off against each other. Thus, the Cruzob survived as long as they could play the British off against Mexico. The Cruzob were the product of a revitalization movement, itself born of a peasant rebellion, in turn born from peasant protest against their fratricidal involvement in a civil war between two cities, Campeche and Merida. Insolents always have local political autonomy, maintained by miniature standing armies of all their adult men. They deal with their own disputes, often through blood feud and mediation of holy men. They may or may not share the religion of regional urban elites.

In contrast, no peasantry ever has political and military independence from the urban state. Open peasantries, like the Irish countryfolk, are linked in some way, along some institutional dimension (kinship and marriage, ritual and organized religion, shopkeeping and markets) to the urban elites. Yet they remain rural, and remain in control of their land in a traditional pattern of inheritance through the stem family system. The pattern of scattered, indivisible homesteads, handed over at marriage to a single heir and new spouse, is an ancient one. At times the Irish peasantry could practice it, if at all, only as tenant farmers on estates belonging to the Anglo-Irish aristocracy. In the late nineteenth century the Irish peasantry reemerged as scattered landowning small farmers. They linked themselves to the towns by marrying their daughters, with dowries, to shopkeepers. They also apprenticed some of their sons to shopkeepers, providing them with the equivalents of dowries.

Closed corporate communities, which may be as old as the cities of Mesopotamia, have always hidden behind a hard shell of symbols and practices that exclude outsiders. Some limit themselves to outside ties through the mediation of a headman or a few elders and to impersonal transactions in safe marketplaces. Their settlement pattern makes perfect ecological sense for a possible Mesopotamian origin in antiquity: Open wheat fields around a nucleated cluster of dwellings allow for common plowing and common grazing of the necessary oxen and other cattle. An open plaza is a threshing floor, a ritual and political assembly place, and the ground for redistribution of grains.

These peasant corporations provide for psychological and physical safety for their members at the cost of innovation or of any sort of adventurous lives. These communities are by nature conservative. But most of all, they attempt to conserve their most vital resource, land, and hand it on intact to a generation no more numerous than its own. They do not always succeed in that, and more pressure on the land, and hence on the community, results. Such communities have a fair degree of internal local political autonomy. They may handle internal legal disputes themselves, but they are never independent economic or military entities. We examined two such communities in widely different culture areas: Castilian Spain and Hispanic Maya Guatemala.

For its part, the elite assumes itself to be the source of benevolent rewards in exchange for rural tributes, especially from closed corporate peasant communities. All states provide their subjects with judges to whom they may take disputes. All states construct public works, without which village agriculture would decline, or even vanish in lands dependent upon irrigation and drainage. State troops and garrisons defend villages from insolent folk tribesmen in the hills or deserts who are ready to lay waste to peasant crops. In addition, state rituals provide symbolic satisfaction without price when peasants partake of them as confirmed participants and true believers.

Finally, many agrarianists are actual town or city dwellers, forced into some face-to-face personal relation with the elites, upon whom they depend, often totally, for access to land to farm. Such dependence can breed explosive tensions, and riots and revolts can result. But such explosions usually serve to let off steam by giving expression to anger, and by lowering population pressure through killings they allow conditions to return rather quickly to the status quo.

Overall, the variety and complexity of folk cultures has only been hinted at in this chapter. We have not discussed the Hindu wheat villages of the north India plains, for example, where each village is divided into members of separate castes, loosely assigned an occupational or craft specialty. Each caste marries its daughters to fellow caste members of other villages in a wide circle over the plain. The villagers almost reincorporate artisans and handcrafts into the folk culture, although they do not make fine luxury goods, which are left to urban specialists, nominally of their same caste.

Such specializations and complications are not limited to India. In traditional highland Guatemala, for example, each Maya-speaking village had its own craft specialty to supplement agricultural production. That of Alotenango was to manufacture native plywood boxes for sweets. This practice has largely died out today. But on the outskirts of Guatemala City, the women of Chinautla, a closed corporate community, have long been potters. As the community's population grows, and the city encroaches, the men have largely become urban laborers or helpers in their wives' cottage workshops. Chinautla is becoming an ethnic urban ward of female potters and their families (Reina, 1960, 1966).

Folk cultures and communities are thus as various and complex as uncivilized tribes. But they differ from tribes by always being conditioned in some sense by the urban elites with whom they are in some sort of dialogue. We must remember that the elites themselves are in flux. They are often at odds with each other, and their wars can draw in peasants to fights not of their making, with outcomes no one expected, as in the birth of the Cruzob.

The modern world since A.D. 1500 is in greater and faster flux than was characteristic of the first 6,000 years of civilized existence in Eurasia. That change is sped by two institutional emergences: legal-rational bureaucracy on the one hand and price-regulated markets on the other. We'll get to these topics in Part V.

SUGGESTED READINGS

Arensberg, Conrad M., and Solon T. Kimball. *Family and Community in Ireland*, rev. ed. Cambridge, Mass.: Harvard University Press, 1968. An excellent account of interplay of peasant families, marketing, marketplaces, and towns.

Barth, Fredrik. *Nomads of South Persia: The Basseri Tribe of the Khamseh Confederacy*. Prospect Heights, Ill.: Waveland Press, 1961. Discusses insolent tribes, kinship, tribal politics, and the political economy of nomadism.

Boehm, Christopher. *Blood Revenge: The Anthropology of Feuding in Montenegro and Other Tribal Societies*. Philadelphia: University of Pennsylvania Press, 1984. A superb ethnography of European mountaineering insolents.

Buechler, Hans C., and Judith-Maria Buechler. *The Bolivian Aymara*. Ft. Worth: Harcourt Brace Jovanovich, 1971. A concise analysis of a peasantry, revolutionary change, and market networks.

Keiser, Lincoln. *Friend by Day, Enemy by Night: Organized Vengeance in a Kohistani Community*. Ft. Worth: Harcourt Brace Jovanovich, 1991. More insolent mountaineers—these are in Pakistan.

Levine, Nancy E. *Dynamics of Polyandry: Kinship, Domesticity and Population on the Tibetan Border*. Chicago: University of Chicago Press, 1988. The most current ethnography on that peculiar stem family, polyandry, in which many husbands jointly marry a single wife.

Moore, Alexander. *Life Cycles in Atchalán: The Diverse Careers of Certain Guatemalans*. New York: Teachers College Press, 1973. Shows closed corporate peasants being proselytized by national bureaucrats, the schoolteachers. Indian ways of getting through life are contrasted with those of nonpeasants.

GLOSSARY

agrotown In the Mediterranean culture area, a large nucleated town, dominated by landowning aristocrats but largely inhabited by landless agrarian laborers, who must manipulate the patrician lords by claims of personal friendship and loyalty in order to get access to land.

cargo In Mexican and Guatemalan Indian closed corporate communities, the notion that a public office is a sacrificial offering, a cargo or burden, to be carried to gain favor with the deities and make the fields prosper.

civil/religious hierarchy In Mexican and Guatemalan Indian closed corporate communities, the organization of adult men into balanced hierarchies, one political, the other ritual. Assuming office in turn on each side is called a cargo, or "burden," and all men must do a minimal service in these inward-looking cults and offices. They are devices of closure.

civilized tribes Not to be confused with uncivilized tribes, the "insolents" on the margins of state-controlled regions, often nomads or pastoralists, who instead of paying tribute strive to force the state to pay *them* a subsidy. They maintain local political and military autonomy. They often terrorize peaceful settled peasants and extract "protection tribute" from them. They are common in the Middle Eastern deserts and mountains and across the "silk route" of central Asia.

closed peasant communities Communities of peasants forming a commune in control of some corporate resource. They are endogamous (refusing to marry outsiders), form one civil body dealing with the state through a single headman, and form one ritual congregation. They have local political autonomy but no military or economic independence.

communes Closed corporate peasant communities that hold communal title to some resource, usually land. An assembly of householders, usually dominated by elders on a principle of seniority, regulates commune affairs. European wheat villages are of this type.

corvée labor Conscripted labor, usually in gangs, to work on public projects or simply to labor on the estates of an aristocrat. A form of labor tribute, commonly exacted from peasants.

elites Urban peoples who are in charge of commanding institutions and who fully participate in the dominant culture politically.

folk Literally, "the people," the rural peoples who provide the food and domesticated animals for civilized societies, often through tribute, but including the marginal insolent peoples who resist state control by force of arms.

folk culture The local versions, often highly reinterpreted, or syncretic, of the official, urban, dominant culture of a civilized region. For example, both the Cruzob Maya and the peasant Maya of Alotenango have a highly particular local culture, drawing much from the ancient Maya past and much from the dominant Hispanic culture.

"insolents" Food producers or pastoralists who resist state control. See *civilized tribes*.

open peasants Peasants who are open to the dominant culture through a number of dimensions, such as marriage and kinship, religion, or placing their children in town and urban economic enterprises in regular patterned ways.

patricians Landowning upper-class elites, associated with Mediterranean towns and cities.

pastoralists People who herd grazing animals in large numbers. They may be fully nomadic, living in tents and constantly moving, or may merely follow their flocks from winter to summer pastures. Nomads tend to be insolent civilized tribesmen.

peasants Literally, "countrymen," agrarian food producers upon whom urban centers depend for a food supply.

plebeians Peasant masses, "urban agrarians," dwelling in agrotowns or even in small cities, dominated by patrician landowners.

stem family household A family unit extended along the lower generation by importing only one marriage partner for the designated heir. The homestead remains intact from generation to generation, thus conserving scarce resources, usually for peasants, but in some cases for aristocrats and royal dynasties as well.

syncretism The combination of elements from different cultures into a new cultural synthesis. For example, the Cruzob combined Latin ritual with the ancient Maya symbol of the cross as the gateway to the divine.

THE ANTHROPOLOGY OF MODERN LIFE

CHAPTER 17

The Market and the Modern Metropolis:
A New System of Exchange and the Rise of Commercial Industrial Cities

CHAPTER 18

Corporate Bureaucracy and the Culture of Modern Work

CHAPTER 19

Modernity and Culture

The modern world is one of constant growth and change at such an accelerated rate that human beings everywhere must come to grips with the pace of development within a single lifetime. Social transformations are channeled within dominant forms of culture and community; today that dominant form is the great metropolitan urban region. Three uniquely modern institutions are the *price-regulated market*, the *legal-rational bureaucracy*, and the *industrial factory system of production*.

The key transformations of modernity (and perhaps beyond into a "postmodern" era) center on the full emergence of these three institutions out of archaic prototypes. Just as human kinship and family emerged out of primate potentials, the capacity for impersonal exchange with strangers, practiced first in safe neutral havens ("ports of trade"), eventually emerged as a *market system*—that is, a system in which prices were self-regulating. (Such systems were swiftly regulated by the state in the interest of public welfare, however, as we shall see.)

Capitalism—the culture formed when price-regulated markets combined with the industrial factory system—favors careers open to talent in business, but it has proved unresponsive to the needs of laborers and to concerns about the environmental impact of technology. Capitalism has dissolved the traditional ties of both peasants and tribal peoples to the land and each other.

The second fully emergent institution was *legal-rational bureaucracy*, whose prototype in dynastic beginnings we have examined with the Ottomans and others. The latter emerged in the sixteenth-century "enlightened absolutist despotisms" of Europe, themselves competing with each other in vain attempts to found world empires, which culminated first with the Napoleonic Wars and then a century later in the two world wars and the Cold War of the twentieth century. Legal-rational bureaucracy has in the capitalist, as well as nonprofit, corporation become the dominant social form in modern life.

In the former socialist and Soviet economies of the "Soviet World" bloc, state legal-rational bureaucracies—unregulated by civil democracy—proved themselves unresponsive to their clients (the people) and to environmental concerns. The people of the former USSR and its Eastern European satellites have rejected that system and are attempting to build another, more responsive, one.

After 1500 A.D. no single absolute royal bureaucracy was ever able to control the developing market economies, as it was international. In fact, the international European market system flourished free of any one despot's control. Its merchants prepared the way for a price-regulated market system that was controlled by the laws of supply and demand and that enabled these same merchants to introduce industrialism and the factory system of production.

Preindustrial urban craft specialization in Eurasian central civilization was organized in workshops, each dominated by a master craftsman, who belonged to a guild. The life cycle of craftsmen began with masses of apprentices, many from peasant homes, all eager to join the age grade of journeymen: wage-earning accomplished workers. They in turn competed with each other to become masters by passing guild exams, demonstrating mastery of all phases of the production process and the capacity to produce a masterpiece. The Industrial Revolution transformed that system, harnessing masses of workers to machines, themselves harnessed to an exterior source of energy, and synchronizing the motions of the workers with those of the ma-

chine in vast assembly lines. Masters were displaced by merchant-capitalists and eventually by corporate managers. We examine what has happened to workers on the line in Chapter 18.

The community form resulting from industrialism was the mill town, the new dominant community of the early nineteenth century. The mill town in turn— when wedded to transport centers and the large-scale organization of trade, finance, transport, and communications in corporate bureaucracies—gave rise to the giant commercial metropolises, vast new cities in the form of giant circles. Chicago represents the archetype, as we shall see in Chapter 17.

The institutional growth of work in the modern world has transformed public life. The dominant form of work is the corporate bureaucracy, within which the factory is just one more bureaucratized and almost militarized workplace. The organization of workers in a factory or in any other corporation resembles that of the Baroque royal army: The precise movements of workers on the assembly line resemble the precise motions of soldiers marching and drilling on parade.

Science and technology—knowledge and material tools—drive modern culture. Merchant-industrialists ("capitalists") shaped the mill town in response to new machines. Baroque monarchs responded to science and laid out their capitals as sundials with themselves in the center to reflect Sir Isaac Newton's discoveries of the laws of gravity.

We shall examine in the next three chapters the currently dominant modern community form, the sprawling urban region (conurbation), and we shall also look at modern work, corporate organizations, and the relations of managers, workers, and machines. The public world of corporate bureaucracies has spawned a culture that philosopher/anthropologist Ernest Gellner (1988) has called "generic Protestantism." This is a culture of efficiency and reliability, in which each individual is literally a priest of order who finds satisfaction in unremitting work as a sign of his or her "vocation," a divinely inspired "calling" to work, and in which the entire fabric of society is pervaded with punctuality, order, and productivity.

In addition, with the rise of the university, professional vocations separated from the priesthood. Ideally, physicians, lawyers, engineers, scientists, and other scholars must be true to the ethics of their callings.

In contrast to the impersonal precision of work, we shall see that the household has become a haven of privacy and togetherness, having turned inward toward personal and private satisfactions. In response to the gap between workplace and household, a new institution—the school—has factored out of the ritualized age grades and apprenticeships of old. Formal schooling is now the bridge that takes young people out of the households of their birth and inducts them into giant corporate bureaucracies of work.

Two other bridges between private individuals and the public world, especially politics, are small informal cliques of friends—which resemble the political teams of primitive tribes—and more formal voluntary associations. These bridges link individuals to each other and to the political process. Universally, in modern nations, politics must first receive and then balance the demands of new groups for participation in the life of the center. Such demands include the conflicting claims of the corporate world and urban regions.

Friendship cliques and newly formed voluntary associations may reflect our human striving for a face-to-face community, something modern urban people have left behind in bands, tribal neighborhoods, and peasant villages.

Thus, the urban region (conurbation), corporate bureaucracies, private households, formal schooling, and voluntary associations make up the constellation of the modern metropolitan world. The spread of this constellation throughout the world is inexorable. In Chapter 19 we examine the impact of modernity on a formerly traditional culture, today's Japan. We also examine the interplay between modern culture and protest movements. Everywhere national and ethnic minorities, workers, women, and now—in the West—gays and lesbians, have formed protest movements bidding for more full access and participation in these modern institutions.

Finally, in the Epilogue, we consider the ongoing problems of parliamentary deliberation, rational policy making, and the prospects for both the citizen and the applied anthropologist in a multicultural, increasingly democratic, and deliberative public world.

The Market and the Modern Metropolis:

A New System of Exchange and the Rise of Commercial Industrial Cities

17

MARKETS AND MARKETPLACES

The Origin of Marketplaces: Ports of Trade

Staggered and Stellar Marketplaces

"Just Prices": Archaic Market Exchange as Generalized or Balanced Reciprocity

ETHNOGRAPHIC CLOSE-UP: WHYDAH, PORT OF TRADE

African-Administered Trade: Immutable "Fair" Prices

European "Market Prices"

MODERN POLITICS AND ECONOMICS: THE NATION-STATE AND MARKET SYSTEMS

Nation-States and the Theory of Economic Mercantilism

Price-Regulated Markets: The Full Emergence of a New Institution

Price-Regulated Markets and the Rise of Industrial Production

INDUSTRIAL MARKET SYSTEMS AND SETTLEMENT PATTERNS: THE SUCCESSION OF MODERN COMMUNITY TYPES

The Mill Town

The Modern Metropolis

    Concentric Circles

    Central Business District

    Urban Processes in a Lower-Class Residential District

    Other Zones

Cities with "Symbolic" Ecology

Conurbations: Sprawling Metropolitan Regions with Many Urban Centers

O ne certainty about the modern world has been the constancy of change. Modern people have been late in realizing this fact. At first, they strove to turn the known world into an empire, an eternal imperium of the Roman sort. They strove to manage public, imperial, economic life on the model of generalized reciprocity, as if the commonwealth were one huge household. An emerging institution, market systems, made that attempt impossible in the context of competing nation-states. Eventually market systems, wedded to machine-run industrialism, gave rise to new urban forms. The first new settlement pattern was the industrial mill town, which gave way to the commercial-industrial metropolis, which today has been succeeded by the seemingly formless sprawling conurbation of vast urban areas where many cities have grown together. Figure 17.1 provides an overview of the emergent institutions at this modern level of civilization.

MARKETS AND MARKETPLACES

Market exchange is quite unlike simple reciprocity, dominant in the world of bands, or redistribution, dominant in competitive feasting complexes and in traditional civilizations in the form of tribute. Rather, **market exchange** is the impersonal exchange of goods among persons who may be strangers. Anyone can trade anything with anyone else. This exchange is difficult to achieve and rare at tribal levels of society, where strangers are by definition dangerous, potential enemies.

Unlike other forms of reciprocity, market exchange is free of domestic, kin, ritual, or political relationships and depends instead entirely on the desire of the two partners for each other's goods. A market system can be represented abstractly as A/B A/C A/D A/E; B/C B/D B/E B/A; C/D C/E C/A C/B . . . All may trade and all combinations of trading partners appear.

The famous laws of supply and demand, formulated by Western economists, operate only in market exchange (although they occurred latently at first, since people thought prices were immutable, determined by divinely inspired tradition). The relative proportions of the goods exchanged depend

Justice
Law codes and state constitutions almost universal. International law and tribunals. Many nation-state governments unwilling to submit selves to their own or international law. In short, a gap between constitutions and "constitutionalism."

Language
Mass communications of modern media in print, film, radio, and television.

Politics
World system of nation-states regulated by balance of power and intermittent warfare. Great diversity of politics from one to another, but world-wide trend for mass participation in politics (Aristotle's "democracy") to compete with rule of the few ("oligarchy"). Protest movements of ethnic groups, labor, women, and gays and lesbians.

Learning
Mass schooling separating juvenile age grades from households. Universities and research institutes create new knowledge explosively.

Modern Metropolitan Civilization
Community field: Consists of enormous urban regions. Urban regions have specialized settlements—central business districts, industrial districts, separate residential areas by social class, and suburbs. The "unicentric" form arranges these parts concentrically around the central business district in a wheel. The other, "polycentric," form strings together many central business districts in accord with geographical features.

Economics
Price-regulated markets vie with state-regulated redistribution world-wide. The "factors of production"—land, labor, and capital, with legal restrictions—enter the market in more capitalistic countries. Economies of urban regions surpass many times that of "underdeveloped areas."

Ritual
Mass secular rituals, often extended through the media. Psychoanalysis and other schools based in psychological theories heal troubled individuals.

Technology
Industrialism—harnessing of sources of energy to machines synchronized with activities of human workers. Electronics make possible dispersal of original assembly lines and an information revolution through computers.

Sociology
Work separated from household. Huge state and private corporations. Division of labor by sex weakens. Proliferation of voluntary associations, a "bridge" between private individual and public roles. Three social classes form in relation to market and to ownership, management, and staffing of corporate bureaucracies.

Figure 17.1 Emergent institutions in modern metropolitan civilizations.

on their quantity (the supply) and on the desire (demand) for them. If I have nets to exchange and you have fish, the fish will be worth so many nets, depending on how plentiful your catch is, how desirable the fish are for eating, how many nets I have on hand, how easily I made the nets, and how great your desire is for them. Other factors operative in supply and demand include competitors also offering fish and nets. In short, the "free market" value of these two goods depends entirely on whatever the two of us are willing to exchange them for, and our calculations can be expected to change over time.

Note that "extraneous" ideas about value have been eliminated by supply-and-demand theory. **"Just price"** theorists, especially tribal or traditional people, might maintain that a certain size net might be worth the number of fish that same net is expected to bring in on an "average" catch. Other theorists, following Karl Marx, might say that the net should be worth the labor that went into it and that all fair prices reflect labor value. For Marx, any person's daily labor ought to earn a "market basket" of food, goods, and services sufficient to support laborer-and-family that day. Neither of these approaches is relevant to supply and demand.

Markets arose only in the right spatial setting. Their origins were dependent on the physical safety of the traders. Thus, essential to the origins of markets were **marketplaces:** safe, bounded, policed, and protected areas dedicated to impersonal market exchange.

The Origin of Marketplaces: Ports of Trade

Marketplaces did not originate in cities. In the earliest cities, such as those of protodynastic Mesopotamia, exchanges were completely dominated by the redistributive mode of allocating goods. Marketplaces originated at the borders of the ancient empires. They were places for politically and ritually supervised exchanges in balanced reciprocity between distant strangers—who needed the assurance of a neutral, safe meeting ground and the symbolic (and supernatural) guarantees of good faith (Polanyi, Arensberg, and Pearson, 1957).

Market trade originated from expeditions that were at first as much for war as for trade. The expedition looked for easy booty and plunder, but if the strangers were strong and militarily prepared, the expedition traded with them. Goods were brought home to Mesopotamian temple households. The first merchants were armed temple servants specializing in long-distance forays. Their task was to procure luxury goods, ritual items, hardwoods, and precious stones for temple construction. These early trading expeditions in some ways resembled those of the kula ring.

Early merchants soon found it useful to have trading partners and trading places. The Greeks reported "silent trade" between Egyptians and Africans along the Red Sea shores in the "land of Punt." In silent trade, even today, the parties leave articles on neutral ground and retreat; there had been no fighting at such places. It has been hypothesized that the ancient empty enclosures on the coast of the eastern Mediterranean were used for such silent trade.

In time, such places turned into **ports of trade,** small city-states far removed from the imperial centers of power, often on the seacoast or at the edges of regions, as where mountains meet the plain. A port of trade was characterized by a neutral political authority—weak compared to the power of the monarchs of the inland empires but strong enough to keep the peace in the city and its surroundings. Traders from the empires, representing their monarchs and their temple priests, could come to these ports without fear that the local authorities would seize their goods. They could trade their manufactured wares with barbarian traders for needed raw materials.

Ports of trade had defenses to keep the market peace, storehouses for goods to be shipped elsewhere, and shrines for ritual and supernatural sanctions to the transactions. Contracts were oaths taken at local shrines. When Alexander the Great, who founded the Greek city of Alexandria on Egyptian soil, had temples erected to his deceased deified friend Hephaestion, "Hephaestion's name was to be engraved on all the legal documents with which the merchants entered into bargains with each other" (quoted in Polanyi et al., 1957, p. 63).

Staggered and Stellar Marketplaces

Since the port of trade was institutionalized as a safe place for balanced exchanges, it has spread widely, especially among warring civilized tribesmen whose usual communication is through weapons. For them a system of regional marketplaces is extremely useful. Market days are *staggered*; that is, there is a market within walking distance of a community on any given day of the week. But the location of the market jumps from one community to another each day, rotating over the countryside in a giant circle (see Figure 17.2).

Fierce Albanian mountaineers and insolent Berbers of the Atlas

Figure 17.2 Abstract view of a regional staggered marketplace system on a weekly schedule, with stellar markets—fairs—on a yearly schedule. This is likely to be a region of insolent civilized tribesmen.

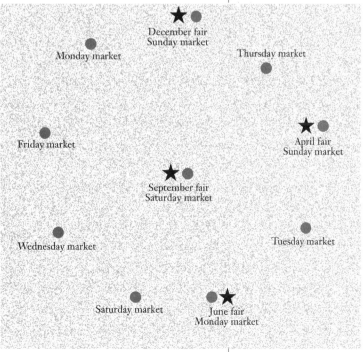

Mountains make great use of **staggered marketplaces** in the midst of on-going blood feuds. Throughout the Berber territories with their isolated cantons, marketplaces are located on the borders of communities. The market peace is in force not only within the market but on the roads leading to it, and a man can walk with impunity through his enemies' territory as long as he is on the road to a market on its market day.

Smaller markets are guaranteed by the elders of the cantons bordering it. In larger markets, where there is a saint's tomb, a lineage of holy men descended from the saint often enforce the market peace. They uphold oaths taken by the shrine, grant asylum within the shrine, and even require men to check their weapons upon entering the market precincts. Markets in Berber North Africa from time to time explode: Old enemies mutter insults, daggers flash suddenly from under robes, and as many as fifty corpses litter the market grounds at the end of the day. Despite such mishaps, markets move goods and provide information over a wide tribal area (Benet in Polanyi et al., 1957).

A system of staggered marketplaces is a useful device in urban societies, as well as for exchanging goods between peasant villages and between villages and cities. In such cases the larger markets become the "stars" of the staggered system, drawing people from a wide circle of smaller, satellite marketplaces to them. Such larger, **stellar markets** are usually at cities, but peasant villages often hold fairs on a yearly schedule (see Figure 17.3). The stellar markets of seasonal fairs, wherever they may be held, draw upon many

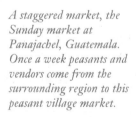

A staggered market, the Sunday market at Panajachel, Guatemala. Once a week peasants and vendors come from the surrounding region to this peasant village market.

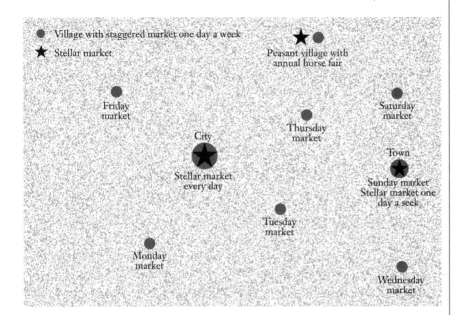

Figure 17.3 *A staggered-stellar regional market-place system with staggered markets at peasant villages and stellar ones at town, city, and village fair sites.*

satellite markets. Such systems are in operation in much of the civilized world today.

Alotenango, the community I studied in Guatemala, has its staggered market on Sundays. Some nearby peasant villages and crossroad settlements have such markets every other day of the week. At the nearby provincial capital, Antigua, there is a stellar market on Thursdays and Saturdays. Friday is the day to make the trip to Guatemala City to sell produce at any one of several marketplaces. These urban markets are all stellar, but they are biggest on Friday. In addition, each peasant community has a fair of sorts when it holds its annual fiesta or major rite of intensification. The December fair of St. Andrew at San Andrés Itzapa is of national importance. It is the largest horse fair in Guatemala, and the place to acquire a horse, mule, or donkey if you are in the equine market.

"Just Prices": Archaic Market Exchange as Generalized or Balanced Reciprocity

You will note that marketplaces have their origins in balanced one-to-one reciprocity between strangers; they are diplomatic places. As you will recall from previous chapters, there are three kinds of reciprocity. Generalized reciprocity occurs in relations within a household, although redistributive relationships in a patrimonial empire may be phrased in the same language. Balanced reciprocity occurs in relations between neighboring but strange peoples. Negative reciprocity occurs when one party gets something valued highly in return for nothing at all or something valued low. It is characteristic of distant peoples locked in a pattern of primitive warfare who take booty, for example, but it is also a latent characteristic of the haggling in a market system.

Strangers who are attracted to marketplaces bring plentiful articles of their own production to exchange for things scarce and valuable. Such persons may go away thinking they have made a killing, gotten something for almost nothing. The other party may likewise have acquired something scarce in return for something plentiful. Satisfaction abounds.

Such rudimentary mutual negative exchange is highly developed in archaic marketplace systems and is best expressed in staggered and stellar market patterns. Nonetheless, individuals buying cheap in times of plenty and selling dear in times of want are usually thought of as *unfair*, and in most archaic empires this practice is quite forbidden. Thus, the laws of supply and demand are never allowed their full effect in traditional societies. Even vendors and merchants who live full time off the marketplace are allowed only their "fair share" by government regulation or the edicts of merchant guilds. Traditionally, most cultures conceived of prices as reflecting values determined by the inherent nature of the goods exchanged.

Marketday in Gualeceo, Ecuador.

For example, the women who sold cooked food in the marketplaces of the kingdom of Dahomey were allowed a commission calculated at 20 percent of the market price. That is, they purchased the raw food at the royal plantations at a base rate of 80 (calculated in cowrie-shell currency) and sold the cooked food at the set price of 100. The 20 percent difference in market price was their commission. Note that it actually represents 25 percent of their cost. Their prices never varied with supply or demand.

In the stellar marketplaces of traditional empires, prices seem remarkably stable and often artificially low to the Western observer trained in supply-and-demand accounting. In addition, because such things as cowrie shells are so plentiful, they allow penny accounts of a sort unimaginable for us today. The stability and lowness of prices in archaic markets reflect a political ideology stressing generalized and balanced reciprocities. The commonwealth is likened to a giant household in which all are expected to contribute to the maintenance of all others, getting back in exchange not necessarily a balanced equivalent, but something in accord with one's social and political status.

In the marketplace, one's return is supposed to be either exactly balanced or, if negative, then negative as a reflection of political standing in the wider redistributive economy. In native theory, this meant that the exchange was supposed to be generalized, balanced out in the long run or in the context of social relations. Thus, Aristotle in his treatise on economics declared that marketplace exchanges ought to be determined by the status of the traders and that important and ranking men should pay less than men of low rank! European philosophies before the work of the eighteenth-century European economists shared Aristotle's "antimarket" ideology.

As a consequence of such ideologies, traditional governments use a number of practices that stabilize market prices in the interest of urban and elite groups. If anyone gets something for nothing in such traditional systems, it is assuredly neither the peasant nor the local marketplace vendor. It is rather the elite urban consumer.

First among such price-fixing practices is a system of tolls at the marketplace itself levied on all vendors, whether peasants or middlemen who enter to sell. Such tolls, typical of farmers' markets in the United States today, pay the expenses of overseeing and maintaining the marketplace. But their payment is also a means by which the state authority controls access to the market and enforces price fixing and price ceilings.

Local or central metropolitan authorities often set price ceilings on goods, especially on the staple foods. Sometimes, as in Dahomey, they set the price on everything, through negotiations with vendors' guilds. Such a "fair price" would be the one-to-one equivalent of the product, possibly with a set commission for the vendor calculated as well.

The practice of regulating sales through state control of vendors' guilds is quite common, as is the practice of allowing too many persons to become full-time vendors. The effect of an overpopulation of middlemen in a marketplace is to keep the prices low, as each strives to capture his or her own customers. This means the lowest possible price above the purchase price sufficient to keep the vendor alive at a modest level of subsistence.

Archaic imperial governments, European mercantilist governments (described later in this chapter), and modern governments interested in welfare often intervene in the supply-and-demand mechanism in the marketplace. Throughout history governments in Latin America have bought up grain from peasants after a plentiful harvest, stored it in public granaries, and then sold it to vendors in the marketplace at set low prices later in the year when the market supply was scarce. The effect is to keep the price of staple foods low and the urban populations fed (and their wages low as well).

Marketplaces, then, are targets for political leaders of all sorts, since they have everything to do with allocating goods and keeping communities in balance with their resources. Let us examine the political role of a historic port of trade in the early modern period.

E T H N O G R A P H I C   C L O S E - U P

WHYDAH, PORT OF TRADE

Ports of trade were common in European expansion during the Age of Discovery and later in unconquered areas that Europe traded with. Whydah, on the west coast of Africa in today's Republic of Dahomey, was a principal port of trade during the centuries of slave trade (Polanyi, 1966). A protected harbor site on an island, originally the home of the Hueda people, Whydah had a monarch who was just strong enough to keep the peace in his region and fend off warlike inland kings, often by paying them tribute and allowing them a safe outlet for exporting their captives to Europe. The slave trade at Whydah is of theoretical concern because on the African side it is an example of **administered trade** conceived of as *balanced*, while on the European side, through the invention of double-entry bookkeeping—that is, of cost accounting—it was conceived of as *profitable*.

The king of Whydah profited from the slave trade in the traditional manner of rulers of ports of trade, like the Phoenicians of old. He allowed Europeans—French, English, Dutch, and Portuguese—to build forts on the island. Whydah soon became a spatially typical port of trade. Around each European fort a native quarter grew up of their African servants. Nearby were the palace of the king and the shrines of Whydah's serpent cult. A great marketplace provisioned the local population—in total isolation, however, from the European trade. The king allowed traders, emissaries of inland kings, to bring slaves to Whydah, detain them there, and sell them to European ships under his supervision. When the European powers were themselves at war, the king of Whydah enforced strict neutrality in his port and waters on pain of expulsion from the island. Warring Europeans mingled peacefully, then, in neutral Whydah.

But Whydah fell to Dahomey, an expanding and militaristic inland kingdom, in 1727. (Dahomey had been established as an independent realm in 1627. It

The Guinea Coast, showing the port of trade Whydah in relation to the kingdom of Dahomey and its capital, Abomey.

was conquered by the French in 1892.) Dahomean troops invaded precisely because Whydah's neutrality was threatened by an empire to the south.

The king of Dahomey needed firearms and gunpowder to maintain his military posture. European firearms were essential to his safety. But the only goods he had to offer in return (besides palm oil) were captive human beings. The European powers were happy to supply firearms, because they needed slaves as laborers in the plantations of the New World. (Millions of Africans participated in the forced emigration of the era, as we know.)

444

After the conquest, Dahomey kept the city as a port of trade. Ordinary subjects of Dahomey were forbidden to go there; it was off limits. The king himself never set foot there, but ruled through a viceroy. The native snake cult, considered an abomination by the Dahomeans, was tolerated within Whydah. Indeed, snake fetishes were dedicated at the four European quarters of the port to impart their supernatural sanction to the trade agreements.

The slave trade at Whydah, apart from its dramatic and tragic implications for modern history, is of great interest to anthropological theory, for it demonstrates that balanced reciprocity is the principle behind administered trade.

African-Administered Trade: Immutable "Fair" Prices

The exchange of slaves for European goods did not take place according to the laws of supply and demand, at least not on the African side. If the African governments were doing the same today, you can be sure that trained accountants would try to measure the cost of the labor (soldiers) invested in the campaigns to acquire a supply of slaves. They would also try to come up with a money figure for capital investment, in this case the cost of the firearms and gunpowder. They would then measure these sums against the price received for the slaves

captured and present the king with a balance sheet showing profit or loss on his slaving expeditions.

But nothing of the sort was ever calculated. The king's annual campaigns were not market pricing transactions but political and redistributive events. They were conducted by levies of unpaid warriors, raised on a rotating basis from the villages of the realm, and by the fierce Amazon warriors of the king's household. Slave raiding was a labor contribution made by the king's subjects.

Great commanders and notables were rewarded with grants of captives at the Annual Customs. If they sold the captives at Whydah, they were allowed to keep the goods received for them. Many captives were kept as laborers on the royal plantations. They raised food that was then cooked and marketed to the general population at a low, set price by market women. This food and the supply of public prostitutes at the marketplaces were among the payoffs of the realm to the common subject.

There were two kinds of money in use: gold and cowrie shells (which the Europeans acquired in the Indian Ocean). An ounce of gold was valued at 32,000 cowrie shells. For centuries along the west coast of Africa, the kings took that price to be immutable. This was true in the 1680s and true in 1892 when the French conquered Dahomey. When a European ship came to Whydah, it was boarded by

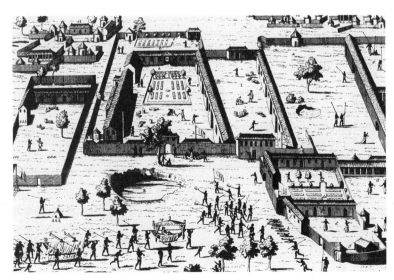

The Royal Palace and the European factories at Savi, Whydah. The factories, or trading posts, of the European powers are each denoted by its flag. Note the European riding in a litter. The palace of the king of Whydah and the royal serpent shrine are also shown.

an official in the harbor before it even dropped anchor. Negotiations followed. The price per able-bodied adult male or female slave was negotiated anew each time with reference to the last price paid. However, the price remained remarkably stable in terms of gold ounces.

European "Market Prices"

The Europeans, who endeavored to turn over as little gold as possible, exchanged weights of cowrie shells and items such as gold dust, manufactured cloth, iron bars, gunpowder, and firearms—a "sorting." For example, according to the records of the French slave ship *Dahomet*, one adult woman slave was sold in 1772 at a value of 8 ounces in gold; but the sorting handed over for her consisted

of three barrels of brandy, 123 pounds of cowrie shells, two pieces of handkerchief stuff, and eight lengths of white cotton fabric (Polanyi, 1966).

The king of Dahomey was not interested in the price of these items in European markets, and the traders valued these goods against gold in the way most profitable to them. Their markup was from eight to fifteen times what the goods had cost them in European money. They bought the slaves and then sold them for far greater sums in the same currencies. Europeans kept account books, but Dahomeans did not; rather, they assumed that the goods they were getting in terms of gold ounces were "correct" equivalents. For them, trade was never a matter of making a profit; it was the exchange of exactly equivalent goods.

MODERN POLITICS AND ECONOMICS: THE NATION-STATE AND MARKET SYSTEMS

Europe after 1600 was unique. Unlike any other great civilized region the world has ever known, it consisted of many fragmented jealous nation-states with a joint economy that was a single market system. This combination had occurred before only in civilized tribal areas where marketplaces were the only safe places for warring tribal republics to communicate. In civilizations, on the contrary, central imperial powers had always contrived to control marketplaces. In modern Europe, each nation-state at first desperately tried to control its market system.

Nation-States and the Theory of Economic Mercantilism

The absolutist bureaucracies that ruled from the new nation-state's center expected the masses to give their unstinting allegiance to the absolutist state, in return for its enlightened benefits. This was most thoroughly expressed in the theory of **mercantilism,** a refined version of generalized reciprocity. Such ideologies are common to empires, but now the theory was made explicit and wedded to a system of market exchange.

The basic mercantilistic notion was that the peripheral provinces and colonies existed for the benefit of the metropolis and must supply it with goods and services through taxes and conscription. Accounts in trade were kept, and market exchanges were viewed as yet another means for the periphery to supply the center. It was held that goods should flow into the center at a low price and go out at a higher price and that the metropolis should maintain a favorable balance of trade with its dependencies.

For the first time, the reciprocities inherent in an imperial system were phrased in terms of the market; moreover, the terms were unintentionally those of negative reciprocity, although the metropolis theoretically returned services for its favorable balance of trade by fending off foreigners, preserving the holy faith, constructing public works, and dispensing justice for all. But the fact remains that for the first time metropolitan balance books had to show a profit. This was in part a result of the perfection of **cost accounting.** All transactions could be measured in money—in this case, in gold and silver; and because of the invention of *double-entry bookkeeping*, any firm could measure costs paid out (column 1) against money received (column 2). Prices were becoming not fixed, "fair" entities, but numbers.

However, in spite of the fact that nation-states were deciding that the (fair or not) correct price should show a profit for the metropolis, international practice was actually leaving mercantilistic theory behind. As historian Immanuel Wallerstein (1974) pointed out, the several mercantilistic systems formed one "world economic system," and the central trading nations—the Dutch United Provinces, Great Britain, France, and some German cities—formed the "core."

After 1600, Spain fell into the economic "semiperiphery"; on the full periphery lay Poland and eastern Europe (except Russia and Turkey); and on the other side of the core were the Spanish and Portuguese Indies in the New World. The Indies provided the core with gold and silver for currency, while Poland and its neighbors provided it with wheat and basic foodstuffs. In exchange, the core countries provided manufactured goods exported to the periphery at a profit. On a multinational scale, the market operated in favor of the merchants of Amsterdam and their neighbors in the core countries.

Price-Regulated Markets: the Full Emergence of a New Institution

In the late 1700s and early 1800s in Europe, market practice and theory slowly changed. By the end of the 1700s economists had formulated a simple and elegant theory of "free," or **price-regulated, market** systems, in which the price of any item on the market is governed not by any set or fair price, or even by the labor that went into it, but by the laws of supply and demand—that is, by how plentiful the supply of similar items is and by how much demand there is for it by consumers. Producers' costs are determined by the prices they pay to produce the item they have for sale, and from their point of view, the price of their products should be higher than their costs of production.

The *costs* of any productive enterprise consist of the price paid for the use of land (rent, taxes), the price paid for labor (wages), and the price paid for capital investments in production—that is, for equipment (tools, farm machinery, and so on) and for money borrowed (interest) to purchase land, equipment, and even labor. These *factors of production* are also subject to the law of supply and demand, which determines their price. Thus, supplies of all commodities and the prices paid for them are constantly fluctuating according to supply and demand, which themselves vary with pricing.

One can figure out formal implications of each factor in economic theory, and that makes it the fascinating intellectual game it is to businessmen and economists.

Price-Regulated Markets and the Rise of Industrial Production

In the early 1800s yet another human institution—a complex of interrelated behaviors—had emerged: the **industrial factory**. Machines were being used for industrial production, among them the steam engine that the Greeks had invented in Hellenistic Alexandria, originally for opening temple doors as if by magic. In the 1800s a new dominant building appeared, the factory, in which there was the totally new combination and synchronization of human effort with machines powered from nonhuman sources. Here for the first time in human history, merchants began manufacturing goods in bulk.

Karl Polanyi (1944), the economic historian who also worked with anthropologist Conrad Arensberg to define the three modes of allocation, argues that the birth of industrialism required that price-regulated markets

An early English factory.

appear simultaneously. He states that in Great Britain conditions were extremely favorable for the appearance of such a price-regulated, or free, system. Influential factors included Britain's cottage industry, or craft manufacture by peasant households; its staggered and stellar markets; and its great fairs at stellar markets, in which huge quantities of particular goods were sold.

Moreover, there was an extraordinarily aggressive and spirited merchant class, recruited in part from the second sons of the nobility (with its stem family primogeniture) and in part from the dissenting Puritans, who treated trade as if it were a spiritual vocation. Instead of investing their profits in personal luxuries, they plowed them back into the firms, creating a perpetual supply of capital. This fact is part of Weber's argument that the Protestant ethic was conducive to the rise of capitalism.

In Great Britain, a portion of the peasantry had always been mobile because of the demands of the inheritance system, which did not grant every young man a share in the village patrimony. Thus, there had always been a potential labor force at hand. Added impetus came from the enclosure movement, in which the gentry began to treat lands theretofore held in feudal or communal title as private property. It took a simple act of Parliament, which was controlled by the gentry, to convert land titles. The gentry thus displaced thousands of peasants as huge tracts were converted to sheep runs or other private uses.

Other factors that gave rise to industrialism included the practices of double-entry bookkeeping and cost accounting and the availability of money for capital investments in machinery provided by banks, loans at interest, and a good supply of gold and silver from the Indies. But here is the rub. Polanyi argues that the changeover to industrial manufacture could take place only if merchants were assured of recouping the cost of their new machines, expensive capital investments, and then some; this required a certain human price.

Because of the "modern world system," merchants were assured of buyers at the periphery of Europe for the vast quantities of goods that machines could produce. But the new manufacturers also needed a supply of laborers at a low or profitable cost whom they could let go when and if sales went down, so as not to be ruined by labor costs not offset by income from sales. The upshot was that in Great Britain land, labor, and capital (the factors of production) were freed in the next three generations from "archaic" state controls and were treated like any other commodity on the market (Polanyi, 1944).

Although for some time British laborers had some form of public relief to protect them from sudden unemployment and wages insufficient to support life, even this recourse was denied them after the Poor Law Amendment of 1834 was passed by a parliament responsive to manufacturers. For a brief period in Great Britain, labor was completely free of any state restraint and was thrown on the open market. But this was not to last, for governments are unable to tolerate the ill effects of a labor force completely at the mercy of a price-regulated market. Great Britain enacted labor laws in the 1850s.

Human labor is not a commodity like any other and cannot be run through and used up as if it were a supply of raw materials. When labor is completely free—that is, sold at whatever the market will bear—inhumanly long work shifts result. During the Industrial Revolution in Britain and New England, shifts were sixteen or more hours a day. Because there were no controls, small children, the aged, and pregnant women all scrambled to sell their labor in sweatshops. The results were great suffering and wasted lives.

Land, too, was "liberated" by the free market system to become a commodity subject to supply and demand like any other. The impact of these changes was revolutionary everywhere European civilization reached, which by the late nineteenth century was over most of the world through Europe's far-flung colonies. We have already seen the immense deportation of slave labor from Africa to the New World, where the Africans worked plantations to produce commodities to be processed by the new industrial factories. The best land through much of the colonial world was taken up by vast estates owned by capitalist landlords. (See Wolf, 1982, for a global view of the impact of European industrial capitalism.)

However, the new institutions of price-regulated markets and industrialism also changed modern community form. Let us see what free markets did to urban settlement patterns. **Capitalism** manufactured its own culture and community first in the mill town, second in the metropolis.

INDUSTRIAL MARKET SYSTEMS AND SETTLEMENT PATTERNS: THE SUCCESSION OF MODERN COMMUNITY TYPES

In the cities, free markets favored the grid plan, an old urban form used by Romans in military camps and by Spaniards in new cities in America. The nineteenth-century version emphasized sales. Long, broad streets expedited commercial unloading and gave maximum frontage for shops. The new form was rectangular rather than square. The market value for each salable unit of land was maximized. The city lot, on a long skinny block, was surveyed and subdivided and given a title. Like a bank note or other commercial paper, it could be bought and sold at will with no restrictions from state or community.

Industrialism and the free market spawned not only differing land use patterns, oriented toward the market, but new communities and new cultures. In these communities, factories, warehouses, transport buildings, department stores, and banks became the dominant architectural features. And people became defined in relation to the settlement. They fell into at least three **social classes:** upper, middle, and lower. Upper classes included factory and business owners, top managers, and genteel descendants of the formerly wealthy; middle classes included small entrepreneurs and middle-level, supervising employees; lower classes included workers of all sorts. Analysts sometimes place the "underclass," the permanently unemployed and marginal populations with multiple social and psychological problems, in this group, but it is probably more correct to place them in a fourth category "below" the other three classes.

This community pattern, with its associated architecture and social organization, first became apparent in the *mill town*, originally shaped by merchant industrialists (capitalists) dealing with new machines. In the rest of this chapter, we shall concentrate on it and the kinds of commercial-industrial cities that came after it.

The Mill Town

The mill town was the first modern industrial city to arise in the West. It appeared in England, but its descendants are everywhere. Its location was determined by the availability of sources of energy for the machines of the factories and mills. In the days before electricity, coal had to be burned to produce steam, and streams were needed for turning waterwheels. A coal-mining town situated on a river had both. The signs of the times were giant waterwheels and smokestacks belching smoke from coal furnaces below. So that the railroad that hauled away coal and manufactured goods did not have to climb steep grades, mill towns were situated in low-lying places, and mining towns were situated in valleys. Towns using water power along a river were often at the fall line, where water power is more efficiently harnessed.

Mill towns have often been studied by social scientists. In "Yankee City" (actually Newburyport, Massachusetts), studied by anthropologist W. Lloyd Warner and his associates in the 1930s (Warner et al., 1963), the spatial elements consist of a downtown area centered on the railroad

A coal town.

station and the river wharves. Close by are the mills and factories. In the same district but ranging out farther are the cottages and tenements of the workers.

As is typical in mill towns, a low-lying area beside the river is the district of the poorest, most dilapidated housing. It is inhabited by "river rats," a lower lower underclass that includes many who do not work because of physical disabilities, alcoholism, and other such problems. (Warner divided each of the three classes into higher and lower sections, thus creating a six-class system.) High above them on the hill, set on large lots with trees and commanding a view of the town and the river, are the well built and beautifully maintained homes of the rich, the upper upper class of mill owners and merchants.

Between these two neighborhoods and the downtown area is a range of neighborhoods. Middle managerial groups live in good homes with less elevated and less prestigious addresses. The solid working class, or upper lower class, live in well-kept cottages in a neighborhood that is a cut above the river and its river rats. The mill town, which long ago became part of a bigger modern metropolis, still survives today.

The Modern Metropolis

Chicago circa 1900.

When the mill town was added to great sea and railroad ports or to the old national capitals such as London and Paris, a new city arose in the form of a giant circle. The Chicago school of urban sociologists, notably Robert Park and Ernest Burgess, studied this form. Chicago from 1890 to 1910 was its best representative, but all modern forms are transitional, and the circular metropolis has given way to the conurbation or urban region. Let us take up the earlier form first.

Concentric Circles. The Chicago school found that metropolitan ecology, or land use, could be represented as a series of banded zones in concentric circles. As you can see from Figure 17.4, these zones are the central business district, lower-class residential districts, manufacturing areas, middle-class residential areas, and higher-class residential areas. Modifications of the original findings have shown that some zones push out along corridors like fingers or sectors, rather than staying in purely concentric bands.

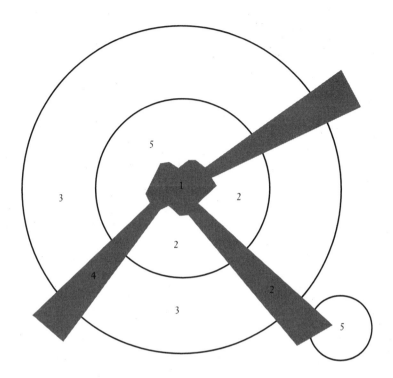

Figure 17.4 Ecological structure of cities as defined by Chicago school: (1) central business district; (2) lower-class residential area; (3) middle-class residential area; (4) higher-class residential area; (5) light and heavy manufacturing district.

Central Business District. The center of the metropolis is literally a transport hub at the center of an asterisk. Such cities are located at the juncture of transportation terminals, especially railroads and waterways. Chicago is located where an inland seaport on the Great Lakes joins enormous railroad yards. Although there are factories in the central district, they were early supplanted by commercial buildings and in most cases pushed out beyond the central zone.

The dominant structure of the central business district was devised early in the 1800s; it consisted of iron frames upholding great open floors and galleries. Mumford (1961) points out that such buildings lent themselves to a number of purposes. By moving partitions around the inner floors, one could have a department store, an office building, or a hotel. Just as the city block and the building lot were being measured with an eye to maximum profit per frontage linear foot, so was the iron-framed commercial building being designed with an eye to cost per abstract unit of space—the cubic foot as well as the front foot. Eventually, the office building became dominant, a development aided by the invention of an office technology, which has been described by Peter Hall (1966):

An extraordinarily concentrated set of inventions created the modern office: commercial shorthand (Pitman's, 1837), electric telegraphy (also 1837), cheap universal postage (1840), the lift or elevator (1857), the typewriter (1867), the skyscraper (ca. 1876), the telephone (1876), the adding machine (developed commercially 1872–1888), the electric light (1880), the steel-frame skyscraper (1883), the mimeograph and the dictating machine (1887), carbon paper (applied to typewriting ca. 1890). And between 1849 and 1893, another whole series of developments in printing and photo-reproduction made modern advertising possible.

The business district was a center for transportation, commerce (selling), and, above all, communicating, managing, and coordinating information. As techniques improved, an intensifying communications net converged on the center. The central business district grew outward, at the expense of other zones of settlement, and upward, in that American invention, the steel-frame skyscraper, creating a skyline that in much of the world is a most coveted status symbol and the surest sign of modernization.

Urban Processes in a Lower-Class Residential District. The ecology, or balance of forces, resulting in different uses of the land is the product of the following **urban processes,** according to the Chicago sociologists: centralization of urban activities; specialization and segregation by function; competition for access to land; invasion of an area by winners of the competition to take it over for a centralized and specialized use; and succession, whereby one invasion gives way to another (Boskoff, 1970). Let us look at these growth processes in the lower-class residential district.

Chicago tenements, 1906.

Worker tenements close to the downtown mills were early torn down to make way for office buildings and department stores. The working classes, forced farther out by the expansion of the central business district, invaded the nearby area of formerly upper- or middle-class housing. The classic image of a slum is a deteriorated, formerly elegant area close to the central business district and in some cases penetrating its side streets. The housing is crowded and left in poor repair.

Working classes thus win the competition for space; middle- and upper-class residents are not willing to pay increased prices (rents) or to crowd in as working classes do to meet the higher prices. Such a situation occurred with the influx of migrant Puerto Rican working-class families into the west side of Manhattan in the late 1950s. The invasion was slowed down by rent control, which protected apartment dwellers who had signed leases in the 1940s; but as that group vacated their apartments, landlords could raise their rents. In a four-bedroom apartment that had once housed a single middle-class family, there might live six or seven Puerto Rican families, one to each room, sharing the apartment kitchen (Padilla, 1958; Rand, 1958).

In urban invasions, the demand for unskilled labor continues in the metropolis, especially for the construction and maintenance of skyscrapers, and also for the seasonal output of light industries in older buildings on the fringes of the central business district. (Heavy industry increasingly demands highly skilled and specialized laborers.) As slum land values become too high and the cost of maintenance increases, landlords sell their properties for astronomical prices per front foot to businesses that erect skyscrapers where laborers once dwelt, thus replacing the slums and pushing them farther out.

What happened recently in the cycle of invasion and succession was unknown in the free market of Chicago in 1900. In Manhattan and other places, slum housing that deteriorated to the point of collapse was declared a "hazard to life and limb" and condemned by city authorities. If the landlord abandoned the property rather than pay for repairs and back taxes, the city claimed it for some urban renewal plan, such as high-rise public housing. Thus, instead of the "natural" sequence of competition and invasion, the old housing was succeeded by publicly owned apartment skyscrapers.

Not all lower-class residential areas are slums, and some "stable working-class areas" also defy the processes of invasion and succession. Often an ethnic working-class population (for example, Italians in the United States) entrenches itself in a neighborhood. After an initial period of overcrowding, the group spaces itself at one family to an apartment in something approaching the middle-class norm. Resident extended families buy up entire tenements and keep them in repair with considerable self-help. Outwardly, the area remains old and less desirable, but inside, the housing is decent. People of the neighborhood become satisfied and conservative (Gans, 1962).

Other Zones. All other zones are dependent on the central business district. Manufacturing depends on the center for the transportation of incoming raw materials and outgoing products for sale. Like the slums, manufacturing districts run the risk of being invaded and displaced by downtown.

A seeming exception to the concentric zones has always been the higher-class residential area. Chicago's is close to the slums and the skid row Hobohemia, but in many metropolises some favored corridor, such as Philadelphia's Main Line, leads from an inner Gold Coast out to the garden suburbs, where spacious mansions sit upon wooded estates within easy commuting distance of the central business district. Fingers of lower-class residences also extend along some transport route to areas of manufacturing and employment. The outer areas of the usual metropolis of 1900 were an almost solid band of middle-class one-family townhouses. Farther out, where the population was less dense, townhouses gave way to garden dwellings on single lots.

Cities with "Symbolic" Ecology

Metropolises of the "symbolic" type have a markedly different pattern—attributed by sociologists to the "stubborn immobility of high-status families" (Boskoff, 1970, p. 89) or to the entrenched attitudes of state authorities. Usually, such cities are nonindustrial or newly industrial and firmly in the grip of a landowning aristocracy. Examples include New Orleans, Bangalore in India (Boskoff, 1970), Guatemala City (Caplow, 1949), and Popoyán in Latin America (Whiteford, 1964).

Much of the charm of New Orleans is its "aristocratic" aura, especially in the historic French Quarter.

These cities generally have a central business district, but close by and perhaps intermingled with the office buildings are the high-status dwellings of the aristocrats. Slums tend to be squatter-settlement shantytowns on the outskirts. If there are squatters downtown, they use leftover unclaimed land on steep hillsides, in swamps, or in deep ravines. Future research on such cities should tell us more about the processes behind their patterns. In the meantime, many of them, especially New Orleans and Charleston, South Carolina, are becoming centers of nostalgic tourism.

Conurbations: Sprawling Metropolitan Regions with Many Urban Centers

Metropolises today have everywhere become **conurbations**—clusterings of several important centers growing together. A sea of urban settlement extends far beyond old formal governmental boundaries, and often beyond what used to be recognized as metropolitan edges. Large suburban areas are often unincorporated areas governed by county jurisdictions or myriad petty local municipalities. Sociologists trained in the Chicago school tend to see in such settlements the old pattern of one central city with suburbs or satellites. Urban regions that take the form of a giant wheel, such as the regions of Atlanta, London, Paris, and Moscow, can be depicted by such a pattern. This is shown in Figure 17.5, which was devised by sociologist Alvin Boskoff.

Even in this relatively conservative pattern, the suburban ring rapidly fills up (everywhere in the world) with solid settlement. It takes the most stringent greenbelt legislation and enforcement to preserve open space beyond the central city. London and Moscow have done just that, and they have open country where the United States has solid suburb. However, in both cases, large satellite settlements have sprung up and promise to fill in solidly around the greenbelt on the other side.

In the United States, new centers have emerged in the suburban zone that are quite independent of the old town centers. They appear along the spokes of the wheel pattern, where highways and other lines lead out of the central city, especially at intersections with beltway highways around the perimeter of the metropolis. New centers at outer-rim junctures tend to duplicate the commercial services of downtown; suburban shopping centers, office areas, and "executive" and industrial parks compete with the inner city.

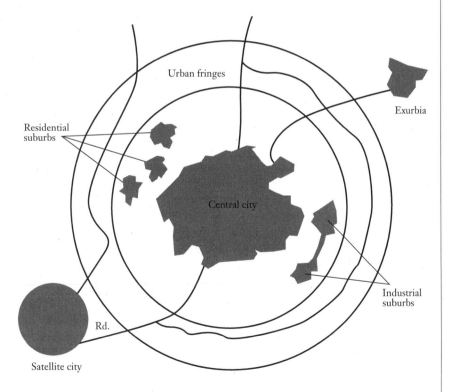

Figure 17.5 Simplified ecological diagram of the urban region.

Even "exurbia" is being urbanized. This is a rural area where upper-class bohemians from the art world, show business, and the mass media live in old farmsteads and commute to the metropolis once a week or so. Whole areas of once rustic countryside in the United States are being taken up by exurban urbanites ranging from summer vacationers to industrial retirees in trailers along rivers. In certain states noted for outdoor living, such as Florida, green cities of a sort unknown to Western civilizations are rapidly developing.

In many cases, it is difficult to differentiate satellites from central cities. Several cities growing together may seem equally central or equally each other's satellites. The Los Angeles area, for example, has not one but many centers. Any service found downtown is sure to be duplicated somewhere else in the region. For example, the seven-county greater metropolitan area has four campuses of the University of California (in Los Angeles, Santa Barbara, Riverside, and Irvine), not to mention a private center of higher education at USC. In Florida the stretch of 100 miles from Homestead north through Miami and Fort Lauderdale to Palm Beach has several central business districts; and the symbolic center, Miami Beach, with its palatial skyscraper hotels, is rivaled by Fort Lauderdale.

The Miami area is an example of a linear polycentric conurbation. But it is by no means unique. In the Netherlands three conurbations form a vast national conurbation, Randstad (Ring City), composed of The Hague and Rotterdam to the south, Amsterdam to the north, and Utrecht to the east. Dutch planners let them all grow together in a horseshoe shape open to the southeast, and they are passing laws to preserve a green interior (Hall, 1966). Similarly, the Rhine-Ruhr, which stretches from Bonn on the Rhine north through Cologne and Dusseldorf into the Ruhr valley, has a concentration of some ten major and ten lesser cities. The urbanized valleys are the two arms of an inverted and lopsided V-shape. Dusseldorf is at the point of the V, but there is no single center (Hall, 1966). Mexico City, perhaps four million persons in 1964, has grown to over 20 million today.

In terms of human numbers, these conurbations are totally unsurpassed by any civilized precedent, and they promise to surpass themselves several times over in the future. In 1800 no European city had a million inhabitants; London came close with over 900,000. By 1900, eleven metropolises had over a million inhabitants, including Chicago (Mumford, 1966). By 1960, however, there were twenty-four metropolitan areas with over 3 million each, four of which had over 10 million. Regional planners were dealing with 11.3 million in administrative Tokyo in 1969 (Honjo, 1975) and with over 22 million in the planning area (Hall, 1966). With full industrialization, however, cities level off. In 1990 Tokyo proper had increased to only 11.6 million.

SUMMARY AND CONCLUSIONS

The progress of human social evolution since the emergence of our species has been along two dimensions: increasing population spread and density, and successive factoring out and explicit emerging of distinct social institutions. That process probably began before the origin of the species, with the factoring out and emergence of human family and kinship from disparate primate precedents.

In this chapter we have seen this factoring out and emergence—this time of markets and of industrial factories—happening before our human collective eyes; we are still trying to make sense of it. Markets first had an archaic stage—just as bureaucracy went through a stage as an appendage to royal dynastic households. Markets were invented as ports of trade, safe havens policed by local authorities on the borders of the ancient empires for neutral exchange to take place freely between official imperial merchants with manufactured goods and tribal barbarians with raw materials. Once invented, the device spread as the marketplace, a small-scale haven for free exchange, ideally balanced, among strangers.

Market and marketplace were from the start devices that defied the ability of priests, tyrants, and monarchs to control exchanges and are thus characteristic of insolent civilized tribal areas on the fringes of civilized states; they are also a means of integration and communication in such areas, which may well lack any central state control.

Markets have the latent tendency to follow the "laws" of supply and demand, whereby persons cheaply exchange goods that they have in plentiful supply for items that are, for them, scarce. Value, therefore, may constantly fluctuate according to these two factors. It took thousands of years for human beings to come to grips, intellectually, with this variability. On the contrary, all societies at first assumed value to be immutable, given by custom, itself enshrined in myth and further legitimized through redistributive rituals. State and local (tribal or peasant) authorities took all manner of measure to fix prices in marketplaces according to traditional standards.

The first explicit philosophy about market economies, Aristotle's, conceived of them as mechanisms that properly upheld the commonwealth as a great household and thus must lawfully follow the model of generalized reciprocity. In this approach the elites, who do so much for society and take on a paternal role in the grand social household, should buy better goods at cheaper prices than the masses, as a reward for their good deeds.

Price-regulated markets are those in which the laws of supply and demand are allowed to operate, thus setting their own "market prices." Such markets were allowed to operate fully only once, in Great Britain for twenty years after 1834. Their rise coincided with the rise of industrialism. Thus we have one of the rare chances to observe, often rather imperfectly in hindsight, the emergence of two institutions. We can see the happenstance nature, the falling together quite coincidentally of a number of factors at once. So it must have been in all such institutional emergences: they are unpredictable, and seemingly random. We can only assert that, given enough time and space, human beings will try out everything, and all possible combinations will occur, some of them then gelling into something new and different—in this case a price-regulated market system in conjunction with factory industrialism.

One invention necessary for price-regulated markets was cost accounting, with double-entry bookkeeping, whereby producers could keep track of the cost of their product (column 1) versus its price (column 2). This invention led to the much touted "bottom line" at the end of the columns. A device for seeing *profits*, the excess of price over costs, had been invented. This concept was first used, however, in mercantilist theory to argue that the metropolis should always show a profit in dealing with the provinces or colonies.

I agree with Polanyi's contention that factory industrialism, the coupling of an external source of energy to machines and human labor, could arise only with price-regulated markets, since merchants needed a chance to recoup their capital investment in the machines even if prices fell. That meant they needed *free* labor, labor that seeks its price on the open market, rather than labor bound by prior social arrangements. However, in the long run no state can live with the consequences of a price-regulated market in labor, and it must take measures—labor laws—protecting the health and life of its laborers.

Max Weber also argues that the culture of capitalism—the *freeing* of capital, money, and equipment to meet its own price on the market—was conditioned by the rise of Protestant culture. We shall examine that thesis in the next chapter.

Industrial market economies also arose in the context of competing nation-states, thus avoiding the official regulations of a world empire that would probably have choked them before they even had a chance to take off.

Once in place, these economies gave rise to new settlement patterns, first in the mill town and later in the commercial metropolis, arranged in concentric circles around a transport hub and central business district. Another zone is a manufacturing one. Various housing zones differentiate the urban three-class system (upper, middle, and lower, with generally an underclass on skid row and elsewhere). These urban classes arose to stand between the peasantry and the landed aristocracy.

The expansion of metropolises is conditioned by ecological forces (centralization, specialization and segregation by function, competition for land, invasion of an area, and succession, one invasion after another). These in turn are conditioned by market forces and also by symbiotic arrangements that we do not fully understand. Jane Jacobs (1984) asserts that the key process is one of import substitution, whereby a backward city substitutes locally manufactured items for those they formerly imported, which occurs in explosive chain reactions.

However we are to understand the processes, they are most certainly with us and most certainly explosive. Human settlements in the great conurbations now surpass in size and scale any aggregated population and activity of even the largest ancient empire.

In the modern conurbation, the elite is now a mass elite. Urban educational levels the world over have risen with the expansion of metropolitan population. In Moscow, heavily populated by peasant migrants in 1900 and still swollen with former peasants today, one-fifth of the working population has a university education, and one-third of the work force has a specialized or technical education (Frolic, 1975). The Moscow regional population is now some 9 million or more, and the university-trained elite consists of hundreds of thousands of men and women. In western Europe and the United States, educational development has been older and steadier, and the number of educated elite is greater.

Time is no longer the repetition of days, seasons, and generations. In industrial factories, time is split-second synchronization with the impersonal rhythm of machines, something we examine in the next chapter. Other machines produce jet lag, the fatigue experienced by travelers who have journeyed faster than the earth has rotated on its axis. Generational time is beset by future shock, young men and women reaching maturity vastly better educated than their parents and facing a vastly different life. In the modern urban life cycle, we see millions leave villages and towns for conurban metropolises. We also see individual social mobility, the chance for better education, better jobs, and higher income and living levels than one's parents had. The adaptations of individuals and whole modernizing cultures, such as Japan, to the wider social functions of the modern metropolis are the subjects of the two chapters that follow.

SUGGESTED READINGS

Cooper, Eugene. *The Wood-carvers of Hong Kong: Craft Production in the World Capitalist Periphery.* Prospect Heights, Ill.: Waveland Press, 1988. Himself apprenticed as a woodcarver, the author examines firsthand the transition from handcraft to industrialism.

Hall, Peter. *The World Cities*, 2nd ed. New York: McGraw-Hill, 1969. Lavishly illustrated and comparative work by a geographer; interesting contrasts between linear polycentric conurbations and those in the form of a wheel.

Jacobs, Jane. *Cities and the Wealth of Nations: Principles of Economic Life*. New York: Random House, 1984. Brilliant and intriguing assertion of the thesis that economic development happens in urban regions, not nation-states, and proceeds by explosive chain reactions of import substitution.

Mumford, Lewis. *The Culture of Cities*. New York: Harcourt Brace Jovanovich (paperback), 1938/1970. This work has been very influential among planners and architects, a classic in its own time.

Padilla, Elena. *Up from Puerto Rico*. New York: Columbia University Press, 1958. Straightforward account of a recent urban migration and invasion.

Wolf, Eric. *Europe and the People Without History*. Berkeley: University of California Press, 1982. An exhaustive examination of the impact of industrial capitalism on the entire globe. It has been criticized as an exercise in the "Leninist thesis on imperialism" but remains a good source for student term papers.

GLOSSARY

administered trade Exchange conducted as official procurement by merchants representing state powers; it follows "just prices" and often takes place in ports of trade.

capitalism Broadly speaking, a culture resulting from the combination of price-regulated markets and factory industrialism. Capitalists (originally merchant-industrialists) favor a culture and political program minimizing government regulation of land, labor, and capital (commercial investments measured in money). They favor careers open to individual talent in business.

conurbation An urban metropolitan region consisting of a number of urban centers growing together, either at exterior transport spokes on a wheel or in linear fashion.

cost accounting A method of marketing brought explicitly to consciousness in double-entry bookkeeping, whereby the costs of production, or of doing business, are measured against the price received for the product.

industrial factory A productive enterprise coupling some exterior source of energy to machines, in turn coupled to the patterned labor of human beings.

"just price" The assumption, common to all traditional societies, that values are fixed and immutable, given by divinely sanctioned custom.

market exchange Impersonal exchange of goods among persons who may be strangers. Anyone can trade anything with anyone else. It is difficult to achieve and rare at tribal levels of society, where strangers are by definition dangerous, potential enemies.

marketplaces Safe, bounded spaces, generally policed and often supervised by judges, where market exchange among strangers may take place.

mercantilism The seventeenth- and eighteenth-century doctrine in Europe which held that all transactions between a central metropolis and its provinces and colonies should properly show a profit for the metropolis.

ports of trade The original marketplaces, neutral grounds controlled by local authorities, where officials from the ancient empires could trade manufactured wares for raw materials from barbarian tribals.

price-regulated market Market exchange in which prices are left to what the market will bear, generally following the laws of supply and demand without state intervention. However, all modern states regulate the prices of land, labor, and capital in the interest of public welfare.

social classes The classification of persons in modern metropolises into upper, middle, and lower classes. Upper classes are factory and business owners and top managers; middle classes include small entrepreneurs and middle-level, supervising employees; lower classes include workers of all sorts. Professionals are middle to upper class. An "underclass" of the permanently unemployed is sometimes listed as a fourth class.

staggered and stellar marketplaces A regional system of marketplaces, each of which is in operation on its day in turn (staggered), and among which some (stellar markets) on certain days are *fairs* or big markets, with many more vendors and greater quantities and varieties of goods than the ordinary markets on ordinary days.

urban processes *Process* generally implies a logically ordained sequence of events, in this case of an ecology or balance of forces in urban growth: centralization of urban activities; specialization and segregation by function; competition for access to land; invasion of an area by winners of the competition to take it over for a centralized and specialized use; and succession, whereby one invasion gives way to another. We have no adequate theory as to why the forces should exist in the first place, but they are clearly linked to the market.

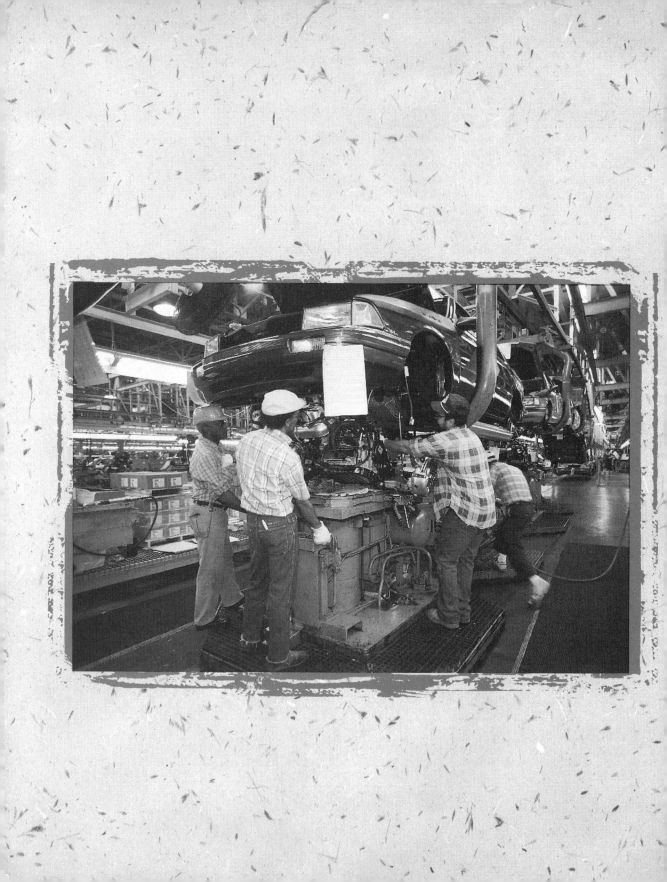

Corporate Bureaucracy and the Culture of Modern Work

LEGAL-RATIONAL BUREAUCRACY:
AN EMERGING INSTITUTION

THE BAROQUE CAPITAL:
MONUMENT TO ABSOLUTE ROYAL
BUREAUCRATIC POWER

Culture of the Baroque Capital

Baroque Royal Rituals: The Parade

Dominant Architectural Forms of the Baroque Capital

Survivals and Revivals of the Baroque Capital

THE MODERN CORPORATION AND
BUREAUCRACY

The New Command Center: The Corporate Board

Institutional Consequences

Social Effects

CORPORATE BUREAUCRATIC
TABLES OF ORGANIZATION

BEHAVIOR IN MODERN
BUREAUCRACIES

Lines of Work

Supervision Down the Line

Staff-Line Behavior

Up-the-Line Behavior

Informal Relations Between Workers

THE CULTURE OF CORPORATE
WORK AND THE CULT OF
EFFICIENCY

The Protestant Ethic and Enlightened Bureaucratic Rationality

The Cult of Efficiency

Taylorism

The Spread of Taylorism

ETHNOGRAPHIC CLOSE-UP:
THE WORKER AND THE GROUP

THE INFORMAL GROUP AND
PRODUCTION

*T*he other key institution beside the market in modern life is *corporate* legal-rational bureaucracy, which has come to control factory industrialism. **Corporations** are legal devices in which several partners may act as one person. Over the last two centuries, corporations have grafted onto themselves the form of the legal-rational bureaucracies perfected in the seventeenth and eighteenth centuries by the absolutist monarchs of Europe. As corporations, legal-rational bureaucracies are now the dominant form of social organization, having spread far beyond government into industrial production, market systems, even religion. In form they consist of corporate boards commanding military-type hierarchies of organization. A model of human activity perfected in factories by managers and engineers has taken hold of the flow of work at all levels. Individuals work in such impersonal places that they are prompted to ask, "Who am I?"

LEGAL-RATIONAL BUREAUCRACY: AN EMERGING INSTITUTION

Max Weber (1864–1920) gave us the theory of bureaucracy, the organization that maximizes efficiency in administration. Weber's theory came over a century after the full perfection of the legal-rational bureaucratic form. The absolute kings of Europe had consolidated their nation-states in the 1400s, had reached their height as "enlightened despots" in the 1700s, and had their grand era from 1500 to 1800. Legal-rational bureaucracy thus arose in the **Baroque age,** the age of these absolutist kings. Clockwork was the metaphor of that age, as we shall see later. Royal bureaucracies were intended to be giant clocks of human beings running smoothly in relation to each other.

When institutions emerge, human beings invariably do not fully understand them. The full ramifications are only slowly brought to consciousness. During the Baroque age, apologists for the absolutist regimes hoped that the social machines that were being perfected would indeed act like giant springs, wound up by the monarch and his council and then left to run in tick-tock fashion perfectly with a minimum of tinkering. Even Weber, generations later, did not understand that such social machines are not springs kicking energy into social clockwork. Weber never grasped that they must *respond* to the changing needs of their clients and not only to their internal charter (where catalytic energy is stored).

Bureaucracy, per se, is any social device enabling one or only a few persons to rule multitudes of other people. In its dynastic, patrimonial form, bureaucracy was a powerful device for shaping huge areas of the earth into empires. Nevertheless, it had not yet fully emerged as a fully realized, independently based organization, as we saw in Chapter 15.

Legal-rational bureaucracy, according to Weber, is a set of government bureaus defined by a legal charter according to a specialized, logical function (see page 372 in Chapter 15). Careers are open to talent, by training, and are rewarded by seniority. Activities are supervised by paperwork and records, revenues are budgeted from a central treasury bureau, and the whole enterprise justifies itself by efficiency.

While Weber—debating the Marxists—correctly foresaw that legal-rational bureaucracy was a more dangerous institution for human liberty than market capitalism, he could never have imagined the totalitarian extremes that Hitler's Germany and Stalin's Soviet Union reached by means of this institution. The Ottoman gate slaves were a corporation recruited, originally cruelly, from the subject populations. They conquered, administered, and defended a vast empire for their sultan, but they left social life to ongoing civil communities, production to the guilds, consumption to marketplaces, and justice and learning to the clergy. Not so in a modern totalitarian regime. In it, a self-perpetuating corporation, such as the Communist party in the former USSR, controls through subsidiary bureaucracies the organs of production, consumption, learning, police, justice, and defense, and all the associations ordinarily associated with a free and responsible citizenry. Fortunately, the Soviet version of this system has collapsed, together with its unwilling empire in Eastern Europe, and the predictions of its most severe internal critics, such as the physicist Andrei Sakharov, have been borne out.

Baroque legal-rational bureaucracy had its own community form, in cities dedicated to the absolute power of legal-rational monarchs, the Baroque capitals.

THE BAROQUE CAPITAL: MONUMENT TO ABSOLUTE ROYAL BUREAUCRATIC POWER

The culture and art of the sixteenth to the eighteenth centuries in Europe is known as *Baroque*, marked by dynamic opposition and energy and curving and plastic forms. In science Sir Isaac Newton discovered the laws of gravity and related them to the motions of the solar system in one grand theory. In technology clockwork was perfected; in social organization legal-rational bureaucracy emerged. In architecture the whole order was given coherence around one giant sundial in the monumental royal residence cities, the **Baroque capitals.** In keeping with our emphasis on culture and community, we shall discuss that form here, as it is indicative of the culture in which corporate bureaucracy was born.

Culture of the Baroque Capital

As a city type, the Baroque capital is most pure in a royal-residence city such as Versailles in France, built in the seventeenth century by Louis XIV, the "Sun King."

During the Baroque age, Sir Isaac Newton's discovery of the laws of gravity accounted for the movements of the solar system. The culture of the Age of Enlightenment reflects that discovery and the solar system itself. The capitals of ancient empires, such as the square around the Forbidden City in dynastic China, had reflected an eternal rectangular universe with the emperor at the sacred mountain close to heaven. In contrast, the Baroque capital reflected a clockwork universe with the "sun king" at the center of a giant sundial. The solar system had replaced heaven. Light and enlightenment was the hopeful symbol of the age.

Mechanical clocks had been perfected and were the rage (indeed the consuming hobby of that unfortunate monarch, Louis XVI, who was to lose his head to another machine, the guillotine). The whole nature of time had changed for Europeans. Time was no longer the rhythms of the life cycle but clock time divided up by the swing of the pendulum and the ticking of the seconds. Philosophers who were largely courtiers and amateurs now understood that the swinging of the pendulum was an expression of the motion of the earth upon its axis; that the earth spins and revolves around the sun by celestial clockwork; that time is an expression of that very same motion.

The Palace Square in St. Petersburg (formerly Leningrad), looking at the Army General Staff Building around the triumphal arch and the Alexander Column, both commemorating Russian victory over Napoleon. This square was used to review troops and to receive vast military parades down the Nevsky Prospect.

Baroque Royal Rituals: The Parade

Royal **military parades** were the great Baroque rites of intensification, and they provided symbolic coherence as only rituals can. Baroque parade and drill were quite different from the war rallies of old. Western parades to this day are the ritual expression of the absolute power of the commander-in-chief, the monarch, over the foot soldiers, with their clockwork motions of marching and saluting, each in perfect timing and rhythm with thousands of others. Fancy dress drill before the reviewing stand and displays of firearms and animals, such as the famous stallions of Vienna, are brought into perfect synchronization in the most elaborate ways in royal parades.

Marching past the vanishing point on the avenue was the symbol of infinite royal power. Such a parade vanished, not by turning a corner, but by extending out of sight. The grand finale of a day of parade and drill was the light of the explosion of gunpowder: fireworks bursting over palace and avenue as if the sun itself were exploding in the night sky to the strains of royal anthems.

Like all rites of intensification, the parade reinforced social and political ties. The power of the monarch was upheld by the symbols of clockwork, gunpowder, marching men, horses, infinity, and the solar system itself. Religious rituals continued, but they took second place to the secular rites of enlightened despots.

Dominant Architectural Forms of the Baroque Capital

The forms that emerged at Versailles had been used before and were favored by military planners. Architect Francesco Martini had drawn up a military plan for an octagonal town in 1500; the republic of Venice founded one in 1593 (Mumford 1961). Let us take up the architectural features of these forms.

Asterisk and Sundial. The master form of the architects who designed royal residences and worked on projects within the older capitals was an asterisk pattern, applied with ruthless and geometric perfection on the terrain and layout of avenues. A miniature asterisk is often found in formal gardens of the era, which are laid out in footpaths around a sundial. In this way, the garden itself becomes a sundial, the rays of the sun falling upon the walkways so that their shadows tell time everywhere, not just on the dial itself. The asterisk was also used for grander purposes in parks and was the favorite design for landscaping royal hunting lodges, for it lent itself to royal pleasure as no other plan can.

The king and his hunting party could start at any point on horseback, galloping after the stag as it disappeared in the distance down another avenue. Dogs and mounted hunters, if not the deer, had splendid sport for hours, chas-

Air view of Versailles, Baroque royal-residence city. Originally a hunting lodge for Louis XIII, it was transformed by the Sun King, Louis XIV, conserving the asterisk-sundial plan. Note the monumental avenue leading straight to the palace in the upper center, and the repetition of the asterisk in the formal gardens in the foreground.

ing endlessly down and around wide avenues through the woods. At the center of the spokes of the asterisk of avenues the lodge itself might stand. This plan was applied to whole towns, to cities, and to projects within cities.

Fortifications. Gunpowder came into its own in Europe in early modern times. Ferdinand and Isabella discovered its effectiveness when they laid siege to Moorish Granada, taking it in 1492. Artillery changed the whole nature of fortifications, for old medieval city walls were now inadequate. Baroque capitals were defended by mounded earthworks past the perimeter of the settlement.

The earthworks enclosed the asterisk, if such was the master plan, making it either a circle or polygon, and spokes of earthworks formed a star (see Figure 18.1). The enclosure limited living space within the city, so that working-class quarters expanded upward in tenements seven or eight stories high. Crowding was worsened by heavy numbers of soldiers in the barracks. There were 21,309 soldiers out of a total population of 90,000 in Berlin in 1740 (Mumford, 1961). The fortifications had gates, affording the kings opportunities to erect triumphal arches for parades celebrating military victories and for royal entries and exits during courtly excursions.

Figure 18.1 Baroque urban fortification patterns.

Monumental Avenue and Parade Ground. Royal designers often took one central avenue of the asterisk as an axis, prolonging it and extending it from some monumental gate to the grand facade of the palace itself at the center.

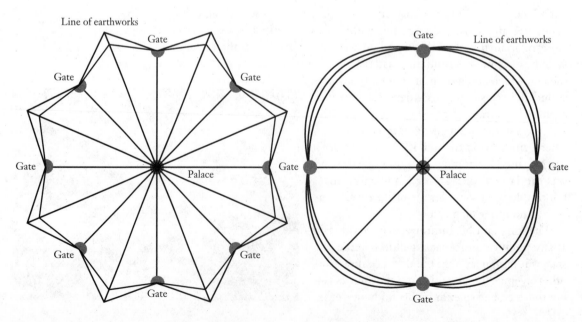

This avenue was closely associated with the discovery of perspective in painting, where the vanishing point gives the illusion of infinity. This illusion was heightened by lining the avenue with palaces of uniform height and ornament.

The Palace and Its Derivatives. At the great royal-residence cities, such as Versailles, Potsdam in Prussia, and Aranjuez in Spain, the great palace occupies the center of the asterisk, the sundial. The Baroque capital spawned a number of palatial buildings with other functions besides housing the monarch. Palace office buildings (and lesser palaces of nobility and new grandees elevated as cabinet ministers in royal bureaucracies) lined great avenues; an example is the Nevsky Prospect in St. Petersburg, lined with palatial shops as well as palaces. Another classic example is the mall extending from the Capitol in Washington, D.C. Block after block of uniform palaces extend to the vanishing point, a bureaucratic infinity.

In addition, nonroyal palaces were needed for foreign embassies, and for visiting notables the palatial hotel appeared. Grand hotels in the capitals of Europe are quite literally palaces; in London, for example, visiting royalty is housed in the Claridge Hotel. Certain palaces housed royal art collections and later became art galleries open to the public. Some of the greatest art museums in the world are royal collections housed in palaces: the Prado in Madrid, the Louvre in Paris, and the Hermitage in St. Petersburg, to name a few. The royal hunting park likewise changed; it grew into the public city park on the one hand—such as the Retiro in Madrid and the Bois de Boulogne in Paris—and amusement gardens on the other, such as the famed Tivoli Gardens in Copenhagen or Vauxhall in London.

Within the complex of royal parks certain other features factored out and are very much with us today. The royal botanical collections gave rise to the public botanical garden. Likewise, the royal zoological park becomes the public zoo.

Architectural Eclipse of the Church. It is curious that in Baroque plans, a church is not usually at the center of any asterisk of avenues. Churches and cathedrals continued to be built, but they were upstaged by palaces. The cathedral of Madrid, for example, is a minor building to one side of the Royal Palace, which completely eclipses it.

Mumford points out that many activities conducted in churches were removed to other places in the early modern period. Pulpit, preaching, and teaching went to the universities or to the brilliant salons, the evening receptions in the drawing rooms of noble palaces that concentrated on talk and philosophy. The choir was displaced by concerts in the royal chambers (chamber music). Church pageants were replaced by theater presentations,

St. Petersburg: A Baroque Capital

St. Petersburg, Russia (formerly Leningrad) was founded in 1703 by Peter the Great (1672–1725), with the laying of the cornerstone of the Peter and Paul Fortress on an island in the Neva River. Three great avenues ("prospects") converge on the center of Peter's sundial city plan, the Admiralty, which was the second building in the new city, designed to be Russia's window on the West. The Admiralty was originally a shipyard, where Peter the Great commanded the construction of something new, a Russian navy fleet. A winter palace (not the current structure, which houses the Hermitage Art Museum) and the Palace Square were among the next elements to appear in the founding of the capital. Note that St. Isaac's Cathedral is on a grand square on the other side of the Admiralty from Palace Square. A final original element, at the other end of the great Nevsky Prospect, was the Alexander Nevsky

Monastery and church, where Peter brought the remains of the warrior tsar and saint, Alexander Nevsky, who had repelled invaders from Russia and who is one of the patron saints of the city (St. Peter is the other). The Peter and Paul Fortress also became a shrine, since within its walls the Cathedral of Saints Peter and Paul holds the tombs of Peter and all the monarchs who succeeded him in his Romanov dynasty, including the last one, Nicholas II (whose murdered remains were interred secretly in Siberia by the Bolsheviks but were reburied in a state funeral in 1998).

When couples get married today in St. Petersburg, they have their photograph taken in front of the great horseman statue of Peter the Great by the Admiralty, then they deposit flowers from the bridal bouquet in the Neva, and finally they leave the rest of the flowers on Peter's tomb. The tsar's legacy remains one of the world's most beautiful cities.

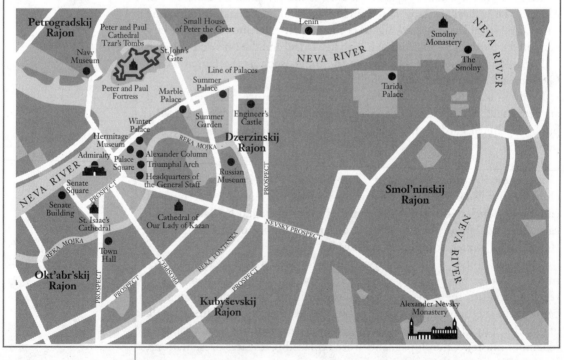

often at the royal palace, where the audience was seated by rank and wealth. The central nave of the church was repeated in the first stock exchanges—the bourse at Antwerp, for example—and later in shopping malls.

Survivals and Revivals of the Baroque Capital

Most pure Baroque capitals were royal-residence cities built outside of older capitals. None of these older capitals was completely done over to the master plan. Some cities were built from scratch, such as St. Petersburg and Washington, D.C., whose original plan was a masterpiece of Baroque design. For 200 years, state planners have been expressing their fascination with that old design, producing Canberra in Australia, New Delhi in India, and Brazil's new capital Brasilia, which was carved imperiously out of the wilderness on the central plateau during the 1950s and 1960s.

Another example of Baroque survival is the Magic Kingdom of the several Disney theme parks around the world whose form is exactly that of the royal-residence city. From the inner gates, a central parade avenue (Main Street) leads to a giant asterisk of pedestrian avenues converging on a circle on an island in front of the Castle, the palace. The entire Magic Kingdom is surrounded by mounded earthworks, which, while not meant to be fortifications, do enclose the whole in an impenetrable circle. By day there are parades down Main Street, and by night fireworks flash over the castle to the strains of "America the Beautiful." Walt Disney knew that a magical "kingdom" had to take the form of the Baroque capital if people were "to believe" (Moore, 1980a).

Modern bureaucratic corporations originated in the civil and military state services of the Baroque capitals; in the joint stock companies, counting houses, and banks of the mercantile nation-states; and in the factories of the mill towns. In 1600 citizens joined the army and went on parade for the monarch. Today we join an organization of the corporate bureaucracy.

THE MODERN CORPORATION AND BUREAUCRACY

The corporation was invented in Roman law as a means of establishing business partnerships in which two or more men could act as one person (the Latin *corpus* means "body") for purposes of making contracts in the marketplace. Monarchs in Baroque Europe discovered that chartering notables (joint

St. Isaac's Cathedral in St. Petersburg. Under the tsars, it was the prime church of the Russian empire.

stockholders) as one body for foreign exploration and colonization proved extremely useful. The corporation could build ships, dispatch them on voyages, import, export, govern colonies, and eventually build and manage factories. Today bureaucracy has become the dominant organizational form in every sphere of human work, spreading via the corporation, in all developed and developing countries.

The first civil government in British North America was by an ordinance of the Virginia Company in 1621 (Kimball and McClellan, 1962). The Virginia Company, which obtained the Virginia charters in 1606 and 1609, was originally a small group of proprietors. Like so many other boards of directors, they soon found they could govern a colony by grafting a state organization on their corporation. Corporate service was then and still is modeled on state service.

In the United States, the corporate form was encouraged by American distrust of state agencies. American corporations claimed the legal privileges and immunities that private persons have under the Constitution. During the last half of the nineteenth century, a series of Supreme Court decisions greatly strengthened such claims and expedited the practices of the robber barons, who industrialized North America with corporately owned railroads, coal and oil fields, and steel mills (Kimball and McClellan, 1962).

The New Command Center: The Corporate Board

Today all that has been added to the old bureaucratic table of organization is the body of persons who compose the "corporation": a board, or council. (I like to use the Latin word for group, *collegium*.) Legal control may be vested in some larger assembly, such as a convention of all the stockholders, but corporate decisions are usually made by small councils or by directors in consultation with top managers. Corporate boards (directors, regents, trustees, and so on) meet regularly with chief executives of corporations to listen to and consider managerial reports.

In public corporations, the collegium is the same as the corporation. Consider your university, for example. Although it imagines itself a community of scholars—faculty, students, and alumni—a public university is controlled through state legislatures and governors by means of state-appointed boards of regents. In a private university, the board is often selected by the alumni. In either case, the collegium *is* the university; it is vested with legal ownership of lands and buildings and with responsibility for the operation of classrooms and research facilities.

Institutional Consequences

No institutional endeavor organized for work is immune from the corporation. In the United States alone, an average of 200,000 new corporations were chartered per year in the early 1960s and late 1950s. Not all these were

474

highly bureaucratized (Kimball and McClellan, 1962), but those that were have spawned their own multiple subagencies or subsidiaries. Our largest corporations are all conglomerates, or multiple organizations, in some sense. Universities changed from simple undergraduate colleges to collections of schools and colleges on one campus (undergraduate, business, law, medicine, and so on) and then to collections of campuses, such as the University of California, which has nine campuses, each with its own collection of schools.

Larger corporations may have subsidiaries that actually compete with each other in the market system, an example being General Motors. Pontiac, Oldsmobile, Buick, and even economy Cadillacs and luxury Chevrolets, the top and bottom of the line, compete with each other. General Motors, like many similar "transnational" corporations (think of Toyota, Honda, Mitsubishi, just to name a few) also has subsidiaries that operate factories in many different nation-states. Yet, in spite of such corporate complexity and in spite of annual profits that for many transnationals are greater than the gross national product and the government income of many nation-states, each such company is *one person* before the law, the same as you and I are.

The modern form of bureaucracy is the corporation, headed by a board of directors.

The corporate form dominates industry, commerce, entertainment, hospitals, transportation, tourism, and hotels. Even traditionally congregational and nonbureaucratic religious denominations now have their associated secretariats and subsidiaries—a board of home missions, for example, or a board of church publications. Agriculture has also been invaded by the corporation. In some cases, land is taken up by commercial firms (agribusinesses). In other cases, farmers are dominated by companies that prepare and pack food (their principal buyers) and are supplied by other companies with machinery, seeds, fertilizers, and insecticides. In addition, the heavily capitalized modern farmer is supplied by banks with short-term credit from harvest to harvest. Farming is not as simple as it used to be!

Social Effects

Socially, the corporate revolution has had two contradictory effects. In capitalist countries, differences in wealth and status have increased because the families that founded the great industrial corporations are now heirs to the greatest fortunes the world has ever known. Such fortunes consist of shares in company stock (industrials, chemicals, utilities, banks) that can never be lost, dissipated, or spent by any one heir. All the descendants of John D. Rockefeller who bear the Rockefeller surname, for example, have inheritances larger than any one individual can spend. Because of expanding national economies, such fortunes grow with growing industries, dividends, and interest rates. It is true that some fortunes do not grow faster than the number of family heirs, but some of these heirs are still richer than the monarchs of the Baroque age. Moreover, every few decades new entrepreneurs create new fortunes, often based on new technologies. Witness the rise of Bill Gates and his Microsoft Corporation.

The other effect of corporations is a socially leveling one. Corporations, like all legal-rational bureaucracies, thrive on trained and competent management. No great private corporation can afford to allow the patrimonial claims of incompetent ownership and the dynastic principle to influence its management or its policy decisions. Members of owning families are preferred for managerial jobs only when they have produced the proper credentials and demonstrated their competency. (Many family members are actively engaged in Du Pont enterprises, for example.)

Silent coalitions of hired managers and family members will act to oust incompetent owner-managers by kicking them "upstairs" or by finding some harmless activity to occupy them. The dynastic principle is not allowed to interfere with the bureaucratic one, and when the two principles come to a test, ownership is divorced from management. (See A. A. Berle, Jr., *Power Without Property*, 1959, for a study of this process.)

Thus, while incomparably wealthy persons now "own" most private corporations, corporate management is vested in an increasingly larger and diverse group of professionals. Managers need have no social connection whatever with owners, and in the long run corporations are quite unconcerned with managers' "irrelevant" and "private" characteristics. Credentials depend increasingly on impersonal demonstrations of competence rather than on social, ethnic, racial, regional, sexual, or religious factors.

CORPORATE BUREAUCRATIC TABLES OF ORGANIZATION

As complex teams managed in ranks of individuals arranged in chains of command, bureaucracies are far more complicated than teams of tribesmen. In the United States, the principal example is the chain of command in the military **table of organization,** which leads directly from the president as commander-in-chief to the lowliest infantry private. The chain branches at each step downward, with each position responsible for many positions below it, thus forming a true hierarchy (see Figure 18.2).

Under the single commander-in-chief at the top are (1) a number of general officers, heads of divisions whose official staff assistants are members of the officer corps, and (2) generals who head their own subunits and who together with their assistants make up the commissioned officer corps. Officers of all modern armed forces are grouped into ranks, or strata. Certain jobs are reserved for certain ranks—that is, certain divisions may be commanded only by colonels, and so on.

Within each rank every individual also has a protocol or precedence ranking at any given post. If a number of majors, for example, are assigned to the same garrison, when they gather for an official function or even to board a vehicle, they follow each other "Indian file" according to their "number" in strict seniority; each knows his exact place in line. (For a discussion of how this kind of strict rank order avoids conflict and orders all army post

Figure 18.2 Corporate bureaucratic table of organization.

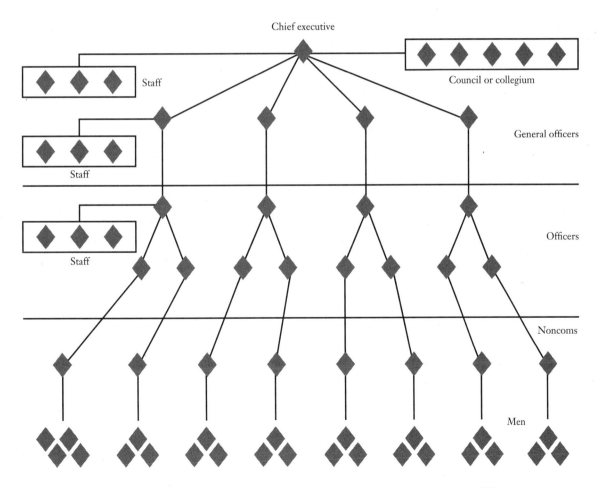

relations, see Kimball and McClellan, 1962, pp. 246–247.) Underneath the officers and assisting them in their staffs are noncommissioned sergeants of various grades. Some are in charge of the next grouping down, the "men," who in the United States Army are divided into corporals and privates, foot soldiers all.

In theory, all Western armies serve the citizens of their nation-state, who are thereby their clients, since the army defends them. In addition, army units are the clients of many units in other branches of the government and of private industries that supply them with munitions and materiel. The table of organization differs drastically among agencies: in numbers of personnel, ratios of officers to subordinates, numbers of subunits, and types of clients.

Most large universities in the Western world, for example, are headed by a chief executive, president, or rector, who is assisted by a number of top-level general officers, such as the vice-president for academic affairs and the university business officer (treasurer). Below them are the deans in charge of divisions, such as schools and colleges, assisted by their own "baby deans." Academic "commissioned officers" are the faculty, which in most North American universities is organized in four or five ranks of professors. The "noncommissioned officers" of the academic world are graduate teaching assistants, and the "men" are students. A university also has clients—parents, alumni, and, in public universities, the people of the state. The research function also brings many clients—agricultural extension services find clients in every farm family, for instance. Faculty members are themselves clients to agencies and foundations that sponsor their research—which is as much a function of a great university as teaching is.

We may easily apply the table of organization to any bureaucracy, including hospitals. Anthropologist Carol Taylor (1970) points out that in hospital wards there are three kinds of officers: a physician; an administrator in charge of services, supplies, and budget; and a nurse. To avoid conflicts, they are supposed to be a decision-making team, but rivalry and squabbles are common because of a built-in professional rivalry between physicians and nurses, who regard themselves as full professionals. In the United States Armed Services Medical Corps, nurses are commissioned officers, but in other medical settings, physicians have traditionally treated nurses as sergeants, not officers.

The relative position of orderlies and patients is ambiguous. In formal terms, orderlies and aides are at the bottom of the table of organization, equivalent in any pay chart to the privates of an army. By the same chart, patients who pay for services are clients. But in fact, patients in hospitals are also at the bottom rung of the hierarchy; they are acted upon and given orders "for their own good." This puts them on the same level as the orderly, and tensions result.

BEHAVIOR IN MODERN BUREAUCRACIES

Beyond the typological and developmental concerns pioneered by Weber is the day-to-day behavior of people in bureaucracies. Conrad Arensberg's framework for viewing behavior in factories applies to all kinds of legal-rational corporate bureaucracies. Arensberg is one of a handful of anthropologists who, along with other social scientists, have done field work in factories. Let us examine his findings (Arensberg and Kimball, 1965).

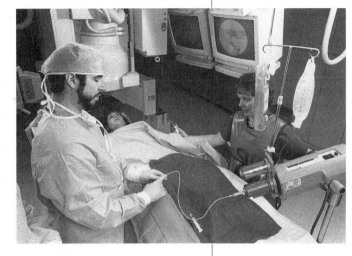

In the hospital bureaucracy, patients are at the bottom of the hierarchy.

Lines of Work

In factories, the minute formal work activities of men at the bottom of the hierarchy in the table of organization are the result of very old informal human patterns of cooperation. For thousands of years in the civilized world, the production of goods was handled by age-graded craft workshops grouped into guilds. Adolescent boys entered a shop to learn tasks by imitating under supervision. These apprentices usually started with lower-ranking, dirtier, more physically demanding tasks that required less precision. When the apprentice became a journeyman, he commanded some larger sequence of the whole job, as when a tailor's apprentice had learned to cut an entire suit of clothes to the measure of a client.

Finally, some workers achieved the final stage and were graduated to the status of master workman, one who commanded all the techniques and separate tasks of the trade. Master workmen could perform the whole process from beginning to end and were judged fit to supervise apprentices and journeymen. As in Ireland in the 1930s, this usually meant setting up one's own shop and finding a wife—assuming adulthood in both public and private life.

Eventually work and supervision were separated. Whereas master craftsmen had originally engaged in the productive enterprise and worked alongside their fellows as well as supervising them, in ancient empires these two activities were separated, both in war and in public works. Lewis Mumford has pointed out that an ancient public project was a kind of factory organization, a vast human machine in which masses of people were thrown together in work gangs; efforts were synchronized within gangs and between gangs. This was before the invention of the steam engine and the utilization of nonanimal sources of power.

Thus, in all line-of-work behavior, gangs of workers do minutely supervised tasks set for them by management, whether they are laboring on ancient monuments, typing at desks in office buildings, or working on industrial assembly lines. This flow of work is repeated in rites of intensification, whether it is the drill of the common foot soldier on the parade ground or the split-second synchronization of band members responding to the baton of their musical director as they produce highly rational Western music.

Supervision Down the Line

All bureaucratic organizations are good at supervisory behavior; decisions made at the top are quickly made known at the bottom through orders and commands. Bureaucratic behavior originates at the top in policy decisions; directives are issued by the board, and executive memorandums implement those directives. Directives are supposed to be consistent with *overall* goals, such as making a profit or providing for national defense, and with *specific* objectives, such as making profitable shoes or winning a battle.

As one goes down the line, officials have less formal discretion in matters of policy and greater responsibility for carrying out directives to the letter. Nineteenth-century European governments were notably rigid and demanding in this respect.

Staff-Line Behavior

Prevalent in industry is a cybernetic device used by management to maintain an optimum level of productivity, work, or preparedness (as in an army). Various supervisors, especially engineers in industry, intervene in the line of work and troubleshoot. Such intervention is often in response to flagging production reports, mechanical failures, breakdowns, and complaints by supervisors that there are problems with workers. Even the advice of reading experts in grade school classes are staff-line activities.

Up-the-Line Behavior

Bureaucracies do not excel at and are not designed for a rapid flow of information or evaluation of performance back to the decision makers. All bureaucracies are designed to implement decisions made at the top by activities that produce quickly measured results: profits, industrial inventories, winning a battle, or some other score. In such organizations, as Chapple and Coon (1942) pointed out, a line of cleavage separates work from supervision and workers from supervisors.

As Arensberg points out, formal up-the-line activity is what union-management grievance procedures involve. Union shop stewards outside the productive chain of command are able to initiate activity and send information back up the line. But it took concerted efforts on the part of the labor movement to institute such procedures, and they are by no means universal in the world today.

Informal Relations Between Workers

Bureaucracies, including industry, largely ignored human contact between peers on the line of work; they did not plan for it and only began to investigate it when social scientists in the 1930s launched studies aimed at improving production by attending to social and psychological factors. Informal worker behaviors vary. In some highly programmed and formal situations, there is no contact between workers; in other situations intense friendships develop, and workers cluster in cliques around leaders, ostracizing certain social isolates.

A machine shop, ca. 1910. Workers interacted with machines, not with each other.

THE CULTURE OF CORPORATE WORK AND THE CULT OF EFFICIENCY

In the previous chapter we saw that capitalism, industrialism, and price-regulated markets all arose at once, an accident that Weber attributes in part to the Protestant ethic among the dissenting Puritans of the merchant and new manufacturing groups. In the rise of corporate bureaucracy we see the mentality necessary for free market capitalism and industrialism wedded with the mentality of the highly educated, professionally identified, rational civil servant who has passed many aptitude and achievement tests and who believes that technical solutions are available for all human problems, especially for the advancement of his or her bureaucratic agency.

The Protestant Ethic and Enlightened Bureaucratic Rationality

These two ethics, Protestant and bureaucratic professional, were combined. They were in fact quite compatible with each other, and their combined influence is a dominant strain in modern culture today.

The **Protestant ethic,** eventually translated into what Ernest Gellner (1988) calls **generic Protestantism,** entails several things. First is the "priesthood of all believers." This means that the full moral and theological implications of a religion have been absorbed by a literate, even learned, set of men and women, who in effect conduct their personal life with the same devotion of monks and nuns in cloistered convents. Only these Puritans live in the world.

Second, productive work is considered a badge of salvation, a sign of God's calling. Yet, because Puritans lived austerely, they reinvested their earnings into their firms.

Third, because of the high degree of internal personality controls, there is little need for a strong state or police power. When they do appear, Puritan police and military forces also tend to be incorruptible, nonavaricious, and completely trustworthy to carry out their chartered mandate, something never known in the original dynastic empires. Moreover, Puritan officials tend to treat bureaucratic office as a trust and are willing to be rotated in office at the expense of building personal power. Finally, the legal machinery of the state—and, by implication, the corporation—is taken unquestioningly as an expression of God's will. (That became the case only when the Puritans and their allies had in fact effected revolutions in Great Britain, affirming the Protestant establishment, and in America, affirming the reign of "natural law," as enshrined in the Declaration of Independence and the Constitution.)

Moreover, legal-rational bureaucracies and all corporations recruit **professionals,** people trained in universities for their jobs. Historically, with the rise of the university, professional vocations separated from the priesthood. Ideally physicians, lawyers, engineers, scientists, and other scholars must be true to the ethics of their callings. Professionals and managers have much more freedom to shape their daily work patterns than do factory workers, whose formal behavior is dictated by managers.

The Cult of Efficiency

The combination of generic Protestantism with professional bureaucratic vocations has bred a mentality that puts technique, productivity, and the company rules above other values. In particular, this mentality has tended to dominate in the managerial—that is, official—ranks of corporations, rather than in the worker ranks. Let us see how this has worked out in practice in modern industry.

An increasing tendency since the 1890s has been to manage human work by a **cult of efficiency** and greater productivity. Informal relations between workers and effective up-the-line behavior are essential for the masses of employees. These behaviors are most closely connected with the private world of household, family, and self. Yet it is precisely these activities that have suffered most from the dehumanizing onslaught of managerial organization.

Sociologist Daniel Bell (1962) identified three types of logic that govern modern industrial organizations: size, hierarchy, and metric time. The logic that gathered workers and machines close to the source of steam-driven power is slowly being overcome. With electricity and mobile gas-engine machines, this centralization is no longer an imperative. In Japan, much industrial production is decentralized and farmed out to individuals who remain at home assembling or processing materials, which are then sent on to other processors. The firm assumes the cost of transporting materials to the workers. The logic of size is still operative in the United States, however, where workers come to the factory at their own cost and where enormous work areas are under one roof. The old General Motors plant at Willow Run, Michigan, for example, is a shed two-thirds of a mile long and one-fourth of a mile wide.

The logic of hierarchy was pointed out by Karl Marx in his studies of the Industrial Revolution in the mid-1800s. Marx called it the "iron law of proportionality." He cited an example in type manufacture: One founder could cast 2000 type an hour, the breaker could break up 4000, and the polisher could finish 8000 in the same time; thus, to keep one polisher busy, the enterprise needed two breakers and four founders, and units were hired or discharged, therefore, in multiples of seven" (Bell, 1962, p. 234).

In factories, time takes on a dimension of clockwork quite unrivaled by even the Baroque army and its drill. Split-second timing and the stopwatch were introduced into industry by American engineer Fredrick Taylor (born in 1856), who called his approach **scientific management.**

Taylorism

Taylor had a vigorous career as a management consultant. He saw all work flows as "problems" because workers had set their own pace. To his puritanical engineer's mind, all workers were guilty of "soldiering," deliberately working below maximum effort. The term comes from the infamous informal behavior of certain soldiers in a standing army who spend little or no time in actual combat and tend to let informal relationships get the upper hand in day-to-day activities. Taylor detested soldiering and set out to abolish it.

Taylor used price-regulated market theory to back up his attack on soldiering. Workers, he said, were mistaken in believing that raised output would mean fewer jobs and greater unemployment. Increased output could only mean lower costs, which in turn meant lower prices, which meant greater sales and more work. (This is, of course, a very partial view of the business cycle.) At any rate, Taylor set himself the task of making human beings and machines produce at optimum capacity.

In staff-line consultations with management in any given plant, Taylor subjected the flow of work to a rigorous time and motion study with the help of a stopwatch. Fixing his attention on the most skillful workman in a shop, he recorded his motions in the smallest units he could isolate, clocked them repeatedly, and also clocked the motions of the machine in relation to the human motions.

In the actual intervention, Taylor took one likely worker and trained him in new techniques thought out on the drawing board in an attempt to eliminate waste motion and arrive at the one most efficient way of performing any task. The worker was rewarded with a bonus and the promise of greater pay in return for the demonstration that productivity could indeed be raised by the new techniques. Often Taylor perfected the machine involved, since he usually had to regulate its timing and sometimes its mechanical proficiency as well.

Once a single worker had demonstrated that a certain high rate of productivity could be achieved, Taylor standardized the new motions and the new work rate. All workers soon found that they had to learn the new motions, increase their productivity, and maintain the new production rates, or be fired. Taylor did insist, however, that workers converting to his methods receive higher wages. He also insisted that his work rates were well within the daily capacities of the normal healthy worker.

The Spread of Taylorism

Taylorism found a wide public. Taylor's books were read avidly in the United States and translated into many languages, including Russian. One of Taylor's readers and admirers was Lenin, who was busy directing the Russian revolution and its aftermath. Taylorism was incorporated into the work code of the Soviet Union at an early date, and scientific management was instituted in Soviet factories. Soviet rate busters were deliberately discovered, heaped with honors, and publicly invested with medals as heroes. These workers set new and seemingly superhuman rates of production, which were then made mandatory for other workers. Such rate busters were called *Stakhanovites* after Stakhanov, the first one to be singled out and decorated.

The labor movement in the United States did not take kindly to Taylorism. Labor critics embarrassed Taylor by raising questions about health and longevity under the new production rates. In truth, Taylor always insisted that management raise wages when they adopted his methods, which he guaranteed to raise productivity. In the long run, that became the bargaining point between trade unions and management. The labor movement today does not usually challenge the postulates of Taylorism. Instead, it bargains for higher wages and other benefits in return for increased productivity.

The contract between U.S. Steel and the CIO Steelworkers Union of May 8, 1946 illustrates the nature of the bargains. It first set a benchmark

Taylorism in action. This industrial worker must synchronize the motions of both hands with the movement of the conveyer belt in a pace predetermined to the split second.

definition of a "fair day's work," with which all particular daily jobs were equated. The benchmark was "that amount of work that can be produced by a qualified employee when working at a normal pace . . . equivalent to a man walking, without load, on a smooth level ground at a rate of three miles per hour" (Bell, 1962, p. 236).

How this normal pace was to be translated into precise amounts of factory work is a mystery of scientific management and collective bargaining, but let us consider the following job specifications that resulted, a translation set forth in the same contract:

Packaging staples

Material: 34 x 14 gauge staples; 1 pound per cardboard box

Equipment: 3-pound capacity metal scoop, platform scale; assembled cardboard boxes with one end open for filling; metal covered working surface

Working condition: inside, seated

Production rate: filling scoop from pile of staples in tray, pouring one pound into tray on scale, picking up tray and pouring into cardboard box, closing flaps on box, placing aside approximately 24 inches—5.9 boxes a minute

Consider what this job specification meant for a worker undertaking it. The pace of work itself in the benchmark was not terribly demanding. The staples packager was seated indoors at a metal working surface. It would

A modern assembly line.

seem from the contract that cardboard boxes were coming toward the worker, perhaps on a conveyer belt, with one end open. Our packager wielded a three-pound scoop in one hand, scooped up staples, and poured them into the tray on the scale exactly to the measure of one pound and then deftly poured that tray into the cardboard box. Then, with one or both hands, the worker closed the box and set it aside where the boxes could conveniently continue on their way in the assembly line.

Note that there was no time for dillydallying and no time for pouring more or less than the exact pound of staples into the tray on the scales, since the packager was obligated to fill 5.9 boxes a minute at the correct weight. The pace may not seem strenuous but the motions demanded were precise and rigorous. Moreover, there was no room in this job description for innovation or for trading off jobs with other workers. The packager was figuratively chained to the metal-covered working surface doing a job designed and planned by others.

Our packager sat scooping and filling boxes at the rate of 5.9 a minute, eight hours a day, five days a week, fifty-two weeks a year (with appropriate vacation time). That is what a lifetime of work came to be. Unlike the apprentice and journeyman in the old craft workshops, our packager was not assured of the possibility of advancement within the line of work. He or she might get other jobs on the assembly line, perhaps more skilled and higher paying than packaging staples, but otherwise he or she was not even assured of being promoted to that ambiguous worker-manager position, foreman, the sergeant of industry.

E T H N O G R A P H I C   C L O S E - U P

THE WORKER AND THE GROUP

One of the most famous studies of informal behavior on the line of work was done in 1931 at the Western Electric Company plant in Hawthorne, Illinois. The study was reported by F. J. Roethlisberger and William J. Dickson in *Management and the Worker* (1940) and restudied exhaustively by George C. Homans in *The Human Group* (1950).

A researcher spent months systematically observing and recording activities in the bank-wiring room at the plant. Nine wiremen placed wires on banks (electrical equipment), three soldermen soldered the wires in place, and two inspectors tested the completed banks to make sure that each was functioning correctly. The workers formed two informal cliques of friends who joked, traded jobs, helped each other, bet on horses, told stories, and bought candy. The incidence of doing such things together was much greater within each clique than outside.

Cliques were spatially determined. Clique A consisted of all of the men at one work table, and Clique B of all those at the work table on the opposite end of the room. Of the men at the third (middle) table, one on each edge fraternized with the men at the adjacent table, while the wireman (W5) and the solderer (S2) who worked in the middle of the table were literal social isolates, if not outcasts (see Figure 18.3).

These two men constituted the social division in the room. The middle wireman (W5) was more disliked. The others considered him a rate buster, since he consistently produced at a higher rate than the group norm. The solderer at the table was neither liked nor disliked but was regarded with indifference. Not so the inspector (I3) who inspected the work of Clique B. Because he took it on himself to report minor infractions to management, he was hated and regarded as a squealer. Eventually the men used informal up-the-line means to have him removed from the job.

The individual most respected by the entire group (W3) was the leader of Clique A. All the men went to him for advice, offered him help, and volunteered to trade jobs with him. This man was the one worker who fulfilled the group production rate or norm *exactly*. In the larger group, in addition to the ostracized and disliked rate buster in the middle, there was a "chiseler" from Clique B (W9) whose output was consistently below the group norm. This man was joshed severely if his output fell too far below group levels.

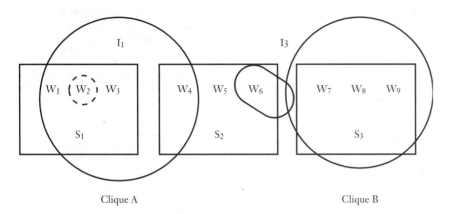

Figure 18.3 Bank-wiring room: division of the group into cliques.

THE INFORMAL GROUP AND PRODUCTION

All told, it was clear that the workers of the bank-wiring room were not producing at optimum capacity. In Taylor's terms, they were all soldiering (although they had not been subjected to a time-motion study). The social psychologists prominent in early industrial studies tended to discount workers' own explanations of limited production as "rationalizations." Workers said they feared layoffs if production went up, since management might select a few to do the work of many. The social psychologists held that production was limited by low morale, which could be remedied by individual attention and recognition from management. When such attention was provided to the workers studied, productivity did increase.

Social psychologists later suggested that industry use the informal group as a means of organizing production and letting the workers set their own goals and pace. Experiments were made with white-collar workers, clerks in a large insurance company (Bell, 1962). Results showed that the control group, which was rigorously managed during the experimental period, produced at a higher rate than the self-directed one but that the latter group expressed greater personal satisfaction with the job. Because management tends to measure all organizational efforts exclusively in terms of productivity, the experiment was not a success for greater worker autonomy and group direction.

Sociologist Eugene Schneider (1969) argues that informal group behavior has many adaptive functions for the individual worker. It provides relief from boredom and fatigue on the job and opportunities for recognition. In the bank-wiring room, for example, other individuals besides the leader were respected. In addition, the informal group allows for a flow of emotional

Many companies in the U.S., such as Westing-house, are using a team approach to motivate workers and boost productivity.

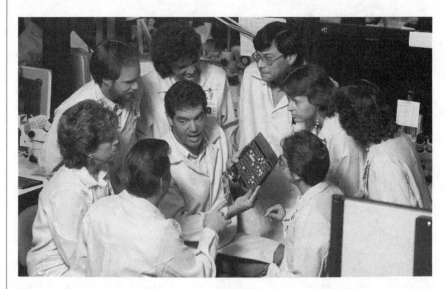

responses and independence from management, and it creates a sense of security.

Such informal groups resemble teams of tribals around a natural leader, as in the case of the Nambicuara. The leader sets the pace and is adept at all group tasks, including informal entertainment and games, without excelling to perfection. It is interesting to note that the leader in the bank-wiring room did not represent the group to management; management was scarcely aware of his identity let alone of his informal role. Yet it was he whose activity implicitly set the production rate of the group.

Suggestions that industry make greater use of informal worker groupings and invest them with greater flexibility on the job have now been taken up by voices within the labor movement in the United States. Moreover, Taylorism itself has been subjected to critical review and testing in plants where time-motion methods have been standardized. Engineer Adam Abruzzi challenged Taylorism through a series of statistical tests to determine whether each standardized motion is indeed independent of the motions immediately before and after it. He concluded that human industrial productivity in fact depends on a whole form, body motions in an entire technique larger than the individual movements (Bell, 1962).

As long as managers are interested first and foremost in productivity, they will be little inclined to listen to arguments for work group autonomy, individual creativity at the job, and natural body movements. This is as true in nationalized (state-owned) socialist industry as it is in capitalist firms. Thus, I must agree with industrial sociologist Eugene Schneider that no informal group of workers is about to exert more than a minor influence on the wider firm. Informal groups find it very difficult to send much information back up the line. To do so, workers have had to join trade unions. The next chapter considers trade unions as one bridge between private and public worlds.

SUMMARY AND CONCLUSIONS

*I*n Chapter 17 we surveyed the impact and importance of first market-places, then price-regulated markets, and finally factory industrialism in the emergence of the dominant modern community form. In this chapter we have surveyed the effects of the emergence of legal-rational bureaucracies, first in the absolutist Baroque age and later, in the context of the market, in the form of corporate boards (collegia) that succeeded in gaining control of their own legal-rational bureaucracies. The Baroque age had its own dominant community form, the royal-residence city built to replicate a giant sundial and to symbolize a clockwork social order in which the monarch was the source of light and enlightenment. That urban form lingers wherever states still build themselves cities as monuments to bureaucratic power.

Much of the beauty of Baroque culture depicted more order and coherence than the world ever actually had. All the developments of the time in science, commerce, and statecraft seemed to bolster such order; Newtonian physics, the dominant landscape of the asterisk and sundial, and clockworks were part of it.

If the rise of price-regulated markets and industrialism depended in part on the rise of the Protestant ethic, the rise of corporate bureaucracy also depended upon the rise of the career bureaucrat, who was highly skilled in passing examinations and who, highly trained, held some professional diploma. The mentality of the professional career bureaucrat coincides in large measure with the Protestant ethic, producing a culture that can be called "generic Protestantism," no longer having anything to do with religious faith but rather everything to do with professional behavior.

This culture encourages austere behavior, which orients all actions toward some goal that embodies productive work, which is entirely self-policing and superficially incorruptible, and which sees all problems as solvable by technical means. When wedded with free market commercialism, this means an identification of all rewards and values with monetary profit, the "bottom line."

Paradoxically, generic Protestantism and its austere behavior bring material success and, in many individual cases, prosperity. Advertising and popular culture, encouraged by the marketing interests of the great corporations, produce consumerism. Austere, hard-working executives are encouraged to buy goods and to "play hard." Wealth and material goods become status symbols. Consequently the annual changes of fashion, designer goods, and even works of art become badges of success. One trait of factory industrialism is its ability to "overproduce"—that is, turn out more goods than a given population can absorb. High-status goods, yearly fashions, and "planned obsolescence" of hard durable goods are one way to try to solve that problem. The contradiction between consumerism and generic Protestantism remains a source of cultural tension in modern society.

Most modern human beings work for a corporate bureaucracy. While modernization has captured the old national symbolic centers for the masses (Eisenstadt, 1966), it is equally true that the center has captured the masses. Modern workers, supervisors (noncoms), and managers come to their jobs with educational credentials demonstrating that they have the necessary skills or can learn them. Management as a consequence is increasingly separated from ownership, and people are hired more and more on the basis of their relevant skills rather than family background, gender, race, ethnicity, or religion.

People take jobs in one of three broad rankings in corporate bureaucracies: on-the-line workers; noncoms as their immediate supervisors; and managers or officers to execute policies decided on in the collegium corporate board, composed of owners and managers who *are* the corporation.

However, the demands of work, especially on the "firing line" or the line of work, are increasingly less professional and less demanding of human initiative and on-the-spot decisions. This is the case with the noncommissioned officer roles—supervisor, teacher, nurse—as well as of the workers whom they supervise. This trend represents a triumph of staff-line and down-the-line supervisory behavior at the expense of autonomy at the line of work itself. Up-the-line behaviors and informal peer behaviors are simply ignored by the cult of efficiency.

In short, true to their origins in the Baroque age, corporate bureaucracies are still very much the instrument of decision makers at the top, members of the board or collegium, who often unconsciously display the culture of generic Protestantism and have no understanding of other values or of the fact that their values may not be shared by workers down the line. Every corporate bureaucracy produces its own "party line," which noncoms and workers may or may not believe in.

It is perhaps only by a conscious cultivation of informal worker-worker relations and by fostering groups as autonomous production teams that human dignity can be restored to work, not only to assembly lines but to teaching, nursing, office jobs, and so on.

In the countries of the former Communist bloc of Eastern Europe, these defects of corporate behavior were greatly intensified by the attempted centralization of control and the creation of a command economy responding to a single collegium, the Central Committee of the Communist Party of each country but most particularly the Central Committee of the Soviet Union. It is now apparent after the astonishingly rapid collapse of the Marxist-Leninist movement in these countries that the corporate system there was statist, monolithic, highly inefficient, and almost completely unresponsive to its various clienteles. The peoples of these countries are now trying to remedy the situation and come to terms with modernity in ways that will guarantee them both prosperity and human dignity. We shall discuss this problem further in the Epilogue.

Modern life is split into two areas. One's *public life* is played out in places of work and marketing; one's *private life* is played out in households, neighborhoods, and the gathering places of relatives and friends, including street corners. The two institutional devices that serve as bridges between the public and private worlds are voluntary associations and the schools (Kimball and McClellan, 1962). In the next chapter we shall consider these as well as the Japanese version of corporate bureaucratic modern culture.

SUGGESTED READINGS

Blau, Peter. *Bureaucracy in Modern Society*. New York: Random House, 1956. A classic study of formal and informal behavior in office settings: the "book" contrasted with the "ropes."

Goffman, Erving. *Asylums: Essays on the Social Situations of Mental Patients and Other Inmates*. Garden City, N.Y.: Doubleday/Anchor, 1961. By now, the classic study of behavior at the bottom of the table of organization in "total institutions," that is, corporate bureaucracies in which one lives full time.

Holston, James. *The Modernist City: An Anthropological Critique of Brasília*. Chicago: University of Chicago Press, 1989. An account of how a planned (revived Baroque) capital dedicated to state power and the uplift of its citizenry has been "recaptured" by Brasilian culture.

Homans, George C. *The Human Group*, 2nd ed. (with introductions by A. Paul Hare and Richard Brian Polley). New Brunswick, N.J.: Transaction Books, 1992. A famous sociologist tries to isolate and analyze social dynamics in five small groups, one of them being the bank-wiring room.

Solzhenitsyn, Aleksandr. *Gulag Archipelago 1918–1956: An Experiment in Literary Investigation*, abridged one vol. ed. New York: Harper & Row, 1985. A literary masterpiece by one of Russia's leading dissidents. It documents the ultimate inhumanity of a corporate system that reduces its citizens to prisoners in state industrial camps.

Westwood, Sallie. *All Day Every Day: Factory and Family in the Ecology of Women's Lives*. Urbana: University of Illinois Press, 1985. A lively ethnography of working women in an English factory; the ethnographer is a radical feminist; her subjects are not.

GLOSSARY

Baroque age The culture and art of the sixteenth to the eighteenth centuries in Europe, marked by dynamic opposition and energy and curving, plastic forms. In science the laws of gravity and the motions of the solar system were related to each other in one grand theory. In technology clockwork was perfected. In social organization legal-rational bureaucracy emerged. In architecture the whole order was given coherence around one giant sundial in the monumental royal-residence cities, the Baroque capitals.

Baroque capitals Royal-residence cities of the Age of Enlightenment, typified by Versailles in France, built in the form of a giant sundial to symbolize clockwork, light, and infinity as parades of drilled men marched past the vanishing point down monumental central avenues, further illuminated by the weapon of the time, gunpowder, in fireworks displays at night. Enlightened despots were supposed to preside over clockwork realms that needed only to be tinkered with to run perfectly.

bureaucracy A social device enabling the one or the few to rule not just the many, but multitudes. Technically, a government apparatus divided into bureaus, or agencies, with special functions.

corporation A legal fiction in which a group of persons can be considered one person before the law. In social organization, the corporation is usually embodied legally in a board or collegium.

cult of efficiency A critical term applied to scientific management, or Taylorism, implying that such techniques are as much rituals meant to allay the anxiety of management about production as they are efficient means to increase it.

generic Protestantism The extension of the Protestant ethic to legal-rational bureaucratic values, without any implication of religious faith. The professional bureaucrat lives for work and holds profit production goals as the foremost value in life.

legal-rational bureaucracy According to Weber, a set of government bureaus defined by a legal charter according to a specialized, logical function. Careers are open to talent, by training, and are rewarded by seniority. Activities are supervised by paperwork and records, revenues are budgeted from a central treasury bureau, and the whole enterprise justifies itself by efficiency.

military parades Rite of intensification of state power perfected in the Baroque age, in which rows of men marched as automatons, timed in response to each other like clockwork, down monumental avenues past the vanishing point, giving the illusion of infinity and eternity. The synchronization of timing, music, and men's motions was also true of the symphony orchestra and ballet, invented at the same time.

professionalism The code of conduct expected of highly educated university graduates in the professions—such as physicians, lawyers, engineers, scientists, and other scholars—who must exercise their duties proficiently and must also live up to a high ethical standard. Professional associations sometimes monitor the behavior of their members. Professionalism favors school systems open to talent, and careers advanced by merit.

Protestant ethic According to Weber, the mentality necessary for the rise of capitalism. It produced a "priesthood of all believers" who internalized self-control, who took work as a badge of salvation and therefore as sacred, and who, living austerely, reinvested all their business profits in their enterprises.

scientific management See *Taylorism*.

table of organization A form borrowed from the military that ranks all employees of a bureaucracy into directors (corporate board or collegium), officers, noncommissioned officers, and "men." Clients are usually not included in company charts, but in fact corporate bureaucracies must respond to them.

Taylorism "Scientific management," or time-motion studies invented by the American engineer Fredrick Taylor, who held that human motions could be coordinated with those of machines in split-second timing. The goal of Taylorism was to maximize worker production.

Modernity and Culture

ETHNOGRAPHIC CLOSE-UP:
MAMACHI, A MIDDLE-CLASS
SUBURB OF TOKYO

Friendship, Informal Cliques, and PTA in Mamachi

Schooling

ANALYSIS: PATTERNS OF MODERN
JAPANESE LIFE

Life Cycle

Individual Achievement: Working with the Group for the
Leader

Safety Valves: Friendly Cliques and Formal Associations

More Safety Valves: Popular Culture in Mass Media

Japanese Values

THE PRIVATE WORLD IN NORTH
AMERICA: DIFFERENTIAL ACCESS
TO MODERNITY

Upper Class: Hereditary Elites

Middle Class: Achieving Elite Status Each Generation

Working Class: Decency and Familism at the Cost of Social
Mobility

The Poor: Living on the Dole

BRIDGES BETWEEN PRIVATE AND PUBLIC WORLDS

Associations as Institutional Shock Absorbers

Associations and the Labor Movement

PROTEST MOVEMENTS

The Youth Movement

The Women's Movement

The Gay and Lesbian Movement

    Homosexual Behavior

    Classical Greek Homosexual Patterns

    Western Prohibition of Homosexuality

    Gays and Cultural Revision

*T*he modern world is dominated by corporate bureaucracies, polycentric metropolitan urban regions, and a transnational market in which nation-states struggle to control prices in the interest of their own national welfare. **Modernity** itself is often phrased as a variant of Weber's legal-rational bureaucracy. That is, it is assumed to be a social and cultural order characterized by increasing specialization by function. Each specialty is defined by some written charter that reflects the influence of science on technology and is staffed by persons highly trained to carry out that function. Charters for action are rational and legal, having passed the scrutiny of professional lawyers.

Many social scientists assume that a central process in modernization has to do with people's gaining access to modern (meaning legal-rational) social structures. S. N. Eisenstadt (1966) asserts that the central drama of the modern age has been the often repeated capture of the center by the masses, which in its first and most dramatic form occurred in the French Revolution when the mob went to Versailles and brought King Louis XVI back to Paris as their prisoner. The dynamic is still with us. In 1917 the masses invaded Palace Square in St. Petersburg to oust the tsar; in August 1991 they rallied there again to protest the attempted Communist coup in Moscow. The masses are constantly bidding for elite status and for political participation.

The world over people are grappling with the implications of modernity. For one thing, people are now more crowded together in larger urban areas than ever before, and they are much more highly organized socially, in the aggregate, than ever before. Communications, through electronic media, are much more intense. Telephones and television screens bring relatives, friends, and distant strangers into the center of one's own home, without one's having to step outside. Paradoxically, urban travel and transport have become more of a chore or even an ordeal, with traffic jams and sardine-tight subway cars, while urban people, as tourists, travel to the far corners of the earth and jostle against members of surviving bands and tribes, who often live surrounded by wide open spaces.

Then there is the problem of participation in modern culture. The masses are no longer undifferentiated working classes. There are now "mass elites" in all the urban centers. People of differing ethnic backgrounds and religions crowd together in the same urban space and compete for advancement in corporations and the job market. Do they become "organization people" in their public life while remaining something else in private? Does the nature of modernity imply a single, uniform modern culture?

The evidence from anthropology is that, while modern social forms are necessarily similar, there is in fact no single modern culture. We saw in Chapter 3 that the Mohawks of Brooklyn engage in highly skilled work soldering the steel frames of skyscrapers. They enjoy the material benefits of modernity and live like the affluent working class anywhere. (That is, they spend money on good food, comfortable home furnishings, automobiles, and appliances, but not on art or education, like the middle classes.) Yet the Mohawk have turned their high-steel adventure into an exercise of both the social organization and the values of their indigenous culture. Like the war and hunting parties of old, they engage in work as if it were a raid intended to exercise individual bravery. Wages and bonuses are treated as game or booty and handed over to women, who live together in matrilineal apartment houses, while men remain at the bar, like a men's house of old, when not working. Outwardly they are in clothing, language, and cuisine no different from the Anglo working class, but in culture they are quite different.

Other ethnic groups are not so fortunate, and they bid to participate in modernity at all levels. Protest is part of the process of modernity. Since the end of the nineteenth century protests have come from labor and youth, in a seemingly institutional process. More recently they have also come from women and gays.

This chapter examines some of the diverse responses to modernity. We shall first survey how the Japanese have become the first thoroughly modern non-Western nation. Then we shall look at Western protesters—labor, youth, women, and gays—before assessing some of the variability that seems inherent in the emerging responses to modernity.

Japan is a highly industrialized, literate nation, with many aggressive corporations, a vast national education establishment, many associations, and a parliamentary democracy built on earlier democratic forms during the United States occupation. In Japan, patterns of modernity are simpler yet no less modern than ours.

ETHNOGRAPHIC CLOSE-UP

MAMACHI, A MIDDLE-CLASS SUBURB OF TOKYO

I n 1958 Ezra Vogel and his wife, two young American social scientists, went to live for two years in Mamachi, a prosperous suburb of Tokyo, where they did an intensive study of six families (Vogel, 1971). (For a recent similar study, see Bestor, 1989.) The single-family houses surrounded by tiny, carefully landscaped gardens on walled lots were small by American standards. Houses were seldom more than four rooms, and elementary kitchen facilities included two gas burners for cooking and a wooden icebox cooled by blocks of ice.

Most houses had running water, but flush toilets and sewage systems did not exist. Neither did central heating, and on cold winter evenings families huddled around a sunken sitting and heating pit. In spite of their lacks by American standards, homes were beautifully kept in an understated way, with great emphasis being placed on the beauty of everyday things, from the family garden to the appearance of the evening meal.

Household heads fell into four occupational groupings. Shopkeepers, professionals, and businessmen in family firms belonged to traditional Japanese stem families or modifications of them. The fourth and most numerous group, "salary men," or managers, belonged to small nuclear families. Shopkeepers kept small food and variety shops along the main avenues. To compete with the department stores of downtown Tokyo, they worked long hours and took almost no holidays. Their wives and elder sons helped with the shop, and the general expectation was that one of the sons would bring in a bride and take over the shop on the retirement of the household head.

Physicians and dentists, the only professionals in Mamachi, lived next to their clinics and wards, which had beds for patients. Private physicians do not refer patients to hospitals in Japan, and they have no rights to attend patients in hospitals. They, too, hoped that one son would eventually take over the father's practice. Businessmen who owned their own firms lived in the most luxurious homes in Mamachi. Their wives often employed maids, and they could always count on company employees for extra help, such as at New Year's Day open house. Husbands rode to work in chauffeured cars provided by the firm.

Businessmen hoped to place all their sons in the family firm if it were large enough; they certainly expected one of the sons to manage it. If several sons entered the business, the more talented and (ideally) more senior one could expect to become its chief executive. Such families provided expensive education for their children. They went to great lengths to enroll them in "escalator" private school systems, which avoided the highly competitive entrance examinations of other Japanese schools, except for the kindergarten entrance examination. Thus they purchased security in the extremely competitive Japanese educational system.

The salary man (Japanese: *sarariiman*, from the English) was a manager or an executive in one of the great corporations or government bureaus of Tokyo. Unlike the others, he could not hand his job over to a selected son in the stem family tradition. He was not even assured that sons could win employment in his firm. Consequently, he strove to give his children the best possible education as their stake in life.

Friendship, Informal Cliques, and PTA in Mamachi

Husband and wife never entertained together in Mamachi, except on formal occasions when they visited senior relatives together. Moreover, the division of labor within the household was extreme by North American standards. Husbands could not cook a meal for themselves and were hard put even to fix a cup of tea in an emergency. A few salary men helped their wives take the children's beds (quilts) out of the closets at night. The work of man and wife was completely separate, as were their leisure and recreational activities.

A wife had a small circle of friends, neighborhood women near the same age and economic standing who visited each other daily to exchange news and advice on rearing children and handling husbands. Such friendships usually endured for life, since once a family was lucky enough to buy land and build a house in Mamachi it was quite unlikely to move until the death of the household head.

A salary man's friends were exclusively his companions at work and likely from the same age group, or class, in the firms. Japanese firms hire new managers on the same date each year, thus forming a "freshman class." The salary man arrived home an average of three hours after work because he amused himself with his friends before catching the commuter train for the hour ride home. Favorite spots were bars, coffee shops, and amusement parlors where groups stopped for refreshment and talk.

Ties between informal companions from work are reinforced by company policy. Companies arrange and pay for group excursions and vacations for employees in a chartered bus or railroad car for a carefree outing to a hot-spring spa or the like. Such

Japanese salary men.

informal groups of male companions also endure for life. Usually, once a man joins a firm he is neither dismissed nor hired away by another firm. Put another way, firms hire their personnel for life, and employees almost never seek employment elsewhere on the job market. (We shall discuss the implications of this personnel practice later.)

One formal association to which all parents of schoolchildren belong is the PTA. Mamachi mothers attended PTA meetings regularly, and older mothers were likely to become PTA officers. However, a study of a Japanese middle school in Nichu, a provincial city, found that mothers formed the rank and file, while the long-term chairman was a self-made millionaire, and retired businessmen and salary men predominated among the officers. In this city, men who attended monthly meetings alongside the mothers were members of the neighborhood's municipal councils (Singleton, 1967).

The PTA is vital for the functioning of Japanese schools, for it helps collect funds. Parents are expected to provide monthly fees, as well as uniforms and supplies. PTAs conduct local drives for special expenses. In Nichu, the PTA raised 11.3 percent of the school's total yearly expenditures, but these funds in fact made up almost the total cash outlays made by the school itself (Singleton, 1967). The PTA is thus very much a link between parents and school and between teachers, school administrators, and local governments. Moreover, it is the one formal organization in which Japanese housewives enthusiastically participate.

Schooling

The Japanese education system at first glance looks much like that of the United States. During the United States occupation, the system was expanded and modeled more closely on ours rather than on Europe's, as had been the case before. The system provides six years of compulsory elementary school; a middle school or junior high of three years, also compulsory; three years of high school, not compulsory; public trade and vocational high schools; academically oriented high schools, many of them private although some of the best are public; and four years of college at excellent universities for a select few (see Figure 19.1).

What makes this educational system different is the **examination system.** Entrance examinations are administered in all private schools and above the elementary level in all public schools. Teachers never fail students in their own schools, but to get into another school, a student must pass a tough, impersonal, and competitive examination. An elementary school is ranked by its rate of success in placing

graduates in good middle schools, which in turn are ranked by their success rate in getting graduates into the ranking high schools.

High schools are similarly rated by their ability to place graduates into the most prestigious universities, especially Tokyo Imperial (Todai), the highest-

Figure 19.1 A schematic view of the Japanese educational system, showing years of schooling, age grading, major kinds of schools, and the relative proportion of each age grade in school.

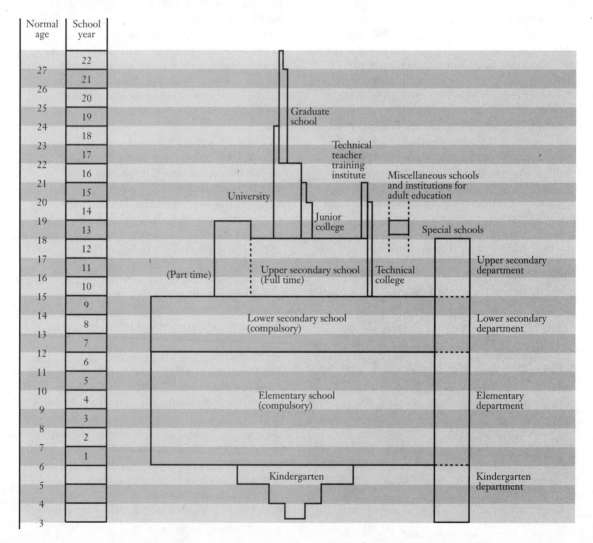

ranking educational institution in Japan. This and the other ranking universities have the most success in placing graduates in the most prestigious corporations and government agencies. In Mamachi, children, especially sons, of salary men are expected to earn a university degree, as that is their only hope of attaining their father's comfortable job status.

Access to neighborhood elementary schools is determined by residence, but access into public schools from middle school on is determined by the entrance examinations alone, not residence. Elementary schools in Mamachi were considered quite good, and many children from other districts were entered in its rolls by parents who registered at the address of relatives in Mamachi. Mamachi schools were relatively successful in getting their graduates into good middle schools that were more centrally located in the greater Tokyo area.

Once a child has been admitted into a school, promotion is automatic with the age grade. Of course, entrance into the next school is not automatic, since it depends on passing that school's entrance examinations. Much of the work of any school, then, is to prepare children to take other schools' examinations. In Mamachi mothers were in charge of supervising this effort, working closely with teachers. If the teacher advised tutoring or special classes after hours, the mother cooperated and found the funds to pay for the tutorials.

Mothers also select a number of lower secondary schools for her child to attempt to enter by taking their examinations. A child cannot apply to two schools that give their exams on the same day. Exams are given in January and February before the start of the school year in April. Usually a child takes exams in several schools, preferring them according to their prestige. The same process is repeated when a student graduates from lower secondary school—although here the competition to get into the best Tokyo high schools is even stiffer. The competition to get into Tokyo University is staggering. In 1957, for example, there were 13,485 applicants, of which 2,004 were admitted (Passin, 1965). In 1987 half of those applying failed the university entrance exam (de Mente, 1987).

Japanese schoolchildren.

At every level, if a student does not get into the school of first choice, he or she may wait a year and take the entrance exam again. During that year, students enroll in private tutoring classes concentrating on the examinations. Such students are called *ronin*, from the knights without lords and masters in Japan's feudal period. Students have been known to remain ronin as long as four, five, and even up to ten years in an effort to get into Tokyo University. Of those 13,485 applicants in 1957, for example, only 34 percent were applying fresh from high school; the remaining 66 percent were ronin repeaters!

Even after Japanese have graduated from the university, the interaction with the examination system is not yet finished, as the great corporations and government services have their own entrance examinations. These exams are not quite as competitive, for graduates of the handful of top universities are virtually assured of a good job somewhere, if not necessarily in the organization of their first choice. Thus, in Mamachi the children of salary men were under great pressure to do well early in the system. The examination months are periods of great stress for the young in Japanese life. The suicide rate for young people is high and peaks annually during and after exams.

ANALYSIS: PATTERNS OF MODERN JAPANESE LIFE

It is clear that Japanese life, for all its success in handling factory industrialism, corporate bureaucracy, and the transnational market, has markedly different cultural patterns from ours in the United States. Let us analyze these patterns.

Life Cycle

Japanese children are highly dependent on their mothers during their first six years of life.

A Japanese child is born into either a traditional stem family household (with resident grandparents) or a more modern nuclear family without resident grandparents. Early childhood is a period of intense maternal attention. Children are usually breast fed for a year and a half, longer in many instances. They sleep with their mothers until they are almost seven years old and take hot baths in the deep Japanese tub with her until they are six.

Through such close dependency, mothers find it easy to train children without any physical punishment whatever. Mothers try to bend a child's habits by concentrating their efforts when the youngster is in a cooperative mood. They never "work against the child." The results are remarkable. The "little terror" of three years is transformed into a polite and well-behaved child of six, quite ready for school. The abrupt transition into a world outside the household is mediated by the mother's unfailing attendance at the PTA meetings.

The teacher, like the mother, never punishes or rejects. The school always promotes each child each year to the next grade. A child is assured of each teacher's benevolent, patient devotion. In return, the child is expected to do as well as possible, especially on the entrance examinations that loom at the end of six years.

Level of schooling attained has much to do with individual merit, but it also has much to do with family traditions, expectations, and ability to pay. Many sons of workers and farmers do not go to high school because their families cannot afford their time away from work. Young men and women who stop school after lower secondary schooling, at age fourteen or fifteen, as well as many high school graduates, enter the labor force directly as factory workers or office clerks.

Firms customarily do much training on the job. Women usually leave the work force upon marriage, and almost certainly at the birth of the first child.

Many of them marry fellow workers, and no firm employs both husband and wife. Men who have completed a university degree compete fiercely with other graduates for a job with a prestigious firm. Although schooling determines one's place in life and one's place in the corporate hierarchy, family and school connections help in the final selection:

> In 1961, one of Japan's great newspapers found itself with 3000 applicants for only 20 openings. The first examination served as a screening device to determine the 100 most promising candidates. In the second stage the final 20 were selected from the successful 100 on the basis of interviews and recommendations. An acquaintance boasted that he had used his "influence" to secure a job for the son of a friend. (Passin, 1965, p. 126)

Thus when all candidates are nearly equal, "personal impression, manners, and recommendations" are allowed to influence decisions.

A man follows one of three employment patterns. He may take over the family patrimony in the stem family tradition; he may enter employment for others at the appropriate level—unskilled, skilled, or managerial; or he may venture forth on his own to try his hand at free enterprise. The stem family pattern is usually followed by sons of farmers and small shopkeepers after minimal education and by the sons of professionals after long education. The sons of private businessmen are usually obliged to take examinations on entrance into the family firm, so as to assure all concerned that the family manager is also competent. As mentioned earlier, it is the sons of such established families who are most likely to avoid competitive public education and follow instead an expensive private school system whose only examination is to enter kindergarten. Some men, often with little education, choose to enter the free sector of Japanese economic life and go into business for themselves in service occupations or new industries. Some such men represent success stories, founding great firms and large fortunes; others have failed miserably.

Because a salary man is employed by a firm or government agency for life and rarely leaves to join a competitor, men who do so are regarded with suspicion in the new firm as disloyal persons. There are several results of **life employment.** First, salaries and promotions are determined by age and seniority rather than by performance. Most companies are sure that they have hired competent individuals in the first place because of company exams. Second, promotion is only within broad rankings. That is, workers are never promoted into the managerial group. Third, salaries and wages tend to be very low by United States standards, but companies do provide accident and health benefits as well as retirement pay. These are of utmost importance for employees, since public welfare programs are little developed in Japan and are thought of as the last resort for the desperate. Retirement pay is low, however, and retirement age is usually fifty-five, early by United States standards. Retirees often take freelance or part-time jobs in the risky enterprises of the free sector.

New employees marry in their late twenties—rather later than in the United States. Formerly, marriages were arranged entirely by the stem family household head. The Western nuclear family ideal has been consciously introduced, however, with the result that some couples do date each other before marriage. But they are formally introduced by family and friends and do not seek each other out in bars or other public places. That is quite unthinkable.

Moreover, when a young man and a young woman are ready for marriage in the judgment of their parents, matchmaking starts in earnest. Families still engage private detectives to investigate the other family and make a report. Although couples now exercise a veto power over their parents' recommendations, courtship is still a family affair in Japan. Even in the most liberal sectors, nothing like a free and open courtship system exists. A girl is particularly responsive to her parents' wishes, for if she should make a mistake in marriage and later divorce her husband, she must rely on her parents for shelter and help.

Although courtship in Japan appears similar to "free" Western courtship, in reality it is governed by family and workplace expectations.

Firms themselves are active in the marriage market. Abegglen (1973) reports that a small factory regularly hired some fifteen country girls, signing contracts with their household heads and putting the girls up in a company dormitory while paying them low wages for three years' apprenticeship and two or three years' work as weavers. The firm provided all girls with bonuses, like dowries, when they left to marry young men investigated by the firm in matches made by the manager.

A more recent study of female office workers in the headquarters of a prestigious Tokyo-based firm found that each year the company hired exclusively from among the graduates of a top secretarial (junior) college (McLendon, 1983). The young women were selected not only for their secretarial skills but also for their poise and beauty. It was the company's expectation that within ten years all these young women should have married young salary men from the company. Indeed, this was one of the incentives it held out to prospective employees. The few women who were not married past age thirty were encouraged to leave and find work elsewhere. (A few stuck it out for career employment.) In this case the company set up the courtship situation for its young employees, and they were expected to carry out the rest for themselves. "Free courtship" in Japan, then, is not what it is in the West.

Divorce in Japan traditionally consisted of returning the woman to her stem family household. Something of that still persists, because there is little opportunity for the divorced or widowed woman to find employment on the Japanese job market. Once a couple are married and launched into domestic life, they are unlikely to divorce. In 1963 the Japanese divorce rate for all marriages was only .7 percent; in 1987 it was 2 percent (de Mente, 1987).

Salary men are likely to find a small home in the suburbs, and workers are likely to find subsidized housing either from their firm or from the government. The preoccupations of the Japanese are improving their standard of living, purchasing appliances and other modern amenities, saving for the inevitable early retirement, and educating their children to do well on the examinations. The total world for most Japanese families is very narrow: the public world of the firm; the small, warm, and intense nuclear family; and the separate cliques of male work companions and female neighbors.

Japanese nuclear family patterns are repeated in schooling and the workplace.

The only other important associations, the PTA and trade unions, which are not in the least voluntary, tell us much about Japanese life. The PTA assumes a much greater importance than in American life because of the emphasis on achievement in impersonal examinations. Trade unions are grouped by firm, not by craft or trade. They include many not ordinarily included in the West—office workers and engineers, for example. At the emphatic insistence of the United States occupation authorities when they encouraged the growth of trade unions in Japan, management was kept out, although they expressed a desire to join alongside the workers!

Individual Achievement: Working with the Group for the Leader

Much of the astonishing vitality of Japan—its successful modernization and industrialization during the late 1800s and its speedy recovery from the devastating defeat after World War II—has had to do with attitudes toward individual achievement, worked out first in the family and repeated in the firm.

According to Chie Nakane (1970), a Japanese social anthropologist, it became fashionable after the war for the stem family to be considered backward. Researchers unconsciously tried to encourage the trend toward the nuclear family, but today many attributes of the old stem family household survive and are of utmost importance. The husband and father, the breadwinner, is the source of authority and the spokesman for all family decisions. Even the college-educated wife lets her husband make all formal decisions, although in fact he always consults her. The wife and mother is always the one to get the ball rolling in decisions about household expenses and children's education, but officially decisions are made in the name of the household head.

Children never question the authority and wisdom of their father, although he always consults them and knows their feelings. Remember that all Japanese children are assured of unquestioning acceptance and love from their parents. They have never been physically punished, for example. Yet in return for this love, benevolence, and wisdom, children are expected to show continuous respect and unlimited dedication to their father and their family name. It is not an exaggeration to say that the father figure is one of the most important symbols in Japanese culture. He is linked with the stem line on the land in peasant families, with Japanese nationality, and with the highest father figure of all, the emperor.

In Japan, fathers are expected to be wise and benevolent and to make major family decisions (although they always consult their wives).

If we turn to the public world of work, we find much that has been carried over from the family. There is the unquestioned acceptance of those who have been admitted as employees that they will never be dismissed. Many firms provide all sorts of private and paternal benefits from the North American point of view: subsidized cafeterias, dormitories for unmarried employees, whole neighborhoods of housing for marrieds.

According to Nakane, the Japanese work well for a boss of unquestioned seniority, experience, and competence—ideally someone who has trained them. In short, they can be counted on to do their best job for a trusted father figure. Even when young employees are naturally more talented or better trained in recent discoveries or techniques, they are quite content to do their best work and let the credit go to the boss, since this usually brings some special distinction to the unit as well as the benevolent commendation of the elder man. All employees are assured of promotions with seniority, and Japanese are happiest doing jobs that make benevolent father figures look good. The result, oddly enough, is an increase in individual self-esteem.

As an example of the need for father figures, Nakane cites the Japanese attempt to send mountaineering expeditions to the Himalayas after World War II. The first team to go, recruited from proven mountain climbers all around Japan who were roughly the same age, proved a failure. The team arrived in Calcutta afterward in a state of bitter feud. Poor teamwork was said to have plagued them as much as bad weather. The next team to go out was put under the direction of a leader over fifty years old:

> It was said that the personal attributes of the leader were of much greater value to the party organization than his physical capability for climbing. The leader was the senior, most experienced member of the Japanese Alpine Club, who was acceptable to all on the grounds of his seniority and warm personality. In addition the members were well known to the leader. The team seemed well integrated and happy and succeeded in conquering the peak. (Nakane, 1970, p. 75)

Because the function of the school in Japanese society is to remove children from their families and prepare them to take a place in the world of work, the school is also a workplace and is dominated by a benefactor who accepts the child totally. (Japanese prefer the term *benefactor* to refer to parents, teachers, and employers.) It is during examinations that both education and the world of work are legal, rational, and impersonal.

The examination is the great rite of passage between home and school, between levels of schools, and between school and job. It is a resurrection and adaptation of the old Confucian imperial examination system of the Chinese mandarinate. The Japanese have applied it to a mass society for the same ends as of old: to find each individual's place in the social system. Once that place is found, the individual never loses it.

Safety Valves: Friendly Cliques and Formal Associations

According to Vogel (1971), the main function of the informal group of job companions is to dispel the competitive tensions of the job. By associating with each other in a relaxed, open atmosphere after the formalities of the workplace and the formalities imposed by the presence of the boss, companions build up strong personal ties. They also handle jealousies. The peer who has been commended, favored, or singled out in some way is joshed by his comrades, who thus deal with minor jealousies and restore good feeling to the group. In cases of sudden and rapid promotion ahead of the age grade, the firm is likely to transfer a favorite son to a different unit, as in a life history reported by Norbeck (1967).

In Japan, where there is little chance for quitting or taking another job, informal friendly relations are a safety valve for on-the-job pressures. Similarly, the informal group of women neighbors helps a wife deal with household personnel problems: how to cope with a first baby; how to handle jealous siblings when new babies come; and above all how to deal with a difficult husband, always authoritarian and often absent. Just as male peers help each other handle the boss, so do the women help each other handle their husbands!

More Safety Valves: Popular Culture in Mass Media

Even with constantly activated cliques and associations, the tensions in Japanese life are deep. Remember that in this society pampered, indulged children are expected to grow up to become rigorous conformists. It is not surprising that a study of Japanese popular culture in mass media of film, television, and comic books shows that they project considerable ambivalence on fictitious heroes, thereby releasing tensions in real life.

We learn from Ian Baruma's *Behind the Mask: On Sexual Demons, Sacred Mothers, Transvestites, Gangsters and Other Japanese Cultural Heroes* (1984), for example, that Japanese adore their mothers, yet they also wish to punish them. In fiction they portray mothers as self-sacrificing, rejected, and suffering ignominiously in a tear-jerking finale. Similarly, they adore transvestite (cross-dressing) players, as well as young male stars of ambivalent gender identification. This is reasonable in a society in which homosexuality, and sexuality in general, is not forbidden but in which marriage with an appropriate partner is rigorously expected of everyone, no matter what their sexual preference.

Surprisingly, we learn that father figures, unlike mother figures, are often reviled and laughed at. Baruma explains this in the rootlessness of salary men. They not only are largely absent from home, but they have no stem family tradition to uphold. Their claims to uphold the family name are hollow, since their families are not rooted in place over three or more generations. *Grandfather* figures, in contrast, are revered, in the figure of the bosses of "good" (as opposed to "evil") gangster organizations. These are always frail, quiet elders who inspire loyalty to the death in their followers.

Popular culture acts as a safety valve, relieving tensions caused by pressure to conform to social traditions.

Gangster heroes, moreover, disclose the limits of the morality of legal rationality in Japanese culture. They often engage in battles, like samurai knights of old, on matters of principle that make no sense in terms of the rights or merits of a particular case but lots of sense in terms of personal obligation to one's master, and to honor to one's name.

Thus, the popular arts of the mass media in modern society at least partly replace the maintenance function of rites of intensification in traditional society. The liminal period becomes "liminoid," the embodiment of fantasies, projections, and cultural creativity (Turner, 1987).

Japanese Values

The Japanese have imbued modernity with their own traditional values. These **Japanese values** are enunciated in the Imperial Rescript of the Meiji Emperor of 1879, *The Great Principles of Education*:

> The essence of education, our traditional national aim, . . . is to make clear the ways of benevolence, justice, loyalty, and filial piety, and to master knowledge and skill and through these to pursue the Way of Man. (In Passin, 1965, p. 227)

These values are in origin Confucian and are drawn from the model of society as properly a patriarchal household, in which patriarchs (and hence all those in authority) are by nature assumed to be *benevolent* and *just*, while subordinates must be *loyal* to their peers and *pious* toward their seniors. Moreover, the society itself aims at justice, in the attempt to find every person's "correct" place in life through the examination system. We have seen these values acted out in our discussion of the individual and the group.

In addition to these Confucian values are some closely related compatible ones that are peculiarly Japanese. Several terms convey these values, but we can discuss them in abbreviated, translated form as *unpayable debt* to one's seniors, and to one's name, and *honor*, the obligation to uphold the good name of oneself, one's seniors, and one's stem family line. Note further that "knowledge and skill," the essence of legal-rational modernity, are simply means to pursue the ends of Confucian values. Thus, modern values in Japan do not have the same content as in the West.

The institutional elements of modern life work very well in Japan, at least when judged by such indicators as speed of postwar recovery, rate of economic growth, and production per capita, which rose from a little over $100 in 1950 to nearly $2,000 in 1970 (Abegglen, 1973) to $23,730 in 1989 (Europa World Yearbook, 1991). These figures have not been adjusted for inflation but are still indicative.

THE PRIVATE WORLD IN NORTH AMERICA: DIFFERENTIAL ACCESS TO MODERNITY

While the private world of family and household in the United States is relatively insulated from the cult of efficiency of the work world, it is influenced by rampant consumerism, the relentless pursuit of leisure, and a turning inward on household, hobbies, and vacation homes. Let's see how this is reflected in the various **social classes.**

Upper Class: Hereditary Elites

At the upper reaches, great families of high society tend to form ancestor-oriented kindreds, uniting the descendants of the founder of the family fortune. This corporateness is often expressed symbolically in the exurban compound of the kindred's country place, with many luxurious separate residences of individual nuclear families. Such families also maintain apartments in high-rise high-security enclaves in central cities. In this world of social register, debutante balls, men's clubs in town, and country clubs in the suburbs, private education in good schools is assured even for those with learning disabilities.

The rituals associated with meals vary from social class to social class.

Socialites may choose a life of idle ease or a life of action. Many enter firms connected with family interests if they have the right educational credentials. Others enter the professions, especially law, act as directors of charitable foundations started in honor of their ancestors, or are active in politics. Wealthy Americans have participated in both political parties, although those who are Democrats may be regarded resentfully by their relatives as "traitors to their class."

Every generation, new entrepreneurs—and recently even corporate CEOs (chief executive officers)—leave their children such great family fortunes. For example the entertainment pioneer Walt Disney, with his brother, Roy, established a wealthy family. Today Michael Eisner, current CEO of the Disney Corporation, is in the process of amassing such a fortune.

Middle Class: Achieving Elite Status Each Generation

The North American middle class, on the other hand, lives well but cannot bequeath their children a patrimony sufficient to maintain them in luxury without working. The true inheritance of the middle class, like that of the Japanese salary men, is an education sufficient to launch young men and women into managerial, official, or professional jobs. Middle-class families tend to live in suburban houses, one to a lot and isolated from its neighbors. The family form is nuclear, and the overwhelming preoccupation of the family is childrearing and the school system. Local schools are academically oriented toward placing as many children as possible in college. PTAs are active, as is the individual mother, who confers at length with teachers about her child's progress.

In suburban schools with middle-class pupils, the educational expert is in great demand. Parents actively encourage academic experimentation and the incorporation of new knowledge and techniques into the curriculum. Middle-class parents *expect* their children to be different from themselves and to live in the constantly changing world of the future. They are not alarmed when children teach new facts to parents. Parents whose lives have been uncertain train their children for a life that will be mobile and surprising (Kimball and McClellan, 1962; Seeley, Sim, and Loosely, 1956). In recent decades, the increasing rates of divorce and remarriage have made life for middle-class parents even more mobile and unpredictable.

Working Class: Decency and Familism at the Cost of Social Mobility

The working classes reside in inner-city older neighborhoods in old commercial metropolises or in less expensive suburban neighborhoods of new conurbations such as Los Angeles and Miami. Sociologist Herbert Gans (1962), who studied Italians in South Boston, characterized the American working class as peer oriented rather than child oriented. Visiting patterns with extended family members, especially adult siblings and cousins, are intense.

What class might this family belong to?

Ideally, working-class people want enough schooling to equip their children for a decent, clean job that provides a comfortable livelihood without requiring geographical or social mobility. Residing within daily visiting distance of parents is desirable, but parents are more likely to keep company with their own age mates. In their authoritarian and unchanging approach, the best teachers were the old-style Roman Catholic nuns who dispensed facts and upheld discipline with the full weight of the bishop and the pope behind them.

The Poor: Living on the Dole

The poor live in poverty in the inner city and other older districts. They are not working and are receiving public or private charitable assistance as the clients of welfare agencies, or they are crowding in on employed relatives and working where they can. Such poverty is a product of world-wide processes of urbanization. Hardest hit are the unskilled and uneducated rural migrants to the cities, especially women and children whose labor is not in demand in the metropolis. Moreover, every mature industrial economy today has the capacity to produce more goods than its nation-state can consume. Exports are critical. Most such economies seldom produce at full capacity; thus, they always fail to employ some percentage of the labor force. This is "structural unemployment," and the long-term unemployed must live on public assistance or fall back on relatives for help.

No necessary link has been established between the poor and the urban ills of society. The books of Oscar Lewis (1959, 1961, 1965) about the urban poor in Mexico City, San Juan, Puerto Rico, and New York City overstate the case for a "culture of poverty," as Valentine (1968) has demonstrated, but they still remain some of the social sciences' most moving human documents.

BRIDGES BETWEEN PRIVATE AND PUBLIC WORLDS

Modern human beings need to face the problem of leaving the private world, into which we all enter at birth, for impersonal, nonfamily activity in the public world. **Schooling** moves individuals of all classes from private households into the public world of work.

Modern men and women must also strike a balance between the two sides of their lives. They do so primarily by means of **voluntary associations.** These range from small informal **cliques** of friends, workers, or neighbors to vast bureaucratized federations of trade unions, businessmen, or professionals. In all countries such complex associations are invariably linked to the political process through pressure groups and political parties. Voluntary associations eventually link the individual to politics by one of the central processes of modernization: the increasing demand by all individuals to share in the symbols and institution of the center.

In modern life, associations provide opportunities for ritual and for social interaction.

Associations as Institutional Shock Absorbers

According to Chapple and Coon (1942), associations are substitutes for individual rites of passage and are institutional shock absorbers that offset tensions and difficulties in other institutions such as family and work. They are first and foremost outlets for sociability denied or upset elsewhere. That is their primary function; any other announced goal or purpose is secondary.

According to Chapple and Coon, associations tide us through times of transition when rites of passage are lacking. Indeed, entry into many associations is exaggeratedly ritualized. It is no accident that sororities and fraternities flourish on college campuses, where there is little ritual and where rational procedures are emphasized. Rushing, pledging, and being initiated into a fraternity or sorority take up the social gap (Leemon, 1972) for young persons newly separated from their parents, and thrust them happily into an intimate group of brothers and sisters.

Associations and the Labor Movement

Although the labor movement in the United States now consists of highly bureaucratized associations of workers, unions do provide for formal grievance procedures. They are initiated by shop stewards, workers representing the union, in up-the-line communications. However, the trade union movement is not closely linked to informal cliques of workers, nor has it been established that informal leadership leads directly to holding union office.

In the United States, the trade union movement was late in gaining official recognition and legal protection and was late in unionizing major industries when compared to other industrial countries. However, trade unions eventually became an essential means for workers to communicate with management. As small corporations are swallowed up by large, often multinational ones, local manager-owners are replaced by outside managers on temporary

Unionization in Yankee City

Laborers did not form trade unions or strike in Yankee City until the 1930s, when to everyone's surprise they organized, went on a long and bitter strike, and successfully brought the shoe manufacturers to their knees. Warner (1962) explains the successful unionization in Yankee City as a delayed response to (1) the collapse of the old age-graded skill hierarchy and (2) the blocking of informal up-the-line communication.

In Yankee City shoes had been made in old craft shops with an age-graded progression of job skills from apprentice to journeyman to master cobbler. In the forty years before 1930, there was a slow change, and as in most highly industrialized enterprises where workers are trapped in one status or ranking for life, the age-skill hierarchy collapsed.

Nevertheless, workers were Protestants who spoke the same language and went to the same churches as the factory owners. The economy had been expanding over the long term; productivity was rising and so were wages. As the depression of 1929 hit, the upper class sold their factories to national firms owned and managed from New York City and Boston. In some cases, former

owners stayed on as hired managers with little real power; in other cases, New Yorkers came to manage the plants. At a time of layoffs and attempted wage cuts, the workers struck with determination and staying power.

Warner reports a case in which a former owner, Caleb Choate, was repeatedly invoked as the symbol of a good manager by the workers. Choate was president of a bank, director of three other business firms, and president of two Unitarian church associations, and he was on the board of directors of the hospital, the schools, and the library. He had been chairman of the local Republican party committee, mayor of Yankee City, a member of the city council, and an officer in several fraternal orders and social clubs.

Any complaints of workers in Choate's factory quickly came to his ears. If an aggrieved worker was not personally associated with the good man, he was bound to have a friend, relative, or club associate who could easily put in a good word on the worker's behalf. It was in factories without such channels, or where channels were blocked, that unionization, strikes, and formal grievance procedures resulted in Yankee City (Warner, 1962; Warner et al., 1963).

assignments. The history of Yankee City's transformation (see Box) is still repeating itself in many places in North America today.

PROTEST MOVEMENTS

In that gap between private and public life we can also see the seeds of protest and change, the demand for access to modernity, the demand for responsiveness of corporate bureaucracies to their clients, and the questioning of modern legal-rational values, such as the cult of efficiency. **Protest movements** include the various revolutionary movements of Western history. Certainly the labor movement is one offspring of revolutionary socialism, although in North America it quickly lost that identification. The civil rights movement in North America and the anti-apartheid struggle in South Africa are protest movements that, like the labor movement, bid for access to corporate bureaucracy and the market under conditions of legal equality for ethnic (termed "racial") minorities. Like the labor movement, these movements have not questioned legal rationality itself.

In terms of cultural protest, the romantic movement of the last century, with its charismatic poetic leaders, is one of the strongest, and its effects linger with us today. Romanticism led to nationalism—Lord Byron was a hero of the Greek War of Independence, for example. Let us review some of the protest movements of the modern era.

In the 1960s the youth movement made itself heard in protests against the Vietnam war.

The Youth Movement

Closely linked to the romantic movement was the protest movement of European youth starting in the last century. S. N. Eisenstadt (1966) sees one side of the youth movement as establishment and mainstream, but also running the risk of turning inward and escaping into its own tiny particularist sects. This mainstream is rooted in the romantic cult of unspoiled individuality of the genius who creates great works and achieves fame and distinction without any prolonged study, instruction, or effort.

The mainstream youth movement is a direct response, like fraternities and sororities, to the growth of large-scale higher education in modern life. Youth has had to confront the ever-lengthening of the age grade to be spent in the university, the increasing requirement of technical and educational specialization, and the increasing possibility that knowledge learned in school may soon be obsolete or outmoded in the world of work.

It is no surprise that periodic protest movements are born among modern university youth the world over. Some groups developed around charismatic leaders ended in sectarian communes like the Bruderhof, born from the German youth movement (Zoblocki, 1971). The remnants of the latter were absorbed by the official Hitler youth movement. In the United States, the youth movement, once safely contained by fraternities and football teams, exploded into mass protest and mass rituals of rock concerts during the 1960s, a time of unprecedented growth of the university population. Youth was also rightly concerned with the political issue of the Vietnam war in which they, like the rest of the country, were called to participate without consultation.

The Women's Movement

In the 1970s the women's movement came into its own, with giant rallies such as this one, in support of the Equal Rights Amendment.

While the labor movement can be seen as a direct bid by workers to economic participation and up-the-line communication in corporate bureaucracy, the youth movement is a manifestation of impatience by youth bidding to get into the managerial levels of the corporate world. It began, romantically, to question the cultural validity of the legal-rational model. The *women's movement* has carried that cultural questioning a step further, for it questions the shape of the *private* world of family while bidding for equal legal access and treatment for women in the corporate world.

The women's movement erupted into national consciousness in the United States in the late 1960s, with a series of strident demonstrations and rallies by large crowds of women in major cities. (The press made much of a short-lived ritual of protest, public bra burning.) These women had charismatic leaders, a rich and

National Rally for Equal Rights

controversial literature, and a pervasive ideology, **feminism:** "In a minimalist definition, feminism could be taken to refer to the awareness of women's oppression and exploitation at work, in the home, and in society as well as to the conscious political action taken by women to change this situation" (H. L. Moore, 1988, p. 10).

The women's movement has generated a host of associations, from small study groups to the National Organization for Women (NOW). Intellectually it has generated not only a bid for political, managerial, and economic access but an intellectual challenge to the continued legitimacy of the division of labor by sex in the household. It espouses reproductive rights for women—that is, the prospective mother's freedom to choose to end a pregnancy.

The women's movement has also launched, rather partially, a cultural critique of the basis of legal rationality as supposedly echoing "masculine" values on competition and dominance. Insofar as such a critique questions such phenomena as the cult of efficiency and corporate policies of mindless growth, it can only be healthy for modern society. Moreover, intellectual feminism encourages a mode of detachment and critical distance very much like the ethnographic one. It encourages new perspectives.

Homosexuals are choosing a number of alternative lifestyles. This lesbian couple have a family with children.

Like all protest movements, the women's is diverse, even chaotic. It ranges from highly articulate mass associations like NOW, with its coherent political agenda, to tiny splinter groups around charismatic figures, including groups calling themselves "witches' covens" and others attempting to institute goddess worship. In all its forms it points to some of the areas in which we can expect dynamic changes in the form of modernity in the future.

The Gay and Lesbian Movement

In the twentieth century homosexual lifestyles have become the basis for a mass movement of "gay" persons. *Gay* was originally a code word used by the oppressed (but never effectively suppressed) minority of homosexuals to refer to themselves. *Gay*, then, is a "native" term associated with a conscious demand for liberation. The appearance of a mass gay and lesbian liberation movement is dated in the United States from 1969. However, the gay movement was first a social movement—the clear emergence of a minority lifestyle—before it became a political one. Gays and lesbians built a series of private, economic, social, and civic organizations before going public with their protests.

Modern life has included a "sexual revolution," since on the one hand medicine seemed to have conquered sexually transmitted diseases and on the other hand modern technology had perfected readily available birth control devices. Men and women could engage in sex without fear of disease or of unwanted pregnancies. It was within these conditions that distinctive sexual liberationist (heterosexual and homosexual) lifestyles emerged. A contemporary emphasis on individual rights, encouraged by the civil rights and women's movements, also has had an impact. In addition, in an economy of factory industrialism it was no longer economically necessary for every adult to have children—people became more likely to depend on cash savings (investments, pensions, social security) in their old age.

A gay lifestyle is characterized first of all by preferential choice of members of one's own sex as sexual partners. In large cities a number of gay institutions also emerge. Most common is the gay bar, a place to meet others and to socialize. Some of these places have evolved into enormous dance halls accommodating over a thousand persons. Others have specialized according to the age or class levels of their clientele. In most major cities of North America—certainly in New York, Los Angeles, and San Francisco—gay and lesbian "ghettos" have emerged as neighborhoods surrounding concentrations of gay bars, coffeeshops, bookstores, and other meeting places. Here residents are heavily gay, many businesses are gay-owned, and tourists even come to see gays as they might come to see ethnic Chinese in Chinatown.

Homosexual Behavior. Homosexuality is a pattern of preferred sexual behavior with members of one's own sex. Since the mid-1950s we have learned a great deal more about the subject than ever before. We now understand, from the laboratory observations of scientists William Masters and Virginia Johnson (1979), that the physiology of homosexual response is identical to that of heterosexual response. It is only the object of sexual desire and attention that differs. These findings of sex researchers have been supplemented by studies by sociologists, psychologists, anthropologists, political scientists, and writers from the gay and lesbian community itself (Blumenthal and Raymond 1988; Levine, 1979; Whitam and Mathy, 1986).

Homosexual persons do not usually take on the characteristics of the other sex. Indeed, the usual pattern of sexual behavior, widely misunderstood, is not for one partner to be "active" and hence "male" and the other "passive" and hence "female." Instead, most homosexual couples, in North America at least, assume both active and passive roles (Tripp, 1987).

In most societies casual homosexual contacts exist, and some societies recognize same-sex marriages. In American society about half the population never have sexual contact with members of their own sex and indeed may be quite averse to doing so. Another group of persons display the opposite or mirror-image preference and have never had an experience with a member of the other sex. Some people, however, are "bisexual," with preference for partners of either sex. Why some persons—perhaps as many as 5 to 10 percent of males in the North American population—should prefer homosexual relations is not clearly understood in terms of preconditions and life experiences (Bell, Weinberg, and Hammersmith, 1981; Masters and Johnson, 1979; Weinrich, 1987).

Homosexuality is not to be confused with *inversion*—the taking on or imitating of characteristics of the other gender. One form of inversion is *transvestism*, or dressing in the costume of the other sex. (In fact, many transvestites are not homosexual in their sexual preference.) In addition, some individuals are so deeply inverted in their self-image that physicians and surgeons are willing to certify them for a sex-change operation, in which their exterior sex organs are surgically transformed into replicas of those of the other sex. Through hormone injections these *transexuals* are able to acquire the "secondary" characteristics of the other sex, such as loss of facial hair and growth of breasts, but are not able actually to have children as an ordinary member of their new sex.

Classical Greek Homosexual Patterns.   In classical Greece, homosexual friendships were a common and regular part of the coming of age of aristocratic youths. A young man was courted by an older youth, and if accepted as a lover, the older of the pair assumed special responsibilities in initiating his beloved in the arts of war and in citizenship. Ideally, the younger partner was around age eighteen, ready to be inducted into the compulsory age grade of warriors—the *ephebia*—of his city-state, and his lover was in his mid-twenties, having already served his two years as a warrior recruit (Dover, 1978; Marrou 1964). Love between two men was idealized by the philosopher Plato and is the origin of the concept of "platonic" love.

Greek homosexual friendships, then, were a part of the life cycle of free Greek citizens. At around age thirty, the elder partner was expected to marry a woman. His younger partner was then free to court his own younger friend. Classical Greek male lifestyles can be described as homosexual at one phase of life and heterosexual in the later, childrearing one. A similar pattern has been described by Herdt for the Sambia of New Guinea (1987).

Western Prohibition of Homosexuality. Since medieval times, homosexuality has been forbidden in Western culture, and most Western systems of law penalized it. In France that changed with the promulgation of the Code Napoleon at the beginning of the 1800s, which did not penalize homosexual practices between consenting adults. In contrast, in Great Britain men were hanged for "sodomy" (the traditional name for anal intercourse) throughout the eighteenth century and the first half of the nineteenth century. The law making sodomy a capital offense was not repealed until 1861. As a consequence, homosexual behavior went underground in most of the West, but was certainly not eliminated. Indeed, being forbidden, homosexual behavior may well have seemed attractive, or at least daring, to some.

Gays and Cultural Revision. Gays have, however, organized into political pressure groups to work against laws forbidding homosexual practices by consenting adults and discriminating against gays in employment. These groups work to support election of candidates who are favorable to their views. Gay news publications, both local and national, support this effort.

In addition, religiously oriented lesbians and gay men have been rethinking theology in many Christian denominations and in Reformed Judaism. The Metropolitan Community Church is a Christian denomination whose clergy and membership are overwhelmingly homosexual. While it has not yet been accepted by the more conservative denominations, many liberal theologians and religious practitioners are coming to affirm that a gay lifestyle—couples, friendship, or fellowship—can be spiritually redeeming. Indeed, such is the position held by many gays and lesbians today who are practicing Christians or Jews.

Religious institutions have been challenged by the gay and lesbian movement.

For many gays, homosexuality is a private matter. Some engage in multiple sexual contacts while cultivating a close circle of friends for emotional satisfaction. Others form long-term unions with a partner of the same sex, committed to building a relationship together. Many such unions last for years, into old age (McWhirter and Mattison, 1984). Some gay couples, especially lesbians, actually raise children, usually born to a previous heterosexual marriage, but sometimes adopted. Some lesbian women undergo artificial insemination to bear a child for the union. Thus, it is evident that the gay movement is challenging the traditional definition of marriage and the family (Warren, 1974).

In sum, gay lifestyles have emerged out of once repressed, but never suppressed, hidden behaviors. In the modern metropolis, gay ghettos, bars, businesses, publications, religious groups, and political organizations have emerged. While lesbians have a lower rate of sexual disease than heterosexuals, AIDS has disproportionately ravaged the gay men's community in the United States. That community has responded by organizing itself for safe-sex education and disease prevention. In the 1990s, most new AIDS infection in the world are occurring among heterosexuals.

Disease and risk, like change and transformations, are parts of the human condition. A new human lifestyle, once it has asserted its prevalence and its dignity, may be transformed in the course of human history, but it is never lost. For example, the monastic movement, which removed large numbers of men and women from heterosexual family life and childrearing, was an important and populous movement in the Middle Ages. Today it is much less important, but monasticism, like every other human institution that has been invented, is here to stay.

SUMMARY AND CONCLUSIONS

*I*n the two previous chapters we surveyed the emergence of two dominant institutions—market systems and corporate bureaucracy—and the emergence of polycentric metropolitan communities. The culture of modernity at first glance seems to be legal rational, with increasing differentiation and specialization by function and professional task. Social class the world over is now conditioned in relation to these two institutions and this community form. Upper-class persons are hereditary elites; middle-class persons bid to enter the managerial elite through education. Schooling also conditions access to the supervisory and line-of-work levels of corporate industrial bureaucracy.

Modernity has spread to non-Western societies, while in the West and its dominions labor and marginalized ethnic (racial) groups have demanded access to schooling and corporate careers on an equal footing with others.

Japan is the first thoroughly modern non-Western society. It has adopted corporate bureaucracy and the market system with great success. Yet it has done so with very different life cycle patterns from those of the West. Workplaces carry over much from the family. Decision making, especially about new product lines and other business developments, is done slowly by large circles of work groups. Once decided, new policies are enacted rapidly, giving Japanese the business motto, "Slow, slow, fast, fast" (Hall and Hall, 1987).

At every stage of life, the individual Japanese is assured of benevolent acceptance by seniors. Children are never physically punished, students are never flunked by teachers, and employees are never fired by firms. Yet Japanese society is pervaded by *rank*, a kind of differentiation not so highly developed in the West, in which access to schools and jobs is by dint of placement through impersonally administered examinations. If Japan has a cult of efficiency, it is in its placement examinations, which are traumatic obstacles weighing on the future of youth.

Thus, while Japanese business performs well in productive competition on world markets, its values are not simply those of the bottom line but rather are those of making each firm a victor. Business is conceived of as a battle, and the bottom line is a battle score, either a trophy or a loss. These victories redound to the credit of bosses, and Japanese live to make their superiors look good.

Legal-rational corporate bureaucracy in Japan, then, is a forum for the exercise of the traditional Confucian values of benevolence, justice (on the part of seniors), and loyalty and filial piety (on the part of juniors). It is further an exercise in loyalty to one's name and the name of one's firm.

Modernity in Japan is no less demanding than anywhere else, perhaps more so, since it functions with a minimum of external discipline and controls. The popular arts in print, film, television, and even comic books have projected Japanese fantasies and ambivalence on a wide variety of fictitious heroes. And to make up for the great tensions generated by the workplace as well as the demands of schooling on the family, adult males and females in Japan spend a great deal of their time with informal cliques of peers, as well as with at least one formal association, the PTA.

Our theory of associations, and the informal cliques they derive from, is that they are institutional shock absorbers that absorb the tensions emanating from other institutions. They can also be substitute rites of passage. Associations are also vehicles of protest. All protest movements take place in an array of informal groups and formal associations (sometimes spilling over, of course, into mobs and crowds at mass events). Protest is a process generated by modernity itself and cannot be avoided. The labor movement generated trade unions and socialist revolutions of various sorts. One brand of socialism, Marxism-Leninism, has been deemed a moral, social, and economic failure by the masses in whose name it attempted to rule. Throughout eastern Europe and the former Soviet Union, Marxism-Leninism has collapsed. One initiative for that collapse arose from a free labor movement, Poland's Solidarity. Protest movements can sweep even "revolutionary" corporate establishments.

Labor movements seek to give workers and their children access to line-of-work positions at "fair" wages, as well as the means for up-the-line communication. In contrast, the youth movement, born of the frustrations of long years of schooling for highly technical careers, often attempted to glorify the romantic ideal of the unfettered, untutored genius. Romanticism, however, seems not to have changed the exigencies of legal-rational modernity.

Like the youth movement, the women's movement has been sparked and led by educated elites. Women have been demanding their rightful place in the corporate world, asking for political, legal, and economic equality on a par with men. They have also been questioning the division of labor by sex in the household and have been demanding a woman's full reproductive rights to control if and when she gives birth.

The gay and lesbian movement emanates from the same middle-class educated elites and demands the legalization, indeed the normalization, if you will, of gay and lesbian lifestyles. Like the women's movement, it has sparked a host of informal and formal organizations, but unlike the former, it has tended to form separate urban residential and business enclaves in the largest cities.

Modernity, while it means legal-rational corporate forms and cost accounting world-wide, does not imply static, one-world structures. The attempt to create them, in Marxism-Leninism, was doomed to failure. Families and associations, and associated protest movements—in short, private cultures, many of them newly forged out of old antecedents—are always going to be with us.

SUGGESTED READINGS

Baruma, Ian. *Behind the Mask: On Sexual Demons, Sacred Mothers, Transvestites, Gangsters and Other Japanese Cultural Heroes.* New York: Meridian Books/New American Library, 1984. A set of lively essays.

Bestor, Theodore C. *Neighborhood Tokyo.* Palo Alto, Calif.: Stanford University Press, 1989. An acclaimed recent ethnography.

Hall, E. T., and Mildred Reed Hall. *Hidden Difference: Doing Business with the Japanese.* Garden City, N.Y.: Doubleday, 1987. Intended as a manual for American businessmen doing business in Japan, this is a very practical guide to interacting with the Japanese.

Herdt, Gilbert, ed. *Gay Culture in America: Essays from the Field.* Boston: Beacon Press, 1991. A cogent ethnographic survey of the subject today.

Kondo, Dorinne, *Crafting Selves: Power, Gender, and Discourses of Identity in a Japanese Workplace.* Chicago: University of Chicago Press, 1990. Beautifully written ethnography of a Tokyo neighborhood of craft workshops and small factories, concentrating on a pastry factory employing women laborers.

McWhirter, David P., and Andrew M. Mattison. *The Male Couple: How Relationships Develop.* Englewood Cliffs, N.J.: Prentice-Hall, 1984. A fascinating account of just how radical a cultural change gay lifestyles can be.

David W. Plath, ed. *Work and Lifecourse in Japan.* Albany: SUNY Press, 1983. A fascinating collection of articles on every aspect of work and life cycles in contemporary Japan.

SUGGESTED VIDEO

The Japanese Version. Louis Alvarez and Andrew Kolker. Hohokus, N.J.: CNAM Film Library, 1991. A hilarious view of the Japanese version of American culture via the popular arts and media.

GLOSSARY

cliques Informal groups of friends that serve as the basis for forming associations.

examination system A system of achievement and placement tests common to all corporate, industrial, scientific countries but carried to an extreme in Japan (and to a slightly lesser extent, in France) governing entrance into schools higher than the school one is leaving. They act as competitive mechanisms of sorting out fewer and fewer persons into each higher echelon of education. In Japan one is examined only for the school one hopes to enter. Tests further act as placement devices on the corporate job market.

feminism The pervasive ideology of the women's movement that seeks to raise consciousness to resist oppression and exploitation of women generally.

Japanese values Core values, derived from Confucian philosophy, exalting *benevolence* and *justice* (for superiors), *loyalty* (toward peers and seniors), and *filial piety* (toward one's seniors and one's name and the name of one's firm). Justice is fulfilled by placing people in their "correct station in life" through examinations. In addition, traditional Japanese values include the notion of a noncancelable, *unpayable debt* to one's parents and all other superiors, and the necessity of upholding the *honor* of one's name.

life employment The Japanese pattern of never firing an employee in most firms. Hiring depends on passing an examination. However, retirement age is fifty-five. In important firms or government agencies, some managers seeing themselves passed over for promotion do "fall from heaven." That is, they take managerial jobs in firms or agencies subsidiary to their first firm.

modernity The cultural expression of legal rationality, characterized by increasing differentiation and specialization of tasks by function, as defined by science and technology, and as set forth by written charters that are both rational and legal.

protest movements Social movements, manifest in informal cliques, crowds, mobs, and formal associations, that seek to "capture the center of modernity"—that is, in some way gain access to or control the nature of corporate bureaucracy and the market system. Aside from liberal-democratic revolutions, protest movements have surged from nationalities (to form nation-states), ethnic and racial minorities, labor, women, and gays and lesbians.

schooling In the modern world, a "bridge" between the private world of home and the corporate world of work. Level of schooling determines one's level of access for entry into the corporate world: line-of-work, supervisory, or managerial.

social class The classification of persons in modern metropolises into upper, middle, and lower classes. These classes can be correlated with educational level and level in corporate bureaucracies. Upper-class persons are hereditary elites who own, but do not manage, corporate firms, and chief executives who have climbed to the top. Middle-class persons are entrepreneurs, professionals, and managerial elites, generally university educated. Supervisory elites may be either middle or working class. Like the lower or working class, they have generally completed a secondary or technical school education. An "underclass" of the permanently unemployed is sometimes listed as a fourth class. These are often grade school dropouts or even illiterates.

voluntary associations Groups of persons, generally not recruited by kinship, who stand "between" other major institutions, such as the school and the home, or the workplace and the home. They are institutional shock absorbers and substitute rites of passage, as well as vehicles for protest movements.

Applied Anthropology and the Policy Process

*ANTHROPOLOGISTS AND THE
POLICY PROCESS*

*ETHNOGRAPHIC CLOSE-UP:
POLICY RECOMMENDATIONS AND
KUNA DEMOCRACY*

Parliamentarianism and Democracy

The Kuna Local Congress

The Kuna General (Tribal) Congress

The Panamanian National Assembly

Awareness of a Dilemma and Some Policy Recommendations

*O*ver time, human communities have increased in number, population density, and specialization and complexity of institutions. This book has examined the emergence of these institutions out of behaviors already present in the previous community forms. Institutions have emerged successively, but only slowly have they entered human consciousness, and then often shrouded in myths that only pretend to explain them. Since about 1500, modern people have been grappling with the implications of three key institutions: markets, legal-rational bureaucracies, and factory industrialism. This Epilogue concentrates on the implications of human awareness of our institutions through the **rational deliberation** of public policies.

I have emphasized the constraints that modern institutions, in their various cultural manifestations, impose on people. The picture has been a sober one. A world-wide culture of generic Protestantism generates impersonal school bureaucracies and seemingly cruel examinations systems. In Japan, and elsewhere, the popular arts provide avenues of escape through fantasy. More concretely, protest and unrest is everywhere inevitable. Yet paradoxically, as this book is written, never has the modern world seemed to hold so much hope for individual and group achievement and fulfillment.

For example, in the last few years the latest attempt at world empire has collapsed in Eastern Europe. A system of nation-states and multiple balances of power politics has replaced the Cold War system of two giant power blocs in armed countervailing pose. Small wars are likely through the next generations, but a world nuclear holocaust seems much less likely than before.

The statist extremes of totalitarian corporate bureaucracy reached their height under Marxism-Leninism as practiced by Stalin and his successors. The fatal deficiencies of that set of institutions, if given a monopoly of all institutional life in a competitive international framework, have been exposed. As a *revitalization movement*, Marxism-Leninism as institutionalized by Stalin simply did not pass the reality test over three generations. It is being swept away by leaders who were among its second generation of schoolchildren.

Yet the entire modern world continues to grapple with a large set of problems. Economic development, the implementation of a factory industrial system in all countries, is perceived as a priority by all the nation-states of the developing world. Countries already industrialized are concerned with keeping up technologically and, more critically, with balancing industrial output with consumption.

We are learning, with Jane Jacobs (1982), the limitations of exporting industrialism in one piece. Huge factories simply plunked down out of context remain that, out of context. In contrast, the origin of Japanese industry is instructive. Small shops dedicated to repairing imported bicycles, for example, set out to manufacture spare parts. Next they began to assemble these parts into bicycles. Bicycles led to motorbikes, and these, finally, to automobiles. (Honda still keeps a strong motorbike division.) As a consequence, Japan also evolved a system of decentralized firms and workshops committed to manufacturing parts, so that the numbers of workers gathered at assembly lines was never as vast as in the United States. Japanese industrialization derived from a process of import substitution, as in this case—first of bike parts and finally of whole automobiles.

One result of this process is that the Japanese work force has a large "independent" array of small firms to work in after retirement from the large firms at age fifty-five. A continued stream of small-scale entrepreneurial activity means the founding of many small firms, some of which do not outlive their founder. The process, however, is vital to continued economic growth and is more effective than simply dictating the construction of large factories from scratch.

Industrial nations also have to grapple with employment policies. The output of an efficient industrial system can easily outstrip the capacity of the population to consume it. A few workers can produce enough for all. Unemployment and idleness for many are a possible result. Questions of welfare payments, even guaranteed national incomes, are therefore urgent matters of public debate in Western Europe and the United States.

This leads to questions of household composition and the entry and staying capacity of women in the labor force. The United States increasingly has a pattern in which women enter the work force at the same age as men and stay there. In Japan they enter at a young age, only to leave a few years later upon marriage. In Great Britain women leave the work force around age twenty-five, but they are likely to reenter it after about age forty. Scandinavian women tend to take only part-time work. In France and Germany women tend to follow the American pattern (Mendras and Cole, 1991).

While feminists in the United States believe that a work career is every woman's right, some experts, such as Marvin Harris (1987), hold that two-income households must be looked at carefully. If two incomes are really only maintaining a household at the level previously attained by one income, then society has not benefited economically by the expansion of the work force. I argue instead that two-income households offer other payoffs by tapping into wider pools of talent.

More broadly yet, we have seen that capitalism (the culture of price-regulated markets combined with factory industrialism) gives rise to vast private bureaucratic corporations that tend to be unresponsive to labor and often heedless of the effect of technology on the environment. Everywhere capitalism tends to dissolve the traditional ties of tribal peoples and peasants to the land and to each other. Likewise, socialism gives rise to vast state-owned public corporate bureaucracies with similar failings.

These examples are all broad problems of public policy in the modern nations. They concern the nature of the large-scale institutions, the market and entrepreneurs, and the world of public and private corporations of both capitalism and socialism.

In modern societies anthropologists observe people as they participate in these institutions at all levels. We also study the local groupings of ethnic groups, rural communities, or part-cultures, whether of neighborhood or institution within metropolitan regions. Bands and tribes, the so-called "native peoples" survive, and their interaction with the vast impersonal corporate bureaucracies of health, schooling, defense, and territorial administration is often mediated today by **applied anthropologists,** brokers between the view from the ground that form the elite centers.

ANTHROPOLOGISTS AND THE POLICY PROCESS

The Phases of the Policy Process
1. Awareness of need
2. Formulation and evaluation of policy choices
3. Implementation of one policy choice
4. Evaluation of that policy

In the United States today 50 percent of new anthropology Ph.D's start applied anthropology careers, contributing to the formulation of policy measures on behalf of the people they study. **Policy** can be defined as a set of moral and legal guidelines for dealing with the solution of a problem. A rational policy argues for one set of solutions over others.

John Van Willigen (1986) sees the **policy process** as one of rational "formulation, implementation, and evaluation of policy" (p. 143). Through ethnographic research, anthropologists can provide information for all stages of the process. Van Willigen elaborates this process further into awareness of need, then formulation and evaluation of alternative solutions, before the "formulation of policy," which is obviously thereby *choice* among the alternatives. Van Willigen and other applied anthropologists strive for enlightened decision making. For example, Michael Angrosino and Linda Whiteford (1986) refine the policy process into no less than eleven stages.

By being aware of policy as a process, anthropologists can judge when to intervene at any stage, including the pre-stage of defining or setting the problem. We can do field work with a specific theoretical framework that may involve the definition of a policy need felt by the field community. Or, conversely, the community may already present the field worker with a policy problem and ask for a solution.

An example of a **policy ethnography** is Paul Driben's *Aroland Is Our Home* (1986). Driben was hired as consultant by a community of Canadian Ojibwa Indians of northern Ontario, who were squatting without legal title on Crown (public) land. Their goal was to gain title; the anthropologist's role was to aid in the formulation of policy alternatives—that is, the several ways they could indeed gain title, with a comparative assessment of each.

The people of Aroland, the Ojibwa community, sought to define themselves as a single landowning entity modeled on Indian reserves elsewhere in Canada. Yet they were not a historic, registered "band" with an inalienable right to ancestral land reserves. Rather, they were an unincorporated group of squatters. Worse, a minority of them were "nonstatus" Indians, a legal accident created by nineteenth-century Canadian Indian policy, which had sought to "emancipate" Indian men by giving them grants of land and absorbing them into Western society. This policy had been ineffective, as very few Indian men ever availed themselves of it. Yet that same policy had fixed Indian identity and descent in the male line. Indian women who married non-Indian men lost Indian status for themselves and their children. Yet in fact most children of Indian women remained Indian. Driben thus depicts the contradictions within Aroland when seen through Canadian legal categories.

Driben gave the Ojibwa Arolanders good advice, setting forth the alternatives from which they might choose. How can you gain title to Crown land in Ontario? Basically the choice he put to the Indians was between "dependent" (meaning tribal reserve) status, and independent status—outright (fee simple) title, to be held either collectively or individually. Driben also pointed out how any choice would affect the internal division of the community, between fully legal ("status") and nonstatus Indians. This distinction was meaningless in terms of internal community identity, but vital in terms of land tenure.

When polled in a referendum, the community was nearly evenly divided in its choice. Consequently, the Aroland Indian Association went into negotiations with federal and provincial authorities with an open slate about what they might achieve: land tenure in any way feasible.

Driben says they attained an "incomplete victory" at first. The Ministry of Resource Management was willing to sell the community some 4,000 acres, but the price was higher than the Arolanders could afford. In any case, the Indians had "achieved notoriety" and would not henceforth be disregarded by the authorities. No one was likely to try to evict them from the public lands where they lived and harvested forest resources. Moreover, the Indians had come to understand the economic, political, and social consequences of land acquisition. Finally, they had hit on a community solution to the conflicting claims of status versus nonstatus Indians. They intended to gain two types of land tenure. One portion of their land would become a tribal reserve, for the legal Indians. The rest of the land would be registered as a corporate holding for the nonstatus group.

However, just as Driben was ending his contract with the Aroland Indian Association, Canadian Indian policy changed by act of Parliament. Loss of Indian status through women marrying out (exogamy) was perceived as sexual discrimination. To correct this abuse, a new law provided for nonstatus Indians to apply for legal status as Indians. Bands could establish their own membership. Aroland quickly incorporated as an Indian band, registered its nonstatus minority as fully Indian, and applied to establish a new tribal land reserve.

In my critique of this and other recent books on the policy process (1991), I noted that Driben has presented simply a project report. A theoretical problem lurks in his material. How does a group derived from hunting-and-gathering band culture, with its rudimentary leadership, come to manage an effective political council? These people had mounted a tribal republic; it would be interesting to know what their meetings were like. Driben runs the risk of becoming a mere technician, rather than an anthropologist, if he has not (and he may have) studied the theoretical implications of his materials.

The policy process is obviously closely linked to the speech events of group deliberation. In the world of tribes and traditional civilization, such deliberation takes place in councils and community assemblies. In the modern world it takes place in committees, task forces, elected and appointed councils, and legislatures. Applied anthropologists must learn to work with such deliberative groups while at the same time studying them. One theoretical framework for ethnographic research can be democracy itself.

ETHNOGRAPHIC CLOSE-UP

POLICY RECOMMENDATIONS AND KUNA DEMOCRACY

Democracy was my theoretical framework in field work among the 40,000 or so Kuna* Indians

*In my previous publications I spelled it *Cuna*. Since then, many Kuna intellectuals have come to prefer *Kuna*, since in the alphabet devised by European linguists for their language, there is no *C*, only *K*. (In Spanish the letter *C* stands for phonemes sounding like *K*, *S*, and *TH* in English.)

of San Blas district, Panama (Moore, 1980b, 1981, 1983, 1984c, 1985). The Kuna have councils and chiefs for each of their approximately fifty local communities, and a tribal council with three high chiefs for the entire district, which comprises some 150 miles of strategic Atlantic coastline. The communities are mainly located on coral islands just offshore. Each council arrives at its decisions by a rule of complete consensus. Their rule is unanimity, not majority. I proposed to study the unanimous decision-making process. I have not yet figured out with any precision how they in fact are able to come to agreements when speakers often enter debates passionately at odds over issues. But I have learned a great deal about how they shape that debate and their council meetings.

When I summarized some of my findings, I compared the parliamentary procedure practiced in Panamá's national assembly with the council procedures of the Kuna tribal congress. Then I became aware of a policy need for greater formalization of tribal politics, while safeguarding indigenous democracy. I then formulated several policy recommendations accordingly.

Parliamentarianism and Democracy

In Western parliaments each item of business must take the form of a motion, made and seconded from the floor and then stated aloud by the chair. Each motion must be either accepted or rejected by means of a vote. This yes or no form of business is, according to political scientist Herbert L. Spiro (1959), the product of an English history in which parliament was originally a "parley" or palaver among king, church, lords, and commoners. It acted as a court of law to decide trouble cases. In English common law every case must be defined by a single issue or point of law. If there is no point of law in question, there is no case; the plaintiff's complaint is dismissed. All decisions must be defined in terms of yes or no answers to the issue in question.

We can readily see that a parley corresponds to the crisis and confrontation phase in conflict theory (Chapter 10). Two contenders challenge each other. Instead of fighting it out in armed battles or duels, they refer to a redressive mechanism, the vote, which is a peaceful way to measure the size of the allies they can muster. In early days (and still in some countries undergoing political crises) the two sides may have indeed left the parliament to take up arms.

Parliamentary procedures and rules of order have been a way to codify this peace-making, deliberative

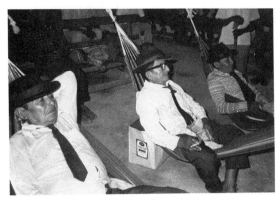

From central hammocks, three local chiefs preside over a Kuna local congress.

process. Most Western countries (but not Sweden) follow British procedures as publicized by the utilitarian philosopher Jeremy Bentham, who wrote to the French Estates General during the French Revolution to instruct them on how to conduct themselves. His manual was widely disseminated in Latin America in 1810 and is repeated in the **standing orders** (*Reglamento Interno*) of the Panamanian national assembly.

The Kuna Local Congress

In contrast, Kuna local community congresses take up business with no formal rules of precedence or order at all, spoken or written. Each local Kuna community has from three to six chiefs, who gather all the adult men to a congress, or talking gathering, some three or more evenings a week to discuss anything of public concern. Much of the business is informative: residents returning from travels deliver a report; visitors state their business. In addition, the gathering takes up action items, or "paths" (*ikar*, pl. *ikarkana*), matters that require resolution.

Matters follow the sense of timing of the first chief. Many action items are trouble cases, disputes between two parties in which the gathering, through the chiefs, acts as a court. Votes are not taken. Instead, each matter is resolved by the sense of the meeting. Thus, in spite of the lack of formal rules, meetings are orderly. (See Howe [1986] for an ethnography of the Kuna local congress.)

At a Kuna tribal congress, a local community chief orates while tribal secretaries sit at the head table.

The Kuna General (Tribal) Congress

Presided over by the three high chiefs, the Kuna tribal congress meets around three times a year in one of the larger communities. Every community sends a delegation consisting of some of its chiefs and any others the local congress has picked. It is convened by an organizing committee, which dissolves when the first high chief announces the composition of the head table. A secretary from the new head table reads correspondence and the agenda, set by the first high chief. There then follow reports from the high chiefs and Kuna delegates to the national assembly. This is followed by action items, the more important ones first. Delegates are unwilling to stay more than three days, so some less important items are never discussed. Votes are not taken; again, resolution is reached by the sense of the meeting. After key action items have been resolved, erstwhile opponents are called forward to sit together for a formal admonishment (*unanaet*), in which a respected elder exhorts them to uphold new agreements and to become friends.

After its own business is exhausted, the congress listens dutifully to reports from Panamanian bureaucrats. At one congress there were no action items, only ten lengthy official reports. When there have been action items, the secretaries of the high table read aloud the Spanish texts of the resolutions they have prepared for each action item resolved. Each text is interpreted in Kuna, debated, and often amended before editing in final form. Finally, by

tacit agreement there is a stir to leave and the congress adjourns without any formal motion.

The Panamanian National Assembly

By the constitution of 1972, amended in 1979, the *Asamblea Nacional* consists of 505 representatives of local electoral districts. (The San Blas Kuna have three representatives.) It meets for one month each year and elects delegates to the national legislative committee, which, when meeting with the cabinet, enacts all legislation.

Procedures follow parliamentary standards. A session is called to order by the president of the assembly, who directs the secretary to ascertain whether there is a quorum. If there is, the session follows the Order of the Day, as set forth in the standing orders. Here is my translation:

> Article 130: The Order of the Day shall by fixed by the Committee of Ways and Means in the following manner:
>
> 1. Reading and discussion of the Minutes;
>
> 2. The correspondence that the Assembly ought to hear, telegrams, petitions, and memorials of whatever nature. . . ;
>
> 3. The elections which must be made by a vote of the Assembly;
>
> 4. The observations of the Executive Organ or its objections to any of the Projects agreed upon by the Assembly;
>
> 5. The Projects which may be read for debate. In the debate the norm to be followed is rigorous chronological order of presentation, . . . ; and
>
> 6. The announcements of committees which do not accompany another project in law. (Panamá, 1979, pp. 37–38)

In spite of parliamentarianism, there are strong limitations to the democratic character of the national assembly, especially during the years (1972–1979) it shared power with the dictator whose constitutional convention created it, General Omar Torrijos. Between 1969 and 1979 the Torrijos regime launched massive economic development in agriculture, mining, hydroelectricity, port facilities, and tourism, investing heavily in these sectors through public and private foreign aid. The regime also invested heavily in education and public health. It wanted to cultivate a citizenry that was hygienic, well nourished, literate, and politically conscious. However, its image of citizen participation did not include active opposition to its projects—quite the contrary. Although the regime encouraged citizen participation in local advisory councils, with the idea that these should be channels for citizen-initiated legislation and policy through the assembly, in fact its projects were born in the bureaucracy and applied from the top down.

Looking at the flow of political action in Torrijos's Panamá, it is clear that the national assembly was not so much a structure for inputs to express popular demands as it was a structure for outputs, a **support structure** designed to mobilize the population and its leadership to the regime's own ends.

In contrast, the Kuna local and tribal congresses are very much input or **demand structures**, articulating grassroots democracy. Yet Panamanian officials tend to treat the Kuna general congress the way cabinet ministers treat the assembly: as a place to deliver reports and to communicate administrative actions, not deliberate them. Therefore, it was almost certain that the Torrijos regime and the Kuna congress should clash. When the national tourist agency tried to incorporate San Blas into national development plans through a project to build a resort on the Kuna coast at a cost of millions, the project was presented to the tribal congress as a report, not an action item (Moore, 1980). When the agency actually tried to carry out feasibility studies, neither the local community nor the tribal congress would allow it, revoking a permit issued by the three high chiefs and precipitating a months' long crisis between the Indians and the government, which eventually tacitly abandoned the project.

Awareness of a Dilemma and Some Policy Recommendations

The dilemma facing the Kuna is this: They will be under increasing pressure to continue the formalization of their general congress, running the risk of converting it into a support structure rather than one

V. P. G. Gonzalez of Panamá, responding to Kuna demands, Kuna general congress, November 1977.

for the articulation of demands and the resolution of issues internal to the district. They themselves want to update and "civilize" native institutions while retaining their intrinsically Kuna character.

I have made some recommendations to resolve this dilemma.* In general, the Kuna are well advised to continue to borrow the best from Western parliamentarianism while conserving Kuna interaction patterns and safeguarding their councils as demand structures.

First, the general congress ought to adopt its own standing orders with an order of the day. To keep and read minutes is to have a useful corporate memory. A specific procedure to differentiate discussion of executive reports as opposed to action items is desirable. It is also essential to have a mechanism to carry over old business from one session to the next; standing orders provide this. The adoption of standing orders would allow the general congress to observe Western forms and conserve Kuna usage. I recommend they keep the current custom of deciding all issues by consensus.

---

*I sent these recommendations in a letter in Spanish to a Kuna group studying tribal institutions. That was at a time when all Panamanians were preoccupied with the crisis of opposition to General Manuel Noriega, former commander of the defense forces. I expect that I and Kuna sociologist Eligio Alvarado shall be presenting them again in the near future for more active local consideration.

The Kuna general congress is open to charges of being unrepresentative and easily manipulated as long as its membership rule is as vague as it is now. The composition of any one congress may be weighted toward the communities particularly concerned with the issues to be debated. They send the most numerous and vociferous delegations. In its standing orders, the general congress could fix the number of delegates per community, leaving their selection, as now, to the local congress. Formal membership would give the tribal congress more credibility in the eyes of other Panamanians.

Second, the general congress, acting as a demand structure, ought to amend the tribal charter (*Carta Orgánica*) and propose Panamanian legislation to give the congress the same financial and police powers that Panamanian municipal councils have. These powers are deeply rooted in Hispanic culture and would be respected by any Panamanian government. That is, municipal councils have the right to levy taxes, fines, and fees. They can hire full-time secretaries and employ constables (who do not generally have the right to bear firearms). They can enforce their decisions on recalcitrant households or hamlets within their jurisdiction. The Kuna tribal government can do none of these things. Since the example is clearly understood by other Panamanians, it is worth exploring.

SUMMARY AND CONCLUSIONS

The modern world everywhere confronts our species with the challenge of coming to terms with three emergent institutions: market, legal-rational bureaucracy, and factory industrialism. If new institutions are to arise in a postmodern era, we are not yet aware of them. (I might speculate that something may emerge out of the social organization of science around the research team or task force, but that is merely speculation, hardly scientific prediction.)

As we become increasingly aware of our social situation, we have the chance to shape our immediate future through policy choices. These are articulated and implemented in many social settings, including but not limited to legislatures and local councils. The policy process starts with the conscious articulation of a need, the formulation and weighing of policy choices to respond to that need, the implementation of one such policy, and its subsequent evaluation.

Applied anthropologists are now 50 percent of new Ph.D's in the field. Anthropologists are becoming more sophisticated about the policy process and our prospective role in it. Originally, many were simply hired to help implement policies already decided on, often with little deliberation or debate, in political councils. Now we realize that we may shape the deliberation from the beginning of the process.

Still, there are inevitable frustrations. Political and ideological predispositions may blind policy makers to the facts as we present them. Elizabeth

Colson (1985), musing over her distinguished career as an applied anthropologist in her speech accepting the Malinowski Award from the Society for Applied Anthropology, recalls that in 1941 her colleague Godfrey Wilson advised the colonial government of Northern Rhodesia (today, Zambia) that migrant black workers in the copper mining towns were not temporary laborers but were settling in to create ongoing, permanent communities. The government rejected his findings and stopped his research funding. They wanted to pursue a policy treating all urban blacks as temporary migrants, soon to return to their native tribal homelands.

This same policy choice was made by the neighboring South African government a few years later, flying in the face of Wilson's published reports (1941, 1942), when they contrived the legal framework of *apartheid*, whereby blacks were to be segregated in native homelands, coming to the towns and cities only as temporary workers, living in segregated areas ("townships") where they could never own land. Almost fifty years later, after much suffering and hardfought protest, this policy is a stunning failure. Not only was its moral premise wrong, but its practical premise was, too. In the face of industrialization, blacks could not be confined to their native homelands but rather migrated to create their own urban communities in the industrial centers, just as Wilson had said.

Thus, the process of open group deliberation at all levels is one to be nurtured. It has its pitfalls, and many failures shall surely continue to happen. Rational deliberation, wherever its arena, and whether or not it is formally constituted, is everywhere to be encouraged. In the example just cited, the Afrikaner South African architects of apartheid enacted their unjust and socially uninformed policies perfectly legally through elected representatives meeting in parliament. The problem there was that blacks had been excluded from the electoral and parliamentary process.

Likewise in Panama, the Kuna Indians practice a largely informal but thoroughly democratic system of local councils, while the national government, formally democratic, is much less so in practice than the Kuna. I have sought to formulate some policy recommendations to strengthen Kuna democracy while formalizing it. But formalities alone are never the answer. Information, carefully and accurately researched, and careful group deliberation of that information, in the making of rational policy choices—whatever they may be—in the long term can provide the best, if often painful, answers to *Homo sapiens*.

SUGGESTED READINGS

Eddy, Elizabeth M., and W. L. Partridge, eds. *Applied Anthropology in America*, 2nd ed. New York: Columbia University Press, 1987. A splendid collection of articles dedicated to the proposition that applied anthropologists are ethnographic researchers as well as policy brokers.

Salvador, Mari Lyn, ed. *The Art of Being Kuna: Layers of Meaning Among the Kuna of Panama*. Los Angeles: UCLA Fowler Museum of Cultural History, 1997. This lavishly illustrated volume covers all of Kuna ethnography while concentrating on the aesthetics of everyday life: designed to accompany the museum exhibit of the same name.

Van Willigen, John. *Applied Anthropology: An Introduction*. South Hadley, Mass.: Bergin & Garvey Publishers, 1986. A clear and thorough guide to the subject.

Wali, Alaka. *Kilowatts and Crisis: Hydroelectric Power and Social Dislocation in Eastern Panama*. Boulder and London: Westview Press, 1989. A detailed policy ethnography about the effects on several ethnic groups of the construction of a massive hydroelectric dam and huge artificial lake.

GLOSSARY

applied anthropologists Cultural anthropologists who put ethnographic findings to use to solve some problem by making recommendations at any phase of the policy process. They are often brokers between communities and corporate structures.

demand structure In political theory, an organization that articulates political demands of citizens and formally asks for actions to meet those demands.

policy Moral and legal guidelines for dealing with the solution of a problem.

policy ethnography A study in which an ethnographer seeks to make recommendations at any phase of the policy process.

policy process Sequence in which people become aware of the need to resolve a problem, formulate and evaluate policy choices, implement one of them, and evaluate the policy implemented.

rational deliberation A formal speech event in which people examine past courses of action and weigh future ones in terms of expected benefits and costs, in order to reach reasonable decisions from available information.

standing orders A set of written, formal parliamentary rules of order adopted by any organization to govern its deliberations. In much of the world they are modeled on Anglo-American traditional parliamentary rules, much as they are in *Robert's Rules of Order* (1915/1979).

support structure In political theory an organization that mobilizes popular support for state initiatives but does not itself articulate initiatives at the request of citizens.

REFERENCES

Abegglen, James C.

1973, *Management and Worker: The Japanese Solution*. Tokyo and New York: Sophia University and Kodansha International Ltd.

Adams, Robert McC.

1966, *The Evolution of Urban Society: Early Mesopotamia and Prehispanic Mexico*. Chicago: Aldine.

Angrosino, Michael V., and Linda M. Whiteford

1987, "Service, Delivery, Advocacy, and the Policy Cycle." In Elizabeth M. Eddy and W. L. Partridge, eds., *Applied Anthropology in America*, 2nd ed. New York: Columbia University Press.

Arens, W.

1980, *The Man-Eating Myth: Anthropology and Anthropophagy*. New York: Oxford University Press.

Arensberg, Conrad M.

1937, *The Irish Countryman*. Garden City, N.Y.: Doubleday, Natural History Press.

1963, "The Old World Peoples: The Place of European Cultures in World Ethnography," *Anthropological Quarterly*, Vol. 36, pp. 75–99. Reprinted as a chapter in *Culture and Community* by C. M. Arensberg and S. T. Kimball.

1968, "The Urban in Cross-cultural Perspective." In Elizabeth M. Eddy, ed., *Urban Anthropology*. Atlanta: Southern Anthropological Society, University of Georgia Press.

1972, "Culture as Behavior: Structure and Emergence," *Annual Review of Anthropology*, Vol. 1, pp. 1–26.

———, and Solon Kimball

1965, *Culture and Community*. New York: Harcourt Brace Jovanovich.

1968, *Family and Community in Ireland*, 2nd ed. Cambridge, Mass.: Harvard University Press.

1968, *The Irish Countryman*. Prospect Heights, Ill.: Waveland Press.

Arlington, L. C., and William Lewisohn

1935, *In Search of Old Peking*. New York: Paragon Book Reprint, 1967.

Bailey, F. G.

1969, *Stratagems and Spoils: A Social Anthropology of Politics*. New York: Schocken Books.

Baruma, Ian

1984, *Behind the Mask: On Sexual Demons, Sacred Mothers, Transvestites, Gangsters and Other Japanese Cultural Heroes*. New York: Meridian Books, New American Library.

Bell, Alan, Martin Weinberg, and Sue Hammersmith

1981, *Sexual Preference: Its Development in Men and Women*. Bloomington: Indiana University Press.

Bell, Daniel

1962, *The End of Ideology*. New York: Free Press.

Bendix, Reinhard

1960, *Max Weber: An Intellectual Portrait*. Garden City, N.Y.: Doubleday/Anchor.

Benet, Francisco

1957, "Explosive Markets: The Berber Highlands." In Karl Polanyi et al., *Trade and Market in the Early Empires: Economics in History and Theory*. New York: Free Press, pp. 188–217.

Berle, A. A., Jr.

1959, *Power Without Property*. New York: Harcourt Brace Jovanovich.

Bestor, Theodore
1989, *Neighborhood Tokyo*. Palo Alto, Calif.: Stanford University Press.
Blumenfeld, Warren, and Diane Raymond
1988, *Looking at Gay and Lesbian Life*. Boston: Beacon Press.
Boehm, Christopher
1992, "Segmentary 'Warfare' and the Management of Conflict: Comparison of East African Chimpanzees and Patrilineal-Patrilocal Humans." In A. Harcourt and F. de Waal, eds., *Cooperation and Competition in Animals and Humans*. New York: Oxford University Press.
Bohannan, Paul
1984, *All the Happy Families*. New York: McGraw-Hill.
———, ed.
1970, *Divorce and After: An Analysis of the Emotional and Social Problems of Divorce*. Garden City, N.Y.: Doubleday/Anchor.
Boskoff, Alvin
1970, *The Sociology of Urban Regions*, 2nd ed. Englewood Cliffs, N.J.: Prentice-Hall.
Boulding, Kenneth E.
1956, "Toward a General Theory of Growth," *General Systems*, Vol I, pp. 66–75.
Buckley, Walter
1967, *Sociology and Modern Systems Theory*. Englewood Cliffs, N.J.: Prentice-Hall.
1968, *Modern Systems Research for the Behavioral Scientist*. Chicago: Aldine.
Burch, Ernest J.
1970, "Marriage and Divorce Among the North Alaskan Eskimos." In Paul Bohannan, ed., *Divorce and After*. Garden City, N.Y.: Doubleday/Anchor.
Callahan, Raymond E.
1962, *Education and the Cult of Efficiency: A Study of the Social Forces That Have Shaped the Administration of the Public Schools*. Chicago: University of Chicago Press.
Campbell, Joseph (with Bill Moyers)
1988, *The Power of Myth*, edited by Betty Sue Flowers. New York: Doubleday.
Caplow, Theodore
1949, "The Social Ecology of Guatemala City," *Social Forces*, Vol. 28, p. 2.
Carter, William E., ed.
1980, *Cannibis in Costa Rica: A Study of Chronic Marijuana Use*. Philadelphia: Institute for the Study of Human Issues.
Carneiro, R. L.
1970, "A Theory of the Origin of the State," *Science*, Vol. 169, pp. 733–738.
Chapple, Eliot D.
1980, "The Unbounded Reaches of Anthropology as a Research Science, and Some Working Hypotheses," *American Anthropologist*, Vol. 82, pp. 741–758.
———, and Carleton Coon
1942, *Principles of Anthropology*. New York: Holt, Rinehart and Winston.
Chase-Ribaud, Barbara
1986, *Valide: A Novel of the Harem*. New York: Morrow.
Childe, Gordon
1954, *What Happened in History*, rev. ed. Baltimore: Penguin Books.
Collier, Peter, and David Horowitz
1976, *The Rockefellers: An American Dynasty*. New York: Holt, Rinehart and Winston.
Colson, Elizabeth
1985, "Using Anthropology in a World on the Move," *Human Organization*, Vol. 44, No. 3, pp. 191–196.

Connor, Linda, Patsy Asch, and Timothy Asch
1986, *Jero Tapakan, Balinese Healer: An Ethnographic Film Monograph*. New York: Cambridge University Press.
Coon, Carleton
1958, *Caravan: The Story of the Middle East*, rev. ed. New York: Holt, Rinehart and Winston.
Daner Francine J.
1976, *The American Children of Krsna: A Study of the Hare Krsna Movement*. New York: Holt, Rinehart and Winston.
Davis, Fanny
1986, *The Ottoman Lady: A Social History from 1718 to 1918*. New York: Greenwood Press (Contributions in Women's Studies, No. 70).
DeBary, William T.
1958, "Chinese Despotism and the Confucian Ideal." In John K. Fairbank, ed., *Chinese Thought and Institutions*. Chicago: University of Chicago Press.
De Mente, Boye
1987, *Passport's Japan Almanac, 1987*. Lincolnwood, Ill.: Passport Books.
DeVore, Irven, ed.
1965, *Primate Behavior: Field Studies of Monkeys and Apes*. New York: Holt, Rinehart and Winston.
Dougherty, Molly C.
1973, "Maturation and Motherhood: Becoming a Woman in Rural Black Culture." Doctoral Dissertation in anthropology, University of Florida.
1978, *Becoming a Woman in Rural Black Culture*. New York: Holt, Rinehart and Winston.
Douglass, William A.
1969, *Death in Murelaga: Funerary Ritual in a Spanish Basque Village*. Seattle: University of Washington Press. American Ethnological Society Monograph 49.
1975, *Echalar and Murelaga: Opportunity and Rural Exodus in Two Spanish Basque Villages*. New York: St. Martin's Press.
Dover, K. J.
1978, *Greek Homosexuality*. Cambridge, Mass.: Harvard University Press.
Driben, Paul
1986, *Aroland Is Our Home: An Incomplete Victory in Applied Anthropology*. New York: AMS Press.
Eddy, Elizabeth M.
1967, *Walk the White Line: A Profile of Urban Education*. Garden City, N.Y.: Doubleday/Anchor.
Eisenstadt, S. N.
1966, *Modernization: Protest and Change*. Englewood Cliffs, N.J.: Prentice-Hall.
———, and Stein Rokkan, eds.
1973, *Building States and Nations*, Vol. 1. Beverly Hills, Calif.: Sage.
Eldredge, Niles, and Ian Tattersall
1982, *The Myths of Human Evolution*. New York: Columbia University Press.
Eldredge, H. Wentworth
1975, *World Capitals: Toward Guided Urbanization*. Garden City, N.Y.: Doubleday/Anchor.
Epstein, David
1973, *Brasilia, Plan and Reality*. Berkeley: University of California Press.
Europa World Yearbook, 1991. London: Europa Publications.

Evans-Pritchard, E. E.
 1940, *The Nuer*. New York: Oxford University Press.
 1951, *Kinship and Marriage Among the Nuer*. New York: Oxford University Press.
Evenson, Norma
 1975, "Brasilia: Yesterday's City Tomorrow." In H. Wentworth Eldredge, ed., *World Capitals*. Garden City, N.Y.: Doubleday/Anchor, pp. 470–508.
Fei, Hsiao-t'ung
 1953, "Peasantry and Gentry: An Interpretation of Chinese Social Structure and Its Changes." In Reinhard Bendix and S. M. Lipset, eds., *Class, Status, and Power*. New York: Free Press, pp. 631–650.
Flannery, Kent V.
 1972, "The Cultural Evolution of Civilizations." *Annual Review of Ecology and Systematics*, pp. 399–426.
Fox, Robin
 1967, *Kinship and Marriage: An Anthropological Perspective*. Baltimore: Penguin Books.
Freeman, Susan Tax
 1970, *Neighbors: The Social Contract in a Castilian Hamlet*. Chicago: University of Chicago Press.
Freilich, Morris
 1958, "Cultural Persistence Among the Modern Iroquois," *Anthropos* (Fribourg, Switzerland), Vol. 53, pp. 473–483.
 1970, *Marginal Natives: Anthropologists at Work*. New York: Harper & Row.
Frolic, B. Michael
 1975, "Moscow: The Socialist Alternative." In H. Wentworth Eldredge, ed., *World Capitals*. Garden City, N.Y.: Doubleday/Anchor, pp. 295–339.
Gans, Herbert J.
 1962, *The Urban Villagers*. New York: Free Press.
Gearing, Fred
 1962, *Priests and Warriors: Social Structures for Cherokee Politics in the 18th Century*. Menasha, Ill.: American Anthropological Association.
Geertz, Clifford
 1963, *Peddlers and Princes: Social Development and Economic Change in Two Indonesian Towns*. Chicago: University of Chicago Press.
 1973, *The Interpretations of Cultures*. New York: Basic Books.
 1983, *Local Knowledge: Further Essays in Interpretive Anthropology*. New York: Basic Books.
Geertz, Hildred
 1961, *The Javanese Family: A Study of Kinship and Socialization*. New York: Free Press.
Goffman, Erving
 1961, *Asylums: Essays on the Social Situations of Mental Patients and Other Inmates*. Garden City, N.Y.: Doubleday/Anchor.
Goodale, Jane C.
 1971, *Tiwi Wives: A Study of the Women of Melville Island, North Australia*. Seattle: University of Washington Press. American Ethnological Society Monograph No. 51.
Goodall, Jane
 1986, *The Chimpanzees of Gombe: Patterns of Behavior*. Cambridge, Mass: The Belknap Press of Harvard University Press.
Gough, E. Kathleen
 1959, "The Nayars and the Definition of Marriage," *Journal of the Royal Anthropological Institute*, Vol. 89.

1961, "Nayar: Central Kerala." In D. M. Schneider and K. Gough, eds., *Matrilineal Kinship*. Berkeley: University of California Press, pp. 298–384.

Greer, Scott
1962, *The Emerging City: Myth and Reality*. New York. Free Press.

Gregory, David D.
1972, *Intra-European Migration and Sociocultural Change in an Andalusian Agro-town*. Ph.D. dissertation, Department of Anthropology, University of Pittsburgh.

Gronewald, Sylvia
1972, "Did Frank Hamilton Cushing Go Native?" In S. T. Kimball and J. B. Watson, eds., *Crossing Cultural Boundaries*. New York: Intext.

Gulick, John
1967, *Tripoli: A Modern Arab City*. Cambridge, Mass.: Harvard University Press.

Hall, Edward T.
1959, *The Silent Language*. Garden City, N.Y.: Doubleday/Anchor.
1966, *The World Cities*. New York: McGraw-Hill.
1969, *The Hidden Dimension*. Garden City, N.Y.: Doubleday/Anchor.
1976, *Beyond Culture*. Garden City, N.Y.: Doubleday/Anchor.
1984, *The Dance of Life: The Other Dimension of Time*. Garden City, N.Y.: Doubleday/Anchor.

———, and Mildred Reed Hall
1987, *Hidden Differences, Doing Business with the Japanese*. Garden City, N.Y.: Doubleday/Anchor.
1990, *Understanding Cultural Differences: Germans, French, and Americans*. Yarmouth, Me.: Intercultural Press.

Hall, Peter
1969, *The World Cities*, 2nd ed. New York: McGraw-Hill.

Harris, Marvin
1987, *Why Nothing Works: The Anthropology of Daily Life*. New York: Simon & Schuster Touchstone.

Hart, C. W. M., Arnold R. Pilling, and Jane C. Goodale
1988, *The Tiwi of North Australia*, 3rd ed. Fort Worth: Harcourt Brace Jovanovich.

Heider, Karl
1991, *Grand Valley Dani: Peaceful Warriors*, 2nd. ed. Fort Worth: Harcourt Brace Jovanovich.

Herdt, Gilbert
1987, *The Sambia: Ritual and Gender in New Guinea*. New York: Holt, Rinehart and Winston.

Herson, L. J. R.
1957, "China's Imperial Bureaucracy: Its Direction and Control," *Public Administration Review*, Vol. 17 (Winter), pp. 44–53.

Hoebel, E. Adamson
1977 (1960), *The Cheyennes: Indians of the Great Plains*, 2nd ed. Fort Worth: Harcourt Brace Jovanovich.

Homans, George C.
1941, *English Villagers in the Thirteenth Century*. Cambridge, Mass.: Harvard University Press.
1950, *The Human Group*. New York: Harcourt Brace Jovanovich.

Honjo, Masahiko
1975, "Tokyo: Giant Metropolis of the Orient." In H. Wentworth Eldredge, ed., *World Capitals*. Garden City, N.Y.: Doubleday/Anchor, pp. 340–390.

Howe, James
    1986, *The Kuna Gathering: Contemporary Village Politics in Panama*. Austin: University of Texas Press.

Iberall, Arthur S.
    1972, *Toward a General Science of Viable Systems*. New York: McGraw-Hill.
    1983, "What Is 'Language' That Can Facilitate the Flow of Information? A Contribution to a Fundamental Theory of Language and Communication," *Journal of Theoretical Biology*, Vol. 102, pp. 347–360.

———, and W. S. McCulloch
    1969, "The Organizing Principle of Complex Living Systems," *Transactions of the ASME (American Society of Mechanical Engineers), Journal of Basic Engineering*, Vol. 91 (June), pp. 290–294.

———, Harry Soodak, and Conrad Arensberg
    1980, "Homeokinetic Physics of Societies—A New Discipline: Autonomous Groups, Cultures, Polities." In H. Reul et al, eds., *Perspectives in Biomechanics*, Vol. I, Part A. New York: Harwood Academic Press, pp. 433–521.

———, and Douglas White
    1988, "Evidence for a Long-Term Process Scale for Social Change in Modern Man Settled in Place via Agriculture and Engaged in Trade and War," *GeoJournal*, Vol. 178, No. 3, pp. 311–388.

———, and David Wilkinson
    1984a, "Human Sociogeophysics—Phase 1: Explaining the Macroscopic Patterns of Man on Earth," *GeoJournal*, Vol. 8, No. 2, pp. 171–179.
    1984b, "Phase 2: The Diffusion of Human Ethnicity by Remixing," *GeoJournal*, Vol. 9, No. 4, pp. 387–391.
    1987, "Dynamic Foundations for Complex Systems." In George Modelski, ed., *Exploring Long Cycles*. Boulder, Col.: Lynne Reinner, pp. 16–55.

Jacobs, Jane
    1984, *Cities and the Wealth of Nations: Principles of Economic Life*. New York: Random House.

Josselin De Jong, J. P.
    1952, *Lévi-Strauss's Theory of Kinship and Marriage*. Leiden, Netherlands: E. J. Brill.

Katz, D., and R. L. Kahn
    1966, "Common Characteristics of Open Systems." In F. E. Emery, ed., *Systems Thinking*. Baltimore: Penguin Books.

Kearney, Michael
    1984, *World View*. Novato, Calif.: Chandler & Sharp.

Kelly, Raymond C.
    1985, *The Nuer Conquest: The Structure and Development of an Expansionist System*. Ann Arbor: University of Michigan Press.

Kenyon, Kathleen
    1957, *Digging Up Jericho*. New York: Praeger.

Kimball, Solon T., and James E. McClellan, Jr.
    1962, *Education and the New America*. New York: Random House.

———, and James B. Watson
    1972, *Crossing Cultural Boundaries: The Anthropological Experience*. New York: Intext.

Kinross, Lord John
    1977, *The Ottoman Centuries: The Rise and Fall of the Turkish Empire*. New York: Morrow.

Krige, Eileen J.
1964, "Property, Cross-Cousin Marriage and the Family Cycle Among the Lovedu." In R. F. Gray and P. H. Gulliver, eds., *The Family Estate in Africa*. London: Routledge & Kegan Paul.
———, and J .D. Krige
1943, *The Realm of the Rain Queen*. New York: Oxford University Press.
Kroeber, Alfred
1952, *The Nature of Culture*. Chicago University of Chicago Press.
Kummer, Hans
1971, *Primate Societies: Group Techniques of Ecological Adaptations*. Chicago: Aldine-Atherton.
Kuper, Hilda
1947, *An African Aristocracy*. New York: Oxford University Press, for International African Institute.
1950, "Kinship Among the Swazi." In A. R. Radcliffe-Brown and Daryll Forde, eds., *African Systems of Kinship and Marriage*. New York: Oxford University Press, for International African Institute.
1986, *The Swazi: A South African Kingdom*, 2nd ed. Fort Worth: Harcourt Brace Jovanovich.
Lee, Richard B.
1979, *The !Kung San: Men, Women, and Work in a Foraging Society*. Cambridge: Cambridge University Press.
1984, *The Dobe !Kung*. Fort Worth: Harcourt Brace Jovanovich.
Leemon, Thomas A.
1972, *The Rites of Passage in a Student Culture: A Study of the Dynamics of Transition*. New York: Teachers College Press.
Lessa, William A., and Evon Z. Vogt
1965, *Reader in Comparative Religion: An Anthropological Approach*, 2nd ed. New York: Harper & Row.
1972, *Reader in Comparative Religion: An Anthropological Approach*, 3rd ed. New York: Harper & Row.
Levine, Martin P., ed.
1979, *Gay Men: The Sociology of Male Homosexuality*. New York: Harper & Row.
Levine, Nancy E.
1988, *Dynamics of Polyandry: Kinship, Domesticity, and Population on the Tibetan Border*. Chicago: University of Chicago Press.
Lévi-Strauss, Claude
1944, "The Social and Psychological Aspects of Chieftainship in a Primitive Tribe: The Nambikuara of North-Western Mato Grosso," *Transactions of the New York Academy of Sciences*, Series 2, Vol. 7, No. 1, pp. 6–32. Reprinted in Ronald Cohen and John Middleton, eds., *Comparative Political Systems*. Garden City, N.Y.: Natural History Press, 1967.
1948, *La Vie Familiale et Sociale des Indiens Nambikwara*. Paris: Musée l'Homme.
1949, *Les Structures Elementaires de la Parente*. Paris: Presses Universitaires France.
1963, *Structural Anthropology*. Claire Jacobson and Brooke Grundfest Schoepf, trans. New York: Basic Books.
Lewis, Oscar
1959, *Five Families*. New York: Basic Books.
1961, *The Children of Sanchez: The Autobiography of a Mexican Family*. New York: Random House.

1965, *La Vida: A Puerto Rican Family in the Culture of Poverty, San Juan and New York.* New York: Random House/Vintage Books.

Lisón-Tolosana, Carmelo
1966, *Belmonte de los Caballeros: A Sociological Study of a Spanish Town.* Oxford: Clarendon Press.

Lomnitz, Larissa, and Marisol A. Perez-Lizaur
1988, *A Mexican Elite Family, 1820–1980: Kinship, Class, and Culture.* Princeton, N.J.: Princeton University Press.

MacKenzie, Norman, ed.
1967, *Secret Societies.* New York: Collier Books.

Malinowski, Bronislaw
1922 (1961), *Argonauts of the Western Pacific.* New York: Dutton.
1944, *A Scientific Theory of Culture and Other Essays.* Chapel Hill: University of North Carolina Press.

Mallowan, M. E. L.
1965, *Early Mesopotamia and Iran.* Library of the Early Civilizations. New York: McGraw-Hill.

Marrou, H. I.
1964, *A History of Education in Antiquity.* George Lamb, trans. New York: Mentor (*Histoire de l'Education dans l'Antiquite*, Paris: Editions du Seuil, 1948).

Marwick, Brian Allan
1940, *The Swazi: An Ethnographic Account of the Natives of the Swaziland Protectorate.* London: Cambridge University Press.

Masters, William H., and Virginia E. Johnson
1979, *Homosexuality in Perspective.* Boston: Little, Brown (reprinted New York: Bantam Books, 1982).

McLendon, James
1983, "The Office: Way Station or Blind Alley?" In David W. Plath, ed., *Work and Lifecourse in Japan.* Albany: SUNY Press, pp.156–182.

McWhirter, David P., and Andrew M. Mattison
1984, *The Male Couple: How Relationships Develop.* Englewood Cliffs, N.J.: Prentice-Hall.

Mellaart, James
1965, *Earliest Civilizations of the Near East.* The Library of Early Civilizations. New York: McGraw-Hill.

Mendras, Henri, with Alistair Cole
1991, *Social Change in Modern France: Toward a Cultural Anthropology of the Fifth Republic.* New York: Cambridge.

Metraux, Alfred
1944, "The Tupinambá," *Handbook of South American Indians*, Vol. III, *The Tropical Forest Tribes*, edited by Julian Steward. Washington, D.C.: Smithsonian Institution.

Michael of Greece, Prince
1983, *Sultana.* Alexis Ullman, trans. New York: Harper & Row.

Miner, Horace
1965, *The Primitive City of Timbuctoo*, rev. ed. Garden City, N.Y: Doubleday/Anchor.

Montaigne, Michel de
1934–1936, *The Essays of Michel de Montaigne.* Jacob Zeitlin, trans. and ed. New York: Knopf.

Moore, A.
1987, *The Neolithic of the Levant*, Vols. 1 and 2. Ann Arbor, Mich.: University Microfilms International.

Moore, Alexander
1967, *Realities of the Urban Classroom: Observations in Elementary Schools*. New York: Praeger.
1973, *Life Cycles in Atchalán: The Diverse Careers of Certain Guatemalans*. New York: Teachers College Press.
1978, *Cultural Anthropology*. New York: Harper & Row.
1979, "Initiation Rites in a Mesoamerican Cargo System: Men and Boys, Judas and the Bull," *Journal of Latin American Lore*, Vol. 5, No. 1, pp. 55–81.
1980a, "Walt Disney World: Bounded Ritual Space and the Playful Pilgrimage Center," *Anthropological Quarterly*, Vol. 53, No. 4, pp. 207–218.
1980b, "Planners, Tourists, and the Indians: National Planning, Regional Development, and the San Blas Cuna," *Practicing Anthropology*, Vol. 2, pp. 5–6, 19–20.
1981, "Basilicas and King Posts: A Proxemic and Symbolic Event Analysis of Competing Public Architecture Among the San Blas Cuna," *American Ethnologist*, Vol. 8, No. 2, pp. 259–277.
1983, "Lore and Life: Cuna Indian Pageants, Exorcism and Diplomacy in the 20th Century," *Ethnohistory*, Vol. 30, No 2, pp. 93–106.
1984a, "Obituary: Solon Toothaker Kimball, 1909–1982," *American Anthropologist*, Vol. 86, No. 2, pp. 386–393.
1984b, "Peoples of the Old World Revisited: Cultures and Communities of Spain." In Owen M. Lynch, ed., *Culture and Community in Europe: Essays in Honor of Conrad M. Arensberg*. Delhi: Hindustan Publishing Corporation; New York: Academic Press.
1984c, "From Council to Legislature: Democracy, Parliamentarianism, and the San Blas Cuna," *American Anthropologist*, Vol. 86, No. 1, pp. 28–42.
1985, "The Form and Context of the Kuna General Congress." In William G. D'Arcy and Mireya D. Correa, eds., *The Botany and Natural History of Panama*. St. Louis: Missouri Botanical Garden, pp. 333–343.
1991, "Discipline or Profession: Anthropology and Its Guilds," *Reviews in Anthropology*, Vol. 18, pp. 115–125.
Moore, Henrietta L.
1988, *Feminism and Anthropology*. Cambridge, Eng.: Polity Press.
Moore, Sally Falk, and Barbara G. Myerhoff
1975, *Symbol and Politics in Communal Ideology: Cases and Questions*. Ithaca, N.Y.: Cornell University Press.
Mumford, Lewis
1938, *The Culture of Cities*. New York: Harcourt Brace Jovanovich, 1970.
1961, *The City in History: Its Origins, Its Transformations, and Its Prospects*. New York: Harcourt Brace Jovanovich.
Murdock, George Peter
1949, *Social Structure*. New York: Macmillan.
Murphy, Robert
1957, "Intergroup Hostility and Social Cohesion," *American Anthropologist*, Vol. 59, pp. 1018–1935.
Murra, John
1962, "Cloth and Its Functions in the Inca State," *American Anthropologist*, Vol. 64, pp. 710–728.
Nairn, C.
1974, *Ongka's Big Moka* (film). London: Grenada Television Disappearing World Series.
Nakane, Chie
1970, *Japanese Society*. Berkeley: University of California Press.

Neville, Gwen Kennedy
1987, *Pilgrimage and Kinship: Rituals of Reunion in American Protestant Culture*. New York: Oxford University Press.
Norbeck, Edward
1967, *Changing Japan*. New York: Holt, Rinehart and Winston.
Oates, Joan
1986, *Babylon*, rev. ed. London: Thames & Hudson.
Oliver, Douglas L.
1955, *A Solomon Island Society: Kinship and Leadership Among the Siuai of Bougainville*. Cambridge, Mass.: Harvard University Press; Boston: Beacon Press, 1967.
Padilla, Elena
1958, *Up from Puerto Rico*. New York: Columbia University Press.
Panamá
1979, *Asamblea Nacional de Representantes de Corregimientos, Reglamento Interno, Ley No. 14, del 30 de octubre*. Panamá: Editora del Poder Popular.
Partridge, William L.
1973, *The Hippie Ghetto: The Natural History of a Subculture*. New York: Holt, Rinehart and Winston.
Passin, Herbert
1965, *Society and Education in Japan*. New York: Teachers College Press.
Pelzel, John C.
1958, "Notes on the Chinese Bureaucracy." In *Systems of Political Control and Bureaucracy in Human Societies*. American Ethnological Society Proceedings (Spring). Seattle: University of Washington Press.
Polanyi, Karl
1944, *The Great Transformation: The Political and Economic Origins of Our Time*. Boston: Beacon Press, 1957.
1966, *Dahomey and the Slave Trade: An Analysis of an Archaic Economy*. Seattle: University of Washington Press. American Ethnological Society Monograph 42.
————, Conrad M. Arensberg, and Harry W. Pearson, eds.
1957, *Trade and Market in the Early Empires: Economies in History and Theory*. New York: Free Press.
Rand, Christopher
1958, *The Puerto Ricans*. New York: Oxford University Press.
Reina, Ruben
1960, *Chinautla, a Guatemalan Indian Community: A Study in the Relationship of a Community Culture and National Change*. Middle American Research Institute Publication 24. New Orleans: Tulane University.
1966, *The Law of the Saints: A Pokomam Pueblo and Its Community Culture*. Indianapolis: Bobbs-Merrill.
Robert, Henry M., III
1979 (1915), *Robert's Rules of Order Revised*. New York: Morrow Quill.
Roethlisberger, F. J., and William J. Dickson
1940, *Management and the Worker*. Cambridge, Mass.: Harvard University Press.
Roscoe, Rev. J.
1911, *The Baganda*. New York: Macmillan.
Roth, Julius A., and Elizabeth M. Eddy
1967, *Rehabilitation for the Unwanted*. New York: Atherton.
Rowe, John
1944a, "An Introduction to the Archaeology of Cuzco," *Papers of the Peabody Museum*, Vol. 27, p. 2. Cambridge, Mass.: Harvard University Press.

1944b, "The Incas at the Time of the Spanish Conquest." In Julian Steward, ed., *Handbook of South American Indians*, Vol. II, *Andean Civilizations*. Washington, D.C.: Smithsonian Institution.

Sahagún, Fray Bernardino de
1950, *Florentine Codex: General History of the Things of New Spain*, Book I. J. O. Anderson and Charles E. Dibble, trans. and eds. Santa Fe, N.M.: School of American Research, University of Utah.

Sahlins, Marshall D.
1961, "The Segmentary Lineage: An Organization of Predatory Expansion." *American Anthropologist*, Vol. 63, pp. 322–345.
1972, *Stone Age Economics*. New York and Chicago: Aldine-Atherton.

Schele, Linda, and Mary Ellen Miller
1986, *The Blood of Kings: Dynasty and Ritual in Maya Art*. Fort Worth: Kimball Art Museum.

Schneider, David M., and Kathleen Gough, eds.
1961, *Matrilineal Kinship*. Berkeley: University of California Press

Schneider, Eugene V.
1969, *Industrial Sociology: The Social Relations of Industry and the Community*, 2nd ed. New York: McGraw-Hill.

Schwarz, Henry F., III
1972, *Trujillo: The Ethnography of a Preindustrial City in Western Spain*. Ph.D. dissertation, Department of Anthropology, University of Pennsylvania.

Seeley, J. R., R. A. Sim, and E. W. Loosley
1956, *Crestwood Heights: A Study of the Culture of Suburban Life*. New York: Wiley.

Service, Elman
1975, *Origins of the State and Civilization*. New York: Norton.

Shevoroshkin, Vitaly
1990, "The Mother Tongue," *The Sciences*. May/June, pp. 20–27.

Shostak, Marjorie
1983, *Nisa: The Life and Words of a !Kung Woman*. New York: Vintage.

Sidenbladh, Goran
1975, "Stockholm: Three Hundred Years of Planning." In H. Wentworth Eldredge, ed., *World Capitals*. Garden City, N.Y.: Doubleday/Anchor, pp. 25–54.

Singleton, John
1967, *Nichu: A Japanese School*. New York: Holt, Rinehart and Winston.

Siskind, Janet
1973, *To Hunt in the Morning*. New York: Oxford University Press.

Spiro, Herbert J.
1959, *Government by Constitution: The Political Systems of Democracy*. New York: Random House.

Staden, Hans
1557, *Hans Staden: The True History of His Captivity*. Malcolm Letts, trans. and ed. London: George Routledge, 1928.

Strathern, Andrew
1971, *The Rope of Moka: Big-Men and Ceremonial Exchange in Mount Hagen, New Guinea*. New York: Cambridge University Press.
1979, *Ongka: A Self-account by a New Guinea Big-man*. New York: St. Martin's Press.

Suttles, Gerald D.
1968, *The Social Order of the Slum: Ethnicity and Territory in the Inner City*. Chicago: University of Chicago Press.

547

Swartz, Marc J., Victor Turner, and Arthur Tuden
    1966, *Political Anthropology*. Chicago: Aldine.
Taylor, Carol
    1970, *In Horizontal Orbit: Hospitals and the Cult of Efficiency*. New York: Holt, Rinehart and Winston.
Trigger, Bruce C.
    1969, *The Huron: Farmers of the North*. New York: Holt, Rinehart and Winston.
Tripp, C. A.
    1987 (1975), *The Homosexual Matrix*, 2nd ed. New York: New American Library.
Turnbull, Colin M.
    1961, *The Forest People: A Study of the Pygmies of the Congo*. New York: Simon & Schuster.
Turner, Victor
    1964, "Betwixt and Between: The Liminal Period in Rites of Passage," *Proceedings of the American Ethnological Society*. Reprinted in William A. Lessa and Evon Z. Vogt, *Reader in Comparative Religion: An Anthropological Approach*, 3rd ed. New York: Harper & Row, 1972, pp. 338–347.
    1969, *The Ritual Process: Structure and Anti-Structure*. Chicago: Aldine.
    1987, "Body, Brain, and Culture," *The Anthropology of Performance*. Preface by Richard Schechner. New York: PAJ Publications, pp. 157–178.
Valentine, Charles A.
    1968, *Culture and Poverty: Critique and Counter-Proposals*. Chicago: University of Chicago Press.
Van Gennep, Arnold
    1960, *The Rites of Passage*. Monika B. Vizedom and Gabrielle L. Caffee, trans. Chicago: University of Chicago Press.
Vayda, Andrew P.
    1968, "Hypotheses About Functions of War." In M. Fried, M. Harris, and R. Murphy, eds., *The Anthropology of Armed Conflict and Aggression*. Garden City, N.Y.: Doubleday.
Vogel, Ezra F.
    1971, *Japan's New Middle Class*, 2nd ed. Chicago: University of Chicago Press.
Vogt, Evon Z.
    1990, *The Zinacantecos of Mexico: A Modern Maya Way of Life*, 2nd ed. Fort Worth: Harcourt Brace Jovanovich.
Wallace, Anthony F. C.
    1956, "Revitalization Movements," *American Anthropologist*, Vol. 58, pp. 264–281. Reprinted in William A. Lessa and Evon Z. Vogt, *Reader in Comparative Religion: An Anthropological Approach*, 3rd ed. New York: Harper & Row, 1972, pp. 503-512.
    1966, *Religion: An Anthropological View*. New York: Random House.
    1969, *The Death and Rebirth of the Seneca*. New York: Random House.
Wallerstein, Immanuel
    1974, *The Modern World System: Capitalist Agriculture and the Origins of the European World Economy in the Sixteenth Century*. New York: Academic Press.
Warner, W. Lloyd
    1962, *American Life: Dream and Reality*, rev. ed. Chicago: University of Chicago Press.
——, et al.
    1963, *Yankee City*, abridged ed. New Haven, Conn.: Yale University Press.
Warren, Carol A. B.
    1974, *Identity and Community in the Gay World*. New York: Wiley.
Weber, Max
    1946, *From Max Weber: Essays in Sociology*. New York: Oxford University Press. Portions of his *Wirtschaft und Gesellschaft*, 2nd ed. (Tubingen: J. C. B. Mohr, 1925) two volumes, H. H. Gerth and C. W. Mills, trans.

1947, *The Theory of Economic and Social Organization*. New York: Free Press.

1951, *The Religion of China: Confucianism and Taoism*. H. H. Gerth, trans. and ed. New York: Free Press.

1952, *Ancient Judaism*. H. H. Gerth and Don Martindale, trans. and eds. New York: Free Press.

Weinreich, James D.

1987, *Sexual Landscapes: Why We Are What We Are, Why We Love Whom We Love*. New York: Scribner's.

Wheatley, Paul

1971, *The Pivot of the Four Quarters: A Preliminary Enquiry into the Origins and Character of the Ancient Chinese City*. Chicago: Aldine.

Whiteford, Andrew H.

1964, *Two Cities in Latin America: A Comparative Description of Social Classes*. Garden City, N.Y.: Doubleday/Anchor.

Whitam, Frederick L., and Robin M. Mathy

1986, *Male Homosexuality in Four Societies: Brazil, Guatemala, the Philippines, and the United States*. New York: Praeger.

Whitten, Norman E., Jr.

1974, *Black Frontiersmen: A South American Case*. New York: Schenkman.

Whyte, William Foote

1955, *Street Corner Society*. Chicago: University of Chicago Press.

Wilkinson, David

1987, "Central Civilization," *Review of Comparative Civilizations*, Fall, pp. 31–59.

———, and Arthur S. Iberall

1991, "The Cultural Evolution of the Ur-Language," paper read at a symposium "Homeokinetic (Self-Organizing) Systems Perspectives on Human Values and Activities," Alexander Moore, organizer-chair, 50th Annual Meeting of the Society for Applied Anthropology, Charleston, South Carolina, March 15.

Wilson, Edmund

1960, *Apologies to the Iroquois, With a Study of the Mohawks in High Steel by Joseph Mitchell*. New York: Random House.

Wilson, Godfrey

1941, *An Essay on the Economics of Detribalization in Northern Rhodesia, I*. London: Rhodes-Livingston Papers 5.

1942, *An Essay on the Economics of Detribalization in Northern Rhodesia, II*. London: Rhodes-Livingston Papers 6.

Wittfogel, Karl A.

1957, *Oriental Despotism: A Comparative Study of Total Power*. New Haven, Conn.: Yale University Press.

Wolf, Eric

1955, "Types of Latin American Peasantry: A Preliminary Discussion," *American Anthropologist*, Vol. 57, No. 3.

1982, *Europe and the People Without History*. Berkeley: University of California Press.

Yates, F. Eugene

1987, *Self-Organizing Systems: The Emergence of Order*. New York and London: Plenum Press.

Zablocki, Benjamin

1971, *The Joyful Community: An Account of the Bruderhof—A Communal Movement Now in its Third Generation*. Baltimore: Penguin Books.

CREDITS

Chapter 1
page 4: Richard Lee, Anthro-Photo; pages 7, 8, 9, 12: excerpts and original woodcuts from Hans Staden, *The True History of His Captivity*, Malcolm Letts, trans. and ed. (London: George Routledge, 1928), used with permission of Routledge and Kegan Paul, London; pages 12–13: excerpts from *The Essays of Michel de Montaigne*, vol. II, Jacob Zeitlin, trans. (New York: Knopf, 1934–1936), pp. 182–183, 186, 187; pages 14–15, 16, 17: excerpts from Fray Bernardino de Sahagún, *Florentine Codex: General History of the Things of New Spain, Book 1*, J. O. Anderson and Charles E. Dibble, trans. (University of Utah and School of American Research, 1950), pp. 2, 27–28, 34–35, 38.

Chapter 2
pages 20, 29: Christopher Boehm.

Chapter 3
page 44: Levon Mardikyan; page 47: Christopher Boehm; page 48: photo courtesy Helena Wayne and the British Library of Political and Economic Science, London School of Economics; page 49: Bronislaw Malinowski, *Argonauts of the Southwest Pacific* (New York: Dutton, 1922); page 53: photo by Roger Keyes; pages 54, 55: Alexander Moore; page 57: Edward Norbeck; page 59: From Solon T. Kimball and J. B. Watson, *Crossing Cultural Boundaries* (New York: Chandler, 1972); page 61: courtesy Morris Freilich; page 62: Michael A. Schwarz.

Chapter 4
page 70: Christopher Boehm; page 80: photo © 1985 David L. Brill, of Lucy reconstruction by Owen Lovejoy and students, Kent State; page 84: adapted from Niles Eldredge and Ian Tattersall, *Myths of Human Evolution* (New York: Columbia University Press, 1982), endpapers; page 86: photo of *Homo erectus* skeleton by David L. Brill © National Geographic Society, National Museum of Kenya, Nairobi.

Chapter 5
pages 106, 114: Irven DeVore, Anthro-Photo; page 118: Jane Goodale.

Chapter 6
page 126: Irven DeVore, Anthro-Photo; page 130: Bruce Silberstein/Peter Arnold, Inc.; page 135: from Jane C. Goodale, *Tiwi Wives* (Seattle: University of Washington, 1971); pages 137, 138: Jane Goodale; page 139: Alexander Moore; page 140: from Colin Turnbull, *The Forest People* (New York: Simon & Schuster/Touchstone, 1961); page 147: Arnold R. Pilling.

Chapter 7
pages 150, 154: Levon Mardikyan; page 157: Dan Bosler, Tony Stone Worldwide Ltd.; page 158: Melvin Kanner, Anthro-Photo.

Chapter 8
pages 172, 175: Richard Lee, Anthro-Photo; page 177: Irven DeVore, Anthro-Photo; page 180: Jane C. Goodale; page 183: Marjorie Shostak, Anthro-Photo; pages 185, 186: Alexander Moore; page 188: AP/Wide World Photos.

Chapter 9
page 202: Pitt Rivers Museum, University of Oxford; page 216: The Bettmann Archive; page 218: S. Bassoula, Sygma; page 219: Pitt Rivers Museum, University of Oxford; page 221: adapted from Raymond C. Kelly, *The Nuer Conquest: The Structure and Development of an Expansionist System* (Ann Arbor: University of Michigan Press, 1985), p. 169; pages 222, 224, 227: Pitt Rivers Museum, University of Oxford; pages 224, 226: diagrams adapted from E. E. Evans-Pritchard, *Kinship and Marriage Among the Nuer* (New York: Oxford University Press, 1951), pp. 75, 11.

Chapter 10
pages 236, 240, 241: Christopher Boehm; pages 247, 248, 249: from Hans Staden, *The True History of His Captivity*, Malcolm Letts, trans. and ed. (London: George Routledge, 1928), used with permission of Routledge and Kegan Paul, London.

Chapter 11
page 256: Courtesy of the Royal British Columbia Museum, Victoria, B.C.; pages 264, 266, 268, 269, 270: Douglas Oliver; pages 274, 275, 276, 277, 278: Bronislaw Malinowski, *Argonauts of the Southwest Pacific* (New York: Dutton, 1922).

Chapter 12
page 282: Western History Collections, University of Oklahoma Library; page 287: The Bettmann Archive; pages 289, 290: Claude Lévi-Strauss; page 298: The American Museum of Natural History; page 300: photo by Elizabeth C. Grinnell, courtesy of Southwest Museum; page 302: photo by Edward S. Curtis, courtesy Southwest Museum.

Chapter 13
page 308: Photo by E. Dossetter, courtesy Department of Library Services, American Museum of Natural History, neg. no. 42314/32960; pages 312, 313, 314: Alexander Moore; page 319: photo by Elizabeth C. Grinnell, courtesy of Southwest Museum; page 320: The Bettmann Archive; page 323: AP/Wide World Photos; page 325: Cranbrook Institute of Science; page 327: (top) Solon T. Kimball and J. B. Watson, *Crossing Cultural Boundaries* (New York: Chandler, 1972); (bottom) © 1982 Kal Mulle, Woodfin Camp & Associates.

Chapter 14
page 338: AP/Wide World Photos; page 345: Hirmer Fotoarchiv; pages 346, 349, 350: adapted from M. Mallowan, *Early Mesopotamia and Iran*, Library of the Early Civilizations (New York: McGraw-Hill, 1965); page 351: Hirmer Fotoarchiv; page 353: AP/Wide World Photos; page 354: adapted from *Beijing Shi* (Beijing: Beijing Publishers, 1985); page 355: AP/Wide World Photos; page 356: adapted from Cyril Aldred, *Akhenaten: King of Egypt* (London: Thames and Hudson); pages 363: from Hilda Kuper, *The Swazi: A South African Kingdom*, 2nd ed. (Fort Worth: Harcourt Brace Jovanovich, 1986).

Chapter 15
page 368: AP/Wide World Photos; page 371: Princess Der Ling, *Two Years in the Forbidden City*; Moffat, Yard, & Co.; page 375: Melville Herskovits, *Dahomey*, J. J. Augustin, 1938; page 377: adapted from Colin Thubron, *Istanbul* (Amsterdam: Time-Life Books), 1978); page 382: AP/Wide World Photos; pages 383, 386, 387, 390: Levon Mardikyan; page 394: Princess Der Ling, *Two Years in the Forbidden City*; Moffat, Yard, & Co.

Chapter 16

page 400: Alexander Moore; page 404: AP/Wide World Photos; page 406: Nelson Reed, *The Caste War of Yucatan* (Stanford, Calif.: Stanford University Press, 1964); page 407: Alexander Moore; page 409: after Conrad M. Arensberg and Solon T. Kimball, *Family and Community in Ireland* (Cambridge, Mass.: Harvard University Press, 1968); page 411: Spencer Grant, Monkmeyer Press; page 413: AP/Wide World Photos; pages 416, 418, 419: Alexander Moore; page 421: David G. Gregory.

Chapter 17

page 434: Audrey Gottlieb, Monkmeyer Press; page 440: Alexander Moore; page 442: Hermine Dreyfuss, Monkmeyer Press; page 444: Karl Polanyi, Conrad Arensberg, and Harry Pearson, *Trade and Market in the Early Empires: Economies in History and Theory* (New York: Free Press, 1957); page 445: Karl Polanyi, *Dahomey and the Slave Trade* (Seattle: University of Washington Press, 1966); page 448: London Library; page 451: New York Public Library; pages 452, 454: Chicago Historical Society; page 453: Alvin Boskoff, *The Sociology of Urban Regions*, 2nd ed. © 1970, p. 89; reprinted by permission of Prentice-Hall, Englewood Cliffs, N.J.; page 456: Jackie Estrada; page 457: Alvin Boskoff, *The Sociology of Urban Regions*, 2nd ed. © 1970, p. 107; reprinted by permission of Prentice-Hall, Englewood Cliffs, N.J.

Chapter 18

page 464: Jim Pickerell, Tony Stone Worldwide; page 468: Levon Mardikyan; page 469: AP/Wide World Photos; page 473: Levon Mardikyan; page 475: John Waterman, Tony Stone Worldwide; page 479: Bob Daemmrich/The Image Works; page 481: The Bettmann Archive; page 484: Paul Conklin/Monkmeyer; page 485: Adam Tanner, Comstock; page 487: adapted from George C. Homans, *The Human Group*, © 1950 by Harcourt Brace Jovanovich, used by permission; page 488: Dan Ford Connolly/Picture Group.

Chapter 19

pages 494, 499, 501, 502, 504, 505, 506, 508: Stephen Dunn; page 500: after Herbert Passin, *Society and Education in Japan* (New York: Teachers College Press, 1965), p. 309, © Columbia University, all rights reserved; page 510: Topham/The Image Works; page 511: Michael Siluk/The Image Works; page 512: Stephen Dunn; pages 514, 515: AP/Wide World; page 516: Catherine Allport/The Image Works; page 519: Stephen Dunn.

Epilogue

page 525: Levon Mardikyan; pages 531, 532, 533: Alexander Moore.

*A*blution, 130
abreaction, 318, 329
Acheulian tool-making
   tradition, 86–87
active research, 58
Adams, Robert, 348, 349
administered trade, 444–
   446
affines, 137
age grading
   in band communities
      111, 134–136
   in modern metropolitan
      civilizations, 40, 499–
      501, 514
   in traditional civiliza-
      tions, 382, 414, 417
aggressive sequences, 239–
   245, 252
agonistic behavior, 121–
   123
agrotowns, 421
AIDS, 519
alliance feasting, 251, 260–
   261
allies, mobilization of, 253
Alotenango, 415–420, 424,
   441
alpha males, 240, 246
ambilineal descent groups,
   210–211
amino acids, 75
ancestor-oriented
   kindreds, 210
Ancient Society (Morgan),
   50
Angkor Wat, 356
animism, 143
annual cycles, in band
   communities, 115–
   117, 124
Anthropoidea, 77
anthropology, 22–23, 40–
   42, 76
   applied, 22, 528, 534–
      535
   defined, 22
   field work in, 46–67
   genetics and, 73–76
antitherapy. *See* witchcraft
apartheid, 535
apical ancestors, 210, 212
Apologies to the Iroquois
   (Wilson), 62–63

archaeology, 22, 76
Arens, W., 14
Arensberg, Conrad, 448,
   479–481
*Argonauts of the Western
   Pacific* (Malinowski),
   272
aristocracy, 287
Aristotle, 287, 296, 304–
   305, 433, 459
Aroland, 529–530
arrow renewal ceremony,
   300
articles, anthropological,
   60
associations, 35, 298–300,
   304, 507, 512
Australopithecus, 79–82
Australopithecus afarensis,
   80–81, 83, 90, 96, 97
Australopithecus africanus,
   81–83, 96, 97
Australopithecus boisei, 83
Australopithecus habilis, 85
Australopithecus robustus, 83
avunculocal residence, 206
Aztecs, 14–17

*B*aboons, 94
Babylon, 351
bachelorhood, in
   Swaziland, 361–362
balanced reciprocity, 183,
   264, 259, 441–443
balanced trade, 251
band communities, 25–26,
   30–32, 108–124, 342
   culture of, 190–191
   cycles of activities in,
      111–119
   economics in, 30–32,
      109, 180–187
   justice in, 31, 109, 121–
      124
   lifestyle and, 191
   language in, 31, 32, 109,
      120–124
   learning in, 31, 109
   politics in, 31, 32, 109,
      120–124
   ritual in, 30, 31, 109,
      124, 128–148
   sociology in, 30, 31, 32,
      109, 152–167
   technology in, 31, 32,
      109

Baroque age, 466–473, 489
Baroque capitals, 467–473
Baruma, Ian, 508
Basque peasant stem
   families, 407–408
*Behind the Mask: On Sexual
   Demons, Sacred
   Mothers, Transvestites,
   Gangsters and Other
   Japanese Cultural
   Heroes* (Baruma), 508
Belize, 340
Bell, Daniel, 482
Belmonte de los
   Caballeros, 421
benefactors, 507
benefices. *See* prebends
Bentham, Jeremy, 531
Berbers, 404
berdaches, 297, 304
bifurcate merging, 214
Big Men, 35, 259–271,
   273, 279, 281, 305
bilateral descent, 210–211
bilocal residence, 206
binuclear families, 170
biologists, 66
bipedalism, 78, 79, 80, 83,
   85
bisexuality, 517
blood feud, 250
bloodwealth, 210, 226–228
Boas, Franz, 190
bonding mechanisms, 241,
   250, 252
bonfires, 132, 133
"Book of Ceremonies"
   (Sahagún), 15
"Book of the Gods"
   (Sahagún), 14–15
books, anthropological, 60
brachiating, 78
brain size, and evolution,
   87–88, 190
breeding populations, 25
   see also communities
bride service, 158
bridewealth
   among Nuer, 225–226,
      230, 231
   in Swaziland, 360
Brooklyn Mohawks, 61–
   66, 67, 497
bull of Nuer village, 225,
   231

bureaucracy
   behavior in, 479–481
   corporate, 473–478
   defined, 467
   legal-rational, 372, 393,
      466–491
   modern corporation
      and, 474–481
   original, 370–397
   royal, 37, 38
   tables of organization
      in, 476–478

*C*alendar, 15
caliphs, 389
campfire talks, 120–121
   see also hearth
Canadian Indians, 528–530
cannibalism, 6–9, 12–14,
   245–247
capitalism, 431, 450, 460
cargo, 417–419
catalysis, ritualistic, 128,
   138–140
catalyst, language as, 89
Catarrhini, 77
central business district,
   453–454, 461
central civilization, 10, 41
Chan Santa Cruz, 405–407
charisma, 331
charismatic domination,
   331
charismatic leadership, 119
Cheyenne Indians, 296,
   297–303, 304–305,
   348
Chicago school of urban
   sociologists, 452–456
chiefdoms, 364
childrearing phase, 156
chimpanzees, 26–29, 78,
   82–83, 120
   aggressive sequences
      among, 240–241
   sexual behavior of, 164
   warfare among, 29, 82–
      83, 241–242
China, 207, 340, 353–355,
   394
Chippewa, 207
Christianity, 9–10, 11, 16–
   17, 389, 407, 414,
   419–420, 519
chromosomes, 73

cities, 347–350
    green, 34–38, 354–364
    nucleated, walled, 34–
        38, 345–347, 352–353
civilizations
    modern metropolitan,
        38–41, 431–522
    traditional, 35–42, 336–
        425
civilized constitutions, 289
civilized tribes, 404–407
civil/religious hierarchy,
    414
clans, 34, 212
cliques, 512
clocks, 468–469
    molecular, 78
closed corporate peasant
    communities, 403,
        411–420, 423
clustering tendency, 347
coalitions, 243, 290, 297–
    298
Code Napoleon, 518
Colson, Elizabeth, 534
commercial metropolises,
    452–456, 460–461
communes, 411–420
communication. See
    language; speech;
    writing
communitas, 147
communities, 24–26, 108–
    111, 210
    see also band communi-
        ties; tribal communi-
        ties
community fields, 25–42
community forms,
    progression of, 42
community proper
    in band communities,
        110
    in tribal communities,
        231
community sponsors, 54–
    55
competitive courtship,
    414–415
competitive feasting, 258–
    281
competitive systems, 258–
    259
complementary opposi-
    tion, 222–223, 231,
        232, 238, 302

concentric-circle form,
    452, 461
conceptus, 73
conflict
    as bonding mechanism,
        250
    as repulsion, 250–251
conflict process, 121–123
conflict theory, 243–244,
    531
consciousness
    family and, 167
    speech and, 94–95
consortship, 164–165, 167
constitutions
    civilized, 289
    unspoken, 288–289, 303
contradictions, resolution
    through symbols,
        139–140
conurbations, 456–458
corporate boards, 474, 475
corporations, 466–491
corvé labor, 403
cost accounting, 447, 460
cottage industry, 449
countervailing tendencies
    phase, 244
courtship, 155–157, 414–
    415, 504
cousins. See cross-cousins;
    parallel cousins
craft specialization, 37, 38,
    343
credit, 178
crisis phase, 244
cross-cousins, 137, 214–
    218
Cruzob Maya, 405–408
cult of efficiency, 482–483,
    490
cult of Judas, 416–417
cults, 41, 327, 328
cultural anthropology, 22–
    23, 41–42, 46
    as natural history, 24–25
cultural cycles, 112–113
cultural evolution, 341–
    348
cultural relativism, 190–
    191
culture, 11, 110, 187–191
    band-level, 190–191
    families and, 152–154
    race and, 189–190
    redefined, 191
culture shock, 18
Cushing, Frank Hamilton,
    59

cycles of activities
    aggressive sequences
        and, 239–243
    in band communities,
        111–119, 121
    exchange and, 181–182
    in modern metropolitan
        civilizations, 502–505
    rituals and, 129–130

Dahomey, 375
daily cycles, 113–115, 121
Dalmations, 189
Dani feasts, 260–261
data, 58
deduction, 47
deliberation, rational, 526,
    535
demagoguery, 287
demand structures, 533
democracy, 287, 305, 530,
    535
deoxyribonucleic acid. See
    DNA
descent groups, 209–212
diffusion, 340, 341–342
diffusionists, 50
disorganized complexity,
    47
division of labor by sex,
    31–32, 86, 111, 166,
        498–499, 521
divorce, 157, 505
DNA, 73–75, 89, 95, 163
doctoral dissertations, 60
dog, domesticated, 187–
    189
dominance hierarchies, 28,
    286
dominance-status
    competition, 239
double-entry bookkeeping,
    447, 460
down-the-line supervisory
    behavior, 490
drainage canals, 340
Driben, Paul, 528–530
dry-season villages, 115
duels, Tiwi, 121
Dunbar, Robin, 87–88, 94
dynastic cycle, 394
dynasties, 37, 38, 365, 371,
    376–394, 395

Economics, 23
    in band communities,
        30–32, 109

in modern metropolitan
    civilizations, 38–40,
        437
    in primate troops, 27, 29
    in traditional civiliza-
        tions, 36, 37, 38, 344
    in tribal communities,
        33–34, 205, 271–272
ego-oriented kindreds, 211
Egypt, 340, 354–356, 375–
    376
Eisner, Michael, 510
elite, 402
    hereditary, 510, 520
    mass, 497
emissary prophets, 320,
    330
encounter phase, 244
epigenetic potential,
    culture as, 152
erect posture, 78, 80–81,
    85, 86, 96
Eskimoan kinship
    terminology, 213–214
Eskimos, 113, 132, 148,
    165
Estepa, 421
estrus, 164
ethics, 59–60
ethnocentrism, 13–18
ethnographies, 46–67
    interpretation of, 12–13,
        16–18
    spontaneous, 6–9, 11–12
ethologists, 66
eukaryotes, 163
eunuchs, 379, 386
European Age of Discov-
    ery, 9–12
Evans-Pritchard, E. E.,
    219, 221, 222
Eve, mitochondrial, 189–
    190
evolution, 72, 76, 189–190
    brain size and, 87–88
    cultural/social, 341–343
    see also speciation
evolutionists, 50
examination system, 500–
    501
exchange
    in band communities,
        174–195
    generalized, 279
    market, 186–187, 436–
        438
    marriage, 181, 193,
        212–219

exemplary prophets, 320, 330
exogamy, 218
extended family households, 161–162

*F*actories
cycles of activities as, 111
industrial, 448
living systems as, 72
factors of production, 448
factory day, 111
factory industrialism, 460
facts, 46–47
fall camps, 116
families
in band communities, 124, 152–170
chimpanzee, 28, 82–83
culture and, 152–154
in Japan, 502–507
nuclear, 155–156, 168, 502
speech and, 94
father figures, 506–507, 508
feasting, 258–281
alliance, 251, 260–261
competitive, 258–281
redistributive, 273–274
as redressive mechanism, 251–252, 253
feminism, 515
fiefs. *See* prebends
field, 46
community, 25–42
field work, 46–67, 528
active research in, 58
conditions for, 48
entry into community, strategy for, 54–55
ethics of, 59–60
field of specialization, selection of, 52–53
funding of, 53
methodological steps in, 56–60
methods for, 49
practical steps for, 52–56
program of study, selection of, 52
scientific aims of, 49–51
spy rumors, combating, 55–56
survival of, physical and psychological, 55

theoretical framework, specification of, 56
writing up findings of, 60
filicide, 392
fire, 86, 96, 131–133
firms, 504, 505–507
Florentine Codex, 14
folk, 402
folk cultures, 402–425
food, 138–139, 174–175
see also feasting
foreign boys, 382–383
foreign relations
in band communities, 110
Nambicuara chief's role in, 292–293
in traditional civilizations, 364
in tribal communities, 232
formal associations, 507
fratricide, 392
free market. *See* price-regulated markets
Freilich, Morris, 51, 61–66, 67
functional equivalence, 66
funding, of field work, 53
funerals, Tiwi, 118, 136–137, 140, 178–182, 195
future shock, 18

*G*ametes, 95, 163
gate slaves, 378–385, 390, 391, 392–393
Gates, Bill, 476
gays, 170, 516–519, 521
gender (grammatical), 166
gender roles, 166
gene pools, 74
generalized exchange, 279
generalized marriage exchange, 218–219
generalized reciprocity, 183–184, 188, 264–264, 441–443, 459
generational cycles, 117–118, 124
generic Protestantism, 482, 489–490
genes, 73
genetic code, 73–76
as language, 89–90, 95
genocide, 191
genotype, 73, 96
ghost marriage, 228

gibbons, 87, 153–154
Goodall, Jane, 29, 47, 70, 240, 241–242
gorillas, 83
grammar, 89, 92, 98
of ritual messages, 91
transformational, 92
grandfather figures, 508
grazers, 83
Great Britain, 449–450
green cities, 34–38, 354–364
grooming, social function of, 94
groups
informal, 487–489
workers and, 486–487
guild regiments, 348

*H*ammurabi, 351
Handbook of South American Indians (Metraux), 249
Handsome Lake, 324–328, 331
harems, 162, 373–375, 385–388
Harris, Marvin, 527
hearth, 113, 116, 131–133, 154–155
hearths of civilization, 340
hereditary elites, 510, 520
heterarchies, 72, 75, 95
hierarchies
civil/religious, 417
evolutionary, 72
in living systems, 95
temple, 348–349
holism, 41
Homans, George C., 486
Hominidae, 76, 79–89, 96
Hominoidea, 76
Homo, 79, 83–89, 96–97
race and, 189–190
Homo erectus, 41, 83, 86–88, 96–97
Homo habilis, 83, 85–86, 96
Homo neanderthalensis, 88, 97
Homo sapiens, 22, 29–30, 41, 77, 88–89, 97–98, 189
Homo sapiens sapiens, 22, 29, 77, 97
homosexuality. *See* gays
horticulturalists, 34
House of Osman, 376–378, 381, 385–386

household structure, Tiwi, 116
households, 116, 155
extended, 161–162, 204–209
matrilocal, 207–209
patrilocal, 206–207
residence decisions for, 206
two-income, 527–528
housing zones, 455–456, 461
Human Group, The (Homans), 486
human sacrifice, 14–17
hunting parties, 111
hunting-and-gathering bands. *See* band communities
Hylobatidae, 77
hypergamy, 411

*I*deology, 231
idolatry, 16
Incans, 375–376
incest tabu, 93, 98, 118, 152–153, 167, 214, 216, 218, 376
Incwala, 362
individual cycles, 112
induction, 24, 47, 66–67
Indus Valley, 340
industrial factory, 448
industrialism, 38, 448–458, 460–461, 489–490, 527
informal group, production and, 487–489
informants, 58
in-laws, 137
insolents, 402–407, 423
institutions, 25, 526–528, 534–535
see also specific institutions
interacting field, 46
interpretationist school, 51, 60
interviewing, 49, 58
inversion, 518
Ireland
open peasantry in, 410–411
stem family households in, 408, 409
Iroquoian kinship terminology, 214–218
Iroquois, 324–329, 331

irrigation, 352–353, 364
Islam, 9–10
  see also Muslims

*J*acobs, Jane, 527
Janissaries, 378, 382–383, 385, 388
Japan, 356, 497–509, 520–521, 527
joint families, 208
Judas, cult of, 419–420
jurisprudence, 23
just prices, 182, 438, 441–443
justice
  in band communities, 31, 109
  in modern metropolitan civilizations, 39, 437, 509
  in traditional civilizations, 36, 344, 351, 391–392
  in tribal communities, 33, 205, 227–229

*K*angaroos, 85
Khmer, 356
kindreds, 210–211, 230
kinetic cycles. *See* cycles of activities
kings, 349–351, 362
kinship, 30, 204
  bilateral, 210–211
  royal, 372–375
kinship systems, 230
  in band communities, 118–119, 124
  in Irish stem families, 408
  language and, 118
  among Nuer, 219–229
  in tribal communities, 34, 209–219
kinship terminologies, 213–215, 219
kula ring, 49, 272–278, 279, 280, 304, 306
kulama yam ceremony, 116–117, 135–136, 138–139
Kuna Indians, 208–209, 530–534, 535
!Kung San, 164, 330
  aggressive sequences among, 243
  cycles of activities among, 113–117, 119

exchange among, 177–178
fire places of, 132–133
marriage among, 158–159, 161, 168
myths of, 141
speech events among, 120–123
values among, 175–176, 177–178

*L*abor, 449–450, 460
labor movement, 484–485, 488, 513–514, 521
Lady Elephant, 357, 359, 360–361
language, 10, 89–95 119–120, 352
  in band communities, 31, 32, 109, 124
  genetic code as, 89–90
  kinship systems and, 118
  kinship systems as, 204, 230, 232
  in modern metropolitan civilizations, 39, 437
  ritual as, 90-91
  in traditional civilizations, 36, 344
  in tribal communities, 33, 205
  ur, 92–93, 120
  see also speech; writing
law codes, 351, 391–392
laws of entail, 410
leader-follower alliances, 303–304
leader-follower unit, 299–302
leadership, 119, 286–296
  natural, 290, 291–296
learning
  in band communities, 31, 109
  in modern metropolitan civilizations, 39, 40, 437
  in primate troops, 27
  in traditional civilizations, 36, 344
  in tribal communities, 33, 205
legal anthropology, 22–23
legal-rational bureaucracy, 372, 393–396, 466–491
  defined, 467
legitimacy, 296
Lenin, 484

leopard-skin chief, 221–222, 231
lesbians, 170, 516–519, 521
Lewis, Oscar, 512
life crisis rites, 30
  see also rites of passage
life cycles, among !Kung San males and females, 159–160
life employment, 503–504
lifetime cycles, 119, 124
limens, 144
liminality, 131
  see also transition, ritual
lineages, 34, 212
line-of-work behavior, 479–480, 521
linguistic analysis, 218
linguistics, 22
Linné Carl von, 76
Linnaean classification, 76
literacy, 95
Lobamba, 357–359, 362, 363
local residence, 110
local villages, 231
Lovedu, 373–374
Lévi-Strauss, Claude, 218, 291–293, 294

*M*acrocommunities, 238
magic, 50–51
Malinowski, Bronislaw, 47–51, 67, 272, 273
Mamachi, 498–501
man of cattle, 221, 231
man of the spear, 221, 231
mandarins, 394
Marginal Natives: Anthropologists at Work (Freilich), 51
market exchange, 187, 436–438
market system, 38–40
markets/marketplaces, 436–446
  defined, 438
  emergence of, 37, 38
  nation-states and, 446–450
  staggered, 439–440, 449
  stellar, 440–441, 442, 449
marriage, 30, 97, 152–153, 168–169, 193
  in band communities, 117–118, 124, 158–160

cross-cousin, 214–218
  ghost, 228
  in modern metropolitan civilizations, 504–505
  among Nuer, 223–226
  preferential cross-cousin, 215–216
  sexual behavior and, 165–166
  trial, 158
  see also families
marriage exchanges, 181, 193, 212–219
Marroquín, Socorro, 311–319
marsupials, 85
Marxism-Leninism, 483, 521, 522, 526
mass elites, 497
mass media, 508
masters essays, 60
matrilineal descent groups, 212, 229–230
matrilocal extended households, 208–209
matrilocal residence, 206, 207–208
Maya, 207, 311–319, 356, 408–410, 415–420
Mbuti Pygmies, 141–143
medical anthropology, 22
meiosis, 74, 163
men's houses, 264–265
mercantilism, 446–447
Mesoamerica, 340
mesolithic period, 212
Mesopotamia, 340, 343, 345–347, 364, 438
messenger RNA, 74
Metraux, Alfred, 248–249
metropolitan civilizations, modern, 38–41, 431–433, 496–522, 526–528
  bureaucracy in, 466–491
  economics in, 38–40, 437–458
  justice in, 39, 437, 509
  language in, 39, 437
  learning in, 39, 40, 437
  markets in, 39, 40, 436–461
  politics in, 39, 40, 437
  ritual in, 39, 40, 437, 468–469
  sociology in, 39, 40, 437
  technology in, 38, 39, 437
  work in, 466–491

middle class, 510–511, 520
military parades, 468–469
mill towns, 451, 460
Mitchell, Joseph, 61, 63, 64
mitochondrial Eve, 189–190
mitosis, 74, 75
mobilization phase, 244
modern metropolitan civilizations. *See* metropolitan civilizations, modern
modernity, 496–522
    differential access to, 509–511
Mohawks, Brooklyn, 61–66, 67, 497
"Mohawks in High Steel" (Mitchell), 61
molecular clock, 78
molimo ritual, 141–143
monarchy, 287
monasticism, 519
money, 264, 279
monogamy, 87, 153–154
Montaigne, 12–14, 17
Moore, Alexander, 53, 54–55, 57, 311–319, 415–420, 530–534
morals. *See* ethics; tabus
Morgan, Lewis Henry, 50
morphemes, 92, 98
movements
    gay and lesbian, 516–519
    labor, 513–514
    protest, 514–529
    women's, 515–516
    youth, 514–515
mufti, 384, 389, 392
multimale groups, 153
Mumford, Lewis, 469, 471
Muslims, 376–394, 391, 396–397
mutations, genetic, 74, 90, 96
myths, 128–129, 132, 141–143, 144, 145–146, 316, 329

*N*ambicuara Indians, 291–296
National Organization for Women (NOW), 515, 516
nation-states, market systems and, 446–450

natural history method, 24–25, 46–47
natural leadership, 290, 291–296
Navajo, 207–208
Neanderthals, 88
negative reciprocity, 185–186, 270, 279, 441–443
neocortex, 87, 88
neolithic transition, 211
neolocal residence, 206
neophytes, 129
New World monkeys, 77
Nisa (!Kung San woman), 158–160
noble savage, 13
nodes, urban, 343, 364
nonunilineal descent groups, 211
norms, 167
nuclear families, 156–157, 168–169, 502
    residence decisions of, 206
nucleated, walled cities, 34–38, 345–347, 353–355
Nuer, 219–229, 231–232, 288–289, 319–320

*O*jibwa Indians, 207, 528–529
Old World monkeys, 77
Oldowan tool-making tradition, 81–82, 86
oligarchy, 287
omnilineal descent groups, 211
"On Cannibalism" (Montaigne), 12–13
on-the-line workers, 490
open peasantries, 403, 407–411, 423
organization, tables of, 476–478
organized complexity, 47
original bureaucracies, 370–397
    as dynamic institutions, 394–395
Other, 60
Ottoman Turks, 376–394

*P*ages (Ottoman), 382, 383–385, 393
palaces, 348–350, 472

palavers, 121
paleoanthropology, 72, 76–77, 78
Panama, 530–534
parade grounds, 470–471
parades, 468–469
parallel-cousins, 214
parental pairs, 153
pari, 276
parley, 531
parliamentarianism, 531
participant-observer, 57
pastoralists, 402–403
patriarchal extended family, 416
patricians, 420
patricide, 392
patrilineal descent groups, 212, 230
patrilocal extended households, 206–207, 416
patrilocal residence, 206
patrimony, 370
patrolling, chimpanzee, 28–29, 241–242
peace chiefs, 300–301, 302–303
peasant communities
    closed corporate, 403, 411–420, 423
    open, 403, 407–411, 423
peasants, 402–403
pebble tools, 82
Peking, 353–355
Peru, 340, 375–376
phenotype, 73
phonemes, 91–92
physical anthropology, 22
Plato, 518
Platyrrhini, 77
plebeians, 420–422
pokala, 276
Polanyi, Karl, 186
policy, 528
policy ethnography, 528–529
policy process, 528, 530, 534
political science, 23
politics
    in band communities, 31, 32, 109
    defined, 289
    in modern metropolitan civilizations, 39, 40, 437

in primate troops, 27, 28, 29
in traditional civilizations, 36, 37, 38, 344, 348, 371–372
in tribal communities, 33, 34–35, 205, 271, 286–306
polity, 287, 305
polyandry, 161, 410fn
polygamy, 161
polygynous households, 161–162, 169–170
polygyny, 155, 161–162
Pongidae, 77, 78
popular culture, 508, 521
population growth, 341–342
population size, neocortex development and, 88
ports of trade, 439, 444–446, 459
poverty, 511
prebendaries, 370, 390, 391
prebends, 370, 387, 388, 391
preferential cross-cousin marriage, 215–216
price fixing, 443, 459
price-regulated markets, 38–40, 447–450, 460, 483, 489
priests, 348
primate troops, 25, 26–29
primates, 77, 82–83, 87–88, 94, 97
    see also chimpanzees; gibbons; gorillas; primate troops
primogeniture, 408, 410
production
    factors of, 448
    industrial, 448–450
    informal groups and, 487–489
professionals, 482
profits, 460
prokaryotes, 163
prophets, 112, 145, 310, 320–328, 330–332
proteins, 75
protest movements, 514–519, 521–522
Protestant ethic, 481–482, 489–490
Protestantism, 481

Proto-World, 92–93
psychology, 23
PTA, 499, 505, 510, 521
public policy, 526–535
Pygmies, Mbuti, 141–143

Qadis, 389
queen mother. See Lady
Elephant

Races, 76, 341
culture and, 189–190
racism, 190
rainy-season villages, 115–
116
rank, 520
rapport, establishment of,
56–57
rational deliberation, 526,
535
rational leadership, 119
reciprocal trading rings.
See trading rings
reciprocity, 183–186, 193,
194
balanced, 183, 264, 259,
441–443
dynamics of, 184–185
generalized, 183–184,
188, 263–264, 441–
443, 459
negative, 185–186, 270,
279, 441–443
redistribution, 38, 186,
260, 340–341, 364
in original bureaucra-
cies, 370–371
temples as centers of,
347
in traditional civiliza-
tions, 352
redistributive feasting,
273–274
redress phase, 244
redressive action, 121–123
reflexive approach, 60
regicide, 392
reincorporation, ritual, 91,
129, 144, 270, 317,
318
relativism, cultural, 190–
191
religion, 23
republics, tribal, 290, 296–
303, 304–305
research, active, 58
research proposals, 53

residence decisions, 206
resolution phase, 245
responsiveness, bureau-
cratic, 372
revitalization movements,
320–328, 526
revitalization prophets,
112, 331
ribonucleic acid. See RNA
rites of intensification, 30,
129, 138, 142, 144,
147, 250, 328, 364,
468–469, 508
Cheyenne, 298–299
see also feasting; kula
ring
rites of passage, 117, 129,
133–137, 138, 142,
158–160, 191, 248–
249, 512, 521
rites of salvation, 141, 310,
311, 315–318, 329
ritual, 30, 98
in band communities,
30, 31, 109, 124, 128–
148
as language, 90–91
in modern metropolitan
civilizations, 39, 40,
437, 468–469
molimo, 141–143
myth and, 140–143
among Neanderthals, 89
in primate troops, 27,
28–29
space dimensions of,
130–137
speech and, 94
symbols in, 138–140
therapeutic process of,
318–319
time dimensions of,
129–130, 133–136
in traditional civiliza-
tions, 36, 37, 38, 344
in tribal communities,
33, 34, 205
ritual cleansing, 130
river valleys, 340
RNA, 74–75, 95
robust australopithecines.
See Australopithecus
robustus
ronin, 501
royal bureaucracy, 37, 38
royal kinship, 372–375

Sacred space, 130–133
sagali, 274

Sahagún, Friar Bernardino
de, 14–17, 18
salary men, 498–499, 503,
508
sanctions, 295, 300, 304
Sargon of Akkad, 350
Saudi Arabia, 396–397
Schneider, Eugene, 487
schooling, 512, 520
Japanese, 499–501, 502–
503, 521
scientific Eve, 88
scientific management,
483–486
score, in tribal warfare,
245
sects, 328
segmentary lineage
systems, 220, 229
self-awareness, speech and,
94–95
Seligman, C. G., 48
Senecas, 326–328
separation, ritual, 91, 129,
131, 144, 269, 317,
318
sepoys, 389–390, 391, 393
serendipity, 56
sex, division of labor by,
31–32, 86, 111, 166,
498–499, 521
sexual behavior, marriage
and, 164–165
sexual dimorphism, 80, 83
sexual revolution, 516
sexuality, 162–165
shamans, 8, 9, 33, 34, 112,
145, 310–319, 328–
332
Shostak, Marjorie, 158–
160
showdown phase, 244
shrines, 353, 364
sibs, 211
silent trade, 11
single-male groups, 153
Siuai, 263–269
slavery, 376–394, 444–446,
450
see also gate slaves
small families. See nuclear
families
Smoking Mirror. See
Tezcatlipoca
social anthropology, 47–48
social classes, 451, 509–
511, 520
social cycles, 112–113

social dramas, 121–123,
140, 243, 252
social evolution, 341–343
social mobility, 461
socialized anthropologists,
58
sociobiology, 96
sociology, 23
in band communities,
30, 31, 32, 109
in modern metropolitan
civilizations, 39, 40,
437
in primate troops, 27, 28
in traditional civiliza-
tions, 36, 37, 38, 346
in tribal communities,
33, 34, 205
sodalities. See associations
solitary species, 153
Solutrean tool-making
tradition, 97
Songi, 267–269, 294, 296,
305
South Africa, 535
Soviet Union, 484, 491,
521
spacing mechanisms,
conflicts as, 251
spatial diffusion, 341–342
speciation, 76–77, 96
species, 76
race and, 189–190
speech, 78 98
as adaptive feature, 93–
95
in band communities,
119–123, 124, 187
in rituals, 128
as structured
extragenetic code,
91–92
Spiro, Herbert L., 531
sponsors, 54–55
spontaneous ethnogra-
phies, 6–9, 11–12
spring camps, 116
spy rumors, combating,
55–56
St. Francis of Assisi, 322,
323
St. Petersburg, 471
Staden, Hans, 6–9, 10, 11–
12, 14, 246, 247
staff-line behavior, 480,
490
staggered marketplaces,
439–440, 449

Stakhanovites, 484
Stalin, Josef, 526
standing orders, 531, 533
state, transformation of through ritual, 90–91
state, political, 286, 304, 305, 343
state cult, 391
stellar marketplaces, 440–441, 442, 449
stem family households, 407–410, 502, 503
stickleback, 90
stimulus diffusion, 340, 363
structural analysis, 218
sublineages, 212
Sudanese kinship terminology, 219, 223, 230
sun dance, 300
supervision, 480
supply and demand, laws of, 186–187, 436–438, 443, 459
support structures, 533
Swaziland, 357–363, 364, 372–373
symbolic association, 62
symbolic ecology, 456
symbols, 315, 317–318
  contradictions and, 139–140
  household, 410
  nature of, 138–139
  in ritual, 138–140, 144
  sacred spaces as, 130
syncretism, 407

Tables of organization, 477–479
tabus, 132, 167
  see also incest tabu
tax farming, 370, 372
taxonomy, 76–77
Taylor, Frederick, 483–486
Taylorism, 483–486, 488–489
technology
  in band communities, 31, 32, 109
  in modern metropolitan civilizations, 38, 39, 437
  in primate troops, 27
  in traditional civilizations, 36, 37, 38, 346

in tribal communities, 33, 34, 205
temples, 345–350, 354
term papers, 60
territoriality, 110, 232
Tezcatlipoca, 14–16, 17
theoretical framework, 56
theories, 46, 66
  working, 49
third-party intervention, 243
thresholds, 130–131, 144
time scales, 425–426
  in metropolitan civilizations, 461
  in tribal civilizations, 342, 364
  see also cycles of activities
Tiwi, 164–165
  cycles of activities among, 113, 116–119
  exchange among, 178–182
  funerals, 136–137, 140, 178–182, 195
  households, 161–162, 169
  life cycle stages, 133
  male initiation rites, 134–136, 138, 145, 147
  marriage among, 168, 169
  speech events among, 120–121
tomboy wantons, 292, 294
tools, 82, 87, 97–98
  chimpanzee use of, 29
Topkapi, 379, 380–381
Torrijos, Omar, 533–534
trade, 11
  administered, 444–446
  silent, 11
  see also exchange
trade unions, 485, 505, 513
trading partners, 264
trading rings, 258–281
traditional civilizations, 35–38
  economics in, 36, 37, 38, 344
  folk cultures, 408–428
  justice in, 37, 344, 351, 391–392
  language in, 37, 344
  learning in, 37, 344

original bureaucracies in, 370–397
  politics in, 36, 37, 38, 344, 348, 371–372, 375, 394
  ritual in, 36, 37, 38, 344
  sociology in, 36, 37, 38, 344, 372–395
  technology in, 36, 37, 38, 344
  warfare in, 348, 350, 353, 364–365
traditional domination, 331
traditional leadership, 119
trance states, 91, 132, 144
transfer RNA, 74–75
transformational grammar, 92
transition, ritual, 91, 129, 130, 131, 144, 269–270, 317, 318
transsexuals, 517–518
transvestism, 517
  see also berdaches
tribal communities, 32–35, 204, 342
  economics in, 33–34, 205, 271–272
  justice in, 33, 205, 227–229
  kinship systems in, 209–221
  language in, 33, 205
  learning in, 33, 205
  politics in, 33, 34–35, 205, 271, 286–306
  ritual in, 33, 34, 205, 309–329
  sociology in, 33, 34, 204–232
  technology in, 33, 34, 205
  trading systems in, 258–281
  warfare in, 34, 229, 238–253, 280, 297–298, 301
tribal republics, 290, 296–303, 304–305
tribes, 204
  civilized, 404–407
tributes, redistributive, 391
Trobrianders, 48, 50–51, 273–278, 304, 306
troops, 25, 26–29
trophies, war, 245
Trujillo, 424–425

Tupinambá, 6–9, 12–14, 245–249, 251
Turnbull, Colin, 141–143
two-income households, 527–528
two-variable analysis, 47
tyranny, 287

Unemployment, structural, 511
unilineal descent groups, 211–212, 218
unions, labor, 513
unspoken constitutions, 286–289, 303
upper class, 510, 520
up-the-line behavior, 480–481, 490
up-the-line communica-tions, 512
ur language, 92–93
urban centers, 343
urban cultures. See traditional civiliza-tions
urban elites, 424–425
urban nodes, 343, 344
urban processes, 448–449
Uruk, 345–347

Valdemora, 414–415
valuables, 272
values, 174–182, 186
  as goods, 175
  Japanese, 509
  leadership and, 296–297
Van Willigen, John, 528
voluntary associations, 512–513

Wallace, A. F. C., 61, 320–324
warfare
  Cheyenne, 297–298, 301
  chimpanzee, 29, 82, 241–242
  modern, 526
  in traditional civiliza-tions, 348, 350, 353, 364–365
  in tribal communities, 34, 229, 238–253, 280, 297–298, 301
  Tupinambá, 245–249
water as sacred symbol, 138

Weber, Max, 370, 372, 397, 460, 466–467
wheat villages, 411–420, 423, 424
Whydah, 438–440
Wilson, Edmund, 62–63
Wilson, Godfrey, 535

witchcraft, 317, 326, 329–330
wolves, 188
women
    in work force, 527
    see also division of labor by sex
women's movement, 515–516, 521

working class, 511
working theory, 49
worldview, 176
writing, 351, 352
written reports, 60, 67

*Y*ankee City, 445–456, 513

Yanomamo Indians, 330
youth movement, 514–515, 521

*Z*injanthropus, 83
zoology, 76–77
Zui Pueblo Indians, 59
zygotes, 73, 74, 95, 163